Complete

NINTH EDITION

Tomorrow's Technology and You

George Beekman
Ben Beekman

Prentice Hall
Upper Saddle River, New Jersey
Columbus, Ohio

To students all over the world –

The promise of the future

lies not in technology

but in you.

—G.B.

—B.B.

Library of Congress Cataloging-in-Publication Data
Beekman, George.
   Tomorrow's technology and you / George Beekman, Ben Beekman. — Complete, 9th ed.
         p. cm.
   Includes index.
   ISBN-13: 978-0-13-504504-6
   ISBN-10: 0-13-504504-5
   1. Computer science. 2. Information technology. I. Beekman, Ben. II. Title.
   QA76.C5628 2010b
   004—dc22

                                                                    2008044054

VP/Editorial Director: Natalie E. Anderson
Editor in Chief: Michael Payne
Associate VP/Executive Acquisitions Editor: Stephanie Wall
Product Development Director: Pamela Hersperger
Product Development Manager: Eileen Bien Calabro
Development Editor, Text and Supplements: Nancy Lamm
Editorial Project Manager: Virginia Guariglia
Editorial Assistant: Terenia McHenry
AVP/Director of Online Programs, Media: Richard Keaveny
Editorial Media Project Manager: Alana Coles
Production Media Project Manager: Lorena Cerisano
Director of Marketing: Kate Valentine
Marketing Manager: Tori Olson Alves
Marketing Assistant: Angela Frey
Senior Managing Editor: Cynthia Zonneveld
Associate Managing Editor: Camille Trentacoste
Production Project Manager: Ruth Ferrera-Kargov

Manager of Rights and Permissions: Charles Morris
Senior Operations Specialist: Nick Sklitsis
Operations Specialist: Natacha Moore
Senior Art Director: Jonathan Boylan
Cover Designer: Christopher Weigand
Interior Designer: Jill Little
Cover Image: Association for Internet Data Analysis, University of California
Director, Image Resource Center: Melinda Patelli
Manager, Rights and Permissions: Zina Arabia
Manager, Visual Research: Beth Brenzel
Manager, Cover Visual Research and Permissions: Karen Sanatar
Image Permission Coordinator: Cynthia Vicenti
Photo Researcher: Abigail Reip
Composition: Aptara, Inc.
Full-Service Project Management: Aptara®, Inc.
Printer/Binder: Worldcolor
Cover Printer: Lehigh Phoenix

Microsoft, Windows, Word, PowerPoint, Outlook, FrontPage, Visual Basic, MSN, The Microsoft Network, and/or other Microsoft products referenced herein are either registered trademarks or registered trademarks of the Microsoft Corporation in the U.S.A. and other countries. Screen shots and icons reprinted with permission from the Microsoft Corporation. This book is not sponsored or endorsed by or affiliated with the Microsoft Corporation.

About the cover: The cover shows a computer-generated image of global internet traffic. The lines represent sample data sent out to 20,000 pre-selected locations. The colors of the lines represent the nationality of that part of the internet: USA (blue); UK (dark blue); Italy (yellow); Sweden (red); and unknown countries (white). Maps like this will make moving around the Internet easier, as well as showing when and where data jams occur. The image was created by the Cooperative Association for Internet Data Analysis, University of California, USA.

Pearson Education Ltd., London
Pearson Education Singapore, Pte. Ltd
Pearson Education, Canada, Inc.
Pearson Education–Japan

Pearson Education Australia PTY, Limited
Pearson Education North Asia Ltd., Hong Kong
Pearson Educación de Mexico, S.A. de C.V.
Pearson Education Malaysia, Pte. Ltd.

Prentice Hall
is an imprint of

10 9 8 7 6 5 4 3 2
ISBN-13: 978-0-13-504504-6
ISBN-10: 0-13-504504-5

Contents

Chapter 4   Software Basics: The Ghost in the Machine   104

Chapter 5   Productivity Applications   142

Chapter 6   Graphics, Digital Media, and Multimedia   186

Chapter 7   Database Applications and Privacy Implications   232

Chapter 8   Networking and Digital Communication   270

Chapter 9   The Evolving Internet   316

Chapter 10   Computer Security and Risks   358

Chapter 11   Computers at Work, School, and Home   396

Chapter 12   Information Systems in Business   436

Chapter 13   Electronic Commerce and E-Business: The Evolving Internet Economy   472

Chapter 14   Systems Design and Development   508

Chapter 15   Is Artificial Intelligence Real?   550

Appendix A   Basics   583

Appendix B   ACM   607

Glossary   615

Credits   635

Index   639

About this Book

In the world of information technology, it seems like change is the only constant. In less than a human lifetime, this technological torrent has transformed virtually every facet of our society—and the transformation is just beginning. As old technologies merge and new technologies emerge, far-fetched predictions routinely come true. This headlong rush into the high-tech future poses a challenge for all of us: How can we extract the knowledge we need from the deluge of information? What must we understand about information technology to survive and thrive in an increasingly technological future? *Tomorrow's Technology and You* is designed to aid travelers on their journey into that future.

Meeting this challenge means going far beyond knowing how to create a budget spreadsheet or find facts on the Internet. A deeper understanding of information technology will help you answer much more meaningful questions. What kind of new media will emerge from the next generation of Internet technology, and how will our lives change as a result? How can you cope with spam and spyware? What should you do to reduce your chances of being a victim of identity theft? What should you consider when setting up a home network? Will automation result in massive, long-term unemployment? Will information technology be a tool to bring the people of the world closer together, or will it drive a permanent wedge between the rich and the poor? *Tomorrow's Technology and You* is designed to help you explore these questions. It goes beyond simply describing the latest gadgets and explains many of the benefits we derive (and risks we tolerate) when we incorporate information technology into our lives.

What Is *Tomorrow's Technology and You?*

Tomorrow's Technology and You explores information technology on three levels:

- Explanations: *Tomorrow's Technology and You* clearly explains what a computer is and what it can (and can't) do; it describes the basics of information technology, from smart phones and multimedia PCs to the Internet and beyond.

- Applications: *Tomorrow's Technology and You* illustrates how computers and networks are—and will be—used as practical tools to solve a wide variety of problems and extend human capabilities in all kinds of new directions.

- Implications: *Tomorrow's Technology and You* puts technology in a human context, illustrating how our ever-growing network of digital devices affects our lives, our world, and our future.

Here's a quick rundown of the book's chapters:

Chapter 1 offers a solid foundation for the chapters that follow by presenting a big-picture view of our digital planet. This chapter provides a perspective for understanding the future by emphasizing trends and storylines rather than historical details and technical trivia. It opens with profiles and perspectives on a particularly powerful digital trend—the Web 2.0 phenomenon. The *Inventing the Future* box near the end of the chapter provides an overview of strategies for predicting the future—strategies that are applied in later chapters.

Chapters 2 through 4 provide clear explanations of the basic concepts of computer hardware and software—concepts that are often misunderstood by students—even those who have considerable computer experience. These chapters, like later chapters in the book, include optional *How It Works* boxes that provide more technical detail for those who want or need to know more.

Chapters 5 through 7 survey a variety of computer and Internet applications, from familiar office tools to cutting-edge multimedia and database applications.

Chapters 8 and 9 go into much greater depth on network technology in general and the Internet in particular. These chapters cover emerging technologies that are rapidly changing the way we use the Internet—technologies that many casual Internet users don't understand. The Web of tomorrow will be vastly different than today's Web, and its impact on our lives is hard to imagine today. Material in these chapters should make it a little easier for students to predict their networked futures.

Chapter 10 provides a focal point for a variety of ethical and social issues related to information technology. Many of these issues—privacy, security, reliability, and more—are discussed throughout the book. This chapter, though, pulls all of these concepts together. The chapter closes with a discussion of big questions about our relationship to technology—important questions for all citizens of the future to think about.

Chapter 11 surveys the applications and implications of digital technology in our three most important social institutions: our homes, our schools, and our workplaces.

Chapters 12 and 13 are targeted at students who have a need or desire to know more about the application of information technology in business. Chapter 12 focuses on digital tools for managing all kinds of businesses. Chapter 13 has been completely rewritten to cover all aspects of electronic commerce, from traditional e-business models to future trends in e-commerce.

Chapter 14 goes beyond Chapter 4's introduction to software technology, exploring programming, systems design, and computer science concepts in more depth.

Chapter 15 covers one of the most intriguing fields of computer science: artificial intelligence. The chapter demystifies AI and at the same time points toward a future in which machine intelligence may radically alter our world.

The Appendix provides a friendly introduction for students who have little or no experience with PCs and the Internet. This unique feature addresses the most commonly reported problem of introductory computer concepts classes—the diverse backgrounds of students in those classes. Most instructors report that the majority of their new students have PC and Internet experience. These students don't need to be told about keyboarding or navigating a Web site. But if these topics aren't covered, the inexperienced students are at a distinct disadvantage. The Appendix is designed for those beginners, so they can fill in gaps in their knowledge before launching into the rest of the book.

In general, the book's focus flows from the concrete to the controversial and from the present to the future. Individual chapters have a similarly expanding focus. After a brief introduction, each chapter flows from basic concepts toward abstract, future-oriented questions and ideas. Most chapters raise ethical issues related to the use and misuse of digital technology. Every chapter asks readers to think about the trade-offs associated with information technology innovations. The book provides a framework to help readers think about ways to use present and future technology as a way to help them achieve their goals.

About the Authors

George Beekman is an Honorary Instructor in the School of Electrical Engineering and Computer Science at Oregon State University. For more than two decades he designed and taught courses in computer literacy, interactive multimedia, computer ethics, and computer programming at OSU. An innovative computer literacy course he created more than two decades ago served as the inspiration for *Tomorrow's Technology and You*. George Beekman has taught workshops in computer literacy and multimedia for students, educators, and economically disadvantaged families from the Atlantic to Alaska. He has written many books on computers, information technology, and multimedia, as well as more than 100 articles and reviews for *Macworld* and other popular publications. George also bikes, hikes, and runs on Oregon trails and roads, shoots and edits photos and videos, produces and plays acoustic and electronic music, and cultivates community connections at home and beyond.

Ben Beekman is a multimedia designer, writer, and technical consultant based in Oregon. Ben has developed multimedia Web sites for businesses, nonprofits, artists, and musicians. He has done extensive desktop publishing, page layout, and design for periodicals and one-shot publications. He has written blogs for the Web and technology reviews for print media. He has worked behind-the-scenes on several books, including previous editions of this one. Ben also composes, mixes, and remixes music and video, tracks the evolving Internet, consumes comedy, plays disc golf, and enjoys the outdoors with friends and his dog Gizmo.

Acknowledgments

We're deeply grateful to all of the people who have come together to make *Tomorrow's Technology and You* a success. Their names may not be on the cover, but their high quality work shows in every detail of this project.

We're especially thankful to Publisher Natalie Anderson, whose clear vision and personal commitment to *Tomorrow's Technology and You* helped elevate this book to a new level of excellence. We're also grateful to Stephanie Wall, the savvy Executive Editor who worked with us to ensure that we had the resources and help we needed to produce a first-rate text. Stephanie, along with Product Development Manager Eileen Calabro, put together a terrific team to work on this book. Special thanks to Project Manager Virginia Guariglia, who skillfully kept this project on course and on schedule from day 1 until the presses rolled. This edition is also far better thanks to the careful, thoughtful, and timely work of Editorial Development Editor Nancy Lamm, Copy Editor Joe Ruddick, and technical editors Jan Snyder, Lynne Bowen, and Jean Kotsiovos.

Many others brought their considerable talents to *Tomorrow's Technology and You*. Art Director Jonathan Boylan turned our cover idea into a beautiful work of art. Ruth Ferrera-Kargov worked on all aspects of production, helping ensure that the project could make all those nearly impossible deadlines. Abigail Reip uncovered many of the new photos in this and many previous editions. Shelley Creager and her team at Aptara compiled the final book from all of the raw materials supplied by the others listed here.

All of this effort would be wasted if *Tomorrow's Technology and You* didn't reach its intended audience. Thankfully, Prentice Hall's amazing marketing and sales team does a phenomenal job of making sure that professors and their students have access to our books, and we can't thank them enough for their efforts.

We both owe special thanks to our family and community, here in Corvallis and all around our digital planet, who provided unbelievable support during the turbulent and challenging period when we were launching this project. We're especially grateful to Susan Grace Beekman, who somehow managed be there whenever we needed her in spite of the fact that she was immersed in an extremely challenging project of her own.

There are others who contributed to *Tomorrow's Technology and You* in all kinds of ways, including critiquing chapters, answering technical questions, tracking down obscure references, guiding us through difficult decisions, and being there when we needed support. There's no room here to detail their contributions, but we want to thank the people who gave time, energy, talent, and support during the years that this book was under development, including: Evan Scheessele, Jeremy Smith, Mina Carson, Micky Hulse, Robert Rose, Gabe Guzman, Skyler Corbett, Johanna Beekman, Maureen Spada, Dave Trenkel, Mark Dinsmore, Stephanie Sireix, Naftali Anderson, Martin Erwig, Otto Gygax, Francisco Martin, Jim Folts, Jan Dymond, Johanna Beekman, Mike Johnson, Margaret Burnett, Sherry Clark, Walter Rudd, Cherie Pancake, Bruce D'Ambrosio, Bernie Feyerherm, Rajeev Pandey, Dave Stuve, Clay Cowgill, Keith Vertanen, Gary Brent, Marion Rose, Megan Slothover, Claudette Hastie Baehrs, Melissa Hartley, Gracewinds Music, Shjoobedebop, Breitenbush, Oregon Public Broadcasting, and all of the editors and others who helped with previous editions. Thanks also to all the hardware and software companies whose cooperation made our work easier.

Visual Walk-Through

Tomorrow's Technology and You is designed to help you to provide students with the background they need to survive and prosper in a world transformed by information technology. The ninth edition comes in two forms, the Introductory Edition and the Complete Edition and both books include a variety of supplements and ancillary materials designed to help you enhance your students' learning experience.

About this Edition

This edition of Tomorrow's Technology and You is one of the most significant and comprehensive revisions we've ever done. Here is a chapter-by-chapter summary of improvements and additions to this edition.

Chapter 1, "Our Digital Planet." This chapter provides a broad overview of the information technology trends that have completely transformed our society, while providing a solid foundation for the chapters that follow. An updated "Digital Technology Time Line" clarifies our changing relationship to computers by describing the eras of institutional, personal, interpersonal, and collaborative computing. New material highlights Web 2.0 as one of the fastest-changing parts of the digital landscape. Placing Web 2.0 in the context of our ever-more-digital time line provides a perspective that makes it easier to understand what kind of changes are ahead—and how those changes are likely to transform our lives.

Chapter 2, "Hardware Basics: Inside the Box," and Chapter 3 "Hardware Basics: Peripherals." Both of these chapters have been updated to clearly describe the latest hardware technology, from processors to peripherals. We've added a new section and feature box on multi-touch technology, reworked and revised tables comparing processors, optical media types, and storage devices, rewrote the section on ports, and added more on flash memory and Blu-ray discs.

Chapter 4, "Software Basics: The Ghost in the Machine." This chapter includes expanded and updated coverage of Web applications and operating systems. A new Working Wisdom box, "When Good Software Goes Bad," suggests strategies for dealing with program freezes, system crashes, and other bugs that plague computer users.

Chapter 5 "Productivity Applications." This chapter has been updated to include current productivity and simulation software, as well as more information on speech recognition, text recognition, and other practical applications of artificial intelligence in productivity software.

Chapter 6, "Graphics, Digital Media, and Multimedia." This chapter has been revised to include new material on graphics, digital audio, digital video, and multimedia, covering both amateur and professional applications. A rewritten Screen Test illustrates the creation of a CD cover using professional Photoshop techniques. A new Screen Test, "Multimedia on a Student Budget," covers low-cost software that can deliver high-end results for Windows and Mac users.

Chapter 7, "Database Applications and Privacy Implications." The material on databases has been updated with a new Access Screen Test. There's additional coverage of databases in other types of computers, from smart phones to mainframes. There's more coverage of intelligent searches, including natural language queries and contextual searches. The section on privacy implications includes timely new material, including tips on protecting personal privacy.

Chapter 8, "Networking and Digital Communication." This chapter has been extensively revised to reflect significant changes in the technology and the way people use networks. The chapter includes expanded and updated coverage of wireless technologies, from Bluetooth to WiMax. The sections on blogs, forums, and other types of collaborative communication have been expanded and updated. There's new coverage of wikis, social bookmarking, media sharing, and crowdsourcing. There is also a new section called "Sharing Resources: Peer-to-Peer, Grid, and Cloud Computing."

Chapter 9, "The Evolving Internet." This chapter has also been extensively rewritten to reflect changes in Internet technology, applications, and implications. The section on Web programming tools now presents PHP, AJAX, and other modern Web development tools in a clearer, more comprehensive way. A new section, "Web 2.0 and You", explores the build-it-yourself technology and philosophy of the emerging Web 2.0. The chapter also has updated and expanded coverage of ethical and political issues, including net neutrality, access, and censorship.

Chapter 10, "Computer Security and Risks." The sections on computer crime, malware, backups, and security have all been updated to reflect current trends and issues.

Chapter 11, "Computers at Work, School, and Home," includes updated material on telecommuting, office automation, educational computing, and home computing, and smart cards. An all-new Inventing the Future box, "Tomorrow's Technology for Today's Child," explores the futuristic technology and the far-reaching implications of One Laptop per Child's XO-2.

Chapter 12, "Information Systems in Business," includes an all-new Inventing the Future box covering "The Virtualization of IT."

Chapter 13, "E-Commerce and E-Business: The Evolving Internet Economy," has been completely rewritten to reflect a new world of twenty-first century electronic commerce. The opening Jeff Bezos profile now focuses on Amazon's shift from selling products to selling cloud-computing services. The coverage of e-business basics, including intranets, extranets, B2C, and C2C, has been streamlined and clarified. A new Working Wisdom box gives practical advice for "Selling Stuff Online." An important new section, "E-Business 2.0: Reinventing Web Commerce," explores the impact of Web 2.0 on sales, marketing, and advertising (including social networks, wikis, user reviews, free services, Web 2.0 C2C technology, and The Long Tail of e-commerce as an alternative to mass-marketing of the pre-digital era). The section on e-commerce ethics has been revised and updated.

Chapter 14, **"Systems Design and Development"** has been updated to reflect changes in technology and techniques of software design and development. A new Screen Test Box covers "Object Oriented Programming in Java." New and updated material on agile development and extreme programming has been included, along with explanations of fourth- and fifth-generation programming languages and an updated section on programming for the Web. The "Systems Development Life Cycle" How It Works feature has been revised with a more timely example.

Chapter 15, "Is Artificial Intelligence Real?," includes updated coverage of applied AI and robotics, along with a new Inventing the Future box, "Microtechnology, Nanotechnology, and Artificial Life."

Appendix, "Basics." The appendix contains introductory material updated to cover the latest software and hardware.

Special Focus Boxes

Tomorrow's Technology and You includes several unique feature boxes that add value for students, instructors, and casual readers. Many of these boxes are new or updated for this edition.

How it Works

How It Works boxes provide additional technical material on more complex topics. For classes where this kind of technical detail isn't necessary, students can skip these boxes. How It Works boxes are numbered so that instructors can create customized reading assignments by specifying which are required and which are optional.

Working Wisdom

Working Wisdom boxes contain relevant and intriguing tips that can help readers produce better results and steer clear of trouble.

Screen Test

Screen Tests show what it's like to use a software application to achieve specific goals. They provide students with a glimpse of programs they might not otherwise experience.

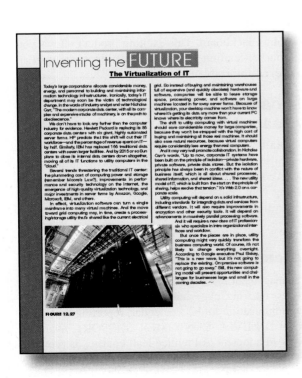

Inventing the Future

Inventing the Future boxes provide futuristic perspectives at the end of every chapter.

Crosscurrents

Completely updated **Crosscurrents** articles are some of the best contemporary, short essays focusing on our complex relationship with technology. Topics include the erosion of personal privacy, the abuse of intellectual property laws, software reliability, and machine intelligence.

Other Resources

Companion Web Site

This text is accompanied by a Companion Web site at www.pearsonhighered.com/beekman. This Web site brings you and your students a richer, more interactive Web experience than ever before. Features of this site include an interactive study guide, end-of-chapter materials, additional Internet exercises, and crossword puzzles to enhance your understanding of key concepts and terms from each chapter.

Instructor Resources

The Prentice Hall Instructor's Resource Center on CD-ROM includes the tools you expect from a Prentice Hall Computer Concepts text, like:
- The instructor's material in Word format
- Solutions to all questions and exercises from the book and Web site
- Customizable PowerPoint slide presentations for each chapter
- Web resources
- Internet exercises
- Discussion questions
- Additional assignments
- Image library of all of the figures from the text

TestGen Software

TestGen is a test generator found on your instructor resource CD that lets you view and easily edit testbank questions, transfer them to tests, and print in a variety of formats suitable to your teaching situation. The program also offers many options for organizing and displaying testbanks and tests. Powerful search and sort functions let you easily locate questions and arrange them in the order you prefer.

QuizMaster, also included in this package, allows students to take tests created with TestGen on a local area network. The QuizMaster utility built into TestGen lets instructors view student records and print a variety of reports. Building tests is easy with TestGen and exams can be easily uploaded into WebCT, Blackboard and CourseCompass.

OneKey

www.pearsonhighered.com/onekey

OneKey lets you in to the best teaching and learning resources all in one place. OneKey for *Tomorrow's Technology and You* is all your students need for anywhere,

anytime access to your course materials, conveniently organized by textbook chapter to reinforce and apply what they've learned in class. OneKey is all you need to plan and administer your course. All your instructor resources are in one place to maximize your effectiveness and minimize your time and effort. OneKey provides convenience, simplicity, and success . . . for you and your students.

CourseCompass

www.coursecompass.com

CourseCompass is a dynamic, interactive online course-management tool powered exclusively for Pearson Education by Blackboard. This exciting product allows you to teach market-leading Pearson Education content in an easy-to-use, customizable format.

Blackboard

www.pearsonhighered.com/blackboard

Prentice Hall's abundant online content, combined with Blackboard's popular tools and interface, results in robust Web-based courses that are easy to implement, manage, and use—taking your courses to new heights in student interaction and learning.

WebCT

www.pearsonhighered.com/webct

Course management tools within WebCT include page tracking, progress tracking, class and student management, a grade book, communication tools, a calendar, reporting tools, and more. GOLD LEVEL CUSTOMER SUPPORT, available exclusively to adopters of Prentice Hall courses, is provided free of charge upon adoption and provides you with priority assistance, training discounts, and dedicated technical support.

Tomorrow's Technology and You

1

Our Digital Planet

After you read this chapter
you should be able to:

▌ Describe how digital technology plays a critical
role in modern life

▌ Discuss several key trends in the evolution
of computers and digital technology

▌ Describe the major types of computers and their
principal uses

▌ Explain how the explosive growth and evolution
of the Internet is changing the way people use
information technology

▌ Explain how our information age differs from any
time that came before

▌ Discuss the social and ethical impact
of information technology on our society

> The **culture of generosity** is the very **backbone of the Internet.**
>
> —Caterina Fake, co-founder of Flickr

Creating Communities on the Living Web

The World Wide Web isn't new; it's been around since the 1990s. But until recently, most people treated it like a television set or a library. They surfed and searched for information, images, and experiences, but they didn't add anything new. That's changing, thanks to Web pioneers who are designing sites that depend on creative contributions of people such as you and me. Today some of the most active and interesting parts of the Web are being built by everyday people working (and playing) together in virtual communities that span the globe.

One of the best known examples of the new, living Web is MySpace. MySpace was founded in 2003 by Tom Anderson and Chris DeWolfe, two Los Angeles entrepreneurs. Inspired by sites such as Match.com and Friendster, they set out to create an online community experience for young people. But unlike other popular social networking sites, MySpace enabled—and encouraged—members to create personal Web sites to share words and pictures with other members. They also designed MySpace so that it was easy for musicians to connect directly with their fans, bypassing the traditional corporate PR portals. According to Anderson, "The idea was that if it was a cool thing to do online, you should be able to do it on MySpace."

MySpace's success was immediate and overwhelming. Within three years it became one of the most

FIGURE 1.1 MySpace founders Tom Anderson and Chris DeWolfe.

3

FIGURE 1.2 Facebook founder Mark Zuckenberg.

FIGURE 1.3 Flickr founders Caterina Fake and Stewart Butterfield on the cover of Newsweek.

popular Web destinations, rivaling Yahoo!, Google, and Amazon in page visits and advertising revenue. Anderson, a "friend" for each of the millions of MySpacers, developed the celebrity status of a rock star. In 2005, MySpace was purchased by Rupert Murdoch's News Corp. for $580 million. Many see MySpace as the new MTV.

MySpace's biggest competitor in the social networking domain is FaceBook, founded in 2004 by Harvard student Mark Zuckenberg. Facebook was originally designed for Harvard students; it later expanded its service to other college students. Today it's open to just about anyone, anywhere—except in a handful of countries where it's banned by dictators who fear the free exchange of ideas. Facebook offers an expanding array of services and features, from games to continual updates on who's doing what.

The online worlds of Facebook and MySpace aren't trouble-free. Unsuspecting users reveal personal information and photographs, naively assuming that all of their "friends" can be trusted, and that only their friends will see their postings. Online stalking, harassment, and bullying incidents have forced both companies to deal with difficult questions about the balance between personal security and privacy—the same kinds of questions that plague communities in the nondigital world.

Flickr is an online community with a different purpose and a different story. Caterina Fake and Stewart Butterfield, a married couple in Vancouver, B.C., Canada, founded their company to create a massive multiplayer Web game. When one of their engineers developed a clever way for players to share pictures, they decided to build a photo-sharing site around that technology. "It turned out the fun was in the photo sharing," Fake says. Their game didn't survive, but Flickr became an instant hit. Within two years it was snapped up by Yahoo! for an estimated $35 million (U.S.).

Flickr members generously share their photographs—from personal portraits to late-breaking news images—with millions of other members. They add tags to photos so they're easy to locate in searches. They decide collectively how Flickr's online galleries should be organized and categorized. They develop a sense of community based on shared interests and trust.

The creators of Flickr, MySpace, FaceBook, and other emerging Web sites aren't just building pages—they're creating communities. And we're all invited to be part of that creative process. These sites, along with YouTube, Del.icio.us, Blogger, and others, are referred to as Web 2.0 because they're transforming the Web into a different kind of experience. As Steven Levy and Brad Stone wrote in *Newsweek,* "MySpace, Flickr, and the other newcomers aren't places to go, but things to do, ways to express yourself, means to connect with others and extend your own horizons." ～

Computers and the Internet are so much a part of modern life that we tend to take them for granted. We hardly notice when some technical marvel—MySpace, Flickr, iTunes, Google, or whatever's next—changes the way we live. And we're even less conscious of the computer-controlled devices humming away in the background, maintaining the infrastructure of our civilization. But we'd certainly notice if they suddenly stopped working. Imagine . . .

Living in a Nondigital World

You wake up with the sun well above the horizon and realize your alarm clock hasn't gone off. You wonder if you've overslept. You have a big research project due today. The TV and radio don't work. The lights don't work either, so that clinches it: there is no power. But that's not all. The face of your digital wristwatch stares back at you blankly. Your laptop isn't just sleeping; it's dead. You can't even get the time by telephone because your phone doesn't work.

The morning newspaper is missing from your doorstep. You'll have to guess the weather forecast by looking out the window. You decide to go out for breakfast, but your car won't start. In fact, the only cars moving are antiques from the 1970s or earlier. Dejected, you pull out the camping stove, carry it out to the deck behind your apartment, and heat some water for coffee. Leaning against the rail of the deck, you notice how quiet the city is.

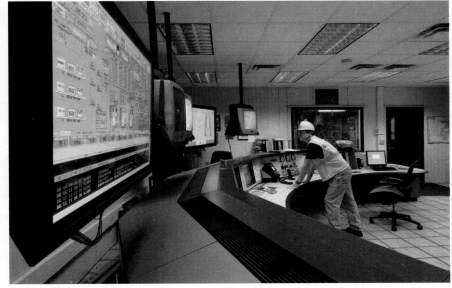

FIGURE 1.4 This utility company control room depends on digital technology.

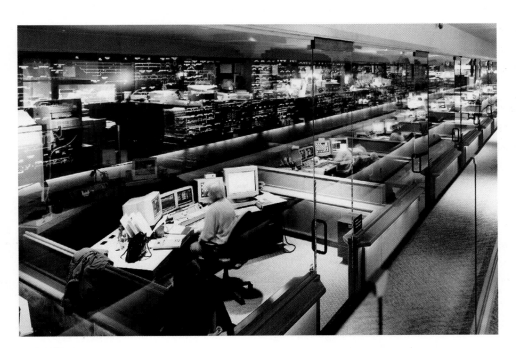

FIGURE 1.5 Computers are used to coordinate thousands of Union Pacific trains in this high-tech Omaha control room.

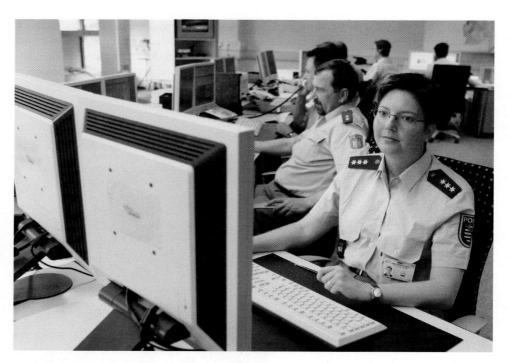

FIGURE 1.6 Police dispatchers depend on digital networks for emergency communications.

By noon the water faucets and toilets no longer work: there is no more fresh water. You've spent a good part of the morning talking to your neighbors about the apparent failure of all things digital. Under normal circumstances you rarely see most of these people, but the techno-crisis seems to have sparked a sense of community.

As you discuss plans with your neighbors, you hear popping sounds from the direction of the nearby mall. Could that be gunfire? Where are the police?

Our story could go on, but the message should be clear enough by now. Computers are everywhere, and our lives are directly affected in all kinds of ways by their operation—and nonoperation. It's truly amazing that computers have infiltrated our lives so thoroughly in such a short time.

Computers in Perspective

Invention breeds invention.

—*Ralph Waldo Emerson*

Although computers have been with us for only about five decades, these extraordinary machines are built on centuries of insight and effort.

Computers grew out of a human need to quantify. Early humans were content to count with fingers, rocks, or other everyday objects. As cultures became more complex, so did their counting tools. The abacus (a type of counting tool and calculator used by the Babylonians, the Chinese, and others for thousands of years) and the Hindu-Arabic number system are examples of early calculating tools that had an immediate and profound effect on the human race. (Imagine trying to conduct business without a number system that allows for easy addition and subtraction.)

By the early nineteenth century, the capitalist culture's appetite for mathematics had outgrown its tools. A "computer" was a person who performed calculations. These human computers labored for many hours to produce mathematical tables. Unfortunately, to err is human, and the tables they produced were riddled with mistakes. A pair of British visionaries, Charles Babbage and Augusta Ada King, the Countess of Lovelace (commonly called Ada Lovelace today), imagined the construction of an Analytical Engine—a mechanical computer that would automatically and reliably perform these tasks. But it took about 125 years for engineers to turn this vision into a reality. Here are a few highlights of the journey from that early vision to the modern computer:

■ In 1939 a young German engineer named Konrad Zuse completed the Z1, the first programmable, general-purpose digital computer. "I was too lazy to calculate and so I invented the computer," Zuse recalled. In 1941, Zuse and a friend asked the German government for funds to build a faster electronic computer to help crack enemy codes during World War II. The Nazi military establishment turned him down, confident that their aircraft would quickly win the war without the aid of sophisticated calculating devices.

■ At about the same time, the British government was assembling a top-secret team of mathematicians and engineers to crack Nazi military codes. In 1943 the team, led by mathematician Alan Turing and others, completed Colossus. This special-purpose computer allowed British military intelligence to eavesdrop on even the most secret German messages throughout the remainder of the war.

■ In 1939, Iowa State University professor John Atanasoff and graduate student Clifford Berry created the Atanasoff-Berry Computer (ABC), which was capable of solving systems of linear equations. When Atanasoff approached International Business Machines for funding, he was told "IBM will never be interested in an electronic computing machine."

■ Harvard professor Howard Aiken was more successful in financing the automatic, general-purpose calculator he was developing. Thanks to a $1 million grant from IBM, he completed the Mark I in 1944. This 51-foot-long, 8-foot-tall monster used noisy, slow, electromechanical relays, but it proved its worth by computing ballistics tables for the U.S. Navy.

■ After consulting with Atanasoff and studying the ABC, John Mauchly teamed up with J. Presper Eckert to help the U.S. war effort by constructing a machine that could calculate ballistics tables for the U.S. Army. The machine was the Electronic Numerical Integrator and Computer (ENIAC), a 30-ton behemoth that broke down, on average, once every seven minutes. When it was running, it could calculate 500 times faster than the existing electromechanical calculators—about as fast as a modern pocket calculator. The ENIAC wasn't completed until two months after the end of World War II in 1945, but it convinced its creators that large-scale computers were commercially feasible. After the war Mauchly and Eckert started a private company and designed the UNIVAC I, the first general-purpose commercial computer built in the United States. Mauchly and Eckert were better engineers than businessmen. Calculator maker Remington Rand bought them out in 1950, completed the UNIVAC I, and delivered it to the U.S. Census Bureau in 1951.

Computer hardware evolved rapidly from those early days, with new technologies replacing old every few years. The first computers were big, expensive, and finicky. Only a large institution such as a major bank or the U.S. government could afford a computer, not to mention the climate-controlled computing center needed to house it and the staff of technicians needed to program it and keep it running. But with all their faults, computers quickly became indispensable tools for scientists, engineers, and other professionals.

The transistor was invented in 1948 as a substitute for the vacuum tube, and transistors first appeared in computers eight years later. Computers that used transistors were radically smaller, more reliable, and less expensive than computers that used vacuum tubes to store and manipulate data.

FIGURE 1.7 J. Presper Eckert (left) describes the UNIVAC I computer to CBS correspondent Walter Cronkite before the 1952 presidential election. When 5 percent of the votes had been reported, UNIVAC correctly predicted that Eisenhower would win the election, but CBS cautiously chose to withhold the prediction until most of the votes were reported.

FIGURE 1.8 A vacuum tube, a transistor, and an integrated circuit.

Because of improvements in software at about the same time, these machines were also much easier and faster to program and use. As a result, computers became more widely used in business, science, and engineering.

The Space Race spurred further developments in computer technology. After the Soviet Union's successful launch of the Sputnik satellite in 1957, the United States was desperate to catch up with its Cold War rival. America's fledgling space program needed computers that were even smaller and more powerful than the transistor-based machines, so researchers developed the integrated circuit: a small silicon chip containing hundreds of transistors and other electronics. By the mid-1960s, transistor-based computers were replaced by smaller, more powerful machines built around these new integrated circuits.

Integrated circuits rapidly replaced transistors for the same reasons that transistors superseded vacuum tubes:

■ *Reliability.* Machines built with integrated circuits were less prone to failure than their predecessors because the chips could be rigorously tested before installation.

■ *Size.* Single chips could replace entire boards filled with hundreds of transistors and other electronics, making it possible to build much smaller machines.

■ *Speed.* Because electricity had shorter distances to travel, the smaller machines were markedly faster than their predecessors.

■ *Efficiency.* Because chips were so small, they used less electrical power. As a result, they created less heat.

■ *Cost.* Mass production techniques made it easy to manufacture inexpensive chips.

Just about every breakthrough in computer technology since the dawn of the computer age has presented similar advantages over the technology it replaced.

The inventions of the vacuum tube, the transistor, and the silicon chip had tremendous impact on our society. But the impact was even bigger when, in 1971, Intel engineers developed the first microprocessor—a single silicon chip containing *all* of a computer's computational components. The research and development costs for the first microprocessor were enormous. But once the assembly lines were in place, silicon computer chips could be mass-produced cheaply. The raw materials were certainly cheap enough; silicon, the main ingredient in beach sand, is the second most common element (after oxygen) in the Earth's crust.

U.S. companies soon flooded the marketplace with watches and pocket calculators built around inexpensive microprocessors. The economic effect was immediate: mechanical calculators and slide rules became obsolete overnight, electronic hobbyists became wealthy entrepreneurs, and California's San Jose area gained the nickname Silicon Valley when dozens of *semiconductor* manufacturing companies sprouted and grew there.

The personal computer revolution began in the late 1970s, when Apple, Commodore, Tandy, and other companies introduced low-cost, microprocessor-based microcomputers as powerful as many of the room-sized computers that had come before. Personal computers, or PCs, are now common in offices, factories, homes, schools, and just about everywhere else. Microprocessors have found their way into countless other devices, from phones and game machines to robots and space stations. Every year brings more silicon surprises.

All of these digital innovations are possible because of Moore's law. In 1965 Gordon Moore, the chairman of chipmaker Intel, predicted that the number of transistors that can be packed into a silicon chip of the same price would roughly double every two years. Moore's Law has been widely misquoted. (The most common misstatement of Moore's Law is that computer power doubles every 18 months; Moore insists he never said that.) Moore's Law has been remarkably accurate through the years. This type of exponential growth has powerful implications over an extended period of time: a quantity that doubles every two years grows by a thousand in two decades—and by a million in four decades.

A microprocessor's performance doesn't necessarily double with its transistor count. Still, the phenomenal growth of computing power over the last few decades is largely due to the effects of Moore's Law. In fact, all of the five factors listed earlier in this section—reliability, size, speed, efficiency, and cost—have continually improved as engineers find ways to pack more transistors into those tiny slabs of silicon. (According to Intel, similar progress in the airline industry would have resulted in one-second trans-atlantic flights that cost about a penny!) Moore's law has also resulted in a steady increase in computer memory capacity. At the same time, technological improvements have resulted in exponential growth in hard disk capacity and network capacity. Software engineers have been in a continual race to keep up with the relentless progress on so many hardware fronts. And there's no reason to believe this exponential progress won't continue for a decade or more.

Computers Today: A Brief Taxonomy

I've come up with a set of rules that describe our **reactions to technologies**.

1. Anything that is in the world when you're born is **normal and ordinary** and is just a natural part of the **way the world works**.
2. Anything that's invented between when you're fifteen and thirty-five is **new and exciting and revolutionary** and you can probably get a **career** in it.
3. Anything invented after you're thirty-five is **against the natural order of things**.

—*Douglas Adams, author of* The Hitchhiker's Guide to the Galaxy

Thanks to an abundance of low-cost microprocessors, today's world is populated with an incredible variety of computers, each particularly well suited to specific tasks. We'll take a quick look at the major computer classes here, starting with the devices that most people don't think of as computers.

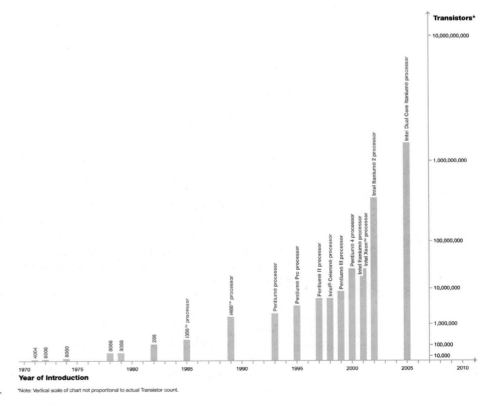

FIGURE 1.9 According to Moore's Law, the number of transistors per chip doubles every two years. Computer power continues to increase as a result.

*Note: Vertical scale of chart not proportional to actual Transistor count.

Embedded Systems

More than 90 percent of the world's microprocessors are hidden inside common household and electronic devices. A microprocessor used as a component of a larger system is called an embedded system. You can find embedded systems inside building thermostats, traffic lights, and all kinds of consumer goods: wristwatches, toys, game machines, stereos, digital video recorders, cars, and ovens. Just about anything that's powered by electricity—battery or house current—has become a candidate for a microprocessor implant.

The microprocessors inside embedded systems are, at their core, similar to those in general-purpose personal computers. But unlike their desktop cousins, these special-purpose machines typically have their programs etched in silicon so they can't be altered. When a program is immortalized on a silicon chip, it becomes known as firmware— a hybrid of hardware and software.

Personal Computers and Workstations

A personal computer (PC) is, generally speaking, designed to be used by one person at a time as a tool for enhancing productivity, creativity, or communication. PCs can be classified as desktop computers, workstations, and laptop computers.

As the name implies, a desktop computer is a personal computer designed to sit on a desk or table for extended periods of time. The most common type of desktop computer has several separate components, including a tower (containing the microprocessor and several other critical components), monitor, keyboard, mouse, and speakers. The tower, or system unit, doesn't really need to sit on the desktop, so it's commonly stashed under or beside the desk. Another type of desktop computer eliminates the tower by hiding all of its components inside the monitor casing. Together, a desktop computer's components may weigh 20 pounds or more. A desktop computer has one or more power cables connecting it to an electrical outlet.

FIGURE 1.10 Embedded computers are so common in today's world that they are all but invisible. The Independence iBOT Transporter is an intelligent wheelchair that allows people to climb up and down stairs, "stand up" on two wheels, and even stroll on the beach (left). Embedded computers in the Toyota Prius integrate the hybrid's gas engine and battery, optimizing gas mileage and providing constant feedback to the driver (middle). Toymaker Sega's 'A.M.P.' (Automated Music Personality) uses embedded computers to move on two wheels and play digital audio (right).

FIGURE 1.11 PCs today come in a variety of shapes and sizes.

A **workstation**—a high-end desktop computer with massive computing power—is used for computationally intensive interactive applications, such as large-scale scientific data analysis. As workstations become less expensive and desktop computers become more powerful, the line that separates them is becoming as much a marketing distinction as a technical one.

A **laptop computer** (sometimes called a **notebook computer**) is a personal computer designed with portability in mind. A typical laptop computer weighs less than seven pounds and relies on an internal battery to power its electronics. Extra-light notebooks are sometimes called **subnotebooks**. To keep size and weight down, manufacturers often leave out some components that would be standard equipment on desktop machines. For example, some laptops don't have built-in optical drives for playing or recording CDs or DVDs. Most have ports that enable external drives, keyboards, mice, and monitor screens, referred to as **peripherals**, to be attached with cables.

Most laptop computers are built around microprocessors similar to those that drive desktop models. But portability comes at a price—laptops generally cost more than comparable desktop machines. They're also more difficult to upgrade when newer hardware components become available.

Handheld Devices

Many computing devices are small enough to tuck into pockets and serve the needs of users who value mobility over a full-sized keyboard and screen. **Personal digital assistants (PDAs)** like the Palm and the Pocket PC were originally designed to serve as pocket-sized

FIGURE 1.12 These handheld digital devices are really multi-purpose computers, even though many are marketed as phones or PDAs.

digital address books and day planners that could share data with PCs, but they quickly evolved into multi-purpose handheld computers.

Today's digital mobile phones incorporate technology pioneered in PDAs. In fact, many people use their mobile phones as PDAs. Some devices, including the popular BlackBerry, add email features to basic PDA/phone functionality. Apple's iPod and other media players also share some of the information storage and retrieval capabilities of PDAs.

The rising star of the handheld computer market is the smart phone, combining features of PDAs, Internet access devices, phones, digital cameras, and media players. Apple's iPhone is the best-known smart phone, but we're likely to see dozens of high-powered devices in this expanding market.

Servers

A **server** is a computer that provides other computers connected to the network with access to data, programs, or other resources. For example, Web servers respond to requests for Web pages, database servers handle database queries, and print servers provide other computers access to a printer. Although just about any desktop computer can be used as a server, some computers are specifically designed with this purpose in mind. Servers may have faster processors, more memory, or faster network connections than typical desktop systems. Servers are often clustered together in groups to increase their processing power.

Mainframes and Supercomputers

Before the microcomputer revolution, most information processing was done on **mainframe computers**—room-sized machines with price tags to match. Today large organizations, such as banks and airlines, still use mainframes for big computing jobs. But their use of microprocessors means that today's

FIGURE 1.13 Rack-mounted servers don't need built-in displays because they can be remotely controlled through other computers.

mainframes are smaller and cheaper than their ancestors; a typical mainframe today might be the size of a refrigerator and cost around 50 thousand U.S. dollars. These industrial-strength computers are largely invisible to the general public because they're hidden away in climate-controlled rooms.

But the fact that you can't see them doesn't mean you don't use them. When you make an online airline reservation or deposit money in your bank account, a mainframe computer is involved in the transaction behind the scenes. Your travel agent and your bank teller might communicate with a mainframe using a computer **terminal** or **thin client**. A terminal is a combination keyboard and screen with little local processing power that transfers information to and from a mainframe computer or server; a smart client is similar, but typically has more on-board processing power than a bare-bones terminal. The mainframe or server might be in another room or even in another country halfway around the globe.

A mainframe computer can communicate with several users simultaneously through a technique called **timesharing**. For example, a timesharing system allows travel agents all over the country to make reservations using the same computer and the same flight information at the same time.

Timesharing also makes it possible for users with diverse computing needs to share expensive computing equipment. Many research scientists and engineers, for example, need more mathematical computing power than they can get from PCs. Their computing needs might require a powerful mainframe computer. A timesharing machine can simultaneously serve the needs of scientists and engineers in different departments working on a variety of projects.

Many researchers can't get the computing power they need from a mainframe computer; traditional "big iron" simply isn't fast enough for their calculation-intensive work, such as weather forecasting, telephone network design, simulated car crash testing, oil exploration, computer animation, and medical imaging. Power users with these special requirements need access to the fastest, most powerful computers made. These superfast, superpowerful computers are called **supercomputers**. Typically, these supercomputers are constructed out of thousands of microprocessors.

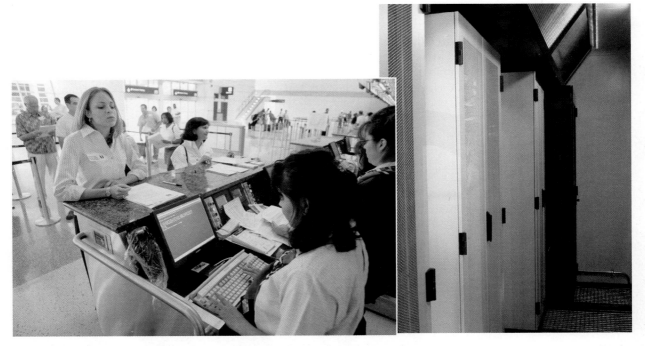

FIGURE 1.14 Terminals like the one in the photo on the left make it possible for ticket agents all over the world to send information to a single mainframe computer like the one shown on the right.

FIGURE 1.15 IBM BlueGene/L supercomputer.

Computer Connections: The Internet Revolution

The **grand design** keeps getting grander. A **global computer** is taking shape, and we're **all connected** to it.

—Stewart Brand, in The Media Lab

We've seen that microprocessors have worked their way into everything from our wristwatches to supercomputers. The microprocessor's impact has been magnified by the development of networks to connect many of those devices together. In the late 1960s, a group of visionary computer scientists and engineers, with financial backing from the U.S.

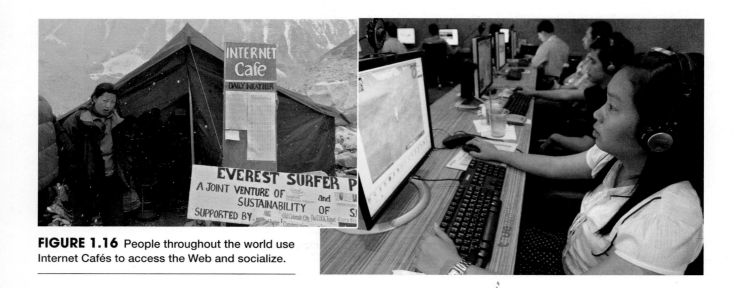

FIGURE 1.16 People throughout the world use Internet Cafés to access the Web and socialize.

government, began work on an experimental network for connecting computers. As the network evolved, it became known as the Internet.

As late as the 1980s, the Internet was still the domain of researchers, academics, and government officials, who used it to transfer files and exchange electronic mail (email) messages. The Internet wasn't designed for casual visitors; users had to know cryptic commands and codes that only a programmer could love.

But in the 1990s, Internet software suddenly took giant leaps forward in usability. The most significant breakthrough was the development of the World Wide Web (or just Web), a vast tract of the Internet accessible to just about anyone who could point to buttons on a computer screen. The led to the Internet's transformation from a text-only environment into a multimedia landscape incorporating pictures, animation, sounds, and video. Millions of people now connect to the Internet each day through browsers—programs like Internet Explorer and Firefox that, in effect, serve as navigable windows into the Web. Hypertext links on Web pages loosely tie together millions of Web pages created by diverse authors, making the Web into a massive, ever-changing global information storehouse.

Widespread email and Web use have led to astounding Internet growth, from a few million users in the mid-1990s to well over a billion today. In the late 1990s, Internet users tended to be young, educated, male, white, and middle-class. But as the Internet's population has grown, it has come to look more like the population at large. More than half of all active Internet users are now female. And while there are still some areas with no Internet access, those areas are becoming harder to find. In just about any city on Earth, you can rent time on a PC to check your email or explore the Web. The Internet is growing faster than television, radio, or any other communication technology that came before it. In the U.S. and many other countries, Internet connections will soon be as common as telephones and televisions.

Internet-based computing goes beyond traditional PCs. Video game consoles, including Microsoft's Xbox 360, Sony's PlayStation 3, and Nintendo's Wii, provide Internet access through TVs sets. Many smart phones and other handheld devices provide easy access to

FIGURE 1.17 This graph is a computer-generated "map" of the Internet—a visualization showing the complex network of interconnecting nodes. In this graph, colors represent geographic regions.

FIGURE 1.18 These people are playing a game with other Internet-connected gamers who might be anywhere in the world.

Digital Timeline

These Time covers represent our changing relationship to computers and digital technology. Notice that the beginning of each new "era" doesn't mean the end of the old ways of computing. Today we live in a world of institutional, personal, interpersonal, and collaborative computing.

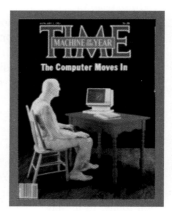

1950   1975

Institutional Computing Era

A few large, expensive, mainframe computers in climate-controlled room

Controlled by experts and specialists

Used mainly for data storage and calculation.

Personal Computing Era

Millions of small, inexpensive PCs in offices, schools, homes, and elsewhere

Controlled mostly by users

Used mostly for document creation, data storage, and calculation.

FIGURE 1.19 Evolution of computing styles.

1995

2005

Interpersonal Computing Era

Networks of interconnected computers in offices, homes, schools, and elsewhere

Controlled by users (clients) and network administrators

Used mostly for communication, document creation, data storage, and calculation

Collaborative Computing Era

Global network of PCs, handhelds, embedded computers, and other clients connected to a "cloud" of servers providing online applications, storage, and other services

Controlled by users, groups, and network administrators

Used mostly for collaborative creation, self expression, information sharing, communication, document creation, data storage, and calculation

Screen Test

Windows into the World of Web 2.0

Web 2.0 sites are built around contributions from Web users. Here are several popular examples.

FIGURE 1.20a MySpace, one of the most popular social networking sites, makes it easy for members to create personalized pages and link up with networks of friends.

FIGURE 1.20b Facebook is another popular social networking site. Facebook members can join groups, keep track of friends, play games with other members, and even write programs to enhance the Facebook experience.

FIGURE 1.20c Vimeo, like YouTube, is an online video hub where members share movies with each other and the rest of the world.

FIGURE 1.20d Users can easily add information to the vast collection of Google Maps, creating custom maps to share with others.

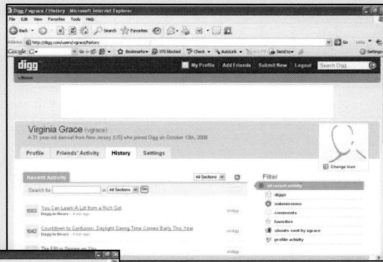

FIGURE 1.20e Blogger invites visitors to sign up, create blogs, and publish them on the Web.

FIGURE 1.20f Digg is one of many social bookmarking sites that makes it easy for members to help each other find the best of the Web by sharing their bookmarks.

FIGURE 1.20g StumbleUpon takes social bookmarking a step farther by helping users "stumble upon" interesting sites.

FIGURE 1.20h Second Life is a virtual world built mostly by members.

<u>Working the Web</u>

The Web is so easy to navigate that it's tempting just to dive in. But like a large library, the Web has more to offer if you learn a few tricks and techniques. Your goals should dictate your Web strategy.

➡ ***Get to know your search engines.*** Try several, choose your favorites, and learn the more advanced search features so you can minimize the time it takes to find what you're looking for. Search Engine Watch (www.searchenginewatch.com) is a good source of information about search engines.

➡ ***Be specific when you search.*** A search engine is more likely to give you the answer you're looking for if you search for "Epson USB scanner" than if you just type "scanner." An even better search would specify the scanner's model number.

➡ ***Know your plusses and minuses.*** In most search engines, you can use a plus sign to signify that you want pages that contain all words. For example, "+Alaska +oil +wildlife" searches pages that contain all three words. On the other hand, a minus sign (or hyphen) usually means "not." For example, "cancer -astrology" locates pages that contain "cancer" but not "astrology." When you use these symbols, you're using basic Boolean algebra—the logical basis of database queries.

➡ ***Be selective.*** As Robert P. Lipshutz wrote in *Mobile Computing*, "A few tidbits of accurate, timely and useful information are worth much more than a ream of random data, and bad information is worse than no information at all." When you're assessing a Web page's credibility, consider the author, the writing, the references, and the page sponsor's objectivity and reliability. Be aware that many search engines charge companies to be listed prominently in their directories and that some give top billing to their own services and partners.

➡ ***Triangulate.*** A traditional navigation technique for sailors, triangulation involves using two different perspectives to establish location. Xerox Chief Scientist John Seely Brown suggests that the same concept should be applied to the turbulent waters of the Web. Don't assume something is true because one Web source tells you so, unless you're sure the source is rock solid.

➡ ***Beware of urban legends.*** The Internet is an amazing information source, but it's also a tremendous source of misinformation. Web sites and email chain letters spread all kinds of "urban legends"—widely-believed stories that may be false, misleading, or sensationalized. Microsoft is giving money to people who forward this message; a prominent politician is secretly allied with terrorists; parking lot thieves use ether-laced perfume samples to render their victims unconscious—these stories are believed by many of the people who read about them in email messages or Web postings. Snopes.com debunks the most popular urban legends; check there if you read something that seems too good—or too fantastic—to be true.

➡ ***Organize your favorites.*** When you find a page worth revisiting, record it on your list of favorites or bookmarks. Browsers enable you to organize your lists by category—a strategy that's far more effective than just throwing them all in a digital shoebox. If you work on several different computers, consider using a Web-based bookmarking site like del.icio.us so you can access them from anywhere.

➡ ***Protect your privacy.*** Many Web servers keep track of all kinds of data about you: which site you visited before you came, where you clicked, and more. When you fill out forms to enter contests, order goods, or leave messages, you're providing more data for your hosts. Don't divulge any private information about yourself. And make sure you don't leave tracks that you're ashamed of as you hop around the Web.

➡ ***Be conscious of cookies and bugs.*** Many Web servers send cookies to your browser when you visit them or perform other actions. Cookies are tidbits of information about your session that can be read later; they enable Web sites to remember what they know about you between sessions. Cookies make personalized portals and customized shopping experiences possible. Unfortunately, cookies can also provide all kinds of possibilities for snoopers who want to know how you spend your time online. It's easy to set the browser's settings to refuse all cookies or ask you before accepting a cookie. Unfortunately, you can't easily turn off Web beacons (also called Web bugs)—one-pixel graphic images that are programmed to send information about your Web use back to their creators.

➡ ***Remember that online shopping isn't always better.*** Online shops and auctions can save you money, especially if you comparison shop. But when a product doesn't work as advertised, or when you have after-sale questions, a Web merchant might not be as helpful as a local shopkeeper. If your purchase will require person-to-person communication before or after the sale, you're probably better off patronizing a local merchant.

➡ ***Shop with care.*** The Web, like the nondigital world, has its share of less-than-honest merchants. Use services such as Bizrate (www.bizrate.com) to check out questionable merchants before you lay your digital money down. If you're dealing with a private party or an unknown merchant, consider using a transaction service, such as PayPal (www.paypal.com), to serve as a safe temporary depository for funds until the purchased product reaches you.

email and other Internet services. Future homes and businesses may have dozens of devices—computers, telephones, televisions, stereos, security systems, and even kitchen appliances—continually connected to the Internet, monitoring all kinds of data that can have an impact on our lives and our livelihoods.

The explosive growth of the Internet is largely fueled by the rapid expansion of commerce on the Web. The Internet economy generates hundreds of billions of dollars in revenues and millions of jobs each year. Online stores, auctions, and service bureaus have transformed the way people do business worldwide. Multiplayer games and virtual communities connect people all over the planet. Internet advertising supports a myriad of free services, from email services and search engines to radio stations and social networks.

But a surprising amount of Internet traffic is still noncommercial. Academics and researchers collect data and collaborate through global networks. Governments, nonprofits, political candidates, and activists communicate through the Web. Ad-hoc communities form to create not-for-profit encyclopedias, art galleries, and software.

The Internet is a work in progress—a work that seems to transform itself into something new every few years. And with each transformation it plays a more important role in the lives of people everywhere.

Into the Information Age

Every so often, civilization dramatically changes course. Events and ideas come together to transform radically the way people live, work, and think. Traditions fall

First we shape our **tools**, thereafter **they shape us**.

—*Marshall McLuhan*

by the wayside, common sense is turned upside down, and lives are thrown into turmoil until a new order takes hold. Humankind experiences a paradigm shift—a change in thinking that results in a new way of seeing the world. Major paradigm shifts take generations because individuals have trouble changing their assumptions about the way the world works.

Roughly ten thousand years ago, people learned to domesticate animals and grow their own food using plows and other agricultural tools. Over the following centuries, a paradigm shift occurred as people gave up nomadic hunter-gatherer lives to live and work on farms, exchanging goods and services in nearby towns. The agricultural age lasted until about two centuries ago, when advances in machine technology triggered what has come to be known as the Industrial Revolution.

The Industrial Revolution ushered in the industrial age. Factory work promised a higher material standard of living for a growing population . . . but not without a price. Families who had worked the land on sustainable farms for generations found it necessary to take low-wage factory jobs for survival. As work life became separate from home life, fathers were removed from day-to-day family life, and those mothers who didn't have to work in factories assumed the bulk of domestic responsibilities. As towns grew into cities, crime, pollution, and other urban problems grew with them.

The convergence of computer and network technology is at the heart of another paradigm shift—the shift from an industrial economy to an information economy. In the information age, most people earn their living working with words, numbers, and ideas. Instead of planting corn or making shoes, most of us shuffle bits in one form or another. As we roar through the information age, we're riding a wave of social change that rivals any that came before.

Living with Digital Technology

In less than a human lifetime, computers have evolved from massive, expensive, undependable calculators into (mostly) dependable, versatile machines that have worked their way into just about every nook and cranny of modern society. The pioneers who created and marketed the first computers did not foresee these spectacular advances in computer technology. Thomas Watson, Sr., the founding father of IBM, declared in 1943 that the world would not need more than five computers! And the early pioneers certainly couldn't have predicted the extraordinary social changes that resulted from the computer's rapid

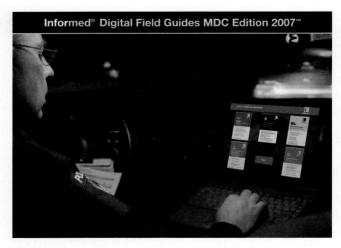

FIGURE 1.21 This onboard computer runs software designed to put critical emergency information at the fingertips of police officers, emergency medical technicians, firefighters, and other first responders.

evolution, not to mention the interconnections among those computers as networks encompass the globe. In the time of UNIVAC, who could have imagined laptop PCs, iPhones, PlayStations, Google, YouTube, eBay, robot moon rovers, or laser-guided "smart bombs"?

Technological breakthroughs encourage further technological change, so we can expect the rate of change to continue to increase in coming decades. It's just a matter of time, and not very much time, before today's state-of-the-art PCs look as primitive as ENIAC looks to us—and before the Web we know seems as quaint as a Model T Ford. Similarly, today's high-tech society just hints at a future world that we haven't yet begun to imagine.

What do you really need to know about digital technology today? The remaining chapters of this book provide answers to that question by looking at the technology on three levels: explanations, applications, and implications.

Explanations: Clarifying Technology

You don't need to be a computer scientist to coexist with computers and networks. But your encounters with digital technology will make more sense if you understand a few basic concepts. Computer hardware and software details change every few years. And the Internet is evolving even faster; some suggest that one normal year is equal to several "Internet years," a phrase coined by Intel co-founder Andy Grove. But most of the underlying concepts remain constant as computers and networks evolve. If you understand the basics, you'll find that it's a lot easier to keep up with the changes.

FIGURE 1.22 Smart bombs, such as those employed in both Gulf wars, helped the U.S. armed forces target enemy installations with greater accuracy than was possible in earlier wars.

Applications: Digital Technology in Action

Application programs, also known simply as **applications**, are the software tools that transform general-purpose computers, from PDAs and smart phones to PCs and mainframes, into special-purpose tools useful for meeting particular needs. Most applications are designed to be stored and run on particular computers. *Web applications* are stored on the Web so they can be accessed and used by multiple computers with Internet access. Many computer applications in science, government, business, and the arts are far too specialized and technical to be of use or interest to people outside the field. And many operate almost invisibly, taking care of business without demanding our attention. On the other hand, some applications are general-purpose tools with mass consumer appeal.

Regardless of your background or aspirations, you can almost certainly benefit from knowing a little about these applications:

■ *Network applications.* A network application is a door into a world of online communication, communities, and commerce. Email, instant messaging, Web browsing,

FIGURE 1.23 PC applications make it possible for people to work in ways that aren't possible otherwise. This marine biologist (left) uses a laptop computer to record research notes and analyze data in the field. This videographer (top right) can capture and edit footage for a music video using portable gear. This blogger (bottom right) can provide timely news and commentary to a worldwide audience.

Web publishing, social networks just scratch the surface of the possibilities that a networked computer offers. For many people, a PC is of no value when it's disconnected from the Internet.

- *Word processing and desktop publishing.* Word processing is a critical skill for anyone who communicates in writing—on paper, via documents, or on the Web. Desktop-publishing software can transform written words into polished, visually exciting publications.
- *Spreadsheets and other number-crunching applications.* In many businesses, the spreadsheet is the PC application that pays the rent—or at least calculates it. If you work with numbers, spreadsheets and statistical software can help you turn those numbers into insights.
- *Databases.* Electronic record-keeping databases reign supreme in the world of mainframes and servers. Of course, databases are widely used on PCs, too. Even if you don't have database software on a PC, you can apply database-searching skills to find just about anything on the Internet.
- *Graphics and image processing.* Computers make it possible to produce and manipulate all kinds of graphics, including charts, drawings, digital photographs—even realistic 3-D animation. As graphics tools become more accessible, visual communication skills become more important for all of us.
- *Audio, video, and multimedia.* Most PCs and many handheld devices and set-top boxes can play music, videos, and games. But audio and video applications can also open up creative possibilities for all kinds of people, from amateur podcasters to professional filmmakers. Multimedia documents and Web sites, by combining graphics, video, audio, and interactivity, open up all kinds of opportunities for entertainment and information exploration.
- *Programming and customized problem solving.* People often use computers to solve problems. Most people use applications written by professional programmers,

but you may want to use computers to solve problems for which off-the-shelf applications or Web applications don't exist. Programming languages allow you to build custom application programs. Many computer users find that their machines become more versatile and valuable when they learn a little about programming.

■ *Artificial intelligence.* Artificial intelligence is the branch of computer science that explores the use of computers in tasks that require intelligence, imagination, and insight—tasks that have traditionally been performed by people rather than machines. Until recently, artificial intelligence was mostly an academic discipline—a field of study reserved for researchers and philosophers. But that research is paying off today with commercial applications that exhibit intelligence, from basic speech recognition to sophisticated expert systems that can solve problems normally requiring the knowledge of a human expert.

Implications: Social and Ethical Issues

Digital technology is transforming the world rapidly and irreversibly. Jobs that existed for hundreds of years are being eliminated by automation, while new careers are built on emerging technology. Start-up businesses create new markets overnight, while older companies struggle to keep pace with "Internet time." Instant worldwide communication changes the way businesses work and challenges the role of governments. Computers routinely save lives in hospitals, keep space flights on course, and predict the weekend weather.

More than any other recent technology, computers and networks are responsible for profound changes in our society. To recognize their impact, all we need to do is imagine a world without them, as we did at the beginning of the chapter. Of course, computer scientists and computer engineers are not responsible for all the technological turbulence. Developments in fields as diverse as genetic engineering, medicine, and atomic physics among others contribute to the ever-increasing rate of social change. But researchers in all these fields depend on computers and the Internet to produce their work and communicate.

Although it's exciting to consider the opportunities arising from advances in artificial intelligence, multimedia, robotics, and other cutting-edge technologies of the electronic revolution, it's just as important to pay attention to the potential risks. Here's a sampling of the kinds of social and ethical issues we'll confront in this book:

FIGURE 1.24 This robot security guard protects a museum from vandals and thieves. But does it threaten the jobs of human security guards?

■ *The threat to personal privacy posed by large databases and computer networks.* When you use a credit card, buy an airline ticket, place a phone call, visit your doctor, send an email message, or explore the Web, you're leaving a trail of personal information in one or more computers. Who owns that information? Is it OK for the business or organization that collected the information to share it with others or make it public? Do you have the right to check its accuracy and change it if it's wrong? Do laws protecting individual privacy rights place undue burdens on businesses and governments?

■ *The hazards of high-tech crime and the difficulty of keeping data secure.* Even if you trust the institutions and businesses that collect data about you, you can't be sure that data will remain secure in their computer systems. Computer crime is at an all-time high, and law enforcement officials are having a difficult time keeping it under control. How can society protect itself from information thieves and high-tech vandals? How can lawmakers write laws about technology that they are just beginning to understand? What kinds of personal risk do you face as a result of computer crime?

■ *The difficulty of defining and protecting intellectual property in an all-digital age.* Software programs, musical recordings, videos, and books can be difficult and expensive to create. But in our digital age, all of these can easily be copied. What rights do the creators of intellectual property have? Is a teenager who copies music files from the Web a computer criminal? What about a shopkeeper who sells pirated copies of Microsoft Office for $10? Or a student who posts a clip from *The Daily Show* on his Web site? Or a musician who uses a two-second sample from a Beatles song in an electronic composition?

■ *The threat of automation and the dehumanization of work.* Computers and the Internet fueled unprecedented economic growth in the last decade of the twentieth century, producing plenty of new jobs for workers with the right skills. But the new information-based economy has cost many workers—especially older workers—their jobs and their dignity. Many workers today find that their jobs involve little more than tending to machines—and being monitored by bosses with high-tech surveillance devices. As machines replace people in the workplace and global networks force workers to compete for jobs in a worldwide market, what rights do displaced workers have? Does a worker's right to privacy outweigh an employer's right to read employee email or monitor worker actions? What is the government's role in the protection of worker rights in the high-tech workplace?

■ *The abuse of information as a tool of political and economic power.* The computer age has produced an explosion of information, and most of that information is concentrated in corporate and government computers. The emergence of low-cost computers and the Internet makes it possible for more people to access information and the power that comes with that information. But the majority of the people on the planet have never made a phone call, let alone used a computer. Will the digital divide between information technology "haves" and "have nots" leave the "have nots" behind? Do information-rich people and countries have a responsibility to share technology and information with the information-poor?

FIGURE 1.25 Though somewhat controversial, cochlear implants use modern technology to help the profoundly deaf hear.

FIGURE 1.26 What impact will computer technology have on traditional cultures that evolved for thousands of years without computers?

Working Wisdom

<u>Computer Ethics</u>

Ethics is moral philosophy—philosophical thinking about right and wrong. Many people base their ethical beliefs on religious rules, such as the Ten Commandments or the Buddhist Eightfold Path. Others use professional codes such as the doctor's Hippocratic oath, which includes the often quoted "First do no harm." Still others use personal philosophies with principles like "It's OK if a jury of observers would approve." But in today's changing world, deciding how to apply the rules isn't always easy. Sometimes the rules don't seem to apply directly, and sometimes they contradict each other. (How should you "Honor thy father" if you learn that he's using the home computer to embezzle money from his employer? Is it OK to allow a friend who's broke to borrow your Microsoft Office CD for a required class project?) These kinds of *moral dilemmas* are central questions in discussions of ethics. Information technology poses moral dilemmas related to everything from sampling music to reporting a coworker's sexist screen saver or racist email.

Computer ethics can't be reduced to a handful of rules; the gray areas are always going to require thought and judgment. But principles and guidelines can help to focus thinking and refine judgments when dealing with technology-related moral dilemmas. The Association for Computing Machinery (ACM) Code of Ethics, reprinted in the appendix of this book, is the most widely known code of conduct specifically for computer professionals. The ACM Code is worth understanding and applying even if you don't plan to be a "computer professional." Who shouldn't "Contribute to society and human well-being" or "Honor confidentiality"? But these principles take on new meaning in an age of Facebook and eBay.

Here are some other guidelines that might help you to decide how to "do the right thing" when faced with ethical dilemmas at school, at work, or at home:

➡ **Know the rules and the law.** Many laws, and many organizational rules, are reflections of moral principles. For example, almost everyone agrees that plagiarism—presenting somebody else's work as your own—is wrong. It's also a serious violation of rules in most schools. And if the work is copied without permission, plagiarism can become copyright infringement, a serious legal offense even if the work is not explicitly copyrighted.

➡ **Don't assume that it's OK if it's legal.** Our legal system doesn't define what's right and wrong. How can it when we don't all agree on morality? The law is especially lax in areas related to information technology because the technology changes too fast for lawmakers to keep up. It's ultimately up to each individual to act with conscience.

➡ **Think scenarios.** If you're choosing between different actions, think about what might happen as a result of your actions. If you suspect your employer is falsifying spreadsheets to get around environmental regulations, what's likely to happen if you snoop around on his computer and blow the whistle on him? What's likely to happen if you don't? What are your other alternatives?

➡ **When in doubt, talk it out.** Discuss your concerns with people you trust—ideally, people with wisdom and experience dealing with similar situations. For example, if you're unsure about the line between getting computer help from a friend and cheating on homework, ask an instructor.

➡ **Make yourself proud.** How would you feel if you saw your actions on YouTube, cable news, the *New York Times*, or your family's hometown newspaper? If you'd be embarrassed or ashamed, you probably should choose another course of action.

➡ **Remember the golden rule:** *Do unto others as you would have them do unto you.* This universal principle is central to every major spiritual tradition, and it is amazingly versatile. One example: Before you download that bootleg MP3 file of that up-and-coming singer, think about how you'd feel about bootleggers if you were the singer.

➡ **Take the long view.** It's all too easy to be blinded by the rapid-fire rewards of the Internet and computer technology. Consider this guiding principle from a Native American tradition: In every deliberation, consider the impact of your decision on the next seven generations. Musician and digital artist Brian Eno coined the phrase "the long now" to represent this kind of future-oriented decision making. (Visit longnow.org for more on the Long Now Foundation that Eno co-founded.)

➡ **Do your part.** In a democratic society, we're responsible for our own actions. But as citizens and voters, we're also responsible for making sure our representative government is acting ethically. Is the government using technology in ways that we can be proud of? Is our country following the golden rule in its relationships with other countries? Is it taking the long view when dealing with information technology, natural resources, national debt, and education policies? If not, it's up to us to do something about it. And thanks to the Internet, it's never been easier to take an active role in our democratic process.

- *The emergence of biodigital technology.* Today thousands of people walk around with computer chips embedded in their bodies, helping them overcome disabilities and lead normal lives. At the same time, researchers are attempting to develop computers that use biology, rather than electronics, as their underlying technology. As the line between organism and machine blurs, what happens to our vision of ourselves? What are the limits of our creative powers, and what are our responsibilities in using those powers?
- *The dangers of dependence on complex technology.* Every once in a while, a massive power blackout, Internet virus, or database crash reminds us how much we have come to depend on this far-from-foolproof digital technology. Are we, as a society, addicted to computer technology? Should we question new technological innovations before we embrace them? Can we build a future in which technology never takes precedence over humanity?

History of the Future

Today's technology raises fascinating and difficult questions. But these questions pale in comparison to the ones we'll have to deal with as the technology evolves in the coming years. Imagine . . .

It's almost impossible to know **which grain of sand** is going to start an **avalanche**.

—*Musician and digital artist Brian Eno*

> *You wake up to the sound of your radio playing songs and news stories that match your personal interest profile. The newscaster is talking about the hacker uprising that has crippled China's infrastructure, but you have other things on your mind.*

FIGURE 1.27 The "Meteor" subway line of the Paris Metro is completely automated. The trains have no drivers.

Today's the day of your big trip. You're looking forward to spending some time in the same room with Tony, your Italian lab partner. Over the past few months you've become close friends, working and chatting by videophone, conquering virtual reality games together, and creating truly terrible music in those late-night long-distance jam sessions. Still, there's no substitute for being in the same space, especially after Tony's accident. Tony says that the chip implant and the prosthetic hand will make him almost as good as new, but you know he can use some moral support while he recovers.

On the way to the airport, your electric car's computer pipes up, "Ben's Bagels ahead on the right is running a special on cinnamon bagels. Nobody is at the drive-up window, so you can pick up a bagel and still make your flight."

"I thought I told you already: I don't like cinnamon bagels," you grumble.

Noting your annoyance, the car responds, "Sorry. I knew you didn't like cinnamon buns. No more cinnamon bagel ads or notifications, either." You wonder if the computer's spam and ad filter needs fixing, or you just forgot to tell it about your bagel preferences. Before you can ask, the computer announces that the next freeway entrance is blocked because of an accident. It suggests another entrance and talks you through the traffic to that entrance.

Once you get on the freeway, you join the "auto train" in the fast lane. Your car, now controlled by a network computer, races along at exactly the same speed as the car that's a few feet in front of it. You take this opportunity to ask your phone, "Which bus do I take to get from the Rome airport to Tony's place?" The phone responds, "Bus 64. Watch out for pickpockets." You shiver when you remember what happened the last time you lost your wallet; it took months to undo the damage from that identity thief.

At the airport, you step out of the car near the shuttle station, remove your suitcase, and tell the car to park itself in the long-term lot. It says "Goodbye" and glides away.

On the shuttle you use your phone to try to learn a few Italian phrases. You say "Translate Italian" then, "I would like to convert dollars into Euros." The phone responds, "Vorrei convertire i dollari in Euro," into your tiny wireless earpiece. You know the phone can translate for you on the fly, but you'd like to be able to say a few things without its help.

At the security station, you insert your passport into the slot, put your hand on the scanner, and put your face into a shielded enclosure. After the system confirms your identity by taking your handprint and scanning your retinas, it issues a boarding pass, baggage claim slip, and routing tag. Under the watchful eye of the security guard, you attach the routing tag to your bag and place it on the conveyer belt leading to the baggage handling area. You notice that a nearby passenger is being vigorously questioned, and you hope that she's not the victim of yet another security system error.

You realize you forgot to pack your jet lag medication. You enter the airport gift shop and insert your medical ID card under the pharmacy scanner. A dispenser issues a vial of pills that should work well with your genetic structure. You also download a best-selling book into your phone for the trip. As you leave the store, a sensor detects your two purchases. Your phone tells you that $33.97 has just been deducted from your account and asks if you want to know the remaining balance. You don't answer; you're trying to remember the last time you bought something from a human cashier.

This isn't far-fetched fantasy. Early versions of most of the devices in this story already exist. And exponential growth in computing power (remember Moore's Law?) makes it likely that you'll see similar technology in your everyday life in just a few years.

For better and for worse, we will be coexisting with information technology until death do us part. As with any relationship, a little understanding can go a long way. The remaining chapters of this book will help you gain the understanding you need to survive and prosper on our digital planet.

FIGURE 1.28 The Kurzweil KNFB Mobile Reader makes it possible for this blind woman to read signs, menus, and money.

Inventing the FUTURE

Tomorrow Never Knows

In the short term, the impact of new technologies like the Internet will be **less than the hype would suggest**. But in the long term, it will be **vastly larger than we can imagine today**.

—*Paul Saffo, technology forecaster*

There is no denying the importance of the future, but the future isn't always easy to see. In 1877, when Thomas Edison invented the phonograph, he thought of it as an office dictating machine and lost interest in it; recorded music did not become popular until 21 years later. A 1900 Mercedes-Benz study estimated that worldwide demand for cars would not exceed 1 million, primarily because of the limited number of available chauffeurs. When the Wright brothers offered their invention to the U.S. government and the British Royal Navy, they were told airplanes had no future in the military. In 1977 Ken Olson, the founder of Digital Equipment Company, said, "There is no reason anyone would want a computer in their home."

History is full of stories of people who couldn't imagine the impact of new technology. Technological advances are hard to foresee, and it is even harder to predict the impact that technology will have on society. Who could have predicted in 1950 the profound effects, both positive and negative, television would have on our world?

Computer scientist Alan Kay has said, "The best way to predict the future is to invent it." Kay's visionary research at XEROX more than three decades ago defined many of the essential qualities of today's PCs. Of course, we can't all invent world-changing tools. But Kay says there are other ways to predict the future. For example, we can look in the research labs today to see the commercial products of the next few years. Of course, many researchers work behind carefully guarded doors, and research often takes surprising turns.

A third way is to look at products from the past and see what made them succeed. According to Kay, "There are certain things about human beings that if you remove, they wouldn't be human any more. For instance, we have to communicate with others or we're not humans. So every time someone has come up with a communications amplifier, it has succeeded the previous technology." The pen, the printing press, the telephone, the television, the PC, the smart phone, and the Internet are all successful communication amplifiers. What's next?

Kay says we can also predict the future by recognizing the four phases of any technology or media business: hardware, software, service, and way of life.

➡ *Hardware.* Inventors and engineers start the process by developing new hardware. But whether it's a television set, a PC, or a global communication network, the hardware is of little use without software.

➡ *Software.* The next step is software development. Television programs, sound recordings, video games, databases, and Web pages are examples of software that give value to hardware products.

➡ *Service.* Innovative hardware and clever software aren't likely to take hold unless they serve human needs. Computer and Internet companies that focus on serving their customers are generally the most successful.

➡ *Way of life.* The final phase happens when the technology becomes so entrenched that people don't think about it anymore; they notice only if it isn't there. We seldom think of pencils as technological tools. They're part of our way of life, so much so that we'd have trouble getting along without them. Similarly, the electric motor, which was once a major technological breakthrough, is now all but invisible; we use dozens of motors every day without thinking about them. Computers are clearly headed in that direction.

Kay's four phases of predicting the future don't provide a foolproof crystal ball, but they can serve as a framework for thinking about tomorrow's technology. In the remaining chapters of this book, we'll examine trends and innovations that will shape future computer hardware and software. Then we look at how this technology will serve users as it eventually disappears into our way of life. ～

FIGURE 1.29 The 1930 movie *Just Imagine* presented a bold, if not quite accurate, vision of the future; here Maureen O'Sullivan sits in her personal flying machine.

The Future Is Now? Pretty Soon, at Least   *by John Tierney*

Ray Kurzweil is famous for many inventions: reading machines for the blind, digital pianos with spectacularly realistic sound, speech recognition products, and more. But he's becoming even more famous for his unabashedly optimistic predictions about a future in which technology solves many of the most difficult problems we face today. This slightly condensed article from the June 3, 2008, New York Times examines Kurzweil's bold view of the future.

Before we get to Ray Kurzweil's plan for upgrading the "suboptimal software" in your brain, let me pass on some of the cheery news he brought to the World Science Festival last week in New York.

Do you have trouble sticking to a diet? Have patience. Within 10 years, Dr. Kurzweil explained, there will be a drug that lets you eat whatever you want without gaining weight.

Worried about greenhouse gas emissions? Have faith. Solar power may look terribly uneconomical at the moment, but with the exponential progress being made in nanoengineering, Dr. Kurzweil calculates that it'll be cost-competitive with fossil fuels in just five years, and that within 20 years all our energy will come from clean sources.

Are you depressed by the prospect of dying? Well, if you can hang on another 15 years, your life expectancy will keep rising every year faster than you're aging. And then, before the century is even half over, you can be around for the Singularity, that revolutionary transition when humans and/or machines start evolving into immortal beings with ever-improving software.

At least that's Dr. Kurzweil's calculation. It may sound too good to be true, but even his critics acknowledge he's not your ordinary sci-fi fantasist. He is a futurist with a track record and enough credibility for the *National Academy of Engineering to publish* his sunny forecast for *solar energy.*

He makes his predictions using what he calls the Law of Accelerating Returns, a concept he illustrated at the festival with a history of his own inventions for the blind. In 1976, when he pioneered a device that could scan books and read them aloud, it was the size of a washing machine.

Two decades ago he predicted that "early in the 21st century" blind people would be able to read anything anywhere using a handheld device. In 2002 he narrowed the arrival date to 2008. On Thursday night at the festival, he pulled out a new gadget the size of a cellphone, and when he pointed it at the brochure for the science festival, it had no trouble reading the text aloud.

This invention, Dr. Kurzweil said, was no harder to anticipate than some of the predictions he made in the late 1980s, like the explosive growth of the Internet in the 1990s and a computer chess champion by 1998. (He was off by a year—Deep Blue's chess victory came in 1997.)

"Certain aspects of technology follow amazingly predictable trajectories," he said, and showed a graph of computing power starting with the first electromechanical machines more than a century ago. At first the machines' power doubled every three years; then in midcentury the doubling came every two years (the rate that inspired Moore's Law); now it takes only about a year.

Dr. Kurzweil has other graphs showing a century of exponential growth in the number of patents issued, the spread of telephones, the money spent on education. One graph of technological changes goes back millions of years, starting with stone tools and accelerating through the development of agriculture, writing, the Industrial Revolution and computers.

Now, he sees biology, medicine, energy and other fields being revolutionized by information technology. His graphs already show the beginning of exponential progress in nanotechnology, in the ease of gene sequencing, in the resolution of brain scans. With these new tools, he says, by the 2020s we'll be adding computers to our brains and building machines as smart as ourselves.

This serene confidence is not shared by neuroscientists like Vilayanur S. Ramachandran. It might be possible to create a thinking, empathetic machine, Dr. Ramachandran said, but it might prove too difficult to reverse-engineer the brain's circuitry because it evolved so haphazardly.

"My colleague *Francis Crick* used to say that God is a hacker, not an engineer," Dr. Ramachandran said. "You can do reverse engineering, but you can't do reverse hacking."

Some experts endorse Dr. Kurzweil's belief that conscious, intelligent beings can be created, but most think it will take more than a few decades.

He is accustomed to this sort of pessimism and readily acknowledges how complicated the brain is. But if experts in neurology and artificial intelligence (or solar energy or medicine) don't buy his optimistic predictions, he says, that's because exponential upward curves are so deceptively gradual at first.

"Scientists imagine they'll keep working at the present pace," he told me after his speech. "They make linear extrapolations from the past. When it took years to sequence the first 1 percent of the human genome, they worried they'd never finish, but they were right on schedule for an exponential curve. If you reach 1 percent and keep doubling your growth every year, you'll hit 100 percent in just seven years."

Discussion Questions

1. Which of Kurzweil's predictions to you agree with, and which do you doubt? Why?

2. Can you think of other examples of the Law of Accelerating Returns in the past or present?

Summary

Mechanical computing devices date back hundreds of years, but the first real computers were developed during the 1940s. Computers have evolved at an incredible pace since those early years, becoming consistently smaller, faster, more efficient, more reliable, and less expensive. At the same time, people have devised all kinds of interesting and useful ways to put computers to use in work and play.

Computers today come in all shapes and sizes, with specific types being well suited for particular jobs. Mainframe computers and supercomputers provide more power and speed than smaller desktop machines, but they are expensive to purchase and operate. Timesharing makes it possible for many users to work simultaneously at terminals connected to these large computers. At the other end of the spectrum, personal computers and handheld devices provide computing power for those of us who don't need a mainframe's capabilities. Microprocessors aren't just used in general-purpose computers; they're embedded in appliances, automobiles, and a rapidly growing list of other products.

Connecting to a network enhances the value and power of a computer; it can share resources with other computers and facilitate electronic communication with other computer users. Some networks are local to a particular building or business; others connect users at remote geographic locations. The Internet is a collection of networks that connects the computers of businesses, public institutions, and individuals around the globe. Email provides hundreds of millions of people with near-instant worldwide communication capabilities. With browsing software, those same Internet users have access to billions of pages on the World Wide Web. This is a distributed network of interlinked multimedia documents. Although it started as a tool for scientists, researchers, and scholars, the has quickly become a vital center for entertainment and commerce. In the last few years there's been a trend toward Web 2.0 sites—sites created by their users—social networks, media sharing sites, blogs, and more.

Computers and information technology have changed the world rapidly and irreversibly. Our civilization is in a transition from an industrial economy to an information economy, and this paradigm shift is having an impact on the way we live and work. Computers and information technology are central to our information age, and we can easily list dozens of ways in which computers now make our lives easier and more productive. PC and Web applications, from word processing and email to multimedia and database applications, have become essential tools for people everywhere. Emerging technologies, such as artificial intelligence, offer promise for future applications. Devices that were the stuff of science fiction novels 50 years ago are appearing on store shelves. At the same time, computers threaten our privacy, our security, and perhaps our way of life. As we rush into the information age, our future depends on computers and on our ability to understand and use them in productive, positive ways.

Key Terms

agricultural age .... (p. 21)
application program
   (application)......................(p. 22)
browers ....(p. 15)
desktop computer ....(p. 10)
digital divide............................(p. 25)
electronic mail (email) ....(p. 15)
embedded system ....(p. 10)
firmware ....(p. 10)
hypertext link..........................(p. 15)
industrial age ....(p. 21)
Industrial Revolution..............(p. 21)
information age ....(p. 21)

integrated circuit........................(p. 8)
Internet ....(p. 15)
laptop computer.......................(p. 11)
mainframe computer ....(p. 12)
microprocessor ....(p. 8)
Moore's law ....(p. 8)
network....................................(p. 14)
notebook computer................ (p. 11)
paradigm shift..........................(p. 21)
peripherals ....(p. 11)
personal computer (PC)............(p. 8)
personal digital assistant
   (PDA)..................................(p. 11)

server ....(p. 12)
silicon chip ....(p. 8)
Silicon Valley............................(p. 8)
subnotebooks ....(p. 11)
supercomputer ....(p. 13)
terminal....................................(p. 13)
thin client.................................(p. 13)
timesharing .... (p. 13)
transistor...................................(p. 7)
workstation ....(p. 11)
World Wide Web
   (Web) ....(p. 15)

Interactive Activities

1. The *Tomorrow's Technology and You* Web site, **www.pearsonhighered.com/beekman**, contains self-test exercises related to this chapter. Follow the instructions for taking a quiz. After you've completed your quiz, you can email the results to your instructor.

2. The Web site also contains open-ended discussion questions called Internet Exercises. Discuss one or more of the Internet Exercises questions at the section for this chapter.

True or False

1. If all computers stopped working, people would use their phones much more to get necessary information.

2. Because it can be programmed to perform various tasks, the PC is a general-purpose tool, not a specialized device with one use.

3. One of the first computers helped the Nazis crack Allied codes during World War II.

4. According to Moore's law, the power of a silicon chip of the same price would double about every 8 years for at least 100 years.

5. A PDA (personal digital assistant) is a software program for managing calendars, contacts, and to-do lists.

6. Timesharing technology allows one person to use several computers at the same time.

7. A smart phone is, in essence, a handheld computer with communication capabilities.

8. More than 90 percent of the world's microprocessors are hidden inside common household and electronic devices.

9. Only about half of the world's countries have Internet connectivity.

10. Computer technology, like any technology, carries significant risks to individuals and society.

Multiple Choice

1. When did the World Wide Web become available?
   a. 1960s
   b. 1970s
   c. 1980s
   d. 1990s
   e. 2000s

2. When did Web 2.0 sites like MySpace and Flickr become popular?
   a. 1960s
   b. 1970s
   c. 1980s
   d. 1990s
   e. 2000s

3. For which of the following do we depend on computer technology?
   a. Controlling our money and banking systems
   b. Keeping our transportation systems running smoothly
   c. Making many of our household appliances and gadgets work properly
   d. All of the above
   e. None of the above

4. PCs are extremely versatile tools because they can accept instructions from a wide variety of
   a. hardware.
   b. software.
   c. network connections.
   d. PDAs.
   e. semiconductors.

5. Many of the most important developments in the earliest days of the computer were motivated by what event?
   a. World War I
   b. The Great Depression

   c. World War II
   d. The first San Francisco earthquake
   e. The launch of Sputnik by the USSR

6. Which of these technologies was developed first?
   a. The PC
   b. The microprocessor
   c. Email
   d. The World Wide Web
   e. The mainframe computer

7. Which of these technologies was developed most recently?
   a. The PC
   b. The microprocessor
   c. Email
   d. The World Wide Web
   e. The mainframe computer

8. Which represents the order in which computer circuitry evolved through three generations of technology?
   a. Silicon chip, vacuum tube, transistor
   b. Vacuum tube, silicon chip, transistor
   c. Transistor, vacuum tube, silicon chip
   d. Vacuum tube, transistor, silicon chip
   e. Transistor, silicon chip, vacuum tube

9. As computers evolved, they
   a. grew in size.
   b. became faster.
   c. consumed more electricity.
   d. became less reliable.
   e. cost more.

10. When a bank clerk transfers money into your account, where is the actual transaction probably being processed and stored?
    a. A supercomputer
    b. A mainframe computer

c. A terminal
d. An embedded computer
e. A Web page

11. Some computers are able to maintain simultaneous connections to many users through a technique called
    a. nanolinking.
    b. hot syncing.
    c. spider sycing.
    d. parallel processing.
    e. timesharing.

12. Silicon Valley is a nickname for
    a. the region in California that contains most of the world's silicon mines.
    b. the part of the Internet where most of the traffic is channeled through silicon cables.
    c. the part of a computer that's used to transport data from the hard drive to the processor.
    d. the dip in productivity on a timeline that inevitably happens when new computer technology is introduced.
    e. the area in Northern California where many of the most important digital technology companies are based.

13. Which of these principles is NOT a useful guideline for making ethical decisions related to technology?
    a. The Golden Rule.
    b. Take the long view.
    c. Think about how you would feel if your actions were widely viewed as a YouTube video.
    d. If it's legal, it's ethical.
    e. If you have any doubts, discuss them with knowledgeable people before taking action.

14. An application program is
    a. a program that lets users create new applications.
    b. a program that lets users apply for jobs.
    c. a program that lets someone use a computer for a particular purpose.
    d. a program that updates the operating system of a computer.
    e. none of the above.

15. Artificial intelligence is
    a. the use of artificial stimulants to improve intelligence.
    b. the use of computers in tasks that require intelligence.
    c. the attempt to reduce all human intelligence to rules.
    d. the result of Google's vast database of knowledge.
    e. the use of robots to write computer programs.

Review Questions

1. List several ways you interact with hidden computers in your daily life.

2. What is the most important difference between a computer and a calculator?

3. How are computers today similar to those from World War II? How are they different?

4. The way people use the Internet has changed since the early days. How?

5. What is the difference between a mainframe and a microcomputer? What are the advantages and disadvantages of each?

6. What kinds of computer applications require the speed and power of a supercomputer? Give some examples.

7. What types of computers typically employ timesharing?

8. What types of applications are particularly well suited for handheld devices? What common applications are particularly well suited for PCs?

9. Why is it important for people to know about and understand computers?

10. Describe some of the benefits and drawbacks of the information age.

Discussion Questions

1. What do people mean when they talk about the information age? Why is it a societal paradigm shift?

2. Do you expect another "age" to follow the information age? What do you think it might be?

3. The Digital Time Line in this chapter divided the information age into four computer-related eras: the Institutional Computing Era, the Personal Computing Era, the Interpersonal Computing Era, and the Collaborative Computing Era. Talk about each of these eras and speculate about what the next era might be.

4. How would the world be different today if a wrinkle in time transported a state-of-the-art notebook computer, complete with software, peripherals, and manuals, onto the desk of Woodrow Wilson? Adolf Hitler? Albert Einstein?

5. The automobile and the television set are two examples of technological inventions that changed our society drastically in ways that were not anticipated by their inventors. Outline several positive and negative effects of each of these two inventions. Do you think, on

balance, that we are better off as a result of these machines? Why or why not? Now repeat this exercise for the computer and the Internet.

6. Over a period of just a few years, digital music downloads, both legal and illegal, have replaced CDs and records as the most popular music source. What were the results (both good and bad) of the download revolution in music?

7. Should all students be required to take at least one computer course? Why or why not? If so, what should that course cover?

8. Computerphobia—fear or anxiety related to computers —is a common malady among people today— especially people who grew up before computers were everywhere. What do you think causes it? What, if anything, should be done about it?

9. How much privacy are you willing to give up in airports to reduce the chance of an airplane being hijacked?

10. Suppose a company were marketing a tiny microprocessor designed to be implanted in your brain behind your right ear. The tiny device is designed to help you remember people's names. It is particularly popular among people who work with the public. You plan to have a career in sales. Would you consider getting such an implant? Why or why not? What questions would you want to have answered before you agreed to have the device implanted in your brain?

Projects

1. Start a collection of news articles, cartoons, or television segments that deal with computers, the Internet, or some other digital technology. Does your collection say anything about popular attitudes toward the technology? Does it reveal any misconceptions about the technology?

2. The title "Inventor of the Computer" has been given to Charles Babbage (for the Analytical Engine), Konrad Zuse (for the Z1, Z2, and Z3), John Atanasoff and Clifford Berry (for the Atanasoff-Berry Computer), John Mauchly and J. Presper Eckert (for the ENIAC), and F. C. Williams, Tom Kilburn, and Geoff Tootill (for the Small-Scale Experimental Machine). Research these inventors and their machines. Draw a table comparing the features of these computing devices. Decide for yourself who deserves the title "Inventor of the Computer."

3. Make a graph that charts how the price of an entry-level personal computer system changed over the last twenty years. Use the Web, back issues of computer magazines, and other sources to determine past pricing. Use the Consumer Price Index inflation calculator, found at http://www.bls.gov/cpi/home.htm, to adjust all the prices to the same real dollar value. Of course, a price graph won't tell the whole story. Attach a short description of how the features and power of the entry-level system changed over time.

4. Develop a questionnaire to try to determine people's awareness of the computers around them. You can ask them about how often they use a computer, the uses to which they put a computer, the most valuable thing a computer does for them, and so on. Once you have collected the answers, analyze them. What percentage of the people assumed you were talking about "personal computers" when you asked them about their computer use? How many of them mentioned embedded computers, such as the computers in cell phones, microwaves, clock radios, ATM machines, and automobile engines?

5. Take an inventory of all the computers you encounter in a single day. Be sure to include embedded computers, such as those in cars, appliances, entertainment equipment, and other machines. *Hint*: If a device has an LCD screen or LED numbers (digital numbers made out of light segments), it contains a microprocessor.

Sources and Resources

Books

Everyware: The Dawning Age of Ubiquitous Computing, by Adam Greenfield (Berkeley, CA: New Riders, 2006). We tend to think of computers as PCs and mainframes—general-purpose devices running programs to do our bidding. But computers are finding their way into all kinds of other devices, from clothing to furniture. We're entering an age of ubiquitous computers—computers everywhere. Designer and writer Adam Greenfield refers to this phenomenon as *everyware*. In this book he explores the implications of everyware in a series of short, thought-provoking essays. Welcome to the future.

The Difference Engine, by William Gibson and Bruce Sterling (New York, NY: Bantam, 1992). How would the world of the nineteenth century be different if Charles and Ada had succeeded in constructing the Analytical Engine 150 years ago? This imaginative mystery novel takes place in a world where the computer revolution arrived a century early. Like other books by these two pioneers of the "cyberpunk" school of science fiction, *The Difference Engine* is dark, dense, detailed, and thought-provoking.

A History of Modern Computing, Second Edition, by Paul E. Ceruzzi (Cambridge, MA: MIT Press, 2003). This book traces the first 50 years of computer history, from ENIAC to Internetworked PCs. The social context of the technology is clear throughout the book.

Crystal Fire: The Invention of the Transistor and the Birth of the Information Age, by Michael Riordan and Lillian Hoddeson (New York, NY: Norton, 1998). One of the defining moments of the information age occurred in 1947, when William Shockley and his colleagues invented the transistor. *Crystal Fire* tells the story of that earthshaking invention, clearly describing the technical and human dimensions of the story.

Accidental Empires: How the Boys of Silicon Valley Make Their Millions, Battle Foreign Competition, and Still Can't Get a Date, Revised Edition, by Robert X. Cringely (New York, NY: Collins, 1996). Robert X. Cringely is the pen name for *InfoWorld's* computer-industry gossip columnist. In this opinionated, irreverent, and entertaining book, Cringely discusses the past, present, and future of the volatile personal computer industry. When you read the humorous, colorful characterizations of the people who run this industry, you'll understand why Cringely didn't use his real name. *Triumph of the Nerds*, a 1996 PBS TV show and video based loosely on this book, lacks much of the humor and insight of the book but includes some fascinating footage of the pioneers reminiscing about the early days.

The Clock of the Long Now: Time and Responsibility: The Ideas Behind the World's Slowest Computer, by Stewart Brand (New York, NY: Basic Books, 2000). Brand is one of the prime movers of the Long Now Foundation, an organization dedicated to promoting the long view and overcoming civilization's "pathologically short attention span." Brand's books are always thought provoking, and the foundation attracts some of the most forward-thinking people on the planet. This book presents many of the basic concepts of the Long Now.

The Black Swan: The Impact of the Highly Improbable, by Nassim Nicholas Taleb (New York, NY: Random House, 2007). One of the hazards of predicting the future is that we need to base our predictions on what's most likely to happen, and that's not always what happens. Taleb's book deals with the phenomenon of the "black swan"—the highly improbable event that can't easily be predicted.

The World is Flat 3.0: A Brief History of the Twenty-first Century, by Thomas Friedman (New York, NY: Picador, 2007). Thomas Friedman's *The World is Flat* described in clear prose the new globalized, interconnected world. The world has changed since he wrote the first edition, and this new edition reflects those changes.

Periodicals

Wired (wired.com). This highly stylized monthly started out as "the first consumer magazine for the digital generation to track technology's impact on all facets of the human condition." Today *Wired* devotes more pages to hawking the latest gear for the techno-chic lifestyle, but it's still one of the most important and influential sources for thought-provoking, future-oriented articles about technology and its impact on our future.

Technology Review (technologyreview.com). This periodical from MIT provides excellent coverage of technology in the labs today that will change our lives tomorrow.

Scientific American (scientificamerican.com). This old standby still provides some of the best writing on science and technology, including emerging information technologies.

PC World (pcworld.com). This periodical is one of the most popular sources for keeping up with developments in the PC world. The companion Web site offers up-to-the-minute information along with archives from past issues.

PC Magazine (pcmag.com). *PC Magazine* is a popular PC periodical, containing news, reviews, and feature articles for a variety of interests.

Macworld (macworld.com). This is the premier periodical for Mac users, covering hardware, software, and Internet issues with clear, easy-to-read articles and reviews.

InfoWorld (infoworld.com). This magazine covers business computing, including applications for mainframes, servers, and other behind-the-scenes machines that aren't typically covered in PC-centric publications.

ComputerWorld (computerworld.com). InfoWorld's older sibling covers the broad spectrum of computers and information technology from the perspective of the computer professional.

2

Hardware Basics
Inside the Box

Objectives

After you read this chapter you should be able to:

▶ Explain in general terms how computers store and manipulate information

▶ Describe the basic structure and organization of a computer

▶ Discuss the functions and interactions of a computer system's principal internal components

▶ Explain why a computer typically has different types of memory and storage devices

> It's **not** like we were all **smart enough** to see a **revolution coming**. Back then I thought there might be a revolution in **opening** your garage door, **balancing** your checkbook, **keeping** your recipes, that sort of thing. There are a **million people** who study markets and analyze economic trends, people who are **more brilliant than I am**, people who worked for companies like Digital Equipment and IBM and Hewlett-Packard. **None of them foresaw** what was going to happen either.
>
> —*Steve Wozniak*

Steve Wozniak, Steve Jobs, and the Garage that Grew Apples

What Steve Wozniak and all those other people failed to foresee was the personal computer revolution—a revolution that he helped start. Wozniak, a brilliant engineer called Woz by his friends, worked days as a calculator technician at Hewlett-Packard; he was refused an engineer's job because he lacked a college degree. At night he designed and constructed a scaled-down computer system that would fit the home hobbyist's budget. When he completed it in 1975, he offered it to HP, but they turned it down.

Wozniak took his invention to the Homebrew Computer Club in Palo Alto, where it caught the imagination of another college dropout, Steve Jobs. A free-thinking visionary, Jobs persuaded Wozniak to quit his job in 1976 to form a company born in Jobs's garage. They marketed the machine as the Apple I.

With the help and financial backing of businessman A. C. Markkula, the two Steves turned Apple into a thriving business. Wozniak created the Apple II, a more refined machine, and in the process invented the first personal computer disk operating system. Because it put computing power within the reach of individuals, the Apple II became popular in businesses, homes, and especially schools. Apple became the first company in American history to join the Fortune 500 in less than five years. Still in his mid-twenties, Jobs was running a corporate giant.

When IBM introduced its PC in 1982, it overshadowed Apple's presence in the business world. Other companies developed PC clones, treating the IBM PC as a standard—a standard that Apple refused to accept. Inspired by a visit to Xerox's Palo Alto Research Center (PARC), Jobs worked with a team of Apple engineers to develop the Macintosh, a futuristic computer Jobs hoped would leapfrog IBM's advantage. When Jobs insisted on focusing most of Apple's resources on the Macintosh, Wozniak resigned to pursue other interests.

Businesses failed to embrace the Mac, and Apple stockholders grew uneasy with Jobs's controversial management style. In 1985, a year and a half after the Macintosh was introduced, Jobs was ousted. He went on to form NeXT, a company that produced expensive

FIGURE 2.1 Steve Wozniak

FIGURE 2.2 Steve Jobs

workstations and software. He also bought Pixar, the computer animation company that later captured the public's attention with *Toy Story,* the first computer-generated full-length motion picture.

After Apple's fortunes declined under a string of CEOs, the company bought NeXT in 1997 and invited an older and wiser Jobs to retake the helm. He agreed to share his time between Pixar and Apple. Under his leadership, Apple has regained its innovative edge, releasing a flurry of elegant and trend-setting products. Though its share of the PC market is relatively small, Apple continues to maintain and expand a fanatically loyal customer base, especially in the consumer, creative, and education markets.

While Apple was cranking out hits such as the iPod, the iPhone, and the iTunes Store, Pixar was producing blockbusters such as *Finding Nemo* and WALLE that redefined the art of animation. In 2006 the Disney Corporation bought Pixar, making Steve Jobs the single largest stockholder in the entertainment giant. His phenomenal success at running Pixar and Apple makes Jobs something of a legend in the business world. Woz, on the other hand, leads a more low-key life, developing technology companies out of the public spotlight. ∼

Computers schedule airline flights, predict the weather, play and even create music, control space stations, and keep the world's economic wheels spinning. How can one kind of machine do so many things?

To understand what really makes computers tick, you would need to devote considerable time and effort to studying computer science and computer engineering. Most of us don't need to understand every detail of a computer's inner workings any more than a parent needs to explain wave and particle physics when a child asks why the sky is blue. We can be satisfied with simpler answers, even if those answers are only approximations of the technical truth. We'll spend the next three chapters exploring answers to the question, "How do computers do what they do?"

The main text of each of these chapters provides simple, nontechnical answers and basic information. How It Works boxes use text and graphics to dig deeper into the inner workings of the computer. Depending on your course, learning style, and level of

FIGURE 2.3 PCs are assembled in highly automated factories such as this one owned by Dell Computer. In this chapter and the next, we'll examine the hardware components that make up a modern computer.

curiosity, you may read these boxes as they appear in the text, read them after you've completed the basic material in the chapter, or (if you don't need the technical details) bypass some or all of them. Use the Sources and Resources section at each chapter's end for further explorations.

What Computers Do

The simple truth is that computers perform only four basic functions:

- *Receive input.* Computers accept information from the outside world.
- *Process information.* Computers perform arithmetic or logical (decision-making) operations on information.
- *Produce output.* Computers communicate information to the outside world.
- *Store information.* Computers store and retrieve information from memory and storage devices.

> Stripped of its interfaces, **a bare computer** boils down to little more than a pocket calculator that can **push its own buttons** and **remember** what it has done.
>
> —*Arnold Penzias, in* Ideas and Information

Every computer system contains hardware components—physical parts—that specialize in each of these four functions:

- **Input devices** accept input from the outside world. The most common input devices today, of course, are keyboards and pointing devices, such as mice.
- **Output devices** send information to the outside world. Most computers use a TV-like display, or video monitor, as their main output device, a printer to produce paper printouts, and speakers to output sounds.
- A **microprocessor**, also called the **processor** or **central processing unit (CPU)**, is, in effect, the computer's "brain." The CPU processes information, performs arithmetic calculations, and makes basic decisions by comparing information values.
- **Memory** and **storage devices** both store information, but they serve different purposes. The computer's memory (sometimes called *primary storage* or **RAM**, for **random**

access memory) is used to store programs and data (information) that need to be instantly accessible to the CPU. Storage devices (sometimes called *secondary storage*), including hard disk drives and a variety of removable media devices, serve as long-term repositories for data. You can think of a storage device, such as a hard disk drive, as a combination input and output device because the computer sends information to the storage device (output) and later retrieves that information from it (input).

These four types of components, when combined, make up the hardware part of a computer system. Of course, the system isn't complete without software—the instructions that tell the hardware what to do. But for now, we will concentrate on hardware. In this chapter we take a look at the central processing unit and the computer's memory; these components are at the center of all computing operations. In the next chapter, we look at the input, output, and storage devices—that is, the peripherals of the computer system. Because every computer hardware component is designed to transport or to transform information, we start with some facts about information.

Storage Device(s)

Input Device(s)

Processor (CPU)

Output Device(s)

Memory

FIGURE 2.4 The basic components of every computer system include the central components (the CPU and memory) and various types of peripherals.

A Bit about Bits

The term information is difficult to define because it has many meanings. According to one popular definition, *information* is communication that has value because it *informs*. This distinction can be helpful for dealing with data from television, magazines, computers, and other sources. But it's not always clear, and it's not absolute. As educator and author Richard Saul Wurman points out, "Everyone needs a personal measure with which to define information. What constitutes information to one person may be data to another. If it doesn't make sense to you, it doesn't qualify."

At the opposite extreme, one communication theory defines information as anything that can be communicated, whether it has value or not. By this definition, information comes in many forms. The words, numbers, and pictures on these pages are symbols representing information. If you underline or highlight this sentence, you're adding new information to the page. Even the sounds and pictures that emanate from a television commercial are packed with information, though it's debatable whether most of that information is useful.

Some people attempt strictly to apply the first definition to computers, claiming that computers turn raw data, which has no value in its current form, into information, which is valuable. This approach emphasizes the computer's role as a business data processing machine. But in our modern interconnected world, one computer's output is often another's input. If a computer receives a message from another computer, is the message worthless data or valuable information? And whose personal measure of value applies?

For our purposes, describing the mechanics of computers in these chapters, we lean toward the second, more objective, approach and use the terms *data* and *information* more or less interchangeably. In later chapters, we present plenty of evidence to suggest that not all computer output has value. In the end, it is up to you to decide what the real information is.

> The great Information Age is really an **explosion of non-information**; it is an **explosion of data**. To deal with the increasing **onslaught of data**, it is imperative to distinguish between the two; information is **that which leads to understanding**.
>
> —*Richard Saul Wurman, in* Information Anxiety

Bit Basics

Whatever you call it, in the world of computers, information is digital: This means it's made up of discrete, countable units—digits—so it can be subdivided. In many situations people need to reduce information to simpler units to use it effectively. For example, a child trying to pronounce an unfamiliar word can sound out each letter or syllable individually before tackling the whole word.

A computer doesn't understand words, numbers, pictures, musical notes, or even letters of the alphabet. Like a young reader, a computer can't process information without dividing it into smaller units. In fact, computers can digest information only if it has been broken into bits. A bit, or binary digit, is the smallest unit of information a computer can process. A bit can have one of two values: 0 and 1. You can also think of these two values as yes and no, on and off, black and white, or high and low.

If you think of the innards of a computer as a collection of microscopic on/off switches, it's easy to understand why computers process information bit by bit. Each switch stores a tiny amount of information: a signal to turn on a light, for example, or the answer to a yes/no question. (In modern integrated circuits, high and low electrical charges represent bits, but these circuits work as if they were really made up of tiny switches.)

Remember Paul Revere's famous midnight ride to warn the American colonists of the British invasion? His co-conspirators used a pair of lanterns to convey a choice between two messages, "One if by land, two if by sea"—a binary choice. It's theoretically possible to send a message like this with just one lantern. But "One if by land, zero if by sea" wouldn't have worked very well unless there had been some way to know exactly when the message was being sent. With two lanterns, the first lantern could say, "Here is the message," when

How It Works

2.1 Binary Numbers

A computer's memory is made up of millions of microscopic switches that can be either "on" or "off." A single switch can represent only two symbols: 0 and 1. Still, two symbols are all a computer needs to represent numbers and perform arithmetic operations on them. Let's look at the inner workings of a calculator to see how this is done.

1. When you use a calculator, you use the keys 0–9 to type numbers. These are decimal (base ten) numbers because there are ten different digits. The microprocessor inside the calculator actually stores the numbers as a series of 0s and 1s. These are binary (base two) numbers because there are only two different digits.

2. Just as we use more than one decimal digit to represent numbers larger than 9, processor designers use more than one binary digit (bit) to represent numbers larger than 1. A collection of 8 bits is called a byte.

3. A byte can represent all the numbers between 0 and 255. The positional values are powers of 2, not 10. They start at 1 (the units' place) and double in value for each additional place. If all bits are 0, the value is 0; if all 8 bits are 1, the value is 255 (1 + 2 + 4 + 8 + 16 + 32 + 64 + 128).

FIGURE 2.5

4. To represent values larger than 255, processor designers combine bytes. Two bytes, with 16 bits, can represent all the numbers from 0 to 65,535.

32768 16384 8192 4096 2048 1024 512 256   128 64 32 16 8 4 2 1

2 bytes

5. Adding binary numbers is much simpler than adding decimal numbers because there are fewer rules to remember. That's good news for hardware designers.

$$
\begin{array}{cccc}
0 & 0 & 1 & 1 \\
+0 & +1 & +0 & +1 \\
\hline
0 & 1 & 1 & 10
\end{array}
$$

6. Using these rules, we can compute the binary sum of twelve and ten:

$$
\begin{array}{r}
1100 \\
+1010 \\
\hline
10110
\end{array}
$$

7. The calculator transforms the sum from binary back into a decimal number displayed on the calculator's screen.

it was turned on. The second lantern communicated the critical bit's worth of information: land or sea. If the revolutionaries had wanted to send a more complex message, they could have used more lanterns ("Three if by subway!").

In much the same way, a computer can process larger chunks of information by treating groups of bits as logical units. For example, a collection of 8 bits, called a byte, can represent 256 different messages ($256 = 2^8$). If you think of each bit as a light that can be either on or off, you can make different combinations of lights represent different messages. (Computer scientists usually speak in terms of 0 and 1 instead of on and off, but the concept is the same either way.) The computer has an advantage over Paul Revere in that it sees not just the number of lights turned on, but also their order, so 01 (off–on) is different from 10 (on–off).

Building with Bits

There's a **runaway market** for bits.

—*Russell Schweickart, astronaut*

FIGURE 2.6 The MITS Altair, the first popular personal computer, came with no keyboard or monitor. It could be programmed only by manipulating a bank of binary switches on the front panel for input. Binary patterns of lights provided the output. *(Source: Courtesy of The Computer History Museum.)*

What does a bit combination such as 01100110 mean to the computer? There's no single answer to that question; it depends on context and convention. A string of bits can be interpreted as a number, a letter of the alphabet, or almost anything else.

Bits as Numbers

Because computers are built from switching devices that reduce all information to 0s and 1s, they represent numbers using the *binary number system*, a system that denotes all numbers with combinations of two digits. Like the 10-digit decimal system you use every day, the binary number system has clear, consistent rules for every arithmetic operation.

The people who worked with early computers had to use binary arithmetic. But today's computers include software that converts decimal numbers into binary numbers automatically, and vice versa. As a result, the computer's binary number processing is completely hidden from the user.

Bits as Codes

Today's computers work as much with text as with numbers. To make words, sentences, and paragraphs fit into the computer's binary-only circuitry, programmers have devised codes that represent each letter, digit, and special character as a unique string of bits.

The most widely used code, ASCII (an abbreviation of American Standard Code for Information Interchange, pronounced "as-kee"), represents each character as a unique 8-bit code. Out of a string of 8 bits, 256 unique ordered patterns can be made—enough to make unique codes for 26 letters (upper- and lowercase), 10 digits, and a variety of special characters.

As the world shrinks and our information needs grow, ASCII's 256 unique characters simply aren't enough. ASCII is too limited to accommodate Chinese, Greek, Hebrew, Japanese, Arabic, and other languages. To facilitate multilingual computing, the computer industry is embracing Unicode, a coding scheme that supports more than 100,000 unique characters—more than enough for all major world languages.

Of course, today's computers work with more than characters. A group of bits can also represent colors, sounds, quantitative measurements from the environment, or just about any other kind of information that we need to process. We explore other types of information in later chapters.

	Decimal representation	Binary representation
	0	0
	1	1
	2	10
	3	11
	4	100
	5	101
	6	110
	7	111
	8	1000
	9	1001
	10	1010
	11	1011
	12	1100
	13	1101
	14	1110
	15	1111

FIGURE 2.7 In the binary number system, every number is represented by a unique pattern of 0s and 1s.

Character	ASCII binary code
A	0 1 0 0 0 0 0 1
B	0 1 0 0 0 0 1 0
C	0 1 0 0 0 0 1 1
D	0 1 0 0 0 1 0 0
E	0 1 0 0 0 1 0 1
F	0 1 0 0 0 1 1 0
G	0 1 0 0 0 1 1 1
H	0 1 0 0 1 0 0 0
I	0 1 0 0 1 0 0 1
J	0 1 0 0 1 0 1 0
K	0 1 0 0 1 0 1 1
L	0 1 0 0 1 1 0 0
M	0 1 0 0 1 1 0 1
N	0 1 0 0 1 1 1 0
O	0 1 0 0 1 1 1 1
P	0 1 0 1 0 0 0 0
Q	0 1 0 1 0 0 0 1
R	0 1 0 1 0 0 1 0
S	0 1 0 1 0 0 1 1
T	0 1 0 1 0 1 0 0
U	0 1 0 1 0 1 0 1
V	0 1 0 1 0 1 1 0
W	0 1 0 1 0 1 1 1
X	0 1 0 1 1 0 0 0
Y	0 1 0 1 1 0 0 1
Z	0 1 0 1 1 0 1 0
0	0 0 1 1 0 0 0 0
1	0 0 1 1 0 0 0 1
2	0 0 1 1 0 0 1 0
3	0 0 1 1 0 0 1 1
4	0 0 1 1 0 1 0 0
5	0 0 1 1 0 1 0 1
6	0 0 1 1 0 1 1 0
7	0 0 1 1 0 1 1 1
8	0 0 1 1 1 0 0 0
9	0 0 1 1 1 0 0 1

FIGURE 2.8 The capital letters and numeric digits are represented in the ASCII character set by 36 unique patterns of 8 bits each. (The remaining 92 ASCII bit patterns represent lowercase letters, punctuation characters, and special characters.)

Bits as Instructions in Programs

So far we've dealt with the ways bits represent data. But another kind of information is just as important to the computer: the programs that tell the computer what to do with the data you give it. The computer stores programs as collections of bits, just as it stores data.

Program instructions, like characters, are represented in binary notation through the use of codes. For example, the code 01101010 might tell the computer to add two numbers. Other groups of bits—instructions in the program—contain codes that tell the computer where to find those numbers and where to store the result. You learn more about how these computer instructions work in later chapters.

Bits, Bytes, and Buzzwords

Trying to learn about computers by examining their operation at the bit level is a little like trying to learn about how people look or act by studying individual human cells; there's plenty of information there, but it's not the most efficient way to find out what you need to know. Fortunately, people can use computers without thinking about bits. Some bit-related terminology does come up in day-to-day computer work, though. Most computer users need to have at least a basic understanding of the following terms for quantifying data:

Even the most **sophisticated** computer is really only a large, well-organized **volume of bits**.

—*David Harel, in* Algorithmics: The Spirit of Computing

■ *Byte:* A logical group of eight bits, also referred to as an octet. If you work mostly with words, you can think of a byte as one character of ASCII-encoded text.

How It **Works**

The United States has long been at the center of the computer revolution; that's why the ASCII character set was originally designed to include only English-language characters. ASCII code numbers range from 0 to 127, but this isn't enough to handle all the characters used in the languages of Western Europe, including accents and other diacritical marks.

The Latin I character set appends 128 additional codes onto the original ASCII 128 to accommodate additional characters.

Both the ASCII and the Latin I character sets can use 8 bits—1 byte—to represent each character, but there's no room left for the characters used in languages such as Arabic, Greek, Hebrew, and Hindi, each of which has its own 50- to 150-character alphabet or syllabary. Asian languages, such as Chinese, Korean, and Japanese, present bigger challenges for computer users. Chinese alone has nearly 50,000 distinct characters, of which about 13,000 are in current use.

The international standard character set called Unicode is designed to facilitate multilingual computing by allowing for more than 100,000 distinct codes. In Unicode the first 256 codes (0 through 255) are identical to the codes of the Latin I character set. The remaining codes are distributed among the writing systems of the world's other languages.

Most major new software applications and operating systems are designed to be transported to different languages. Making a software application work in different languages involves much more than translating the words. For example, some languages write from right to left or top to bottom. Pronunciation, currency symbols, dialects, and other variations often make it necessary to produce customized software for different regions even where the same language is spoken.

Computer keyboards for East Asian languages don't have one key for each character. Using phonetic input, a user types a pronunciation for a character using a Western-style keyboard then chooses the character needed from a menu of characters that appears on the screen. The software can make some menu choices automatically based on common language-usage patterns.

FIGURE 2.9 After entering a phonetic pronunciation of a Japanese character, a user can choose the correct character from a pop-up menu.

- **Kilobyte (KB or K):** About 1,000 bytes of information. For example, about 5K of storage is necessary to hold 5,000 characters of ASCII text. (Technically, 1K is 1,024 bytes because 1,024 is 2^{10}, which makes the arithmetic easier for binary-based computers. For those of us who don't think in binary, 1,000 is often close enough.)
- **Megabyte** or **meg (MB):** Approximately 1,000KB, or 1 million bytes.
- **Gigabyte** or **gig (GB):** Approximately 1,000MB, or 1 billion bytes.
- **Terabyte (TB):** Approximately 1 million MB or 1 trillion bytes. This massive unit of measurement applies to the largest storage devices commonly available today.
- **Petabyte (PB):** This astronomical value is the equivalent of 1,024 terabytes, or 1 quadrillion bytes. While it's unlikely that anyone will be able to store 1PB of data on their home PC anytime soon, we're definitely heading in that direction.

The abbreviations K, MB, GB, TB, and PB describe the capacity of memory and storage components. You could, for example, describe a computer as having 2GB of memory (RAM) and a hard disk as having a 1TB storage capacity. The same terms are used to quantify sizes of computer files as well. A *file* is an organized collection of information, such as a term paper or a set of names and addresses, stored in a computer-readable form. For example, the text for this chapter is stored in a file that occupies about 169KB of space on a hard disk drive.

To add to the confusion, people often measure data transfer speed or memory size in *megabits (Mb or Mbits)* rather than megabytes (MB). A megabit, as you might expect, is approximately 1,000,000 bits—one-eighth the size of a megabyte. When you're talking in bits and bytes, a little detail such as capitalization can make a significant difference.

The Computer's Core: CPU and Memory

It may seem strange to think of automated teller machines, video game consoles, and supercomputers as bit processors. But whatever it looks like to the user, a digital computer is, at its core, a collection of on/off switches designed to transform information from one form to another. The user provides the computer with patterns of bits—input—and the computer follows instructions to transform that input into a different pattern of bits—output—to return to the user.

> The **microprocessor** that makes up your personal computer'scentral processing unit, or CPU, is the **ultimate computer brain**, **messenger**, **ringmaster**, and **boss**. All the other components— RAM, disk drives, the monitor—exist only to bridge the gap between you and the processor.
>
> —*Ron White, in* How Computers Work

The CPU: The Real Computer

The CPU, often just called the *processor*, performs the transformations of input into output. Every computer has at least one CPU to interpret and execute the instructions in each program, to perform arithmetic and logical data manipulations, and to communicate with all the other parts of the computer system indirectly through memory.

A modern *microprocessor*, or CPU, is an extraordinarily complex collection of electronic circuits. In a desktop computer, the CPU is housed along with other chips and electronic components on a circuit board. The circuit board that contains a computer's CPU is called the motherboard.

Many different kinds of CPUs are in use today; when you choose a computer, the type of CPU in the computer is an important part of the decision. Although there are many variations in design among these chips, only two factors are important to a casual computer user: compatibility and performance.

Working Wisdom

Green Computing

When compared with heavy industries, such as automobiles and energy, the computer industry is relatively easy on the environment. But the manufacturing and use of computer hardware and software does have a significant environmental impact, especially now that so many of us are using the technology. Fortunately, you have some control over the environmental impact of your computing activities. Here are a few tips to help minimize your impact:

➡ **Buy green equipment.** Today's computer equipment uses relatively little energy, but as world energy resources dwindle, less is always better. Many modern computers and peripherals are specifically designed to consume less energy. Look for the Environmental Protection Agency's Energy Star certification on the package.

➡ **Use a notebook.** Portable computers use far less energy than desktop computers. They're engineered to preserve precious battery power. But if you use a laptop, keep it plugged in when you have easy access to an electrical outlet. Batteries wear out from repeated usage, and their disposal can cause environmental problems of a different sort. (If you're the kind of person who always needs to have the latest and greatest technology, a notebook isn't the best choice because notebooks are difficult or impossible to upgrade.)

➡ **Take advantage of energy-saving features.** Most systems can be set up to go to sleep (a sort of suspended animation state that uses just enough power to preserve RAM) and turn off the monitor or printer when idle for more than an hour or so. If your equipment has automatic energy-saving features, use them. You'll save energy and money.

➡ **Turn it off when you're away.** If you're just leaving your computer for an hour or two, you won't save much energy by turning the computer off. But if you're leaving it for more than a few hours and it's not

FIGURE 2.10 Windows and Mac OS X systems have advanced energy-saver control panels that can be used to switch the monitor, hard drive, and CPU to lower-power sleep modes automatically after specified periods of inactivity.

Compatibility

Not all software is compatible with every CPU; that is, software written for one processor will usually not work with another. Every processor has a built-in instruction set—a vocabulary of instructions the processor can execute. CPUs in the same product family are generally designed so newer processors can process all instructions handled by earlier models. For example, chips in Intel's Core 2 Duo microprocessor family are backward compatible with the Core, Celeron, Pentium, 486, 386, and 286 chips that preceded it, so they can run most software written for those older CPUs. (Likewise, many of the processors designed by Advanced Micro Devices—AMD—are purposefully made to be compatible with those made by Intel.) In contrast, PowerPC processors used in many gaming consoles and older Macintosh computers have a different instruction set from Intel CPUs. A PowerPC CPU can't decipher Intel Pentium instructions, and vice versa.

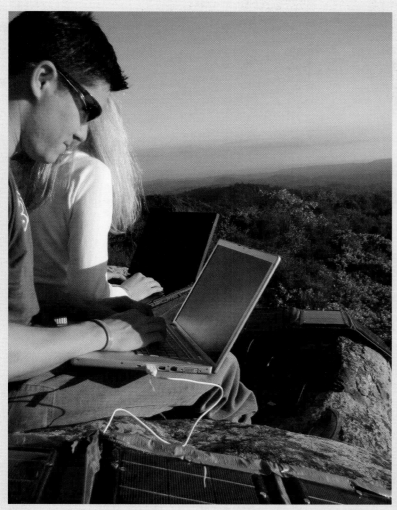

FIGURE 2.11 Laptop computers consume far less energy than desktop PCs. This makes it possible to use solar panels to power them in remote locations.

on duty receiving faxes and email, you'll do the environment a favor by turning it off or putting it to sleep.

➡ *Save energy, not screens.* Your monitor is probably the biggest power guzzler in your system, especially if it's not a flat-panel display. A screen saver can be fun to watch, but it doesn't save your screen, and it doesn't save energy, either. As long as your monitor is displaying an image, it's consuming power. Use sleep.

➡ *Print only once.* Don't print out a rough draft just to proofread; try to get it clean on-screen. (Most people find this one hard to follow 100 percent of the time; some errors just don't seem to show up until you proofread a hard copy.)

➡ *Recycle your waste products.* When you reprint that 20-page report because of a missing paragraph on page 1, recycle the flawed printout. When your laser printer's toner cartridge runs dry, ship or deliver it to one of the many companies that recycles cartridges. They may even pay you a few dollars for the empty cartridge. When your portable's battery dies, follow the manufacturer's instructions for recycling it. While you're in recycling mode, don't forget all those computer magazines and catalogs.

➡ *Pass it on.* When you outgrow a piece of hardware or software, don't throw it away. Donate it to a school, civic organization, family member, or friend who can put it to good use.

➡ *Send bits, not atoms.* It takes far more resources to send a letter by truck, train, or plane than to send an electronic message through the Internet. Whenever possible, use your internet connection instead of your printer.

A related issue involves the software systems that run on these hardware processors. Programs written for Linux, a popular operating system, can't run on Windows, even though both operating systems can be installed on PCs powered by an Intel microprocessor. In Chapter 4 you will learn more about these issues and see how virtual machine software can often overcome incompatibility problems by translating instructions written for one CPU or software system into instructions that another can execute.

Performance

When it comes to handling information, some processors are much faster than others. Most computer applications, such as Web browsing, are more convenient to use on a faster machine. Many applications that use multimedia or perform computations, such as statistical

FIGURE 2.12 The motherboard of a typical PC has places for the CPU, memory, and several other important chips and components.

programs, graphic design programs, and many computer games, require faster machines to produce acceptable results.

A computer's overall performance is determined in part by the speed of its micro-processor's internal *clock*—the timing device that produces electrical pulses to synchro-nize the computer's operations. A computer's clock speed is measured in units called

FIGURE 2.13 This chip specialist is examining a silicon wafer before it is sliced into many silicon chips.

FIGURE 2.14 The Intel Pentium-M (left) and Pentium 4 chips contain circuitry that looks like geometric patterns when magnified.

gigahertz (GHz), for billions of clock cycles per second. Ads for new computer systems often emphasize gigahertz ratings as a measure of speed. But these numbers can be somewhat misleading; judging a computer's speed by its gigahertz rating alone is like measuring a car's speed by the engine's RPM (revolutions per minute). For example, two processors may have the same clock speed, but one processor may outperform the other if its memory accesses are faster.

PC performance can also be limited by the **architecture** of the processor—the design that determines how individual components of the CPU are put together on the chip. For example, newer chips can manipulate more bits simultaneously than older chips can, which makes them more efficient, and therefore faster, at performing most operations. The number of bits a CPU can process at one time—typically 32 or 64—is sometimes called the CPU's *word size*. More often, though, people use the number without a label, as in "The Itanium was Intel's first mainstream 64-bit processor." Some embedded and special-purpose computers still use 8- and 16-bit processors because their performance needs are smaller.

The amount of heat generated by a CPU increases as the clock speed increases. The fastest CPUs need large heat sinks and fans to keep them from overheating. The heat dissipation problem is one reason manufacturers have realized it is impractical to keep increasing the performance of CPUs by increasing clock speeds. Instead, chip makers now offer **multicore processors**—putting multiple CPUs, which run simultaneously, on a single chip. **Parallel processing** (sometimes called **symmetric multiprocessing** or just **multiprocessing** in the PC world) has been used in high-end servers and workstations for some time. The advent of low-cost multicore processors means parallel processing is going mainstream. Dual-core CPUs such as the Intel Core 2 Duo are common on today's PCs and game consoles and quad-core processors are increasing in popularity. More powerful experimental *manycore* machines may have tens or hundreds of processors per chip.

Another way to improve performance on high-end server systems is simply to add more machines to the mix. This way, the processing resources of multiple servers can be grouped together in a **cluster** to improve rendering speeds in lifelike computer graphics or calculate the sums of complex financial trading computations more quickly. Google uses a cluster of more than 15,000 PCs to handle hundreds of millions of search queries a day. Server clusters are also used for reliability reasons: If one machine in a cluster shuts down because of errors, or to be serviced, the other servers can pick up the slack.

How It **Works**

2.3 The CPU

The central processing unit (CPU) is the hardware component that executes the steps in a software program, performing math and moving data from one part of the system to another. The CPU contains the circuitry to perform a variety of simple tasks called *instructions*. An individual instruction does only a tiny amount of work. A typical instruction might be "Read the contents of memory location x and add the number y to it." Most CPUs have a vocabulary of fewer than 1,000 distinct instructions.

All computer programs are composed of instructions drawn from this tiny vocabulary. The typical computer program is composed of millions of instructions, and the CPU can execute millions of instructions every second. When a program runs, the rapid-fire execution of instructions creates an illusion of motion in the same way a movie simulates motion out of a sequence of still pictures.

The typical CPU is divided into several functional units: control, arithmetic logic decode, bus, and prefetch. These units work together like workers on an assembly line to complete the execution of program instructions.

Control Unit

Arithmetic Logic Unit

Decode Unit

Bus Unit

Prefetch Unit

1. In most cases the actual execution of an instruction is performed by the CPU's *arithmetic logic unit (ALU)*. The ALU includes *registers*, each usually 32 or 64 bits in size.

2. Program instructions are stored in primary storage (memory), which is usually on chips outside the CPU. The CPU's first task is to read an instruction from memory. The bus unit handles all communication between the CPU and primary storage.

3. The *prefetch unit*, or prefetcher, instructs the bus unit to read the instruction stored at a particular memory address. This unit fetches not only the next instruction to execute but also several subsequent instructions to ensure that an instruction is always ready to be executed.

FIGURE 2.15

4. The *decode unit* takes the instruction read by the prefetcher and translates it into a form suitable for the CPU's internal processing. It does this by looking up the steps required to complete an instruction in the control unit.

**Bus
(group of wires)**

**Memory
(RAM)**

**Bus
Interface Unit**

5. If an instruction requires that information be sent out from the CPU—for example, written into memory—then the final phase of execution is *writeback*, in which the bus unit writes the results of the instruction back into memory or to some other device.

6. Microprocessor manufacturers use many techniques to eliminate bottlenecks and speed up processing. For example, in the same way it prefetches the next likely instructions to be read, the CPU prereads the next likely data to be used into a cache in memory, called a *Level 2 cache (L2 cache)*, or, for faster access, in the CPU itself (a *Level 1 cache*).

Popular CPUs and Where to Find Them

CPUs are commonly classified according to the instructions that are used to program them—their instruction set architecture (ISA). It's hard to tell the relationship between chips based on their names, because the chips are often named for reasons related more to marketing than engineering. Word size—the number of bits a CPU can process at one time–is another important factor in classifying CPUs. Today most new CPUs have either 32- or 64-bit word sizes.

ISA and Word Size	Photo	Examples	Used In	Primary Developer/ Manufacturer
x86 (8-bit, 16-bit, and 32-bit)		286, 386, 486, Pentium, Athlon	Older PCs	Intel
x86-64/AMD64 (64-bit)		AMD Phenom, AMD Opteron, AMD Athlon 64, Intel Core 2	New PCs and notebooks	AMD, Intel
IA-64 (64-bit)		Itanium	Enterprise servers and workstations	Intel, HP
POWER (32-bit and 64 bit)		PowerPC G3, G4, and G5	Embedded applications, older Macintoshes, game consoles (including original Xbox)	IBM
Cell (32-bit)		Cell	Embedded applications, high definition displays and recording equipment, game consoles (including Playstation 3)	IBM
ARM (32-bit)		ARM11, Xscale	Mobile phones, PDAs, handheld computers (including iPhone and Blackberry)	Many companies
SPARC (32-bit and 64-bit).		UltraSparc	Sun servers	Sun

FIGURE 2.16

The Computer's Memory

The CPU's main job is to follow the instructions encoded in programs. But like Alice in *Through the Looking Glass*, the CPU can handle only one instruction and a few pieces of data at a time. The computer needs a place to store the rest of the program and data until the processor is ready for them. That's what RAM is for.

> "**What's one** and **one** and **one** and **one** and **one** and **one** and **one** and **one** and **one** and **one**?" "**I don't know**," said Alice. "I lost count." "**She can't do addition**," said the Red Queen.
>
> —*Lewis Carroll, in* Through the Looking Glass

Random access memory (RAM) is the most common type of primary storage, or computer memory. RAM chips contain circuits that store program instructions and data temporarily. The computer divides each RAM chip into many equal-sized memory locations. Memory locations, like houses, have unique addresses so the computer can tell them apart when it is instructed to save or retrieve information. You can store a piece of information in any RAM location—you can pick one at random—and the computer can, if so instructed, quickly retrieve it. Hence the name random access memory.

The information stored in RAM is nothing more than a pattern of electrical current flowing through microscopic circuits in silicon chips. This means that when the power goes off, the computer instantly forgets everything it was remembering in RAM. RAM is sometimes referred to as volatile memory because information stored there is not held permanently.

This could be a serious problem if the computer didn't have another type of memory to store information that you don't want to lose. This **nonvolatile memory** is called **read-only memory (ROM)** because the computer can only read information from it; it can never write any new information on it. The information in ROM was etched in when the chip was manufactured, so it is available whenever the computer is operating, but it can't be changed except by replacing the ROM chip. All modern computers use ROM to store start-up instructions and other critical information. You can also find ROM inside preprogrammed devices with embedded processors, such as pocket calculators and microwave ovens. Printers use ROM to hold information about character sets.

Other types of memory are available; most are seldom used outside of engineering laboratories. There are two notable exceptions:

- *Complementary metal-oxide semiconductor (CMOS)* is a special low-energy kind of RAM that can store small amounts of data for long periods of time on battery power. CMOS RAM stores the date, time, and calendar in a PC along with other system settings. (CMOS RAM is called *parameter RAM* in Macintoshes.)
- *Flash memory* chips, like RAM chips, can be written and erased rapidly and repeatedly. But unlike RAM, flash memory is nonvolatile; it can keep its contents without a flow of electricity. Digital cameras, cell phones, pagers, portable computers, handheld computers, PDAs, and other digital devices use flash memory to store data that needs to be changed from time to time. Data flight recorders also use it. In spite of its relatively high cost, flash memory is used as a substitute for the spinning hard drive in some computers. Unlike a disk-based hard drive, a flash-based solid state drive (SSD) has no moving parts.

It takes time for the processor to retrieve data from memory—but not very much time. The *access time* for most memory is measured in *nanoseconds (ns)*—billionths of a second. Compare this with hard disk access time, which is measured in *milliseconds (ms)*—thousandths of a second. Memory speed (access time) is another factor that affects the computer's overall speed.

FIGURE 2.17 Slots and ports enable the CPU to communicate with the outside world via peripheral devices. Here an add-on card is being inserted into an internal slot in the PC. (The circuit board containing the slot has been removed for easier viewing.)

How It Works

2.4 Memory

Memory is the work area for the CPU. In order for the CPU to execute instructions or manipulate data, these instructions or data must be loaded into memory. Think of memory as millions of tiny storage cells, each of which can contain a single byte of information. Like mailboxes in a row, bytes of memory have unique addresses that identify them and help the CPU keep track of where things are stored. PCs contain a large amount of random access memory (RAM) and a small amount of read-only memory (ROM).

The CPU can store (write) information into RAM and retrieve (read) information from RAM. The information in RAM may include program instructions, numbers for arithmetic, codes representing text characters, digital codes representing pictures, and other kinds of data. RAM chips are usually grouped on small circuit boards called *dual in-line memory modules (DIMMs)* and are plugged into the motherboard. RAM is volatile memory, meaning that all the information is lost when power to the computer is turned off.

On the other hand, information is permanently recorded on the ROM, meaning the CPU can read information from the ROM, but cannot change its contents. On most computer systems, part of the operating system is stored in ROM. Programs stored in ROM are called firmware.

1. When you turn on the computer, the CPU automatically begins executing operating system instructions stored in ROM.

2. The executing instructions help the system start up and tell it how to load the operating system—copy it from disk into RAM.

3. Once instructions for the operating system are loaded into RAM, the CPU is able to execute them.

FIGURE 2.18

Buses, Ports, and Peripherals

In a desktop computer, the CPU, memory chips, and other key components are attached to the motherboard. Information travels between components on the motherboard through groups of wires called **system buses**, or just **buses**. Buses typically have 32 or 64 wires, or data paths; a bus with 32 wires is called a *32-bit bus* because it can transmit 32 bits of information at a time, twice as many as a 16-bit bus. Just as multilane freeways allow masses of automobiles to move faster than they could on single-lane roads, wider buses can transmit information faster than narrower buses. Newer, more powerful computers have wider buses so they can process information faster.

FIGURE 2.19 Most laptop computers have ports and slots for attaching external storage devices and other peripherals.

Buses connect to storage devices in **bays**—open areas in the system box for disk drives and other devices. Buses also connect to **expansion slots** (sometimes just called *slots*) inside the computer's housing. Users can customize their computers by inserting special-purpose circuit boards (called **expansion cards**, or just *cards*) into these slots. Buses also connect to **ports**—sockets on the outside of the computer chassis. These ports are generally used to attach peripherals—external devices that enable the CPU to communicate with the outside world and store information for later use. The peripherals are connected to the ports through *external buses*—cables designed to transmit data back and forth between computers and peripherals.

A computer typically has a variety of ports to meet diverse needs: one or more video ports for connecting monitors; audio jacks for connecting speakers and/or headphones; *USB ports* for connecting keyboards, mice, printers, cameras, disk drives, portable storage devices, and more; and Firewire ports for connecting video cameras, external hard drives, and other peripherals. Some ports are connected directly to the system board. Others, such as the video port, may be attached to an expansion card. In fact, many expansion cards do little more than provide convenient ports for attaching particular types of peripherals. In many computers—especially portable computers, where size is critical—most ports go directly to the system board. Because portable computers don't have room for full-sized cards, many have slots for **Express cards**, **PC cards**, or small removable cards that contain memory, miniature peripherals, or additional ports. PC cards are credit-card-sized; newer express cards are considerably smaller. PC cards and express cards are *hot-swappable*—they can be inserted or removed from a computer's slot while the system is running.

Slots and ports make it easy to add peripherals to the computer system. Without peripherals, CPU and memory together are like a brain without a body. Some peripherals, such as keyboards and printers, serve as communication links between people and computers. Other peripherals link the computer to other machines. Still others provide long-term storage media. In the next chapter, we explore a variety of input, output, and storage peripherals and then revisit the buses, slots, and ports that connect those peripherals to the CPU and memory.

Inventing the FUTURE

Tomorrow's Processors

The only thing that has consistently **grown faster** than hardware in the last 40 years is **human expectation**.

—*Bjarne Stroustrup, AT&T Bell Labs, designer of the C++ programming language*

Many research labs are experimenting with alternatives to today's silicon chips. For example, IBM researchers have developed plastic chips that are more durable and energy efficient than silicon chips. Intel, Motorola, and AMD are working with the U.S. government to develop new laser etching technology called *extreme ultraviolet lithography* (EUVL) that could reduce chip size and increase performance radically. Motorola researchers have created chips that combine silicon with gallium arsenide, a semiconductor that conducts electricity faster than silicon and emits light that can be used for information applications; the research should soon produce chips that are much faster than any currently available. IBM and Motorola researchers are making progress producing chips based on carbon rather than silicon. Carbon-based nanoscale processors would be much smaller and consume far less electricity than conventional silicon-based microprocessors. Scientists at HP Labs are experimenting with an alternative to transistors made out of nanowires only 100 atoms in diameter.

Researchers are pursuing other radical research technologies, too. Superconductors that transmit electricity without heat loss could increase computer speed a hundredfold. Unfortunately, superconductor technology generally requires a supercooled environment, which isn't

Five Steps to a Petaflop Computer

Blue Gene

Tower

Board — 1 Petaflop

Chip — 16 Teraflops

2 Teraflops

Processor — 32 Gigaflops

1 Gigaflop

FIGURE 2.20b This illustration shows how IBM researchers envision the evolution of high-performance computers from simple processors to Blue Gene, IBM's next-generation supercomputer.

practical for most applications. A more realistic alternative is the **optical computer**, which transmits information in light waves rather than in electrical pulses. Optical computers outside research labs are currently limited to a few narrow applications, such as robot vision. But when the technology is refined, general-purpose optical computers may process information hundreds of times faster than silicon computers do.

Some of the most revolutionary work in computer design involves not what's inside the processors, but how computers are put together. One example is IBM's Blue Gene supercomputer. The Blue Gene architecture is designed around small, simple processors, each capable of handling eight threads of instructions simultaneously. The processors don't have power-hungry embedded caches, but they do have built-in memory to improve speed. The network of processors is self-heading; it detects failed components, seals them off, and directs work elsewhere. The first computer in the Blue Gene series, Blue Gene/L, is already in operation at Lawrence Livermore National Laboratory, where it is being used for nuclear weapons–related research. Blue Gene/L is currently the fastest computer in the world. The eventual goal is to create a system with one million processors, capable of executing one quadrillion (1,000,000,000,000,000) instructions per second—tens of thousands of times faster than today's PCs! ∼

FIGURE 2.20a Researchers are exploring ways to apply fiber-optic technology to circuit board and chip design to produce faster processors.

The Clock of the Long Now   *by Stewart Brand*

According to one Native American tradition, it's important to think about each decision in terms of its impact seven generations into the future. In today's fast-paced technology-driven society, few people take the time to think more than a few years—or even days—ahead. The Long Now Foundation is a visionary group dedicated to encouraging long-term thinking. Its pioneering members include writer and consultant Stewart Brand, musician and artist Brian Eno, and computer scientist and inventor Danny Hillis. (The organization's name was coined by Eno, who noticed when he moved to New York City that "here" and "now" meant "this room" and "this five minutes," as opposed to the bigger here and longer now of his native England.) In this short essay from The Long Now Foundation's Web site, Brand describes the rationale behind the group's most well-known artifact: The Clock of the Long Now.

The Clock and Library Projects

Civilization is revving itself into a pathological short attention span. The trend might be coming from the acceleration of technology, the short-horizon perspective of market-driven economics, the next-election perspective of democracies, or the distractions of personal multi-tasking. All are on the increase. Some sort of balancing corrective to the short-sightedness is needed-some mechanism or myth which encourages the long view and the taking of long-term responsibility, where 'long-term' is measured at least in centuries. Long Now proposes both a mechanism and a myth. It began with an observation and idea by computer scientist Daniel Hillis:

"When I was a child, people used to talk about what would happen by the year 2000. For the next thirty years they kept talking about what would happen by the year 2000, and now no one mentions a future date at all. The future has been shrinking by one year per year for my entire life. I think it is time for us to start a long-term project that gets people thinking past the mental barrier of an ever-shortening future. I would like to propose a large (think Stonehenge) mechanical clock, powered by seasonal temperature changes. It ticks once a year, bongs once a century, and the cuckoo comes out every millennium."

Such a clock, if sufficiently impressive and well engineered, would embody deep time for people. It should be charismatic to visit, interesting to think about, and famous enough to become iconic in the public discourse. Ideally, it would do for thinking about time what the photographs of Earth from space have done for thinking about the environment. Such icons reframe the way people think.

Hillis, who developed the 'massive parallel' architecture of the current generation of supercomputers, devised the mechanical design of the Clock and is now building the second prototype (the first prototype is on display in London at the Science Museum). The Clock's works consist of a binary digital-mechanical system which is so accurate and revolutionary that we have patented several of its elements. (With 32 bits of accuracy it has precision equal to one day in 20,000 years, and it self-corrects by 'phase-locking' to the noon Sun.) For the way the eventual Clock is experienced (its size, structure, etc.), we expect to keep proliferating design ideas for a while. In 01999 Long Now purchased part of a mountain in eastern Nevada whose high white limestone cliffs may make an ideal site for the ultimate 10,000-year Clock. [The Long Now Foundation uses five digit dates, the extra zero is to solve the deca-millennium bug which will come into effect in about 8,000 years.] In the meantime Danny Hillis and Alexander Rose continue to experiment with ever-larger prototype Clocks.

Long Now added a "Library" dimension with the realization of the need for content to go along with the long-term context provided by the Clock—a library of the deep future, for the deep future. In a sense every library is part of the 10,000-year Library, so Long Now is developing tools (such as the Rosetta Disk, The Long Viewer the Long Server) that may provide inspiration and utility to the whole community of librarians and archivists. The Long Bets project—whose purpose is improving the quality of long-term thinking by making predictions accountable—is also Library-related.

The point is to explore whatever may be helpful for thinking, understanding, and acting responsibly over long periods of time.

Discussion Questions

1. Do you think the Long Now Clock is a good idea? Why or why not?

2. Can you think of other ways to encourage long-term thinking?

Summary

Whether it's working with words, numbers, pictures, or sounds, a computer is manipulating patterns of bits—binary digits of information that it can store in switching circuitry and that are represented by two symbols. Groups of bits can be treated as numbers for calculations using the binary number system. Bits can be grouped into coded messages that represent alphabetic characters, pictures, colors, sounds, or just about any other kind of information. Even the instructions computers follow—the software programs that tell the computer what to do—must be reduced to strings of bits before the computer accepts them. Byte, kilobyte, megabyte, terabyte, and other common units for measuring bit quantities are used in descriptions of memory, storage, and file size.

The microprocessor, or central processing unit (CPU), follows software instructions to perform the calculations and logical manipulations that transform input data into output. Not all CPUs are compatible with each other; each is capable of processing a particular set of instructions, so a software program written for one family of processors can't necessarily be understood by a processor from another family. Engineers are constantly improving the clock speed and architecture of CPUs, making computers capable of processing information faster.

The CPU uses RAM (random access memory) as a temporary storage area—a scratch pad—for instructions and data. Another type of memory, ROM (read-only memory), contains unchangeable information that serves as reference material for the CPU as it executes program instructions.

The CPU and main memory are housed in silicon chips on the motherboard and other circuit boards inside the computer. Buses connect to slots and ports that enable the computer to communicate with internal devices and external peripherals.

Key Terms

architecture ....(p. 51)
ASCII ....(p. 44)
backward compatible ....(p. 48)
bay ....(p. 57)
binary ....(p. 41)
bit ....(p. 41)
bus ....(p. 57)
byte ....(p. 44)
central processing unit
   (CPU) ....(p. 39)
cluster ....(p. 51)
compatible ....(p. 48)
data ....(p. 40)
digit ....(p. 41)
digital ....(p. 41)
expansion card ....(p. 57)

expansion slots ....(p. 57)
express card ....(p. 57)
file ....(p. 47)
gigabyte (gig or GB) ....(p. 47)
information ....(p. 41)
input device ....(p. 39)
kilobyte (KB) ....(p. 47)
megabyte (meg or MB) ....(p. 47)
memory ....(p. 39)
microprocessor ....(p. 39)
motherboard ....(p. 47)
multicore processor ....(p. 51)
multiprocessing ....(p. 51)
nonvolatile memory ....(p. 55)
optical computer ....(p. 58)
output device ....(p. 39)

parallel processing ....(p. 51)
PC card ....(p. 57)
peripheral ....(p. 40)
petabyte (PB) ....(p. 47)
port ....(p. 57)
processor ....(p. 39)
random access memory
   (RAM) ....(p. 39)
read-only memory (ROM) ......(p. 55)
sleep ....(p. 48)
storage device ....(p. 39)
symmetric multiprocessing ....(p. 51)
system bus ....(p. 57)
terabyte (TB) ....(p. 47)
Unicode ....(p. 44)

Interactive Activities

1. The *Tomorrow's Technology and You* Web site, www.pearsonhighered.com/beekman, contains self-test exercises related to this chapter. Follow the instructions for taking a quiz. After you've completed your quiz, you can email the results to your instructor.

2. The Web site also contains open-ended discussion questions called Internet Explorations. Discuss one or more of the Internet Exploration questions for this chapter.

True or False

1. In order for a computer to add two numbers, the numbers first must be converted to ASCII code.

2. A simple on/off switch can store exactly one bit of information.

3. The data processed by digital computers is made up of discrete units, or digits.

4. The contents of ROM cannot be changed.

5. If a processor is backward compatible with another, older processor, it can run older programs written for that processor.

6. A megabyte (MB) is ten times as big as a gigabyte (GB).

7. The information stored in RAM is nothing more than a pattern of electrical current flowing through microscopic circuits in silicon chips.

8. If two different CPUs have exactly the same clock speed, they take exactly the same amount of time to accomplish identical tasks.

9. Slots and ports make it possible for the CPU to communicate with the outside world through peripherals.

10. The access time for most memory is slower than the access time for a typical hard disk.

Multiple Choice

1. Why will software written for the Core CPU generally run on the Core 2 Duo CPU?
   a. Microsoft uses special encoding techniques that work only with Core CPUs.
   b. The Core 2 Duo has special compatibility registers in RAM.
   c. The Core 2 Duo is designed to be backward compatible with earlier Core chips.
   d. Every CPU is, by definition, compatible with the Core processor.
   e. All software written for the Core 2 Duo is compiled on Core processors.

2. Express cards are
   a. cards that are designed to be inserted into expansion slots on desktop PCs.
   b. high-speed cards that are designed to work with workstations.
   c. compact cards that are designed to work with notebook computers.
   d. cards that attach directly to the PC motherboard.
   e. None of the above

3. One megabyte equals approximately
   a. 1,000 bits.
   b. 1,000 bytes.
   c. 1 million bytes.
   d. 1 million bits.
   e. 2,000 megabits.

4. How many values can be represented by a single byte?
   a. 2
   b. 8
   c. 16
   d. 64
   e. 256

5. Transformation of input into output is performed by
   a. peripherals.
   b. memory.
   c. storage.
   d. the CPU.
   e. the ALU.

6. A coding scheme that supports 100,000 unique characters has the name
   a. ASCII.
   b. EBCDIC.
   c. Esperanto.
   d. Unicode.
   e. URL.

7. What does the speed of a computer depend on?
   a. The architecture of the processor
   b. The clock speed of the processor
   c. The word size of the processor
   d. The number of processors
   e. All of the above

8. Why are program instructions represented in binary notation within the computer?
   a. Binary notation is more compact than other representations.
   b. Computer memory is made out of binary digits (bits).
   c. There are only two different directions for electricity to move along a wire.
   d. Computer programmers prefer to think in binary.
   e. A CPU can execute no more than two instructions at one time.

9. A computer's internal bus can be connected to an external bus through
   a. a depot
   b. a CPU

c. a port
d. a flash
e. a megabit

10. When you first turn on a computer, the CPU is preset to execute instructions stored in
   a. RAM.
   b. ROM.
   c. flash memory.
   d. the CD-ROM.
   e. the ALU.

11. When you are working on an unsaved document on a PC, where is the document temporarily stored?
   a. RAM
   b. ROM
   c. The CPU
   d. The Internet
   e. The CD-ROM

12. Information travels between components on the motherboard through
   a. flash memory.
   b. CMOS.
   c. bays.

d. buses.
e. peripherals.

13. Nonvolatile memory
   a. can be thrown in a fire without exploding.
   b. cannot be used to store programs.
   c. can keep its contents without a flow of electricity.
   d. loses its contents without a flow of electricity.
   e. dissolves in water.

14. A collection of bits in the computer's memory might be treated as
   a. binary numbers that can be added and subtracted.
   b. ASCII codes representing letters and other characters.
   c. program instructions that tell the computer what to do.
   d. Any of the above
   e. None of the above

15. Storage devices can be connected to the CPU and memory via
   a. expansion slots.
   b. ports.
   c. bays.
   d. All of the above
   e. None of the above

Review Questions

1. Provide a working definition of each of the keywords listed in the "Key Terms" section. Check your answers in the glossary.

2. What is the main hardware obstacle to running Sony PlayStation software on a PC?

3. Draw a block diagram showing the major components of a computer and their relationships. Briefly describe the function of each component.

4. Why is the international computer industry shifting from ASCII to Unicode for representing text?

5. Why is information stored in some kind of binary format in computers?

6. Clock speed is only one factor in determining a CPU's processing speed. What is another?

7. Explain how symmetrical multiprocessing can increase a computer's performance; use an example or a comparison with the way people work if you like.

8. Why do computer manufacturers typically make their new processors backward compatible with earlier processors?

9. What is the main architectural difference between the Intel Core 2 Duo and the Core and Pentium processors that preceded it?

10. Describe several ways you can minimize your negative impact on the environment when you purchase and use a computer.

Discussion Questions

1. How is human memory similar to computer memory? How is it different?

2. Why are computer manufacturers constantly releasing faster computers? How do computer users benefit from the increased speed?

3. Does information always have value? Explain your answer.

4. Do you think the computer industry has more of a positive or negative effect on preserving global ecosystems?

Projects

1. Collect computer advertisements from newspapers, magazines, and other sources. Compare how the ads handle discussions of speed. Evaluate the usefulness of the information in the ads from a consumer's point of view.

2. Use the World Wide Web to window shop for a computer. Try to determine how the choice of CPU and memory affect price and performance.

3. Interview a salesperson in a computer store. Find out what kinds of questions people ask when buying a computer. Develop profiles for the most common types of computer buyers. What kinds of computers do these customers buy, and why?

4. Systems supporting the keyboard input of Chinese can be put into three types, depending on whether they rely on encoding, pronunciation, or the structure of the characters. Research these systems, and report on the relative strengths and weaknesses of each system type.

Sources and Resources

Books

Apple Confidential 2.0: The Definitive History of the World's Most Colorful Company, by Owen Linzmayer (San Francisco, CA: No Starch Press, 2004). This may be the most comprehensive history of Apple you'll find. The author has covered Apple from the early days through the dark years to its spectacular re-emergence under Steve Jobs.

iWoz: Computer Greek to Cult Icon: How I Invented the Personal Computer, Co-founded Apple, and Had Fun Doing It, by Steve Wozniak with Gina Smith (New York, NY: W. W. Norton, 2006). This is the story of Apple's slightly less famous Steve in (mostly) his own words.

Insanely Great: The Life and Times of Macintosh, the Computer That Changed Everything, Reissue Edition, by Steven Levy (New York, NY: Penguin, 2000). There are dozens of books about Apple's colorful history. This is one of the best. Apple fan and *Newsweek* columnist Steven Levy recounts the first 10 years of the Macintosh's history in breathless detail.

The Second Coming of Steve Jobs, by Alan Deutschman (New York, NY: Broadway Books, 2001). This book focuses on Apple's controversial CEO in the years at NeXT and his return to Apple. Jobs is a contentious, complex, and private person who has achieved fame that rivals rock stars. His story makes good reading.

How Computers Work, Ninth Edition, by Ron White (Indianapolis, IN: Que, 2008). The first edition of How Computers Work launched a successful series that inspired many imitators. Now in its ninth edition, this book is still a great tool for people who want to know more about what's going on inside their PCs. By combining beautiful illustrations with clear prose, *How Computers Work* takes much of the mystery out of the machine.

How Computers Work: Processor and Main Memory, by Roger Young (1st Book Library, Bloomington, IN: 2002). This book is much more technical than *How Computers Work* by Ron White. If you're interested in decoding the circuit diagrams that serve as blueprints for silicon chips, this book may be a good place to start.

Inside the Machine: An Illustrated Introduction to Microprocessors and Computer Architecture, by John Stokes (San Francisco, CA: No Starch Press, 2006). Computer architecture is a complex and highly technical field. Most books on the subject are written in a language only engineers can understand. This book uses color illustrations and clear prose to make the material accessible to a larger audience.

The Soul of a New Machine, by Tracy Kidder (New York, NY: Back Bay Books, 2000). This Pulitzer Prize–winning book provides a journalist's inside look at the making of a new computer in the late 1970s, including lots of insights into what makes computers (and computer people) tick. It's still a good read—and highly relevant—more than two decades after it was first published.

High Tech Trash: Digital Devices, Hidden Toxics, and Human Health, Second Edition, by Elizabeth Grossman (Washington, D.C.: Island Press, 2007). We don't like to talk about it, but we're leaving a toxic trail of digital discards behind us as we rush into the future. In this book, the author makes the case that the environmental impacts of our high-tech tools and toys "are now being felt by communities from the Arctic to Australia, with poorer countries and communities receiving a disproportionate share of the burden." Parts of the book are fairly technical, but there's also a practical appendix: How to Recycle a Computer, Cell Phone, TV, or Other Digital Device.

3

Hardware Basics
Peripherals

Objectives

After you read this chapter you should be able to:

▶ List several examples of input devices and explain how they can make it easier to get different types of information into the computer

▶ List several examples of output devices and explain how they make computers more useful

▶ Explain why a typical computer has different types of storage devices

▶ Diagram how the components of a computer system fit together

> **No one gets to vote** on whether technology
> is going to **change our lives.**
>   —*Bill Gates*

Bill Gates Rides the Digital Wave

In the early days of the PC revolution, Bill Gates and Paul Allen formed a company called Microsoft to produce and market a version of the BASIC programming language for personal computers, then commonly referred to as microcomputers. Microsoft BASIC quickly became the standard language installed in virtually every microcomputer.

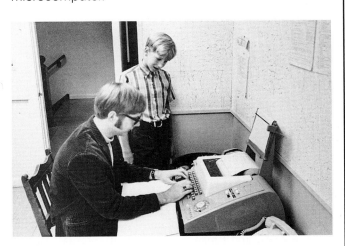

FIGURE 3.1 Bill Gates and Paul Allen as students.

When IBM went shopping for an operating system for its PC, Microsoft moved aggressively to get IBM's business. Microsoft purchased an operating system from a small company, reworked it to meet IBM's specifications, renamed it MS-DOS (for Microsoft Disk Operating System), and charged IBM only $80,000 for a nonexclusive, royalty-free license to use MS-DOS forever. Gates's goal was to make money by licensing MS-DOS to other manufacturers making PC-compatible computers. His gamble paid off. MS-DOS became the dominant operating system for the IBM PC, and Microsoft made billions of dollars providing it to other PC makers and users. In the years that followed, Microsoft's Windows replaced MS-DOS, PC shipments soared, and Microsoft became a giant corporation.

Today Microsoft dominates the PC software industry, selling operating systems, application programs, server software, and software development tools. Software has made Gates one of the richest men on Earth.

Microsoft's desktop dominance was threatened in the mid-1990s by the Internet explosion. For many people, computers became little more than portals into the Internet. Gates responded by making the Internet a critical part of Microsoft's software strategy. Today Microsoft's Internet Explorer web browser is a central component of the Windows OS, Microsoft desktop applications have links to the Internet, and Microsoft has partnerships with dozens of web-related businesses worldwide.

According to writer Steven Levy, Gates "has the obsessive drive of a hacker working on a tough technical dilemma, yet has an uncanny grasp of the marketplace, as well as a firm conviction of what the future will be like and what he should do about it." To prepare for an all-digital future, Microsoft has extended its reach into all kinds of information-related business ventures, from online banking and shopping to the MSNBC cable TV network.

Many competitors and customers insist that Microsoft has used unethical business practices to ruthlessly—and sometimes illegally—stomp out competition and choice. In 1998, 20 states joined the U.S. government in a widely publicized lawsuit against Microsoft's anticompetitive practices. That same year the European Union filed two antitrust lawsuits against the company. Microsoft responded with arrogant denials and a massive PR campaign; one state official received pro-Microsoft form letters from hundreds of people, including some who had died years before. The company was found guilty of antitrust violations in the United States and the EU, but the resulting penalties had little effect on the company's dominance.

Ironically, Microsoft's digital domain is more threatened by the rise of another near-monopoly, Google. Microsoft has so far had little success in controlling the online world, where operating systems and PC applications are less important than emerging web applications.

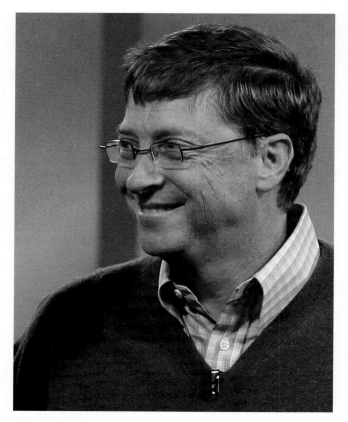

FIGURE 3.2 Bill Gates

In early 2000 Gates stepped aside as CEO of Microsoft to become the company's chairman and chief software architect. That same year he formed the Bill and Melinda Gates Foundation to channel his unprecedented wealth into global causes such as public health, education, libraries, and at-risk families. In 2008 he left behind most of his duties at Microsoft so that he could focus full time on philanthropy work. However, he still continues to serve as Microsoft's chairman and an advisor on key development projects. When Bill Gates applies his relentless, results-driven approach to solving problems that plague the poor, he gives hope to people all over the world. ∼

In this chapter we'll complete the tour of hardware we started in the previous chapter. We've seen the CPU and memory at the heart of the system unit; now we'll explore the peripherals that radiate out from those central components. We'll start with input devices, then move on to output devices, and finish with a look at external storage devices. As usual, the main text provides the basic overview; if you want or need to know more about the inner workings, consult the How It Works boxes scattered throughout the chapter.

Input: From Person to Processor

The nuts and bolts of information process-ing are usually hidden from the user, who sees only the input and output, or as the pros say, *I/O*. This wasn't always the case. Users of the first computers communi-cated one bit at a time by flipping switches on massive consoles or plugging wires into switchboards; they had to be intimately familiar with the inner workings of the machines before they could successfully communicate with them. In contrast, today's users have a choice of hundreds of input devices that make it easy to enter data and commands into their machines. Of these input devices, the most familiar is the computer **keyboard**.

> A computer terminal is **not** some **clunky old** television with a typewriter in front of it. It is an **interface** where the **mind** and **body** can **connect** with the **universe** and **move bits** of it about.
>
> *—Douglas Adams, author of* The Hitchhiker's Guide to the Galaxy

The Keyboard

In spite of nearly universal acceptance as an input device, the QWERTY keyboard (named for the top row of letter keys) seems strangely out of place in a modern computer system. The weird arrangement of letters dates back to the earliest manual typewriters. The letter placement was chosen to reduce typing speed, making it less likely that a typist would hit two keys at the same time and cause the machine to jam. Technological traditions die hard, and the QWERTY keyboard became standard equipment on typewriters and later on virtually all PCs.

Some modern computer keyboards stray from the traditional typewriter design, however. Typing on a standard keyboard, with keys lined up in straight rows, forces you to hold your arms and wrists at unnatural angles. Evidence sug-gests that long hours of typing this way may lead to medical problems, including repetitive-stress injuries, such as ten-donitis and carpal tunnel syndrome. Ergonomic keyboards place the keys at angles that are easier on your arms and hands without changing the ordering of the keys.

FIGURE 3.3 A standard wireless computer keyboard (top) has a straight row of keys. An ergonomic keyboard (left) puts the keys at an angle to allow your wrists to assume a more natural posi-tion while you type.

Whether it's straight or ergonomic, a typical keyboard sends signals to the computer through a cable of some sort. A battery-powered *wireless keyboard* doesn't need a cable connecting it to the rest of the system. Most wireless keyboards use a radio technology called Bluetooth (described in Chapter 8).

Other variations on keyboard design include, miniature keyboards built into pocket-sized devices, screens on phones or laser projections that display keys that react to touch or movement, one-handed keyboards for people who need to (or prefer to) keep one hand free

FIGURE 3.4 Many pocket computers and phones, such as the BlackBerry, have QWERTY keyboards, even though they are too small for touch typing. The iPhone's keyboard appears on the touch-sensitive screen when needed to input text.

FIGURE 3.5 The Virtual Laser Keyboard (VKB) can turn just about any flat sur-face into a QWERTY keyboard.

for other work, and keyboards printed on membranes that can be rolled or folded like paper. Innovative ideas are still emerging from that ancient typewriter technology.

Pointing Devices

Computer users today use their keyboards mostly to enter text and numeric data. For other traditional keyboard functions, such as sending commands and positioning the cursor, they typically use a **mouse**. The mouse is designed to move a pointer around the screen and point to specific characters or objects. The typical mouse uses reflected light and an optical sensing device to detect movement. Most mice have two or more buttons. In a standard configuration, the left button sends standard "click" and "drag" messages, while the right button is used to issue additional commands. A mouse may contain a scroll wheel between the two buttons to streamline the process of scrolling through documents. Apple's Mighty Mouse has no visible buttons—only a tiny scroll ball embedded in a smooth touch-sensitive shell that can detect left-clicks, right-clicks, and other standard button actions. Software can be used to customize the functions of various mouse buttons. *Wireless mice* use Bluetooth technology (see Chapter 8) to send their signals; they require batteries to power tiny radio transmitters.

It's virtually impossible to find a new computer today that doesn't come with a mouse as standard equipment, but there is one exception: The mouse is impractical as a pointing device on laptop computers because these machines are often used where there's no room for a mouse to roam across a desktop. Laptop computer manufacturers provide a variety of alternatives to the mouse as a general-purpose pointing device, and some of these devices are becoming popular as desktop solutions as well:

FIGURE 3.6 The Microsoft mouse (left), like most others, has multiple buttons and a scroll wheel to streamline the process of scrolling through documents or graphical windows. Apple's Mighty Mouse (right) has no visible buttons, but the pressure-sensitive surface responds like a multibutton mouse.

■ The **touchpad** (sometimes called **trackpad**) is a small flat panel that's sensitive to light pressure. The user moves the pointer by dragging a finger across the pad.

■ The **pointing stick** (often called **TrackPoint**, Lenovo's brand name for the device) is a tiny handle that sits in the center of the keyboard, responding to finger pressure by moving the pointer in the direction in which you push it. It's like a miniature embedded joystick.

■ The **trackball** resembles an upside-down mouse. It remains stationary while the user moves the large protruding ball to control the pointer on the screen.

Other pointing devices offer advantages for specific types of computer work (and play). Here are some examples:

■ *Game controllers* come in a verity of forms. A *joystick* is a gearshift-like device used to control movement in arcade games and flight simulators. A *gamepad* is a multi-button device that is held in both hands and typically includes a small joystick. The Nintendo Wii remote is an innovative three-dimensional pointing device that sends position and movement information to the game machine.

■ The **graphics tablet** is popular with artists and designers. Most touch tablets are pressure sensitive, so they can send different signals depending on how hard the user presses on the tablet with a stylus. The *stylus* performs the same point-and-click functions as a mouse does. A similar screen used on Tablet PC devices uses a screen with an active digitizer to track a specially made stylus, letting users input data in their own handwriting.

■ The **touch screen** responds when the user points to or touches different screen regions. Computers with touch screens are frequently used in public libraries, airports, and shopping malls, where many users are unfamiliar with computers. Touch screens are also used in many handheld computers, PDAs, and smart displays; a stylus can be used for pointing or writing on these small screens.

FIGURE 3.7 Mouse Alternatives. Clockwise from top left: a. Many laptops, including this HP Pavilion, include a built-in touchpad as a pointing device. b. The Lenovo ThinkPad has a tiny pointing stick, called a TrackPoint, embedded in the center of its keyboard. c. A trackball is an alternative pointing device for a PC. d. A joystick can be used to control movements in arcade games and flight simulators. e. A game controller typically includes several buttons and joystick-like controls. f. A graphics tablet uses a stylus as a pointing, writing, and drawing tool. g. Touch screen displays are often used in kiosks, ATM machines, and self-service retail devices.

Multi-Touch Input Devices

Sometimes pointing with a mouse or stylus isn't enough. With a **multi-touch** input device, it's possible to use multi-finger or multi-hand gestures to accomplish complex tasks quickly. A multi-touch device might be a touch-sensitive screen, a touch tablet, or a trackpad that can recognize the position, pressure, and movement of more than one finger or hand at a time.

Probably the best known example of a multi-touch device is the screen of Apple's iPhone. Multi-touch technology enables the iPhone's tiny screen to recognize two-fingered movements and gestures; the iPhone can interpret those movements and gestures as complex commands. For example, zooming in for a close-up view of part of a map is as simple as spreading two fingers apart on the map.

Apple and other computer manufacturers also use multi-touch technology in many laptop trackpads. A multi-touch trackpad is more than a simple pointing device. Multi-touch gestures and movements can trigger a variety of complex operations, depending on how the computer's software interprets them. For example, you might be able to rotate a photo by simply touching opposite corners of the picture and rotating your fingers, just as you would with a physical photograph on a smooth table.

Multi-touch input is also useful in many professional applications. For example, the Lemur Jazz Mutant gives a musician or multimedia artist the freedom to control multiple devices, sounds, or images simultaneously. An audio or video technician can replace a myriad of knobs, switches, and sliders with a well-designed multi-touch device.

One of the most ambitious products based on multi-touch technology is Microsoft's Surface. Surface is, in essence, a computer embedded in a table with a large touch-sensitive tabletop that serves as the monitor. Surface is initially designed for use by restaurants, hotels, retail stores, and military applications. Surface can recognize 50 or more touches at a time, and can be programmed to recognize many physical objects. For example, it might display a wine menu when a diner sets a wine glass on its surface.

Futuristic multi-touch technology has appeared in science fiction films such as *Minority Report* and *The Island*. As the technology develops and prices drop, it will undoubtedly appear in our businesses, schools, and homes.

Pinch fingers to shrink or zoom out

Expand fingers to enlarge or zoom in

Rotate fingers to rotate picture or view

Swipe fingers to quickly navigate a multi-page or large document

FIGURE 3.8 Common multi-touch gestures.

FIGURE 3.9 Multitouch Input Devices (clockwise from top) a. The glass screen on the iPhone recognizes a variety of one- and two-fingered movements. b. Apple's Macbook Air has a large multi-touch trackpad that can interpret a variety of multi-digit gestures as commands. c. Lemur's Jazz Mutant is a popular multi-touch control surface for musicians, multimedia artists, and technicians. d. In this mockup of a future application, pictures pour out of a camera phone placed on Microsoft Surface, where they can be sorted, rearranged, and resized using simple hand gestures.

FIGURE 3.10 Computers use specialized input devices to read information stored as optical marks, bar codes, and specially designed characters.

Reading Tools

In spite of their versatility, pointing devices are woefully inefficient for the input of large quantities of text into computers, which is why the mouse hasn't replaced the keyboard on the standard personal computer. Still, there are alternatives to typing for entering numbers and words into computers. Some types of devices, specifically designed for computer input, allow computers to read marks rapidly that represent codes:

■ **Optical mark readers** use reflected light to determine the location of pencil marks on standardized test answer sheets and similar forms.

■ **Magnetic ink character readers** read those odd-shaped numbers printed with magnetic ink on checks.

■ **Bar code readers** use light to read *universal product codes (UPCs)*, inventory codes, and other codes created from patterns of variable-width bars. In many stores, bar code readers are attached to **point-of-sale (POS) terminals**. These terminals send scanned information to a mainframe computer. The computer determines the item's price, calculates taxes and totals, and records the transaction for future use in inventory, accounting, and other areas.

■ **Radio frequency identification (RFID) readers** use radio waves to communicate with **radio frequency identification (RFID) tags**. When energized by a nearby RFID reader, an RFID tag broadcasts its unique identification number to the reader, which digitizes the information for input into a computer. An RFID tag can be as large as a deck of cards or as small as a grain of rice. Larger tags can be read from a greater distance. The hard plastic antitheft cards attached to clothes at department stores contain RFID tags. RFID tags are also used to identify railroad cars, automobiles at toll booths, library books at checkout counters, and pallets of goods being shipped to stores.

Because test forms, magnetic ink characters, bar codes, and RFID tags were designed to be read by computers, the devices that read them are extremely accurate. Reading text from books, magazines, and other printed documents is more challenging because of the great variety of printed text. **Optical character recognition (OCR)** is the technology of recognizing individual characters on a printed page, so they can be stored and edited as text.

FIGURE 3.11 This self-service POS terminal uses three input devices for gathering information about a purchase: A touch screen for entering commands and answering questions, a bar code reader for scanning product information, and a scale for security and accuracy. Before the transaction is completed, another input device reads information encoded in the magnetic strip on the customer's credit card.

FIGURE 3.12 A pen scanner can capture text from a printed document and transfer it to a PC.

FIGURE 3.13 A Tablet PC is a Windows computer with stylus input capabilities.

Before a computer can recognize handwriting or printed text, it must first create a digital image of the page that it can store in memory. This is usually done with an input device known as a *scanner*. There are many types of scanners, as you'll see in the next section. A scanner doesn't actually read or recognize letters and numbers on a page—it just makes a digital "picture" of the page available to the computer. The computer can then use OCR software to interpret the black-and-white scanned patterns as letters and numbers.

Actually, a few special-purpose scanners take care of the OCR work themselves. *Pen scanners* look like highlighters, but they're actually wireless scanners that can perform character recognition on the fly. When you drag a pen scanner across a line of printed text, it creates a text file in its built-in memory, where it's stored until you transfer it into your computer's memory through a cable or infrared beam. A wireless pen scanner actually contains a small computer programmed to recognize printed text. This kind of optical character recognition isn't 100 percent accurate, but it's getting better all the time.

Handwriting recognition is far more difficult and error-prone than printed character recognition is. But handwriting recognition has many practical applications today, especially in **pen-based computers**, such as the Tablet PC. A pen-based computer can work without a keyboard and can accept input from a stylus applied directly to a flat-panel screen. The computer electronically simulates the effect of using a pen and pad of paper. **Handwriting recognition software** translates the user's handwritten forms into ASCII characters. In the past such systems required users to modify their handwriting so that it was consistent and unambiguous enough for the software to decipher reliably, but Tablet PCs have dramatically increased the accuracy and efficiency of this machine type.

Personal digital assistants (PDAs) are handheld computers that serve as pocket-sized organizers, notebooks, appointment books, and communication devices. These popular, versatile devices can also be programmed for specialized work, ranging from sports score-keeping to medical analysis. Newer models feature multimedia functionality, such as music playback and video and photo viewing, and may even be GPS-enabled.

Handwriting recognition software can even be applied to notes scrawled on a white-board in a meeting room or classroom. A *smart whiteboard* can serve as an input device for a PC, so each board full of information is stored as a digital image on the

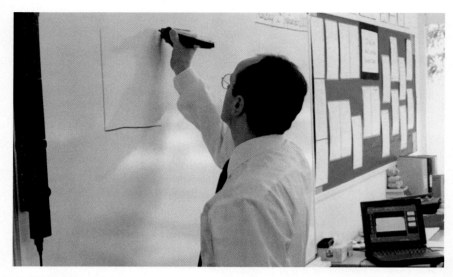

FIGURE 3.14 A smart whiteboard can send its contents to a PC, simplifying and streamlining the note-taking process for meetings and classes.

The … **number-one peripheral device** is not a drive. It's not a printer, scanner, hub, or network. It's you, the user.

—*John K. Rizzo and K. Daniel Clark, in* How the Mac Works

computer's disk. If the writing is clear enough, handwriting recognition software can turn the whiteboard notes into a text file that can be emailed to meeting or class participants. (OCR and handwriting recognition are covered in more detail in later chapters.)

Digitizing Devices

Before a computer can recognize handwriting or printed text, a scanner or other input device must digitize the information—convert it into a digital form. Because real-world information comes in so many forms, a variety of input devices have been designed for capturing and digitizing information. In this section we'll examine several of these devices, from common scanners to exotic sensors.

A scanner is an input device that can create a digital representation of typed text, handwritten text, graphics, and objects. The most common models today are *flatbed scanners*, which look and work like photocopy machines, except that they create computer files instead of paper copies. Inexpensive flatbed scanners are designed for home and small-business use. More expensive models used by graphics professionals are capable of producing higher-quality reproductions and, with attachments, scanning photographic negatives and slides. Some scanners, called *film scanners* (slide scanner), can scan only slides and negatives, but generally produce higher-quality results than flatbed scanners do when scanning transparencies. *Drum scanners* are larger and more expensive than flatbeds are; they're used

FIGURE 3.15 Flatbed scanners (left) capture and digitize images from external paper sources, while slide and photo scanners (right) can reproduce photographs from slides and negatives. A slide scanner can produce high-quality digital reproductions from photographic negatives and slides.

FIGURE 3.16 Consumer cameras, such as the one shown in the top-left photo, sell for a few hundred dollars or less; professional models, such as the one in the top-right photo, can cost much more. Many cell phones, such as the one in the center, include picture- and movie-taking capabilities and can send these images to other phone users. Digital video cameras, such as the one in the bottom-left photo, can deliver video directly to a PC or Mac. A webcam, such as the one shown in the lower-right photo, can continuously feed still pictures or video directly to a PC or Mac.

for museum archival and high-end publishing, where image quality is critical. Regardless of its type or capabilities, however, a scanner converts photographs, drawings, charts, and other printed information into bit patterns that can be stored and manipulated in a computer's memory, usually using graphics software.

In the same way, a **digital camera** can capture snapshots of the real world as digital images. Instead of capturing images on film, a digital camera stores bit patterns on flash memory cards or other digital storage media.

A *video digitizer* is a collection of circuits that can capture input from an analog video camera, television, or other analog video source and convert it to a digital signal. A *digital video camera* can send video signals directly into a computer without a video digitizer because its video images are digitized when they're captured by the camera. Digital video input makes it possible for professionals, hobbyists, and consumers to capture and edit videos with a PC. Videos created this way can be easily packaged as DVDs or uploaded to the web. These video applications are discussed in more detail in later chapters.

One type of digital video camera, commonly called a *webcam*, is either attached to or built into a computer monitor; it can't function as a standalone camera. Webcams are typically used for capturing and posting images or videos to the web and for desktop *videoconferencing*. With videoconferencing software and hardware, people in diverse locations can see and hear each other while they conduct long-distance meetings; their video images are transmitted through networks.

Audio digitizers contain circuitry to digitize sounds from microphones and other audio devices. Digitized sounds can be stored in a computer's or PDA's memory and modified with software. Of course, audio digitizers can capture spoken words as well as music and

How It **Works**

3.1 **Digitizing the Real World**

We live in an analog world, where we can perceive smooth, continuous changes in color and sound. Modern digital computers store all information as discrete binary numbers. To store analog information in a computer, we must digitize it—convert it from analog to digital form.

Digitizing involves using an input device, such as a digital camera or sound card, to take millions of tiny samples of the original image or sound. A sample of an image might be one pinpoint-sized area of the image;

each sample from an audio source is like a brief recording of the sound at a particular instant.

The value of a sample can be represented numerically and, therefore, stored on a computer. A representation of the original image or sound can be reconstructed by assembling all the samples in sequence.

In the example below, you can see how a digital camera and a microphone connected to a computer's sound card can capture photographs and sound recordings of a wolf.

Analog Input

A digital camera captures the wolf's image.

Inside the digital camera, the image is divided into a grid of tiny cells called pixels. Filters separate light into the three primary colors: red, blue, and green. A CCD *(charge-coupled device)* or CMOS *(complimentary metal oxide semiconductor)* converts light into electrons. An ADC *(analog-to-digital converter)* converts the electrical charges into discrete values. A single byte (eight bits) represents the intensity of each primary color; a three-byte code represents the color of each pixel. After compression, the byte codes are stored as a JPEG file.

A microphone transmits the wolf's howl to a sound card inside the computer.

An ADC samples the wave frequently—44,000 or more times per second—and stores the sound level as a number. The faster the sampling frequency is, the better the sound recording. Using more storage to represent the sound level also improves quality. An 8-bit sample can represent 256 different levels; a 16-bit sample can represent 65,536 different levels.

A DSP *(digital signal processing)* chip compresses the stream of bits before it is transmitted to the CPU.

FIGURE 3.17

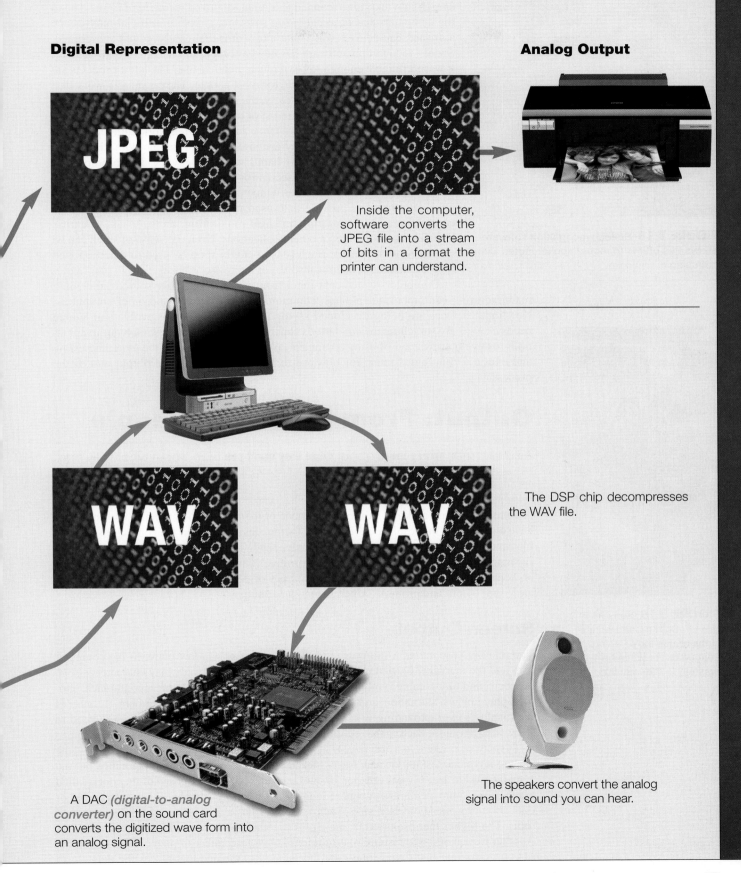

Digital Representation

Analog Output

Inside the computer, software converts the JPEG file into a stream of bits in a format the printer can understand.

The DSP chip decompresses the WAV file.

A DAC *(digital-to-analog converter)* on the sound card converts the digitized wave form into an analog signal.

The speakers convert the analog signal into sound you can hear.

FIGURE 3.18 Speech recognition software allows this officer to record spoken notes without using a keyboard.

FIGURE 3.19 Sensors in this LifeShirt monitored life signs of this Indy Racing League driver when he crashed in the Indy 500.

sound effects. But digitizing spoken input isn't the same thing as converting speech into text. Like scanned text input, digitized *voice input* is just data to the computer. *Speech recognition* software, a type of artificial intelligence software, can convert voice data into words that can be edited and printed. Speech recognition software has been available for years, but until recently it wasn't reliable enough to be of much practical use. The latest products are too limited to replace keyboards for most people. They generally work best when the speaker articulates clearly, the program has been trained to recognize an individual's speech patterns, or input is limited to preset vocabulary (such as in a telephone menu system), and they often work with only a limited vocabulary. However, they are invaluable for people with disabilities and others who can't use their hands while they work. The promise and problems of automated speech recognition will be explored in later chapters.

Sensors designed to monitor temperature, humidity, pressure, and other physical quantities provide data used in robotics, environmental climate control, weather forecasting, medical monitoring, biofeedback, scientific research, and hundreds of other applications. Even our sense of smell can be simulated with sensors. Such sensors might soon be used to detect spoiled foods, land mines, chemical spills, or halitosis.

Computers can accept input from a variety of other sources, including manufacturing equipment, telephones, communication networks, and other computers. New input devices are being developed all the time as technologies evolve and human needs change. By stretching the computer's capabilities, these devices stretch our imaginations to develop new ways of using computers. We'll consider some of the more interesting and exotic technologies later; for now we turn our attention to the output end of the process.

Output: From Pulses to People

As a rule, men **worry more** about **what they can't see** than about what they can.

—Julius Caesar

A computer can do all kinds of things, but none of them is worth anything to us unless we have a way to get the results out of the box. Output devices convert the computer's internal bit patterns into a form that humans can understand. The first computers were limited to flashing lights, teletypewriters, and other primitive communication devices. Most computers today produce output through two main types of devices: display screens for immediate visual output and printers for permanent paper output.

Screen Output

The **display**, also called a **monitor**, serves as a one-way window between the computer user and the machine. Early computer displays were designed to display characters—text, numbers, and tiny graphic symbols. Today's displays are as likely to present graphics, photographic images, animation, and video as they are to display text and numbers. Because of the display's ever-expanding role as a graphical output device, computer users need to know a bit about the factors that control image size and quality.

Display size, like television size, is measured as the length of a diagonal line across the screen; a typical desktop display today measures from 17 to 30 inches diagonally, but the actual viewable area is often smaller. Images on a display are composed of tiny dots, called *pixels* (for picture elements). A square inch of an image on a display is typically a grid of dots about 96 pixels on each side. Such a monitor has a **resolution** of 96 dots per inch (dpi). The higher the resolution is, the closer together the dots and the clearer the image. Another way to describe resolution is to refer to the total number of pixels displayed on the screen. Assuming that two displays are the same size, the one that places the dots closer

FIGURE 3.20 These four images show the same photograph displayed in four different bit depths: 1, 4, 8, and 24 bits.

together displays more pixels and creates a sharper, clearer image. When describing resolution in this way, people usually indicate the number of columns and rows of pixels rather than the total number of pixels. For example, a 1,024 × 768 image is composed of 1,024 columns by 768 rows of pixels, for a total of 786,432 pixels.

Resolution isn't the only factor that determines image quality. Computer displays are limited by *color depth*—the number of different colors they can display at the same time. Color depth is sometimes called *bit depth* because a wider range of colors per pixel takes up more bits of space in video memory. If each pixel is allotted 8 bits of memory, the resulting image can have up to 256 different colors on screen at a time. (There are 256 unique combinations of 8 bits to use as color codes.) In other words, 8-bit color, common in older PCs, has a color depth of 256. Most graphics professionals use 24-bit color, or *true color*, because it allows more than 16 million color choices per pixel—more than enough for photorealistic images. Older *monochrome monitors* can display only monochrome images. *Gray-scale monitors*, which can display black, white, and shades of gray but no

FIGURE 3.21 Most desktop computers have historically used CRT monitors because they're inexpensive and they produce high-quality images at a variety of resolutions. However, sales of flat-panel LCD monitors have now surpassed sales of CRT monitors (right). LCDs are also used in projectors that allow computer screen images to be projected for large viewing audiences (left).

How It **Works**

3.2 Color Display

An image on a computer display is made up of rows of tiny colored pixels. LCD pixels are square and CRT pixels are round, but they're so small that they don't appear as individual circles or squares to us. A monitor's image is refreshed many times per second; with each refresh, the color displayed by each pixel might change.

Each pixel is made up of a mixture of red, green, and blue light. A pixel with maximum values of red, green, and blue appears white; a pixel with maximum red and blue but no green appears magenta; and so on. By varying the luminosity (brightness) of the three colored lights that make up each pixel, a monitor can display millions of unique colors. This process of creating colors by combining colored lights is called additive color synthesis.

FIGURE 3.22

Red, green, and blue are the three additive primary colors. Additive color synthesis that's based on red, green, and blue uses the RGB color model.

The RGB color model is device dependent—an image might look different on two different monitors because of the way the primary colors are generated. Graphic designers and photographers depend on color management hardware and software to fine tune displays so they're consistent with each other and with other output devices. Image editing programs like Photoshop have controls for adjusting RGB values in individual images.

Additive color synthesis is really a kind of optical illusion. Pixels that combine red and green light appear to the human eye to be yellow, even though the light they produce is not truly yellow.

other colors, and *color monitors*, which can display a range of colors, have greater color depth. A modern PC or Mac can portray different combinations of resolution and color depth on the same display.

The monitor is connected to the computer by way of the *video adapter*, which is typically a circuit board installed in a slot inside the main system unit. An image on the monitor exists inside the computer in video memory, or *VRAM*, a special portion of RAM on the video adapter dedicated to holding video images. The amount of VRAM determines the maximum resolution and color depth that a computer system can display. The more video memory a computer has, the more detail it can present in a picture. Many Macs and PCs include additional video hardware to support multiple monitors.

Most displays fall into one of two classes: television-style **cathode-ray tube (CRT) monitors** and flat-panel **liquid crystal displays (LCDs)**. Once used primarily in laptop computers, LCDs are now more popular than the older, bulky, CRT monitors on the desktop. **Video projectors** also use LCDs to project computer screen images for meetings and classes.

Paper Output

Output displayed on a monitor is immediate but temporary. A **printer** can produce a hard copy on paper of any static information that can be displayed on the computer's screen. Printers come in several varieties, but they all fit into two basic groups: *impact printers* and *nonimpact printers*.

Older **impact printers** include line printers and dot matrix printers. Printers of this type share one common characteristic: They form images by physically striking paper, ribbon, and print hammer together, the way a typewriter does. Mainframes use line printers to produce massive printouts; these speedy, noisy beasts hammer out thousands of lines of text per minute. You might have seen form letters from banks and stores, bills from utility companies, and report cards from schools that were printed with **line printers**. Because they're limited to printing characters, line printers are inadequate for applications such as desktop publishing in which graphics are essential.

Dot matrix printers print text and low-resolution graphics with equal ease. Instead of printing each character as a solid object, a dot matrix printer uses pinpoint-sized hammers to transfer ink to the page.

Except for those applications, such as billing, where multipart forms need to be printed, **nonimpact printers** have replaced impact printers in most offices, schools, and homes. The two main types of nonimpact printers are laser printers and inkjet printers. **Laser printers** can quickly print numerous pages per minute of high-quality text and graphical output. Because of their speed, durability, and reliability, they're often shared among PCs in office environments. Laser printers use the same technology as photocopy machines: A laser beam creates patterns of electrical charges on a rotating drum; those charged patterns attract black toner and transfer it to paper as the drum rotates. Color laser printers can print multicolor images by mixing different toner shades.

People who work in color tend to use less-expensive **inkjet printers**, which spray ink directly onto paper to produce printed text and graphic images. Inkjets generally print fewer pages per minute than laser printers do. But high-quality color inkjet printers cost far less than color laser printers cost, and many are less expensive than the cheapest black-and-white laser printers. Inkjet printers are also smaller and lighter than laser printers. Portable inkjet printers designed to travel with laptops weigh only a couple of pounds each. **Photo printers** are designed to print high-quality photos captured with digital cameras and scanners; these printouts are often indistinguishable from the photos you might order from a professional photo-printing service.

FIGURE 3.23 A portable photo printer (top), an inkjet printer (center), and a laser printer (bottom) all provide different types of hard copy output.

How It **Works**

3.3 Color Printing

Printed colors can't be as vivid as video colors because printed images don't produce light the way monitors do; they only reflect light. Most color printers use subtractive synthesis to produce colors: they mix various amounts of cyan (light blue), magenta (reddish purple), yellow, and black pigments to create a color. Colors mixed this way follow the CYMK color model (for Cyan, Yellow, Majenta, and blacK)

Most printers, like monitors, are raster devices; they form images from tiny dots. Each dot is made up of a mixture of the primary subtractive colors.

Matching on-screen color with printed color is difficult because monitors use additive color synthesis to obtain the color, whereas printers use subtractive synthesis. Monitors are able to display more colors than printers can, although printers can display a few colors that monitors can't. But the range of colors that humans can perceive extends beyond either technology.

You can demonstrate subtractive synthesis by painting overlapping areas of cyan, magenta, and yellow ink. The combination of all three is black; combinations of pairs produce red, green, and blue, which are secondary colors of the subtractive system.

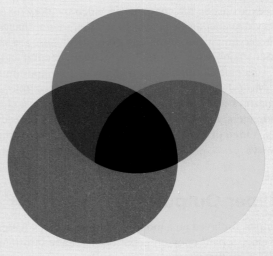

FIGURE 3.24

Both laser and inkjet printers produce high resolution output—usually 600 or more dots per inch. At these resolutions, it's hard to tell with the naked eye that characters and pictures are, in fact, composed of dots.

Multifunction printers (**MFP**, also called *all-in-one devices*) take advantage of the fact that different tools can use similar technologies. A multifunction printer usually combines a scanner, a laser or inkjet printer, and a fax modem (described in the next section). Such a device can serve as a printer, a scanner, a color photocopy machine, and a fax machine.

For certain scientific and engineering applications, a **plotter** is more appropriate than a printer for producing hard copy. A plotter is an automated drawing tool that can produce large, finely scaled drawings, engineering blueprints, and maps by moving the pen and/or the paper in response to computer commands.

FIGURE 3.25 A multifunction printer combines a printer with a scanner and a fax modem so that it can print, scan, fax, and photocopy.

Fax Machines and Fax Modems

A **facsimile (fax) machine** is a fast and convenient tool for transmitting information stored on paper. When you send a fax of a paper document, the sending fax machine scans each page, converting the scanned image into a series of electronic pulses and sending those signals over phone lines to another fax machine. The receiving fax machine uses the signals to construct and print black-and-white facsimiles, or copies, of the original pages. In a sense, when combined, fax machines and telephone lines serve as a long-distance photocopy machine.

A computer can send on-screen documents through a fax modem to a receiving fax machine. The **fax modem** translates the document into signals that can be sent over phone wires and decoded by the receiving fax machine. In effect, the receiving fax machine acts like a remote printer for the document. A computer can also use a fax modem to receive transmissions from fax machines, treating the sending fax machine as a kind of remote scanner. A faxed letter can be displayed on-screen or printed to paper, but it can't immediately be edited with a word processor the way an email message can. Like a scanned document, a digital facsimile is nothing more than a collection of black-and-white dots to the computer. Before a faxed document can be edited, it must be processed by optical character recognition (OCR) software.

Output You Can Hear

Modern PCs include sound cards. A **sound card** enables the PC to accept microphone input, play music and other sound through speakers or headphones, and process sound in a variety of ways. (All Macs and some PCs have audio circuitry integrated with the rest of the system, so they don't need separate sound cards.) With a sound card, a PC can play digital recordings of all kinds of sounds, from personal recordings made with the PC and a microphone to music downloaded from the Internet.

Most sound cards also include synthesizers—specialized circuitry designed to generate sounds electronically. These *synthesizers* can be used to produce music, noise, or anything in between. A computer can also be connected to a stand-alone music synthesizer so that the computer has complete control of the instrument. Computers can also generate synthesized speech with the right software. Of course, to produce any kind of sound, the computer needs to include or be attached to speakers or headphones.

FIGURE 3.26 Daft Punk, like many modern musical groups uses computers and electronic synthesizers for composing and performing music.

Controlling Other Machines

In the same way that many input devices convert real-world sights and sounds into digital pulses, many output devices work in the other direction, taking bit patterns and turning them into nondigital movements or measurements. Robot arms, telephone switchboards, transportation devices, automated factory equipment, spacecraft, and a host of other machines and systems accept their orders from computers.

FIGURE 3.27 Using output devices that operate on similar principles, computers control the movements of spacecraft and virtual reality arcade games.

In one example familiar to computer gamers, an enhanced input device delivers output. Controllers with *force feedback* can receive signals from a computer and give tactile feedback—jolts, scrapes, and bumps—that matches the visual output of the game or simulation. Many video arcades take the concept further by having the computer shake, rattle, and roll the gamer's chair while displaying on-screen movements that match the action. Output devices that generate synthetic smells are also beginning to appear. If these devices catch on, Web sites might commonly include smells as well as sights and sounds. While you're virtually visiting your favorite beach resort, you might smell synthetic surf, sand, and sunblock.

Of course, computers can send information directly to other computers, bypassing human interaction altogether. The possibilities for computer output are limited only by the technology and the human imagination, both of which are stretching further all the time.

CHAPTER 3 | Hardware Basics   **85**

Storage Devices: Input Meets Output

Some computer peripherals are capable of performing both input and output functions. These devices, which include tape and disk drives, are the computer's **storage devices**. They're sometimes referred to as *secondary storage* devices because the computer's memory is its *primary storage*. Unlike RAM, which forgets everything when the computer is turned off, and ROM, which can't learn anything new, storage devices enable the computer to record information semipermanently so it can be read later by the same computer or by another computer.

A **retentive memory** may be a good thing, but **the ability to forget** is the true token of greatness.

—*Elbert Hubbard*

Magnetic Tape

Tape drives are common storage devices on most mainframe computers and some PCs. A tape drive can write data onto, and read data off of, a magnetically coated ribbon of tape. The reason for the widespread use of **magnetic tape** as a storage medium is clear: a magnetic tape can store massive amounts of information in a small space at a relatively low cost. The spinning tape reels that symbolized computers in so many old science fiction movies have for the most part been replaced by tape cartridges based on similar technology.

FIGURE 3.28 This backup device stores large quantities of data on magnetic tape cartridges. *(Source: Photo courtesy of Iomega Corporation.)*

Magnetic tape has one clear limitation: Tape is a **sequential-access** medium. Whether a tape holds music or computer data, the computer must zip through information in the order in which it was recorded. Retrieving information from the middle of a tape is far too time-consuming for most modern computer applications because people expect immediate response to their commands. As a result, magnetic tape is used today primarily for backing up data and a few other operations that aren't time sensitive.

Magnetic Disks

Like magnetic tape, a *magnetic disk* has a magnetically coated surface that can store encoded information; a *disk drive* writes data onto the disk's surface and reads data from the surface. But unlike a tape drive, a disk drive can rapidly retrieve information from any part of a magnetic disk without regard for the order in which the information was recorded, in the same way you can quickly select any track on an audio compact disc. Because of their **random access** capability, disks are the most popular media for everyday storage needs.

Many computer users are familiar with the 3.5-inch *diskette* (also called *floppy disk*)—a small, magnetically sensitive, flexible plastic wafer housed in a plastic case. The diskette was once

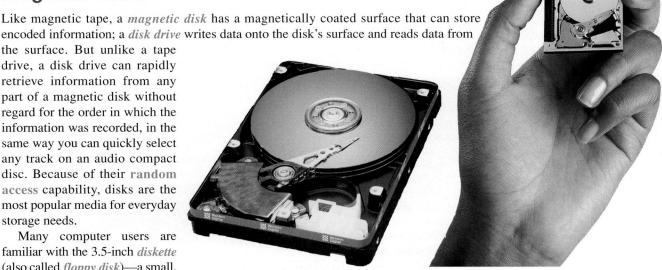

FIGURE 3.29 Internal hard drives and smaller microdrives are based on very similar technologies, despite the differences in size.

Working Wisdom

Ergonomics and Health

Along with the benefits of computer technology comes the potential for unwelcome side effects. For people who work long hours with computers, the side effects include risks to health and safety due to radiation emissions, repetitive-stress injuries, or other computer-related health problems. Inconclusive evidence suggests that low-level radiation emitted by CRT monitors and other equipment might cause health problems, including miscarriages in pregnant women and leukemia. The scientific jury is still out, but the mixed research results so far have led many computer users and manufacturers to err on the side of caution.

More concrete evidence relates keyboarding to occurrences of *repetitive-stress injuries*, such as *carpal tunnel syndrome*, a painful affliction of the wrist and hand that results from repeating the same movements over long periods. Prolonged computer use also increases the likelihood of headaches, eyestrain, fatigue, and other symptoms of "techno-stress."

Ergonomics (sometimes called *human engineering*) is the science of designing work environments that enable people and things to interact efficiently and safely. Ergonomic studies suggest preventative measures you can take to protect your health as you work with computers:

➡ *Choose equipment that's ergonomically designed.* When you're buying computer equipment, look beyond functionality. Use Web site and magazine reviews, manufacturer's information, and personal research to check on health-related factors, such as monitor radiation and glare, noise levels, and keyboard layout. Flat-panel LCD monitors reduce eyestrain in addition to saving desk space. A growing number of computer products, such as split, angled ergonomic keyboards, are specifically designed to reduce the risk of equipment-related injuries.

➡ *Create a healthful workspace.* Keep the paper copy of your work at close to the same height as your screen. Position your monitor and lights to minimize glare. Sit at arm's length from your monitor to minimize radiation risks.

➡ *Build flexibility into your work environment.* Whenever possible work with an adjustable chair, an adjustable table, an adjustable monitor, and a removable keyboard. Change your work position frequently.

➡ *Let the technology work for you.* If your work involves frequent repetitive typing, consider using a software utility to automate the repetition. If you do lots of typing, consider voice recognition software.

➡ *Rest your eyes.* Look up from the screen periodically and focus on a faraway object or scene. Blink frequently. Take a 15-minute break every two hours.

➡ *Stretch.* While you're taking your rest break, do some simple stretches to loosen tight muscles. Occasional stretching of the muscles in your arms,

Adjustable flat-panel display, arm's length and 15° to 30° below line of sight

Screen positioned to avoid glare and backlighting

Wrist pad or ergonomic keyboard

Horizontal forearm

Lower back support

Dog

Feet flat on the floor

FIGURE 3.30a A healthful workspace can reduce the chances of developing computer-related injuries.

hands, wrists, back, shoulders, and lower body can make hours of computer work more comfortable and less harmful.

➡ *Listen to your body.* If you feel uncomfortable, your body is telling you to change something or take a break. Don't ignore it.

➡ *Seek help when you need it.* If your wrists start hurting when you work, you have persistent headaches, or you are feeling some other problem that may be related to excessive computer work, talk to a professional. A medical doctor, chiropractor, physical therapist, or naturopath may be able to help you to head off the problem before it becomes chronic.

FIGURE 3.30b This unusual keyboard is designed to minimize strain on wrists and possibility of injury.

routinely used for transferring data files between machines, though their limited capacity—typically just 1.44MB—and slow speed make them less useful today. Few PCs sold today include floppy diskette drives as standard equipment.

Virtually all PCs include hard disks as their main storage devices. A **hard disk** is a rigid, magnetically sensitive disk that spins rapidly and continuously inside the computer chassis or in a separate box connected to the computer housing. This type of hard disk is usually not removed by the user. Information can be transferred to and from a hard disk much faster than from a floppy disk. A hard disk might hold hundreds of gigabytes (thousands of megabytes) of information—more than enough room for every word and picture in this book, an entire music collection, several movie-length video clips, and years of photographs.

To fill the gap between low-capacity, slow floppy disks and nonremovable, fast hard disks, manufacturers in the 1990s developed a variety of high-capacity transportable storage solutions based on magnetic disk technology, including the Zip disk. But today, magnetic cartridge drives have all but disappeared as a result of advances in optical disc and flash memory storage technology.

	Sequential-access media	Random-access media
Video	VHS tape	DVD, or Blu-ray disk
Data	Cassette tape	CD

FIGURE 3.31 Many home theater systems include sequential-access devices—VHS tape decks—and random-access devices—DVD players. The advantages of random access are the same for video and audio players as for computers.

Optical Discs

An **optical disc drive** uses laser beams rather than magnets to read and write bits of data on a reflective aluminum layer of the disk. A transparent plastic disc surface protects the aluminum layer from routine physical damage while letting laser light through. Access speeds are slower for optical discs than for magnetic hard disks. While optical discs are generally reliable for long-term storage, they can deteriorate. A severe scratch in the plastic coating can allow air to reach the aluminum layer, leading to oxidation and a loss of information. Surprisingly, the upper surface of the disc (with the label) is more sensitive to scratching than the lower surface because the protective plastic layer is thinner on that side.

From CD-ROM to BD-RW, there's an alphabet soup of choices in optical disc drives for PCs today. The names can be especially confusing because they aren't consistent. Does R stand for Read, Recordable, Rewritable, or Random? It depends on the context. Many of these drive types will fall by the wayside as the cost of all-purpose drives comes down. But until then, it's helpful to know something about these oddly named devices.

The oldest type of optical drive in computers is the *CD-ROM drive*. A CD-ROM drive can read data from **CD-ROM** (compact disc—read-only memory) discs—data discs that are physically identical to music compact discs. The similarity of audio and data CDs is no accident; it makes it possible for CD-ROM drives to play music CDs under computer control. A CD-ROM can hold up to about 800MB of data—more raw text than you could type in your lifetime. But because CD-ROM drives are read-only devices, they can't be used as storage devices. That's why they're seldom found in PCs today; they've been replaced by drives that can write as well as read optical discs.

Like a CD-ROM drive, a *CD-RW drive* can read data from CD-ROMs and play music from audio CDs. But a CD-RW drive can also *burn*, or record, data onto CD-R and CD-RW disks. **CD-R** (compact disc-recordable) disks are *WORM* (write-once, read-many) media. That is, a drive can write onto a blank (or partially filled) CD-R disk, but it can't erase the data after it's burned in. **CD-RW** (compact disc-rewritable) discs have the advantage of being erasable. A drive can write, erase, and rewrite a CD-RW disk repeatedly.

How It **Works**

3.4 Disk Storage

MAGNETIC DISKS

Both hard disks and floppy disks are coated with a magnetic oxide similar to the material used to coat cassette tapes and videotapes. The read/write head of a disk drive is similar to the record/play head on a tape recorder; it magnetizes parts of the surface to record information. The difference is that a disk is a digital medium—binary numbers are read and written. The typical hard disk consists of several *platters*, each accessed via a read/write head on a movable *armature*. The magnetic signals on the disk are organized into concentric tracks; the tracks in turn are divided into sectors. This is the traditional scheme used to construct addresses for data on the disk.

Hard disks spin much faster than floppy disks do and have a higher storage density (number of bytes per square inch). The *read/write head* of a hard disk glides on a thin cushion of air above the disk and never actually touches the disk.

CD-ROM

A CD-ROM drive contains a small laser that shines on the surface of the disk, "reading" the reflections. Audio CDs and computer CD-ROMs have similar formats; that's why you can play an audio CD with a CD-ROM drive. Information is represented optically—the bottom surface of the CD, under a protective layer of plastic, is coated with a reflective metal film. A laser burns unreflective pits into the film to record data bits. After a pit is burned, it can't be smoothed over and made shiny again; that's why CD-ROMs are read-only.

FIGURE 3.32

DVD AND BLU-RAY DRIVES

The main difference between DVD and CD technology is that the pits are packed much closer together on a DVD, so about seven times as many can fit on the DVD's surface. (To read these tightly packed bits, the DVD-ROM uses a narrower laser beam.) A DVD can hold even more data—up to 8.5 GB—if it has a second layer of data. On a layered DVD, the top layer is semireflective, allowing a second readback laser to penetrate to the layer below. The laser can "see through" the top layer, just as you can see through a picket fence when you look at it from exactly the right angle. For massive storage jobs, a DVD can have data on both sides— up to 17GB. Two-sided usually have to be turned over for the reader to read both sides; future drives may allow additional readback lasers to read the second side without flipping the disk. A Blu-ray disc can pack almost six times as many bits on a disc as a DVD by using a blue-violet laser, which has a shorter wavelength than the lasers used in DVD drives.

RECORDABLE DRIVES

Recordable CD, DVD, and Blu-ray drives use laser beams to write data on recordable disks. But recordable optical media have layers with chemical structures that react to different temperatures created by different types of lasers. To write data, a high-intensity laser beam produces high temperatures that break down the crystalline structure of the original surface. The resulting pits dissipate, rather than reflect, low-level lasers during the process of reading recorded data. To erase data, a laser heats the pits to about 400 degrees, causing them to revert to their original reflective crystalline state.

FIGURE 3.33 This drive can record DVD-R, DVD-RW, DVD+R, DVD+RW, CD-R, and CD-RW discs. It can play discs in all of the above formats, plus CD-ROM and DVD-ROM discs.

Today, CD-R and CD-RW media are commonly used to make backup copies of data files and personal music CDs and for transporting data between machines. But CD-ROM and CD-RW *drives* have been replaced by drives that can work with DVDs as well as CDs. DVD originally stood for *digital video disc,* because the discs were designed to replace VHS tapes in video stores. Today, many people say DVD stands for *digital versatile disc* because these high-capacity discs are used to store and distribute all kinds of data.

A DVD is the same size, physically, as a standard CD-ROM but can hold between 4.7 and 17 GB of information, depending on how the information is stored. A single-layer DVD can hold up to 4.7 GB of information. A second layer approximately doubles the

	CD-ROM (read-only CD)	CD-RW	DVD-ROM (read-only DVD)	DVD/RW	BD/ROM (read-only Blu-ray)	BD/RW
Capacity	700MB	700MB	4.7GB (single-layer disc), 9.4GB (dual-layer disc)	4.7GB (single-layer disc), 9.4GB (dual-layer disc)	27GB (single-layer disc), 50GB (dual-layer disc)	27GB (single-layer disc), 50GB (dual-layer disc)
Play Audio CD	●	●	●	●	●	●
Play DVD Movie			●	●	●	●
Play HD Blu-ray Movie					●	●
Read CD-R, CD-RW	●	●	●	●	●	●
Write CD-R, CD-RW		●		●		●
Read Data on DVDs			●	●	●	●
Write Data on DVDs				●		●
Read Data on Blu-ray Disc					●	●
Write Data on Blu-ray Disc						●
Record DVD Video				●		●
Record HD Video						●

FIGURE 3.34 This chart summarizes the capabilities of different types of optical drives. (Older drives may require specific + or – media formats for compatibility.)

data capacity of the disc. Most commercial DVD movies are encoded on dual-layer DVDs. It's possible to double the capacity again by recording on both sides of the disc. *DVD-ROM drives* can play DVD movies, read DVD data discs, read standard CD-ROMs, and play audio CDs. They're seldom found in PCs today; they're mostly used in home DVD players.

A combination *DVD/CD-RW drive* offers the advantages of a DVD-R drive and a CD-RW drive in a single unit that can play DVD movies and audio CDs, record and erase data on CD-RW disks, and burn audio CDs and CD-ROMs. But this type of drive can't record movies or other large files on blank DVDs; it can only record on CD-R and CD-RW media. Fortunately, rewritable DVD drives, or *DVD burners*, are inexpensive and commonplace today. These versatile drives can read and write on CD and DVD media. They may be called *DVD-RW*, *DVD+RW*, *DVD+/-RW*, or *DVD/RW* drives. Discs for DVD/RW drives come in write-once (*DVD-R* or *DVD+R*) or rewritable (DVD-RW or DVD+RW) forms. Within each of these categories, it's possible to choose single-layer or more expensive dual-layer media, although not all DVD burners can burn dual-layer discs. In the early days of rewritable DVD drives (just a few years ago), two competing formats, DVD-RW and DVD+RW, were incompatible. Fortunately, newer drives can read and write data on both DVD-RW and DVD+RW disks. (A relatively new format, *DVD-RAM*, is less popular and less compatible with other types of drives. It is used primarily for data backups and digital video recorders.)

With the right software, most of these recordable DVD drives can be used to create DVD videos that you can play on DVD movie players. Unfortunately, some older DVD players have trouble reading DVDs burned on computer drives. Single-layer, write-once discs are the least likely to cause compatibility problems on other machines, including DVD players.

Early DVD burners were rated with speeds of 1X—it might take as long to record a movie as it does to watch it. Today's drive speeds are measured in multiples of 1X. For example, a 16X drive might record data 16 times faster than a 1X drive. Speed can also be affected by the type of media, the type of connection to the computer, and the computer's software.

DVD drives are gradually being supplanted by **Blu-ray** drives (*BD*) that can read and write on media that hold up to 50 gigabytes on two layers—enough for full-length high-definition (HD) movies with plenty of room to spare. *BD-R* drives can read data from Blu-ray discs, DVDs, and CDs; *BD-RW* drives can read and record on all of those types of media. In time, BD drives are likely to be standard equipment in most PCs.

Internal and External Drives

Hard disk drives and optical disc drives come in two basic forms: internal drives and external drives. **Internal drives** generally reside in *bays* inside the system unit. A new tower PC often includes a hard disk in one bay and some kind of optical drive in a second bay. Some PCs have extra bays for additional internal hard drives or removable media. Non-tower desktop systems and laptops generally lack expansion bays for adding additional drives.

But even if there's no room in the system unit for additional internal drives, **external drives** can be connected to the system through USB or Firewire ports, discussed later in this chapter. Because they're contained in their own cases, external drives are relatively easy to transport between locations and share between computers. For example, a photographer might copy a large photo library from an office PC's internal hard drive onto an external hard drive, take the drive home, attach it to a Macintosh, and copy the photo library onto the Mac's internal hard drive. (This kind of *cross-platform* data transfer is generally simple, provided that the disk format is recognizable by both Macs and PCs. Disk formatting and operating systems are discussed in the next chapter.)

Most external drives include their own power supplies that must be plugged into separate AC outlets. Some portable hard drives are designed to draw their power from their host computers through their USB or Firewire connections.

FIGURE 3.35 This SD flash memory card represents one of the most popular kinds of solid-state storage used in digital cameras and other digital media devices.

FIGURE 3.36 An Apple iPod Touch stores music and other data using flash memory. It can connect to a Mac or Windows PC through a USB port.

Flash Memory Storage Devices

In spite of their popularity, disk drives present problems for today's computer users. The moving parts in disk drives are more likely to fail than other computer components. Experienced computer users know that it's not a question of *if* their hard drives will fail, but *when* they'll fail. For airline travelers and others who must depend on battery power for long periods of time, spinning drives consume too much energy. Disk drives can be noisy—a problem for musicians and others who use computers for audio applications. And disk drives are bulky when compared with computer memory; they're often not practical for palm-sized computers and other applications where space is tight and battery life is at a premium.

Until recently, disk drives were the only realistic random-access storage devices for most computer applications. Solid-state storage devices—rewritable memory devices with no moving parts—were far too expensive to be practical for most uses. But that's changing rapidly with the declining cost of flash memory—a type of erasable memory chip that can serve as a reliable, low-energy, quiet, compact storage alternative for many applications. *Flash memory cards*, including SD (Secure Digital) cards, Compact Flash cards, Memory Sticks, and other cards, are used to store images in digital cameras and sounds in digital recorders. A flash memory card can also be read and written to by a PC, provided it's connected to the PC through a connected camera, recorder, or *flash media card reader*. (Some PCs, monitors, and keyboards have built-in flash media card readers.) Flash memory is also used in MP3 players, smart phones, PDAs, and many other electronic devices.

USB flash drives (also called *thumb drives* and *jump drives*) are popular for storing and transporting data files. A key-sized flash drive can plug directly into a USB port; from the computer's point of view, it looks and acts like a small removable hard drive. It can be loaded with data, removed, and plugged into another computer's USB port—regardless of the make and model of each computer. Many people carry flash drives on their keychains so they can easily transport documents, pictures, songs, and even movies between computers. The capacity of early flash memory drives and cards was measured in megabytes. Today's devices hold gigabytes of data.

Flash memory is still too expensive to replace hard drives in most computers. The first diskless laptops—machines with internal flash drives instead of hard drives—cost hundreds of dollars more than their hard-drive-equipped counterparts. But as prices drop and production rises, flash drives will chip away at the dominance of hard drives in the storage market.

FIGURE 3.37 USB flash drives can store gigabytes of data; they plug into a computer's USB port. This Swiss Army knife has a built-in USB flash memory device.

The Computer System: The Sum of Its Parts

The computer is by all odds the most **extraordinary** of the **technological clothing** ever devised by man, since it is an **extension** of our **central nervous system**. Beside it **the wheel is a mere hula hoop** …

—*Marshall McLuhan, in* War and Peace in the Global Village

Most personal computers fall into one of four basic design classes:

- *Tower systems*—tall, narrow boxes that generally have more expansion slots and bays than other designs
- Flat *desktop systems* (sometimes called "pizza box" systems) designed to sit under the monitor like a platform
- *All-in-one systems* (such as the iMac) that combine monitor and system unit into a single housing

Storage Medium	Capacity	Advantages	Disadvantages
Hard Disk	100GB–2TB or more	Relatively high capacity, fast, and inexpensive per GB.	Not easily portable. Moving parts make data more vulnerable to drive failure.
CD (CD-R and CD-RW)	700MB	Can contain audio data compatible with audio CD players. Data CDs can be read by nearly any optical drive.	Smallest capacity of all optical discs. CD-R discs can't be erased and rewritten. CD-RW discs must be reformatted before being rewritten.
DVD (DVD-R, DVD+R, DVD-RAM, DVD-RW, and DVD+RW)	4.7GB–9.4GB	Can contain DVD video compatible with most consumer DVD players.	Smaller capacity than Blu-ray discs. Discs can't be used in CD drives. DVD-R and DVD+R discs can't be erased and rewritten. DVD discs that can be rewritten must be reformatted first.
Blu-ray (BD-ROM, BD-R and BD-RE/BD-RW)	27GB–50GB	Highest capacity optical media option. Can contain HD video playable in many home theater systems.	Relatively expensive. Discs can't be used in CD or DVD drives. BD-ROM and BD-R discs can't be erased and rewritten. BD-RE discs must be reformatted before being rewritten.
Flash Drive	1GB–16GB or more	No card reader required; works with any computer with a USB port. Extremely portable.	Relatively expensive per GB of storage. Requires a spare USB port.
Flash Memory Card	1GB–16GB or more	Can be used in most digital cameras, recorders, and other portable devices. Slightly cheaper than flash drive per GB.	Relatively expensive per GB of storage. May require a card reader to connect to computer.

FIGURE 3.38 Popular storage media compared.

■ *Laptop computers*, which include all the essential components, including keyboard and pointing device, in one compact box

Whatever the design, a PC must allow for the attachment of input, output, and storage peripherals. That's where slots, ports, and bays figure in. Now that we've explored the peripherals landscape, we can look again at the ways of hooking those peripherals into the system.

Ports and Slots Revisited

From the earliest days of the PC's history, designers recognized the need to have standard ports for connecting peripherals. In general, these ports followed interface standards agreed on by the hardware industry so that devices made by one manufacturer could be attached to systems made by other companies. For many years industry standard PCs had *serial ports* that could send and receive data one bit at a time and *parallel ports* for attaching printers and other devices that send and receive bits in groups, rather than sequentially. Additional ports were typically included for keyboard, video displays, and audio equipment.

Working Wisdom

Computer Consumer Concepts

Any brand-specific advice on choosing computer equipment quickly becomes outdated, but some general principles remain constant while the technology races forward. Here are some consumer criteria worth considering if you plan to buy your own computer:

➡ **Cost.** Don't make the mistake of spending your entire budget on the computer itself. Save some funds for peripherals. Depending on how you're going to use the system, you may need one or more of these peripherals: printer, scanner, high-quality microphone, webcam, digital camera, digital video camera, upgraded sound card, and upgraded graphics card. You'll almost certainly need some commercial software, too. Don't be tempted to copy copyrighted software from your friends or public labs; software piracy is against the law. When comparing computers, think about the software that comes bundled with them. A computer that costs a little bit less but doesn't include a word processor, spreadsheet program, and presentation software may be a worse value than a slightly more expensive system that includes that software.

➡ **Capability.** Is it the right tool for the job? Buy a computer that's powerful enough to meet your needs, but don't think that you have to have the fastest processor available. The difference in performance between one system with a 3.8 GHz CPU and an otherwise identical system with a 4.0 GHz CPU may not be worth paying an extra several hundred dollars. What's more likely to be a barrier to high performance is having inadequate RAM. Many applications today don't run well on computers with less than 2 GB RAM, and some of these applications exhibit much better performance on computers with 4 GB or more of RAM. If you want to create state-of-the-art multimedia programs, make sure the computer has FireWire 800 (IEEE 1394) ports.

➡ **Capacity.** If you plan to do graphic design, publishing, or multimedia authoring, you'll be surprised how quickly you can fill up a 160 GB disk. Make sure your machine has enough disk storage to support the resource-intensive applications you'll need. Consider adding removable media drives for backing up and transporting large files.

➡ **Creativity.** If you want to burn your own DVDs, make sure the system has a DVD-RW, DVD+RW, or Blu-ray drive (BD) drive. Otherwise, you can save money by purchasing a system without this capability.

➡ **Customizability.** Computers are versatile, but they don't all handle all jobs with ease. If you'll be using word processors, spreadsheets, and other mainstream software packages, a low-end computer will probably do fine. If you have off-the-beaten-path needs (advanced video editing, instrument monitoring, etc.), choose a system with enough slots and ports to enable it to be expanded for your work.

➡ **Compatibility.** Will the software you plan to use run on the computer you're considering? Most popular computers have a good selection of compatible software, but if you have specific needs, such as being able to take your software home to run on Mom's computer, study the compatibility issue carefully. Total compatibility isn't always possible or necessary. Many people don't care if all their programs will run on another kind of computer; they just need data compatibility—the ability to move documents back and forth between systems on disk or through a network connection. It's common, for example, for Windows users and Mac users to share documents over a network.

➡ **Connectivity.** Some low-end computers do not have fast Ethernet ports as standard features. If you plan to connect your computer to a campus LAN or a cable modem, make sure it has the network connectivity you need.

➡ **Convenience.** Just about any computer can do most common jobs, but which is the most convenient for you? Do you value portability over having all the peripherals permanently connected? Is it important to you to have a machine that's easy to install and maintain so you can take care of it yourself? Or do you want to choose the same kind of machine as the people around you so you can get help easily when you need it? Which user interface makes the kind of work you'll be doing easiest?

➡ **Company.** If you try to save money by buying an off-brand computer, you may find yourself the owner of an orphan system. Even well-constructed computers may need parts and service at some point. Some small companies have provided superior sales and service for many years, but others vanish overnight. Buy from companies that you judge will be around for a while.

➡ **Conservation.** Ivan Illich warned, "In a consumer society there are inevitably two kinds of slaves: the prisoners of addiction and the prisoners of envy." Avoid becoming a prisoner to consumerism. Will the latest model computer really make a difference in how productively you use your time, or are you making the purchase to satisfy an impulse or keep up with others? Conservationists do the planet a favor (and save a lot of money) by using things until they are no longer useful then disposing of them properly. If your computer is obsolete, you'll know it.

FIGURE 3.39 This tower system has its side panel removed so you can see the storage bays containing disk drives (top left) and the expansion boards inserted into slots (lower right).

The downside of industry standards is that they can sometimes hold back progress. By today's standards those serial, parallel, and keyboard ports—often referred to as *legacy ports*—are far too slow for today's needs. It's rare to find a new PC containing those pokey ports today.

From the beginning, most standard PCs had an open architecture—a design that enabled users and technicians to add expansion cards and peripherals as needed. For example, a computer owner might install a network card into an older machine so that the computer could communicate with other computers through an Ethernet port (discussed in Chapter 8). Many hobbyists, taking advantage of open architecture and interface standards, have used the same computers for years; they just swap in new cards, drives, and even CPUs and motherboards to keep their systems up to current standards. But most computer users today don't want to take their computers apart. And many of today's desktop and laptop machines are closed systems, not intended to have their internal hardware modified by consumers. Fortunately, new interface standards enable casual computer users to add the latest and greatest devices to their systems without cracking the box.

Today, most external peripherals (except for monitors and speakers) are connected to desktop and laptop computers using two newer industry standard interfaces: USB 2.0 and Firewire.

The original USB (universal serial bus) standard allowed for data to be transmitted at approximately 11 megabits per second (Mbps)—roughly 100 times faster than the legacy PC serial port. USB 1.0 is fast enough for transmitting signals from keyboards and mice, but not for transferring large amounts of data (such as media files) to and from hard drives. Fortunately, USB 1.0 has been all but replaced by USB 2.0, which has data transfer rates of up to 480 Mbps. Theoretically, up to 126 devices, including keyboards, mice, digital cameras, scanners, and storage devices, can be chained together from a single USB port. USB devices can be hot swapped—removed and replaced without powering down—so the system instantly recognizes the presence of a new device when it is plugged in. And USB is *platform independent*, so USB devices can often work on both PCs and Macs.

Virtually all new PCs and Macs include one or more USB 2.0 ports. Although it is common for some of these ports to be on the back of the

Legacy ports
FireWire
USB
Ethernet
Line out
Headphones
Line in
Monitor

FIGURE 3.40 This rear view of a tower system unit shows several ports, including some (below) that are included in add-on-boards in slots.

box so cables that are seldom removed can be kept out of sight, newer models have USB ports on the front to accommodate frequent use. With a USB port in plain sight on the front of the box, flash drives, cameras, MP3 players, and other temporary peripherals can be plugged in quickly and easily. It's easy to expand the number of available USB ports by attaching a *USB hub* so several USB peripherals can share the same port. Many monitors and keyboards include USB hubs. USB can supply small amounts of power to peripherals, so many low-power USB devices don't need AC connections or batteries. There's a practical limit to the number of USB devices that can draw power from a single port, however. That's why many USB hubs are powered; when plugged into AC outlets, they can overcome the power limitations of their host computer's USB ports.

Another important interface standard is *FireWire*, a high-speed connection standard developed by Apple. Some PC makers refer to FireWire by the less friendly designation, *IEEE 1394*, assigned by the Institute of Electrical and Electronic Engineers when they approved it as a standard. (Sony calls its version iLink.) FireWire can move data between devices at 400Mbps—faster than most peripheral devices can handle. This high speed makes it ideal for working with data-intensive applications such as digital video. Most professional and consumer digital video cameras have FireWire ports, so they can be connected directly to FireWire-equipped PCs or Macs. (Some consumer camcorders have USB 2.0 ports instead.) Like USB, FireWire allows multiple devices to be connected to the same port and to be hot swapped. FireWire can also supply power to peripherals so they don't need an external power supply. A faster version, FireWire 800, offers 800 Mbps data transfer speeds.

A relatively new interface standard for connecting computers to hard drives and optical drives is *Serial-ATA* or *SATA* (Serial Advanced Technology Attachment). Serial ATA can transfer data at up to 1200Mbps. SATA ports aren't as common as USB and Firewire ports on PCs, but the SATA protocol is becoming increasingly common for connecting internal storage devices in PCs.

USB, Firewire, and SATA are likely to go through several speed-enhancing improvements in coming years. Eventually, though, they'll probably be replaced by other technologies that make these standards seem as quaint as the legacy ports on early PCs seem today.

Another trend suggests that we may need fewer ports on tomorrow's PCs. Wireless technology makes it possible for many peripherals to communicate with PCs—and with each other—through radio, infrared, and other technologies. Wireless keyboards and mice are commonplace today. Some cameras (and even some flash memory cards) can send pictures wirelessly to nearby computers. Some researchers are even experimenting with wireless power connections that allow low-power computers to recharge their batteries through thin air connections!

We'll explore wireless technology in more detail in Chapter 8. That chapter also covers networking technologies that enable computers to treat far-away digital devices as if they were directly connected peripherals. The next few chapters will focus on the software that drives all of this hardware.

Inventing the FUTURE

Tomorrow's Peripherals

You can count how many **seeds are in the apple**, but not how many **apples are in the seed**.

—*Ken Kesey, author of*
One Flew over the Cuckoo's Nest

Silicon chips aren't the only parts of computers that are evolving. Here's a sampler of peripheral technologies that are making their way from research labs into products.

TOMORROW'S STORAGE

Magnetic disks continue to shrink in size and cost and increase in capacity. This trend threatens the dominance of tape backup systems because disks are more reliable and offer quicker retrieval of lost data files. But new solid-state storage breakthroughs will seriously challenge disks. For example, Cambridge University researchers funded by Hitachi have developed a single-electron memory chip the size of a thumbnail that can store all the sounds and images of a full-length feature film. This experimental chip consumes very little power and retains memory for up to 10 years when the power is switched off.

The capacity of optical discs will continue to increase as well. InPhase Technologies is developing holographic-encoded discs with about 10 times the capacity of current DVDs.

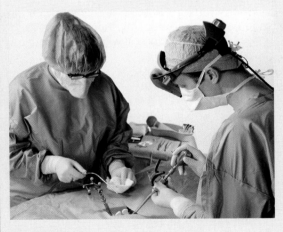

FIGURE 3.41a This surgeon's retinal scanner display makes video images and the patient's vital signs continually visible throughout the surgical procedure.

TOMORROW'S OUTPUT

Flat-panel screens are replacing desktop CRTs at an ever-increasing rate. Soon we'll be using ultra-high-resolution displays that are thin enough to hang on walls like pictures and efficient enough to run on batteries for days. LCD goggle displays—the visual equivalent to headphones—may soon be common for laptop PC users who want to shut the rest of the world out. Those who need to see what's going on around them and inside their computer can wear eyeglasses with built-in transparent heads-up displays. Researchers at the University of Washington have developed a *retinal display* that works without a screen; it shines a focused beam of light through the wearer's pupil, moving across the field of vision to draw pixels directly on the retina. Fighter pilots, neurosurgeons, and people with limited vision are using these displays to see critical computer data without taking their eyes off of their work. We may eventually see these displays attached to PDAs and mobile phones.

Researchers at Oregon State University have developed a transparent transistor. Possible spin-offs of this technology include displays embedded in automobile windshields and new 3-D output devices.

TOMORROW'S INPUT: SENSORS

Technology forecaster Paul Saffo predicts that the next major breakthroughs will occur as researchers develop—and companies market—inexpensive sensors that enable digital devices to monitor the analog world. Temperature sensors, optical sensors, motion sensors, and other types of sensors already make it possible for computers to track a variety of real-world activities and conditions. But as these technologies mature, more sophisticated devices will serve as eyes, ears, and other types of sense organs for computer networks. Saffo wrote in a special anniversary issue of the *Communications of the ACM*:

Two parallel universes currently exist—an everyday analog universe that we inhabit, and a newer digital universe created by humans, but inhabited by digital machines. We visit this digital world by peering through the portholes of our computer screens, and we manipulate with keyboard and mouse much as a nuclear technician works with radioactive material via glovebox and manipulator arms.... Now we are handing sensory organs and manipulators to the machines and inviting them to enter into analog reality. The scale of possible surprise this may generate over the next several decades as sensors, lasers, and microprocessors co-evolve is breathtakingly uncertain. ~

FIGURE 3.41b "Smart dust" computers at the University of California at Berkeley help monitor and control heating and cooling systems using environmental sensors and wireless communication links.

Crosscurrents

Psst! You're Wasting Electricity! *by Clive Thompson*

Many of the technological tools and toys we use everyday, from thermostats to video games, depend on feedback loops to operate properly. Temperature too low? Turn on the furnace. Joystick turned right? Steer that way. Inspired by an unusual gadget that can be used as a computer peripheral, Wired writer Clive Thompson suggests in this August, 2007 column that the right kind of ambient feedback might have global implications for the better.

Mark Martinez couldn't get Southern California Edison customers to conserve energy. As the utility's manager of program development, he had tried alerting them when it was time to dial back electricity use on a hot day—he'd fire off automated phone calls, zap text messages, send emails. No dice.

Then he saw an Ambient Orb. It's a groovy little ball that changes color in sync with incoming data—growing more purple, for example, as your email inbox fills up or as the chance of rain increases. Martinez realized he could use Orbs to signal changes in electrical rates, programming them to glow green when the grid was underused—and, thus, electricity cheaper—and red during peak hours when customers were paying more for power. He bought 120 of them, handed them out to customers, and sat back to see what would happen.

Within weeks, Orb users reduced their peak-period energy use by 40 percent. Why? Because, Martinez explains, the glowing sphere was less annoying and more persistent than a text alert. "It's nonintrusive," he says. "It has a relatively benign effect. But when you suddenly see your ball flashing red, you notice."

Electricity is invisible. That's why we waste so much of it in the home—leaving rechargers permanently plugged in and electronic devices idling in power-slurping "sleep" modes. We can't see that our houses account for nearly a quarter of the nation's energy appetite; we don't know when the grid is nearing capacity and expensive to use.

So Martinez hacked his customers' perceptual apparatuses. He made energy *visible*.

That's the power of "ambient information," which tries to combat data overload by moving information off computer screens and into the world around us. The Orb was originally sold as a tool for monitoring financial portfolios. You could set it to shine a serene sky blue when your stocks were going up or pulse an alarming red when they were tanking. Studies showed that people were two to three times more likely to actively manage their investments, selling off deadbeat stocks and buying better-performing ones, when they used the Orb. This is the psychological paradox of ambient information: We're more likely to act on a subtle but continuously present message than an intermittent one we're forced to stare at.

So here's the radical idea: Maybe the real killer app for ambient information isn't alleviating data overload or tracking investments. Maybe it's taming global warming. To improve energy efficiency and reduce emissions, we first need to make omnipresent the hidden facts about our usage—paint them on the world around us.

After all, we already *know* we're energy hogs, right? We talk about our personal carbon footprint, argue the finer points of buying carbon credits, tut-tut over Al Gore's energy-bingeing McMansion. Ambient display of our actual usage might just get us to cut back.

There's already solid evidence that feedback mechanisms can change eco-behavior. Think about how hybrid-car owners become obsessed with the dashboard display showing an on-the-fly calculation of gas mileage. The result? They change the way they drive, specifically trying to maximize mileage. It becomes a game, an enjoyable challenge, complete with quantifiable personal bests.

Here's an even wilder idea: How about making our energy use visible to everyone? Imagine if your daily consumption were part of your Facebook page—and broadcast to your friends by RSS feed. That would trigger what Ambient Devices CEO David Rose calls the sentinel effect: You'd work harder to conserve so you don't look like a jackass in front of your peers.

This isn't as far-fetched as it sounds. The design firm DIY Kyoto (as in Kyoto Protocol) recently began selling a device called the Wattson, which not only shows your energy usage but can also transmit the data to a Web site, letting you compare yourself with other Wattson users worldwide. In a Borg-like way, users can see how much they've collectively reduced their carbon impact.

The hope is that it could spawn a cascade of conservation. It's fun seeing your personal energy tab go down by kilowatts—but just imagine watching the world's usage plunge by terawatts or petawatts. It would be like a global Prius, with millions worldwide tweaking the Earth for maximum mileage. Now *that's* fun.

Discussion Questions

1. How do you think it would affect your behavior if you had ambient information about your energy usage? What about if that information were publicly posted on the Web for your friends to see?

2. Is the possible benefit to the environment of Thompson's suggestion worth the potential loss of privacy? Why or why not?

3. Do you have other ideas for providing ambient information to help save energy and curb global warming?

Summary

A computer with just a CPU and internal memory is of limited value; peripherals allow that computer to communicate with the outside world and store information for later use. Some peripherals are strictly input devices. Others are output devices. Some are external storage devices that accept information from and send information to the CPU.

The most common input devices today are the keyboard and the mouse, but a variety of other input devices can be connected to the computer. Trackballs, touch-sensitive pads, touch screens, and joysticks provide alternatives to the mouse as a pointing device. Bar code readers, optical mark readers, and magnetic ink readers are designed to recognize and translate specially printed patterns and characters. Scanners and digital cameras convert photographs, drawings, and other analog images into digital files that the computer can process. Sound digitizers do the same thing to audio information. All input devices are designed to do one thing: convert information signals from an outside source into a pattern of bits that the computer can process.

Output devices perform the opposite function: They accept strings of bits from the computer and transform them into a form that is useful or meaningful outside the computer. Video displays, including CRT monitors and LCDs, are almost universally used to display information continu-

ally as the computer functions. A variety of printers are used for producing paper output. Fax machines and fax modems let you share printed information using standard phone lines. Sound output from the computer, including music and synthesized speech, is delivered through audio speakers. Output devices also allow computers to control other machines.

Unlike most input and output peripherals, storage devices such as disk drives and tape drives are capable of two-way communication with the computer. Because of their high-speed random-access capability, and their large capacity, magnetic hard disks are the most common forms of storage on modern computers. Sequential-access tape devices are generally used to archive only information that doesn't need to be accessed often. Optical discs are the most common form of removable storage. Most optical drives can read and write data. In the future, solid-state storage technology will probably replace disks and tapes for most applications.

The hardware for a complete computer system generally includes at least one processor, memory, storage devices, and several I/O peripherals for communicating with the outside world. With the hardware components in place, a computer system is ready to receive and follow instructions encoded in software.

Key Terms

Interactive Activities

1. The *Tomorrow's Technology and You* Web site, **www.pearsonhighered.com/beekman**, contains self-test exercises related to this chapter. Follow the instruc-tions for taking a quiz. After you've completed your quiz, you can email the results to your instructor.

True or False

1. Blu-ray discs can be used with any DVD drive. F

2. Flash memory cards can store digital photos but not computer data. F

3. USB 2.0 ports on standard PCs are used to attach monitors, keyboards, and other peripherals. T

4. Because bar codes were designed to be read by computers, the devices that read them are extremely accurate. T

5. A scanner creates an analog representation of a printed digital image. F

6. The display quality of a monitor is determined in large part by the monitor's resolution and color depth. T

7. The touchpad on a notebook computer serves the same function as a QWERTY keyboard on a desktop PC. T

8. Most PC printers today are laser printers because color laser printers are far less expensive to buy than color inkjet printers. F

9. A DVD-RW drive can be used to store and back up data files. T

10. Multitouch technology enables your computer to be connected to several peripherals at the same time. F

Multiple Choice

1. The mouse is standard equipment on virtually all modern PCs *except*
   a. PCs without USB or FireWire ports.
   b. IBM PCs.
   c. iMacs.
   d. laptop PCs.
   e. workstation PCs.

2. Which of these is both an input and an output device?
   a. A bar-code reader
   b. A flatbed scanner
   c. A touch screen
   d. A sensor
   e. A plotter

3. Serial, parallel, and keyboard ports are also known as
   a. SCSI ports.
   b. FireWire ports.
   c. Plug & Play ports.
   d. Legacy ports.
   e. Next-gen ports.

4. Why was the arrangement of keys on the QWERTY keyboard chosen?
   a. Because it corresponds to alphabetical order in the Esperanto language
   b. Because it corresponds to alphabetical order in the Polish language

   c. To reduce typing speed
   d. To minimize finger motion to reach the most commonly typed characters
   e. To make it easy for the inventor to type his name and address

5. Optical character recognition can be used to extract text from writing on
   a. smart whiteboards.
   b. tablet PCs.
   c. PDAs.
   d. scanned letters.
   e. all of the above

6. Which of these input devices is least likely to use multi-touch technology?
   a. A touch-sensitive display.
   b. A touch tablet.
   c. A mouse with a scroll wheel.
   d. A trackpad.
   e. None of the above

7. LCD technology is used in
   a. notebook computer displays.
   b. many desktop computer displays.
   c. video projectors.
   d. all of the above
   e. none of the above

8. The size of a display is measured
   a. across the top of the display.
   b. down the left side of the display.
   c. across the middle of the display.
   d. down the center of the display.
   e. from the upper-left corner to the lower-right corner of the display.

9. Which of these is most like the open architecture of the modern PC?
   a. A modern car with a computer-controlled emissions system that can be adjusted by factory-authorized mechanics
   b. A "smart" microwave with an embedded computer that allows for complex recipes and scheduling
   c. A stereo system that allows speakers, disc players, and other components to be replaced by the owner
   d. A handheld computer with built-in firmware for all of the most common PDA tasks
   e. A music keyboard that includes a built-in synthesizer and an LCD display

10. External drives are typically connected to the computer by
    a. USB.
    b. FireWire.
    c. VGA.
    d. both A and B.
    e. all of the above

11. A multifunction printer generally includes several devices, including
    a. a scanner.
    b. a CRT monitor.
    c. a DVD drive.
    d. a mouse.
    e. all of the above

12. USB flash drives have all of the following advantages over other storage options *except*
    a. they are small and portable.
    b. they are cheaper per MB than other storage options.
    c. they can be used to access and store your data on virtually any computer with a USB port.
    d. you can save and delete files on a flash drive without having to reformat the drive.
    e. they are less prone to being damaged if dropped or scratched.

13. Hard disk drives have the disadvantage that
    a. they hold less information than CDs do.
    b. they are more likely to fail than other computer components.
    c. they cannot be backed up.
    d. their contents are lost when they lose power.
    e. all of the above

14. Most digital cameras today store images using
    a. DVD-RAM.
    b. CD-ROM.
    c. flash memory.
    d. digital ink.
    e. none of the above

15. Which of these technologies was found on almost all early PCs, but is almost never included in new PCs today?
    a. USB 2.0
    b. FireWire 800
    c. The parallel printer port
    d. Expansion slots
    e. Hot-swappable devices

Review Questions

1. List five input devices and three output devices that might be attached to a PC. Describe a typical use for each.

2. Provide a working definition for each of the key terms listed in the "Key Terms" section. Check your answers in the glossary.

3. Describe the advantages of storing your data on Blu-ray discs instead of DVD discs. Are there any disadvantages?

4. Name and describe three special-purpose input devices people commonly use in public places, such as stores, banks, and libraries.

5. Many people find that the mouse is impractical for use as a pointing device on a laptop computer. Describe at least three alternatives that are more appropriate.

6. What are the advantages of LCD displays over CRTs?

7. What are the advantages of nonimpact printers, such as laser printers, over impact printers? Are there any disadvantages?

8. Describe how multi-touch technology can make common input tasks more efficient.

9. Some commonly used peripherals can be described as both input and output devices. Explain.

10. List several devices that might be connected to a PC through USB and FireWire ports.

Discussion Questions

1. What kinds of new input and output devices do you think future computers might have? Why?

2. If we think of the human brain as a computer, what are the input devices? What are the output devices? What are the storage devices?

3. Imagine you need to work on a term paper in a computer lab as well as on your home computer. Would a flash drive or a Blu-ray disc be a more appropriate storage option, and why?

4. Many computer users have become addicted to multiplayer online role-playing games. Some of them spend 8 hours or more a day playing these games, even though the interactions are through a keyboard, mouse, and video display. Do you think computer addiction will become a bigger problem when more sophisticated peripherals such as LCD goggle displays become commonplace?

Projects

1. The keyboard is the main input device for computers today. If you don't know how to touch-type, you're effectively handicapped in a world of computers. Fortunately, many personal computer software programs are designed to teach keyboarding. If you need to learn to type, try to find one of these programs and use it regularly until you are a fluent typist.

2. Using a web browser to research prices, try to break down the cost of a computer to determine, on the average, what percentage of the cost is for the system unit (including CPU, memory, and disk drives), what percentage is for input and output devices, and what percentage is for software. How do the percentages change as the price of the system goes up?

3. Visit several local businesses. Find and write about unusual input and output devices that you wouldn't find on a typical home PC.

4. Visit a bank, store, office, or laboratory. List all the computer peripherals you see, categorizing them as input, output, or storage devices.

Sources and Resources

Books

Hard Drive: Bill Gates and the Making of the Microsoft Empire, by James Wallace and Jim Erickson (New York, NY: Collins, 1993). This book covers the early years of the Bill Gates story. It doesn't pull punches, often painting Gates as ruthless and difficult. This is a good read on an important era in the Gates legacy. Still, the world is due for a serious biography of the older, wiser, and more generous Bill Gates—the one whose charitable work is changing lives the world over.

How Digital Photography Works, Second Edition, by Ron White and Timothy Edward Downs (Indianapolis, IN: Que, 2007). Ron White's phenomenally popular *How Computers Work* (see Chapter 2 Sources and Resources) has helped countless people figure out what's going on inside their PCs. This book takes a similar approach to digital cameras. White's clear explanations combine with Timothy Edward Downs's illustrations to produce a visually appealing way to understand digital camera technology. As with most technology, an understanding of the inner workings can produce a more satisfying user experience—and better results.

Disclosure, by Michael Crichton (New York, NY: Ballantine Books, 1994). This book-turned-movie provides an inside look at a fictional Seattle corporation that manufactures computer peripherals. Even though the author has clearly tampered with credibility for the sake of a suspenseful plot, the story provides insights into the roles money and power play in today's high-stakes computer industry.

Real World Scanning and Halftones, Third Edition, by David Blanner, Conrad Chavez, Glenn Fleishman, and Steve Roth (Berkeley, CA: Peachpit Press, 2004). It's easy to use a scanner, but it isn't always easy to get high-quality scans. This illustrated book covers scanner use from the basics to advanced tips and techniques.

The Digital Photography Book, Volumes 1 and 2, by Scott Kelby (Berkeley, CA: Peachpit Press, 2006 and 2008). In these two books, master photographer and writer Kelby shares his expertise without getting bogged down in the theory of photography. In his words these books are about "you and I shooting, and I answer the questions, give you advice, and share the secrets I've learned just like I would with a friend, without all the technical explanations and without all the techno-photo-speak." Each page covers a single trick or tip for taking pictures like the pros.

Photopedia: The Ultimate Digital Photography Resource, by Michael Miller (Indianapolis, IN: Que, 2008). Tools, techniques, and tips, from camera to computer. This easy-to-read book contains a wealth of information for anyone interested in digital photography.

Desktop Yoga, by Julie T. Lusk (New York, NY: Perigee, 1998). Like any activity, computer work can be hazardous to your health if you don't exercise care and common sense. This book describes stretching and relaxation exercises for deskbound workers and students. If you spend hours a day in front of a computer screen, these activities can help you to take care of your body and mind.

Software Basics
The Ghost in the Machine

After you read this chapter you should be able to:

▶ Describe three fundamental categories of software and their relationships

▶ Explain the relationship of algorithms to software

▶ Discuss the factors that make a computer application a useful tool

▶ Describe the role of the operating system in a modern computer system

▶ Describe how file systems are organized

▶ Outline the evolution of user interfaces from early machine-language programming to futuristic virtual reality interfaces

▶ Explain why the unauthorized copying of software is against the law

> I had **no idea** what I was doing. I knew I was the **best programmer in the world.** Every 21-year-old programmer knows that. *"How hard can it be,* it's just **an operating system**?"
>
> —*Linus Torvalds*

Linus Torvalds and the Software Nobody Owns

When Linus Torvalds bought his first PC in 1991, he never dreamed it would become a critical weapon in a software liberation war. He just wanted to stop waiting in line to get a terminal to connect to his university's mainframe. Torvalds, a 21-year-old student at the University of Helsinki in Finland, had avoided buying a PC because he didn't like the standard PC's "crummy architecture with this crummy MS-DOS operating system." But Torvalds had been studying operating systems, and he decided to try to build something on his own.

He based his work on Minix, a scaled-down textbook version of the powerful UNIX operating system designed to run on PC hardware. Little by little, he cobbled together pieces of a kernel, the part of the system where the real processing and control work is done.

When he mentioned his project on an Internet discussion group, a member offered him space to post it on a university server. Others copied it, tinkered with it, and sent the changes back to Torvalds. The communal work-in-progress eventually became known as Linux (pronounced "Linn-uks" by its creator). Within a couple of years, it was good enough to release as a product.

Instead of copyrighting and selling Linux, Torvalds made it freely available under the GNU General Public License (GPL) developed by the Free Software Foundation. According to the GPL, anyone can give away, modify, or even sell Linux, as long as the source code—the program instructions—remain freely available for others to improve. Linux is the best-known example of open-source software, and now it spearheads the popular open-source software movement.

Thousands of programmers around the world have worked on Linux, with Torvalds still at the center of the activity. Some do it because they believe there should be alternatives to expensive corporate products; others do it because they can customize the software; still others do it just for fun. As a result of all their efforts, Linux has matured into a powerful, versatile product with millions of users.

Today Linux powers Web servers, film and animation workstations, scientific supercomputers, a handful of handheld computers, some general-use PCs, and even Internet-savvy appliances such as refrigerators.

105

FIGURE 4.1 Linus Torvalds talking to Linux fans.

penguin that has become the Linux mascot. In 1996 he completed his master's degree in computer science and went to work for Transmeta Corp., a chip design company in Silicon Valley. In 2003 he moved to the Open Source Development Labs, which merged with the Free Standards Group to become the Linux Foundation. He has become wealthy thanks to stock options donated by grateful companies that built their products on Linux. He maintains a relatively low profile, but still champions the open source cause. ∼

FIGURE 4.2 A novel use of the Linux operating system is in the NASA personal satellite assistant, currently under development. The six-inch sphere will float around the International Space Station and act as an environmental monitor and communications device. Its design was inspired by the light saber training droid used by Luke Skywalker in the movie *Star Wars*.

Linux is especially popular among people who do computing on a tight budget—particularly in debt-ridden Third World countries.

The success of Linux has inspired Apple, Sun, Hewlett-Packard, and other software companies to release products with open-source code. Even the mighty Microsoft is paying attention as this upstart operating system grows in popularity, and the company has responded with a pseudo–open-source strategy covering its embedded products that compete directly with Linux.

Today Torvalds is an Internet folk hero. Web pages pay homage to him, his creation, and Tux, his stuffed

Chapters 2 and 3 told only part of the story about how computers do what they do. Here's a synopsis of our story so far:

On one side we have a person—you, me, or somebody else—it hardly matters. We all have problems to solve—problems involving work, communication, transportation, finances, and more. Many of these problems cry out for computer solutions.

On the other side, we have a computer—an incredibly sophisticated bundle of hardware capable of performing all kinds of technological wizardry. Unfortunately, the computer hardware *recognizes only zeros and ones*.

A great chasm separates the person who has a collection of vague problems from the stark, rigidly bounded world of the computer. How can humans bridge the gap to communicate with the computer?

That's where software comes in. Software enables people to communicate certain kinds of problems to computers and makes it possible for computers to communicate solutions back to those people.

Modern computer software didn't materialize out of the atmosphere; it evolved from the plug boards and patch cords and other hardware devices that were used to program early computers such as the ENIAC. Mathematician John von Neumann, working with ENIAC's creators, J. Presper Eckert and John Mauchly, wrote a 1945 paper suggesting that program

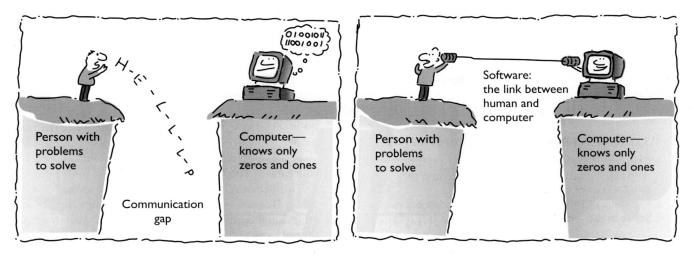

FIGURE 4.3 The communication gap ...

instructions could be stored with the data in memory. Every computer created since has been based on the *stored-program concept* described in that paper. That idea established the software industry.

Instead of flipping switches and patching wires, today's programmers write *programs*—sets of computer instructions designed to solve problems—and feed them into the computer's memory through keyboards and other input devices. These programs are the computer's software. Because software is stored in memory, a computer can switch from one task to another and back to the first without a single hardware modification. For instance, the computer that serves as a word processor for writing this book can, at the click of a mouse, turn into an email terminal, a browser into the World Wide Web, a reference library, an accounting spreadsheet, a drawing table, a video-editing workstation, a musical instrument, or a game machine.

What is software, and how can it transform a mass of circuits into an electronic chameleon? This chapter provides some general answers to that question along with details about each of the three major categories of software:

- Compilers and other translator programs, which enable programmers to create other software
- Software applications, which serve as productivity tools to help computer users solve problems
- System software, which coordinates hardware operations and does behind-the-scenes work the computer user seldom sees

Processing with Programs

Software is invisible and complex. To make the basic concepts clear, we start our exploration of software with a down-to-earth analogy.

> **Leonardo da Vinci** called music **"the shaping of the invisible"** and his phrase is even more apt as a description of **software**.
>
> —*Alan Kay, conceiver of the notebook computer, and user-interface architect*

Food for Thought

Think of the hardware in a computer system as the kitchen in a short-order restaurant: It's equipped to produce whatever output a customer (user) requests, but it sits idle until an order (command) is placed. Robert, the computerized chef in our imaginary kitchen, serves as the Central Processing Unit (CPU), waiting for requests from the users/customers.

When somebody provides an input command—say, an order for a plate of French toast—Robert responds by following the instructions in the appropriate recipe.

As you may have guessed, the recipe is the software. It provides instructions telling the hardware what to do to produce the output the user desires. If the recipe is correct, clear, and precise, the chef turns the input data—eggs, bread, and other ingredients—into the desired output—French toast. If the instructions are unclear, or if the software has **bugs**, or errors, the output may not be what the user wanted.

For example, suppose Robert has this recipe for "Suzanne's French Toast Fantastique."

This seemingly foolproof recipe has several trouble spots. Because step 1 doesn't say otherwise, Robert might include the shells in the "slightly beaten eggs." Step 2 says nothing about separating the six slices of bread before dipping them in the batter; Robert would be within the letter of the instruction if he dipped all six at once. Step 3 has at least two potential bugs. Because it doesn't specify what to fry in butter, Robert might conclude that the mixture, not the bread, should be fried. Even if Robert decides to fry the bread, he may let it overcook while waiting for the butter to turn golden brown, or he may wait patiently for the top of the toast to brown while the bottom quietly blackens. Robert, like any good computer, just follows the instructions he's given.

SUZANNE'S FRENCH TOAST FANTASTIQUE

1. Combine 2 slightly beaten eggs with 1 teaspoon vanilla extract, $^{1}/_{2}$ teaspoon cinnamon, and $^{2}/_{3}$ cup milk.
2. Dip 6 slices of bread in mixture.
3. Fry in small amount of butter until golden brown.
4. Serve bread with maple syrup, sugar, or tart jelly.

FIGURE 4.4 Suzanne's French Toast Fantastique

SUZANNE'S FRENCH TOAST FANTASTIQUE: THE ALGORITHM

1. Prepare the batter by following these instructions.
   1a. Crack 2 eggs so whites and yolks drop in bowl; discard shells.
   1b. Beat eggs 30 seconds with wire whisk, fork, or mixer.
   1c. Mix in 1 teaspoon vanilla extract, $^{1}/_{2}$ teaspoon cinnamon, and $^{2}/_{3}$ cup milk.
2. Place 1 tablespoon butter in frying pan and place on 350° heat.
3. For each of six pieces of bread, follow these steps:
   3a. Dip slice of bread in mixture.
   3b. For each of the two sides of the bread do the following steps:
      3b1. Place the slice of bread in the frying pan with this (uncooked) side down.
      3b2. Wait 1 minute then peek at underside of bread; if lighter than golden brown, repeat this step.
   3c. Remove bread from frying pan and place on plate.
4. Serve bread with maple syrup, sugar, or tart jelly.

FIGURE 4.5 Suzanne's French Toast Fantastique: The algorithm

A Fast, Stupid Machine

The **most useful** word in any computer language is **"oops."**

—David Lubar, in It's Not a Bug, It's a Feature

Our imaginary automated chef may not seem very bright, but he's considerably more intelligent than a typical computer's CPU. Computers are commonly called "smart machines" or "intelligent machines." In truth, a typical computer is incredibly limited, capable of performing only the most basic arithmetic operations (such as $7 + 3$ and $15 - 8$) and a few simple logical comparisons ("Is this number less than that number?" "Are these two values identical?").

Computers *seem* smart because they can perform these arithmetic operations and comparisons quickly and accurately. A typical desktop computer can perform millions of calculations in the time it takes you to pull your pen out of your pocket. A well-crafted program can tell the computer to perform a sequence of simple operations that, when taken as a whole, print a term paper, organize the student records for your school, or simulate a space flight. Amazingly, everything you've ever seen a computer do is the result of a sequence of extremely simple arithmetic and logical operations done very quickly. The challenge for software developers is to devise instructions that put those simple operations together in ways that are useful and appropriate.

Suzanne's recipe for French toast isn't a computer program; it's not written in a language that a computer can understand. But it could be considered an algorithm—a set of step-by-step procedures for accomplishing a task. A computer program generally starts as an algorithm written in English or some other human language. Like Suzanne's recipe, the initial algorithm is likely to contain generalities, ambiguities, and errors.

The programmer's job is to turn the algorithm into a program by adding details, hammering out rough spots, testing procedures, and debugging—correcting errors. For example, if we were turning Suzanne's recipe into a program for our electronic-brained short-order cook, we might start by rewriting it like the recipe shown in Figure 4.5.

We've eliminated much of the ambiguity from the original recipe. Ambiguity, while tolerable (and sometimes useful) in conversations between humans, is a source of errors for computers. In its current form, the recipe contains far more detail than any human chef would want but not nearly enough for a computer. If we were programming a computer (assuming we had one with input hardware capable of recognizing golden brown French toast and output devices capable of flipping the bread), we'd need to go into excruciating detail, translating every step of the process into a series of absolutely unambiguous instructions that could be interpreted and executed by a machine with a vocabulary smaller than that of a two-year-old child!

The Language of Computers

Every computer processes instructions in a native machine language. Machine language uses numeric codes to represent the most basic computer operations—adding numbers, subtracting numbers, comparing numbers, moving numbers, repeating instructions, and so on. Early programmers were forced to write every program in a machine language, tediously translating each instruction into binary code. This process was an invitation to insanity; imagine trying to find a single mistyped character in a page full of zeros and ones!

> The programmer, **like the poet**, works only slightly removed from **pure thought-stuff**. He builds **castles in the air**, created by exertion of the **imagination**. Yet the program construct, unlike the poet's words, is **real** in the sense that **it moves and works**, producing visible outputs **separate from the construct itself**.
>
> —*Frederick P. Brooks, Jr., in* The Mythical Man Month

Today most programmers use programming languages, such as C++, C#, Java, and Visual Basic.NET, that fall somewhere between natural human languages and precise machine languages. These languages, referred to as high-level languages, make it possible for scientists, engineers, and businesspeople to solve problems using familiar terminology and notation rather than cryptic machine instructions. For a computer to understand a program written in one of these languages, it must use a translator program to convert the English-like instructions to the zeros and ones of machine language. The most common type of translator program is called a compiler because it compiles a complete translation of the program from a high-level computer language (such as C#) into machine language before the program runs for the first time. The compiled program can run again and again; it doesn't need to be recompiled unless instructions need to be changed.

To clarify the translation process, let's go back to the kitchen. Imagine a recipe translator that enables our computer chef to look up phrases such as "fry until golden brown." Like a reference book for beginning cooks, this translator fills in all the details about testing and flipping foods in the frying pan, so our computer cook, Robert, understands what to do whenever he encounters "fry until golden brown" in any recipe. As long as Robert is equipped with the translator, we don't need to include so many details in each recipe. We can communicate at a higher level. The more sophisticated the translator, the easier the job of the programmer.

Programming languages have steadily evolved during the past few decades. Each new generation of languages makes the programming process easier by taking on, and hiding from the programmer, more of the detail-oriented work. The computer's unrelenting demands for technical details haven't gone away; they're just handled automatically by

4.1 Executing a Program

Most programs are composed of millions of simple machine-language instructions. Here we'll observe the execution of a tiny part of a running program: a series of instructions that computes the 5 percent sales tax on a $99.00 purchase. The machine instructions are similar to those in actual programs, but the details have been omitted. The computer has already loaded (copied) the program from disk into RAM so that the CPU can see it.

The Program Counter inside the CPU keeps track of the address of the next instruction to be executed. The instruction execution cycle has a three-step rhythm: fetch the instruction, increment the Program Counter, and perform the specified task. In this example, four instructions tell the CPU to read two numbers from memory (locations 2000 and 2004), multiply them, and store the result in memory (location 2008). The CPU goes through 12 steps to execute these four instructions.

2. The CPU increases the value of the Program Counter to contain the address of the next instruction.

5. The CPU increases the value of the Program Counter to contain the address of the next instruction.

3. The CPU loads the contents of memory location 2000 into register A.

1. The Program Counter is 100. The CPU loads the instruction at address 100 into the Instruction Register.

4. The Program Counter is 104. The CPU loads the instruction at address 104 into the Instruction Register.

6. The CPU loads the contents of memory location 2004 into register B.

FIGURE 4.6

Translated into English, the instructions at memory addresses 100–112 look like this:

- (100) Copy the number stored in memory location 2000 into register A inside the CPU.
- (104) Copy the number stored in memory location 2004 into register B inside the CPU.
- (108) Multiply the contents of registers A and B, putting the result in register C.
- (112) Copy the contents of register C into memory location 2008.

In this example, memory location 2000 contains the purchase price (99.00), and memory location 2004 contains the sales tax rate (0.05).

The computer actually stores all instructions and data values as binary numbers, but we have represented them as letters or decimal numbers to make the example easier to follow.

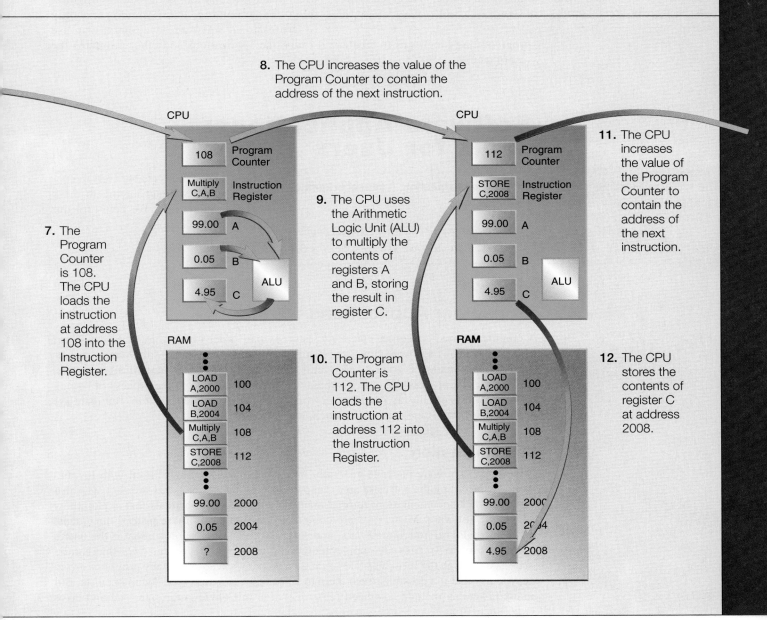

8. The CPU increases the value of the Program Counter to contain the address of the next instruction.

7. The Program Counter is 108. The CPU loads the instruction at address 108 into the Instruction Register.

9. The CPU uses the Arithmetic Logic Unit (ALU) to multiply the contents of registers A and B, storing the result in register C.

10. The Program Counter is 112. The CPU loads the instruction at address 112 into the Instruction Register.

11. The CPU increases the value of the Program Counter to contain the address of the next instruction.

12. The CPU stores the contents of register C at address 2008.

FIGURE 4.7 Compilers enable programmers to write in high-level languages, such as Java (shown), C# or C++.

translation software. As a result, programming is easier and less error prone. As translators become more sophisticated, programmers can communicate in computer languages that more closely resemble natural languages—the languages people speak and write every day.

Even with state-of-the-art computer languages, programming requires a considerable investment of time and brainpower. Fortunately, many tasks that required programming two decades ago can now be accomplished with spreadsheets, graphics programs, and other easy-to-use software applications.

Programming languages are still used to solve problems that can't be handled with off-the-shelf software, but virtually all computer users manage to do their work without programming. Programming today is done mainly by professional software developers, who use programming languages to create and refine the applications and other programs the rest of us use.

Software Applications: Tools for Users

The computer is only a **fast idiot**; it has **no imagination**; it **cannot originate** action. It is, and will remain, **only a tool to man**.

—*American Library Association reaction to the UNIVAC computer exhibit at the 1964 New York World's Fair*

Software applications enable users to control computers without having to think like programmers do. We now turn our attention to applications.

Consumer Applications

Computer stores, consumer electronics stores, mail-order houses, and Internet stores sell thousands of software titles: publishing programs, accounting software, personal-information managers, graphics programs, multimedia tools, educational titles, games, and more. The process of buying computer software is similar to the process of buying movies (DVDs or Blu-ray discs) to play on a home entertainment system. But there are some important differences; we'll touch on a few here.

Documentation

A computer software package generally includes printed documentation with instructions for installing the software on a computer's hard disk. Some software packages also include other documentation: tutorial manuals and reference manuals that explain how to use the software. Many software companies have replaced these printed documents with tutorials, reference materials, and *help files* that appear on-screen at the user's request. Most help files are supplemented and updated with *online help* that can be accessed through the local help files or at the company's Web site. Many programs are so easy to use that it's possible to put them to work without reading the documentation. But many programs include advanced features that aren't obvious through trial-and-error experimentation.

Updating and Upgrading

Most software companies continually improve their programs by removing bugs and adding new features. A typical company might release minor **updates** (containing bug fixes and minor enhancements) several times a year and major **upgrades** (with significant new features and/or improvements) every year or two. Program updates with minor revisions are typically made available for free. Microsoft and other companies occasionally release free *service packs* containing bundled updates. An upgrade to the next major version of a program typically costs an upgrade fee. To distinguish between versions, program names often include version numbers, as in FileMaker Pro 9. Most companies use decimals to indicate minor revisions and whole numbers to indicate major revisions. For example, iTunes 8.0.1 is only slightly different than iTunes 8.0.0 but it's a major improvement over iTunes 7. Many product names, such as Quicken 2009, use years to indicate versions. Still others use name

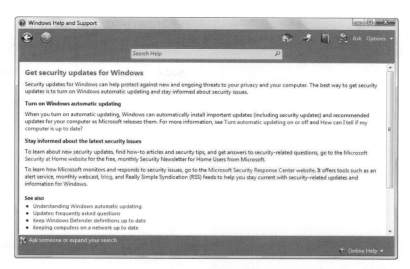

FIGURE 4.8 Most modern computer software provides some kind of online help on demand. Microsoft Windows provides context-sensitive help—help windows with content that depends on what else is currently on the screen. Many software companies, including Microsoft, use Web databases to augment the help included with the system.

changes. For example, the last several consumer versions of Microsoft's operating system have been marketed as Windows 98, Windows Millennium Edition (Windows Me), Windows XP Home Edition, and Windows Vista Home (Basic or Premium).

Compatibility

A computer software buyer must be concerned with **compatibility**. When you buy an audio CD, you don't need to specify the brand of your CD player because all manufacturers adhere to common industry standards. But no complete, universal software standards exist in the computer world, so a program written for one type of computer system may not work on another. Software packages contain labels with statements such as "Requires Windows XP or Vista with 2GB of RAM." These demands should not be taken lightly; without compatible hardware and software, most software programs are worthless.

Disclaimers

According to the little-read warranties included with many software packages, some applications might technically be worthless even if you have compatible hardware and software. Here's the first paragraph from a typical software warranty, which is part of a longer **end-user license agreement** (**EULA**, pronounced "yoo-la"):

> *This program is provided "as is" without warranty of any kind. The entire risk as to the result and performance of the program is assumed by you. Should the program prove defective, you—and not the manufacturer or its dealers—assume the entire cost of all necessary servicing, repair, or correction. Further, the manufacturer does not warranty, guarantee, or make any representations regarding the use of, or the result of the use of, the program in terms of correctness, accuracy, reliability, for being current, or otherwise, and you rely on the program and its results solely at your own risk.*

Software companies hide behind disclaimers because nobody's figured out how to write error-free software. Remember our problems providing our cook, Robert, with a foolproof set of instructions for producing French toast? Programmers who write applications such as word proccessing programs must try to anticipate and respond to all combinations of commands and actions users might perform under any conditions. Given the difficulty of this task, most programs work amazingly well—but not perfectly.

FIGURE 4.9 Thousands of software applications for the iPhone can be downloaded from the iTunes store, including this one from www.hotels.com which enables users to research and book hotels anytime, anywhere.

Licensing

When you buy a typical computer software package, you're not actually buying the software. Instead, you're buying a software license to use the program. While end-user licensing agreements vary, most include limitations on your right to install and use the software on multiple computers, copy discs, install software on hard drives, and transfer information to other users. Many companies offer *volume licenses*—special licenses for families, companies, schools, or government institutions. Some companies even rent software to corporate and government clients.

Virtually all commercial software is copyrighted. Copyrighted software can't be legally duplicated for distribution to others. Some software CDs and DVDs (mostly entertainment products) are physically *copy protected* so they can't be copied *at all* using conventional means. A milder, more common form of copy protection is to require the user to type his or her name and a product serial number before a newly installed program will work. Between these two extremes, many software companies require new owners to complete an authorization process through the Internet.

Because programming is so difficult, software development is expensive. Software developers use copyrights and copy protection to ensure that they sell enough copies of their products to recover their investments and stay in business to write programs.

Software piracy is the term frequently used to describe the unauthorized copying and selling of software. By some estimates, global software piracy costs U.S. companies tens of billions of dollars in lost revenues every year. At the end of the chapter, we'll discuss laws protecting the rights of software developers.

Distribution

Software is distributed through direct sales forces to corporations and other institutions. Software is sold to consumers in computer stores and other retail outlets. Much software is sold through mail-order catalogs and Web sites. Web distribution makes it possible for companies to offer software without packaging or disks. For example, you might download (copy) a demo version of a commercial program from a company's Web site or some other source; the demo program is identical to the commercial

FIGURE 4.10 The Adobe Creative Suite combines Photoshop, Illustrator, InDesign, and other applications used by designers, publishers, and other creative professionals.

version, but with some features disabled or a time limit placed on its usage. After you try the program and decide you want to buy it, you can often contact the company (by phone or through its Web site), pay (by credit card) for the full version of the program, and receive (by email) a code that you can type in to unlock the disabled features of the program.

Not all software is copyrighted and sold through commercial channels. Web sites, user groups, and other sources commonly offer **public-domain software** (free for the taking) and **shareware** (free for the trying, with a send-payment-if-you-keep-it honor system) along with demonstration versions of commercial programs. The term *open source* refers to freely accessible software in which the program's source code is part of the distribution. (Linux, discussed at the beginning of this chapter, is open source software.) Unlike copyrighted software, public-domain software, shareware, demo software, and open-source software can be legally copied and shared freely.

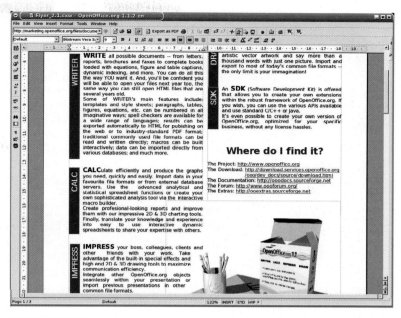

FIGURE 4.11 The open-source application suite OpenOffice.org provides compatibility with Microsoft Office documents but runs on a variety of platforms, including Windows, Linux, and the Mac OS.

Web Applications

A PC equipped with a Web browser has access to thousands of software applications hosted by remote Web servers on the Internet. Most Web applications are developed using browser-friendly languages including HTML, XML, ASP, PHP, Perl, Java, and JavaScript. A Web application typically (but not always) requires a Web browser to work. It might be designed for use by the general public via the Internet, or by a smaller group of individuals on a corporate or institutional network.

Web applications have several advantages over traditional PC applications installed on a computer's local hard drive. Web applications can allow hundreds of people in diverse locations to communicate and interact with each other. Most (but not all) Web applications are designed to work without modification on computers running Windows, Mac OS, Linux, or other operating systems. Using a Web application, a person can start and save a job on a Windows PC at work, continue it on a Mac at home, complete it on a Linux machine in an Internet café, and recheck it on an iPhone while waiting for a ride home. Users of Web applications have immediate access to upgrades when they are installed on the host site's Web server. Most Web applications can be used free of charge (although some sites pay their bills by barraging users with advertisements).

Some Web applications look and perform like PC applications. Google Docs includes full-featured word processor, spreadsheet, and presentation graphics software. Photoshop Express is a photo editing and organization program. All of these programs enable users to edit documents and save them on remote servers using standard Web

FIGURE 4.12 Google Spreadsheets is an example of a Web application quite similar to a traditional application program running on a stand-alone PC.

FIGURE 4.13 Some news-oriented Web applications deliver up-to-the-minute weather forecasts.

browsers. Webmail programs, including Gmail, Hotmail, and Yahoo! Mail, perform the same functions as the mail programs that come with Microsoft Office or Mac OS X. Web reference tools, such as language translation sites and quotation collections, mimic similar PC applications.

Other Web applications take care of business that can't be handled by standard desktop applications. A multiplayer online game turns the Internet into a playing field, enabling global competition and cooperation. A wiki—a collection of Web pages that can be edited by anyone who accesses it—is a type of interactive, collaborative document that can't exist on an isolated PC; the encyclopedia Wikipedia is the best-known example. Retail sites such as amazon.com and gap.com use complex Web applications to make shopping simple for their customers. Online auctions such as eBay connect buyers and sellers all around the world. Online communities such as Facebook and MySpace are built on ever-growing clusters of Web applications that link members to each other. Other Web applications provide instant access to maps, driving directions, weather reports, newsfeeds, Internet radio stations, on-demand video, and much more.

Vertical-Market and Custom Software

Because of their flexibility, word processing, spreadsheet, database, and graphics programs are used in homes, schools, government offices, and all kinds of businesses. But

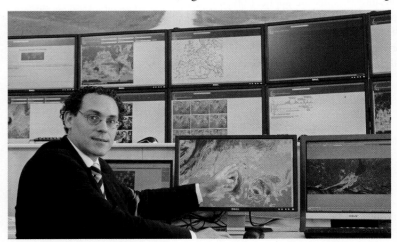

FIGURE 4.14 Vertical-market software helps this researcher track geographic information.

many computer applications are so job specific that they're of little interest or use to anybody outside a given profession. Medical-billing software, library-cataloging software, legal-reference software, restaurant-management software, and other applications designed specifically for a particular business or industry are called **vertical-market applications** or **custom applications**.

Vertical-market applications tend to cost far more than mass-market applications because companies that develop the software have very few potential customers through which to recover their development costs. In fact, some custom applications are programmed specifically for single clients. For example, the software used to control the space shuttle was developed with a single customer—NASA—in mind.

System Software: The Hardware-Software Connection

Originally, **operating systems** were envisioned as a way to handle one of the **most complex** input/output operations: **communicating** with a variety of **disk drives**. But, the operating system quickly **evolved** into an **all-encompassing bridge** between your PC and the software you run on it.

— *Ron White, in* How Computers Work

When you're typing a paper or writing a program, you don't need to concern yourself with low-level details, such as which parts of the computer's memory hold your document, the segments of the word processing software currently in the computer's memory, or the output instructions sent by the computer to the printer. System software, a class of software that includes the *operating system* and *utility programs*, handles these details and hundreds of other tasks behind the scenes.

What the Operating System Does

Every general-purpose computer today, whether it's a timesharing supercomputer or a laptop PC, depends on an operating system (OS) to keep hardware running efficiently and to make the process of communication with that hardware easier. Operating-system software runs continuously whenever your computer is on, providing an additional layer of insulation between you and the bits-and-bytes world of computer hardware. Because the operating system stands between the software application and the hardware, application compatibility is usually defined by the operating system, as well as by the hardware.

The operating system, as the name implies, is a system of programs that performs a variety of technical operations, from basic communication with peripherals to complex networking and security tasks.

- In order to support multitasking—the concurrent execution of multiple applications—the operating system creates dozens of processes (also called tasks). For example, there is usually at least one process associated with every window on the computer's screen. Because the CPU can execute only one process at a time, the operating system must do task scheduling, allocating blocks of CPU time to the processes to enable them to make progress.
- Modern operating systems manage virtual memory, which means the number of memory addresses is much larger than the amount of physical memory available. Virtual memory is divided into same-sized blocks called pages. When a process is not running on the CPU, its pages can be held temporarily on a hard disk. When a process is running, the pages containing the instructions and data needed by the CPU are brought into RAM, displacing pages used by an idle process.
- The operating system maintains the file system that keeps track of the location on the hard drive of all programs and data files.
- On multiuser systems, the operating system is responsible for *authentication* (determining that users are who they claim to be) and *authorization* (ensuring that users have permission to perform a particular action). An example of an authentication mechanism is requiring a user to enter a login name and password before using the computer. An example of an authorization mechanism is allowing only those with administrative privileges to install or uninstall application programs.

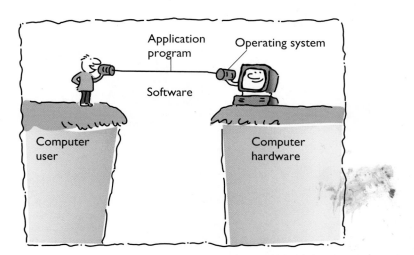

FIGURE 4.15 The user's view: When a person uses an application, whether a game or an accounting program, the person doesn't communicate directly with the computer hardware. Instead, the user interacts with the application, which depends on the operating system to manage and control hardware.

How It Works

4.2 The Operating System

Most of what you see on-screen when you use an application program and most of the common tasks you have the program perform, such as saving and opening files, are being performed by the operating system at the application's request.

When a computer is turned off, there's nothing in RAM (random access memory), and the CPU isn't doing anything. The operating system (OS) programs must be in memory and running on the CPU before the system can function. When you turn on the computer, the CPU automatically begins executing instructions stored in ROM (read-only memory). These instructions help the system boot, and the operating system is loaded from disk into part of the system's memory.

Using the mouse, you "ask" the operating system to load a word-processing application program into memory so it can run.

FIGURE 4.16

The loaded application occupies a portion of memory, leaving that much less for other programs and data. The OS remains in memory, so it can provide services to the application program, helping it to display on-screen menus, communicate with the printer, and perform other common actions. Because the OS and application are in constant communication, control—the location in memory where the CPU is reading program instructions—jumps around. If the application calls the OS to help display a menu, the application tells the CPU, "Go follow the menu display instructions at address × in the operating system area; when you're done, return here and pick up where you left off."

To avoid losing your data file when the system is turned off, you save it to the disk, meaning you have the OS write it into a file on the disk for later use. The OS handles communication between the CPU and the disk drive, ensuring that your file doesn't overwrite other information. (Later, when you reopen the file, the OS locates it on the disk and copies it into memory so the CPU—and, therefore, any program—can see it and work with it.)

Utility Programs and Device Drivers

Even the best operating systems leave some housekeeping tasks to other programs and to the user. **Utility programs** serve as tools for doing system maintenance and repairs that aren't automatically handled by the operating system. Utilities make it easier for users to copy files between storage devices, repair damaged data files, translate files so that different programs can read them, guard against viruses and other potentially harmful programs (as described in Chapter 10), compress files so they take up less disk space, and perform other important, if unexciting, tasks.

The operating system can directly invoke many utility programs, so they appear to the user to be part of the operating system. For example, **device drivers** are small programs that enable I/O devices—keyboard, mouse, printer, and others—to communicate with the computer. Once a device driver—say, for a new printer—is installed, the printer driver functions as a behind-the-scenes intermediary whenever the user requests that a document be printed on that printer. Some utility programs are included with the operating system. Others, including many device drivers, are bundled with peripherals. Still others are sold or given away as separate products.

Where the Operating System Lives

Some computers—mostly game machines, handheld computers, smart phones, and special-purpose computers—store their operating systems permanently in ROM (read-only memory) so they can begin working immediately when the user turns them on. But because ROM is

FIGURE 4.17 Norton 360 (above left) is a popular Windows utility package that includes software tools for protecting PCs from viruses, spyware, and other Internet risks. It also includes tools for disk backup and recovery (lower left). TechTool Pro (above) performs a variety of hardware and software diagnostic and repair functions for Mac OS.

unchangeable, operating systems on these machines can't be modified or upgraded without hardware transplants. Some computers, including many handheld devices, store their operating system in flash memory so it can be upgraded. But most computers, including all modern PCs, hold only a small portion of the operating system in ROM. The remainder of the operating system is loaded into memory in a process called booting, which occurs when you turn on the computer. (The term *booting* is used because the computer seems to pull itself up by its own bootstraps.)

Most of the time the operating system works behind the scenes, taking care of business without the knowledge or intervention of the user. But occasionally it's necessary for a user to communicate directly with the operating system. For example, when you boot a PC, the operating system takes over the screen, waiting until you tell it—with the mouse, the keyboard, or some other input device—what to do. If you tell it to open a graphics application, the operating system locates the program, copies it from disk into memory, turns the screen over to the application, and accepts commands from the application while you draw pictures on the screen.

Interacting with the operating system, like interacting with an application, can be anywhere from intuitive to challenging. It depends on something called the *user interface*. Because of its profound impact on the computing experience, the user interface is a critically important component of almost every piece of software.

The User Interface: The Human–Machine Connection

Early computer users had to spend tedious hours writing and debugging machine-language instructions. Later users programmed in languages that were easier to understand but still technically challenging. Today users spend much of their time working with preprogrammed applications, such as word processing that simulate and amplify the capabilities of real-world tools. As software evolves, so does the user interface—the look and feel of the computing experience from a human point of view.

The anthropologist Claude Levi-Strauss has called human beings **tool makers** and **symbol makers**. The user interface is potentially **the most sophisticated** of these constructions, one in which the **distinction between tool and symbol is blurred**.

—*Aaron Marcus and Andries van Dam, user interface experts*

Desktop Operating Systems

The earliest PC operating systems, created for the Apple II, the original IBM PC, and other machines, looked nothing like today's Mac and Windows operating systems. When IBM introduced its first personal computer in 1981, a typical computer monitor displayed 24 80-column lines of text, numbers, and/or symbols. The computer sent messages to the monitor telling it which character to display in each location on the screen. To comply with this hardware arrangement, the PC's dominant operating system, MS-DOS, was designed with a character-based interface—a user interface based on characters rather than on graphics.

MS-DOS (Microsoft Disk Operating System, often simply called DOS) became the standard operating system on IBM-compatible computers—computers functionally identical to IBM personal computers and, therefore, capable of running IBM-compatible software. Unlike the Windows desktop, MS-DOS used a command-line interface that required the user to type commands to which the computer responded. Some MS-DOS-compatible applications had a command-line interface, but it was more common for applications to

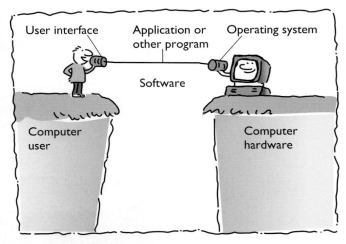

FIGURE 4.18 The user's view revisited: The user interface is the part of the computer system that the user sees. A well-designed user interface hides the bothersome details of computing from the user.

FIGURE 4.19 When typing commands to the OS or selecting options from menus in applications, MS-DOS users work with a character-based interface.

FIGURE 4.20 Many consumer devices today, including VCRs, cell phones, and pagers, have character-based user interfaces.

have a **menu-driven interface** that enabled users to choose commands from on-screen lists called **menus**.

In the years since the introduction of the original IBM PC, graphic displays have become the norm. A computer with a graphic display is not limited to displaying rows and columns of characters; it can individually control every dot on the screen. When the Apple Macintosh was introduced in 1984, it was the first low-cost computer that had an operating system designed with a **graphical user interface**—abbreviated **GUI**, and pronounced "gooey." The **Mac OS**, however, was eclipsed by a product from Microsoft, the company that produced MS-DOS. Today **Microsoft Windows** is far and away the most popular operating system for PCs.

FIGURE 4.21 Mac OS X refines the traditional graphical user interface with a modern take on windows, icons, and directories.

Windows and the Mac OS have evolved over the years, adding new features to their GUIs to make them easier to use. The Windows **taskbar** provides one-click access to open applications, making it easy to switch back and forth among different tasks. **Hierarchical menus** in Windows and Mac OS organize frequently needed commands into compact, efficient submenus, and **pop-up menus** can appear anywhere on the screen. **Context-sensitive menus** offer choices that depend on which on-screen object the user has currently selected.

While there are many differences between Windows and Mac OS, the two now have user interfaces that are more alike than different. Many applications, including Adobe Photoshop and Microsoft Office, are almost identical on Windows and the Mac OS.

Both Windows and the Mac OS started as single-user operating systems. But today both support multiple users. Both are available in server versions that can be used as alternatives to UNIX, the OS that has ruled the server market for decades. (For a more thorough introduction to Windows and Mac OS, see Appendix A).

FIGURE 4.22 Many versions of Linux, including Ubuntu Linux, use menus and icons in ways that would be familiar to Windows and Macintosh users.

UNIX and Linux

Because of its historical ties to academic and government research sites, the Internet is still heavily populated with computers running the **UNIX** operating system. UNIX, developed at Bell Labs more than a decade before the first PCs, enables a timesharing computer to communicate with several other computers or terminals at one time. UNIX has long been the operating system of choice for workstations and mainframes in research and academic settings. In recent years it has taken root in many business environments. In spite of competition from Microsoft, UNIX is still favored by many who require an industrial-strength, multi-user operating system. Some form of UNIX is available for personal computers, workstations, servers, mainframes, and supercomputers.

Because of widespread licensing, commercial brands of UNIX are available from many companies, including Sun (Solaris), Hewlett-Packard (HP-UX), and IBM (AIX). Most Mac users don't know it, but Mac OS X is built around a version of UNIX. Linux, a UNIX clone described at the beginning of this chapter, is widely distributed for free and supported without cost by a devoted, technically savvy group of users.

At its heart, in all its versions, UNIX is a command-line, character-based operating system. The command-line interface (or **shell**) is similar to that of MS-DOS, although the commands aren't the same. For most tasks the UNIX command-line interface feels like a single-user system, even when many users are *logged in*—connected to and using the system. But today's UNIX systems work

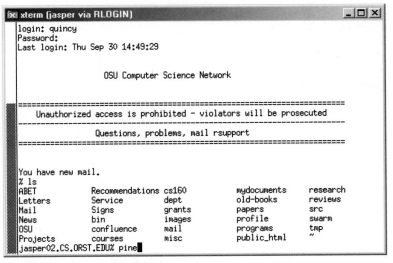

FIGURE 4.23 In its basic form, UNIX is a character-based operating system. This screen shows the beginning of a session on a school's multi-user UNIX mainframe. After the user (quincy) types his login name and password, the system responds with some introductory messages and a prompt (in this case, %). Quincy types the "ls" command to view the names of files in his home directory. The system lists the files and displays a new prompt. Quincy types "pine" to run the pine email program. The session continues this way until quincy responds to a prompt with a command to log off the system. In practice, many UNIX users never see this type of command-line interface because of software shells with GUIs similar to Windows or Mac OS.

Working Wisdom

When Good Software Goes Bad

Even the best software can fail when you need it most. These tips should help you deal with program freezes, system crashes, and other bugs that plague computer users.

➡ **Restart the application.** If the application you're running starts misbehaving, you can often solve the problem by saving your work, closing the application, and re-launching it. If you can't close it because it's frozen, use the system's **force quit** option. In Windows, press the Ctrl + Alt + Del keys at the same time, and then click Task Manager; then select the frozen program and click End Task. On a Mac, press Command-Option-Esc or choose Force Quit from the Apple menu; then select the frozen app from the list and click Force Quit. You may lose the last of your work with that application, but that's better than losing all of your work in every open application.

FIGURE 4.24a When an application freezes, the you can use the Windows Task Manager to select the errant application and press End Task to terminate it.

➡ **Recover your work.** If the application is frozen, you may not be able to save your work before closing. Fortunately, many applications can **autosave** your work every few minutes, so you don't lose more than a few minutes of work in a freeze or crash. Plan ahead: Save each document the minute you start working on it, and make sure you have your applications configured to autosave.

➡ **Reboot the system.** A surprising number of problems can be solved with a simple restart of the computer. A reboot can clear memory of bad data and reset parameters that might have been messed up by "buggy" software. If the computer is completely locked up, you can force a reboot by holding down the power button on your computer for a few seconds.

FIGURE 4.24b Microsoft Word, like many applications, includes an autosave option in Preferences. Here the program is set to automatically save each open document every 10 minutes.

FIGURE 4.24c Windows Update (in the Control Panel) checks the Web to see if there are any updates or patches for the currently running Windows OS. It's generally wise to install any updates soon after they're available.

➡ **Recheck for updates.** Sometimes the problem is out-of-date software. Check the Web to make sure you're using the current version of the misbehaving program and the OS. If you're not, download and install the latest patches.

➡ **Reboot in safe mode.** Some problems can be traced to hidden utilities, widgets, drivers, and other programs that run in the background while you're working with your computer. One of these hidden programs may have become corrupted, or may be clashing with some other program. You can start your machine in safe mode to disable most of these extra programs temporarily. On a Windows machine, press and hold the F8 key on the keyboard as the machine is booting, then use the arrow keys to select Safe Mode in the Windows Advanced Options Menu that appears. On a Mac, hold down the Shift key while restarting until the Apple logo appears. If everything works fine in safe mode, but not otherwise, you'll probably need to do some detective work to identify the suspect software. (On a PC, you may also want to try loading the last known good configuration from the Windows Advanced Options Menu.)

➡ **Research your problem.** Check the Web for similar problems. Try using a few keywords in a search engine. If the program displayed an error message, you might try typing that into the search engine in quotes. You might also want to check forums and FAQs on the software company's Web site, or check popular sites that specialize in troubleshooting.

➡ **Request help.** Software technical support varies in quality and price from company to company.

Sometimes it's free and very good; sometimes it's neither. But in some situations, it's your best shot at solving the problem.

➡ **Reinstall the program.** If all the easy fixes fail, try uninstalling and reinstalling the software. Many programs can be downloaded from the Web, but you may need to type in your original serial number or perform some kind of initialization.

➡ **Restore the operating system.** The most serious problems may require you to back up your data onto another drive, wipe your hard disk clean, and perform a clean install of the OS and applications to start fresh.

➡ **Repair the hardware.** If all your software fixes fail, you may be dealing with hardware problems—a faulty circuit board, a failing hard drive, a short in a connector, or something else. You may need to ask a technician whether it's cost effective to troubleshoot and fix the problem. If it's an older computer or the problem is severe, you may need to look at the final solution—replace the system.

➡ **Replace the system.** If nothing else works, you'll have to start over with fresh hardware, and take consolation in the fact that your new system is faster and more powerful than your old one. But before you move on, don't forget to recycle your old computer.

➡ **Recycle your old computer.** Return it to the company through their recycling program or pass it on to someone who can recover any usable or recyclable parts.

with more than just typed commands. Several companies, including Apple, Sun, and IBM, market UNIX variations and shells with graphical interfaces.

Hardware and Software Platforms

In most electronic devices, the operating system operates invisibly and anonymously. But some operating systems, especially those in PCs, are recognized by name and reputation. The most well-known operating systems include:

- *Microsoft Windows Vista.* This is Microsoft's flagship product. Microsoft sells five different versions of Vista, including Vista Home Basic, for simple home computing needs; Vista Home Premium, which includes Windows Media Center software; Vista Business, for business users; Vista Enterprise, for global organizations with complex IT infrastructures; and Vista Ultimate, the most feature-rich version of the operating system, with capabilities for home computing, mobile computing, and entertainment. All versions share the same code base. Windows Vista is distinguished from earlier versions of Windows by a new user interface, refined navigation and searching tools, beefed-up security, and somewhat slower performance (on many older PCs).

- *Microsoft Windows Server 2008.* Essentially the server-based counterpart to Windows Vista, this version of Windows runs on everything from small Web servers to the mightiest hardware on the planet. This product competes with UNIX and Linux.

- *Microsoft Windows XP.* Windows XP was Microsoft's principal operating system from 2001 until 2006. Microsoft based Windows XP on an earlier operating system that was called Windows NT.

- *Windows Embedded CE.* This stripped-down Windows variant is designed for embedded, connected devices, such as robots, voting machines, music players, and medical equipment. Another Windows CE–based operating system, called Windows Mobile, targets cell phones and Pocket PCs, which means it competes directly with Palm's operating system.

- *Mac OS X (10).* OS X is the standard operating system for the Mac. It sports a stylish, animated user interface that makes many complex tasks surprisingly simple to accomplish. Underneath its friendly exterior, OS X is built on UNIX, the powerful OS known for security and stability rather than simplicity. OS X runs on all modern Macs. A tiny variant of OS X is installed in the iPhone. Apple has released several major upgrades to OS X since its 2001 introduction. Each upgrade has a unique decimal number and informal name. For example, the version introduced in 2007 is known both as OS X 10.5 and as Leopard.

FIGURE 4.25 Compatibility issues: Applications are designed to run on particular operating systems. Operating systems are designed to run on particular hardware platforms.

- *Mac OS 9.* This is the last in a long line of Mac operating systems that started with the original Mac system in 1984. OS 9 and its predecessors run only on older Macs.

- *Linux, Sun Solaris, and other UNIX variations.* Some forms of UNIX or Linux can be found on PCs, Macs, workstations, supercomputers, mainframes, and a variety of other devices. Linux is especially popular because it is free—and freely supported by its partisans. Because Linux doesn't offer as many application programs as Windows does, some people use *dual-boot PCs* that can switch back and forth between Windows and Linux by simply rebooting.

- *BlackBerry OS.* The BlackBerry is a wireless personal digital assistant (PDA) manufactured by Canadian company Research in Motion (RIM). The BlackBerry is especially popular with travellers who want to access email everywhere. The BlackBerry has a proprietary multitasking operating system that supports wireless communication with PCs and takes advantage of the PDA's unique input devices, especially its thumbwheel.

- *Palm OS.* This OS is used in many PDAs and smart phones. It has communication capabilities that make it easy to transfer data between a Palm device and another computer.

Operating systems by themselves aren't very helpful. They need applications so they can do useful work. But application software can't exist by itself; it needs to be built on some kind of **platform**. People often use the term *platform* to describe the combination of hardware and operating system software on which application software is built. *Cross-platform applications*, such as Microsoft Office and Adobe Photoshop, are programs that are available in similar versions for multiple platforms.

The trends are unmistakable. In the early days of the personal computer, there were dozens of different platforms—machines from Apple, Atari, Coleco, Commodore, Tandy, Texas Instruments, and other companies. All of these products have vanished from the marketplace, sometimes taking their parent companies with them. Today's market for new PC hardware and software is dominated by three general platforms: Windows in all its variations, the Mac OS, and various versions of UNIX/Linux. UNIX is mostly used in servers and high-end workstations. While the Mac OS commands a decent share of specialized markets such as education, graphic design, publishing, music, video, and multimedia, it runs far behind Windows in the massive corporate and government markets.

Most personal computers today are built on what's sometimes called the "Wintel" platform: some form of the Windows OS running on an Intel (or compatible) CPU. The Mac platform—Mac OS software running on PowerPC processors (older Macs) or Intel processors (post-2006 Macs)—makes up a smaller segment of the market. The Linux OS can run on many hardware platforms, including Intel and PowerPC processors, but different versions of Linux aren't necessarily compatible.

Even though Windows software isn't designed to run on the Mac platform, software solutions make it possible for Mac users to run most Windows programs. A software emulation program can create a simulated Windows computer within the Mac environment. An *emulation* program translates all Windows-related instructions into instructions the Mac's operating system and CPU can understand. Translation takes time, however, so emulation isn't adequate when speed is critical. Newer Macs use the same Intel CPUs that power Windows machines. On these machines, it's possible to install the Windows OS alongside the Mac OS and choose at system boot-up time which operating system to use. Many Intel and AMD chips support *virtualization*, which allows multiple operating systems to run simultaneously. The CPU can switch rapidly between these partitions. Because software doesn't need to translate instructions to a different CPU's native language, there's no loss

of speed when running Windows software on Intel Macs. With virtualization, it's possible to have Windows, Mac OS, and Linux all running simultaneously on one Mac. (Because the Mac OS is designed to work with specific hardware configurations, this trick doesn't work in the other direction: a standard Windows PC can't run the Mac OS.)

With the growing importance of networks, future applications may be more tied to networks than to desktop computer platforms. Computer users are spending less time dealing with information stored locally on their desktop computers and more time on the Web. Microsoft has responded to that trend with .NET, a strategy that blurs the line between the Web and Microsoft's operating systems and applications. As .NET evolves, more and more software components will be delivered by the network rather than residing on the desktop.

Microsoft's .NET strategy is a response to the popularity of **Java**, a platform-neutral computer language developed by Sun Microsystems for use on multiplatform networks. Programs written in Java can run on computers running Windows, Mac,

FIGURE 4.26 Virtualization software, such as Parallels, lets users run Windows and Linux environments inside of a window on the host OS (in this case, Mac OS X) and move data between the virtual machine and the host OS.

UNIX, and other operating systems, provided those computers have *Java virtual machine* software installed. Like emulation software, Java applications run more slowly than applications targeted to a specific OS platform do. In 2007 Sun made Java available for free to other companies. Similar technologies are emerging from the open source community. If this trend continues, it may someday be possible for computer users to do their work without knowing—or caring—where in the world their software is.

File Management: Where's My Stuff?

The first principle of human interface design, whether for a **doorknob** or a **computer**, is to keep in mind the **human being** who wants to use it. **The technology is subservient to that goal**.

—*Donald Norman, in* The Art of Human–Computer Interface Design

You've seen how the modern operating system provides an interface layer between the computer user and the user's data. In this section we'll look behind the Windows and Mac GUIs to see how information is stored and organized on a computer's hard disk.

Organizing Files and Folders

As we've seen, Windows and the Mac OS employ a user interface that makes an analogy between a computer system and a business office. The monitor becomes a virtual desktop, and the reports, photographs, and other objects manipulated by the computer become files appearing on the desktop. To prevent the desktop from becoming too cluttered, files may be placed inside folders. After a while, the number of folders can become overwhelming, so operating system designers stretch the analogy a little bit and allow users to place a folder inside another folder.

A computer's files and folders are actually stored on a nonvolatile storage device, such as a hard disk, or optical disc. The Windows operating system uses letters to refer to particular storage devices. A Windows PC's primary hard disk is usually given the letter *C*. Every file and folder has a unique **pathname**, which describes the nesting of folders containing it. Within the pathname, the backslash character "\" separates the names of the folders.

FIGURE 4.27 Because many folders and files may be put into the same folder, you can think of the file directory structure as a kind of tree, where the root directory is the trunk, the folders are the branches, and the files are the leaves. In this particular file directory structure the pathname C:\Users\padilla\Documents\budget.xls refers to an Excel spreadsheet.

For example, on a Windows Vista system, the files and folders appearing on the desktop of user "padilla" are most likely kept in the directory

C:\Users\padilla\Desktop

Let's interpret this pathname. The main folder on the C drive, called the **root directory**, contains all the other files and folders kept on the disk. The beginning of the pathname, "C:\", refers to the root directory. The root directory contains a folder named "Users." Within folder "Users" is another folder named "padilla." Within folder "padilla" is another folder named "Desktop." Within folder "Desktop" is a list of the files and folders appearing on the Windows desktop of user "padilla." (Pathnames on Macs are similar to Windows pathnames, except that there's no requirement that drives be given one-letter names. As a result, most drives have names such as "Macintosh HD" and "Backup drive" rather than C and D.)

File-Management Utilities

A **file-management utility** lets you view, rename, copy, move, and delete files and folders. In the Mac OS, the file-management utility is called the Finder; in Windows it is called Windows Explorer. In both cases the file-management utility is included with the operating system; few computer users know they're using a separate program when they use these utilities.

You can use a file-management utility to see the location of a file or folder in a storage device's hierarchy and view its pathname. You can also configure the utility to display information about a particular file, such as its size, its type, and the last time it was modified.

File-management utilities simplify copying, moving, and deleting files and folders. Each of these operations, as well as creating new folders, is reduced to a few simple mouse operations. Renaming a file or folder is as simple as clicking the object's icon and typing the new name.

FIGURE 4.28 Windows Explorer allows you to see both the contents of a folder and the location of the folder in the storage device's hierarchy.

Managing Files from Applications

Most applications manipulate objects that can be stored in files. For example, a word processor allows you to type a new document or start with a previously saved document. In either case, you have the ability to save a copy of the new or revised document. An email program allows you to save some or all of the emails you have sent or received. An entertainment application may give you the opportunity to save the state of a game and restart the game from that point. Most applications support four basic file-management operations: Open, Save, Save As, and Close.

The *Open* operation allows you to select the file containing the project you would like to work on. After you select the file, the application reads its contents into memory. The state of the application changes to reflect the contents of the file. For example, when you open a file containing a spreadsheet, the contents of the spreadsheet file are displayed for you to view and manipulate.

The *Save* operation writes the current state of the application as a disk file. Suppose you are enhancing a spreadsheet that has been in existence for a while. You used the Open operation to retrieve the previous version of the spreadsheet. After adding some new formulas to the spreadsheet, you replace the previous version with the new, improved version. The Save operation overwrites the prior version of the spreadsheet with the enhanced version.

The *Save As* operation allows you to choose the location and name of the file you want to contain the current state of the application. The Save As operation must be used when a new object has been created. For example, suppose you are running a word processor to create a report from scratch. Because you began with a blank document, there is no filename associated with it. The first time you save the report, the application must be given the name and location of the file. Another time to use the Save As operation is when you do not want to overwrite the previously saved version. Suppose you open a file containing a digital photograph and use a photo editor to touch it up. You would like to save your work, but you do not want to lose the original in case you've accidentally made a mistake with your retouching. You can keep the original copy and save the new copy by using the Save As operation to give the new copy a different name than the original.

FIGURE 4.29 The Save As operation lets you choose the location and the name of the file that will store the current state of the application.

FIGURE 4.30 This Windows Vista virtual folder shows all of the user's most recently changed documents, regardless of where they're stored. If the user changes any document, that document will automatically be added to this virtual folder.

The *Close* operation allows you to stop working on a project but remain in the application program. A Close operation is often followed by an Open operation to read in a new project. When you Close a project, its current state is not saved to a file. Changes you have made to the project since the last Save or Save As operation are lost. If you attempt to close a modified project without saving it, the application probably will display a pop-up window that asks you if you would like to save the project before closing it.

Locating Files

Even if you start with a brand-new computer, it doesn't take long to create a huge number of files scattered all over the file system. It's hard to manage data that you can't even find. Of course, it's easier to find files if they're organized logically. To this end, both Windows and the Mac OS support common system folders with self-explanatory names. For example, your documents might be stored in a folder called *Documents*. Likewise, digital photos can be stored in *Pictures* and digital music files can be stored in *Music*. These folders are specific to each user, so multiple users on a single PC will each have unique data in their system folders.

Modern operating systems include search tools that can help you find files wherever they're stored. You can search for filenames, but you can also search for words or phrases inside a file. So if you don't know the name of a file but do know some text that might be contained in that file, you can use the search tool to find your data.

The Search and Find commands are designed to help answer the common computer user's question, "Where's my stuff?" Windows and Mac operating systems were originally designed when low-capacity floppy disk drives seemed spacious. Today's massive hard drives can hold thousands of files, from email messages to media files. In recent years, Apple and Microsoft have developed new file-management tools to help computer users keep track of their music libraries, photograph collections, email messages, and other files.

Today's Windows and Mac operating systems go beyond the limitations of the folders-and-windows GUI for cataloging, organizing, and finding files. They enable you to create virtual folders (smart folders in Mac OS X) that can display collections of files located all over your hard drive that match specific criteria, and automatically update those collections. For example, a virtual folder might "contain" all of the Word documents on your hard drive that contain your school name and were created in the last 3 months. You can access these files without knowing what folders they're actually stored in. If you create a new Word document with your school's name in it, it's automatically added to the virtual folder.

This type of organizational tool—essentially a database interface—can help users find their stuff more quickly and easily, while shielding them from the intricacies of the underlying system. And as we move toward distributed computing environments, where data might be stored on different systems on a network or across the Internet, these technologies will become even more valuable.

Defragmentation: The Cure for Fragmented Files

Before the operating system can store files on a hard disk, the disk must be formatted. Formatting a disk means putting electronic marks on the disk, dividing the disk into a series of concentric *tracks* and dividing each track into a collection of *sectors*. (You may never have had to format a hard disk yourself because computer manufacturers format the hard disks of new computers in order to install the operating system and application programs.) Formatting removes any information that was previously stored on the disk, so you should make sure you never reformat a disk that contains important information.

Sectors are quite small compared to the size of the files most frequently stored on a disk. For this reason disk drives usually bundle sectors into *clusters* or *blocks*. Because many files are larger than a single cluster, the file system must provide a way to link multiple clusters to store larger files. To keep track of the files kept on a disk, the file system maintains a table (also stored on the disk) that indicates which clusters are assigned to each file. The file system also maintains a list of empty clusters. It dips into the pool of empty clusters when you want to create a new file or add to an existing file.

Accessing the information in a file is faster if the file is assigned to contiguous clusters. That way, the disk head reading the information does not have to move from track to track as often. Moving the disk head takes several milliseconds, a long time on PCs that can perform more than a million instructions every millisecond! Assigning a file to contiguous clusters minimizes the movement of the disk head when the contents of the file are read into memory.

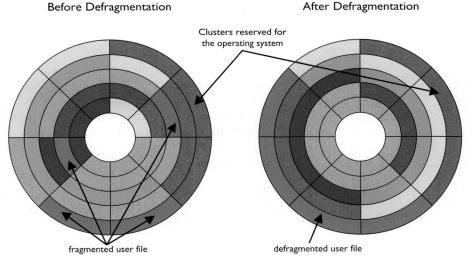

Before Defragmentation

After Defragmentation

Clusters reserved for the operating system

fragmented user file

defragmented user file

FIGURE 4.31 Having a lot of fragmented files can degrade the performance of a hard disk. In this figure, clusters reserved for operating system files are red. Other colors represent application and user files (one file per color). After defragmentation, files are assigned to contiguous clusters whenever possible. For example, before defragmentation, the four sectors holding the user file shown in light blue are scattered over three tracks. After defragmentation, all four sectors occupy a single track.

As you work with a file, its contents may become scattered over distant clusters. Suppose you have been editing a Word document, and you ask the file system to save a newer, longer version of the document. If the document no longer fits in the cluster(s) to which it was assigned, the file system looks to see whether the next cluster is empty. If so, it can allocate that cluster to the document, keeping it stored in contiguous clusters. If the next cluster is already allocated to another file, however, the operating system must find another empty cluster. A fragmented file is a file allocated to noncontiguous clusters. As you create, edit, and delete files, more and more of them become fragmented, degrading the performance of the hard disk.

A defragmentation utility eliminates (as much as possible) fragmented files by changing the assignment of clusters to files. Depending on how fragmented a disk is, the defragmentation process may take hours. For this reason, it's a good idea to let a defragmentation program run overnight. Because defragmentation can significantly improve the performance of a disk drive, some experts recommend that PC users defragment their disks occasionally. (The Mac OS handles routine defragmentation automatically.) If the defragmentation process fails for some reason, a file system can be left in a corrupted state, and the information stored on a disk can be lost. For this reason, it's a good idea to make sure that you've backed up the important files on your hard drive before you defragment the file system, just in case.

Software Piracy and Intellectual Property Laws

Information wants to be free. Information also wants to be expensive. Information wants to **be free** because it has become so cheap to distribute, copy, and recombine—**too cheap to meter. It wants to be expensive** because it can be **immeasurably valuable** to the recipient. **That tension will not go away**.

—*Stewart Brand, in* The Media Lab

Software piracy—the illegal duplication of copyrighted software—is rampant. Millions of computer users have made copies of programs they don't legally own and distributed them to family members, friends, and, sometimes, total strangers. Because so few software companies use physical copy protection methods such as dongles to protect their products, copying software is as easy as duplicating an audio CD or photocopying a chapter of a book. Unfortunately, many people aren't aware that copying software, recorded music, and books can violate federal laws protecting intellectual property. Many others simply look the other way, convinced that software companies, music companies, and publishers already make enough money.

The Piracy Problem

The software industry, with a world market of more than $50 billion a year, loses billions of dollars every year to software pirates. The Business Software Alliance (BSA) estimates that more than one-third of all software in use is illegally copied, costing the software industry tens of thousands of jobs. Piracy can be particularly hard on small software companies. Developing software is just as difficult for them as it is for big companies such as Microsoft and Oracle, but they often lack the financial and legal resources to cover the losses they suffer through piracy.

Software industry organizations, including the BSA and SPA Anti-Piracy (a division of the Software & Information Industry Association), work with law enforcement agencies to crack down on piracy. At the same time, they sponsor educational programs to make computer users aware that piracy is theft because laws can't work without citizen understanding and support.

Software piracy is a worldwide problem, with piracy rates highest in developing nations. In China approximately 95 percent of all new software installations are pirated; in Vietnam the piracy rate is 97 percent. A few Third World nations refuse to abide by international copyright laws. They argue that the laws protect rich countries at the expense of underdeveloped nations. In 1998 the Argentine Supreme Court ruled that the country's copyright laws don't apply to computer software.

Intellectual Property and the Law

Legally, the definition of intellectual property includes the results of intellectual activities in the arts, science, and industry. Copyright laws have traditionally protected forms of literary expression, including books, plays, songs, paintings, photographs, and movies. Trademark law has protected symbols, pictures, sounds, colors, and smells used by a business to identify goods. Patent law has protected mechanical inventions, and contract law has covered trade secrets. Software doesn't fit neatly into any of these categories under the law. Copyright laws protect most commercial software programs, but a few companies have successfully used patent laws to protect software products.

The purpose of intellectual property laws is to ensure that mental labor is justly rewarded and to encourage innovation. Programmers, inventors, scientists, writers, editors, filmmakers, and musicians depend on ideas and the expression of those ideas for their incomes. Ideas are information, and information is easy to copy—especially in this electronic age. Intellectual property laws are designed to protect these professionals and encourage them to continue their creative efforts so society can benefit from their future work.

Most of the time, these laws help them to achieve their goals. A novelist can devote two or three years of her life to writing a masterpiece, confident that she won't find bootleg copies for sale on street corners when she finishes it. A movie studio can invest millions of dollars in a film, knowing that the investment will be returned, a little at a time, through ticket sales and video rentals. An inventor can work long hours to create a better mousetrap and know that MegaMousetrap City won't steal her idea.

But sometimes intellectual property laws are applied in such a way that they may stifle the innovation and creativity they're designed to protect. In 1999 Amazon.com was awarded a controversial patent for "one-click shopping," preventing other e-commerce sites from giving their customers a similar, simple shopping experience. Similarly, SightSound patented all paid downloads of "desired digital video or digital audio signals." RealNetworks patented streaming audio and video, and British Telecom claims to hold a 1976 patent that covers every Web hyperlink! Most experts agree that these ideas are too simple and broad to be owned by one company. And in many cases, the patent owner isn't the inventor of the concept; Douglas Engelbart demonstrated hyperlinking as early as 1967 at Stanford Research Institute. Such broad patents generally end up in court, where legal experts and technology experts debate the merits and scope of the ideas and the laws designed to protect them. Meanwhile, legislators attempt to update the laws to address ever-changing technological advances.

Most existing copyright and patent laws, which evolved during the age of print and mechanical inventions, are outdated, contradictory, and inadequate for today's information technology. Many laws, including the Computer Fraud and Abuse Act of 1984, clearly treat software piracy as a crime. The NET (No Electronic Theft) Act of 1997 closed a narrow loophole in the law that allowed people to give away software on the Internet.

FIGURE 4.32 In 1999 Moscow police attempted to make a dent in the illegal software market by destroying mountains of pirated software. Their efforts were largely unsuccessful, however. At this time, Russia has one of the highest software piracy rates in the world, close to that of China.

The Digital Millennium Copyright Act (DMCA) of 1998 represents the most comprehensive reform of U.S. copyright law in a generation. The DCMA includes several controversial provisions that need to be clarified by the courts. According to the law, it is illegal to write a program that circumvents copy protection schemes, no matter if that program is used to copy DVDs, electronic books, or other protected material illegally. The DMCA also makes it a crime to share information about how to crack copy protection. Critics argue that the law suppresses freedom of speech, academic freedom, and the principle of fair use—the time-honored right to make copies of copyrighted material for personal and academic use and for other noncompetitive purposes.

In 2001 the Recording Industry Association of America (RIAA) used the DMCA to shut down the Napster music-sharing service; by 2003 the RIAA was invoking the DMCA to force Internet service providers to reveal the identities of individual song pirates. While the courts eventually ruled that Internet service providers did not have to give this information to the RIAA, questions about the scope and reach of the DMCA remain. Meanwhile, millions of people continue to exchange music, movies, and other copyrighted works over Kazaa and other file-sharing networks. Some organizations, such as the Electronic Frontier Foundation, are advocating reforms of the copyright system that would legalize file sharing while still providing a way for musicians and other content creators to receive a fair financial return for their creative efforts.

In matters of software, the legal system is sailing in uncharted waters. Experts debate online and off about whether current intellectual property laws encourage or stifle innovation. Whether dealing with issues of piracy or monopoly, lawmakers and judges must struggle with difficult questions about innovation, property, freedom, and progress. The questions are likely to be with us for quite a while.

Inventing the FUTURE

Tomorrow's User Interfaces

*I **hate** computers. **Telepathy** would be better.*

—*John Perry Barlow, writer and cofounder of the Electronic Frontier Foundation*

Twenty years ago, the typical computer could be operated only by a highly trained professional, and using a computer was pretty much synonymous with programming a computer. Today computers are so easy to use that they're sold at shopping malls and operated by preschoolers.

The graphical user interface pioneered by Xerox and popularized by Apple and Microsoft has become an industry standard, making it possible for users to move between computer types almost as easily as drivers can adjust to different brands of cars. But experts expect user interfaces to continue to evolve before they settle down into the kind of long-lasting standard we're used to in automobiles. Today's WIMP (windows, icons, menus, and pointing devices) interface is easier to learn and use than earlier character-based interfaces, but it's not the end of the user interface evolution.

Researcher Raj Reddy uses another acronym to describe emerging user interface technologies: SILK, for speech, image, language, and knowledge capabilities. SILK incorporates many important software technologies:

➡ ***Speech and language.*** Although we still don't have a language-translating telephone or a foolproof dictation-taking "talkwriter," speech technology is maturing into a practical alternative to keyboard and mouse input. Voice-recognition systems are used for security systems, automated voicemail systems, hands-free Web navigation, and other applications. New applications are being developed and marketed every day. With or without speech, natural-language processing will be part of future user interfaces. It's just a matter of time before we'll be able to communicate with computers in English, Spanish, Japanese, or some other natural language. Today many computers can reliably read subsets of these languages or can be trained to understand spoken commands and text. Tomorrow's machines should be able to handle much day-to-day work through a natural-language interface, written or spoken. Researchers expect that we'll soon be using programs that read documents as we create them, edit them according to our instructions, and file them based on their content.

FIGURE 4.33 Virtual reality user interfaces can enhance science and recreation. In Argonne's CAVE, a scientist can interactively study the relationships between the nucleic acids of the molecule.

➡ ***Image.*** In the past decade, computer graphics have become an integral part of the computing experience. Tomorrow's graphics won't be still, flat images; they'll include three-dimensional models, animation, and video clips. Today's two-dimensional desktop interfaces will give way to three-dimensional workspace metaphors complete with 3-D animated objects—virtual workspaces unlike anything we use today. **Virtual reality (VR)** user interfaces will create the illusion that the user is immersed in a world inside the computer—an environment that contains both scenes and the controls to change those scenes. (Virtual reality is discussed in more detail in the Chapter 6 "Inventing the Future".)

➡ ***Knowledge.*** Many experts predict that knowledge will be the most important enhancement to the user interface of the future. Advances in the technology of knowledge will enable engineers to design self-maintaining systems that can diagnose and correct common problems without human intervention. Advances in knowledge will make user interfaces more friendly and forgiving. Intelligent applications will be able to decipher many ambiguous commands and correct common errors as they happen. But more important, knowledge will enable software **agents** to really be of service to users. Software agents are discussed in next chapter's "Inventing the Future". ∿

Copyrights—and Wrongs *by Sascha Segan*

Do our copyright laws encourage or discourage creativity? That's the question at the center of this PC Magazine column from July, 2008.

Did you break the law today? If you've created something on the Internet, probably. Artists, librarians, tech geeks, and software engineers are now fighting over a miserably shrinking public domain. This isn't what copyright was supposed to be about, and only a popular uprising will stop the current trend.

Copyright law was designed to "promote the Progress of Science and useful Arts, by securing for limited Times to Authors and Inventors the exclusive Right to their respective Writings and Discoveries." That's from the U.S. Constitution, thus the weird capitalization.

The way "the exclusive Right" promotes progress is by giving creators a monopoly over selling their works, or letting them sell the rights to someone else, so they can make a living and thus keep creating.

There's an amusing utopian argument against all copyright, but it assumes too many random acts of generosity. Before copyright, only the wealthy, or those with wealthy patrons, could afford to spend time making art. In our market-oriented world, people will buy things if they consider them affordable and valuable—and if there's a punishment for stealing them. When the price and restrictions are too high, people will steal. The record labels still claim to be shocked—shocked!—that their unacceptable terms lead to thievery. But if there's no punishment at all for stealing, nobody will pay, and fewer things will be created because artists will spend time finding ways to feed their families instead.

One of the great tech stories of the past decade has been how technology has enabled a tremendous explosion of creativity. This is why the Electronic Frontier Foundation (EFF), the Consumer Electronics Association, and the Center for Democracy and Technology are involved in the debate over a new Orphan Works Act, which is supposed to expand the public domain. Your camera-phone photos, YouTube mashups, blog posts, home-burned DVDs, iMovies of your kids—even your Facebook status updates—are creative works.

Right now, more Americans are creating lasting works than ever before, and if you borrow content, you're likely violating copyright law. That's nothing new—do you think Shakespeare had an original plot? If you're concerned about legality, the pool of stuff in the public domain that you can legally use to create new brilliance has gotten proportionally smaller with time.

At some point in the 20th century, most works went from being created by people (who die) to being created by corporations (which are immortal). The immortal corporations wanted their rights to extend to their immortal lifespans. The Constitution prohibits an unlimited copyright term, so they just keep extending the term. They're immortal and you aren't, so they'll keep doing this until people make them stop.

As a creator, I don't see why I should keep profiting from something I wrote even 50 years down the line. There needs to be some term of exclusivity to give the work value, but beyond a certain point, that exclusivity discourages creativity. If I can live off one book for 90 years, I have no incentive ever to write another book, and nobody else can use my creativity as a springboard to build the next masterpiece.

So now we get to fighting over scraps. Because copyrights now extend until the fall of Western civilization, the Orphan Works Act is supposed to let people reuse stuff whose provenance they can't identify. An example: If you find an old studio photograph of your grandmother as a young girl, Wal-Mart won't copy it for you, because the estate of the photographer (presumably dead) still holds the copyright. The new law would let you rescue Grandma from the depths of time. If you could tell who created the photo, you'd have to pay for the privilege, but if not, you could still use the image.

This sounds good, but the law's opponents, mostly visual artists and photographers, say that all someone needs to do is pretend not to be able to find the creator. You could submit your work to a registry to protect yourself, but that basically amounts to paying protection money.

Yes, a well-written Orphan Works Act that would accommodate everyone is not impossible. The EFF suggests mandating that the copyright registry be free, and that people have to look very, very hard for the original creator. The artists, of course, fear smooth-talking lawyered folks who can convince a judge that they're looking very, very hard when they aren't. The Orphan Works Act isn't the answer. Returning to a sensible copyright regime is.

The power to create that technology gives us is a heady drink, and a vibrant public domain is the best chaser for it. Endless copyright terms don't encourage creativity or protect individual creators. Tell Congress to cut through all this nonsense and enhance the public domain by shortening the length of copyright terms, not by throwing a few scraps and bones to the public.

Discussion Questions

1. What do you think is a "sensible copyright regime?" Why?

2. How have you broken copyright laws?

Summary

Software provides the communication link between humans and their computers. Because software is soft—stored in memory rather than hard-wired into the circuitry—it can easily be modified to meet the needs of the computer user. By changing software, you can change a computer from one kind of tool into another.

Most software falls into one of three categories: compilers and other translator programs, software applications, and system software. A compiler is a software tool that enables programs written in English-like languages such as Visual Basic, Java, and C# to be translated into the zeros and ones of the machine language the computer understands. A compiler frees the programmer from the tedium of machine language programming, making it easier to write quality programs with fewer bugs. But even with the best translators, programming is a little like communicating with an alien species. It's a demanding process that requires more time and mental energy than most people are willing or able to invest.

Fortunately, software applications make it easy for most computer users today to communicate their needs to the computer without learning programming. Applications simulate and extend the properties of familiar real-world tools such as typewriters, paintbrushes, and file cabinets, making it possible for people to do things with computers that would be difficult or impossible otherwise. Integrated software packages combine several applications in a single unified package, making it easy to switch between tools. Web applications are tools that users typically access through Web browsers. For situations in which a general commercial program won't do the job, programmers for businesses and public institutions develop vertical-market and custom packages.

Whether you're writing programs or simply using them, the computer's operating system is functioning behind the scenes, translating your software's instructions into messages that the hardware can understand. Popular operating systems today include several versions of Microsoft Windows, the Mac OS, and several versions of Linux. An operating system serves as the computer's business manager, taking care of the hundreds of details that need to be handled to keep the computer functioning. A timesharing operating system has the particularly challenging job of serving multiple users concurrently, monitoring the machine's resources, keeping track of each user's account, and protecting the security of the system and each user's data. One of the most important jobs of the operating system is managing the program and data files stored on nonvolatile memory devices, such as hard disks and optical discs. Utility programs can handle many of those system-related problems that the operating system can't solve directly.

Applications, utilities, programming languages, and operating systems all must, to varying degrees, communicate with the user. A program's user interface is a critical factor in that communication. User interfaces have evolved over the years to the point where sophisticated software packages can be operated by people who know little about the inner workings of the computer. A well-designed user interface shields the user from the bits and bytes, creating an on-screen façade, or shell, that makes sense to the user. Today the computer industry has moved away from the tried-and-true command-line interfaces toward a friendlier graphical user interface that uses windows, icons, mice, and pull-down menus in an intuitive, consistent environment. Tomorrow's user interfaces are likely to depend more on voice, three-dimensional graphics, and animation to create an artificial reality.

One of the challenges of working with a computer is keeping track of the masses of information that can be collected, edited, and stored on discs. Most computers use some kind of hierarchical file system involving directories, or folders, to organize files. But modern operating systems have built-in search functions that make it easy to locate files without knowing their exact locations.

Commercial software programs enjoy copyright protection. The purpose of granting copyrights to the owners of intellectual property is to stimulate creativity. Copyright law can stifle creativity if it prevents people from building on the work of others, however. For this reason, a tension exists between the needs and desires of producers and the needs and desires of consumers. Despite copyright protections for computer programs, software piracy has flourished, particularly in countries such as China and Russia.

Key Terms

Interactive Activities

1. The *Tomorrow's Technology and You* Web site, **www.pearsonhighered.com/beekman**, contains self-test exercises related to this chapter. Follow the instructions for taking a quiz. After you've completed your quiz, you can email the results to your instructor.

2. The Web site also contains open-ended discussion questions called Internet Exercises. Discuss one or more of the Internet Exercises questions at the section for this chapter.

True or False

1. Microsoft Windows is the best-known example of an operating system that primarily uses a command-line interface. F

2. An algorithm is a computer program written in a higher-level programming language. F

3. When you buy a software program, you're really buying a license to use the program according to rules specified by the software company. T

4. Shareware is a type of software application used for sharing files over a network or the Internet. F

5. Operating system software is a necessary part of every PC, but it is not used in handheld computers. F

6. Your computer can't print documents unless it has a device driver that allows it to communicate with your printer. T

7. The first low-cost operating system with a graphical user interface was an early version of Linux. F

8. It is impossible to run Windows applications on a Mac computer. F

9. A PC can have only one operating system installed on its hard disk at a time. F

10. Cross-platform Web applications can be run using Web browsers on computers with different operating systems. T

Multiple Choice

1. Which of the following is the most famous example of open-source software?
   a. Microsoft Windows
   b. Mac OS X
   c. UNIX
   d. Linux
   e. Google

2. What is correcting errors in a program called?
   a. Compiling
   b. Debugging
   c. Grinding
   d. Interpreting
   e. Translating

3. A compiler translates a program written in a high-level language into
   a. machine language.
   b. an algorithm.
   c. Java.
   d. C#.
   e. natural language.

4. What does a program's end-user license agreement (EULA) typically include?
   a. Rules specifying how the software may be used
   b. Warranty disclaimers
   c. Rules concerning the copying of the software
   d. All of the above
   e. None of the above

5. When you buy a typical computer software package, you are purchasing
   a. a guarantee that the software has no bugs in it.
   b. a share of stock in the company making the software.
   c. the software.
   d. a license to use the software.
   e. free upgrades to the software.

6. Microsoft Office is
   a. a Web application.
   b. an operating system.
   c. a collection of utility programs.
   d. a vertical-market application.
   e. an application suite.

7. When a PC crashes or freezes while you're using it, the problem might be caused by
   a. a bug in the application program that you were using.
   b. a bug in the operating system.
   c. a clash between two pieces of software that were running at the same time.
   d. a hardware failure.
   e. Any of the above.

8. Which of the following can handle most system functions that aren't handled directly by the operating system?
   a. Vertical-market applications
   b. Utilities
   c. Algorithms
   d. Integrated software
   e. Compilers

9. The operating system is stored in ROM or flash memory in most
   a. Windows and Mac computers.
   b. mainframes and supercomputers.
   c. handheld computers.
   d. open-source and public-domain computers.
   e. computers, regardless of size or function.

10. What happens when you boot up a PC?
    a. Portions of the operating system are copied from disk into memory.
    b. Portions of the operating system are copied from memory onto disk.
    c. Portions of the operating system are compiled.
    d. Portions of the operating system are emulated.
    e. None of the above.

11. Device drivers are
    a. small, special-purpose programs.
    b. tiny power cords for external storage devices.
    c. experts who know how to maximize the performance of devices.
    d. the innermost part of the operating system.
    e. substitutes for operating systems.

12. What is the main folder on your PC's hard drive called?
    a. GUI
    b. Start
    c. Root directory
    d. Hope page
    e. Device driver

13. UNIX is
    a. a multiuser operating system designed more than three decades ago.
    b. at the heart of Mac OS X.
    c. the operating system that is widely used for Internet servers.
    d. All of the above.
    e. None of the above.

14. Future PC user interfaces will almost certainly involve more use of
    a. machine language.
    b. natural language.
    c. high-level language.
    d. assembly language.
    e. algorithmic language.

15. Most commercial software programs enjoy a form of intellectual property protection called
    a. copyright.
    b. open source.
    c. patent.
    d. trademark.
    e. trade secret.

Review Questions

1. What is the relationship between higher level languages and machine language?

2. Most computer software falls into one of three categories: compilers and other translator programs, software applications, and system software. Describe and give examples of each.

3. Which must be loaded first into the computer's memory—the operating system or software applications? Why?

4. Write an algorithm for doing a load of laundry. Check your algorithm carefully for errors and ambiguities. Then have a classmate or your instructor check it. How did your results compare?

5. Describe several functions of an operating system. Do all of these apply to all operating systems?

6. What does it mean when we say that software is written for a particular platform? Give specific examples of several platforms.

7. What is the relationship between a utility and an operating system?

8. What is a graphical user interface? How does it differ from a character-based interface? What are the advantages of each?

9. Describe several steps you might take to solve the problem if your word processing program locks up while you're writing a paper.

10. How do Web applications differ from PC-based applications? What are some advantages of each?

Discussion Questions

1. In what way is writing instructions for a computer more difficult than writing instructions for a person? In what way is it easier?

2. How would using a computer be different if it had no operating system? How would programming be different?

3. Speculate about the user interface of a typical computer in the year 2020. How would this user interface differ from those used in today's computers?

4. Some people believe Web applications will soon replace PC applications for most purposes. What do you think? What would it take to make this practical?

5. How do you feel about the open-software movement? Would you be willing to volunteer your time to write software or help users for free?

6. Suppose you've spent all your spare time for the past eight months programming a new PC game. Your friends have tried it and say it is great. They have started bugging you for copies of the game. Would you give the game away or try to sell it?

7. Suppose Whizzo Software Company produces a program that looks, from the user's point of view, exactly like the immensely popular BozoWorks from Bozo, Inc. Whizzo insists that it didn't copy any of the code in BozoWorks; it just tried to design a program that would apeal to BozoWork users. Bozo cries foul and sues Whizzo for violation of intellectual property laws. Do you think the laws should favor Bozo's arguments or Whizzo's? Why?

Projects

1. Write a report about available computer applications in your field of study or in your chosen profession.

2. Take an inventory of computer applications available in your computer lab. Describe the major uses for each application.

3. Interview five people who own a PC running a version of the Windows operating system, and interview five people who own a PC running a version of the Mac OS. Ask each person to explain what he or she likes best about the computer's operating system, as well as what he or she dislikes the most about the computer's operating system. After you are done with your interviews, look for similarities and differences between the likes and dislikes of Windows and Mac users.

Sources and Resources

Books

Just for Fun: The Story of an Accidental Revolutionary, by Linus Torvalds and David Diamond (New York, NY: HarperBusiness, 2002). The executive editor of Red Herring convinced Linus Torvalds to tell his story. The result is this book, a quirky collection of tidbits from the life of the creator of Linux.

Rebel Code: Linux and the Open Source Revolution, by Glyn Moody (New York, NY: Perseus, 2002). This book tells the Linux story in a style that's more conventional, and for many readers, more readable, than the Torvalds/Diamond book.

The Cathedral and the Bazaar: Musings on Linux and Open Source by an Accidental Revolutionary, by Eric S. Raymond (Sebastopol, CA: O'Reilly, 2001). This widely praised book is an expanded version of the original manifesto for the open-source software movement—the movement that threatens to revolutionize the software industry. Tom Peters calls it "wonderful, witty, and, ultimately, wise."

Windows Vista for Dummies, Special DVD Edition, by Andy Rathbone (Hoboken, NJ: John Wiley & Sons, 2008). The *Dummies* series that started with *DOS for Dummies* has expanded to cover everything from antiquing to yoga. The quality varies from book to book, but the best titles in the Dummies family have served as easy-to-read tutorials for millions of people, dummies or not. This popular package combines a dummies introduction to Windows Vista with a DVD that walks viewers through many of the basic processes. Of course, the Dummies series doesn't have a Windows monopoly. There are hundreds of books on Windows for dummies and nondummies alike.

Microsoft Windows Vista Visual Quickstart Guide, by Chris Fehily (Berkeley, CA: Peachpit Press, 2008). This book covers the basics of Vista, from setup to security, using the popular VQS formula: short, step-by-step tutorials explaining how to do each task, liberal use of screen shots, and plenty of bonus tips.

The Little Mac Book, Leopard Edition, by Robin Williams (Berkeley, CA: Peachpit Press, 2008). Robin Williams has written many great books about computers, desktop publishing, graphic design, Web design, and (especially) the Mac. She's known for her clear, approachable writing style. In this book she explains the ins and outs of the Mac and its operating system. It's one of the best gentle introductions to the Mac you'll find anywhere.

Switching to the Mac: The Missing Manual, Leopard Edition, by David Pogue (Sebastopol, CA: Pogue Press, 2008). If you're already Windows-savvy but you feel a little lost on a Mac, this book should help. David Pogue's book combines an intimate knowledge of both Mac and Windows with a clear, humorous writing style.

Running Windows on your Mac, by Dwight Silverman (Berkeley, CA: Peachpit Press, 2008). Now that Macs use Intel processors, they can easily switch back and forth between the Mac OS and Windows. This book is a helpful guide for Mac users who want or need to spend part of their time in a Windows world.

UNIX: Visual QuickStart Guide, by Deborah S. Ray and Eric J. Ray (Berkeley, CA: Peachpit Press, 2006). Many UNIX books assume that you speak fluent technojargon and that you want to know all about the operating system and how it works. This book is designed for people who want to (or need to) use UNIX but don't particularly want to read a massive volume of UNIX lore. No book can make mastering UNIX simple, but this one at least makes getting started with UNIX simpler.

Linux in a Nutshell, by Ellen Siever, Aaron Weber, Stephen Figgins, Robert Love, and Arnold Robbins (Sebastopol, CA: O'Reilly Media, 2005). O'Reilly has a large list of quality computer books, including the excellent *Missing Manual* series. O'Reilly is especially strong in its coverage of open-source software, including Linux. This massive multiauthor book is one of their most popular titles. It's a useful reference manual, rather than an introductory tutorial.

How to Do Everything with Google Tools, by Donna L. Baker (San Francisco, CA: McGraw-Hill Osborne, 2008). Google is steadily transforming itself from a search engine into an online platform for Web applications of all types. This book provides a practical overview of the growing Google toolbox.

Things That Make Us Smart: Defending Human Attributes in the Age of the Machine, by Donald A. Norman (New York, NY: Perseus, 1994). Norman left his position as the founding chairman of the Department of Cognitive Science at the University of California, San Diego, to work in the computer industry. His research on the relationship between technology and the human cognitive system is especially relevant in an industry where user interface decisions affect millions of users every day. This book, like Norman's others, is informative, thought provoking, and enjoyable. His argument for a more human-centered technology should be required reading for all software designers.

Ethics for the Information Age, Second Edition, by Michael J. Quinn (Boston, MA: Pearson Addison-Wesley, 2006). This book contains in-depth discussions of many ethical issues raised by the introduction of information technology. One of its chapters focuses on intellectual property and debates issues related to the rights of producers and consumers, including whether creators of computer programs and music have a right to own their creations and whether consumers have an obligation to respect copyright laws.

The Pirate's Dilemma: How Youth Culture Is Reinventing Capitalism, by Matt Mason (New York, NY: Free Press, 2008). Are pirates terrorists or freedom fighters? That's the question at the heart of Matt Mason's book. He argues that many of the most important advancements in culture have occurred as a result of what we now call piracy. Everybody from Thomas Edison to Andy Warhol has been accused of piracy. Today's intellectual property laws are, on the surface, designed to encourage innovation. But according to Mason, they may have just the opposite effect. Today's youth culture, steeped in hip hop and open source ideas, may transform our capitalistic system into one that encourages collaboration and openness. It should come as no surprise that the author's Web site includes viral video mashups extolling the ideas in the book.

The Myths of Innovation, by Scott Berkum (Sebastopol, CA: O'Reilly Media, Inc., 2007). O'Reilly has a well-established catalog of books on software design, development, and use. Many of their most popular titles deal with open source technology. In this highly praised book, Scott Berkum explores the nature of innovation, including software innovation. Dozens of examples from technology, business, and the arts show how ideas can become successful, world-changing innovations.

Legal Guide to Web and Software Development, Fifth Edition (book with CD-ROM), by Stephen Fishman (Berkeley, CA: NOLO Press, 2007). NOLO Press specializes in books about law for non-lawyers. This book, like many NOLO books, can demystify legal contracts and concepts, making it easier for creators of intellectual property to protect that property.

Getting Permission: How to License and Clear Copyrighted Materials Online and Off, Third Edition (book with CD-ROM), by Stephen Fishman (Berkeley, CA: NOLO Press, 2007). This NOLO book looks at the other side of the coin: How to get permission to use intellectual property of others. It doesn't have to be hard, as long as you understand the law. That's where this book comes in.

The Public Domain: How to Find and Use Copyright Free Writings, Music, Art, and More, by Stephen Fishman (Berkeley, CA: NOLO Press, 2008). If you don't want to—or can't—get permission to use copyrighted materials in your work, you might want to go the tried and true route of exploring the public domain. If you do, this book should tell you what you need to know about the law as it applies to public domain works.

5

Productivity Applications

Objectives

After you read this chapter you should be able to:

▶ Describe how word processing and desktop publishing software have revolutionized writing and publishing

▶ Discuss the potential impact of desktop publishing and Web publishing on the concept of freedom of the press

▶ Speculate about future developments in word processing and digital publishing

▶ Describe the basic functions and applications of spreadsheets and other types of statistical and simulation programs

▶ Explain how computers can be used to answer what-if questions

▶ Explain how computers are used as tools for simulating mechanical, biological, and social systems

> If you **look out in the future**, you can see how best to **make right choices**.
> —*Doug Engelbart*

Doug Engelbart Explores Hyperspace

On a December day in 1950, Doug Engelbart looked into the future and saw what no one had seen before. Engelbart had been thinking about the growing complexity and urgency of the world's problems and wondering how he could help solve those problems. In his vision of the future, Engelbart saw computer technology augmenting and magnifying human mental abilities, providing people with new powers to cope with the urgency and complexity of life.

Engelbart decided to dedicate his life to turning his vision into reality. Unfortunately, the rest of the world wasn't ready for Engelbart's vision. His farsighted approach didn't match the prevailing ideas of the time, and most of the research community denounced or ignored Engelbart's work. In 1951 there were only about a dozen computers in the world, and those spent most of their time doing military calculations. It was hard to imagine ordinary people using computers to boost their personal productivity. So Engelbart put together the Augmentation Research Center at the Stanford Research Institute to create working models of his visionary tools.

In 1968 he demonstrated his Augment system to an auditorium full of astonished computer professionals and changed forever the way people think about computers. A large screen showed a cascade of computer graphics, text, and video images, controlled by Engelbart and a coworker several miles away. "It was like magic," recalls Alan Kay, one of the young computer scientists in the audience. Augment introduced the mouse, video-display editing (the forerunner to word processing), mixed text and graphics, windowing, outlining, shared-screen video conferencing, computer conferencing, groupware, and hypermedia. Although Engelbart used a large computer, he was really demonstrating a futuristic "personal" computer—an interactive multimedia workstation for enhancing individual abilities.

Today many of Engelbart's inventions and ideas are commonplace. He is widely recognized for one small part of his vision: the mouse. But Engelbart hasn't stopped looking into the future. He now heads the Bootstrap Institute, a nonprofit think tank dedicated to helping organizations make decisions with the future in mind. In a world where automation can dehumanize and eliminate jobs, Engelbart is still committed to replacing automation with augmentation. But now he focuses more on the human side of the equation, helping people chart a course into the future guided by intelligent,

FIGURE 5.2 Doug Engelbart's visionary 1968 presentation showed the world how computers could be used as collaborative tools.

FIGURE 5.1 Doug Engelbart

positive vision. He talks about turning organizations into "networked improvement communities" and focuses on the concept of the collective IQ. If anyone understands how to build the future from a vision, Doug Engelbart does. ∼

Doug Engelbart was one of the first people to recognize that computer technology could be used to augment human capabilities. Thanks in large part to his visionary work, people all over the world use computer applications to enhance their abilities to write papers and articles, publish periodicals and books, perform complex calculations, conduct scientific research, and even predict the future.

In this chapter we survey a variety of applications that people use to manipulate words and numbers. We consider software tools for working with words, from outliners to sophisticated reference tools, and numbers, from spreadsheets to statistical packages and money managers. We look at how desktop publishing technology has transformed the publishing process and provided more people with the power to communicate in print. We examine how scientific visualization software can help us understand relationships that are invisible to the naked eye and how computers simulate reality for work and pleasure.

The Wordsmith's Toolbox

I ... **cannot imagine** now that I **ever** wrote with a typewriter.

—*Arthur C. Clarke, author and scientist*

The way in which we write has forever been transformed by software. Instead of suffering through the painful process of typing and retyping in pursuit of a "clean" draft, a writer can focus on developing ideas and let the machine take care of laying out the words neatly on the page. Word processing technology makes it possible for just about any literate person to communicate effectively in writing.

Word Processing Tools and Techniques

Working with a word processor involves several steps:

- Entering text
- Editing text
- Formatting the document
- Proofreading the document
- Saving the document
- Printing the document

Early word processing systems generally forced users to follow these steps in a strict order. Some systems still in use—mainly on mainframes and other timesharing systems—segregate these processes into steps that can't easily be mixed. Most writers today use word processors that allow them to switch freely between editing and formatting, in some cases doing both at the same time. With virtually all modern word processors, words appear on the screen almost exactly as they will appear on a printed page. This feature is often referred to as *WYSIWYG*, short for "what you see is what you get" and pronounced "wizzy-wig."

Text formatting commands enable you to control the format of the text—the way the words will look on the page. Most modern word processors include commands for controlling the formats of individual characters and paragraphs as well as complete documents.

With character formatting commands, you can select the font and the font size of the document's characters. Other character formatting commands let you do such things as change the color of a character, put it in boldface and/or italics, or underline it.

Other formatting commands apply to paragraphs rather than characters: those commands that control margins, space between lines, indents, tab stops, and justification. Justification refers to the alignment of text on a line. Four justification choices are commonly available: align text left (with a smooth left margin and ragged right margin), align text right, justify (both margins are smooth), and center justification.

Some formatting commands apply to entire documents. For example, Microsoft Word's Page Setup command enables you to control the margins that apply throughout the document. Other commands enable you to specify the content, size, and style of headers and footers—text that appears at the top and bottom of every page, displaying repetitive information, such as chapter titles, author names, and automatically calculated page numbers.

Advanced formatting features enable you to perform the following tasks:

- Define stylesheets containing custom styles for each of the common elements in a document. (For example, you can define a style called "subhead" as a paragraph that's left-justified in a boldface, 12-point Helvetica font with standard margins and apply that style to every subhead in the document without re-selecting all three of these commands for each new subhead. If you decide later to change the subheads to 14-point Futura, your changes in the subhead style are automatically reflected throughout the document.)
- Define alternate headers, footers, and margins so left- and right-facing pages can have different margins, headers, and footers.
- Create documents with multiple variable-width columns.
- Create, edit, and format multicolumn tables.
- Incorporate graphics created with other applications.

FIGURE 5.3 Many word processors are able to convert formatted documents to HTML so they can be published as Web pages.

5.1 Font Technology

When a computer displays a character on a monitor or prints it on a laser, inkjet, or dot matrix printer, the character is nothing more than a collection of dots in an invisible grid. Bitmapped fonts store characters in this way, with each pixel represented as a black or white bit in a matrix. A bitmapped font usually looks fine on screen in the intended point size but doesn't look smooth when printed on a high-resolution printer or enlarged on screen.

A bitmapped font becomes pixelated when enlarged.

Most computer systems now use scalable outline fonts to represent type in memory until it is displayed or printed. A scalable font represents each character as an outline that can be scaled—increased or decreased in size without distortion. Curves and lines are smooth and don't have stair-stepped, jagged edges when they're resized. The outline is stored inside the computer or printer as a series of mathematical statements about the position of points and the shape of the lines connecting those points.

This outline for a lowercase *a* retains its original shape at any size or resolution.

Downloadable fonts (soft fonts) are stored in the computer system (not the printer) and downloaded to the printer only when needed. These fonts usually have matching screen fonts and are easily moved to different computer systems. Most important, you can use the same downloadable font on many printer models.

Laser printers are really dedicated computer systems that contain their own CPU, RAM, ROM, and specialized operating system. Printer fonts are stored in the printer's ROM and are always available for use with that printer, but you may not be able to achieve WYSIWYG if your computer doesn't have a screen font to match your printer font. And if you move your document to a different computer and printer, the same printer font may not be available on the new system.

Until recently, fonts were most commonly available in two scalable outline forms: Adobe PostScript and Apple's TrueType. Because Apple and Microsoft have included TrueType downloadable fonts with their operating systems for many years, TrueType fonts are more popular among general computer users. PostScript fonts usually require additional software but are the long-time standard among many graphics professionals. PostScript is actually a complete page description language particularly well suited to the demands of professional publishers.

In recent years thousands of fonts have been released in a format that combines TrueType and PostScript technology: OpenType, codeveloped by Adobe and Microsoft. According to Adobe, "The two main benefits of the OpenType format are its cross-platform compatibility (the same font file works on Macintosh and Windows computers), and its ability to support widely expanded character sets and layout features, which provide richer linguistic support and advanced typographic control." OpenType enables character shapes to travel with documents in compressed forms so a document transmitted electronically or displayed on the Web will look like the original even if the viewer's system doesn't include the original document's fonts.

1st, 2nd, 3rd	1st, 2nd, 3rd
Rectangle	Rectangle
Quick Brown Fox	*Quick Brown Fox*

FIGURE 5.4 Many OpenType fonts (right) contain expanded character sets and layout features that make them more flexible than their TrueType equivalents (left).

- Use **automatic footnoting** to save you from having to place footnotes and endnotes; the program automatically places them where they belong on the page.
- Use **automatic hyphenation** to divide long words that fall at the ends of lines.
- Use **automatic formatting (autoformat)** to apply formatting automatically to your text; for example, to number lists automatically (such as the exercises at the end of this chapter) and apply proper indentation to those lists.
- Use **automatic correction (autocorrect)** to correct common typing errors. For example, if you type *THe* or *Teh*, the software will automatically change it to *The*.
- Generate tables of contents and indexes for books and other long works (with human help for making judgments calls).
- Attach hidden comments that aren't visible in the final printed document.
- Use coaching or help features (sometimes called **wizards**) to walk you through complex document formatting procedures.
- Convert formatted documents to **HTML (hypertext markup language)** so they can be easily published on the Web.
- Record and reuse **macros**—multi-step sequences of instructions that can save time and effort by automating repetitive task. (More on macros in the spreadsheet section of this chapter.)

In addition to basic editing and formatting functions, a typical word processor includes a built-in outliner, spelling checker, and thesaurus.

Outliners and Idea Processors

If any man wishes to **write** in a **clear style**, let him first **be clear** in his **thoughts**.

—Johann W. von Goethe

For many of us, the hardest part of the writing process is collecting and organizing our thoughts. Traditional English-class techniques, including outlines and 3-by-5 note cards, involve additional work. But when computer technology is applied, these time-honored techniques are transformed into high-powered tools for extending our minds and streamlining the process of turning vague thoughts into solid prose.

Outliners, such as the *Outline View* option built into Microsoft Word, are, in effect, idea processors. Outliners are particularly effective at performing three functions:

1. Arranging information into hierarchies, or levels, so each heading can be fleshed out with more detailed subheads, which can then be broken into smaller pieces
2. Rearranging ideas and levels so subideas are automatically moved with their parent ideas
3. Hiding and revealing levels of detail as needed so you can examine the forest, the trees, or an individual leaf of your project

For a project that requires research, you can use an outliner as a replacement for note cards. Ideas can be collected, composed, refined, rearranged, and reorganized much more efficiently when they're stored in an outline. When the time comes to turn research into a research paper, you don't need to retype the notes; you can polish them with standard text-editing techniques. If the outliner is built into the word processor, the line between notes and finished product blurs to the point where it almost disappears.

FIGURE 5.5 Microsoft Word's Outline View enables you to examine and restructure the overall organization of a document, while showing each topic in as much detail as you need. When you move headlines, the attached subheads and paragraphs follow automatically.

Digital References

The difference between the **right word** and the **almost-right word** is the difference between the **lightning** and the **lightning bug**.

— *Mark Twain*

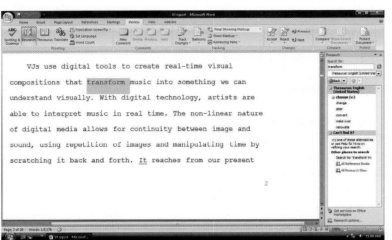

FIGURE 5.6 Microsoft Word's Thesaurus feature puts synonyms at your fingertips. In this case, the computer is providing synonyms for the word *transform*.

Writers rely on dictionaries, quotation books, encyclopedias, atlases, almanacs, and other references. Just about all of these resources are now available in digital form on CD-ROM, DVD, and the Web. Microsoft Office and many other applications include dictionary and thesaurus tools.

Searching for subjects or words by computer is usually faster than thumbing through a book. Well-designed electronic references make it easy to jump between related topics in search of elusive facts. In addition, copying quotes electronically takes a fraction of the time it takes to retype information from a book. Of course, this kind of quick copying makes plagiarism—using someone else's words without giving credit—easier than ever and may tempt more writers to violate copyright laws and ethical standards. If you're tempted to plagiarize someone else's writing, remember that electronic references make detecting plagiarism easier than ever, too!

The classic synonym finder, or **thesaurus**, is an invaluable tool for finding the right word, but it's not particularly user-friendly. A computerized thesaurus is another matter altogether. With a good thesaurus, it's a simple matter to select a word and issue a command for a synonym search. The computerized thesaurus provides almost instant gratification, displaying all kinds of possible replacements for the word in question. If you find a suitable substitute in the list, you can indicate your preference with a click or a keystroke; the software even makes the switch for you.

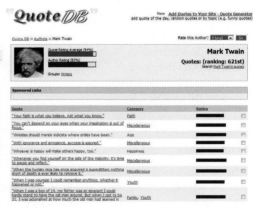

FIGURE 5.7 Students and other researchers can save time when searching for facts, quotes, ideas, or inspiration by using specially designed reference sites on the Web.

Because pictures, maps, and drawings take up so much disk space (and Internet transmission time), they're sometimes removed or modified in computerized references. On the other hand, many digital references include sound, animation, video, and other forms of information that aren't possible to include in books.

Reference materials are everywhere on the Web. Unfortunately, not all of those sources are useful or reliable. Still, the Web offers a combination of timeliness and cross-referencing that can't be found in any other reference source. We'll revisit Web references in later chapters.

Spelling Checkers

It is a **damn poor mind** indeed which can't think of at least **two ways** to spell any word.

—Andrew Jackson

Although many of us sympathize with Jackson's point of view, the fact remains that correct spelling is an important part of most written communication. That's why a word processor typically includes a built-in spelling checker. (The Macintosh OS includes a spelling checker that works in most applications.) A spelling checker compares the words in your document with words in a disk-based dictionary. Every word that's not in the dictionary is flagged as a suspect word—a potential misspelling. In many cases the spelling checker suggests the corrected spelling and offers to replace the suspect word. Ultimately, though, it's up to you to decide whether the flagged word is, in fact, spelled incorrectly.

Spelling checkers are wonderful aids, but they can't replace careful proofreading by alert human eyes. When you're using a spelling checker, it's important to keep two potential problems in mind:

1. *Dictionary limitations and errors.* No dictionary includes every word, so you have to know what to do with unlisted words—proper names, obscure words, technical terms, foreign terms, colloquialisms, and other oddities. If you add words to your spelling checker's dictionary, you run the risk of adding an incorrectly spelled word, making future occurrences of that misspelling invisible to the spelling checker and to you.

FIGURE 5.8 Most spelling checkers, including the one in Microsoft Word, offer the user several choices for handling words that aren't in the dictionary.

2. *Errors of context.* The fact that a word appears in a dictionary does not guarantee that it is correctly spelled in the context of the sentence. The following passage, for example, contains eight spelling errors, none of which would be detected by a spelling checker:

I wood never have guest that my spelling checker would super seed my editor as my mane source of feed back. I no longer prophet from the presents of an editor while I right.

Grammar and Style Checkers

The errors in the preceding quote would have slipped by a spelling checker, but many of them would have been detected by a grammar and style checker. In addition to checking

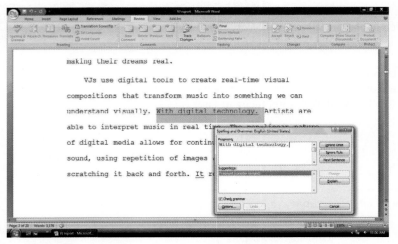

FIGURE 5.9 Grammar-and-style-checking software flags possible errors and makes suggestions about how they might be fixed. Here, Microsoft Word points out a sentence fragment.

spelling, grammar-and-style-checking software analyzes each word in context, checking for errors of context (I wood never have guest), common grammatical errors (Ben and me went to Boston), and stylistic foibles (Suddenly the door was opened by Bethany). In addition to pointing out possible errors and suggesting improvements, it can analyze prose complexity using measurements such as sentence length and paragraph length. This kind of analysis is useful for determining whether your writing style is appropriate for your target audience.

Grammar-and-style-checking software is, at best, imperfect. A typical program misses many true errors, while flagging correct passages. Still, it can be a valuable writing aid, especially for students who are mastering the complexities of a language for the first time. But software is no substitute for practice, revision, editing, and a good English teacher.

Form-Letter Generators

Congratulations, Mr. <last name>. You may already have won!

—Junk mail greeting

Most word processors today have **mail merge** capabilities for producing personalized form letters. When used with a database containing a list of names and addresses, a word processor can quickly generate individually addressed letters and mailing labels. Many programs can incorporate custom paragraphs based on the recipient's personal data, making each letter look as if it were individually written. Direct-mail marketing companies exploited this kind of technology for years before it became available in inexpensive PC software.

Collaborative Writing Tools

Writing only leads to **more writing**.

—Colette

Most large writing projects, including the one that produced this book, involve groups of people working together. Computer networks make it easy for writers and editors to share documents, but it's not always easy for one person to know how a document has been changed by others. Groupware—software designed to be used by a workgroup—can keep track of a document's history as it's passed among group members and make sure that all changes are incorporated into a single master document. Using groupware, each writer can monitor and make suggestions concerning the work of any other writer on the team. Editors can "blue pencil" corrections and attach notes directly to the electronic manuscript. The notes can be read by any or all of the writers—even those who are on another continent. This kind of collaborative writing and editing doesn't require specialized software anymore; it can be done with many word processing and publishing programs. For example, Microsoft Word's Track Changes option can record and display contributions from several writers and editors; it can also compare document

FIGURE 5.10 The Track Changes feature in Microsoft Word enables writers, editors, and other collaborative document creators to contribute to the same document and see each other's changes.

versions and highlight differences between versions. Word's Track Changes feature does not allow multiple users to make changes *simultaneously*. Instead, team members pass the document back and forth, making sequential changes. Some programs, such as Google Documents, Gobby and SubEthaEdit, allow many writers to work on a document at the same time through a network.

Emerging Word Tools

Word processing software has evolved rapidly in the past few years. The evolution isn't over; current trends suggest big changes are coming in word processing technology.

> The **real technology**—behind all of our other technologies—is **language**. It actually creates **the world our consciousness lives in**.
>
> —*Norman Fischer, Abbot, Green Gulch Farm Zen Center*

Processing Handwritten Words

For a small but growing population, pen-based systems provide an alternative tool for entering text. Handwriting recognition doesn't come easy to computers; it requires sophisticated software that can interpret pen movements as characters and words. The diversity in handwriting makes it difficult for today's software to translate all of our scribbles into text. Powerful pen-based systems such as the Tablet PC work reliably because they use all the processing punch of modern notebook PCs and advanced handwriting-recognition algorithms. Simpler pen-based systems, such as those based on the Palm OS, require users to print characters using a carefully defined system that minimizes errors.

Processing Words with Speech

I think that the **primary means of communication** with computers . . . will be **speech**.

—Nicholas Negroponte, director of MIT's Media Lab

FIGURE 5.11 Speech recognition software enables this doctor to dictate notes and other documents into his computer.

Ultimately, most writers long for a computer that can accept and reliably process *speech* input—a *talkwriter*. With such a system, a user can tell the computer what to type—and how to type it—by simply talking into a microphone. The user's speech enters the computer as a digital audio signal. Speech recognition software looks for patterns in the sound waves and interprets sounds by locating familiar patterns, segmenting input sound patterns into words, separating commands from the text, and passing those commands to the word processing software.

Speech recognition software systems have been around for many years, but until recently, most were severely limited. It takes a great deal of knowledge to understand the complexities of human speech. A computer, lacking a child's experience with English, might interpret, say, "recognize speech" as "wreck a nice beach." Research in speech recognition today focuses on producing systems that can:

- Recognize words reliably without being trained to an individual speaker, an ability known as *speaker independence*
- Handle speech without limiting vocabulary
- Handle continuous speech—natural speech in which words run together at normal speed

Researchers are making great strides toward these goals, making speech recognition practical for applications in health care, the military, telephony, and elsewhere. Most of us have navigated through automated customer-service menus by speaking commands rather than punching phone buttons. Many cars and cell phones have speech recognition systems designed to recognize basic commands and names. Speech-recognition systems are especially important for people who can't use their hands because of physical limitations, injuries, or job restrictions.

Dictation software—software designed to turn continuous speech into written text—can achieve accuracy approaching 100 percent under ideal conditions. Accuracy generally improves as the program "trains" to the speaker's voice and mannerisms. The best dictation software integrates seamlessly with word processors, email programs, and other applications. Some Web sites (such as jott.com) offer dictation services via cell phone, translating spoken passages into email messages. For many writers, speech recognition software increases productivity while reducing the risk of repetitive strain injuries.

Intelligent Word Processing Software

Speech recognition is just one aspect of artificial intelligence research that's likely to end up in future word processing software. Many experts foresee word processing software that are able to anticipate the writer's needs, acting as an electronic editor or coauthor. Today's grammar and style checkers are primitive forerunners of the kinds of electronic writing consultants that might appear in a few years.

Here are some possibilities:

- As you're typing a story, your word processing software reminds you (via a pop-up notification message on the screen or an auditory message) that you've used the word *delicious* three times in the past two paragraphs and suggests that you choose an alternative from the list shown on the screen.
- Your word processing software continuously analyzes your style as you type, determines your writing habits and patterns, and learns from its analysis. If your writing tends to be technical and formal, the software modifies its thesaurus, dictionary, and other tools so they're more appropriate for that style.
- You're writing a manual for a large organization that uses specific style guidelines of documentation. Your word processing software modifies your writing as you type so it conforms to the organizational style.
- You need some current figures to support your argument on the depletion of the ozone layer. You issue a command, and the computer does a quick search of the literature on the Web and reports to you with several relevant facts.

All these examples are technically possible now. The trend toward intelligent word processors is clear. Nevertheless, you're in for a long wait if you're eager to buy a system with commands such as Clever Quote, Humorous Anecdote, and Term Paper.

The Desktop Publishing Story

Freedom of the press belongs to the person who **owns** one.

—A. J. Liebling, the late media critic for The New Yorker

Just as word processing changed the writer's craft in the 1970s, the world of publishing was radically transformed in the 1980s when Apple introduced its first LaserWriter printer and a new company named Aldus introduced PageMaker, a Macintosh program that could take advantage of that printer's high-resolution output capabilities. Publishing—traditionally an expensive, time-consuming, error-prone process—instantly became an enterprise that just about anyone with a computer and a little cash could undertake.

What Is Desktop Publishing?

The process of producing a book, magazine, or other publication includes several steps:

- Writing text
- Editing text
- Producing drawings, photographs, and other graphics to accompany the text
- Designing a basic format for the publication
- Typesetting text
- Arranging text and graphics on pages
- Typesetting and printing pages
- Binding pages into a finished publication

In traditional publishing, many of these steps required expensive equipment, highly trained specialists to operate the equipment, and lots of time. With desktop publishing (DTP) technology, the bulk of the production process can be accomplished with tools that are small, affordable, and easy to use. A desktop publishing system generally includes one

FIGURE 5.12 A typical desktop publishing system includes a personal computer, a high-resolution printer, a scanner and other imaging hardware, and a variety of graphical software programs.

Creating Professional-Looking Documents

Many first-time users of WYSIWYG word processing and desktop publishing systems become intoxicated with all the power at their fingertips. It's easy to get carried away with all those fonts, styles, and sizes and to create a document that makes supermarket tabloids look tasteful. Although there's no substitute for a good education in the principles of design, it's easy to avoid tacky-looking documents if you follow a few simple guidelines:

➡ **Plan before you publish.** Design (or select) a simple, visually pleasing format for your document, and use that format throughout the document.

➡ **Use appropriate fonts.** Limit your choices to one or two fonts and sizes per page, and be consistent throughout your document.

➡ **Don't go style-crazy.** Avoid overusing *italics*, **boldface**, ALL CAPS, underlines, and other styles for emphasis. When in doubt, leave it out.

BAD

Title is out of proportion to rest of page

Page uses too many different fonts.

Underlining adds no value here.

Center-justified text is harder to read.

Colors are garish and distracting.

There's not enough white space around image

If the audience includes readers over 50 years old, a 9-point font is too small.

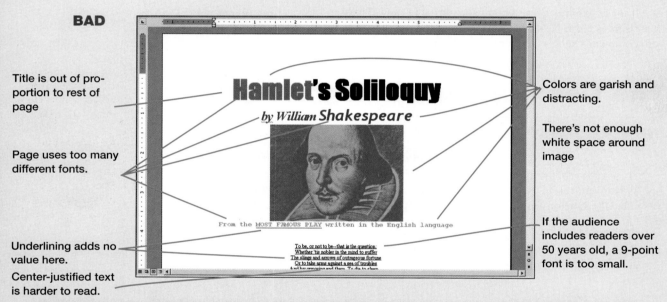

Rules of Thumb for Text Justification		
Justification	When to Use	When to Avoid
This text illustrates full justification. For fully justified text, spaces between words are adjusted to make both margins straight.	Formal documents, such as textbooks and academic reports	Informal documents or documents with narrow columns
This text illustrates left justification. For left-justified text, the left margin is straight and the right margin is ragged.	Informal documents, such as letters and newsletters	Formal documents
This text illustrates right justification. For right-justified text, the right margin is straight and the left margin is ragged.	Headers and footers	Body of a document (entire paragraphs)
This text illustrates centered justification. For centered text both margins are ragged.	Titles and subtitles	Body of a document (entire paragraphs)

FIGURE 5.13

- **Don't go color crazy.** Sometimes less is more. Choose a limited palette of colors that work together and stick to it.
- **Look at your document through your reader's eyes.** Make every picture say something. Don't try to cram too much information on a page. Don't be afraid of white space. Use a format that speaks clearly to your readers. Make sure the main points of your document stand out.
- **Learn from the masters.** Study the designs of successful publications. Use design books, articles, and classes to develop your aesthetic skills along with your technical skills. With or without a computer, publishing is an art.
- **Know your limitations.** Desktop publishing technology makes it possible for anyone to produce high-quality documents with a minimal investment of time and money. But your equipment and skills may not be up to the job at hand. For many applications, personal desktop publishing is no match for a professional design artist or typesetter. If you need the best, work with a pro.
- **Remember the message.** Fancy fonts, tasteful graphics, and meticulous design can't turn shoddy ideas into words of wisdom, or lies into the truth. The purpose of publishing is communication; don't try to use technology to disguise the lack of something to communicate.

GOOD

The Economist magazine inspires this design.

Color enlivens the black-and-white etching without dominating the text.

The heading is in proportion to the rest of the page.

A 12-point font and left-justified text make Shakespeare's words easy to read.

Font Category	Examples	Appropriate Use	Inappropriate Use
Serif fonts	Times New Roman Georgia Book Antiqua Palatino	Just about anywhere	Small text intended to be read on screen
Sans serif fonts	Arial Helvetica Futura Lucida Sans	Titles, subtitles, captions, and boxed text	Body of a document (pages of text)
Monospaced fonts	Courier Courier New Lucida Console	Representing computer programs or user input to a computer with a character-based interface	Anywhere else
Display fonts	Comic Sans MS Birch Tekton	Posters and flyers	Body of a document (entire paragraphs)
Symbol fonts	Σψμβολ (Symbol) ✦✠■ϒ♎✠■ϒ♦ (Wingdings)	When special characters are needed or as dingbats at end of stories in newsletters	Anywhere else

or more Macs or PCs, a scanner, a digital camera, a high-resolution printer, and software. It's now possible for a single person with a modest equipment investment to do all the writing, editing, graphic production, design, page layout, and typesetting for a desktop publication. Of course, few individuals have the skills to handle all of these tasks, so most publications are still the work of teams that include writers, editors, designers, artists, and supervisors. But even if the titles remain the same, each of these jobs is changing because of desktop publishing technology.

The first steps in the publishing process involve producing **source documents**—articles, chapters, drawings, maps, charts, and photographs that are to appear in the publication. Desktop publishers generally use standard word processing and graphics programs to produce most source documents. Scanners with image-editing software are used to transform photographs and hand-drawn images into computer-readable documents. **Page-layout software**, such as QuarkXPress, Microsoft Publisher, Adobe PageMaker, or Adobe InDesign, is used to combine the various source documents into a coherent, visually appealing publication. Pages are generally laid out one at a time on-screen, although most programs have options for automating multiple-page document layout.

Page-layout software provides graphic designers with control over virtually every element of the design, right down to the spacing between each pair of letters (*kerning*) and the spacing between lines of text (*leading*). Today's word processing programs include basic page-layout capabilities, too; they're sufficient for creating many types of publications. But to produce more complex layouts for newspapers, newsletters, magazines, and flyers, publishers need the kind of advanced formatting capabilities found only in dedicated desktop publishing applications. (Word processing and desktop publishing software often works hand in hand: For example, writers usually use word processing software to create the text that is poured into a desktop publishing layout.)

For users without backgrounds in layout and design, most page-layout and word processing programs include **templates**—professionally designed "empty" documents that can easily be adapted to specific user needs. Even without templates, it's possible for beginners to create professional-quality publications with a modest investment of money and time.

FIGURE 5.14 Source documents are merged in a publication document, which can be printed on a laser or inkjet printer, printed on a high-resolution phototypesetter, or published on the Web.

Screen Test

Desktop Publishing
with Adobe InDesign

GOAL *To create a four-page newsletter for ultimate frisbee players*

TOOLS *Adobe Photoshop, Adobe InDesign*

1. Fill in the newsletter length.

2. Select the page size.

3. Select the page orientation.

4. Select number of text columns per page.

5. Adjust the margin size.

6. Click OK to approve your design choices.

7. Import a graphic containing the newsletter's masthead you created with Adobe Photoshop.

8. Import photos you captured with a digital camera and edited with Adobe Photoshop.

9. Draw a box framing the lower two photos, and tint it the same shade as the background of the masthead.

10. Create text boxes to hold the cover story.

11. Use the Get Text command to import text from a Word document.

12. Modify the size of the article's title.

13. Add another text box between the photos at the bottom and type a quote into it. Color the text white.

14. Continue the layout process on the remaining pages, and print the finished document.

FIGURE 5.15

Desktop publishing becomes more complicated when color is introduced. *Spot color—* the use of a single ink color (or sometimes two) to add interest—is relatively easy. But *full-color* desktop publishing, including color photos, drawings, and paintings, must deal with the inconsistencies of different color output devices. Because printers and monitors use different types of color-mixing technologies, as described in the How It Works boxes in Chapter 3, what you see on the screen isn't always what you get when you print it. It's even difficult to get two monitors (or two printers) to produce images with exactly the same color balance. Still, color desktop publishing is big business, and advances in *color-matching* technology are making it easier all the time.

Most desktop publications are printed on color laser printers capable of producing output with a resolution of at least 600 dots per inch (dpi). The number of dots per inch influences the resolution and clarity of the image. Output of 600 dpi is sufficiently sharp for most applications, but it's less than the 1,200 dpi that is the traditional minimum for professional typesetting. High-priced devices, called phototypesetting machines or imagesetters, enable desktop publications to be printed at 1,200 dpi or higher. Many desktop publishers rely on outside service bureaus with phototypesetting machines to print their final camera-ready pages—pages that are ready to be photographed and printed.

Why Desktop Publishing?

Desktop publishing offers several advantages for businesses. Desktop publishing saves money. Publications that used to cost hundreds or thousands of dollars to produce through outside publishing services can now be produced in-house for a fraction of their former cost. Desktop publishing also saves time. The turnaround time for a publication done on the desktop can be a few days instead of the weeks or months it might take to publish the same thing using traditional channels. Finally, quality control is easier to maintain when documents are produced in-house.

The real winners in the desktop publishing revolution might turn out to be not big businesses, but everyday people with something to say. With commercial TV networks, newspapers, magazines, and book publishers increasingly controlled by a few giant corporations, many media experts worry that the free press guaranteed by our First Amendment is seriously threatened by de facto media monopolies. Desktop publishing technology offers new hope for every individual's right to publish. Writers, artists, and editors whose work is shunned or ignored by large publishers and mainstream media now have affordable publishing alternatives. The number of small presses and alternative, low-circulation periodicals is steadily increasing as publishing costs go down. If, as media critic A. J. Liebling suggested, freedom of the press belongs to the person who owns one, that precious freedom is now accessible to more people than ever before.

Beyond the Printed Page

Paper, often underrated as a communication medium, **will not be eliminated** by the growth of electronic media. It remains **inexpensive**, extremely **portable**, and **capable** of carrying very high-resolution images.

—*Mark Duchesne, Vice President, AM Multigraphics*

The first books were so difficult to produce that they were considered priceless. They were kept in cabinets with multiple locks so they couldn't be removed without the knowledge and permission of at least two monks. Today we can print professional-quality publications in short order using equipment that costs less than a used car. But the publishing revolution isn't over yet.

Paperless Publishing and the Web

A common prediction is that desktop publishing—and paper publishing in general—will be replaced by paperless electronic media. Paper still offers advantages for countless communication tasks. Reading printed words on pages is easier on the eyes than reading from a screen. Paper documents can be read and scribbled on almost anywhere, with or

FIGURE 5.16 Adobe Acrobat is a cross-platform software program that enables the electronic sharing of PDF documents, eliminating the need for paper in many publishing projects. People who worked on *Tomorrow's Technology and You* attached their comments to PDF pages and shared them electronically using Acrobat.

without electricity. And there's no electronic equivalent for the aesthetics of a beautifully designed, finely crafted book. Predictions aside, the printed word isn't likely to go away anytime soon.

Still, digital media forms are likely to eclipse paper for many applications. Email messages now outnumber post office letter deliveries. Online and disc-based encyclopedias have all but replaced their overweight paper counterparts. Adobe's *PDF (Portable Document Format)* enables documents of all types to be stored, viewed, or modified on virtually any PC making it possible for organizations to reduce paper flow.

The Web offers unprecedented mass publishing possibilities to millions of Internet users. Programs as diverse as Microsoft Word, InDesign, and PageMaker can save documents in HTML format, so they can be published on the Web. Other programs, specifically designed for Web publishing, offer advanced capabilities for graphics, animation, and

FIGURE 5.17 Mountains of waste paper such as this one should become less common as paperless publishing grows in popularity. That's the theory, anyway.

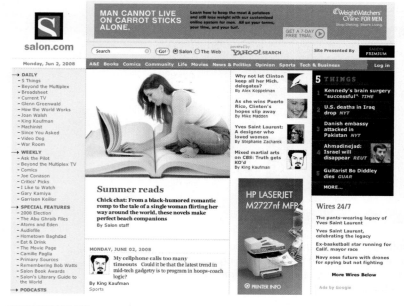

FIGURE 5.18 Many popular periodicals, from *Newsweek* to *Rolling Stone*, are published electronically on the Web. *Salon* is an example of a high-quality, popular magazine that is available only on the Web.

multimedia publishing. (We'll explore some of these tools in later chapters when we discuss multimedia and the Web in greater depth.)

Never before has a communication medium made it so easy or inexpensive for an individual to reach such a wide audience. For a few dollars a month, an Internet service provider can supply you with space to publish your essays, stories, reviews, and musings. It doesn't matter whether you're a student, a poet, an artist, a government official, a labor organizer, or a corporate president; on the Web all URLs are created equal.

Of course, the most popular commercial Web sites cost their owners more than a few dollars a month. A typical Web storefront costs a million dollars just to build. And one of the biggest challenges in Web publishing is attracting people to your site once it's online. Copyright protection is another problem for Web publishers; anything that's published on the Web for the world to see is also available for all the world to copy. How can writers and editors be paid fairly for their labors if their works are so easy to duplicate?

Still, the Web is far more accessible to small-budget writers and publishers than any other mass medium. And many experts predict that Web technology will eventually include some kind of mechanism for automatic payment to authors whose works are downloaded. In any case, the free flow of ideas may be more significant than the flow of money. In the words of writer Howard Rheingold, the World Wide Web "might be important in the same way that the printing press was important. By expanding the number of people who have the power to transmit knowledge, the Web might trigger a power shift that changes everything."

Electronic Books and Digital Paper

Science fiction writers have long predicted the electronic book, or ebook—a handheld device that can contain anything from today's top news stories to an annotated edition of *War and Peace*. Until recently, these types of devices have been commercial failures for two reasons: First, the screens were hard to read and second, content for them was not easily accessible.

LCD technology has made great strides in recent years, and screens are brighter and easier to read than ever before. Recent advances in font technologies from Microsoft and Adobe should help, too. Microsoft's ClearType enhances the clarity of text on flat-panel LCD screens, reducing pixel "blockiness." Adobe has developed a similar technology called Precision Graphics. Easy-on-the-eyes ebooks are likely to take advantage of these technologies soon.

To make it easier for ebook owners to find content—books, periodicals, and other software to download into their devices—several companies are cooperating to develop an open ebook standard. After industrywide standards are in place, electronic book publishing will be more practical—and popular. Future students may download texts rather than carry them out of bookstores. Everybook CEO Daniel Munyan predicts that college freshmen will load their ebooks with their notes and texts for the next four years and receive future updates via the Internet.

Ebooks today are mostly read on devices with rigid LCD screens—laptop computers, handheld computers, and special-purpose ebook readers that resemble tablets. But researchers may soon perfect a form of digital paper that will enable ebooks (as well as emagazines and enewspapers) to look and feel more like their paper counterparts.

FIGURE 5.19 Amazon's Kindle is an electronic book designed to work with Amazon.com's digital bookstore in the same way that Apple's iPod works with the iTunes store.

Electronic paper, or **epaper**, is a flexible, portable, paperlike material that can dynamically display black-and-white text and images on its surface. Unlike traditional paper, digital paper can erase itself and display new text and images as the reader "turns" the page. A busy commuter might soon be able to carry a complete morning newspaper and several important business documents in a sheet of digital paper stuffed in his pocket!

FIGURE 5.20 Compared to an LCD display, electronic paper looks more like real paper, making for a reading environment that is easier on the eyes. Electronic paper is beginning to appear in consumer products. Sony's Reader (left) uses electronic paper to present book pages. This Lexar flash drive (right) uses electronic paper as a storage capacity indicator. The display can be read even when the drive is not plugged in.

The Spreadsheet: Software for Simulation and Speculation

Compare the **expansion of business** today to the **conquering of the continent** in the nineteenth century. The spreadsheet in that comparison is like **the transcontinental railroad**. It **accelerated the movement**, made it possible, and **changed the course** of the nation.

—Mitch Kapor, creator of the Lotus 1-2-3 spreadsheet software

From the earliest days of the PC revolution, the spreadsheet has changed the way people do business. In the same way word processing software can give a computer user control over words, spreadsheet software enables the user to take control of numbers, manipulating them in ways that would be difficult or impossible otherwise. A spreadsheet program can make short work of tasks that involve repetitive calculations: budgeting, investment management, business projections, grade books, scientific simulations, checkbooks, and so on. A spreadsheet can also reveal hidden relationships between numbers, taking much of the guesswork out of financial planning and speculation.

The Malleable Matrix

The goal was that it had to be better than the **back of an envelope**.

—Dan Bricklin, inventor of the first spreadsheet program

Almost all spreadsheet programs are based on a simple concept: the malleable matrix. A spreadsheet document, called a worksheet, typically appears on the screen as a grid of numbered rows and lettered columns. The box representing the intersection of a row and a column is called a cell. Every cell in this grid has a unique address made up of a column letter and row number. For example, the cell in the upper-left corner of the grid is called cell A1 (column A, row 1) in most spreadsheet applications. All the cells are empty in a new worksheet; it's up to the user to fill them. Each cell can contain a numeric value, an alphabetic label, or a formula representing a relationship with numbers in other cells.

Values (numbers) are the raw material the spreadsheet software uses to perform calculations. Numbers in worksheet cells can represent wages, test scores, weather data, polling results, or just about anything that can be quantified.

To make it easier for people to understand the numbers, most worksheets include labels at the tops of columns and at the edges of rows, such as "Monthly Wages," "Midterm Exam 1," "Average Wind Speed," or "Final Approval Rating." To the computer, these labels are meaningless strings of characters. The label "Total Points" doesn't tell the computer to calculate the total and display it in an adjacent cell; it's just a road sign for human readers.

To calculate the total points (or the average wind speed or the final approval rating), the worksheet must include a formula—a step-by-step procedure for calculating the desired number. The simplest spreadsheet formulas are arithmetic expressions using symbols, such as + (addition), − (subtraction), * (multiplication), and / (division). For example, cell B5 might contain the formula =(B2+B3)/2. This formula tells the computer

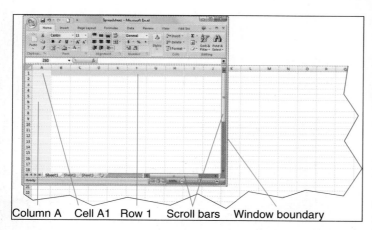

Column A　Cell A1　Row 1　Scroll bars　Window boundary

FIGURE 5.21 The worksheet may be bigger than what appears on your screen. The program enables you to scroll horizontally and vertically to view the larger matrix. (After column Z, columns are labeled with double letters: AA, BB, and so on.)

Creating a Worksheet with Microsoft Excel

GOAL *To create a computerized version of a worksheet showing projected expenses for one college student's fall term.*

TOOLS *Microsoft Excel*

1. Each column represents a month. Type descriptive labels for the month names. The last column will contain total expenses, category by category.

2. Each row represents an expense category. Type labels for these categories. The last row will contain total expenses, month by month.

3. Type numeric values representing the dollars spent in a particular category in a particular month. For example, the September tuition bill is $1,300, so you type 1300.

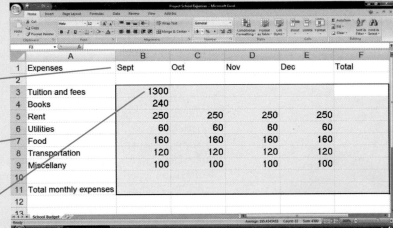

	A	B	C	D	E	F
1	Expenses	Sept	Oct	Nov	Dec	Total
2						
3	Tuition and fees	1300				
4	Books	240				
5	Rent	250	250	250	250	
6	Utilities	60	60	60	60	
7	Food	160	160	160	160	
8	Transportation	120	120	120	120	
9	Miscellany	100	100	100	100	
10						
11	Total monthly expenses					
12						

4. After typing all the values, click-and-drag the mouse to select all the cells containing numbers. Click the Currency icon on the Ribbon to indicate that all the cell values should be considered dollar amounts.

5. Click cell F3.

6. Enter a formula to calculate the total tuition expenses.

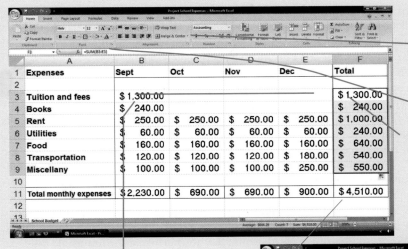

	A	B	C	D	E	F
1	Expenses	Sept	Oct	Nov	Dec	Total
2						
3	Tuition and fees	$ 1,300.00				$ 1,300.00
4	Books	$ 240.00				$ 240.00
5	Rent	$ 250.00	$ 250.00	$ 250.00	$ 250.00	$ 1,000.00
6	Utilities	$ 60.00	$ 60.00	$ 60.00	$ 60.00	$ 240.00
7	Food	$ 160.00	$ 160.00	$ 160.00	$ 160.00	$ 640.00
8	Transportation	$ 120.00	$ 120.00	$ 120.00	$ 180.00	$ 540.00
9	Miscellany	$ 100.00	$ 100.00	$ 100.00	$ 250.00	$ 550.00
10						
11	Total monthly expenses	$ 2,230.00	$ 690.00	$ 690.00	$ 900.00	$ 4,510.00
12						

7. Replicate this formula in cells F4 through F9 using the Fill Down command.

8. A similar two-step process creates the last row of totals.

9. Use the Chart Wizard to tell Excel to create a pie chart from the data in your spreadsheet.

FIGURE 5.22

to add the numbers in cells B2 and B3, divide the result by 2, and display the final result in the cell containing the formula, cell B5.

You don't see the formula in cell B5; you see only its effect. It doesn't matter whether the numbers represent test scores, dollars, or nothing at all; the computer obediently calculates their average and displays the results. If the number in cell B2 or B3 changes, the number displayed in B5 automatically changes, too. In many ways, this is the most powerful feature of a spreadsheet.

Different brands of spreadsheets, such as those included in Microsoft Office, Google Docs, StarOffice, OpenOffice.org, and iWork, are distinguished by their features, their user interfaces, and which operating system platforms they support. In spite of their differences, all popular spreadsheet programs work in much the same way and share most of these features:

■ *Lists.* Despite the availability of powerful and advanced features in virtually all spreadsheets, most individuals still use these applications for fairly mundane tasks, such as making and managing lists of grocery items, to-do tasks, phone numbers, and other related information. For most of these lists, the spreadsheet's calculation capabilities will go untapped; however, because spreadsheets have sophisticated data-formatting capabilities, they are often used like this.

■ *Automatic replication of values, labels, and formulas.* Most worksheets contain repetition: budgetary amounts remain constant from month to month; exam scores are calculated the same way for every student in the class; a scheduling program refers to the same seven days each week. Many spreadsheet commands streamline the entry of repetitive data, labels, and formulas. **Replication** commands are, in essence, flexible extensions of the basic copy-and-paste functions found in other software. The most commonly used replication commands are the Fill Down and Fill Right commands. Formulas can be constructed with *relative references* to other cells, as in the example on the previous page, so they refer to different cells when replicated in other locations, or as *absolute references* that don't change when copied elsewhere.

■ *Automatic recalculation.* **Automatic recalculation** is one of the spreadsheet's most important capabilities. It not only makes possible the easy correction of errors, but also makes it easy to try different values while searching for solutions.

■ *Predefined functions.* The first calculators made computing a square root a tedious and error-prone series of steps. On today's calculators a single press of the square-root button tells the calculator to do all the necessary calculations to produce the square root. Spreadsheet programs contain built-in **functions** that work like the calculator's square-root button. A function in a formula instructs the computer to perform some predefined set of calculations. For example, the formula =SQRT(C5) calculates the square root of the number in cell C5. Spreadsheet applications include libraries of predefined functions. Many, such as SUM, AVERAGE (or AVG), MIN, and MAX, represent simple calculations that are performed often in all kinds of worksheets. Others automate complex financial, mathematical, and statistical calculations that would be extremely difficult to calculate manually. The IF function enables the worksheet to decide what to do based on the contents of other cells, giving the worksheet logical decision-making capability. (For example, if the number of hours worked is greater than 40, calculate pay using the overtime schedule.) Like the calculator's square-root button, these functions can save time and reduce the likelihood of errors.

■ *Macros.* A spreadsheet's menu of functions, like the menu in a fast-food restaurant, is limited to the most popular selections. For situations in which the built-in functions don't fill the bill, most spreadsheets enable you to capture sequences of steps as reusable **macros**—custom-designed procedures that you can add to the existing menu of options. Some programs require you to type macros using a special macro language; others enable you to turn on a macro recorder that captures every move you make with the keyboard and mouse and records those actions in a macro transcript. Later, you can ask the computer to carry out the instructions in that macro. Suppose, for example, you use the same set of calculations every month when preparing a statistical analysis of environmental data. Without macros, you'd have to repeat the same sequence of key-strokes, mouse clicks, and commands each time you created the monthly report. But by creating a macro called, for instance, Monthstats, you can effectively say, "Do it again" by issuing the Monthstats command.

■ *Formatting.* Most spreadsheets enable you to control typefaces, text styles, cell dimensions, and cell borders. They also enable you to include pictures and other graphic embellishments in documents.

■ *Templates and wizards.* Even with functions and macros, the process of creating a complex worksheet from scratch can be intimidating. Many users take advantage of worksheet templates that contain labels and formulas but no data values. These reusable templates produce instant answers when you fill in the blanks. Some common templates are packaged with spreadsheet software; others are marketed separately. A similar feature, called a wizard, automates the process of creating complex worksheets that meet particular needs. Well-designed templates and wizards can save considerable time, effort, and anguish.

■ *Validation.* Some spreadsheets incorporate artificial intelligence to guide users through complex procedures. To help users check complex worksheets for consistency of entries and formula logic, spreadsheet programs now include *validators*— the equivalent of spelling and grammar checkers for calculations. For example, suppose you enter six numbers into consecutive cells of a Microsoft Excel spreadsheet; then you create a formula that finds the sum of only the first five of these values. Excel produces a warning message suggesting that you may have left out a value from the sum.

■ *Linking.* Sometimes a change in one worksheet produces changes in another. For example, a master sales summary worksheet for a business should reflect changes in each department's sales summary worksheet. Most spreadsheet programs can create **automatic links** among worksheets so when values change in one, all linked worksheets update automatically. Some programs can create three-dimensional worksheets by stacking and linking several two-dimensional sheets. Some spreadsheet programs can create links to Web pages so data can be downloaded and updated automatically.

■ *Database capabilities.* Many spreadsheet programs can perform basic database functions: storage and retrieval of information, searching, sorting, generating reports, merging mail, and such. With these features, a spreadsheet can serve users whose database needs are modest. For those who require a full-featured database management system, spreadsheet software might still be helpful; many spreadsheet programs support automatic two-way communication with database software.

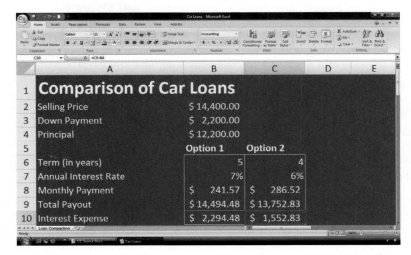

FIGURE 5.23 This simple spreadsheet calculates the true cost of car loans.

"What If?" Questions

The purpose of computation is not **numbers** but **insight**.

—*R. W. Hamming*

A spreadsheet program is a versatile tool, but it's especially valuable for answering "what if?" questions: "What if I don't complete the third assignment? How will that affect my chances for getting an A?" "What if I put my savings in a high-yield, tax-sheltered IRA account with a withdrawal penalty? Will I be better off than if I leave it in a low-yield passbook account with no penalty?" "What if I buy a car that gets only 15 miles per gallon instead of a car that gets 40? How much more will I pay altogether for fuel over the next four years?" Because it enables you to change numbers and instantly see the effects of those changes, spreadsheet software streamlines the process of searching for answers to these questions.

Some spreadsheet programs include equation solvers that turn "what if?" questions around. Instead of forcing you to manipulate data values until formulas give you the numbers you're looking for, an equation solver enables you to define an equation, enter your target value, and watch while the computer determines the necessary data values. For example, an investor might use an equation solver to answer the question "What is the best mix of these three stocks for minimizing risk while producing a six percent return on my investment?"

Spreadsheet Graphics: From Digits to Drawings

Our work … is to present things that are **as they are**.

—*Frederick II (1194–1250), King of Sicily*

Most spreadsheet programs include charting and graphing functionality that can turn worksheet numbers into charts and graphs automatically. The process of creating a chart is usually as simple as filling in a few blanks in a dialog box.

The growth in election campaign spending seems more real as a line shooting toward the top of a graph than as a collection of big numbers on a page. The federal budget makes more (or less?) sense as a sliced-up dollar pie than as a list of percentages. The correct chart can make a set of stale figures come to life, awakening our eyes and brains to trends and relationships that we might not have otherwise seen. The charting and graphing functionality in spreadsheet programs offers a variety of basic chart types and options for embellishing charts. The differences among these chart types are more than aesthetic; each chart type is well-suited for communicating particular types of information.

Pie charts show the relative proportions of the parts to a whole. Line charts are most often used to show trends or relationships over time or to show relative distribution of one variable through another. (The classic bell-shaped normal curve is a line chart.) Bar charts are similar to line charts, but they're more appropriate when data falls into a few categories. Bars can be stacked in a stack chart that shows how proportions of a whole change over time; the effect is similar to a series of pie charts. Scatter charts are used to discover, rather than display, a relationship between two variables. A well-designed chart can convey a wealth of information, just as a poorly designed chart can confuse or mislead.

FIGURE 5.24 Line and bar charts show trends over time and/or distribution over categories. Scatter charts show relationships between variables.

Working Wisdom

Eradicating Spreadsheet Errors

Spreadsheet errors are easy to make and easy to overlook. When creating a worksheet, you can minimize errors by following a few basic guidelines:

➡ **Plan the worksheet before you start entering values and formulas.** Think about your goals, and design the worksheet to meet those goals.

➡ **Make your assumptions as accurate as possible.** Answers produced by a worksheet are only as good as the assumptions built into the data values and formulas. A worksheet that compares the operating costs of a gas guzzler and a gas miser must make assumptions about future trips, repair costs, and, above all, gasoline prices. The accuracy of the worksheet is tied to all kinds of unknowns, including the future of Middle East politics. The more accurate the assumptions, the more accurate the predictions.

➡ **Double-check every formula and value.** Values and formulas are input for worksheets, and input determines output. Computer professionals often describe the dark side of this important relationship with the letters **GIGO—garbage in, garbage out**. One highly publicized spreadsheet transcription error for Fidelity Investments resulted in a $2.6 billion miscalculation because of a single missing minus sign! You may not be working with values this big, but it's still important to proofread your work carefully.

➡ **Make formulas readable.** If your software can attach names to cell ranges, use meaningful names in formulas. It's easier to create and debug formulas when you use readily understandable language, such as payrate*40+1.5*payrate*overtime, instead of a string of characters, like C2*40+1.5*C2*MAX(D2-40,0).

➡ **Check your output against other systems.** Use another program, a calculator, or pencil and paper to verify the accuracy of a sampling of your calculations.

➡ **Build in cross-checks.** Compare the sum of row totals with the sum of column totals. Does everything add up?

➡ **Change the input data values and study the results.** If small input adjustments produce massive output changes, or if major input adjustments result in few or no output changes, something may be wrong.

➡ **Take advantage of preprogrammed functions, templates, and macros.** Why reinvent the wheel when you can buy a professionally designed vehicle?

A chart can clarify, confuse, mislead, or confound....

CLEAR

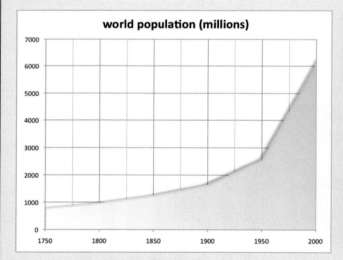

The data values come first, and the trend is clear: Human population has grown exponentially since 1750.

CLUTTERED

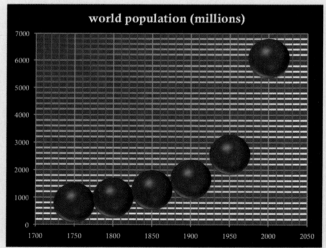

This chart confuses the viewer by applying glitz and gimmicks liberally.

FIGURE 5.25

- **Use a spreadsheet as a decision-making aid, not as a decision maker.** Don't put too much faith in an answer just because it was produced by a computer. Stay alert and skeptical. Some errors aren't obvious, and others don't show up immediately.
- **Take advantage of built-in error-checking tools.** Modern spreadsheet programs have a variety of built-in tools to help you identify errors and track down faulty formulas.
- **Good charts help readers draw the right conclusions from spreadsheet data.** A chart can be a powerful communication tool if it's designed intelligently. If it's not, the message may miss the mark. Here are some guidelines for creating charts that are easy to read and understand:
  - **Keep your goal in mind.** The role of a figure may be to describe a trend, facilitate exploration of the data, or tabulate values. A chart is better than a table of numbers for the first two purposes.
  - **Choose the right chart for the job.** Think about the message you're trying to convey. Line charts, bar charts, and scatter charts are not interchangeable. Pie charts are rarely appropriate.
  - **Put the data first.** Avoid adding elements to your charts that obscure the data values. Too many grid lines make the data values hard to see. If your purpose is tabulating values, perhaps you should be creating a table.
- **Do not distract the reader.** The chart should encourage the reader to think about the meaning of the data values, not which program was used to create the chart or its interesting color scheme. Avoid filling in blank spaces with clip art or other design elements that have nothing to do with the data.
- **Make it easy to compare data.** If the chart illustrates a single trend, make sure the trend is clear. If the chart shows multiple trends, make sure the reader can distinguish among trends and compare them.
- **Do not distort the data.** By hiding the baseline, you can deceive a reader into thinking that the actual change in a data value is larger or smaller than it really is. Your goal should be to reveal the truth, not hide it.
- **Relate to the rest of the document.** If your chart is part of a written report, make sure that the information you provide in your chart is consistent with the descriptions and analyses in your report.
- **Learn from the experts.** Use high-quality charts in magazines, books, and newspapers as models.

MISLEADING

This chart shows one way data can be distorted to lead viewers to a different conclusion. The data is the same, but the horizontal axis has changed—and with it, the apparent rate of population growth.

CONFUSING

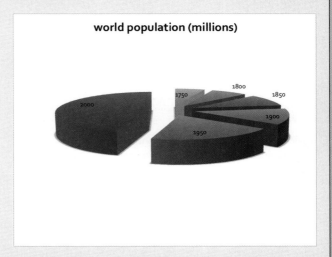

This pie chart displays the same data, but confuses rather than clarifies the trend. A pie chart is not an appropriate way to show a trend over time. The only use for a pie chart is to show how various parts add up to a whole. Even then, pie charts reveal little information for the amount of space they occupy.

Statistical Software: Beyond Spreadsheets

Science is what we understand well enough to **explain to a computer; art** is **everything else**.

—*Donald Knuth, author of* The Art of Computer Programming

Spreadsheet software is remarkably versatile, but no program is perfect for every task. Other types of number-manipulation software are available for situations in which spreadsheets don't quite fit the job.

Money Managers

Spreadsheet software has its roots in the accountant's ledger sheets, but spreadsheets are seldom used for business accounting and bookkeeping. Accounting is a complex concoction of rules, formulas, laws, and traditions, and creating a worksheet to handle the details of the process is difficult and time-consuming. Instead of relying on general-purpose spreadsheets for accounting, most businesses (and many households) use professionally designed accounting and financial-management software.

Whether practiced at home or at the office, accounting involves setting up accounts—monetary categories to represent various types of income, expenses, assets, and liabilities—and keeping track of the flow of money among those accounts. An accountant routinely records transactions—checks, cash payments, charges, and other activities—that move money from one account to another. Accounting software, such as Intuit's popular Quicken, automatically adjusts the balance in every account after each transaction. What's more, it records every transaction so you can retrace the history of each account step by step. This audit trail is a necessary part of business financial records, and it is one reason accountants use special-purpose accounting packages rather than spreadsheet programs.

In addition to keeping records, financial-management software can automate check writing, bill paying, budgeting, and other routine money matters. Periodic reports and charts can provide detailed answers to questions such as "Where does the money go?" and "How are we doing compared to last year?"

Through an Internet connection, a home-accounting program can recommend investments based on up-to-the-hour performance statistics, track investment portfolios, comparison shop for insurance and mortgages, and link to specialized online calculators and advisors. Hundreds of financial institutions offer online banking services, making it possible to pay bills, check account balances, and transfer funds using software.

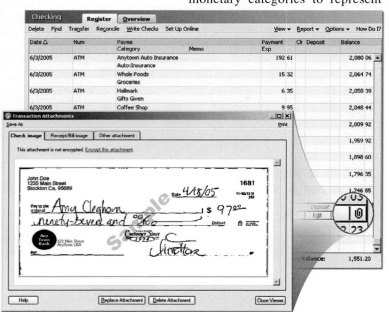

FIGURE 5.26 Inexpensive personal financial-management programs such as Quicken make the accounting process easier to understand by simulating the look of checks and other familiar documents on the screen.

Most accounting and financial-management programs don't calculate income taxes, but they can export records to programs that do. Tax-preparation software works like a prefabricated worksheet. As you enter numbers into the blanks in on-screen forms, the program automatically fills in other blanks. Every time you enter or change a number, the bottom line is recalculated automatically. When the forms are completed, they're ready to print, sign, and mail to the Internal Revenue Service. Many taxpayers now bypass paper forms altogether by sending the completed forms electronically to the IRS.

Automatic Mathematics

Most of us seldom do math more complicated than filling out our tax forms. But higher mathematics is an essential part of the work of many scientists, researchers, engineers, architects, economists, financial analysts, teachers, and other professionals. Mathematics is a universal language for defining and understanding natural phenomena as well as a tool for creating all kinds of products and structures. Whether or not we work with it directly, our lives are constantly being shaped by mathematics.

Many professionals and students whose mathematical needs go beyond the capabilities of spreadsheets depend on symbolic **math-processing software** to grapple with complex equations and calculations. Math processors make it easier for mathematicians to create, manipulate, and solve equations in much the same way word processing software helps writers. Features vary from program to program, but a typical math processor can do polynomial factoring, symbolic and numeric calculus, real and complex trigonometry, matrix and linear algebra, and three-dimensional graphics.

Math processors generally include an interactive, wizardlike question-and-answer mode, a programming language, and tools for creating interactive documents that combine text, numerical expressions, and graphics. Since math processors were introduced in the late 1980s, they've already changed the way professionals use mathematics and the way students learn it. By handling the mechanics of mathematics, these programs enable people to concentrate on the content and implications of their work.

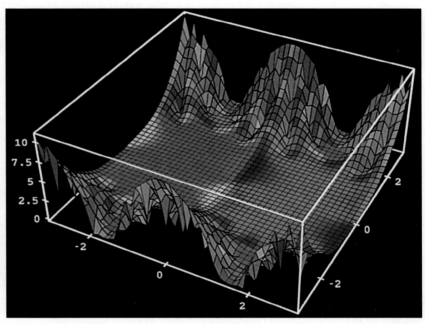

FIGURE 5.27 An abstract mathematical relationship is easier to understand when it is turned into a visible object with software, such as Mathematica.

Statistics and Data Analysis

Yet **to calculate** is not in itself **to analyze**.

—*Edgar Allan Poe, 1841*

One branch of applied mathematics that has become more important in the computer age is **statistics**—the science of collecting and analyzing data. Modern computer technology provides us with mountains of data—census, political, consumer, economic, sports, weather, scientific, and more. We often refer to the data as statistics. ("The government released unemployment statistics today.") But the numbers by themselves tell only part of the story. The analysis of those numbers—the search for patterns and relationships among them—can provide meaning for the data. ("Analysts note that the rise in unemployment is confined to cities most heavily impacted by the freeze on government contracts.") Statisticians in government, business, and science depend on computers to make sense of raw data.

Do people who live near nuclear power plants run a higher cancer risk? Does the current weather pattern suggest the formation of a tropical storm? Are rural voters more likely to support small-town candidates? These questions can't be answered with absolute certainty; the element of chance is at the heart of statistical analysis. But **statistical-analysis** software can suggest answers to questions such as these by testing the strength of data relationships. Statistical software can also produce graphs showing how two or more variables relate to each other. Statisticians can often uncover trends by browsing through two- and three-dimensional graphs of data, looking for unusual patterns in the dots and lines that appear on the screen. This kind of visual exploration of data is an example of a type of application known as scientific visualization.

Scientific Visualization

The **wind blows** over the lake and **stirs the surface** of the water. Thus, **visible effects** of the **invisible** are manifested.

—*The* I Ching

FIGURE 5.28 These two visualizations, created at the Laboratory of Neuro Imaging (LONI), map physical differences between a normal human brain and one with a form of dementia.

Scientific-visualization software uses shape, location in space, color, brightness, and motion to help us understand relationships that are invisible to us. Like mathematical and statistical software, scientific-visualization software is no longer confined to mainframes and supercomputers; some of the most innovative programs have been developed for use on high-end personal computers and workstations, working alone or in conjunction with more powerful computers.

Scientific visualization takes many forms, all of which involve the graphical representation of numerical data. The numbers can be the result of abstract equations, or they can be data gleaned from the real world. Either way, turning the numbers into pictures enables researchers and students to see the unseeable and sometimes, as a result, to know what was previously unknowable. Here are two examples:

■ Margaret Geller of Harvard University created a 3-D map of the cosmos from data on the locations of known galaxies. While using her computer to "fly through" this three-dimensional model, she saw something that no one had seen before: the mysterious clustering of galaxies along the edges of invisible bubbles.

FIGURE 5.29 Using a tool called Access Grid, researchers (shown in the lower right window) work with a shared visualization called the Visible Human (visible in the other two windows).

How It **Works**

5.2 Fractal Geometry and Simulation

Computers have long been used to analyze and visualize scientific data collected through experiments and observation. A computer can also serve as a virtual laboratory that simulates a physical process without real-world experiments. Of course, an inaccurate simulation can give incorrect results. The problems of creating an accurate simulation helped initiate the study of chaos and fractals. Chaos is now a vast field of study with applications in many disciplines.

The "Chaos Game" illustrates how computers can quickly complete repetitive tasks in experiments that would otherwise be impractical or impossible. You could perform the first few steps of such an experiment with pencil, paper, and ruler, like this:

1. Draw three widely separated points on the paper to form a triangle; label the points A, B, and C. Draw a random starting point anywhere on the paper. This will be the first "current" point.

2. Repeat the following process four times: Randomly choose from among points A, B, and C, and draw a new point halfway (on an imaginary straight line) between the current point and the chosen point. The newly drawn point then becomes the new current point.

3. If you use a simple computer program to plot 100,000 repeats of step 2 (excluding the first few points from the drawing), you'll see a pattern emerge rather than a solid mass of dots. This pattern, called a Sierpinski gasket, is a fractal—an object in which pieces are miniatures of the whole figure. You will see a pattern like this.

The Mandelbrot set, discovered by the mathematician Benoit Mandelbrot (who coined the term fractal) while he was working at IBM's Thomas J. Watson Research Facility, is one of the most famous fractals to emerge from chaos theory.

FIGURE 5.30 Because some fractal formulas mimic the patterns of natural objects, such as coastlines and mountains, chaos has found applications in computer-generated scenery and special effects for movies and television shows.

■ Dr. Mark Ellisman of the University of California, San Diego, School of Medicine used a 30-foot electron microscope to collect data from cells of the brain and enter it into a supercomputer, which rendered a 3-D representation of the brain cell. When Ellisman's team displayed the data on a graphic workstation, they saw several previously undiscovered aberrations in brains of patients who had Alzheimer's disease—aberrations that may turn out to be clues for discovering the cause and cure for this disease.

In these examples and hundreds of others like them, visualization helps researchers see relationships that might have been obscure or even impossible to grasp without computer-aided visualization tools.

Calculated Risks: Computer Modeling and Simulation

We have the ability to **model**—to prototype—**faster, better, and cheaper** than ever before. The old back-of-the-envelope is becoming **supercomputer driven** louver!

—*Michael Schrage, author of* Serious Play

Whether part of a simple worksheet or a complex set of equations, numbers often symbolize real-world phenomena. Computer modeling—the use of computers to create abstract models of objects, organisms, organizations, and processes—can be done with spreadsheets, mathematical applications, or standard programming languages. A business executive who creates a worksheet to project quarterly profits and losses is trying to model the economic world that affects the company. An engineer who uses a math processor to test the stress capacity of a bridge is modeling the bridge mathematically. Even a statistician who starts by examining data collected in the real world creates statistical models to describe the data.

FIGURE 5.31 These two popular strategic life-simulation games created by Will Wright put sophisticated simulation technology in the hands of gamers. The Sims and its sequels simulate the daily activities of virtual people, called Sims. Spore is drawn on a much bigger canvas—it simulates the creation and evolution of life, civilization, and technology in the universe.

FIGURE 5.32 Flight simulators for home computers and video game consoles (above) are based on the same simulation technology that's used in professional flight trainers (below).

Computer models aren't always serious; most computer games are models. Chessboards, pinball games, battlefields, sports arenas, ant colonies, cities, medieval dungeons, interplanetary cultures, and mythological societies have all been modeled in computer games. Students use computer models to travel the Oregon Trail, explore nuclear power plants, invest in the stock market, and dissect digital frogs.

Whether it's created for work, education, or play, a computer model is an *abstraction*— a set of concepts and ideas designed to mimic some kind of system. But a computer model isn't static; you can put it to work in a computer simulation to see how the model operates under certain conditions. A well-designed model should behave like the system it imitates.

Suppose, for example, an engineer constructs a computer model of a new type of airplane to test how the plane will respond to human commands. In a typical flight simulation, the "pilot" controls the plane's thrust and elevator angle by feeding input data to the model plane. The model responds by adjusting air speed and angle of ascent or descent, just as a real plane would. The pilot responds to the new state of the aircraft by adjusting one or more of the controls, which causes the system to respond by revising the aircraft's state again. This feedback loop, where plane and pilot react to data from each other, continues throughout the simulation.

A flight simulator might have a graphical user interface that makes the computer screen look and act like the instrument panel of a real plane so human pilots can run it intuitively. Or it might display nothing more than numbers representing input and output values, and the input values might be generated by a simulated pilot—another computer model! Either way, it can deliver a wealth of information about the behavior of the plane, provided the model is accurate.

Computer Simulations: The Rewards

We are reaching the stage where **problems** that we **must solve** are going to become **insolvable** without computers. **I do not fear computers**; I fear the **lack of them**.

—Isaac Asimov, scientist and science fiction writer

Computer simulations are widely used for research in the physical, biological, and social sciences and in engineering. Schools, businesses, and the military also use simulations for training. There are many reasons:

- *Safety.* Although it's safer to learn piloting skills while sitting in front of a computer rather than actually flying in the air, it's still possible to learn to fly without a computer simulation. Some activities, however, are so dangerous that they aren't ethically possible without computer simulations. How, for example, can scientists study the effects of a nuclear power plant meltdown on the surrounding environment? Unless a meltdown occurs, there's only one practical answer: computer simulation.
- *Economy.* It's far less expensive for an automobile manufacturer to produce a digital model of a nonexistent car than to build a prototype out of steel. The company can test the computer model for strength, handling, and efficiency in a series of simulations before it builds and tests a physical prototype. The cost of the computer model is small when compared with the expense of producing a possibly defective car.
- *Projection.* Without computers, it could take decades for biologists to determine whether the rising deer population on an island threatens other species, and by the time they discover the answer, it would be too late to do anything about it. A computer model of the island's ecosystem could speed up natural biological processes so scientists could measure their effects over several generations in a matter of minutes. A computer simulation can, in effect, serve as a time machine for exploring one or more possible futures.
- *Visualization.* Computer models make visualization possible, and visualization enables researchers and students to see and understand relationships that might otherwise go unnoticed. Computer models can speed time up or slow it down; they can make subatomic particles big and the universe small.
- *Replication.* In the real world, it can be difficult or impossible to repeat a research project with slightly different conditions. But this kind of repetition is an important part of serious research. An engineer needs to fine-tune dimensions and angles to achieve peak performance. A scientist studies the results of one experiment and develops a new hypothesis that calls for further testing. An executive needs to test a business plan under a variety of economic scenarios. If the research is conducted on a computer model, replication is just a matter of changing input values and running a new simulation.

Computer Simulations: The Risks

All information is **imperfect**.

—*Jacob Bronowski*

The downside of computer simulation can be summed up in three words: Simulation isn't reality. The real world is a subtle and complex place, and capturing even a fraction of that subtlety and complexity in a computer simulation is a tremendous challenge.

GIGO Revisited

The accuracy of a simulation depends on how closely its mathematical model corresponds to the system being simulated. Mathematical models are built on assumptions, many of which are difficult or impossible to verify. Some models suffer from faulty assumptions; others contain hidden assumptions that may not even be obvious to their creators; still others go astray simply because of clerical or human errors.

The daily weather report is the result of a complex computer model. Our atmosphere is far too complex to capture exactly in a computer model; that's why the weather forecast is sometimes wrong. Occasionally simulation errors produce disastrous results. Faulty computer models have been responsible for the deadly flooding of the Colorado River, the collapse of the roof of a Salt Lake City shopping mall, and the crash of a test plane on its first flight. These kinds of disasters are rare. It's much more common for computer models to help avert tragedies by pointing out design flaws. In fact, sometimes things go wrong because people *ignore* the results of accurate simulations. Still, *garbage in, garbage out* is a basic rule of simulation.

Making Reality Fit the Machine

Simulations are computation intensive. Some simulations are so complex that researchers need to simplify models and streamline calculations to get them to run on the best hardware available. Even when there's plenty of computing power available, researchers face a constant temptation to reshape reality for the convenience of the simulation. In one classic example, a U.S. Forest Service computer model reduced complex old-growth forests to "accumulated capital." Aesthetics, ecological diversity, and other hard-to-quantify factors didn't exist in this model.

Sometimes this simplification of reality is deliberate; more often it's unconscious. Either way, information can be lost, and the loss may compromise the integrity of the simulation and call the results into question.

The Illusion of Infallibility

Risks can be magnified because people take computers seriously. People tend to emphasize computer-generated reports, often at the expense of other sources of knowledge. Executives use worksheets to make decisions involving thousands of jobs and millions of dollars. Politicians decide the fate of military weapons and endangered species based on summaries of computer simulations. Doctors use computer models to make life-and-death decisions involving new drugs and treatments. All of these people, in some sense, are placing their trust in computer simulations. Many of them trust the data precisely because a computer produced it.

A computer simulation, whether generated by a PC spreadsheet or churned out by a supercomputer, can be an invaluable decision-making aid. The risk is that the people who make decisions with computers will turn over too much of their decision-making power to the computers.

Inventing the FUTURE

Truly Intelligent Agents

*I don't want to sit and move stuff around on my screen all day and look at figures and have it recognize my **gestures** and listen to my **voice**. I want to tell it what to do and then go away; I don't want to babysit this computer. I want it to act **for me, not with me**.*

—*Esther Dyson, computer industry analyst and publisher*

At Xerox PARC Alan Kay and his colleagues developed the first user interface based on icons—images that represent tools to be manipulated by users. Their pioneering work helped turn the computer into a productivity tool for millions of people. According to Kay, future user interfaces will be based on agents rather than tools.

Agents are software programs designed to be managed rather than manipulated. An intelligent software agent can ask questions as well as respond to commands, pay attention to its user's work patterns, serve as a guide and a coach, take on its owner's goals, and use reasoning to fabricate goals of its own.

Many PC applications include *wizards* and other agent-like software entities to guide users through complex tasks and answer questions when problems arise. The computer opponents you interact with in games, such as *Civilization IV,* are also intelligent agents. The Internet is home to a rapidly growing population of bots—software robots that crawl around the Web collecting information, helping consumers make decisions, answering email, and even playing games. But today's wizards, bots, and agents aren't smart enough to manage the many details that a human assistant might juggle.

Tomorrow's agents will be better able to compete with human assistants, though. Today's software can perform many of the tasks listed here, but tomorrow's software agents might be able to do all of these things transparently:

➡ *Remind you that it's time to get the tires rotated on your car, and make an appointment for the rotation*
➡ *Distribute notes to the other members of your study or work group, and tell you which members opened those notes*
➡ *Keep you posted on new articles on subjects that interest you, and know enough about those subjects to be selective without being rigid*
➡ *Manage your appointments and keep track of your communications*
➡ *Teach you new applications and answer reference questions*
➡ *Defend your system and your home from viruses, intruders, and other security breaches*
➡ *Help protect your privacy on and off the Net*

Agents are often portrayed with human characteristics; *2001*'s Hal and the computers on TV's *Star Trek* are famous examples. Of course, agents don't need to look or sound human—they just need to possess considerable knowledge and intelligence.

Future agents may possess a degree of sensitivity, too. Researchers at MIT and IBM are developing *affective computers* that can detect the emotional states of their users and respond accordingly. Affective computers use sensors to determine a person's emotional state. Sensors range from simple audiovisual devices to mouse-embedded sensors that work like lie detectors, monitoring pulse or skin resistance. Early research has shown limited success at identifying emotions, but the machines still have much to learn. They can't, for example, tell the difference between love and hate because, from a physiological point of view, they look pretty much the same! ～

FIGURE 5.33 We still don't have the truly intelligent agents many experts predicted a decade or two ago, but many Web sites perform some of the functions of an intelligent agent. Yapta travel assistant tracks flight pricing and notifies shoppers of price drops. Amazon provides shoppers with product recommendations based on previous purchases and purchases of other shoppers with similar interests.

The Sad Fate of the Comma *by Robert J. Samuelson*

Is technology a passport to a more leisurely lifestyle or a ticket to the fast lane? In this Aug 15, 2007, Newsweek article, Robert J. Samuelson looks to the comma for answers.

I have always liked commas, but I seem to be in a shrinking minority. The comma is in retreat, though it is not yet extinct. In text messages and e-mails, commas appear infrequently, and then often by accident (someone hits the wrong key). Even on the printed page, commas are dwindling. Many standard uses from my childhood (after, for example, an introductory prepositional phrase) have become optional or, worse, have been ditched.

If all this involved only grammar, I might let it lie. But the comma's sad fate is, I think, a metaphor for something larger: how we deal with the frantic, can't-wait-a-minute nature of modern life. The comma is, after all, a small sign that flashes PAUSE. It tells the reader to slow down, think a bit, and then move on. We don't have time for that. No pauses allowed. In this sense, the comma's fading popularity is also social commentary.

It is true that Americans have always been in a hurry. In "Democracy in America" (1840), Alexis de Tocqueville has a famous passage noting the "feverish ardor" with which Americans pursue material gains and private pleasures. What's distinctive about our era, I think, is that new technologies and astonishing prosperity give us the chance to slacken the pace. Perish the thought. In some ways, it seems, we Americans have actually become more frantic.

Evidence to support this hunch hasn't been hard to find. Exhibit A is a story a few months ago in The Washington Post headlined, TEENS CAN MULTITASK, BUT WHAT ARE COSTS? We meet Megan, a 17-year-old honors high-school senior. After school, she begins studying by turning on MTV and booting up her computer. The story continues:

Over the next half an hour, Megan will send about a dozen instant messages discussing the potential for a midweek snow day. She'll take at least one cellphone call, fire off a couple of text messages, scan Weather.com, volunteer to help with a campus cleanup [at the local high school], post some comments on a friend's Facebook page and check out the new pom squad pictures another friend has posted on hers.

Whew! And remember, she's also studying. Naturally, the story includes the obligatory quote from a brain scientist, who worries that so much multitasking will turn young minds into mush. "It's almost impossible," says the scientist, "to gain a depth of knowledge of any of the tasks you do while you're multitasking."

In reality, multitasking isn't confined to the young. It's hard to go anywhere these days—including restaurants and business meetings—without seeing people punching furiously on their BlackBerrys, cell phones or other hand-held devices. More mush, maybe. At the least, serious questions of etiquette have arisen. In one survey, almost a third of the executives polled said it is *never* appropriate to check e-mails during meetings.

Next, there's work. Unlike most rich nations, the United States hasn't reduced the average workweek over the past quarter century. In 2006, annual hours for U.S. workers averaged 1,804, barely different from 1,834 in 1979, reports the Organization for Economic Cooperation and Development. By contrast, the Japanese cut annual hours by 16 percent to 1,784, the Germans 20 percent to 1,421 and the French 16 percent to 1,564. One commentator in the London-based Financial Times calls America "the republic of overwork." A study by economists Daniel Hamermesh of the University of Texas and Joel Slemrod of the University of Michigan argues that long working hours, especially among the well paid, may be an addiction, akin to alcoholism and smoking. (The paper is titled "The Economics of Workaholism: We Should Not Have Worked on This Paper.")

I could go on, but the column's only 800 words, and more evidence would simply reinforce the point: de Tocqueville's "feverish ardor" endures. There's always too much to do, not enough time to do it. The comma is a small victim of our hustle-bustle. If we can save a few seconds a day by curtailing commas, why not? Commas are disparaged as literary clutter. They're axed in the name of stylistic "simplicity." Once, introductory prepositional phrases ("In 1776, Thomas Jefferson . . .") routinely took commas; once, compound sentences were strictly divided by commas; once, sentences that began with "once," "naturally," "surprisingly," "inevitably" and the like usually took a comma to set them apart.

No more. These and other usages have slowly become discretionary or unacceptable. Over the years, copy editors have stripped thousands of defenseless commas from my stories. I have saved every last one of them and piled them all on a secluded corner of my desk. They deserve better than they're getting. So here are some of my discarded commas, taking a long-overdue bow: ,,,,,,,,,,,,,,,,,,,,,,,,,,,,,,,,

I'm not quitting quietly. By my count, this column contains 104 commas. Note to copy desk: leave them be.

Discussion Questions

1. Do you think the comma's decline represents a change in our culture? Explain.

2. Do you think any of the changes discussed here are positive? Why?

Summary

Even though the computer was originally designed to work with numbers, it quickly became an important tool for processing text as well.

Word processing software enables the writer to use commands to edit text on the screen, eliminating the chore of retyping pages until the message and the appearance is right. With word processing software, you can control the typefaces, spacing, justification, margins, columns, headers, footers, and other visual components of your documents. Most professional word processing programs automate footnoting, hyphenation, and other processes that are particularly troublesome to traditional typists. Outlining tools turn the familiar outline into a powerful, dynamic organizational tool. Spelling checkers and grammar and style checkers partially automate the proofreading process, although they leave the more difficult parts of the job to literate humans. Online thesauruses, dictionaries, and other computer-based references automate reference works.

As word processing software becomes more powerful, they take on many of the features previously found only in desktop publishing software. Still, many publishers use word processing and graphics programs to create source documents that can be used as input for page-layout programs. Desktop publishing has revolutionized the publishing process by enabling publishers and would-be publishers to produce professional-quality text-and-graphics documents at a reasonable cost. Amateur and professional publishers everywhere use desktop publishing technology to produce everything from comic books to reference books.

The near-overnight success of desktop publishing may foreshadow other changes in the way we communicate with words as new technologies emerge. Computer networks in general and the Web in particular have made it possible for potential publishers to reach mass audiences without the problems associated with printing and distributing paper documents. Typing may no longer be a necessary part of the writing process as handwriting and speech recognition technologies improve, and word processing software that incorporates other artificial intelligence technologies may become as much a coach as a tool for future writers.

Spreadsheet programs, first developed to simulate and automate the accountant's ledger, can be used for tracking financial transactions, calculating grades, forecasting economic conditions, recording scientific data, and just about any other task that involves repetitive numeric calculations. Spreadsheet documents, called worksheets, are grids with individual cells containing alphabetic labels, numbers, and formulas. Changes in numeric values can cause the spreadsheet to update any related formulas automatically. The responsiveness and flexibility of spreadsheet software make it particularly well suited for providing answers to "what if" questions. Most spreadsheet programs include charting commands to turn worksheet numbers into a variety of graphs and charts. The process of creating a chart from a spreadsheet is automated to the point where human drawing isn't necessary; the user simply provides instructions concerning the type of chart and the details to be included in the chart, and the computer does the rest.

Number crunching often goes beyond spreadsheets. Specialized accounting and tax preparation software packages perform specific business functions without the aid of spreadsheets. Symbolic mathematics processors can handle a variety of higher mathematics functions involving numbers, symbols, equations, and graphics. Statistical-analysis software is used for data collection and analysis. Scientific visualization can be done with math processors, statistical packages, graphics programs, or specialized programs designed for visualization.

Modeling and simulation are at the heart of most applications involving numbers. When people create computer models, they use numbers to represent real-world objects and phenomena. Simulations built on these models can provide insights that might be difficult or impossible to obtain otherwise, provided that the models reflect reality accurately. If used wisely, computer simulation can be a powerful tool for helping people understand their world and make better decisions.

Key Terms

Interactive Activities

1. The *Tomorrow's Technology and You* Web site, **www.pearsonhighered.com/beekman**, contains self-test exercises related to this chapter. Follow the instructions for taking a quiz. After you've completed your quiz, you can email the results to your instructor.

2. The Web site also contains open-ended discussion questions called Internet Exercises. Discuss one or more of the Internet Exercises questions at the section for this chapter.

True or False

1. OpenType fonts are identical to TrueType fonts, but are open source.

2. WYSIWYG stands for "what you see is what you get."

3. Text editing and text formatting are two different terms for the same process.

4. A monospaced font assigns equal vertical space to all characters of the same point size.

5. One of the biggest problems with desktop-publishing technology is that its high cost makes it impractical for small businesses and individuals.

6. Charting software, such as the chart tools built into spreadsheet software, generally contains safeguards that prevent the misrepresentation of information.

7. Most accounting and financial-management programs automatically calculate income and capital gains taxes.

8. Statistical-analysis software can suggest answers to scientific questions by testing the strength of data relationships.

9. Electronic publishing is replacing some forms of print publishing, but paper documents aren't likely to go away anytime soon.

10. People tend to be more skeptical of computer-generated reports than they are of other types of reports.

Multiple Choice

1. Which of these is a text-formatting feature of a word processing program?
   a. Drag and drop
   b. Cut and paste
   b. Word wrap
   c. Stylesheets
   e. None of the above

2. Which of these is a text-editing feature of a word processing program?
   a. Copy and paste
   b. Font choice
   c. Justification tools
   d. Stylesheets
   e. None of the above

3. To which of the following does justification generally apply?
   a. Individual characters
   b. Words
   c. Paragraphs
   d. Fonts
   e. All of the above

4. Left justification is particularly useful when formatting
   a. a column of numbers representing your daily expenses.
   b. the paragraphs of a document.
   c. text in font sizes larger than 72 point.
   d. the title of a document.
   e. All of the above

5. When might full justification be a poor choice?
   a. The column is very narrow.
   b. The column is very wide.
   c. The characters are printed in a serif font.
   d. The characters are printed in italics.
   e. None of the above. Full justification is always a good choice.

6. According to the experts, a serif font is better than a sans serif font when formatting
   a. titles and subtitles.
   b. the body of a document (pages of text).
   c. figure captions.
   d. text boxes (sidebars).
   e. All of the above

7. A document created with a desktop publishing system can be
   a. printed on a color printer.
   b. converted into a PDF document for electronic distribution.
   c. displayed on the Web.
   d. printed on a phototypesetting machine at a service bureau.
   e. All of the above

8. Which of the following is a fundamentally important principle of spreadsheets?
   a. They eliminate the need for any other kind of programming language.
   b. They never change the values of cells unless explicitly instructed to by the user.
   c. They provide a bar-chart graphical user interface for data input.
   d. Formulas automatically recalculate results when any of their inputs change.
   e. All of the above

9. To represent full-color images accurately, what must desktop publishing systems use?
   a. Laser printers
   b. Service bureaus
   c. Color-matching technology
   d. Spot color
   e. Phototypesetting machines

10. If you change the value of numbers in a spreadsheet,
    a. nothing else changes unless the spreadsheet is linked to other spreadsheets.
    b. the spreadsheet macros will check for data-entry errors.
    c. the labels at the column heads should automatically change to reflect the new values.
    d. cells containing formulas may change to reflect the new numeric values.
    e. the WYSIWYG checker will apply a template to your changes.

11. Which type of chart is most appropriate for showing the changes in the average annual temperature of a mountain lake over a 100-year period?
    a. Bar chart
    b. Line chart
    c. Scatter chart
    d. Pie chart
    e. Bullet chart

12. Which of these types of software is used for creating models?
    a. Spreadsheet software
    b. Accounting software
    c. Math-processing software
    d. All of the above
    e. None of the above

13. Scientific-visualization software
    a. requires visual input devices to work properly.
    b. is the scientific equivalent of desktop publishing software.
    c. creates pictures from numbers.
    d. requires supercomputer power to run.
    e. doesn't exist yet, but it will be a reality before the end of the decade.

14. Simulation software offers many advantages, including all of these *except*:
    a. It can save money.
    b. It can be much safer than "real-world" experience.
    c. It is generally more accurate than standard experimental research.
    d. It can save time.
    e. It makes experimental replication easier.

15. A wizard inside a PC application is a primitive example of
    a. an intelligent agent.
    b. a spreadsheet program.
    c. a scientific simulation.
    d. a computer virus.
    e. a fractal.

Review Questions

1. Provide a working definition for each of the key terms listed in the "Key Terms" section.

2. How is working with an outliner (or idea processor) different from working with a word processor?

3. Describe three different ways a spelling checker might give incorrect feedback.

4. How is word processing different from text editing?

5. How does desktop publishing differ from word processing?

6. How many different ways can a paragraph or line of text be justified? When might each be appropriate?

7. What kinds of basic reference tools are included in popular word processing programs?

8. An automated speech-recognition dictation system might have trouble telling the difference between a "common denominator" and a "comedy nominator." People who use these programs heavily tend to have fewer of these types of errors over time. Why?

9. In what ways are word processing and spreadsheet programs similar?

10. What are some advantages of using a spreadsheet over using a calculator to maintain a record of sports scores or workout summaries? Are there any disadvantages?

11. If you enter "=A1*B1" in cell C1 of a worksheet, the formula is replaced by the number 125 when you press the Enter key. What happened?

12. List several advantages and disadvantages of using computer simulations for decision making.

13. Explain the difference between a numeric value and a label.

14. Describe or draw examples of several different types of charts, and explain how they're typically used.

15. Describe several software tools used for numeric applications too complex to be handled by spreadsheets. Give an example of an application of each.

Discussion Questions

1. Like Gutenberg's development of the movable-type printing press more than 500 years ago, the development of desktop publishing puts powerful communication tools in the hands of more people. What impact will desktop-publishing technology have on the free press and the free exchange of ideas guaranteed in the United States Constitution? What impact will the same technology have on free expression in other countries? Answer the same questions about publishing on the Web.

2. What do you think of the arguments that word processing reduces the quality of writing because it makes it easy to write in a hurried and careless manner and it puts the emphasis on the way a document looks rather than on what it says?

3. The statement "Computers don't make mistakes, people do" is often used to support the reliability of computer output. Is the statement true? Is it relevant?

4. Spreadsheets are sometimes credited with legitimizing the personal computer as a business tool. Why do you think they had such an impact?

5. Word processing and spreadsheet software were invented before the Internet explosion; both these types of applications were conceived as tools for producing paper documents. Do you think that the Web will eventually make these software categories irrelevant? Explain your answer.

Projects

1. Buy four magazines from your local newsstand. Create a table that documents the text fonts and styles each magazine uses for titles, subtitles, figure captions, text boxes, and the body of each article. For each magazine, create a collage that shows the color scheme used inside the magazine (excluding advertisements). Evaluate the similarities and differences among the magazines.

2. Use a word processing or a desktop publishing system to produce a newsletter, brochure, or flyer in support of an organization or cause that is important to you. Base your design on an attractive, mass-marketed publication.

3. Use a spreadsheet to track your grades in this (or another) class. Apply weightings from the course syllabus to your individual scores, calculating a point total based on those weightings.

4. Use a spreadsheet or a financial-management program to develop a personal budget. Try to keep track of your income and expenses for the next month or two, and record the transactions with your program. At the end of that time, evaluate the accuracy of your budget, and discuss your reactions to the process.

5. Scan the graphics appearing in some newspapers or magazines. Find a graphic that distorts the data values by hiding the baseline. Find a graphic containing superfluous elements that distract from the data values. Find a graphic in which it is difficult to compare data values (for example, a pie chart used inappropriately).

6. Use a spreadsheet to search for answers to a "what if" question that's important to you. Possible questions: If I lease a car instead of buying it, am I better off? If I borrow money for school, how much does it cost me in the long run?

Sources and Resources

Books

Bootstrapping: Douglas Engelbart, Coevolution, and the Origins of Personal Computing, by Thierry Bardini (Palo Alto, CA: Stanford University Press, 2000). This long-overdue book shines a spotlight on the visionary, revolutionary work of Douglas Engelbart at SRI.

Office 2007: The Missing Manual, by Chris Grover, Matthew MacDonald, and E. Vander Veer (Cambridge, MA: Pogue Press, 2007). There are hundreds of books on Microsoft Office. This one is part of David Pogue's highly successful Missing Manual series. It follows a tried-and-true formula that should help you learn the ins and outs of this complex software suite. Microsoft Office 2008 for Macintosh: Visual QuickStart Guide, by Steve Schwartz (Peachpit Press, 2008). Peachpit's Visual Quickstart series covers a variety of applications for multiple platforms, but they're particularly strong on Mac programs because of Peachpit's emphasis on design and creativity titles. This book covers the latest Mac version of Office.

The Non-Designer's Design and Type Book, Deluxe Edition, by Robin Williams (Berkeley, CA: Peachpit Press, 2008). In this perennially popular book, Robin Williams provides a friendly introduction to the basics of design and page layout in her down-to-earth style. The first section of the book illustrates the four basic design principles (proximity, alignment, repetition, and contrast). The second section focuses on using type as a design element. This edition combines two previously separate books and adds full-color illustrations. This book is highly recommended for anyone new to graphic design.

Designing for Print: An In-Depth Guide to Planning, Creating, and Producing Successful Design Projects, by Charles Conover (New York, NY: Wiley, 2003). This book clearly explains and shows how to design successful publications using type, photos, illustrations, and other elements in creative ways.

Bugs in Writing: A Guide to Debugging Your Prose, Second Edition, by Lyn Dupre (Boston, MA: Addison-Wesley, 1998). This entertaining little book is designed to help computer science and computer information systems students, who presumably already know how to debug their programs, debug their prose. It's a friendly, readable tutorial that can help almost anybody to be a better writer.

The Elements of Style, Fourth Edition, by William Strunk, Jr., and E. B. White (Boston, MA: Allyn & Bacon, 2000). Through a half century and four editions, this book has been helping writers to communicate more clearly.

The Chicago Manual of Style, Fifteenth Edition (Chicago, IL: University of Chicago Press, 2003). This is considered by many to be the definitive writing style guide. The latest edition includes much new material on electronic publishing and online publication.

Adobe Acrobat 8 Classroom in a Book, by Adobe Creative Team (Berkeley, CA: Adobe Press, 2007). Adobe's PDF is the industry standard for paperless publishing, and Acrobat is the standard tool for creating and editing PDF documents. This tutorial, like others in Adobe's excellent *Classroom in a Book* series, explains the ins and outs of the software in an easy-to-follow format.

Scrolling Forward: Making Sense of Documents in the Digital Age, by David M. Levy (New York, NY: Arcade Publishing, 2003). How are computers, the Internet, and digital technology changing the notion of documents? The future of books, paper, copyrights, and libraries are discussed in this thought-provoking book. Print is Dead: Books in Our Digital Age, by Jeff Gomez (New York, NY: Macmillan, 2008). The title raises the question; the book attempts to answer that question. What is the future of the book in the age of electronics? You may not agree with Gomez, but this book should at least start some interesting conversations about our future.

Quicken 2008: The Official Guide, by Maria Langer (New York, NY: McGraw-Hill, 2008). Quicken is far-and-away the most widely used personal accounting and money management program. This "official" book covers the basics of the Windows version of the program, with tips for setting up accouns, creating a budget, recording transactions, banking online, investing, and more.

Super Crunchers: Why Thinking-by-Numbers is the New Way to Be Smart, by Ian Ayres (New York, NY: Bantam, 2007). There's a wealth of numeric data out stored in computers today. Ian Ayers argues that intelligent analysis on this data is the right way to make smart decisions today. He uses a variety of real-world examples to illustrate the power of thinkin statistically and analytically.

The Visual Display of Quantitative Information, Second Edition, by Edward R. Tufte (Graphics Press, 2001). Tufte is widely recognized as the master of statistical graphics. In this book he presents his rules for good design and illustrates them with dozens of wonderful (and terrible) graphics that have actually appeared in print.

How to Lie with Statistics, by Darrell Huff (New York, NY: W. W. Norton, 1993). This classic book, first published in 1954, has more relevance in today's computer age than it did when it was written.

The Sum of Our Discontent: Why Numbers Make Us Irrational, by David Boyle (New York, NY: Texere, 2004). Computers, television, and other media bombard us with more numbers than most of us can digest. Boyle argues that all those numbers make it harder, not easier, to understand what's going on around us.

Serious Play: How the World's Best Companies Simulate to Innovate, by Michael Schrage (Cambridge, CA: Harvard Business School Press, 1999). "When talented innovators innovate, you don't listen to the specs they quote. You look at the models they've created," says Michael Schrage, MIT Media Lab fellow and *Fortune* magazine columnist. In this book Schrage looks at the kind of "serious play" being done at innovative companies, such as Disney, 3M, Sony, and Hewlett-Packard.

6

Graphics, Digital Media, and Multimedia

Objectives

After you read this chapter you should be able to:

▶ Explain the difference between painting software, image processing software, drawing software, and 3-D modeling software

▶ Explain effective techniques for improving the quality of slides prepared with presentation-graphics software

▶ Explain the difference between analog video and digital video

▶ Describe how data compression works

▶ Describe several present and future applications for multimedia technology

> The whole idea you can have some idea and **make it happen** means that **dreamers** all over the world should **take heart** and **not stop.**
>
> —*Tim Berners-Lee, creator of the World Wide Web*

Tim Berners-Lee Weaves the Web for Everybody

The Internet has long been a powerful communication medium and a storehouse of valuable information. But until recently, few people mastered the cryptic codes and challenging languages that were required to unlock the Internet's treasures. The Net was effectively off-limits to most of the world's people. Tim Berners-Lee changed all that when he single-handedly invented the World Wide Web and gave it to all of us.

Tim Berners-Lee was born in London in 1955. His parents met while programming the Ferranti Mark I, the first commercial computer. They encouraged their son to think unconventionally. He developed a love for electronics and even built a computer out of spare parts and a TV set when he was a physics student at Oxford.

Berners-Lee took a software engineering job at CERN, the European Particle Physics Laboratory in Geneva, Switzerland. While he was there, he developed a program to help him track all his random notes. He tried to make the program, called Enquire, deal with information in a "brainlike way." Enquire was a primitive hypertext system that allowed related documents on his computer to be linked with numbers rather than mouse clicks. (Back in 1980, PCs didn't have mice.)

Berners-Lee wanted to expand the concept of Enquire so he could link documents on other computers to his own. His idea was to create an open-ended, distributed hypertext system without boundaries, so scientists everywhere could link their work.

Over the next few years, he single-handedly built a complete system to realize his dream. He designed the URL scheme for giving every Internet document a unique address. He developed HTML, the language for encoding and displaying hypertext documents on the Web. He created HTTP, the set of rules that allows hypertext documents to be linked across the Internet. And he built the first software browser for viewing those documents from remote locations.

When he submitted the first paper describing the Web to a conference in 1991, the conference organizers

187

rejected it because the Web seemed too simple to them. They thought that Berners-Lee's ideas would be a step backward when compared to hypertext systems that had been developed by Ted Nelson, Doug Engelbart, and others over the previous 25 years. It's easy to see now that the simplicity of the Web was a strength, not a weakness.

Rather than try to own his suite of inventions, Berners-Lee made them freely available to the public. Suddenly, vast tracts of the Internet were open to just about anyone who could point and click a mouse. Other programmers added multimedia capabilities to the Web, and its popularity spread like a virus. In a few short years, the Internet was transformed from a forbidding fortress of cryptic codes into an inviting multimedia milieu for the masses.

When he created the Web, Tim Berners-Lee created a new medium of communication. Few people in history have had so great an impact on the way we communicate. In the words of writer Joshua Quittner, Tim Berners-Lee's accomplishments are "almost Gutenbergian."

In 1994, Tim Berners-Lee founded the World Wide Web Consortium (W3C). The W3C is a standards-setting organization dedicated to helping the Web evolve in positive directions rather than disintegrate into incompatible factions. The work of Tim Berners-Lee will help ensure that the World Wide Web continues to belong to everyone. ～

FIGURE 6.1 Tim Berners-Lee, the inventor of the World Wide Web. *(Source: © Sam Ogden.)*

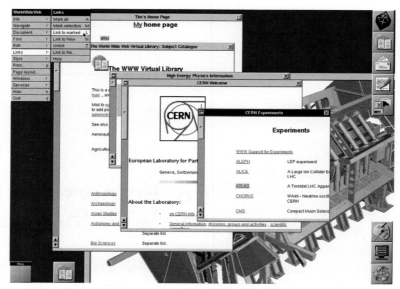

FIGURE 6.2 Berners-Lee implemented the first Web browser on a NeXT workstation in 1990.

The work of Tim Berners-Lee brought multimedia to millions of people around the world. Today, the Web is a source of images, sounds, animations, video clips, and rich interactive documents that merge multiple media types. Even without the Web, though, today's PC can serve as a digital hub for a network of creative media tools, from digital cameras and graphics tablets to musical instruments and video systems. In this chapter we look into these technologies and see how they're changing the ways we create and communicate.

Focus on Computer Graphics

The previous chapter explored a variety of computer applications, from basic word-processing programs to powerful mathematical software packages that can analyze data and generate quantitative charts and graphs from numbers. But computer graphics today go far beyond page layouts and pie charts. In this section we explore a variety of graphical applications, from simple drawing and painting tools to complex programs used by professional artists and designers.

Mastering technology is only part of what it means **to be an artist** in the twenty-first century. The other hurdle is **mastering creative expression**, so that art has **something substantial** to say. **Expression** has been **the one constant** among artists **from the Stone Age** until now. The only thing that has changed is the **technology**.

—*Steven Holtzman, author of* Digital Mantras

Painting: Bitmapped Graphics

Everything you **imagine** is real.

—*Pablo Picasso*

An image on a computer screen is made up of a matrix of **pixels**—tiny dots of white, black, or color arranged in rows. The words, numbers, and pictures we see on the computer display are nothing more than patterns of pixels created by software. Most of the time, the user doesn't directly control those pixel patterns; software creates the patterns automatically in response to commands. For example, when you press the *e* key while word processing, the software constructs a pattern that appears on the screen as an *e*. Similarly, when you issue a command to create a bar chart from a spreadsheet, software automatically constructs a pixel pattern that looks like a bar chart. Automatic graphics are convenient, but they can also be restrictive. When you need more control over the details of the screen display, another type of graphics software might be more appropriate.

Painting software enables you to "paint" pixels on the screen with a pointing device. A typical painting program accepts input from a mouse, joystick, trackball, touch pad, or stylus, translating the pointer movements into lines and patterns on-screen. A professional artist might prefer to work

FIGURE 6.3 When it's used with compatible software, a stylus on a pressure-sensitive tablet can simulate the feel of a paintbrush on paper. As the artist presses harder on the stylus, the line becomes thicker and denser on the screen.

with a stylus on a pressure-sensitive tablet because it can, with the right software, simulate a traditional pen or paintbrush more accurately than other pointing devices can. A painting program typically offers a **palette** of tools on-screen. Some tools mimic real-world painting tools, while others can do things that are difficult, even impossible, on paper or canvas.

FIGURE 6.4 Natural painting programs such as Corel Painter X allow artists and nonartists to create paintings with digital tools that simulate real-world tools such as watercolors, oil paints, and charcoal.

Painting programs create **bitmapped graphics**, or, as they're sometimes called, *raster graphics*. To the computer, these pictures are simple maps showing how the pixels on the screen should be represented. For the simplest bitmapped graphics, a single bit of computer memory represents each pixel. Because a bit can contain one of two possible values, 0 or 1, each pixel can display one of two possible colors, usually black or white. Allocating more memory per pixel, so each pixel can display more possible colors or shades, produces even higher-quality graphics. **Gray-scale graphics** allow each pixel to appear as black, white, or one of several shades of gray. A program that assigns 8 bits per pixel allows up to 256 different shades of gray to appear on the screen—more than the human eye can distinguish.

Realistic color graphics require more memory. Many older computers have hardware to support 8-bit color, allowing 256 possible colors to be displayed on the screen at a time— enough to display rich images, but not enough to reproduce photographs exactly. Photorealistic color requires hardware that can display millions of colors at a time—24 or 32 bits of memory for each pixel on the screen. Modern personal computers are equal to this task.

The number of bits devoted to each pixel—called **color depth** or **bit depth**—is one of two technological factors limiting an artist's ability to create realistic on-screen images with a bitmapped graphics program. The other factor is **resolution**—the density of the pixels, usually described in *dots per inch*, or *dpi*. Not surprisingly, these are also the two main factors controlling image quality in monitors, as described in Chapter 3, "Hardware Basics: Peripherals." But some graphics images are destined for the printer after being displayed on-screen, so the printer's resolution comes into play, too. When displayed on a 96-dpi computer screen—on a Web page, for example—a 96-dpi picture looks fine. But when printed on paper, that same image lacks the fine-grained clarity of a photograph. Diagonal lines, curves, and text characters have tiny "jaggies"—jagged, stair-step-like bumps that advertise the image's identity as a collection of pixels.

FIGURE 6.5 This painting served as the cover art for a Herbie Hancock CD called *Dis is de Drum*. Photographer Sanjay Kothari created the image through the process of digital photographic manipulation. Several of the photos used in the final collage are shown along the side of the main image. At the bottom of the collage, three small images show how the photos were merged to create the final image.

Painting programs get around the jaggies by allowing you to store an image at 300 dots per inch or higher, even though the computer screen can't display every pixel at that resolution and normal magnification. Of course, these high-resolution pictures demand more memory and disk space. But for printed images, the results are worth the added cost. The higher the resolution, the harder it is for the human eye to detect individual pixels on the printed page.

Creating a CD Cover with Photoshop

GOAL *To create a CD cover by modifying a digital photograph of the artist.*

TOOL *Adobe Photoshop, part of the Adobe Creative Suite.*

1. You open two images you'd like to use, and resize the canvas of one of the photos to fit the front of a CD jewel case.

2. You copy and paste the image of the clouds into a new *layer* on the other document.

3. You duplicate and mirror the veiled part of the artist photo to extend the veil up to the edge of the canvas.

4. You use the paintbrush tool to "paint" a *mask* (indicated in red) onto the artist layer. The masked area becomes transparent, hiding the veil and allowing the clouds underneath to shine through.

5. You apply the mask to the image.

6. You import the logo, created earlier with Adobe Illustrator.

7. You add stylized text for the album title.

FIGURE 6.6

Practically speaking, resolution and bit-depth limitations are easy to overcome with today's hardware and software. Artists can use paint programs to produce works that convincingly simulate watercolors, oils, and other natural media, and transcend the limits of those media. Similarly, bitmapped image-editing software can be used to edit photographic images.

Image Processing: Photographic Editing by Computer

Like a picture created with a high-resolution paint program, a digitized photograph or a photograph captured with a digital camera—often simply referred to as a *digital photo*—is a bitmapped image. **Image processing software** enables the photographer to manipulate digital photos and other high-resolution images with tools similar to those found in paint programs. Image processing software, such as Adobe Photoshop, is in many ways similar to paint software; both are tools for editing high-resolution bitmapped images.

> The aim of every artist is to **arrest motion**, which is **life**, by artificial means and **hold it fixed** so that **a hundred years later**, when a stranger looks at it, **it moves again** since it is life.
>
> —*William Faulkner*

Digital image processing software makes it easier for photographers to remove unwanted reflections, eliminate "red eye," and brush away facial blemishes. These kinds of editing tasks were routinely done with magnifying glasses and tiny brushes before photographs were digitized. But digital photographic editing is far more powerful than traditional photo-retouching techniques. With image processing software, it's possible to distort photos, apply special effects, and fabricate images that range from artistic to otherwordly. It's also possible to combine photographs into composite scenes that show no obvious evidence of tampering. Supermarket gossip tabloids routinely use these tools to create sensationalistic cover photos. Many experts question whether photographs should be allowed as evidence in the courtroom now that they can be doctored so convincingly.

A digital camera typically stores images on a flash memory card. Images are usually downloaded from camera to computer via a USB connection or memory card reader. Digital *photo management software* programs such as Apple iPhoto and Google Picasa simplify and automate common tasks associated with capturing, organizing, editing, and sharing digital images. Most consumer-oriented digital photo managers make it easy to import photos from digital cameras, remove red eye, adjust color and contrast, fix small errors, print photos on a color printer, upload images to a Web site, email copies to friends and family, store photo libraries on CD or DVD, and order paper prints or hardbound photo albums online.

FIGURE 6.7 Apple's iPhoto, like many PC photo applications, makes it easy to import, edit, and organize photos. iPhoto also automates the creation of custom photo albums that can be turned into professionally bound books via an online store.

Creating Smart Art

Modern graphics software isn't just for professional artists. Almost anybody can create pictures and presentations. Here are some guidelines to help you make the most of the computer as a graphic tool:

➡ ***Reprogram yourself . . . relax.*** For many of us, the hardest part is getting started. We are all programmed by messages we received in our childhood, which for many of us included "You aren't creative" and "You can't draw." Fortunately, a computer can help us overcome this early programming and find the artist locked within us. Most drawing and painting programs are flexible, forgiving, and fun. Allow yourself to experiment; you'll be surprised at what you can create if you're patient and playful.

➡ ***Choose the right tool for the job.*** Will your artwork be displayed on the computer screen or printed? Does your output device support color? Would color enhance the finished work? Your answers to these questions will help you determine which software and hardware tools are most appropriate. As you're thinking about options, don't rule out low-tech tools. The best approach may not involve a computer, or it may involve some combination of computer and nonelectronic tools.

➡ ***Know your graphics file formats.*** By default, a typical graphic application saves files in a native format—one that's specifically designed for that application. But sometimes it's necessary to save files in standard formats that can be read by a variety of applications. The most common graphics file types are JPEG (or JPG), generally used for photographs; GIF, generally used for Web art; PNG, a newer format generally used for Web art and photographs; and PDF, a general-purpose format especially well-suited for documents that combine graphics and text. (There's more on these file types later in this chapter).

➡ ***Borrow from the best.*** Art supply stores sell *clip art*—predrawn images that artists can legally cut out and paste into their own pictures or posters. Computer artists can choose from countless digital clip art collections. Computer clip art images can be cut, pasted, and edited electronically. Some computer clip art collections are in the public domain (that is, they are free); others can be licensed for a small fee. Computer clip art comes in a variety of formats, and it ranges from simple line drawings to scanned color photographs. If you have access to a scanner, you can create your own digitized clip art from your photos and drawings.

➡ ***Don't borrow without permission.*** Computers, scanners, and digital cameras make it all too easy to create unauthorized copies of copyrighted photographs, drawings, and other images. There's a clear legal and ethical line between using public domain or licensed clip art and pirating copyrighted material. If you use somebody else's creative work, make sure you have written permission from the owner.

➡ ***Understand your rights.*** Copyright laws aren't just to protect other people's work. Your creative work is copyrighted, too. The papers you write, the photographs you take, the doodles you put down on napkins—as soon as your creative work takes on a fixed form, it is your property and enjoys copyright protection. (If an employer is paying you to create the work, the employer is considered to be the author for copyright purposes.) If one of your creations is particularly valuable, you may want to register it with the U.S. Copyright Office. For more information, go to the U.S. Copyright Office Web site: (**www.copyright.gov**).

➡ ***Consider letting others build on your work.*** Under current copyright law, you can't use someone else's work without asking their permission. That means others can't use your work either without asking your permission. If you want to allow certain uses of your creative work, or if you want it to become **public domain** (freely usable by anyone), you can give your permission up front by associating a Creative Commons license with your work. See the Creative Commons Web site for more details (**www.creativecommons.org**).

FIGURE 6.8 The Web offers a multitude of sources for photos and other digital images. Images on iStockPhoto.com are contributed by users; contributors receive royalties when other users buy those images.

Drawing: Object-Oriented Graphics

Because high-resolution paint images and photographs are stored as bitmaps, they can make heavy storage and memory demands. Another type of graphics program can economically store pictures with virtually *infinite* resolution, limited only by the capabilities of the output

> Actually, a root word of technology, **techne**, originally meant "**art**." The ancient Greeks never separated **art** from **manufacture** in their minds, and so never developed **separate words** for them.
>
> *—Robert Pirsig, in* Zen and the Art of Motorcycle Maintenance

device. Drawing software stores a picture not as a collection of dots, but as a collection of lines and shapes. When you draw a line with a drawing program, the software doesn't record changes in the underlying pixels. Instead, it calculates and remembers a mathematical formula for the line. A drawing program stores shapes as shape formulas and text as text. Because pictures are collections of lines, shapes, and other objects, this approach is often called object-oriented graphics or vector graphics. In effect, the computer is remembering "a blue line segment goes here and a red circle goes here and a chunk of text goes here" instead of "this pixel is blue and this one is red and this one is white."

Many drawing tools—line, shape, and text tools—are similar to painting tools in bitmapped programs. But the user can manipulate objects and edit text without affecting neighboring objects, even if the neighboring objects overlap. On the screen, an object-oriented drawing looks similar to a bitmapped painting. But when it's printed, a drawing appears as smooth as the printer's resolution allows. (Of course, not all drawings are designed to be printed. You may, for example, use a drawing program to create images for publication on a Web page. Because many Web browsers recognize only bitmapped images, you'll probably convert the drawings to bitmaps before displaying them.)

Many professional drawing programs, including Adobe Illustrator, store images as PDF (portable document format) documents. PDF is a file format developed by Adobe that enables digital documents to be exchanged between programs independent of application software, hardware, or operating system. A PDF file is, in effect, a complete description of a two-dimensional document, including text, fonts, images, and vector graphics. PDF has become an open standard, and is widely used in illustration programs, desktop publishing programs, and other applications. Web browsers can display PDF documents using Adobe's Acrobat Reader plug-in. A PDF document might be created in Microsoft Word on a Windows PC, embellished with Adobe Illustrator on a Mac, and posted on the Web using a Linux server.

Object-oriented drawing and bitmapped painting each offer advantages for certain applications. Bitmapped image editing programs give artists and photo editors unsurpassed control over textures, shading, and fine detail; they're widely used for creating screen displays (for example, in video games, multimedia presentations, and Web pages), for simulating natural paint media, and for

FIGURE 6.9 This DJ logo was created in minutes with Adobe Illustrator, a professional drawing and illustration program. Each element of the design can be moved as an independent object in the drawing.

Pixels versus Objects How do you edit a picture? It depends on what you're doing and how the picture is stored.		
The task . . .	**Using bitmapped graphics**	**Using object-oriented graphics**
Moving and removing parts of pictures	Easier to work with regions rather than objects, especially if those objects overlap	Easier to work with individual objects or groups of objects, even if they overlap
Working with shapes	Shapes stored as pixel patterns can be edited with eraser and drawing tools	Shapes stored as math formulas can be transformed mathematically
Magnification	Magnifies pixels for fine detail editing	Magnifies objects, not pixels
Text handling	Text "dries" and can't be edited, but can be moved as a block of pixels	Text can always be edited
	When paint text "dries" it can't be edited like other text	Draw text always can be changed
Printing	Resolution of printout can't exceed the pixel resolution of the stored picture	Resolution is limited only by the output device
Working within the limits of the hardware	Photographic quality is possible but requires considerable memory and disk storage	Complex drawings require considerable computational power for reasonable speed

FIGURE 6.10 Pixels versus objects.

embellishing photographic images. Object-oriented drawing and illustration programs are better choices for creating printed graphs, charts, and illustrations with clean lines and smooth shapes. Some programs merge features of both in a single application, blurring the distinction and offering new possibilities for amateur and professional illustrators.

FIGURE 6.11 This scene was created using 3-D modeling software. The upper screen shows three different views of the scene being modeled. The lower screen shows the completed scene, including lighting and surface textures.

3-D Modeling Software

Working with a pencil, an artist can draw a representation of a three-dimensional scene on a two-dimensional page. Similarly, an artist can use a drawing or painting program to create a scene that appears to have depth on a two-dimensional computer screen. But in either case, the drawing lacks true depth; it's just a flat representation of a scene. With **3-D modeling software** graphic designers can create 3-D objects with tools similar to those found in conventional drawing software. You can't touch a 3-D computer model; it's no more real than a square, a circle, or a letter created with a drawing program. But a 3-D computer model can be rotated, stretched, and combined with other model objects to create complex 3-D scenes.

Illustrators who use 3-D software appreciate its flexibility. A designer can create a 3-D model of an object, rotate it, view it from a variety of angles, and take two-dimensional "snapshots" of the best views for inclusion in final printouts. Similarly, it's possible to "walk through" a 3-D environment that exists only in the computer's memory, printing snapshots that show the simulated space from many points of view. For many applications, the goal is not a printout, but an animated presentation on a computer screen or DVD.

FIGURE 6.12 Animated 3-D figures using technology from LifeFX can simulate human expressions for use in Internet-based video communications.

Animation software, presentation-graphics software, and multimedia-authoring software (all described later in this chapter) can display sequences of screens showing 3-D objects being rotated, explored, and transformed. Many modern television and movie special effects involve combinations of live action and simulated 3-D animation. Techniques pioneered in *The Matrix, Jurassic Park, Ratatouille*, other films, and video games continually push computer graphics to new levels of realism.

CAD/CAM: Turning Pictures into Products

Three-dimensional graphics also play an important role in the branch of engineering known as **computer-aided design (CAD)**—the use of computers to design products. CAD software allows engineers, designers, and architects to create designs on-screen for products ranging from computer chips to public buildings. Today's software goes far beyond basic drafting and object-oriented graphics. It allows users to create three-dimensional "solid" models with physical characteristics such as weight, volume, and center of gravity. These models can be visually rotated and viewed from any angle. The computer can evaluate the structural performance of any part of the model by applying imaginary force to the object. Using CAD, an engineer can crash-test a new model of an automobile before it ever leaves the computer screen. CAD tends to be cheaper, faster, and more accurate than traditional design-by-hand techniques. What's more, the forgiving nature of the computer makes it easy to alter a design to meet project goals.

Computer-aided design is often linked to **computer-aided manufacturing (CAM)**. When the design of a product is completed, the numbers are fed to a program that controls the manufacturing or prototyping of products. For electronic parts, the design translates directly into a template for etching circuits onto chips. The emergence of CAD/CAM has streamlined many design and manufacturing processes. The combination of CAD and CAM is often called **computer-integrated manufacturing (CIM)**; it's a major step toward a fully automated factory.

FIGURE 6.13 Engineers use CAD software running on powerful workstations to design everything from microscopic electronic circuits to massive structures.

Presentation Graphics: Bringing Lectures to Life

One common application for computer graphics today is the creation of visual aids—slides, transparencies, graphics displays, and handouts—to enhance presentations. Although drawing and painting programs can create these aids, they aren't as useful as programs designed with presentations in mind.

Presentation-graphics software helps automate the creation of visual aids for lectures, training sessions, sales demonstrations, and other presentations. Presentation-graphics programs are most commonly used for creating and displaying a series of on-screen "slides" to serve as visual aids for presentations. Slides might include photographs, drawings, spreadsheet-style charts, or tables. These different graphical elements are usually integrated into a series of **bullet charts** that list the main points of a presentation. Slides can be output as 35-mm color slides, overhead transparencies, or handouts. Presentation-graphics programs can also display "slide shows" directly on computer monitors or LCD projectors, including animation, audio, and video clips along with still images. Some can convert presentations into Web pages automatically.

Because they can be used to create and display on-screen presentations with animated visual effects and video clips, presentation-graphics programs, such as Microsoft's PowerPoint and Apple's Keynote, are sometimes called multimedia-presentation tools. These programs make it easy for nonartists to combine text, graphics, and other media in simple multimedia presentations. Slide show presentations can be converted to video files that can be published on the Web or on DVD.

We now turn our attention to several types of media that go beyond the limitations of the printed page or the static screen; then we look at how multimedia-authoring software can combine these diverse media types to produce dynamic, interactive documents.

Making Powerful Presentations

You've probably had to suffer through at least one terrible computer-assisted presentation—a speech or lecture that used ugly, hard-to-understand computer-generated slides to distract from, rather than drive home, the basic messages of the talk. Presentation-graphics software makes it easy to create presentations, but it doesn't guarantee that those presentations will be good. These guidelines will help you produce first-rate presentations.

Before you create any slides . . .

➡ *Remember your goal.* Know what you're trying to communicate. Keep your goal in mind throughout the process of creating the presentation.

➡ *Remember your audience.* How much do they know about your topic? How much do they need to know? Do key terms need to be defined?

➡ *Plan a story.* Determine the best way to take your listeners from where they are to where you want them to be. A powerful presentation smoothly guides the audience from one point to the next, as if it were telling a story.

➡ *Determine your slide count.* Depending on your topic and speaking style, you'll probably spend between 30 seconds and 2 minutes per slide. Figure out how many slides you need to create to match the total presentation time. Then estimate how many slides to devote to each point you want to make.

➡ *Tell them what you're going to tell them, then tell them, then tell them what you told them.* It's the speechmaker's fundamental rule, and it applies to presentations, too.

As you create the slides . . .

➡ *Outline your ideas.* If you can't express your plan in a clear, concise outline, you probably won't be able to create a clear, concise presentation. After your outline is done, you can import it into your presentation-graphics software and massage it into a presentation.

➡ *Don't expect too much from one slide.* A single page of this book has more pixels than 200 computer screens. A visual presentation is not a replacement for a detailed written report with data-rich diagrams.

➡ *Keep each slide focused.* Each screen should convey one idea clearly, possibly with a few concrete supporting points.

➡ *Be stingy with words.* Limit yourself to seven lines per list and no more than seven words per line. Whenever possible, eliminate low-information-content words such as "a," "an," "and," and "the."

The presentation software converts an outline into slides.

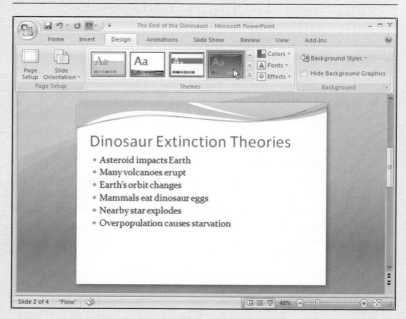

You can choose a professionally designed template from a collection provided with the software.

FIGURE 6.14

- **Use signposts.** Help listeners keep track of where you are in the presentation through the use of signpost slides. A signpost slide lists the major topics and indicates which one is going to be covered next.
- **Use a consistent design.** Make sure all your slides look like they belong together. Use the same fonts, backgrounds, and colors throughout your presentation. Consider using predesigned templates.
- **Cool colors make better backgrounds.** Blues and greens are better than yellows, oranges, and reds. It's hard to go wrong with a dark blue background.
- **Use large letters.** The smallest letters on the slide should be at least 24 point to ensure readability for audience members in the back of the room.
- **Avoid use of all capital letters.** TEXT PRINTED IN ALL CAPITAL LETTERS IS HARDER TO READ.
- **Be smart with art.** Don't clutter your presentation with random clip art. Make sure each illustration contributes to your message. Use simple graphs that support your main points. When you do use illustrations, make sure you coordinate them with the colors and design of the rest of the presentation.
- **Keep it simple.** Avoid useless decorations and distractions. Avoid fancy borders and backgrounds. Don't use a different transition on each slide.

- **Don't go font crazy.** It's generally wise to use one or two fonts and use them throughout your presentation.

When you make your presentation . . .

- **Stand to the left of the screen.** The eyes of the audience members won't have to cross the screen when they shift their gaze from you to a new slide or list item.
- **Do not read your slides.** Talk in complete sentences but only put short phrases on the slides.
- **Reveal no line before its time.** If you unveil the entire contents of a slide all at once, expect audience members to read the slide rather than listen to you.
- **Use wipe right to reveal lines.** The wipe right animation allows audience members to begin reading the text before it is completely written.
- **Pause when you reveal a new slide or bullet.** Give your listeners a chance to read the slide title or list item before you elaborate on it.
- **Vary pace or volume to make a point.** To emphasize a particular point, you can repeat yourself, pause for a moment after saying it, or noticeably change the volume of your voice.

BAD

Blue on red and red on blue are among the worst color combinations.

Each bullet contains a complete sentence. The audience will be tempted to read the sentences, not listen to you speak.

The excessive number of words causes text to be too small.

Background is a hot color.

Title is too long, forcing letter size to be too small.

Graphic images do not add information. Images distract from text.

Images are taken from different libraries and do not match each other.

GOOD

High contrast between letters and background improves readability.

Because there are only six lines and only three or four words per line, text is large and easy to read.

Background is a cool color.

Short title allows large text size.

The graphic contributes information. An animation in which the "No" symbol stamps out the dinosaur would be a nice touch.

201

Dynamic Media: Beyond the Printed Page

The world is **complex, dynamic, multidimensional;** the paper is **static, flat**. How are we to represent the **rich visual world** of experience and measurement on mere **flatland**?

—*Edward R. Tufte, in* Envisioning Information

Most PC applications—painting and drawing programs, word processors, desktop publishers, and so on—are designed to produce paper documents. But many types of modern media can't be reduced to pixels on printouts because they contain dynamic information—information that changes over time or in response to user input. Today's multimedia computers enable us to create and edit animated sequences, video clips, sound, and music along with text and graphics. Just as words and pictures serve as the raw materials for desktop publishing, dynamic media such as animation, video, audio, and hypertext are important components of interactive multimedia projects.

Animation: Graphics in Time

We're on the threshold of a moment in cinematic history that is unparalleled. **Anything** you can **imagine** can be done. If you can **draw it**, if you can **describe it**, we can **do it**. It's just a matter of cost.

—*James Cameron, filmmaker*

Creating motion from still pictures—this illusion is at the heart of all animation. Before computers, artists drew animated films by hand, one still picture, or frame, at a time. Modern computer-graphics technology has transformed amateur and professional animation by automating many of the most tedious aspects of the animation process.

In its simplest form, the techniques used in creating computer-based animation are similar to traditional frame-by-frame animation techniques; each frame is a computer-drawn

FIGURE 6.15 Pixar has created a string of blockbuster feature films, including Wall-E, that use digital animation to create compelling characters and engaging stories.

Screen Test

Creating a Flash Animation

GOAL *To create an animated spaceship for a science fiction fan Web site.*

TOOLS *Flash from Adobe.*

1. You draw the ship and thrusters using the line, shape, and paint tools in the tools palette.

2. You draw the flame using the same tools. The spaceship, thrusters, and the flame are stored as separate objects—graphic symbols that can be manipulated over time in the animation.

3. Each object has its own timeline. You move the playback head through the flame's timeline, slightly changing the flame's shape at a few key frames.

4. To smooth the flame's motion, you use the Shape Tweening command between each pair of key frames.

5. Returning to the stage (main) timeline, you create keyframes for the beginning and end points of the spaceship's journey across the screen. You apply motion tweening to create a smooth movement between these two points. You preview the animation in Onion Skin mode to see multiple points in time on a single screen.

6. Using a masking effect, you cause text to appear in the wake of the moving ship. Your animation is now ready to publish on a Web page.

FIGURE 6.16

picture, and the computer displays those frames in rapid succession. With an animation program, an animator can create key frames and objects and use software to help fill in the movement of the objects in the in-between frames—a process known as *tweening*. The most powerful animation programs include tools for working with animated objects in three dimensions, adding depth to the scene on the screen.

Animation on the Web ranges from simple GIF animations to complex cartoon animations created with programs such as Adobe's Flash and Director. An animated GIF is simply a bundle of bitmapped GIF images that appear in a sequence similar to the pages of a children's flip book. A more sophisticated way to represent an animation is through the use of vector graphics. A vector graphics animation describes a collection of objects and how they change over time. The two most popular vector graphics formats are *Shockwave Flash Format (SWF)*, associated with the Adobe Flash player, and *Scalable Vector Graphics (SVG)*, an open standard promoted by the W3C.

As a way of representing Web animations, vector graphics animations have several advantages over animated GIFs. Vector graphics animations occupy less space, which means they can be downloaded faster. Because vector graphics animations describe images in terms of objects and locations, rather than colored pixels, it is possible to write software that makes the images look good on a wide variety of displays, such as those found on personal computers, pocket PCs, and cell phones. Finally, SVG files represent the words inside images as plain text characters. Future versions of Web search engines may include the contents of animations in their indexes, making it easier for them to return animations in response to queries.

Computer animation has become commonplace in everything from television commercials to feature films. Sometimes computer animation is combined with live-action film; Harry Potter, Spider-Man, the Terminator, and a host of other characters depend on computer animation to make their larger-than-life actions seem real. Other films, including *Toy Story, Shrek, Ratatouille,* and WALL-E use computer animation to create every character, scene, and event, leaving only the soundtrack for live actors and musicians to create.

FIGURE 6.17 The Lord of the Rings trilogy of films combined live action with computer-generated animation to bring J.R.R. Tolkein's fantasy world to life.

Desktop Video: Computers, Film, and TV

Digital technology is the **same revolution** as adding **sound** to pictures and the same **revolution** as adding **color** to pictures. **Nothing more** and **nothing less**.

—George Lucas, filmmaker

There's more to the digital video revolution than computer animation. Computers can be used to edit video, splice scenes, add transitions, create titles, and do other tasks in a fraction of the time—and at a fraction of the cost—of precomputer techniques. The only requirement is that the video be in a digital form so the computer can treat it as data.

Analog and Digital Video

In the twentieth century and the first part of the twenty-first century, almost all television programs, videos, and movies were stored and broadcast as analog (smooth) electronic waves. But analog video technology is rapidly being replaced by digital video technology. In the U.S., all new televisions (as of 2009) are digital. They receive signals that are broadcast as digital data. Many of these digital TVs are **HDTVs**—high definition televisions capable of receiving and displaying high-resolution images, videos, and broadcasts. New camcorders, from consumer grade to professional, are mostly all digital. Many big-screen films are captured using digital camcorders. And analog VHS videotapes have little relevance in a world of DVDs, Blu-Ray discs, and digital movie downloads. (Analog videos and broadcasts can be digitized—converted to a newer digital format—with a *video digitizer*. A video digitizer can be part of a consumer home entertainment system or part of a computer system.)

A digital camcorder might store data on mini-DV tapes, digital-8 tapes, rewritable optical discs, flash memory cards, or a hard disk—different models have different storage capabilities. Most digital video cameras have FireWire (IEEE 1394) ports (see Chapter 3) that can be used to copy raw video footage from camera to computer and later copy the edited video back from computer to camera. (Some consumer camcorders use USB 2.0 instead of FireWire for data transfer.) A camera connected to a computer can also bypass its own tape or disc storage and transfer images directly to a computer in *real time*—at the same time they're being captured by the camera's lens. Because digital video can be reduced to a series of numbers, it can be copied, edited, stored, and played back without any loss of quality.

Video Production Goes Digital

A typical video project starts with an outline and a simple *storyboard* describing the action, dialogue, and music in each scene. The storyboard serves as a guide for shooting and editing scenes.

Today, most video editing is done using *nonlinear editing (NLE)* technology. Because the video and audio clips are stored on the computer's

FIGURE 6.18 Software can turn a desktop or laptop computer into a video-editing and production station. Programs such as Apple's iMovie and iDVD (above right) make it easy for nonprofessionals to capture and edit video footage, add special effects and audio, and publish the finished movie on a DVD, tape, CD-ROM, or Web site. Professional programs, such as Apple's Final Cut Pro (above) and DVD Studio Pro (right), perform the same functions to the exacting standards of industry professionals.

hard disk(s), the editing can happen in any sequence—it isn't limited to the linear sequence of the video footage. Nonlinear editing is faster and easier than older editing techniques, and it allows filmmakers to do things that aren't possible without computers. Video editing makes massive storage and memory demands on a computer. Until recently, nonlinear editing technology was available only to professionals. But thanks to falling hardware prices and technological advances, even an off-the-shelf laptop PC or Mac can serve as a digital video studio.

Video-editing software, such as Adobe Premiere, Apple iMovie, and Microsoft Windows Movie Maker, makes it easy to eliminate extraneous footage, combine clips from multiple takes into coherent scenes, splice together scenes, insert visual transitions, superimpose titles, synchronize a soundtrack, and create special effects. High-end programs such as Final Cut Studio and Avid Media Composer go beyond the basics, providing professionals and serious amateurs with state-of-the-art video production tools. Just about anything is possible with these tools: color correction to compensate for a setting sun in a long shoot, chroma keying an ancient Roman background into a scene shot in front of a green screen, morphing a man into a werewolf, painting one or two frames with a surrealistic effect and applying that effect to an entire scene, and much more.

After it's edited, a video can be turned into a DVD or Blu-ray movie using software such as Apple's iDVD or Sonic's MyDVD. Video clips can also be imported into multimedia presentations using PowerPoint and other presentation programs. But many videos reach their widest audiences through the Web. TV networks, movie studios, and other businesses are distributing countless videos online—often for free. Many amateur videographers and performers distribute their works as video podcasts—programs delivered on demand or by subscription through iTunes or other Web outlets. And countless others post their work—and play—on YouTube.com and other video-friendly Web sites. YouTube has democratized video distribution like nothing that has come before it, creating instant celebrities, capturing politicians making compromising statements, and spreading ideas like viruses.

Data Compression

Digital movies can make heavy hardware demands; even a short full-screen video clip can quickly fill a large hard disk or CD-ROM. To save storage space and allow the processor to

FIGURE 6.19 Many Web sites deliver streaming video content to viewers with fast broadband Internet connections (left). Compressed video can also be displayed on a variety of pocket-sized devices, from iPods to cell phones (right).

keep up with the quickly changing frames, digital movies designed for the Web or CD-ROM are often displayed in small windows with fewer frames per second than the standard 30. In addition, data compression software and hardware squeeze data out of movies so they can be stored in smaller spaces, often with a slight loss of image quality, though formats such as MPEG-4 and Windows Media Video 9 lessen this problem. General data compression software can be used to reduce the size of almost any kind of data file; specialized *image-compression software* is generally used to compress graphics and video files. Modern media players, such as QuickTime and Windows Media Player, include several common software compression schemes. Some compression schemes involve specialized hardware as well as software.

Even highly compressed video clips gobble up storage space quickly. As compression and storage technologies continue to improve, digital movies will become larger, longer, smoother, and more common in everyday computing applications.

Professionals in the motion picture, television, and video industries create their products using graphics workstations that cost hundreds of thousands of dollars. Today, it's possible to put together a Windows- or Macintosh-based system that can perform most of the same graphics functions for a fraction of the cost. Low-cost desktop video systems are transforming the film and video industry in the same way that desktop publishing has revolutionized the world of the printed word. They're also making it possible for individuals, schools, and small businesses to create near-professional-quality videos.

The Synthetic Musician: Computers and Audio

Sound and music can turn a visual presentation into an activity that involves the ears, the eyes, and the whole brain. For many applications, sound puts the *multi* in *multimedia*. Computer sounds can be sampled—digitally recorded—or synthesized—

> It's **easy to play** any musical instrument: all you have to do is **touch the right key** at the right time and **the instrument will play itself**.
>
> —*J. S. Bach*

synthetically generated. Today's computers can produce sounds that go far beyond the basic beeps of early computers; most of them can also digitize sounds.

Digital Audio Basics

An audio digitizer can record just about any sound as a sample—a digital sound file. Digitized sound data, like other computer data, can be loaded into the computer's memory and manipulated by software. Sound-editing software can change a sound's volume and pitch, add special effects such as echoes, remove extraneous noises, and even rearrange musical passages. Sound data is sometimes called *waveform audio* because this kind of editing often involves manipulating a visual image of the sound's waveform. To play a digitized sound, the computer must load the data file into memory, convert it to an analog sound, and play it through a speaker.

Recorded sound can consume massive amounts of space on disk and in memory. As you might expect, higher-quality sound reproduction generally requires more memory. The difference is due in part to differences in *sampling rate*—the number of sound "snapshots" the recording equipment takes each second. A higher sampling rate produces more realistic digital sounds in the same way that higher resolution produces more realistic digital photographs; it allows for more accurate modeling of the analog source. The number of bits per sample—usually 8, 16, or 24 also affects the quality of the sound; this is similar to a digital photograph's bit depth.

Music is digitized on audio CDs at a high sampling rate and bit depth—high enough that it's hard to tell the difference between the original analog sound and the final digital recording. Because computers can read standard audio CDs, it's easy to *rip*, or copy, songs from a CD to the computer's hard drive, and *burn*, or create, audio CDs containing ripped songs.

But CD audio is memory intensive; a three-minute song takes about 30 megabytes of space on a compact disc. Files that large can be expensive to store and slow to transmit through

How It Works

6.1 Data Compression

Graphic images, digital video, and sound files can consume massive amounts of storage space on disk and in memory; they can also be slow to transmit over computer networks. Data-compression technology allows large files to be temporarily squeezed to reduce the amount of storage space and network transmission time they require. Before you can use them, you must decompress compressed files. (In the physical world, many companies "compress" goods to save storage and transportation costs: When you "just add water" to a can of concentrated orange juice, you're "decompressing" the juice.)

All forms of compression involve removing bits; the trick is to remove bits that can be replaced when the file can be restored. Different compression techniques work best for different types of data.

Suppose you want to store or transmit a large text file. Your text compression software might follow steps similar to those shown here:

1. Each character in the uncompressed ASCII file occupies eight bits; a seven-character word—*invoice,* for example—requires 56 bits of storage.

i n v o i c e

(space) p a y a b l e

Portion of a dictionary		
A	○○○○○○○○	○○○○○○○●
a	○○○○○○○○	○○○○○○●○
aback	○○○○○○○○	○○○○○●○○
abacus	○○○○○○○○	○○○○○●○○
. . .		
invoice	○○●○○●○●	○○●●●○○●
invoiced	○○●○○●○●	○○●●●○●○
invoke	○○●○○●○●	○○●●●○●●
. . .		
pay	○●○●○●●●	●○●○○○●○
payable	○●○●○●●●	●○●○○○●●
. . .		
zygote	●●●●●●●●	●●●●●●●●

2. A two-byte binary number can contain code values ranging from 0 to 65,535—enough codes to stand for every commonly used word in English. This partial code dictionary shows the code values for a few words, including *invoice* and *payable.*

3. To compress a file using a code dictionary, the computer looks up every word in the original file; in this example, *invoice* and *payable.* It replaces each word with its two-byte code value. In this example, they are % 9 and V ú. The seven-character word now takes up only 16 bits—less than one-third of its original size.

4. In a compressed file, these two-byte code values would be used to store or transmit the information for *invoice* and *payable,* using fewer bits of information either to increase storage capacity or to decrease transmission time.

% 9 V ú

5. To reverse the process of compression, the same dictionary (or an identical one on another computer) is used to decompress the file, creating an exact copy of the original. A computer program quickly performs all the tedious dictionary lookup.

FIGURE 6.20

Compression programs work on patterns of bits rather than on English words. One type of video compression stores values for pixels that change from one frame to the next; there's no need to store values repeatedly for pixels that are the same in every frame. For example, the only pixels that change in these two pictures are the ones that represent the unicycle and the shadows. In general, compression works because most raw data files contain redundancy that can be "squeezed out."

Lossless compression systems allow a file to be compressed and later decompressed without any loss of data; the decompressed file will be an identical copy of the original file. Popular lossless compression systems include ZIP, TAR, and DMG. GIF is a specialized lossless compression system for graphical images. A *lossy compression* system can usually achieve better compression than a lossless one, but it may lose some information in the process; the decompressed file isn't always identical to the original. This is tolerable in many types of sound, graphics, and video files but not for most program and data files. JPEG is a popular lossy compression system for graphics files.

MPEG is a popular compression system for audio and video. (MP3 and AAC are forms of MPEG compression that are widely used for digital audio.) An MPEG file takes just a fraction of the space of an uncompressed audio or video file. Because decompression programs demand time and processing power, the playback of compressed video files can sometimes be jerky or slow. Many professional video workstations get around the problem with MPEG hardware boards that specialize in compression and decompression, leaving the CPU free for other tasks.

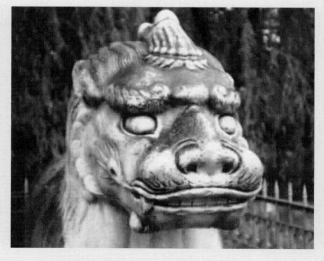

The original photographic image (above) has an uncompressed size of 725 KB. With aggressive JPEG compression, the image on the right occupies only 1/38 as much disk space (19 KB), but looks almost as good.

FIGURE 6.21 You can edit waveform audio files in a variety of ways using software tools such as Peak, from Bias, Inc.

networks. That's why many sound files are compressed during or after the recording process. Sound data compression, like image compression, can significantly shrink a file's size with little loss of quality from the listener's point of view. Several popular compression technologies, including **MP3** (MPEG-1 Audio Layer 3), *AAC* (Advanced Audio Codec), and *WMA* (Windows Media Audio), can squeeze audio files to a fraction of their original CD file sizes with only a slight loss of fidelity. Compression makes it practical to transmit recordings through the Internet, store them on hard disks, and play them on phones and other pocket-sized devices.

Free music files are available on hundreds of Web sites. Many are contributed by undiscovered musicians who want exposure. Others are ripped from CDs and distributed through illicit *peer-to-peer (P2P) file sharing* networks (giving a new meaning to the old phrase *ripped off*). Internet music piracy has taken a serious toll on the industry, robbing musicians and record companies and forcing the closure of countless record stores. But the net has also provided new legal channels for distributing music. Apple's iTunes Music Store, the giant of this emerging industry, has sold billions of songs at 99 cents each, becoming one of the world's biggest music retailers in the process. Customers play their purchases on their computers, burn them to CDs, and download them into iPods and other portable music players. Many competitors follow Apple's pay-by-the-song model; others rent access to music libraries on a month-by-month basis. Audio files are also distributed as **podcasts**—radio-style programs that can be downloaded on demand or automatically by subscription. (Ethical and legal issues raised by digital audio files will be discussed in more detail in Chapters 9 and 10.)

Samplers, Synthesizers, and Sequencers: Digital Audio and MIDI

Multimedia computers can control a variety of electronic musical instruments and sound sources using Musical Instrument Digital Interface (**MIDI**)—a standard interface used to send commands between computers and musical instruments. MIDI commands can be interpreted by a variety of music *synthesizers* (electronic instruments that synthesize sounds using mathematical formulas), *samplers* (instruments that can digitize, or sample, audio sounds, turn them into notes, and play them back at any pitch), and hybrid instruments that play sounds that are part sampled and part synthesized. But most PCs can also interpret and execute MIDI commands using sampled sounds built into their sound cards or stored in software form. Whether the sounds are played back on external instruments or internal devices, the computer doesn't need to store the entire recording in memory or on disk; it just has to store commands to play the notes in the proper sequence. A MIDI file containing the MIDI messages for a song or soundtrack requires only a few kilobytes of memory.

Anyone with even marginal piano-playing skills can create MIDI music files. A piano-style keyboard sends MIDI signals to the computer, which interprets the sequence of MIDI commands using **sequencing software**. (While the keyboard is the most common MIDI controller for sequencing, MIDI communication capabilities are built into other types of instruments, including drums, guitars, and wind instruments.) Sequencing software turns a computer into a musical composing, recording, and editing machine. The computer records MIDI signals as a musician plays each part on a MIDI controller. The musician can use the computer to layer instrumental tracks, substitute instrument sounds, edit notes, cut and paste passages, transpose keys, and change tempos, listening

Working Wisdom

Digital Audio Dos and Don'ts

Whether you are digitizing your audio CD collection or are subscribed to an online music service, your digital audio experiences will go more smoothly if you understand a few simple rules.

➡ **Don't steal.** It's OK to copy audio CDs to your PC, use those songs on portable audio devices, and mix CDs you create, but only if you own the originals. Don't "borrow" music from a friend or steal music online.

➡ **Understand downloading and streaming.** Music is typically delivered from the Web to your computer in one of three ways: downloadable audio, streaming audio, and pseudo-streaming audio. When you download an audio file (for example, from the iTunes Music Store or a band's Web site), your computer stores the entire file on its hard disk. Once the file is transferred from the server to your computer, it can be played by an application (such as iTunes), copied to another device (such as an iPod), backed up, used in a video project, burned to a CD, or edited, depending on the rights granted by the DRM (see below). Streaming audio—the type typically used by Internet radio stations—isn't downloaded to your computer's hard disk. Instead, it's played as it is being delivered to your computer. Once a segment of the audio file is played, it disappears from your computer's memory. Pseudo-streaming audio is downloaded to your hard disk, but it begins playing shortly after the first part of the file is transmitted.

➡ **Know your file formats.** Uncompressed audio CD files can gobble up hard disk space at an alarming rate. The MP3 compression format is popular because it produces files that sound almost identical to uncompressed audio files. But MP3 isn't the

FIGURE 6.22b The iTunes Music Store enables Mac and Windows users to purchase music by their favorite artists in a protected digital format. The purchases can be automatically synced onto an iPod.

only popular audio compression format. Many audio files are stored in the relatively new AAC format, which includes *digital rights management (DRM)* technology designed to protect the artists' intellectual property. Many Windows users prefer Microsoft's WMA format, which can offer quality comparable to MP3 at smaller file sizes; WMA also offers DRM capabilities.

➡ **Don't overcompress.** Audio compression is lossy, so there's always a loss of quality when you compress a sound file. There's no way to put back the bits that you squeeze out in the compression process. Most people can't distinguish between a 160 Kbps MP3 file or a 128 Mbps AAC or WMA file and an original audio CD recording. But if you choose too low a bit rate when compressing a file, you may squeeze the life out of the music.

Format	Description
WAV, AIFF	Standard formats for uncompressed audio for Windows and the Mac OS, respectively. Both formats are supported on Windows, Mac OS, and Linux. Both create large files. Both are lossless—a CD track encoded with WAV or AIFF sounds identical to the original.
MP3	A popular format for transmitting audio on the Internet. A CD track converted to MP3 format can be 1/10 the size of the original—or smaller—but still sound very similar.
WMA	An alternative to MP3 developed by Microsoft for Windows. WMA compression can result in smaller files of higher fidelity. WMA files may be protected by DRM.
AAC	Apple's alternative to MP3 and WMA is used primarily by iTunes and the iTunes Music Store. AAC compression is sonically superior to MP3 compression. AAC files may be protected with DRM.
OGG	Similar to WMA and AAC in sound quality and compression, Ogg Vorbis is open source and freely available — not controlled by any company.

FIGURE 6.22a Popular Digital Audio Formats.

FIGURE 6.23 Digital audio technology has revolutionized the music recording process for hobbyists and professionals alike.

to each change as it's made. The finished composition can be played by the sequencing software or exported to any other MIDI-compatible software, including a variety of multimedia applications.

Music recording and composition software isn't limited to sequencing MIDI commands; most programs can record digital audio tracks as well as MIDI tracks, making it possible to include voices and non-electronic instruments in the mix. The audio and MIDI data is recorded directly onto the computer's hard disk, making tape unnecessary.

A typical electronic music studio includes a variety of synthesizers, samplers, and other instruments. But the trend today is to replace many bulky, expensive hardware devices with *virtual instruments*—instruments that exist only in software. With today's powerful CPUs and massive storage devices, it's possible to have a professional-level multitrack recording and editing studio that fits in a suitcase.

Most musicians today use *DAW (digital audio workstation)* software that incorporates sequencing, recording, and mixing capabilities in a single program. Mixing involves combining multiple tracks, adding audio effects, and balancing volumes and audio placement for the best possible recording. The final mix might take the form of a mono recording for a podcast, a stereo recording for a CD, a multi-channel surround sound mix for a DVD soundtrack, or something else. Some audio artists specialize in creating *remixes*—complete reworking of songs using fresh instrumentation, rhythms, and audio samples.

Professional musicians use computers for composing, performing, recording, mixing, and publishing music, and for educating would-be musicians. Digital audio technology cuts across genres; it's used for everything from Bach to rock. The technology has spawned whole new branches of music that fit loosely into a category called *electronica*—music designed from the ground up with digital technology. Just as computer graphics technology has changed the way many artists work, electronic music technology has transformed the world of the musician. What's more, computer music technology has the power to unleash the musician in the rest of us.

FIGURE 6.24 Music software allows musicians to put Mac and Windows PCs to work in a variety of ways. Serato Scratch Live (top) is a software and hardware-based tool that allows DJs to mix music from hard drives using turntables as control devices. Pro Tools (middle) is widely used for recording, sequencing, and editing music. Sibelius (bottom) is a music notation program that can create sheet music from MIDI files and other sources.

How It **Works**

6.2 Computer-Based Music Production

Music-processing software comes in a variety of forms, but most programs are built on the same fundamental concepts. A musical composition is typically made up of several tracks that represent individual instrumental and vocal parts. For example, a song might have a lead vocal track, a guitar track, a bass track, a drum track, and three backup vocal tracks. You can record and edit each of these tracks separately; you can play them back in any combination.

A software mixer can adjust the relative volumes to achieve the desired balance before you mix the piece down to a final digital stereo recording. The same principles apply for acoustic, electric, or electronic music; the differences between these types of music are reflected mainly in the way the individual tracks are created and stored. Most software can work with two kinds of tracks: digital audio samples, represented as waveforms, and MIDI sequences, depicted as a series of bars representing notes.

1. Real-world instruments and sounds can be sampled by plugging an instrument or microphone into the sound in port on the computer. You can also buy professionally-recorded samples and legally use them in your music productions.

2. Any sample, such as this recording of a percussionist playing a drum kit, can be looped, so that the sample repeats as many times as necessary to reach the desired length.

3. Because waveforms are stored as a series of numbers, many music production tools use math to manipulate those numbers and alter qualities, such as the tempo, pitch, and volume of the recording.

4. Software-based filters can be used to manipulate the sonic qualities of your samples and loops; this particular effect lends an acoustic, echo-filled, ethereal quality to the guitar part.

5. MIDI instruments send performance information, such as when and where each note is played in a sequence and how hard each note is struck. Because MIDI stores your performance as a series of notes rather than an audio sample, you are able to later correct notes, transpose to a different key, alter the tempo, and even change the instrument used to play back your performance. You can easily correct for human error using a feature known as quantizing, which cleans up the timing of a passage by "rounding off" performance data to the nearest points on the rhythmic grid.

FIGURE 6.25

6. Software allows you to control characteristics of sound over time. For example, the master volume controller fades the song out as it nears the song's end.

7. A finished composition can be output in a variety of forms.

8. The final mix can be exported as a stereo waveform.

11. Compression software can produce a much smaller sound file.

12. You can download the compressed audio file into an iPod or other portable music player.

9. Speakers or headphones attached to the computer provide the most direct output, giving the composer and performers immediate sonic feedback.

13. You can upload a compressed audio file to the Web and share it with the online community as a podcast.

10. You can burn the stereo file onto an audio CD.

14. You can import the audio file into a video-editing program for use in a movie soundtrack.

Screen Test

Multimedia on a Student Budget

Professional multimedia software can be very expensive. It's not unusual to pay hundreds—or even thousands—of dollars for state-of-the-art software tools for creating and manipulating graphic images, animation, video, or audio files. If you're creative but cash-poor, you can take advantage of many low-cost or free alternatives to the big-ticket packages. Here's a sampler:

For photo library organization and basic image editing, it's hard to beat iPhoto (left), part of the iLife suite that ships with every Mac. Windows users can download Google Picasa (above), a free program with similar capabilities.

For more advanced photo retouching, Adobe offers a cross-platform browser-based tool called Photoshop Express.

Google SketchUp is a cross-platform 3-D modeling tool. Google provides a 3-D warehouse for searching, sharing, and downloading 3-D models.

FIGURE 6.26

Apple's iTunes is hard to beat for organizing large libraries of music and sounds. It's free for Macs and Windows PCs, and it integrates seamlessly with the iTunes Store. It can also handle movies, TV shows, and video and audio podcasts.

Audacity is a free cross-platform program with a rich selection of audio recording and editing tools. (Mac users also have Garage Band, a popular and powerful multitrack recording studio that's included with iLife; see "Computer-Based Music Production," page 214.)

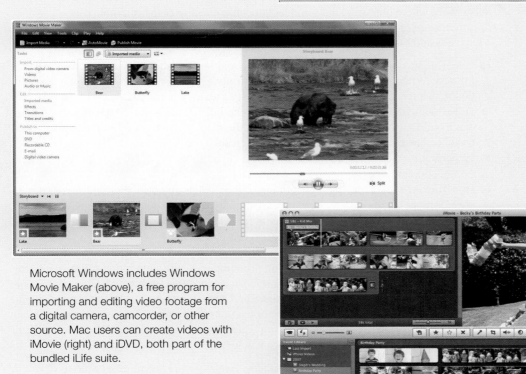

Microsoft Windows includes Windows Movie Maker (above), a free program for importing and editing video footage from a digital camera, camcorder, or other source. Mac users can create videos with iMovie (right) and iDVD, both part of the bundled iLife suite.

Hypertext and Hypermedia

Human beings are naturally predisposed **to hear, to remember, and to tell stories**. The **problem**—for teachers, parents, government leaders, friends, and **computers**—is to have **more interesting stories** to tell.

—*Roger Schank et al., in* Tell Me a Story: Narrative and Intelligence

Word processors, drawing programs, and most other applications today are WYSIWYG—what you see (on the screen) is what you get (on the printed page). But WYSIWYG isn't always necessary or desirable. If a document doesn't need to be printed, it doesn't need to be structured like a paper document. If we want to focus on the relationship between ideas rather than the layout of the page, we may be better off with another kind of document—a dynamic, cross-referenced super document that takes full advantage of the computer's interactive capabilities.

Since 1945 when President Roosevelt's science advisor, Vannevar Bush, first wrote about such an interactive cross-referenced system, computer pioneers such as Doug Engelbart and Ted Nelson, who coined the term hypertext, pushed the technology toward that vision. Early efforts were called hypertext because they allowed textual information to be linked in *nonsequential* ways. Conventional text media, such as books, are linear, or *sequential*: They are designed to be read from beginning to end. A hypertext document contains links that can lead readers quickly to other parts of the document or to other related documents. Hypertext invites readers to cut their own personal trails through information.

Hypertext first gained widespread public attention in 1987 when Apple introduced HyperCard, a hypermedia system that could combine text, numbers, graphics, animation, sound effects, music, and other media in hyperlinked documents. (Depending on how it's used, the term hypermedia might be synonymous with interactive multimedia.) Today, millions of Windows and Macintosh users routinely use hypertext whenever they consult online Help files, and handheld computer and Tablet PC users navigate hypermedia-enabled ebooks. But the biggest hotbed of hypertext/hypermedia activity is the World Wide Web, where hypertext links connect documents all over the Internet.

But in spite of its popularity, hypertext isn't likely to replace paper books any time soon. Web users and others who use hypertext have several legitimate complaints:

- Hypermedia documents can be disorienting and leave readers wondering what they've missed. When you're reading a book, you always know where you are and where you've been in the text. That's not necessarily true in hypermedia.
- Hypermedia documents don't always have the links readers want. Hypermedia authors can't build every possible connection into their documents, so some readers are frustrated because they can't easily get "there" from "here."
- Hypermedia documents sometimes contain "lost" links, especially on the Web, where even a popular page can disappear without a trace.
- Hypermedia documents don't encourage scribbled margin notes, highlighting, or turned page corners for marking key passages. Some hypermedia documents provide controls for making "bookmarks" and text fields for adding personal notes, but they aren't as friendly and flexible as traditional paper mark-up tools.
- Hypermedia hardware can be hard on humans. Most people find that reading a computer screen is more tiring than reading printed pages, although modern font-rendering software such as Microsoft ClearType seeks to reduce this problem. Many people complain that extended periods of screen-gazing cause eyestrain, headache, backache, and other ailments. It's not always easy to stretch out under a tree or curl up in an easy chair with a Web-linked computer, though notebooks and Tablet PCs are making anywhere/everywhere computing more viable.

The art of hypermedia is still in its infancy. Every new art form takes time to develop. How can writers develop effective plot lines if they don't know what path their readers will choose through their stories? This is just one of the hundreds of questions with which hypermedia authors are struggling. Still, hypermedia is not all hype. As the art matures, advances in software and hardware design will take care of many of these problems. Even today hypermedia documents provide extensive cross-referencing, flexibility, and instant keyword searches that simply aren't possible with paper media.

Interactive Multimedia: Eye, Ear, Hand, and Mind

We live in a world rich in sensory experience. Information comes to us in a variety of forms: pictures, text, moving images, music, voice, and more. As information-processing machines, computers are capable of delivering information to our senses in many forms. Until recently, computer users could work with only one or two forms of information at a time. Today's multimedia computers allow users to work with information-rich documents that intermix a variety of audiovisual media.

> The hybrid or the meeting of two media is a **moment of truth and revelation** from which a **new form** is born.
>
> —*Marshall McLuhan, in* Understanding Media: The Extensions of Man

Interactive Multimedia: What Is It?

The term multimedia generally means using some combination of text, graphics, animation, video, music, voice, and sound effects to communicate. By this definition an episode of *Sesame Street* or the evening news might be considered multimedia. In fact, computer-based multimedia tools are used heavily in the production of *Sesame Street*, the evening news, and hundreds of other television programs. Entertainment-industry professionals use computers to create animated sequences, display titles, construct special video effects, synthesize music, edit soundtracks, coordinate communication, and perform dozens of other tasks crucial to the production of modern television programs and motion pictures.

So when you watch a typical TV program, you're experiencing a multimedia product. With each second that passes, you are bombarded with millions of bits of information. But television and video are passive media; they pour information into our eyes and ears while we sit and take it all in. We have no control over the information flow. Modern computer technology allows information to move in both directions, turning multimedia into interactive multimedia. Unlike TV, radio, and video, interactive multimedia allows the viewer/listener to take an active part in the experience. The best interactive multimedia software puts the user in charge, allowing that person to control the information flow.

Interactive multimedia software is delivered to consumers on a variety of platforms. Today, multimedia computers equipped with fast processors, large memories, CD-ROM or DVD-ROM drives, speakers, and sound cards are everywhere. Thousands of education and entertainment multimedia programs are available on

FIGURE 6.27 Interactive multimedia CD-ROMs and DVDs often combine education with entertainment. Google Sky extends Google's ambitious mapping projects to the heavens. The World Book combines an encyclopedia with other reference tools in an easy-to-use interactive package.

CD-ROM and DVD-ROM for these machines. Many more multimedia software titles are designed to be used with television sets and controlled by game machines and other *set-top boxes* from Sony, Microsoft, Nintendo, and other companies. Many multimedia documents are created for use in kiosks in stores, museums, and other public places. A typical multimedia kiosk is a PC-in-a-box with a touch screen instead of a keyboard and mouse for collecting input.

Interactive multimedia materials are all over the Web, too. But multimedia on the Web today is full of compromises because many of today's Web pipelines can't deliver large media files quickly enough. Still, Web technology is improving rapidly, and more people are connecting to the Net with faster broadband technology, making many experts wonder whether disk-based multimedia will eventually be unnecessary. In the meantime, cable, telephone, and other companies are rushing to provide multimedia services, including video on demand.

Multimedia Authoring: Making Mixed Media

Style used to be an interaction between the **human soul** and **tools** that were **limiting**. In the digital era, it will have to come from **the soul alone**.

—*Jaron Lanier, virtual reality pioneer*

Multimedia-authoring software is used to create and edit multimedia documents. Similar to desktop publishing, interactive multimedia authoring involves combining source documents—including graphics, text files, video clips, and sounds—in an aesthetically pleasing format that communicates with the user. Multimedia-authoring software, like page-layout software, serves as glue that binds documents created and captured with other applications. But since a multimedia document can change in response to user input, authoring involves specifying not just *what* and *where* but also *when* and *why*. Some authoring programs are designed for professionals. Others are designed for children. Many are used by both.

FIGURE 6.28 Multimedia authoring involves programming objects on the screen to react, or behave, in particular ways under particular circumstances. Adobe Flash allows you to create advanced interactivity using scripts and prewritten behaviors that can be attached to on-screen buttons, images, and other objects.

Some authoring programs, including HyperStudio and MetaCard, use the card-and-stack user interface originally introduced with Apple's HyperCard. According to this metaphor, a multimedia document is a stack of cards. Each screen, called a card, can contain graphics, text, and **buttons**—hot spots that respond to mouse clicks. Buttons can be programmed to transport the user to another card, play music, open dialog boxes, launch other applications, rearrange information, perform menu operations, send messages to hardware devices, or do other things. Some authoring programs, including ToolBook, use a similar user interface with a book-and-page metaphor: A book replaces the stack and a page replaces the card. The World Wide Web uses metaphorical pages to represent screens of information; many authoring tools are designed specifically to create Web pages. The most widely used professional multimedia-authoring tool, Adobe's Director, has a different kind of user interface. A Director document is a movie rather than a stack of cards or a book of pages. A button can transport a user to another frame of a movie rather than to another card or page. Adobe Flash, a popular tool for adding multimedia to the Web, is based on an interface similar to

Working Wisdom

Creating an Effective Interactive Experience

Whether you're creating a simple presentation or a full-blown multimedia extravaganza, your finished product will communicate more effectively if you follow a few simple guidelines:

➡ **Be consistent.** Group similar controls together, and maintain a consistent visual appearance throughout the presentation.

➡ **Make it intuitive.** Use graphical metaphors to guide viewers, and make your controls do what they look like they should do.

➡ **Strive for simplicity.** A clean, uncluttered screen is more inviting than a crowded one—and easier to understand, too.

➡ **Keep it lively.** If your presentation doesn't include motion, sound, or user interaction, it probably should be printed and distributed as a paper document.

➡ **The message is more important than the media.** Your goal is to communicate information, not saturate the senses. Don't let the bells and whistles get in the way of your message.

➡ **Put the user in the driver's seat.** Include controls for turning down sound, bypassing repetitive animation, and turning off annoying features. Provide navigation aids, search tools, bookmarks, online help, and "Where am I?" feedback. Never tell the user, "You can't get there from here."

➡ **Let real people test your designs.** The best way to find out whether your multimedia works is to test it on people who aren't familiar with the subject. If they get lost or bored, find out why, fix the problem, and test it again.

These two screens from a multimedia CD-ROM portfolio use interactive motion menus and a consistent, intuitive user interface to guide the user through the disk's contents.

FIGURE 6.29

Director's. Some authoring tools, such as Authorware, use flowcharts as tools for constructing documents.

The authoring tool's interface metaphor is important to the person creating the multimedia document, but not to the person viewing the finished document, who sees only the user interface that was built into the document by the author. When you're using a well-designed multimedia document, you can't tell whether it was created by Director, Authorware, or another authoring tool.

With the growing interest in the Internet, many people expect the Web to replace CD-ROMs for most multimedia delivery. Most multimedia-authoring tools can create Web-ready multimedia documents. For example, by using Adobe's Shockwave technology, you can convert documents created by Authorware and Director into Web documents. Shockwave software compresses multimedia documents so they can appear and respond more quickly on the Web. But even with compression, the Internet isn't fast enough to deliver the high-quality audio and video that's possible with CD-ROM and DVD-ROM. On the other hand, the contents of a disc are static; they can't be continually updated like a Web site. And CD-ROMs don't offer opportunities for communication with other people the way a Web site can. Many multimedia manufacturers today produce hybrid discs—media-rich CD-ROMs and DVD-ROMs that automatically draw content and communication from the Web. Hybrid discs hint at the types of multimedia experiences that will be possible without discs through tomorrow's faster Internet.

Multimedia-authoring software today puts a great deal of power into the hands of computer users, but it doesn't solve all the technical problems in this new art form. Many of the problems with hypertext and hypermedia outlined earlier are even more serious when multiple media are involved. Still, the best multimedia productions transcend these problems and show the promise of this emerging technology.

Interactive Media: Visions of the Future

For most of recorded history, the **interactions of humans with their media** have been **primarily passive** in the sense that marks on paper, paint on walls, even motion pictures and television, **do not change** in response to the viewer's wishes. (But computers can) **respond to queries and experiments**—so that the message may involve the learner in a **two-way conversation**.

—Alan Kay

For hundreds of thousands of years, two-way interactive communication was the norm: One person talked, another responded. Today television, radio, newspapers, magazines, and books pour information into billions of passive people every day. For many people, one-way passive communication has become more common than interactive discourse.

According to many experts, interactive multimedia technology offers new hope for turning communication back into a participatory sport. With interactive multimedia software, the audience is a part of the show. Interactive multimedia tools can give people control over the media—control traditionally reserved for professional artists, filmmakers, and musicians. The possibilities are far-reaching, especially when telecommunication enters the picture. Consider these snapshots, all of which are possible with today's technology.

- Instead of watching your history professor flip through overhead transparencies, you control a self-paced interactive presentation complete with video footage illustrating key concepts.
- Using an electronic whiteboard, a professor's writings are automatically transmitted to your wireless notebook or Tablet PC, allowing you to take notes on what he says, not what he writes. Students can present questions in real time, using an electronic ballot.
- In your electronic mailbox you find a "letter" from your sister. The letter shows her performing all of the instrumental parts for a song she composed, followed by a request for you to add a vocal line.
- Your favorite Internet show is an interactive thriller that allows you to control the plot twists and work with the main characters to solve mysteries.

■ While working on a biology project in the field, you come across an unusual bird with a song you don't recognize. Using a pocket-sized digital device, you record some audio/video footage of the bird as it sings. Using the same device, you dial your project partner's phone number and send the footage for editing and analysis. You legally download tracks from several of your favorite bands and remix them into a mashup combining elements from all of those tracks; then you use that as the soundtrack for a re-edited scene from one of your favorite movies.

■ You share your concerns about a proposed factory in your hometown at the televised electronic town meeting. Thousands of others respond to questions from the mayor by pressing buttons on their remote control panels. The overwhelming citizen response forces the city council to reconsider the proposal.

Of course, the future of interactive multimedia may not be all sunshine and roses. Many experts fear that these exciting new media possibilities will further remove us from books, other people, and the natural world around us. If television today can mesmerize so many people, will tomorrow's interactive multimedia TVs cause even more serious addiction problems? Or will interactive communication breathe new life into the media and the people who use them? Will interactive electronic media make it easier for abusers of power to influence and control unwary citizens, or will the power of the push button create a new kind of digital democracy? Will interactive digital technology just turn "sound bites" into "sound bytes," or will it unleash the creative potential in the people who use it? For answers, stay tuned.

FIGURE 6.30 Animators at Pixar Studios work on film projects, including *Finding Nemo* and *The Incredibles*. Many of these projects spawn games, educational software programs, and other interactive multimedia products.

Inventing the FUTURE

Shared Virtual Spaces

What I'm hoping is that **inside virtual worlds**, eventually, people can both have the **power and excitement of imagination** while also **being connected** with other people because the virtual world is really **shared with the real world**, even though you make it up.

—*Jaron Lanier, virtual reality pioneer*

Tomorrow's multimedia is likely to extend beyond the flat screen, creating immersive experiences that challenge our notion of reality.

VIRTUAL REALITY

Since the 1960s researchers have experimented with *virtual worlds*—computer-generated worlds that create the illusion of immersion. Virtual worlds typically involve special hardware; for input, a glove or body suit equipped with motion sensors, and for output, a head-mounted display—a helmet with eye-sized screens with views that change as the helmet moves. This equipment, when coupled with appropriate software, enables the user to explore an artificial world of data as if it were three-dimensional physical space. Virtual reality combines virtual worlds with networking, placing multiple participants in a virtual space. People see representations of each other, sometimes called *avatars*. Most avatars today are cartoonish, but they convey a sense of presence and emotion.

TELE-IMMERSION

Jaron Lanier, who coined the term *virtual reality*, is a multimedia artist and computer scientist known for his research in tele-immersion. Tele-immersion uses multiple cameras and high-speed networks to create an environment in which multiple remote users can interact with each other and with computer-generated objects. (Lanier was a consultant for Spielberg's *Minority Report*, a movie that shows a similar technology.) Tele-immersion combines virtual reality techniques with new vision technologies that allow participants to move around in shared virtual spaces, while maintaining their unique points of view. Today's systems require participants to wear special glasses; future versions may not.

Tele-immersion systems, when coupled with high-speed internet connections, will allow engineers, archaeologists, and artists,

FIGURE 6.31a Virtual reality (VR) pioneer Jaron Lanier.

FIGURE 6.31b Using an experimental system at Columbia University, this student explores the campus with a unique historical perspective. He can see and walk around a 3-D image of the Bloomingdale Asylum—the previous occupant of the campus space—in its original location; additional historical information is displayed on his handheld tablet.

among others, to collaborate long-distance in shared virtual workspaces. It may allow musicians and actors to give personal interactive performances. Tele-immersion may significantly reduce the need for business travel within a decade.

AUGMENTED REALITY

Another promising offshoot of VR research is augmented reality (AR)—the use of computer displays that add virtual information to a person's sensory perceptions. Unlike VR, AR supplements rather than replaces the world the user sees.

The first-down line that's superimposed on TV football fields is a simple example of AR, but the future offers many more practical applications. With AR, a repair person might see instructions superimposed on a machine part; a surgeon might see inside a patient with live ultrasound scans of internal organs overlaid on the patient's body; a firefighter might see the layout of a burning building.

AR researcher Steven K. Feiner predicts "the overlaid information of AR systems will become part of what we expect to see at work and at play: labels and directions when we don't want to get lost, reminders when we don't want to forget and, perhaps, a favorite cartoon character popping out from the bushes to tell a joke when we want to be amused. When computer user interfaces are potentially everywhere we look, this pervasive mixture of reality and virtuality may become the primary medium for a new generation of artists, designers, and storytellers who will craft the future." ∼

Bits, Bands and Books *by Paul Krugman*

The digitization of intellectual property is having a profound impact on businesses old and new. In this June 6, 2008 Op-Ed column for the New York Times, *Paul Krugman ties together newspapers, electronic books, Esther Dyson, and the Grateful Dead. The results are thought provoking.*

Do you remember what it was like back in the old days when we had a New Economy? In the 1990s, jobs were abundant, oil was cheap and information technology was about to change everything.

Then the technology bubble popped. Many highly touted New Economy companies, it turned out, were better at promoting their images than at making money—although some of them did pioneer new forms of accounting fraud. After that came the oil shock and the food shock, grim reminders that we're still living in a material world.

So much, then, for the digital revolution? Not so fast. The predictions of '90s technology gurus are coming true more slowly than enthusiasts expected—but the future they envisioned is still on the march.

In 1994, one of those gurus, Esther Dyson, made a striking prediction: that the ease with which digital content can be copied and disseminated would eventually force businesses to sell the results of creative activity cheaply, or even give it away. Whatever the product—software, books, music, movies—the cost of creation would have to be recouped indirectly: businesses would have to "distribute intellectual property free in order to sell services and relationships."

For example, she described how some software companies gave their product away but earned fees for installation and servicing. But her most compelling illustration of how you can make money by giving stuff away was that of the Grateful Dead, who encouraged people to tape live performances because "enough of the people who copy and listen to Grateful Dead tapes end up paying for hats, T-shirts and performance tickets. In the new era, the ancillary market is the market."

Indeed, it turns out that the Dead were business pioneers. *Rolling Stone* recently published an article titled "Rock's New Economy: Making Money When CDs Don't Sell." Downloads are steadily undermining record sales—but today's rock bands, the magazine reports, are finding other sources of income. Even if record sales are modest, bands can convert airplay and YouTube views into financial success indirectly, making money through "publishing, touring, merchandising and licensing."

What other creative activities will become mainly ways to promote side businesses? How about writing books?

According to a report in *The Times*, the buzz at this year's BookExpo America was all about electronic books. Now, e-books have been the coming, but somehow not yet arrived, thing for a very long time. (There's an old Brazilian joke: "Brazil is the country of the future—and always will be." E-books have been like that.) But we may finally have reached the point at which e-books are about to become a widely used alternative to paper and ink.

That's certainly my impression after a couple of months' experience with the device feeding the buzz, the Amazon Kindle. Basically, the Kindle's lightness and reflective display mean that it offers a reading experience almost comparable to that of reading a traditional book. This leaves the user free to appreciate the convenience factor: the Kindle can store the text of many books, and when you order a new book, it's literally in your hands within a couple of minutes.

It's a good enough package that my guess is that digital readers will soon become common, perhaps even the usual way we read books.

How will this affect the publishing business? Right now, publishers make as much from a Kindle download as they do from the sale of a physical book. But the experience of the music industry suggests that this won't last: once digital downloads of books become standard, it will be hard for publishers to keep charging traditional prices.

Indeed, if e-books become the norm, the publishing industry as we know it may wither away. Books may end up serving mainly as promotional material for authors' other activities, such as live readings with paid admission. Well, if it was good enough for Charles Dickens, I guess it's good enough for me.

Now, the strategy of giving intellectual property away so that people will buy your paraphernalia won't work equally well for everything. To take the obvious, painful example: news organizations, very much including this one, have spent years trying to turn large online readership into an adequately paying proposition, with limited success.

But they'll have to find a way. Bit by bit, everything that can be digitized will be digitized, making intellectual property ever easier to copy and ever harder to sell for more than a nominal price. And we'll have to find business and economic models that take this reality into account.

It won't all happen immediately. But in the long run, we are all the Grateful Dead.

Discussion Questions

1. Do you agree that "Everything that can be digitized will be digitized"?

2. What kinds of businesses will be hurt the most by the digitization of intellectual property? What kinds will be helped?

Summary

Computer graphics today encompass more than quantitative charts and graphs generated by spreadsheets. Bitmapped painting programs enable users to "paint" the screen with a mouse, pen, or other pointing device. The software stores the results in a pixel map, with each pixel having an assigned color. The more possible colors there are and the higher the resolution (pixel density) is, the more the images can approach photorealism. Object-oriented (vector) graphics programs also allow users to draw on the screen with a pointing device, with the results stored as collections of geometric objects rather than as maps of computer bits.

Bitmapped graphics and object-oriented graphics each offer advantages in particular situations; trade-offs involve editing and ease of use. Both types of graphics have applications outside the art world. Bitmapped graphics are used in high-resolution image-processing software for on-screen photo editing. Object-oriented graphics are at the heart of 3-D modeling software and computer-aided design (CAD) software used by architects, designers, and engineers. Presentation-graphics software, which may include either one or both graphics types, automates the process of creating slides, transparencies, handouts, and computer-based presentations, making it easy for nonartists to create visually attractive presentations.

With today's computers, you aren't limited to working with static images; they're widely used to create and edit documents in media that change over time or in response to user interaction. For animation and digital video work, PCs mimic many of the features of expensive professional workstations at a fraction of the cost. Similarly, today's PCs can perform a variety of sound- and music-editing tasks that used to require expensive equipment and numerous musicians.

The interactive nature of the computer makes it possible to create nonlinear documents that enable users to take individual paths through information. Early nonlinear documents were called hypertext because they could contain only text. Today, we can create or explore hypermedia documents—interactive documents that mix text, graphics, sounds, and moving images with on-screen navigation buttons—on disk and on the World Wide Web.

Multimedia computer systems make a new kind of software possible—software that uses text, graphics, animation, video, music, voice, and sound effects to communicate. Interactive multimedia documents are available for desktop computers, video game machines, set-top boxes connected to televisions, and (especially) the Web. Regardless of the hardware, interactive multimedia software enables the user to control the presentation rather than watch or listen passively. Only time will tell whether these new media will live up to their potential for enhancing education, training, entertainment, and cultural enrichment.

Key Terms

3-D modeling software ....(p. 197)
animation ....(p. 202)
audio digitizer.......................(p. 207)
augmented reality (AR).........(p. 224)
bit depth..................................(p. 190)
bitmapped graphics ....(p. 190)
bullet charts ....(p. 198)
button......................................(p. 220)
color depth.............................(p. 190)
compression...........................(p. 207)
computer-aided design
 (CAD)................................(p. 198)
computer-aided manufacturing
 (CAM) ....(p. 198)
computer-integrated manufacturing
 (CIM)................................(p. 198)

digital video...........................(p. 204)
drawing software ....(p. 195)
frame.......................................(p. 202)
gray-scale graphics ....(p. 190)
hypermedia ....(p. 218)
hypertext.................................(p. 218)
image processing software ....(p. 193)
interactive multimedia..........(p. 219)
MIDI......................................(p. 210)
mixing....................................(p. 212)
MP3 ....(p. 210)
multimedia.............................(p. 219)
multimedia-authoring
 software ....(p. 220)
object-oriented graphics ....(p. 195)
painting software ....(p. 189)

palette ....(p. 189)
PDF (portable document
 format) ....(p. 195)
pixel.......................................(p. 189)
podcast...................................(p. 210)
presentation-graphics
 software ....(p. 199)
public domain.......................(p. 194)
resolution...............................(p. 190)
sample....................................(p. 207)
sequencing software ....(p. 210)
synthesized ....(p. 207)
tele-immersion......................(p. 224)
vector graphics ....(p. 195)
video-editing software...........(p. 206)
virtual reality ....(p. 224)

Interactive Activities

1. The *Tomorrow's Technology and You* Web site, **www.pearsonhighered.com/beekman**, contains self-test exercises related to this chapter. Follow the instructions for taking a quiz. After you've completed your quiz, you can email the results to your instructor.

True or False

1. PDF is a standard format that allows various applications, including illustration and desktop publishing programs, to freely exchange documents.

 2. Photographic image-editing software can produce images so realistic that some now question the validity of photographic evidence in the courtroom.

3. Based on trends in animation technology today, it's likely that the first fully computer-animated feature-length film will be released in the second decade of the twenty-first century.

4. <u>Sequencing</u> software allows musicians to record audio and <u>MIDI</u> tracks, edit them, and play them back.

5. Because uncompressed video requires massive amounts of storage, virtually all digital video files are compressed.

6. Through the use of mathematical formulas, vector graphics represent lines, shapes, and characters as objects.

7. Hypermedia is a term referring to a fast-paced computer animation style.

8. Most successful interactive multimedia user interfaces are based on metaphors of real-world experiences.

9. Presentation-graphics programs, such as Microsoft PowerPoint, can automatically generate pie charts and bar charts but not bullet charts.

10. The Web is the major delivery medium for interactive multimedia today.

Multiple Choice

1. Computer animation today
   a. is almost always 2-D animation.
   b. is not 3-D because the computer's display is limited to two dimensions.
   c. is almost always indistinguishable from live action.
   d. is routinely combined with live action to create television special effects.
   e. All of the above.

2. Which kind of technology are photographic image-editing programs largely based on?
   a. Object-oriented graphics
   b. Presentation graphics
   c. Bitmapped graphics
   d. Quantitative graphics
   e. CAD/CAM graphics

3. If a photographic image looks fine when displayed on a computer screen but appears jagged and rough when printed, the problem has to do with the image's
   a. bit depth.
   b. dimensions.
   c. vector.
   d. raster.
   e. resolution.

4. Which of the following might professional artists, seeking an input device that can more accurately simulate a pen or paintbrush, choose to draw with?
   a. A mouse
   b. A joystick
   c. A trackball
   d. A stylus on a pressure-sensitive pad
   e. An infrared system that tracks their eye movements

5. Which technology is 3-D graphics software based largely on?
   a. Object-oriented graphics
   b. Presentation graphics
   c. Bitmapped graphics
   d. Photographic image-editing software
   e. Hypermedia

6. A well-designed slide for a presentation typically
   a. contains at least eight bullet points.
   b. uses at least three different fonts.
   c. contains most or all of the words in the accompanying speech.
   d. has a focal point for drawing in the viewer's eyes.
   e. has at least two different animated objects to keep viewer interest.

7. Data compression is commonly used for reducing the file size of
   a. digital photographs.
   b. digital video clips.
   c. digital music files.
   d. digital text files.
   e. All of the above.

8. The process of tweening in animation is similar to which of these video concepts?
   a. Mixing
   b. Morphing
   c. Sequencing
   d. Synthesizing
   e. Sampling

9. What must you do to use a computer to edit footage captured with a digital video camera?
   a. Install a video digitizer in the PC.
   b. Import the video footage using a FireWire cable or the equivalent.
   c. Digitize the video footage.
   d. Store the video clips on a DVD.
   e. All of the above

10. During the nonlinear video editing process, the edited video and audio clips are typically stored on
    a. tape.
    b. optical disks.
    c. CD-ROM.
    d. thumb drives.
    e. hard disk(s).

11. When a musician plays an electronic keyboard in a music studio, the sounds that it plays might be
    a. synthesized sounds generated by the keyboard.
    b. sampled sounds stored in the instrument's memory.
    c. generated by another electronic instrument connected to the keyboard via MIDI.
    d. created using virtual instruments in a PC.
    e. Any or all of the above.

12. Why is MP3 a popular format for music file sharing?
    a. MP3 files typically contain video as well as audio data.
    b. MP3 files work equally well for text, graphics, and music.
    c. MP3 compression reduces file sizes considerably with minimal loss of music quality.
    d. MP3 compression is lossless.
    e. MP3 files contain DRM technology.

13. Why is a MIDI file of a Beethoven piano concerto much smaller than a CD audio file of the same piece?
    a. MIDI uses efficient MP3 technology.
    b. MIDI uses MPEG-4 compression.
    c. MIDI uses software rather than hardware for compression.
    d. The MIDI file contains only instructions for playing notes; the note sounds are stored in the computer or musical instrument.
    e. Actually, MIDI files are larger than MP3 files.

14. What does hypermedia software give computer users?
    a. Nonsequential access to text, numbers, graphics, music, and other media
    b. Incredibly fast access to documents stored anywhere on the Web
    c. Instantaneous downloading of full-length feature movies
    d. Immersive virtual-reality interaction with other computer users
    e. All of the above

15. What is the most important difference between an interactive multimedia version of *Sesame Street* and a *Sesame Street* television program?
    a. The interactive multimedia version allows the viewer to have more control over the experience.
    b. The interactive multimedia version offers a richer mix of media types.
    c. The interactive multimedia version requires a joystick or game controller.
    d. The interactive multimedia version can't be displayed on a standard TV screen.
    e. The interactive multimedia version exists only in theory; it's not technically possible yet.

Review Questions

1. Define or describe each of the key terms listed in the "Key Terms" section. Check your answers using the glossary.

2. Describe several practical applications for 3-D modeling and CAD software.

3. Why is compression an important part of digital audio technology?

4. Remixing songs has become popular as a result of the emergence of digital audio technology. Explain why these two trends are related.

5. What is the difference between bitmapped graphics and object-oriented graphics? What are the advantages and disadvantages of each?

6. Which two technological factors limit the realism of a bitmapped image? How are these related to the storage of that image in the computer?

7. What are the main disadvantages of hypermedia when compared with conventional media such as books and videos?

8. Is it possible to have hypermedia without multimedia? Is it possible to have multimedia without hypermedia? Explain your answers.

9. What is the main advantage of storing a graphic image as a PDF file?

10. How do hypertext and other hypermedia differ from linear media?

11. Explain how virtual instruments make it possible to create and edit music tracks without using physical musical instruments.

12. Presentation graphics software can produce good presentations and bad presentations. Describe several factors that distinguish the two.

Discussion Questions

1. How does modern digital image-processing technology affect the reliability of photographic evidence? How does digital audio technology affect the reliability of sound recordings as evidence? How should our legal system respond to this technology?

2. Many people enjoy creating mashups—hybrid songs or videos combining pieces of many other songs or videos. Because many of the original songs and videos are copyrighted, this kind of activity can violate copyright laws. Do you think the law should allow this kind of creative expression?

3. Thanks to modern electronic music technology, one or two people can make a recording that would have required dozens of musicians 20 years ago. What impact will electronic music technology ultimately have on the music profession?

4. Digital technology makes it easier than ever for people to violate copyright laws. What, if anything, should be done to protect the intellectual property rights of the people who create pictures, videos, and music? Under what circumstances do you think it's acceptable to copy sounds or images for use in your own work?

5. Try to answer each of the questions posed at the end of the "Interactive Media: Visions of the Future" section.

Projects

1. Draw a familiar object or scene using a bitmapped painting program. Draw the same object or scene with an object-oriented drawing program. Describe how the process changed using different software.

2. Produce a ten-minute video on a subject related to one of your classes. Begin by creating a storyboard outlining the action, dialogue, and music in each scene. Use a digital video camera to record the scenes. Download the video and music files into a computer. Edit the movie using a video-editing software package such as Adobe Premier, Apple iMovie, or Microsoft Windows Movie Maker 2. Save the finished movie onto videotape or DVD. Reflect on the movie production process. Describe possible improvements to the software that would have made your job easier.

3. Compose some original music using a synthesizer, a computer, and a sequencer. Reflect on the process of producing the piece of music. Describe possible improvements to the software that would have made your job easier.

4. Modify a photograph using an image-processing software package, such as Adobe Photoshop. If the photograph is not already in digital form, use a scanner to create a digitized image. With the image-processing software, add some special effects that demonstrate the power of a computer to create images that cannot be seen in the "real world." Which image-processing tools were easiest to use? Which tools were hardest to use?

5. Create visual aids for a speech or lecture using presentation-graphics software. In what ways did the software make the job easier? What limitations did you find?

Sources and Resources

Books

Most of the best graphics, video, music, and multimedia applications books are software specific. When you decide on a software application, choose books based on your chosen software and on the type of information you need. If you want quick answers with a minimum of verbiage, you'll probably be delighted with a book from Peachpit's *Visual Quickstart* series. Most of the titles in the following list aren't keyed to specific applications.

Weaving the Web: The Original Design and Ultimate Destiny of the World Wide Web, by Tim Berners-Lee. (San Francisco, CA: Harper San Francisco, 1999). This is the story of the creation of the Web straight from the word processor of the man who did it. Few people in history have had more impact on the way we communicate than this unassuming man.

Graphic Communications Dictionary, by Daniel J. Lyons (Upper Saddle River, NJ: Prentice Hall, 2000). This is an excellent alphabetic reference for anyone wrestling with the terminology of graphic design.

The New Drawing on the Right Side of the Brain: A Course in Enhancing Creativity and Artistic Confidence, by Betty Edwards and Jeremy P. Tarcher (Los Angeles, CA: J. P. Tarcher, 1999). If you're convinced you have no artistic ability, give this book a try; you might surprise yourself.

Digital Photography Top 100 Simplified Tips & Tricks, Third Edition, by Rob Sheppard (Hoboken, NJ: John Wiley & Sons, 2007). If you want to take pictures that are more than snapshots, this highly graphical book can help. It's packed with useful tips accompanied by clear illustrations.

Photoshop CS3 for Windows and Macintosh: Visual Quickstart Guide, by Elaine Weinmann and Peter Lourekas (Berkeley, CA: Peachpit Press, 2007). Peachpit's *Visual Quickstart Guides* are popular because they provide maximum instruction for a minimal investment of time. This Photoshop guide is one of the best. Using lots of pictures and few words, it unlocks the secrets of the program that is the industry standard for professional photo- and bitmap-editing software.

Adobe Creative Suite 3 Bible, by Ted Padova and Kelly L. Murdock (Hoboken, NJ: John Wiley & Sons, 2007). The Adobe Creative Suite includes Photoshop, InDesign, Acrobat, Illustrator, Flash, and other industrial-strength digital media applications. Many books cover individual applications; this one provides an overview of the entire package.

The Art of 3-D Computer Animation and Effects, Third Edition, by Isaac V. Kerlow (New York, NY: John Wiley & Sons, 2004). Films such as *Shrek* and *Finding Nemo* have turned 3-D graphics into a big business and a popular art form. This book clearly explains the technology that makes it all possible.

Presentation Zen: Simple Ideas on Presentation Design and Delivery, by Garr Reynolds (Indianapolis, IN: New Riders, 2008). There's more to a successful presentation than bullet charts. This book deals with the entire presentation experience. Audiences everywhere will be better served if their presenters read this book before turning on the projector.

Becoming a Digital Designer: A Guide to Careers in Web, Video, Broadcast, Game and Animation Design, by Steven Heller and David Womack (Hoboken, NJ: John Wiley & Sons, 2008). The title says it all: This is the book to read if you want to break into the field of digital design.

Real World Digital Video, Second Edition, by Pete Shaner and Gerald Everett Jones (Berkeley, CA: Peachpit Press, 2004). This book covers the entire video production process, from buying equipment to producing a final video product. You can avoid many of the pitfalls of video production by reading this book before you start.

Developing Digital Short Films, by Sherri Sheridan (Indianapolis, IN: New Riders, 2004). This illustrated guide is a great companion for budding digital filmmakers. The focus is on the art of storytelling through video, rather than technical trivia. An accompanying CD-ROM includes a music video project, tools, and demo software.

Real World Digital Audio: Industrial-Strength Production Techniques, by Peter Kirn (Berkeley, CA: Peachpit Press, 2006). This excellent book covers an amazing amount of ground—the basics of sound, choosing audio gear, setting up a studio, recording, mixing, sound editing, adding sound to video, performing with laptops, and more. It includes a disk full of software, sounds, and other resources. Great for beginners and more experienced audio creators.

Sound Unbound: Sampling Digital Music and Culture, edited by Paul D. Miller (Cambridge, MA: MIT Press, 2008). This wide-ranging collection of essays puts 21st century digital culture in perspective. In this book Paul Miller, aka DJ Spooky, asks artists to describe their experiences and thoughts related to the digital arts revolution. The result is a thought-provoking mashup of ideas.

Secrets of Podcasting: Audio Blogging for the Masses, Second Edition by Bart G. Farkas (Berkeley, CA: Peachpit Press, 2006). The podcast is one of the most democratic of the new media. With a minimal hardware investment, just about anybody can create a personalized audio or video program and distribute it through the net to computers, iPods, and other digital delivery devices all around the world. This book clearly explains the technology and provides instructions for creating and distributing your own audio podcasts.

Crafting Multimedia Text: Websites and Presentations, by Barbara Moran (Upper Saddle River, NJ: Prentice Hall, 2005). Writing for computer screens is different than writing for paper. Writer Barbara Moran draws on her experience as a journalist, a dot-com editor, and an educator to produce this clear, concise guide to writing for new media.

Digital Media: An Introduction, by Richard Lewis and James Luciana (Upper Saddle River, NJ: Prentice Hall, 2005). This text, specifically written for students of art and design, provides a broad overview of digital media, including history, hardware, applications, and lots of colorful examples.

Understanding Media: The Extensions of Man, by Marshall McLuhan (Cambridge, MA: MIT Press, 1994). This classic, originally published in 1964, explores the relationship of mass media to the masses. The new introduction in this thirtieth anniversary reissue reevaluates McLuhan's visionary work 30 years later.

In the Realm of the Circuit: Computers, Art, and Culture, by Charles H. Traub and Jonathan Lipkin (Upper Saddle River, NJ: Prentice Hall, 2004). This colorful book roams far and wide to put digital media in a bigger context. The authors argue that digital technology is radically transforming the ways we create, design, and communicate. By creatively juxtaposing images and ideas from the worlds of technology and art, they provide powerful insights into the digital cultural revolution.

Multimedia: From Wagner to Virtual Reality, Expanded Edition, edited by Randall Packer and Ken Jordan (New York, NY: Norton, 2002). This collection of essays by William Burroughs, John Cage, Tim Berners-Lee, and others offers a broad overview of the historical roots of multimedia.

7

Database Applications and Privacy Implications

Objectives

After you read this chapter you should be able to:

▌ Explain what a database is and describe its basic structure

▌ Identify the kinds of problems that can best be solved with database software

▌ Describe different kinds of database software, from simple file managers to complex relational databases

▌ Describe database operations for storing, sorting, updating, querying, and summarizing information

▌ Give examples of ways in which large, easily accessible databases make our lives safer or more convenient

▌ Explain how databases threaten our privacy

The Google Guys Search for Tomorrow

By any measure Google is one of the great success stories of the Internet age. The Google search engine handles hundreds of millions of queries a day—the majority of all Web search requests. To many Web users, the term "google" is synonymous with "search" (as in, "Have you googled yourself lately?") People use Google to find facts, search for images, shop, locate other people, and even do background checks on blind dates. Today, Google is far more than a search engine—it's the most visited Web site on the planet.

Google was launched by two Stanford Ph.D. computer science students from opposite sides of the globe. Sergey Brin was born in Moscow; Larry Page was from Michigan. In 1996, Page started a research project to improve Web search engines. Early search engines ranked pages by counting how many times the searched-for word or phrase appeared on the page. Sites could fool these search engines by repeating a particular phrase hundreds of times.

Page teamed up with Brin to write BackRub, a search engine that determined a Web page's relevance by counting the number of times *other* related Web pages linked to it.

Page borrowed money and built a Web server in his dorm

FIGURE 7.1 Sergey Brin and Larry Page

room; Brin's dorm room became the business office. In 1998, Page and Brin raised $1 million and officially launched Google. (The name Google is a play on the huge number *googol*—a 1 followed by 100 zeroes.) The start-up operated out of a garage. Today, Google has thousands of employees around the globe.

In 2004, Google offered shares to the public, making Brin and Page instant billionaires. Google's management defied convention by establishing procedures to keep the company focused on long-term strategies rather than short-term profits. In their letter to potential investors, Brin and Page wrote, "Google is not a conventional company. We do not intend to become one."

Google's relaxed corporate culture is anything but conventional, but it has placed the company at the top of *Fortune*'s list of the hundred best places to work. According to Google's philosophy, "work should be challenging and the challenge should be fun." Engineers are encouraged to spend 20 percent of their time on projects that interest them. One personal project turned into Gmail, the free email service; another became Google News, a widely-used news and blog reader; many other pet projects have become successful products.

Today Google products and services include Google AdWords and AdSense, leading online advertising services; YouTube, the hub of the Web's video culture; Google Maps and Google Earth, 2D and 3D interactive global mapping tools; GoogleDocs, an online suite of office applications; Google Desktop, a PC file searching tool; and a rapidly-growing fleet of PC, Web, and enterprise applications. In 2008, Google opened its digital doors to outside developers, providing them with a free

FIGURE 7.2 Google headquarters viewed using Google Earth, a free application that combines satellite imagery, maps, and Google's search engine.

platform for building and sharing their projects. In every venture, Google tries to honor its do-no-evil mission statement.

But Google's phenomenal growth has occasionally challenged that mission. For example, in 2005 Google, like many other companies, agreed to allow the Chinese government to censor certain searches made by Chinese citizens; company officials decided that it was better to have a restricted presence in the most populous country in the world than not to be there at all. Google has also been criticized as a threat to personal privacy, copyright laws, and the environment (because of the massive amounts of energy consumed by their servers).

In spite of occasional growing pains, the company continues to soar. By combining database technology with a seemingly endless supply of creative ideas, Google is having an enormous impact on our lives. ∼

We live in an information age. We're bombarded with information by television, radio, newspapers, magazines, books, and computers. It's easy to be overwhelmed by the sheer quantity of information we're expected to deal with each day. Computer applications, such as word processors and spreadsheets, can aggravate the problem by making it easier for people to generate more documents full of information.

A *database program* is a data manager that can help alleviate information overload. Databases make it possible for people to store, organize, retrieve, communicate, and manage information in ways that wouldn't be possible without computers. To control the flood of information, people use databases of all sizes and shapes—from massive mainframe database managers that keep airliners filled with passengers, to computerized appointment calendars on palmtop computers, to public database kiosks in shopping malls.

First the good news: information at your fingertips can make your life richer and more efficient in a multitude of ways. Ready cash from street-corner ATMs, instant airline reservations from the Web at any time of the day, catalog shopping with overnight mail-order delivery, exhaustive online searches in seconds—none of these conveniences would be possible without databases.

Now the bad news: Some of the information stored in databases is about you and your activities, and you have little or no control over who has it and how it is used. Ironically, the database technology that liberates us in our day-to-day lives is, at the same time, chipping away at our privacy. We explore both sides of this important technology in this chapter.

The Electronic File Cabinet: Database Basics

The next best thing to **knowing**, is knowing **where to find it**.

—Samuel Johnson

We start by looking at the basics of databases. Like word processors, spreadsheets, and graphics programs, database programs are applications—programs for turning computers into productive tools. If a word processor is a computerized typewriter and a spreadsheet is a computerized ledger, you can think of a database program as a computerized file cabinet.

While word processors and spreadsheets generally are used to create printed documents, database programs are designed to maintain *databases*—collections of information stored on computer disks. A database can be as simple as a list of names and addresses, or as complex as an airline reservation system. A recipe file, a library's card catalog, a business inventory file, a school's student grade records, an index file of business contacts, a catalog of your music collection, or a list of Web sites—just about any collection of information can be turned into a database.

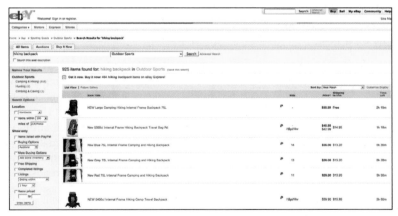

FIGURE 7.3 Internet auction Web sites, such as eBay, wouldn't be possible without database technology.

What Good Is a Database?

Why do people use computers for information-handling tasks that can be done with index cards, three-ring binders, or file folders? Computerized databases offer several advantages over their paper-and-pencil counterparts:

- *Databases make it easier to store large quantities of information.* If you have only 20 or 30 albums, it may make sense to catalog them in a notebook. But if you have 2,000 or 3,000 albums, your notebook may become as unwieldy as your music collection. The larger the mass of information, the bigger the benefit of using a database.
- *Databases make it easier to retrieve information quickly and flexibly.* It might take a minute or more to look up a phone number in a card file or telephone directory, but the same job can be done in seconds with a database. If you look up 200 numbers every week, the advantage of a database is obvious. That advantage is even greater when your search doesn't match your file's organization. For example, suppose you have a phone number on a scrap of paper and you want to find the name and address of the person

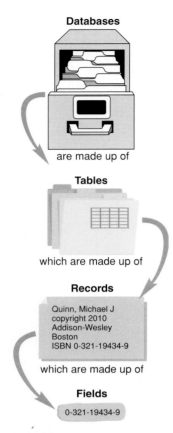

Databases

are made up of

Tables

which are made up of

Records

Quinn, Michael J
copyright 2010
Addison-Wesley
Boston
ISBN 0-321-19434-9

which are made up of

Fields

0-321-19434-9

FIGURE 7.4

with that number. That kind of search may take hours if your information is stored in a large address book or file alphabetized by name, but the same search is almost instantaneous with a computerized database.

■ *Databases make it easy to organize and reorganize information.* Paper filing systems force you to arrange information in one particular way. Should your book catalog be organized by author, by title, by publication date, or by subject? There's a lot riding on your decision because if you decide to rearrange everything later, you will waste a lot of time. With a database, you can instantly switch between these organizational schemes as often as you like; there's no penalty for flexibility.

■ *Databases make it easy to print and distribute information in a variety of ways.* Suppose you want to send letters to hundreds of friends inviting them to your postgraduation party. You'll need to include directions to your place for out-of-towners but not for home-towners. A database, when used with a word processor, can print personalized form letters, including extra directions for those who need them, and print preaddressed envelopes or mailing labels in a fraction of the time it would take you to do it by hand and with less likelihood of error. You can even print a report listing invitees sorted by ZIP code so you can suggest possible car pools. (And if you want to bill those who attend the party, your database can help with that, too.)

Database Anatomy

As you might expect, a specialized vocabulary is associated with databases. Unfortunately, some terms take on different meanings depending on their context, and different people use these words in different ways. We'll begin by charting a course through marketing hype and technical terminology to find our way to the definitions most people use today.

For our purposes, a **database** is a collection of information stored in an organized form in a computer, and a **database program** is a software tool for organizing storage and retrieval of that information. A variety of programs fit this broad definition, ranging from simple address book programs and other list managers to massive inventory-tracking systems. We explore the differences between types of database programs later in the chapter, but for now we treat them as if they are more or less alike.

Early PC databases were simple file managers; they made it easy for users to store, organize, and retrieve information—names, numbers, prices, whatever—from structured data files. This type of data management is really list management since these files are just structured lists. Today's spreadsheet software can easily handle this kind of simple list management. Today's database software isn't limited to this kind of simple file management; it can handle complex tasks involving multiple data files.

A database is typically composed of one or more tables. A **table** is a collection of related information; it keeps that information together the way a folder in a file cabinet does. If a database is used to record sales information for a company, separate tables might contain the relevant sales data for each year. For an address database, separate tables might hold personal and business contacts. It's up to the designer of the database to determine whether information in different categories is stored in separate tables, which are, in turn, stored in files on the computer's disk.

A database table is organized into records. A **record** is the information related to one person, product, or event. In the library's card catalog database, a record is equivalent to one card with information about a book. In an address book database, a record contains information about one person. A photo catalog database would have one record per picture.

Each discrete chunk of information in a record is called a **field**. A record in the library's card catalog database would contain fields for author, title, publisher, address, date, and title code number. Your music database could break records into fields by title, artist, and so on.

The type of information a field can hold is determined by its *field type* or *data type*. For example, the author field in the library database would be defined as a text field, so it could contain text. A field specifying the number of copies of a book would be defined as a *numeric field*, so it could contain only numbers—numbers that can be used to calculate totals and other arithmetic formulas, if necessary. A date-of-purchase field might be a *date field* that could contain only date values. In addition to these standard field types, many database programs allow fields to contain graphics, digitized photographs, sounds, or video clips. **Computed fields** contain formulas similar to spreadsheet formulas; they display values calculated from values in other numeric fields. For example, a computed field called GPA might contain a formula for calculating a student's grade point average using the grades stored in other fields.

Most database programs provide you with more than one way to view the data, including *form views*, which show one record at a time, and *list views*, which display several records in lists similar to a spreadsheet. In any view, you can rearrange fields without changing the underlying data.

FIGURE 7.5 The two windows, created with FileMaker's Bento, show the form (front) and list (back) views of a database.

Database Operations

Information has **value**, but it is as **perishable** as fresh fruit.

—*Nicholas Negroponte, founder and director of the MIT Media Lab*

After the structure of a database is defined, it's easy to enter information; it's just a matter of typing. Typing may not even be necessary if the data already exists in some computer-readable form. Most database programs can easily **import data** or receive data in the form of text files created with word processors, spreadsheets, or other databases. When information changes or errors are detected, records can be modified, added, or deleted.

Browsing

The challenging part of using a database is retrieving information in a timely and appropriate manner. Information is of little value if it's not accessible. One way to find information is to **browse** through the records of the database just as you would if they were paper forms in a notebook. Most database programs provide keyboard commands, on-screen buttons, and other tools for navigating quickly through records. But this kind of electronic page turning offers no particular advantage over paper, and it's painfully inefficient for large databases. Fortunately, most database programs include a variety of commands and capabilities that make it easy to get the information you need when you need it.

Database Queries

The alternative to browsing is to ask the database for specific information. In database terminology, an information request is called a **query**. A query may be a simple **search** for a specific record (say, one containing information on Abraham Lincoln) or a request to **select** *all* records that match a set of criteria (for example, records for all U.S. presidents who served more than one term). After you've selected a group of records, you can browse

Screen Test

Creating a Database
Running Log

GOAL *To create a database to track your running that will allow you to record your improvement over time and track your progress.*

TOOL *Microsoft Access and Microsoft Excel, parts of Microsoft Office*

1. You create a simple list in Excel containing one column for every field you'd like to have in your database, using the information about your most recent run. Excel guesses the format of each column from the data you enter. For example, Calories Burned is recognized as a number, and Start is automatically recognized as a time.

2. You import the spreadsheet into Microsoft Access as a table.

3. Access uses the spreadsheet as a model for the new database, and creates labels and fields to match the spreadsheet's structure and format.

4. Your database is now structurally sound, but it's not very pretty or easy to use. You create a new "Form view" layout that will allow you to quickly and easily record data from your runs.

5. You've rearranged the layout and sequence of the fields, but it contains the same fields.

6. You might add another view of the data—perhaps one that calculates your running time, miles per hour, and distance over time. You might share the database with your running buddies so you can compare statistics. This basic database can be customized in all kinds of ways.

FIGURE 7.6

through it, produce a printout, or do just about anything else you might do with the complete table. Many databases allow you to record, or store, commonly used queries so you can access them quickly in the future. The ability to generate a *stored query* is a powerful feature that helps databases blur the line between application programs and development tools.

Sorting Data

Sometimes it's necessary to rearrange records to make the most efficient use of data. For example, a mail-order company's customer file might be arranged alphabetically by name for easy reference, but it must be rearranged in order by ZIP code to qualify for postal discounts on bulk catalog mailings. A sort command allows you to arrange records in alphabetic or numeric order based on values in one or more fields.

Printing Reports, Labels, and Form Letters

In addition to displaying information on the screen, database programs can produce a variety of printouts. The most common type of database printout is a report—an ordered list of selected records and fields in an easy-to-read format. Most business reports arrange data in tables with rows for individual records and columns for selected fields; they often include summary lines containing calculated totals and averages for groups of records.

You can also use database programs to produce mailing labels and customized form letters. Many database programs don't actually print letters; they simply export data, or transmit the necessary records and fields, to word processors with mail merge capabilities, which then take on the task of printing the letters.

Complex Queries

Queries may be simple or complex, but either way they must be precise and unambiguous. With appropriate databases, queries could be constructed to find the following:

- In a hospital's patient database, the names and locations of all of the patients on the hospital's fifth and sixth floors
- In a database of airline flight schedules, the least expensive way to fly from Boston to San Francisco on Tuesday afternoon
- In a politician's database, all voters who contributed more than $1,000 to last year's legislative campaign and who wrote to express concern over gun control laws since the election

These may be legitimate targets for queries, but they aren't expressed in a form that most database programs can understand. The exact method for performing a query depends on the user interface of the database software. Most programs enable the user to specify the rules of the search by filling in a dialog box or a blank on-screen form. Some require the user to type the request using a special query language that's more precise than English is. For example, to view the records for males between 18 and 35, you might type

Select * From Population Where
Sex = 'M' and Age $>=$ 18 and Age $<=$ 35

Many database programs include programming languages, so queries can be included in programs and performed automatically when the programs are executed. Although the details of the process vary, the underlying logic is consistent from program to program.

Most modern database-management programs support a standard language called SQL (from *Structured Query Language*; often pronounced "sequel") for programming complex queries. Because SQL is available for many different database-management systems, programmers and sophisticated users don't need to learn new languages when they work with different hardware and software systems. Users are usually insulated from the complexities of the query language by graphical user interfaces that allow point-and-click queries.

Querying a Web Search Database

GOAL *To research the use of solar and micro hydro energy to provide electricity for remote indigenous communities.*

TOOL *Any Web browser*

1. You go to google.com and type ecuador OR micro OR hydro OR indigenous to find Web sites that contain those four words.

2. The search reveals that more than four hundred million pages contain at least one of the four target words. Your search strategy was flawed. Most of the articles listed for "solar" probably have nothing to do with indigenous peoples, so you've selected a large collection of mostly irrelevant titles.

3. You put "micro hydro" in quotes so Google will show only pages that contain that whole phrase. You also remove the ORs, knowing that Google assumes AND between words or phrases, so it will show only pages that contain "solar" AND "micro hydro" AND "indigenous."

4. The search reveals 1,160 pages that contain all three phrases, including some at the top of the list that look relevant.

5. Switching OR to an assumed AND in this example reminds you of the importance of choosing every word carefully when defining a database query. If you don't find what you're looking for in this list, you might need to try different search strategies or search engines.

FIGURE 7.7

Special-Purpose Database Programs

Specialized database software is preprogrammed for specific data storage and retrieval purposes. Users of special-purpose databases don't generally need to define file structures or design forms because these details have been taken care of by the software's designers. In fact, some special-purpose database programs are not even sold as databases; they have names that more accurately reflect their purposes.

Directories and Geographic Information Systems

For example, an electronic phone directory can pack millions of names and phone numbers onto a Web site or CD-ROM. Using an *electronic phone directory* for the United States, you can track down phone numbers of people and businesses all over the country—even if you don't know where they are. You can look up a person's name if you have the phone number or street address. You can generate a list of every dentist in town—any town. Then using another type of specialized database, an *electronic street atlas*, you can pinpoint each of your finds on a freshly printed map. Many street atlases are designed to work with global positioning system (GPS) receivers on laptop, handheld, or automobile-based computers. GPS satellites feed location information to GPS receivers; mapping software uses that information to provide location feedback for travelers and mobile workers.

Geographical information systems (GISs) go beyond simple mapping and tracking programs. A GIS allows a business to combine tables of data, such as customer sales lists with demographic information from the U.S. Census Bureau and other sources. The right combination can reveal valuable strategic information. For example, a stock brokerage firm can pinpoint the best locations for branch offices based on average incomes and other neighborhood data; a cable TV company can locate potential customers who live close to existing lines. Because GISs can display geographic and demographic data on maps, they enable users to see data relationships that might be invisible in table form.

Personal Information Managers

One type of specialized database program is often called a **personal information manager (PIM)**. This type of program can automate some or all of the following functions:

- *Address/phone book.* Software address books provide options for quickly displaying specific records and printing mailing labels, address books, and reports. Some include automatic phone-dialing options and fields for recording phone notes.
- *Appointment calendar.* A typical PIM calendar enables you to enter appointments and events and display or print them in a variety of formats, ranging from one day at a time to a monthly overview. Many include built-in alarms for last-minute reminders and ways to share your calendar electronically with other users.
- *To-do list.* Most PIMs enable users to enter and organize ongoing lists of things to do and archive lists of completed tasks.
- *Miscellaneous notes.* Some PIMs accept diary entries, personal notes, and other hard-to-categorize tidbits of information.

PIMs have long been popular among people with busy schedules and countless contacts. They're easier to understand and use than general-purpose database programs, and they're faster and more flexible than their leather-bound paper counterparts. For people on the go, PIMs work especially well with notebook computers or handheld computers. For example, software in Blackberries, iPhones, Windows Mobile and Palm PDAs enables those devices to synchronize with PIM software on desktop computers. This instant data linking makes it easy to keep up-to-date personal information in and out of the office.

Many organizations use networkable tools such as Microsoft Outlook that go beyond the basic features of PIM software. These systems enable networked coworkers to share calendars and contacts easily and often include email and other communication tools along with basic PIM features. The Web offers another alternative: several Web sites provide free PIM software that you can access from any Web-accessible computer; many of these applications also permit workgroups to share calendars and other information.

How It **Works**

7.1 The Language of Database Queries

Years ago, the number of incompatible database languages made it difficult for people using different applications to access the same database. In the mid-1970s, IBM's E. F. Codd proposed a standardized Structured English Query Language, which evolved into SQL. With SQL, users and programmers have a standard way to create, access, and update databases. SQL is not a database-management system. Instead, it's the most important standard database language. SQL statements are understood by MS Access, MS SQL Server, DB2, Oracle, Sybase, MySQL (a popular open-source database), and many other database programs.

SQL is not a full-featured programming language like Java or C#. It's a sublanguage tailored for the database environment. Sometimes SQL statements are embedded inside computer programs written in COBOL, C, or other programming languages. Database-management systems also support a call-level interface that accepts individual SQL commands.

The selection rules for SQL are consistent and understandable whether queries are simple or complex. This simple example is designed to give you an idea of how they work.

SQL combines the familiar database concepts of tables, rows (records), and columns (fields), and the mathematical idea of a set. We will illustrate a simple SQL command using the Rental Vehicles database from Clem's Transportation Rental ("If it moves, we rent it."). Here's a complete listing of the database records.

Vehicle_ID	Vehicle_Type	Transport_Mode	Num_Passengers	Cargo_Capacity	Rental_Price
1062	Helicopter	Air	6	500	$1,250.00
1955	Canoe	Water	2	30	$5.00
2784	Automobile	Land	4	250	$45.00
0213	Scooter	Land	1	0	$10.00
0019	Minibus	Land	8	375	$130.00
3747	Balloon	Air	3	120	$340.00
7288	HangGlider	Air	1	5	$17.00
9430	Sailboat	Water	8	200	$275.00
8714	Powerboat	Water	4	175	$210.00
0441	Bicycle	Land	1	10	$12.00
4759	Jet	Air	9	2300	$2,900.00

A typical SQL statement filters the records of a database, capturing only those that meet the specific criteria. For example, suppose you wanted to list the ID numbers and types of the vehicles that travel on land and cost less than $20.00 per day. The SQL statement to perform this task would look like this:

```
SELECT Vehicle_ID, Vehicle_Type FROM Rental_Vehicles WHERE
Transport_Mode = 'Land' AND Rental_Price < 20.00
```

FIGURE 7.8

In English, this SQL statement says, "Show me (from the Rental Vehicles database) the vehicle IDs and vehicle types for those vehicles that travel by land and cost less than $20.00 per day to rent."

Two rows in the database meet these criteria, the scooter and bicycle:

```
0213 Scooter
0441 Bicycle
```

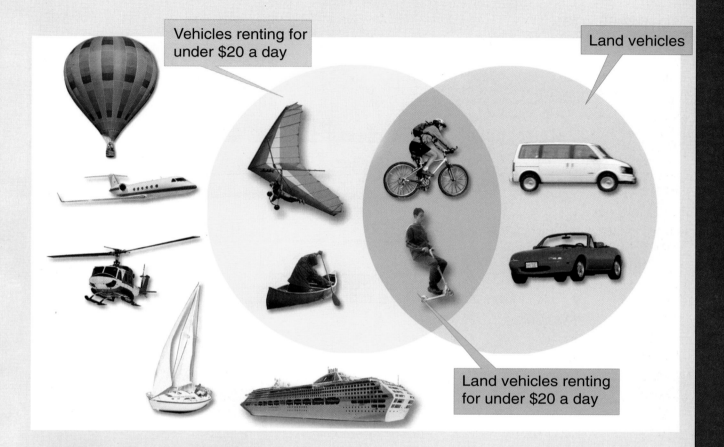

Many factors have led to the success of SQL, including its high-level, easy-to-understand statements, its relational database orientation, and its portability across a wide range of systems ranging from personal computers to mainframes. Interestingly, SQL has benefitted both from being vendor independent and from being supported by products from IBM and Microsoft. The large number of SQL databases in place around the world, combined with the multitude of software professionals familiar with SQL, guarantees that SQL will play an important role in the database scene for many years to come.

Screen Test

Synchronizing Data Between Outlook and Portable Devices

GOAL *To ensure the calendar and contacts list on your PC and all of your portable devices are up to date.*

HARDWARE TOOLS *PC computer, Apple iPod Touch Nokia 6682 phone, Palm Tungsten E2 personal digital assistant (PDA), connector cables*

SOFTWARE TOOLS *Microsoft Outlook, iPodSync, Nokia PC Suite, Palm Outlook Conduits*

1. Microsoft Outlook contains your contact list of names and phone numbers.

2. Outlook also maintains your calendar containing appointments and important dates.

3. You need third-party synchronization software to exchange data between Outlook and your portable devices. You can acquire synchronization utilities from portable device manufacturers or independent software companies.

4. Each portable device has a cable connecting it to a USB port on the PC.

5. A third-party program, such as iPodSync, can connect your iPod to Outlook and download the calendar and contact list.

FIGURE 7.9

6. Nokia's PC Sync program synchronizes the Nokia 6682's contacts list and calendar with the information on your PC.

7. Palm Outlook Conduit synchronizes the Tungsten E2 with the information on the PC.

Beyond the Basics: Database-Management Systems

So far we've used simple examples to illustrate concepts common to most database programs. This oversimplification is useful for understanding the basics, but it's not the whole story. In truth, database programs range from simple mailing label programs to massive financial information systems, and it's important to know a little about what makes them different as well as what makes them alike.

> When we try to pick out **anything**, we find it hitched to **everything else in the universe**.
>
> —*John Muir, first director of the National Park Service*

What Is a Database-Management System?

Technically speaking, many consumer databases and PIM programs aren't really database managers at all. This type of program (which used to be referred to as a file manager) is designed to manage the information in one collection of data, or table, at a time. A true **database-management system (DBMS)** is a program or system of programs that can manipulate data in a large collection of tables—the database—cross-referencing between tables as needed. You can use a DBMS interactively or control it directly

Transcript table

```
Student ID
Name
Local Street Address
Apartment No.
City
State
Zip
Permanent Street Address
Apartment No.
City
State
Zip
Gender
Citizenship
Year Admitted
Class Standing
Major
GPA

(Course 1 information)
Department
Number
Credits
Grade
Date

(Course 2 information)
Department
```

Financial info table

```
Student ID
Name
Local Street Address
Apartment No.
City
State
Zip
Permanent Street Address
Apartment No.
City
State
Zip
Gender
Citizenship
Year Admitted
Class Standing
Major
GPA

Tuition
Deposits
Registration Fees
Parking Fees
Housing Fees
Lab Fees
```

Class list table

```
Course Number
Department
Section Number
Instructor
Time
Location
Number of Students

(Student 1 Information)
Student ID
Name
Class Standing
Major

(Student 2 Information)
Student ID
Name
Class Standing
Major
```

FIGURE 7.10 Student information is duplicated in several different tables of this poorly designed, error-prone database.

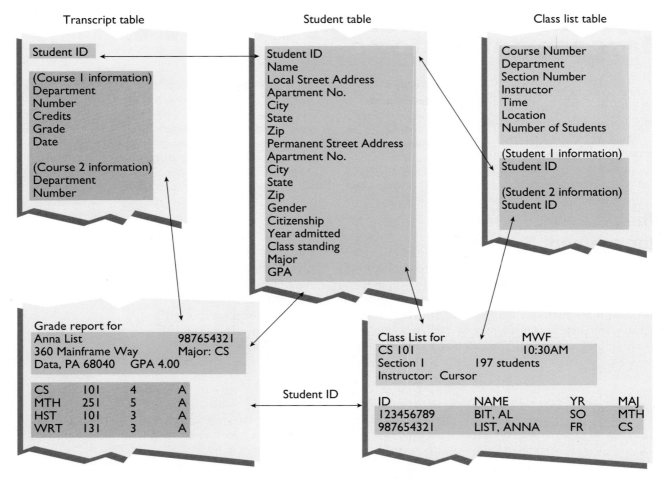

FIGURE 7.11 The Student table serves as a reference when grade reports and class lists are created. The Student ID fields in the Transcript table and the Class List table are used as keys for locating the necessary student information in the Student table.

through other programs. For many large, complex jobs, there's no substitute for a true database-management system.

Consider, for example, the problem of managing student information at a college. It's easy to see how databases might be used to store this information: a table containing one record for each student, with fields for name, student ID number, address, phone, and so on. But a typical student generates far too much information to store practically in a single table.

Most schools choose to keep several tables containing student information: one for financial records, one for course enrollment and grade transcripts, and so on. Each of these tables has a single record for each student. In addition, a school must maintain class enrollment tables with one record for each class and fields for information on each student enrolled in the class. Three of these tables might be organized as shown in the accompanying figure.

In this database, each of the three separate tables contains basic information about every student. This redundant data not only occupies expensive storage space, but also makes it difficult to ensure that student information is accurate and up to date. If a student moves to a different address, several tables must be updated to reflect this change. The more changes, the greater the likelihood of a data-entry error.

With a DBMS there's no need to store all this information in every table. The database can include a basic student table containing demographic information—information that's unique for each student. Because the demographic information is stored in a separate table, it doesn't need to be included in the financial information table, the transcript table, the class list table, or any other table. The student ID number, included in each table, serves as

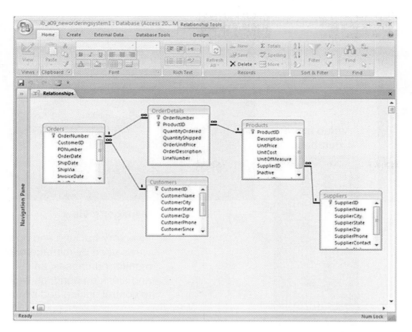

FIGURE 7.12 Microsoft Access provides a visual representation of a relational database.

a *key field*; it unlocks the relevant student information in the student table when it's needed elsewhere. The student ID field is, in effect, shared by all tables that use data from this table. If the student moves, the change of address need be recorded in only one place. Databases organized in this way are called *relational databases*.

What Makes a Database Relational?

To most users, a **relational database** program is one that allows tables to be related to each other so that changes in one table are reflected in other tables automatically. To computer scientists, the term *relational database* has a technical definition related to the underlying structure of the data and the rules specifying how that data can be manipulated.

The structure of a relational database is based on the relational model—a mathematical model that combines data in tables. Other kinds of database-management systems are based on different theoretical models, with different technical advantages and disadvantages. But the majority of DBMSs in use today, including virtually all PC-based database-management systems, use the relational model. So from the average computer user's point of view, the distinction between the popular and technical definitions of *relational* is academic.

In the late 1970s Oracle Corporation produced the first commercial relational database system. Large companies with massive amounts of information to store and retrieve discovered that the relational database model was much more versatile than previous systems were. Oracle Corporation quickly became an industry powerhouse. Today almost all of the FORTUNE 100 companies use Oracle software to manage their databases.

The Many Faces of Databases

Large databases often contain hundreds of interrelated tables. This maze of information could be overwhelming to users if they were forced to deal with it directly. Fortunately, a database-management system can shield users from the complex inner workings of the system, providing them with only the information and commands they need to get their jobs done. In fact, a well-designed database puts on different faces for different classes of users.

Video store database

Clerk's view

Customer service view used by clerks to access customer information, scan bar codes on products, ring up sales, and print receipts

Manager's view

Inventory-tracking and policy views used by managers to monitor purchases, sales, and stock on hand, as well as to control pricing and policy

Technician/programmer's view

Technical view used by programmer to create other user interfaces and custom queries

FIGURE 7.13 Clerks, managers, programmers, and customers see different views of a music store's database. The clerk's view allows for simple data-entry and checkout procedures. The manager, working with the same database, has control over pricing, policies, and inventory but can't change the structure or user interface of the database. The programmer can work under the hood to fine-tune and customize the database so it can better meet the needs of other employees and customers.

Retail clerks don't need to be able to access every piece of information in the store's database; they just need to enter sales transactions on point-of-sale terminals. Databases designed for retail outlets generally include simple, straightforward terminal interfaces that give the clerks only the information, and the power, they need to process transactions. Managers, accountants, data processing specialists, and customers see the database from different points of view because they need to work with the data in different ways.

Database Trends

It is better to ask **some of the questions** than to know **all of the answers**.

—*James Thurber, in* Fables for Our Time

Database technology isn't static. Advances in the past two decades have changed the way most organizations deal with data, and current trends suggest even bigger changes in the near future.

Real-Time Computing

The earliest file-management programs could do only batch processing, which required computer operators to accumulate transactions and feed them into computers in large batches. These batch systems weren't able to provide the kind of immediate feedback we expect today. Questions such as "What's the balance in my checking account?" or "Are there any open flights to Denver next Tuesday?" were likely to be answered "Those records will be updated tonight, so we'll let you know tomorrow."

Today disk drives, inexpensive memory, and sophisticated software have allowed interactive processing to replace batch processing for most applications. Users can now interact with data through terminals, viewing and changing values online in real time. Batch processing is still used for printing periodic paychecks, bills, invoices, and reports and for making backup copies of data files—jobs for which it makes sense to do a lot of transactions at once. But for applications that demand immediacy, such as airline reservations, banking transactions, and the like, interactive, multiuser database systems have taken over. These systems are typically run on powerful servers and accessed by users remotely. Oracle, IBM, Microsoft, and other companies create the *database servers* used by businesses of all sizes around the world.

This trend toward real-time computing is accelerated by the Internet, which makes it possible to have almost instant access to information stored in databases from anywhere on Earth, inside or outside the boundaries of the enterprise.

Downsizing and Decentralizing

In the pre-PC days, most databases were housed in mainframe computers accessible only to information-processing personnel. But the traditional hard-to-access centralized database on a mainframe system is no longer the norm.

Today many businesses use a client/server approach employing database servers: *Client* programs in desktop computers, notebooks, PDAs, or other devices send information requests through a network or the Internet to database servers or mainframe databases. These *servers* process queries and send the requested data back to the client. A client/server system enables users to take advantage of the PC's simple user interface and convenience, while still having access to data stored on large server systems.

Some corporations keep copies of all corporate data in integrated data warehouses. In some respects, data warehouses are similar to old-style systems: They're large, relatively expensive, and centralized. But unlike older, centralized systems, data warehouses give users more direct access to enterprise data. Data warehouses are most commonly found in large corporations and government departments.

Some companies use distributed databases, which spread data across networks on several different computers rather than store it in one central site. Many organizations have data warehouses and distributed databases. From the user's point of view, the differences between these approaches may not be apparent. Connectivity software, sometimes called middleware, links the client and server machines, hiding the complexity of the interaction between those machines and creating a three-tier design that separates the actual data from the programming logic used to access it. No matter how the data is stored, accessed, and retrieved, the goal is to provide quick and easy access to important information.

Data Mining

Today's technology makes it easy for a business to accumulate masses of information in a database. Many organizations are content to retrieve information using queries, searches, and reports. But others are finding that there's gold hidden in their large databases—gold that can be extracted only by using a new technology called *data mining*. **Data mining** is the discovery and extraction of hidden predictive information from large databases. It uses statistical methods and artificial intelligence technology to locate trends and patterns in data that would have been overlooked by normal database queries. For example, a grocery chain used data mining to discover differences between male and female shopping patterns so they could create gender-specific marketing campaigns. (In an industry ad, they announced that some men habitually buy beer and diapers every Friday!) In effect, data-mining technology enables users to "drill down" through masses of data to find valuable veins of information.

Databases and the Web

Many businesses are retooling to take advantage of Internet technology on their internal networks. These *intranets* enable employees to access corporate databases using the same Web browsers and search engines they use to access information outside the company networks. As Internet tools rapidly evolve, database access becomes easier and more transparent.

HTML, the language used to construct most Web pages, wasn't designed to build database queries. But a newer, more powerful data description language called **XML** is designed with industrial-strength database access in mind. Most database manufacturers have retooled their products so they can process data requests in XML. Because XML can serve as a query language and as a Web page construction tool, it's likely to open up all kinds of databases to the Web, making it easy for you to request and receive information online.

For many organizations, Web database strategies revolve around *directories*. Directories were originally little more than repositories for user phone numbers, addresses, and passwords, and they were commonly buried inside network operating systems. But the explosive growth of the Internet and of e-commerce has expanded the roles of directories for many organizations. Directories can be used to store basic employee and customer information, along with access policies, identity proof, payment information, and security information. Directories are at the heart of many *customer relationship management (CRM)* systems—software systems for organizing and tracking information on customers.

The Web makes it possible for employees and customers alike to have instant access to databases, opening up all kinds of rapid-response e-commerce possibilities. But this kind of broad real-time database access also increases the probability of data errors and the importance of eliminating those errors as quickly as possible.

Data records containing errors are called **dirty data**. Examples of dirty data are records with spelling or punctuation mistakes, incorrect values, or obsolete values. If you receive a mail order catalog addressed to the prior resident at your address, that's an example of dirty data in the mail order company's database.

High data quality is a critical factor in successful e-commerce. Dirty data can lead to inefficiency, incomplete or incorrect record matching, and bad business decisions. Most large databases use data-checking routines whenever data is entered. But many organizations also depend on software to correct errors that make it though the entry checks. **Data scrubbing** (also called **data cleansing**) is the process of going through a database and eliminating dirty data. For errors that aren't corrected by automated cleansing tools, the

Working Wisdom

Dealing with Databases

Whether you're creating an address file with a simple file manager or retrieving data from a full-blown relational database–management system, you can save yourself a great deal of time and grief if you follow a few common-sense rules:

➡ *Choose the right tool for the job.* Don't invest time and money in a programmable relational database to computerize your address book, and don't try to run the affairs of your multinational corporation with a spreadsheet list manager.

➡ *Think about how you'll get the information out before you put it in.* What kinds of tables, records, and fields will you need to create to make it easy to find things quickly and print things the way you'll want them? For example, use separate fields for first and last name if you want to sort names alphabetically by last name and print first names first.

➡ *Start with a plan, and be prepared to change your plan.* It's a good idea to do a trial run with a small amount of data to make sure everything works the way you think it should.

➡ *Make your data consistent.* Inconsistencies can mess up sorting and make searching difficult. For example, if a database includes residents of Minnesota, Minn., and MN, it's hard to group people by state.

➡ *Databases are only as good as their data is.* When entering data, take advantage of the data-checking capability of your database software. Does the first name field contain nonalphabetic characters? Is the birth date within a reasonable range? Automatic data checking is important, but it's no substitute for human proofreading or for a bit of skepticism when using the database.

➡ *Query with care.* In the words of Aldous Huxley, "People always get what they ask for; the only trouble is that they never know, until they get it, what it actually is that they have asked for." Here's a real example: A student searching a database of classic rock albums requested all records containing the string "Dylan," and the database program obediently displayed the names of several Bob Dylan albums ... plus one by Jimi Hendrix called *Electric Ladyland*. Why? Because "dylan" is in Ladyland! Unwanted records can go unnoticed in large database selections, so it's important to define selection rules very carefully.

➡ *If at first you don't succeed, try another approach.* If your search doesn't turn up the answers you were looking for, it doesn't mean the answers aren't there; they may just be wearing a disguise. If you search a standard library database, such as Questia, for "Vietnam War" references, you might miss hundreds of them. Why? Because the government officially classifies the Vietnam War as a conflict, so many references are stored under the subject "Vietnam Conflict." Technology meets bureaucracy!

FIGURE 7.14 Library database Questia returns more than 20,000 hits for the search "Vietnam conflict."

last wall of defense is typically a human customer service representative who can provide rapid response to customer complaints.

Object-Oriented Databases

Some of the biggest changes in database technology in the next few years may take place under the surface, where they may not be apparent to most users. For example, many computer scientists believe that the relational data model will be supplanted in the next decade by an object-oriented data model and that most future databases will be **object-oriented databases** rather than relational databases. Instead of storing records in tables and hierarchies, object-oriented databases store *objects*. Every object is an instance of a *class*. The class specifies the data contained in the object as well as the kinds of operations that may be performed on the data.

For example, imagine an object-oriented database containing various kinds of images. Within the database is a class for photographs. There is one instance of this class—one object—for every photograph in the database. The data associated with this object are the name of the photographer, a description of the photograph, its copyright status, and the image itself. One of the operations associated with this class is producing a thumbnail-sized miniature of the photo. The association of actions along with the data distinguishes object-oriented databases from relational databases, which do not have this capability.

Compared to relational databases, object-oriented databases make it easier to manipulate many different types of data. They can store and retrieve unstructured data, such as audio and video clips, more efficiently. Programmers developing a new database can save time by reusing objects. For these reasons, designers of multimedia information-management systems are taking a hard look at object-oriented databases. Many companies are experimenting with databases that combine relational and object concepts into hybrid systems. Users will find databases more flexible and responsive as object technology becomes more widespread, even if they aren't aware of the underlying technological reasons for these improvements.

Multimedia Databases

Today's databases can efficiently store all kinds of text and numeric data. But today's computers are multimedia machines that routinely deal with pictures, sounds, animation, and video clips. Multimedia databases can handle graphical and dynamic data along with text and numbers. Multimedia professionals use databases to catalog art, photographs, maps, video clips, sound files, and other types of media files. Media files aren't generally stored in databases because they're too large. Instead, a multimedia database serves as an *index* to all of the separately stored files. Multimedia databases have applications in law enforcement, medicine, entertainment, and other professions where information needs go beyond words and numbers.

Intelligent Searches

Future databases will undoubtedly incorporate more artificial intelligence technology. We're already seeing databases and data-mining software that can respond to simple *natural language* queries—queries in English or some other human language. But natural language Web search engines haven't (so far) made much headway.

Another trend in database queries, also based on artificial intelligence research, may have a bigger impact on the way we use search engines and other database tools. Some search engines, such as Ask.com, try to put queries in context. Rather than just dumping thousands of possible links on your screen, a contextual search tool might classify results into dictionary definitions, encyclopedia articles, media titles, products, and other

FIGURE 7.15 Ask.com returns search results organized into categories based on concepts rather than a simple list.

categories. Or they might, in effect, respond with questions in an attempt to clarify context and meaning: Did you mean *Casablanca* the movie or Casablanca the city? As these tools become smarter, they'll become far more useful for dealing with the glut of information in our digital world.

No Secrets: Computers and Privacy

Advanced technology has created **new opportunities** for America as a nation, but it has also created the possibility for **new abuses** of the individual American citizen. Adequate safeguards must always **stand watch** so that man remains **master** and never the **victim of the computer**.

—*Richard Nixon, 37th president of the United States, February 23, 1974*

Instant airline reservations, all-night automated banking, overnight mail, instant library searches, Web shopping—databases provide us with conveniences that were unthinkable a generation ago. But convenience isn't free. In the case of databases, we pay with our privacy.

What, exactly, is privacy? While experts may disagree on the definition, a common theme in privacy discussions is the notion of access, where *access* means physical proximity to a person or knowledge about that person. People need a certain amount of privacy to maintain their dignity and freedom. (How much freedom and dignity would you have if everyone could read your mind?) On the other hand, information about people can have great value to a society. Direct mail companies can save a great deal of money, and reduce waste, by sending catalogs only to those people who may make purchases. Many parents want to know the identities of convicted sex offenders living in their neighborhoods. These conflicting desires lead to some interesting dilemmas, especially when computers make gathering, storing, and retrieving information easier than ever.

JOHN ASHCROFT...
They Know Where You Are!

The unsung benefits of a database nation
(see next page)

FIGURE 7.16 Subscribers to *Reason* magazine received a personalized issue in June 2004 that had a satellite photo of their home or workplace on the cover.

Personal Data: All about You

You have **zero privacy** anyway. **Get over it**.

— *Scott McNealy, founder and CEO of Sun Microsystems*

We live in an information age, and data is one of the currencies of our time. Businesses and government agencies spend billions of dollars every year to collect and exchange information about you and me. Thousands of specialized marketing databases contain billions of consumer names, along with a surprising amount of personal information. The typical American consumer is on at least 25 marketing lists. Many of these lists are organized by characteristics, such as age, income, religion, political affiliation, and even sexual preference, and they're bought and sold every day.

Marketing databases are only the tip of the iceberg. Credit and banking information, tax records, health data, insurance records, political contributions, voter registration, credit card purchases, warranty registrations, magazine and newsletter subscriptions, phone calls, passport registration, airline reservations, automobile registrations, arrests, and Internet explorations are all recorded in computers, and we have little or no control over what happens to most of those records after they're collected.

For most of us, this data is out of sight and out of mind. But lives are changed because of these databases. Here are some examples:

■ In 2007, a University of Colorado student was branded as a sex offender and kicked off of MySpace. The aspiring law student, fearing that her name and reputation would be permanently stained, appealed the decision. MySpace refused to reinstate her and clear her name, claiming that her records had already been removed. The company that built the database eventually acknowledged the error, which occurred because database searches turned up a sex offender with the same name and a birthday two years and two days apart from the student.

FIGURE 7.17 The Internal Revenue Service workers shown here enter taxpayers' financial information into massive computer databases. When you shop by phone, respond to a survey, or fill out a warranty card, it's likely that a clerk somewhere will enter that data into a computer.

- When a credit bureau mistakenly placed a bankruptcy filing in the file of a St. Louis couple, banks responded by shutting off loans for their struggling construction business, forcing them into real bankruptcy. They sued but lost because credit bureaus are protected by law from financial responsibility for "honest" mistakes!

- A Los Angeles thief stole a wallet and used its contents to establish an artificial identity. When the thief was arrested for a robbery involving murder, the crime was recorded under the wallet owner's name in police databases. The legitimate owner of the wallet was arrested five times in the following 14 months and spent several days in jail before a protracted court battle resulted in the deletion of the record.

- In a recent, more typical example of identity theft, an imposter had the mail of an innocent individual temporarily forwarded to a post office box so he could easily collect credit card numbers and other personal data. By the time the victim discovered an overdue Visa bill, the thief had racked up $42,000 in bogus charges. The victim wasn't liable for the charges, but it took the better part of a year to correct all of the credit bureau errors.

As these examples indicate, there are many ways that abuse and misuse of databases can take away personal privacy. Sometimes privacy violations are due to government surveillance activities. Sometimes they're the result of the work of private corporations. Privacy breaches may be innocent mistakes, strategic actions, or malicious mischief. The explosive growth of identity theft, which claims millions of victims each year, makes it clear that database technology can be a powerful criminal tool.

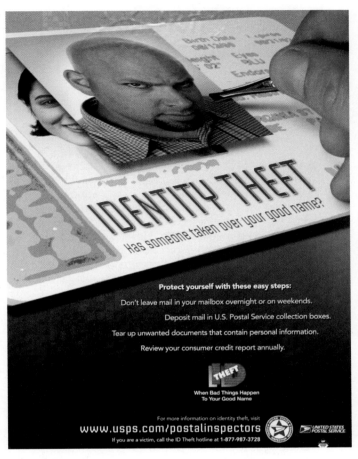

FIGURE 7.18 This poster was part of a campaign to educate the public about identity theft.

Privacy violations aren't new, and they don't always involve computers. The German Nazis, the Chinese Communists, and even Richard Nixon's 1972 campaign committee practiced surveillance without computers. But the privacy problem takes on a whole new dimension in the age of high-speed computers and databases. The same characteristics that make databases more efficient than other information storage methods—storage capacity, retrieval speed, organizational flexibility, and ease of distribution of information—also make them a threat to our privacy.

The Privacy Problem

In George Orwell's *1984*, information about every citizen was stored in a massive database controlled by the ever-vigilant Big Brother. Today's data warehouses in many ways resemble Big Brother's database. Data-mining techniques can be used to extract information about individuals and groups without their knowledge or consent. And database information can be easily sold or used for purposes other than those for which it was collected. Most of the time this kind of activity goes unnoticed by the public. Here are some examples where public knowledge changed privacy policy:

> What has taken me **a lifetime to build**—my trust, my integrity and my identity—has been **tainted**. I don't know if I'm dealing with a **14-year-old messing around with a computer** or if I'm dealing with **organized crime**.
>
> —*Identity theft victim*

Working Wisdom

Your Privacy Rights

Sometimes computer-aided privacy violations are nuisances; sometimes they're threats to life, liberty, and the pursuit of happiness. Here are a few tips for protecting your right to privacy.

➡ ***Your Social Security number is yours; don't give it away.*** Since your SSN is a unique identifier, it can be used to gather information about you without your permission or knowledge. For example, you could be denied a job or insurance because of something you once put on a medical form. Never write it (or your driver's license number or phone number, for that matter) on a check or credit card receipt. Don't give your SSN to anyone unless they have a legitimate reason to ask for it.

➡ ***Don't give away information about yourself.*** Don't answer questions about yourself just because a questionnaire or company representative asks you to. When you fill out any form—coupon, warranty registration card, survey, sweepstakes entry, or whatever—think about whether you want the information stored in somebody else's computer. Pay attention to check boxes that allow companies to share information you have provided them. On many Web forms these boxes are checked by default. You have to make a special effort to remove the check mark.

➡ ***Say no to direct mail, phone, and email solicitations.*** Businesses and political organizations pay for your data so they can target you for mail, phone, and email campaigns. You can remove yourself from many lists using forms from the Direct Marketing Association (**www.the-dma.org**). You can block most telemarketers by enrolling in the U.S. Federal Trade Commission's Opt Out program (**www.donotcall .gov**). If these steps don't stop the flow, you might want to try a more direct approach. Send back unwanted letters along with "Take me off your list" requests in the postage-paid envelopes that come with them. When you receive an unsolicited phone marketing call, tell the caller, "I never purchase or donate anything as a result of phone solicitations," and ask to be removed from the list. If they call within 12 months of being specifically told not to, you can sue and recover up to $500 per call according to the Telephone Consumer Protection Act of 1991. Unfortunately, the federal antispam law (the CAN SPAM Act) has proven to be ineffective, so you should be especially careful about giving out your email address if you don't like receiving unsolicited email.

➡ ***Say no to sharing your personal information.*** If you open a private Internet account, tell your Internet service provider that your personal data is not for sale. If you don't want credit agencies sharing personal information, let them know. The Federal Trade Commission's Privacy Web site (**www.ftc.gov/privacy**) includes clear guidelines and forms for contacting your DMV and credit agencies. The Financial Modernization Act of 1999 allows you to tell your banks and other financial institutions not to share your personal information with other institutions; check with those institutions for details.

➡ ***Think before you post.*** Social networks, blogs, and media sharing sites make it all too easy to share your personal feelings, photos, videos, and more. This isn't necessarily bad, but it's not without risk. Before you post anything, think about whether you want it to be seen tomorrow or twenty years from now by your mother, your blind date, your future employer, or your children.

➡ ***Mobilize technology to protect your privacy.*** There are many software and hardware tools to help you

■ In 2005 hospitals became aware that the Joint Commission on Accreditation of Healthcare Organizations had established a data-mining contract with the Blue Cross and Blue Shield Association. The JCAHO was providing the insurance companies with performance reports on the hospitals that included data hospitals had provided to the JCAHO in order to be accredited. After the American Hospital Association and other groups protested what they called an obvious conflict of interest, the JCAHO agreed to terminate its data-analysis service.

■ In 2004 protests from privacy advocates blocked the implementation of the Computer Assisted Passenger Prescreening System (CAPPS II) in the United States. The CAPPS II system would have required airline passengers to provide name, address, phone number, and birth date. It would have used this information to access commercial databases and government intelligence files to determine whether a passenger ought to be screened more closely at the airport or even prevented from boarding the aircraft.

snoop-proof your email, hide your return address, surf anonymously, send instant messages securely, and lock down your data. Use them as needed. (**www.epic.org** maintains a list of useful resources.)

➡ *If you think there's incorrect or damaging information about you in a file, find out.* The Freedom of Information Act of 1966 requires that most U.S. government agencies records be made available to the public on demand. The Privacy Act of 1974 requires federal agencies to provide you with information in your files related to you and to amend incorrect records. The Fair Credit Reporting Act of 1970 allows you to see your credit ratings—for free if you have been denied credit—and correct any errors. The three big credit bureaus are Equifax (**www.equifax.com**), TransUnion (**www.transunion.com**), and Experian (**www.experian.com**).

➡ *To maximize your privacy, minimize your profile.* If you don't want a financial transaction recorded, use cash. If you don't want your phone number to be public information, use an unlisted number. If you don't want your mailing address known, use a post office box.

➡ *Know your electronic rights.* Privacy protection laws in the United States lag far behind those of other high-tech nations, but they are beginning to appear. For example, the 1986 Electronic Communications Privacy Act provides the same protection that covers mail and telephone communication to some—but not all—electronic communications. The 1988 Computer Matching and Privacy Protection Act regulates the use of government data in determining eligibility for federal benefits.

➡ *Support organizations that fight for privacy rights.* If you value privacy rights, let your representatives know how you feel, and support the American Civil Liberties Union, Computer Professionals for Social Responsibility, the Electronic Frontier Foundation, the Electronic Privacy Information Center, the Center for Democracy and Technology, and other organizations that fight for those rights.

FIGURE 7.19 Tens of millions of households receive fewer telemarketing calls because they put their phone numbers in the free National Do Not Call Registry.

■ Prior to February 2001, N2H2, an Internet filtering software company, sold to other companies "class clicks," which were made up of marketing research based on Web usage patterns of children. The company insisted that its data didn't threaten any individual's privacy. Still, in response to protests, it stopped selling its data.

■ After the terrorist attacks of September 11, 2001, the U.S. Department of Defense established the Information Awareness Office. The goal of the office was to identify potential terrorists by gathering information about people's activities in a central database and looking for patterns of suspicious activity. Privacy advocates were outraged to think that the credit card receipts, utility bills, travel reservations, and tax records of ordinary Americans would be collected and inspected by a government agency. Responding to the public outcry, Congress cut off funding to the Information Awareness Office in February 2003.

Centralized data warehouses aren't necessary for producing computerized dossiers of private citizens. With networked computers, it's easy to compile profiles by combining

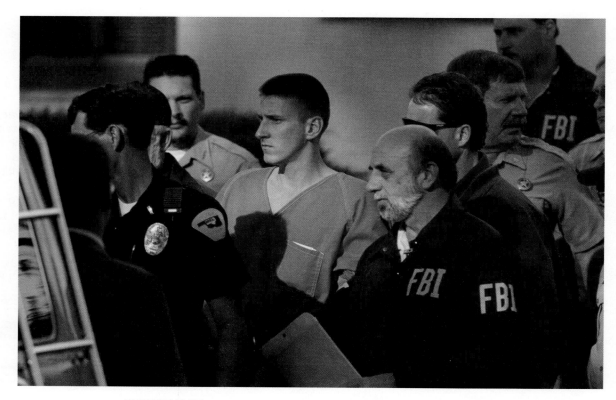

FIGURE 7.20 The National Crime Information Center database helped the FBI apprehend Timothy McVeigh, later convicted for his role in the bombing of the federal building in Oklahoma City.

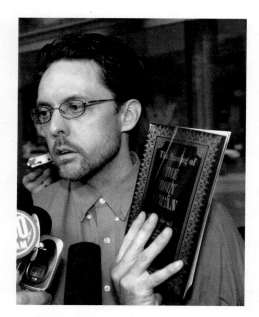

FIGURE 7.21 A partial fingerprint match led the FBI to arrest Portland, Oregon, attorney Brandon Mayfield as a material witness to the bombings of commuter trains in Madrid, Spain. Mayfield was held for two weeks before a judge ordered him to be released. The FBI apologized for the misidentification.

information from different databases. As long as the tables in the databases share a single unique field, such as a Social Security number field, record matching is trivial and quick. And when database information is combined, the whole is often far greater than the sum of its parts.

Sometimes the results of record matching are beneficial. The National Crime Information Center, managed by the FBI, contains more than 39 million records related to stolen automobiles, stolen or missing guns, missing persons, wanted persons, convicted persons, suspected terrorists, and more. The NCIC provided the FBI with the information it needed to identify James Earl Ray as the assassin of Dr. Martin Luther King, Jr. It helped the FBI track down Timothy McVeigh, the person convicted of bombing the Alfred P. Murrah Federal Building in Oklahoma City. Because the NCIC is accessible by state and local law enforcement agencies, it facilitates more than 100,000 arrests and the recovery of more than 100,000 stolen cars every year.

Another benefit of record matching is its use in establishing reputations. Because credit bureaus collect data about us, our financial trustworthiness becomes established in cyberspace. Businesses around the globe have access to this information, meaning we can use credit cards almost anywhere in the world. If we want to borrow money to purchase a house, banks around the nation will compete for our business. More competition means lower interest rates and lower monthly payments.

But these benefits come with at least three problems:

■ *Data errors are common.* Studies show that the average credit report contains at least one error.

■ *Data can become nearly immortal.* Because files are commonly sold and copied, it's impossible to delete or correct erroneous records with absolute certainty.

■ *Data isn't secure.* News sources routinely report thefts of credit card numbers, Social Security numbers, and other sensitive information from businesses and government agencies. Countless other thefts go unreported or undetected.

The word *privacy* does not appear in the U.S. Constitution. While U.S. Supreme Court decisions have recognized that a **right to privacy** is implied by other constitutional guarantees, legal scholars continue to debate the extent of privacy rights.

The creation of computerized databases led to a general concern about an erosion of individuals' privacy rights. In the early 1970s, a panel of experts produced a report to Congress, which included a *Code of Fair Information Practices*. The code suggested that there be no secret government databases, that individuals be able to access and correct information about themselves kept in government databases, and that agencies ensure the reliability and security of information kept in the databases.

Surprisingly, the report had a much greater impact in Europe than in the United States. Nearly every European nation passed laws based on the code of Fair Information Practices. State legislatures have been reluctant to pass laws based on the code because of intense lobbying by business interests. Legislation passed by the U.S. Congress, called the Privacy Act of 1974, fell far short of the ambitions of privacy advocates. For

U.S. Laws Protecting Personal Privacy		
Year	**Law**	**Description**
1970	Fair Credit Reporting Act	Promotes accuracy and privacy of information used by credit bureaus to produce credit reports. Puts a seven-year limit on how long most kinds of negative information can be kept.
1974	Family Education Rights and Privacy Act	Provides students 18 years and older the right to examine their educational records and the right to request changes to erroneous records. Restricts information that may be released without the consent of the student.
1988	Video Privacy Protection Act	Forbids video rental services from disclosing rental records without the written consent of the customer. Requires that information about who has rented what must be destroyed within a year of the date when the information is no longer needed.
1988	Employee Polygraph Protection Act	Most private employers cannot suggest, request, or require pre-employment polygraph tests of job applicants. An employee cannot be fired for refusing to take a polygraph test.
1994	Drivers Privacy Protection Act	Prohibits state DMVs from releasing or using personal information contained in motor vehicle records.
1998	Children's Online Privacy Protection Act	Forbids online services from collecting information from children 12 years old and younger without parental consent.
1999	Financial Services Modernization Act	Allows banks to offer insurance and brokerage services. Requires financial institutions to disclose their privacy policies to customers at least once per year. Gives customers the right to prevent their confidential information from being shared with other companies.
2003	Health Insurance Portability and Accountability Act	Directs health care providers to limit the exchange of patient information to that necessary for the care of the patient. Forbids health care providers from releasing information to banks, life insurance companies, or other businesses without written authorization from the patient.

FIGURE 7.22

example, it applies only to databases managed by the federal government; no one in the federal government is responsible for enforcing its provisions, and agencies can opt out of its requirements.

However, several key pieces of U.S. legislation have provided individuals with a cluster of privacy rights. The Fair Credit Reporting Act promotes the accuracy and privacy of information used by credit bureaus to create consumer credit reports. It puts limits on how long negative information can be kept on a person's credit report. The Family Education Rights and Privacy Act lets students (or the parents of minor students) access their educational records and request changes to erroneous records. The Video Privacy Protection Act prohibits videotape service providers from disclosing rental records without the consumer's written consent. The Children's Online Privacy Protection Act prohibits Internet-based businesses from collecting information from children 12 years old and younger without their parents' consent. The Health Insurance Portability and Accountability Act limits how doctors, hospitals, pharmacies, and insurance companies can use the medical information they collect from patients.

On the other hand, the USA PATRIOT Act, passed by the U.S. Congress in response to the September 11, 2001, attacks on the World Trade Center and the Pentagon, has made it easier for the FBI to collect certain kinds of information about individuals. The FBI can get a search warrant for educational, medical, business, library, and church/mosque/synagogue records simply by stating that they are related to an ongoing investigation. In other words, the FBI does not need to show probable cause. It is illegal for someone who has supplied such records to reveal the existence of the warrant. Critics of the USA PATRIOT Act, including the governments of more than 100 cities and several states, argue that the legislation weakens constitutional guarantees against unreasonable searches and seizures. In 2006, Congress reauthorized the USA PATRIOT Act, extending most of its provisions beyond their original expiration dates. Since then, the controversial act has been used in cases having nothing to do with terrorism. In one high profile case, the governor of New York was forced to resign because his financial records were traced to a prostitution ring. There's little doubt that this act will continue to generate controversy for years to come.

Big Brother and Big Business

If **all records** told the same tale, then **the lie** passed into history and **became truth**.

—George Orwell, in 1984

Database technology clearly poses a threat to personal privacy, but other information technologies amplify that threat:

- Networks make it possible for personal data to be transmitted almost anywhere instantly. The Internet is particularly fertile ground for collecting personal information about you. And the Web makes it alarmingly easy for anyone with a connected computer to examine your personal information.
- Workplace monitoring technology enables managers to learn more than ever before about the work habits and patterns of workers. Supervisors can (and do) count keystrokes, monitor Web activity, screen email, and remotely view what's on the screens of employees.
- Surveillance cameras, increasingly used for nabbing routine traffic violators and detecting security violators, can be combined with picture databases to locate criminals and others. Florida law enforcement officials came under fire from privacy groups because they used cameras, face-recognition software, and criminal databases to find and arrest several attendees of the 2001 Super Bowl. After the terrorist attacks of September 11,

FIGURE 7.23 Surveillance cameras can be used with facial-recognition software to locate criminals, but they may also threaten the privacy of law-abiding citizens.

2001, surveillance cameras were installed in hundreds of businesses and government agencies to guard against future attacks.

■ Surveillance satellites can provide permanent peepholes into our lives for anyone willing to pay the price.

■ Cell phones are now required by law to include technology to determine and transmit their locations to emergency personnel responding to 911 calls. Privacy advocates point out that the same technology can easily be used for less noble purposes.

In George Orwell's *1984,* personal privacy was the victim of a centralized Communist police state controlled by Big Brother. Today our privacy is threatened by many Big Brothers—with new threats emerging almost every day. As Simson Garfinkel says in *Database Nation,* "Over the next 50 years, we will see new kinds of threats to privacy that don't find their roots in totalitarianism, but in capitalism, the free market, advanced technology, and the unbridled exchange of electronic information."

Democracy depends on the free flow of information, but it also depends on the protection of individual rights. Maintaining a balance is not easy, especially when new information technologies are being developed at such a rapid pace. With information at our fingertips, it's tempting to think that more information is the answer. But in the timeless words of populist philosopher Will Rogers, "It's not the things we don't know that get us into trouble, it's the things we do know that ain't so."

Inventing the FUTURE

Embedded Intelligence and Ubiquitous Computing

Computers are disappearing into more of our tools all the time. Information appliances, including cell phones, fax machines, and GPS devices, perform their specialized functions while hiding the technological details from their users. Dozens of household appliances and tools have invisible computers. Even our cars process megabytes of information as we drive down the road.

Some car computers are invisible; others are more obvious. Several companies have introduced dashboard computers that can play music and movies, recognize spoken commands, alert the driver to incoming email messages, read those messages aloud, store and retrieve contacts and appointments, dial phone numbers, recite directions using GPS-based navigation systems, report mechanical problems, and even track stolen vehicles. In 2001 Volkswagen AG became the first automobile company to mass-produce a car with an Internet connection.

Innovation continues in computerized automobile safety systems. Computer-controlled antilock braking systems have become a standard feature on many automobiles. An ABS requires a human actually to hit the brake pedal, but Honda has introduced an automatic braking system to its high-end Inspire sedan sold in Japan. The Collision Mitigation Brake System uses radar to detect objects in front of the car. It warns the driver if it believes a collision is imminent. If the driver does not react quickly enough, the CMS can automatically apply the brakes and even tighten the seat belts in anticipation of a crash. IBM researchers are developing an in-dash "artificial passenger" to make long drives safer. This intelligent agent carries on conversations, watching for signs of fatigue in the driver. If it finds them, it might change the radio station, open a window, or even spray the driver with cold water.

Computers may soon be part of our clothing, too. Most of today's *wearable computers* are strap-on units for active information gatherers. But researchers at MIT and elsewhere are stitching CPUs, keyboards, and touchpads right into clothes, turning their wearers into wireless Internet nodes. These digital outfits aren't just high-tech fashion statements—when worn with eyeglass monitors (described in Chapter 3's Inventing the Future Box [p. 97]), they might be invaluable for any number of jobs that require both activity and connectivity.

In Japan, computer technology has even found its way into the bathroom. A number of Japanese fixture manufacturers sell computer-controlled smart toilets. Some models automatically collect and store information on blood pressure, pulse, temperature, urine, and weight. The information can be displayed on an LCD display, accumulated for months, and even transmitted by modem to a medical service. Users of these smart toilets get a minicheckup whenever they visit the bathroom. Body-monitoring features give the toilet an entirely new function—a function that will undoubtedly save lives.

When computers show up in our toilets, we're clearly entering an era of ubiquitous computers—computers everywhere. For several years, researchers at Xerox PARC, Cambridge University, Olivetti, and elsewhere have been experimenting with technology that will make computers even more ubiquitous. PARC's Mark Weiser describes an experimental office equipped with intelligent devices, including smart badges described in Chapter 10: "Doors open only to the right badge wearer, rooms greet people by name, telephone calls can be automatically forwarded to wherever the recipient may be, receptionists actually know where people are, computer terminals retrieve the preferences of whoever is sitting at them, and appointment diaries write themselves." ~

FIGURE 7.24 A dashboard GPS-based navigator is an example of a visible embedded computer system, unlike the computers controlling the engine and the airbags, which are invisible to the driver.

Are You Part of the Urban Scramble? *by Emily Steel*

Like it or not, you're the target of advertisers who know quite a bit about you. But Emily Steel discovered that the high-tech ad targeting often misses the mark. A longer version of this article first appeared in the September 20, 2008 issue of the Wall Street Journal.

Revenue Science, one of the leading players in the business of targeted advertising, gathers information about consumers and then sells it to marketers. According to the company's "file" on me, I'm a "hip homemaker" who probably trades stocks and buys expensive clothes and boats.

Actually, I'm 24, single and I live in a cramped New York City apartment where my television sits on top of my refrigerator. I sometimes dog-sit for extra spending money and have never bought or sold a single stock. As for luxury boats, the closest I've come to one most recently was during a run past a yacht club in St. Petersburg, Fla., three years ago when I was an intern at a newspaper there.

Some big companies that use targeted advertising report a tripling in the number of clicks on their Web ads, a jump they attribute to having better information about consumers' interests and shopping preferences.

But for all the excitement about this emerging field, as I surf the Web I'm struck by how few of the ads that appear along the way are relevant to me. Marketers don't seem to be targeting me very effectively.

To better understand why, I asked Revenue Science to open up its vault so I could see what the company has gleaned about me. To provide a comparison, I put in a similar request to Acxiom, a Little Rock, Ark.-based company.

Revenue Science and Acxiom, along with a handful of other companies in the field including Yahoo and Time Warner's AOL, make deals with hundreds, sometimes thousands, of Web publishers for permission to collect data about visitors to those sites. When a person lands on one of the sites, the targeting technology places a "cookie," or small string of tracking data, on his or her hard drive. The technology can read the codes embedded in the cookies to see which other sites in the network the person has already visited. Based on that information, it automatically decides which ads to display.

Both Revenue Science and Acxiom label consumers according to things like shared interests or common demographic traits, but their methodologies differ. Revenue Science uses data it gathers from Web traffic only. When it put together my profile for me, it definitely got some things right, correctly pegging me as a woman, a shopper, a moviegoer and a health fanatic living in New York City. But there were also some serious gaps in the profile—my supposed interest in luxury boats, for instance.

Acxiom places individuals into one of more than 70 demographic "clusters" that it creates by sifting through hundreds of pieces of information it collects about consumers offline, and then combines with online data. Clusters include "Apple Pie Families," for example, homeowners between the age of 46 and 65, usually married, with school- age kids, living in an urban setting, with a net worth of $100,000 to $499,000; "Young Workboots" (under 30, predominantly single, living in rural areas and with a net worth of less than $25,000); and "Trucks and Trailers" (age 30 to 45, no children, living in rural areas and with a net worth of under $100,000). Acxiom accurately put me in its "Mixed Singles-Urban Scramble" basket, which contains just over two million U.S. households, or 1.57% of the total.

One reason behavioral targeting is still such an imperfect science is that firms can easily make false assumptions, especially if they are relying on Web-only information.

Another barrier to precision: The data that the firms collect for their clients aren't tied to individually identifiable consumers, but rather to the Internet Protocol addresses of their computers. Families often share computers, and individuals often use more than one machine.

Acxiom seemed to have a better handle than Revenue Science on the kinds of ads that might get my attention. The company correctly labeled me as someone who spends time exercising and socializing at bars and nightclubs; is interested in foreign travel; and likes to go to the movies. Based on my profile, Acxiom said I would likely get pitches from trendy clothing retailers and health clubs, or see ads touting impromptu travel offers, movies or fitness gear. In fact, I spend money on all of these things.

As they try to refine their technology, targeted marketing companies aren't aiming to create profiles of every individual consumer. Instead, they want to make sure that the profiles they have created about consumers actually fit. Separately, these companies also have to find a way to deal with the growing privacy concerns—among lawmakers, privacy advocates and consumers—surrounding the field of ad targeting.

Discussion Questions

1. Do you have privacy concerns about this kind of targeted advertising? Explain.

2. Do you think there should be legal controls on what kind of information can be collected and used for targeting ads? Explain.

Summary

Database programs enable users to store, organize, retrieve, communicate, and manage large amounts of information quickly and efficiently. Each database is made up of tables, which are, in turn, collections of records, and each record is made up of fields containing text strings, numbers, and other chunks of information. Database programs enable users to view data in a variety of ways, sort records in any order, and print reports, mailing labels, and other custom printouts. A user can search for an individual record or select a group of records with a query.

While most database programs are general-purpose tools that can be used to create custom databases for any purpose, some are special-purpose tools programmed to perform a particular set of tasks. Geographical information systems, for example, combine maps and demographic information with data tables to provide new ways to look at data. Personal information managers provide automated address books, appointment calendars, to-do lists, and notebooks for busy individuals.

Many database programs are, technically speaking, file managers because they work with only one file at a time. Database-management systems can work with several data sources at a time, cross-referencing information among files when appropriate. A DBMS can provide an efficient way to store and manage large quantities of information by eliminating the need for redundant information in different tables. A well-designed database provides different views of the data to different classes of users so each user sees and manipulates only the information necessary for the job at hand.

The trend today is clearly away from large, centralized databases accessible only to data processing staff. Instead, most organizations are moving toward a client/server approach that enables users to access data stored in servers throughout the organization's network. While relational databases have been the norm for the past twenty years, a new focus on multimedia records and other complex data sets has sparked the development of object-oriented database systems.

The accumulation of data by government agencies and businesses is a growing threat to our right to privacy. Massive amounts of information about private citizens are collected and exchanged for a variety of purposes. Today's technology makes it easy to combine information from different databases, producing detailed profiles of individual citizens. Although there are many legitimate uses for these procedures, there's also a great potential for abuse. It's encouraging to reflect on the number of times that groups of citizens or their elected representatives have halted the deployment of systems that went too far.

Key Terms

batch processing ....(p. 249)
browse ....(p. 237)
centralized database...............(p. 249)
client/server ....(p. 249)
computed fields ....(p. 237)
data mining.............................(p. 250)
data scrubbing
   (data cleansing)................(p. 250)
data warehouse ....(p. 249)
database ....(p. 236)
database-management system
   (DBMS)..........................(p. 245)
database program...................(p. 236)
dirty data...............................(p. 250)

distributed database ....(p. 249)
export data ....(p. 239)
field.......................................(p. 236)
geographical information system
   (GIS).................................(p. 241)
identity theft ....(p. 255)
import data............................(p. 237)
interactive processing............(p. 249)
object-oriented database........(p. 252)
personal information manager
   (PIM) ....(p. 241)
privacy ....(p. 253)
query.....................................(p. 237)
query language ....(p. 239)

real time.................................(p. 249)
record.....................................(p. 236)
record matching.....................(p. 258)
relational database ....(p. 247)
report ....(p. 239)
right to privacy ....(p. 259)
search.....................................(p. 237)
select (records) ....(p. 237)
sort...(p. 239)
SQL ....(p. 239)
table ....(p. 236)
XML..(p. 250)

Interactive Activities

1. The *Tomorrow's Technology and You* Web site, www.pearsonhighered.com/beekman, contains self-test exercises related to this chapter. Follow the instructions for taking a quiz. After you've completed your quiz, you can email the results to your instructor.

2. The Web site also contains open-ended discussion questions called Internet Exercises. Discuss one or more of the Internet Exercises questions at the section for this chapter.

True or False

1. Because the address book in a typical cell phone is a simple list of names and numbers, it is an ideal application for relational database technology.

2. In a database, a numeric field can contain only computed formulas similar to formulas in spreadsheets.

3. Typical database software allows you to view one record at a time in form view or several records at a time in list view.

4. The most common type of database printout is called a sort.

5. A database-management system (DBMS) can manipulate data in a large collection of files, cross-referencing them as needed.

6. In a typical database, a table contains the information related to one person, product, or event.

7. Democracy depends on the free flow of information and on the protection of individual rights; database technology threatens to upset the balance between these two principles.

8. XML (eXterior Middleware License) is a legal protocol for protecting data from copyright infringement.

9. The right to privacy is not explicitly guaranteed by the U.S. Constitution, but legal experts believe that it is implied.

10. To query a database, you must learn at least some SQL, the universal query language of databases.

Multiple Choice

1. Identity theft might involve
   a. stealing of personal data from a database.
   b. conning an innocent person on the phone.
   c. creating fraudulent documents to forward the mail of an unsuspecting person.
   d. any or all of the above.
   e. none of the above; identity theft is a myth propagated on the Internet.

2. Why do people use databases rather than paper-based filing systems for information-handling tasks?
   a. Databases make it easier to store large quantities of information.
   b. Databases make it easier to retrieve information quickly and flexibly.
   c. Databases make it easy to organize and reorganize information.
   d. Databases make it easy to print and distribute information in a variety of ways.
   e. All of the above.

3. Which of these is the correct hierarchy for a standard database?
   a. Database, record, table, field
   b. Database, field, record, table
   c. Database, table, record, field
   d. Database, record, field, table
   e. Database, table, field, record

4. Which of these is not a specialized database program?
   a. A geographic information system.
   b. A personal information manager (PIM).
   c. A program for organizing and managing photos.
   d. iTunes, the program used to manage music and video libraries.
   e. All of these are specialized database programs.

5. Which of these software tools would work for maintaining a searchable, sortable list of professional contacts?
   a. PIM (personal information manager) software.
   b. A basic file management program.
   c. A relational database manager.
   d. A spreadsheet program with list management capability.
   e. Any of these would work, although some would be easier to set up and use than others.

6. What is the purpose of a database query?
   a. To update information kept within a record
   b. To test the security and integrity of the database
   c. To rearrange the order of the records in a database
   d. To convert a relational database into an object-oriented database
   e. To retrieve information from all appropriate records

7. When you use Google's search engine you're taking advantage of the software's ability to do rapid real-time
   a. batch processing.
   b. file processing.
   c. PIM processing.
   d. interactive processing.
   e. word processing.

8. A college's database administrator writes a program to examine the records of all its students over the past decade, looking for patterns that might explain why some students drop out. What is the administrator's program an example of?
   a. Browsing
   b. Interactive processing
   c. Data exporting
   d. Data importing
   e. Data mining

9. Data warehouses are similar in some ways to old-style centralized databases, but unlike those older systems, data warehouses
   a. depend on middleware to produce reports.
   b. give users more direct access to enterprise data.
   c. are built on distributed database systems.
   d. are powered by simple file-management software.
   e. all of the above.

10. Which of the following defines a relational database?
    a. A database that contains several related records
    b. A database that contains several related fields
    c. A database that has a relationship with other databases
    d. A database whose structure combines data in tables based on the relational model
    e. A database with more than 1,000 records

11. Which of these Web applications depends on database technology?
    a. Online auctions, such as eBay
    b. Search engines, such as Google
    c. Online stores, such as Amazon
    d. Social networking sites, such as Facebook
    e. All of the above

12. An object-oriented database
    a. is a specialized database for tracking and organizing a group of physical objects, such as a collection or an inventory.
    b. is, by definition, a relational database.
    c. cannot function properly without a distributed server.
    d. is based on a different mathematical model than a relational database.
    e. is, at this point, still theoretical.

13. Even without centralized data warehouses, how can government agencies quickly produce detailed dossiers on millions of private citizens?
    a. By using Social Networking Technology (SNT)
    b. By using XML technology
    c. Through record matching
    d. Through identity theft
    e. With middleware

14. What is the act of removing erroneous data from a database called?
    a. Data scrubbing
    b. Data deletion
    c. Data synchronization
    d. Data doodling
    e. Record matching

15. The USA PATRIOT Act has generated controversy because some say it weakens Constitutional guarantees against
    a. the separation of church and state.
    b. freedom of the press.
    c. self-incrimination.
    d. unreasonable searches and seizures.
    e. all of the above.

Review Questions

1. Define or describe each of the key terms listed in the "Key Terms" section. Check your answers in the glossary.

2. Describe how record matching is used to obtain information about you. Give an example.

3. Describe the structure of a simple database. Use the terms *table, record,* and *field* in your description.

4. What is a query? Give examples of the kinds of questions that might be answered with a query.

5. Batch processing isn't as common as it used to be, but it still serves some useful functions. Describe one or two.

6. What are the advantages of personal information management software over paper notebook organizers? What are the disadvantages?

7. What is the difference between a file manager and a database-management system? How are they similar?

8. Explain the difference between searching and sorting data records.

9. How can a database be designed to reduce the likelihood of data-entry errors?

10. Do we have a legal right to privacy? On what grounds?

Discussion Questions

1. Why is there sometimes a loss of privacy associated with increased efficiency?

2. What have you done this week that directly or indirectly involved a database? How would your week have been different in a world without databases?

3. "The computer is a great humanizing factor because it makes the individual more important. The more information we have on each individual, the more each individual counts." Do you agree with this statement by science fiction writer Isaac Asimov? Why or why not?

4. Suppose you have been incorrectly billed for $100 by a mail-order house. Your protestations are ignored by the company, which is now threatening to report you to a collection agency. What do you do?

5. The National Crime Information Center (NCIC) allows local, state, and federal law enforcement personnel to share information with each other. What advantages and disadvantages does a computerized law enforcement system have for law-abiding citizens?

6. How important is it to you to have instant access to your credit card and checking account balances? How often do you inquire about your balances?

7. Do you believe it's possible to maintain security in our society without sacrificing fundamental privacy rights?

8. Would you be upset or worried if the FBI obtained copies of your educational, medical, and library records?

9. In what ways were George Orwell's "predictions" in the novel *1984* accurate? In what ways were they wrong?

Projects

1. Design a database for your own use. (If you're having a hard time thinking of a theme for the database, think about a database related to one of your hobbies.) For example, if you like to bowl, you could create a database in which each record contains the date, the location where you bowled, the lane number(s), and your score(s).) Create several records, sort the data, and print a report.

2. Find out as much as you can about someone (for example, yourself or a public figure) from public records such as tax records, court records, voter registration lists, and motor vehicle files. How much of this information were you able to get directly from the Web? How much was available for free?

3. Find out as much as you can about your own credit rating. The three major credit bureaus are Equifax (www.equifax.com), Experian (www.experian.com), and TransUnion (www.transunion.com).

4. The next time you order something by mail or phone, try encoding your name with a unique middle initial so you can recognize when the company sells your name and address to other companies. Use several different spellings for different orders if you want to do some comparative research.

5. Determine what information about you is stored in your school computers. What information are you allowed to see? What information are others allowed to see? Exactly who may access your files? Can you find out who sees your files? How long is the information retained after you leave school?

6. Keep track of your purchases for a few weeks. If other people had access to this information, what conclusions might they be able to draw about you? For example, could they estimate your income? Could they determine your hobbies? Would they be able to make an educated guess about your favorite kinds of food?

Sources and Resources

Books

Like word processors, spreadsheet software, and multimedia programs, databases have inspired hundreds of how-to tutorials, user's guides, and reference books. If you're working with a popular program, you should have no trouble finding a book to help you develop your skills.

The Search: How Google and Its Rivals Rewrote the Rules of Business and Transformed Our Culture, by John Battelle (New York, NY: Portfolio, 2006). This popular book explores the past, present, and future of Google and other search-driven companies. Battelle sees the search engine as "the database of our intentions." *The Search* is as much cultural anthropology as history.

Googlepedia: The Ultimate Google Resource, 2nd Edition, by Michael Miller (Indianapolis, IN: Que, 2007). This massive book is a manual for a wealth of Google tools, from the basic search engine to specialized tools such as Blogger, Google Checkout, and YouTube. There's plenty here to keep you busy until Google introduces a bevy of new products.

Database Design for Mere Mortals: A Hands-On Guide to Relational Database Design, Second Edition, by Michael J. Hernandez (Boston, MA: Addison-Wesley Professional, 2003). This book can save time, money, and headaches for anyone who's involved in designing and building a relational database. After defining all the critical concepts, the author clearly outlines the design process using case studies to illustrate important points.

SQL Queries for Mere Mortals: A Hands-On Guide to Data Manipulation in SQL, Second Edition, by Michael J. Hernandez and John L. Viescas (Boston, MA: Addison-Wesley Professional, 2007). SQL queries start out as human questions about the real world. This book can help you learn how to translate those questions into SQL so you can extract the data you need from a database.

PHP 6 and MySQL 5 for Dynamic Web Sites: Visual QuickPro Guide, Third Edition, by Larry Ullman (Berkeley, CA: Peachpit Press, 2007). MySQL is the world's most popular open source database. A combination of PHP and MySQL can turn a static Web site into a dynamic, database-driven site. This book provides an introduction to this dynamic duo.

Glut: Mastering Information Through the Ages, by Alex Wright (Washington, DC: Joseph Henry Press, 2007). It's possible to have too much information at your fingertips. This book provides a historical perspective for the information overload we feel today, exploring the ways people managed information throughout history.

Keeping Found Things Found: The Study and Practice of Personal Information Management, by William Jones (San Francisco, CA: Morgan Kaufmann, 2008). As the sea of information swells, we need tools and techniques to keep from being swept away. This book provides useful information about managing information.

Privacy Lost: How Technology Is Endangering Your Privacy, by David H. Holtzman (Hoboken, NJ: Jossey-Bass, 2006). Data never disappears. In this book, David H. Holtzman explores the privacy problem in depth. What is privacy, why is it important, how does technology threaten it, and what can we do about it? These are questions that we all need to consider.

Privacy in Peril: How We Are Sacrificing a Fundamental Right in Exchange for Security and Convenience, by James B. Rule (New York, NY: Oxford University Press, 2007). This book is more of a philosophical exploration than a political document. The title pretty much sums up the tradeoffs we're making.

The Digital Person: Technology and Privacy in the Information Age, by Daniel Solove (New York, NY: NYU Press, 2006). This is a widely praised review of privacy issues and laws in flux.

Computer Privacy Annoyances: How to Avoid the Most Annoying Invasions of Your Personal and Online Privacy, by Dan Tynan (Cambridge, MA: O'Reilly, 2005). This book, part of O'Reilly's popular *Annoyances* series, provides easy-to-understand advice for protecting your privacy at home, on the Net, at work, and in public spaces.

Periodicals

The Privacy Journal (http://www.privacyjournal.net). This widely quoted monthly newsletter covers all issues related to personal privacy.

Organizations

Privacy Foundation (http://www.privacyfoundation.org). The Privacy Foundation isn't an advocacy group; its mission is to report on technology-based privacy threats and circulate alerts.

Privacy Rights Clearinghouse (http://www.privacyrights.org). This nonprofit consumer information and advocacy organization provides a wealth of information about identity theft, workplace privacy, financial privacy, Internet privacy, medical privacy, and more.

Computer Professionals for Social Responsibility (http://www.cpsr.org). CPSR provides the public and policymakers with realistic assessments of the power, promise, and problems of information technology. Much of their work deals with privacy-related issues. Their newsletter is a good source of information.

The Electronic Frontier Foundation (http://www.eff.org). EFF strives to protect civil rights, including the right to privacy, on emerging communication networks.

Electronic Privacy Information Center (http://www.epic.org). EPIC serves as a watchdog over government efforts to build surveillance capabilities into the emerging information infrastructure.

American Civil Liberties Union (http://www.aclu.org). The ACLU tirelessly defends constitutional rights, including privacy rights.

Private Citizen (http://www.private-citizen.com). This organization can help keep you off junk phone and junk mail lists—for a price.

8

Networking and Digital Communication

Objectives

After you read this chapter you should be able to:

▌ Describe the basic types of technology that make telecommunication possible

▌ Describe the nature and function of local area networks and wide area networks

▌ Discuss the uses and implications of email, instant messaging, blogging, teleconferencing, and other forms of online communication

▌ Explain how wireless network technology is transforming the ways people work and communicate

▌ Describe current and future trends in telecommunications and networking

> If an elderly but distinguished scientist says that something is possible he is almost **certainly right**, but if he says that it is impossible he is **very probably wrong**. The only way to find the **limits of the possible** is to go beyond them into the impossible. Any sufficiently advanced technology is **indistinguishable from magic**.
>
> —*Clarke's Three Laws*

Arthur C. Clarke's Magical Prophecy

Besides coining Clarke's laws, British writer Arthur C. Clarke has written more than 100 works of science fiction and nonfiction. His most famous work was the monumental 1968 film *2001: A Space Odyssey,* in which he collaborated with director Stanley Kubrick. The film's villain, a faceless English-speaking computer with a lust for power, sparked many public debates about the nature and risks of artificial intelligence. These debates continue today.

Clarke's most visionary work, however, may be a paper published in 1945 in which he predicted the use of *geostationary communications satellites*—satellites that match the Earth's rotation so they can hang in a stationary position relative to the spinning planet below and relay wireless transmissions between locations. Clarke's paper pinpointed the exact height of the orbit required to match the movement of the satellite with the planetary rotation. He also suggested that these satellites could replace many telephone cables and radio towers, allowing electronic signals to be beamed across oceans, deserts, and mountain ranges, linking the people of the world with a single communications network.

A decade after Clarke's paper appeared, powerful rockets and sensitive radio receiving equipment made communications satellites realistic. In 1964 the first synchronous TV satellite was launched, marking the beginning of a billion-dollar industry that has changed the way people communicate.

FIGURE 8.1 Arthur C. Clarke

FIGURE 8.2 Geostationary communications satellite.

Today Clarke is often referred to as the father of satellite communications. He spent the last half of his life living in Sri Lanka, where he continued to work as a writer, beaming his words around the globe to editors using the satellites he envisioned earlier in his life. He received numerous awards and recognitions, including knighthood, before he died in 2008 at the age of 91. Shortly before his death he said, "I have had a diverse career as a writer, underwater explorer, and space promoter. I would like to be remembered as a writer." ~

The Battle of New Orleans, the bloodiest battle of the War of 1812, was fought two weeks after the war officially ended; it took that long for the cease-fire message to travel from Washington, D.C. to the front line. In 1991, 179 years later, six hard-line Soviet communists staged a coup to turn back the tide of democratic and economic reforms that were sweeping the U.S.S.R. Within hours, messages zipped between the Soviet Union and Western nations on telephone and computer networks. Cable television and computer conferences provided up-to-the-minute analyses of events—analyses that were beamed to

FIGURE 8.3 The telegraph was the first electronic networking technology.

computer bulletin boards inside the Soviet Union. Networks carried messages among the resisters, allowing them to stay steps ahead of the coup leaders and the Soviet military machine. People toppled the coup and ultimately the Soviet Union—not with guns, but with courage, will, and timely information.

Telecommunication technology—the technology of long-distance communication—has come a long way since the War of 1812, and the world has changed dramatically as a result. After Samuel Morse built an electronic telegraph in 1844, people could, for the first time, send long-distance messages instantaneously. Alexander Bell's invention of the telephone in 1876 extended this capability to the spoken word. Today systems of linked computers enable us to send data and software across the room or around the world. Technological transformation has changed the popular definition of the word *telecommunication,* which today means long-distance electronic communication in a variety of forms.

In this chapter, we take a closer look at the networks that connect computers. We examine the hardware and software technologies that make computer networks possible and discuss ways in which such linked computers are used for communication, information gathering, and sharing resources. We also consider how networks are changing the way we live and work. In the next chapter, we'll delve deeper into the technology behind the Internet—the global computer network at the heart of the latest telecommunication revolution. We'll see how this technology will continue to transform our culture in ways that are hard to imagine today. But for now let's start by looking at the building blocks that make up all computer networks.

Basic Network Anatomy

A computer network is any system of two or more computers that are linked together. Why is networking important? The answers to this question revolve around the three essential components of every computer system:

> After more than a century of electric technology, we have **extended our central nervous system** itself in a global embrace, **abolishing both space and time** as far as our planet is concerned.
>
> —*Marshall McLuhan, in Understanding Media*

- *Hardware.* Networks enable people to share computer hardware resources, reducing costs and making it possible for more people to take better advantage of powerful computer equipment.
- *Software.* Networks enable people to share data and software programs, increasing efficiency and productivity.
- *People.* Networks enable people to work together, play together, and communicate in ways that are otherwise difficult or impossible.

Important information is hidden in these three statements. But before we examine them in more detail, we need to look at the hardware and software that make computer networks possible.

Networks Near and Far

In Chapters 2 and 3, you saw how information travels among the CPU, memory, and other components within a computer as electrical impulses that move along collections of parallel wires called buses. A network extends the range of these information

> Pretty soon you'll have no more idea of **what computer you're using** than you have an idea of **where your electricity comes from**.
>
> —*Danny Hillis, computer designer*

pulses, allowing them to travel to other computers. Computer networks come in all shapes and sizes, but most can be categorized as either local area networks or wide area networks.

A local area network (LAN) is a network in which the computers are physically close to each other, usually in the same building. A typical LAN includes a collection of computers and peripherals; each computer and networked peripheral is an individual *node* on the network. Nodes are connected to *hubs* or *switches*, which allow any node on the network to communicate with any other node. A hub broadcasts messages to all devices connected to the network; a switch transmits data to only the destination node. The practical consequence of this difference is that a hub allows only a single message at a time to move across the LAN, whereas a switch can carry multiple messages simultaneously. For this reason, a switch provides a significant advantage over a hub on a busy LAN.

One way to connect a node to a hub or a switch is by using a physical cable. The most common type of LAN cable, known as *twisted pair*, contains copper wires that resemble those in standard telephone cables. Most networked computers today are connected to networks via Ethernet cables plugged into Ethernet ports. Ethernet is a popular networking architecture developed in the 1970s at Xerox PARC; it has become an industry standard. Almost every new PC includes an Ethernet port on the main circuit board; older PCs have network cards that contain Ethernet ports. Circuitry on the motherboard or the network card controls the flow of data between the computer's RAM and the network cable. At the same time, it converts the computer's internal low-power signals into more powerful signals that can be transmitted through the network.

Some networks, mostly in homes, use existing household electrical or telephone wiring to transmit data. (Networks that use power lines are sometimes called *power-line networks*.) For these types of networks, Ethernet cables generally connect each computer's network port to a device that attaches to the phone line or power line.

FIGURE 8.4 A LAN can contain a variety of interconnected computers and peripherals using wired and wireless connections.

But the biggest trend in LAN technology today is the explosive growth in wireless networks. In a **wireless network**, each node has a tiny radio transmitter so it can send and receive data through the air rather than through cables. Wireless network connections are especially convenient for people who are constantly on the move. They're also good to use for creating small networks in homes and small businesses because they can be installed without digging or drilling. Wireless networks are generally slower than wired LANs are. A LAN can include a mix of hard-wired connections and wireless connections.

All computers on a LAN do not have to use the same operating system. For example, a single network might include Macs, Windows PCs, and Linux workstations. The computers can be connected in many different ways, and many rules and industry-defined standards dictate what will and won't work. Setting up a basic home LAN can be simple and straightforward. But large enterprise network systems may typically require the expertise of *network administrators* to take care of the configuration details so others can focus on using the network.

A **wide area network (WAN)**, as the name implies, is a network of LANs that extends over a long distance. In a WAN, each individual network site is a node on the wide area network. The largest and best known WAN is the Internet. By connecting to a network that's part of the Internet, a computer can connect to millions of other computers that are connected to the Internet.

Large WANs are possible because of the Web of telephone lines, microwave relay towers, and satellites that span the globe. Most WANs are private operations designed to link geographically dispersed corporate or government offices. WANs can be built using leased lines, or they can transmit signals using the Internet's packet-switching infrastructure (described in the next chapter).

FIGURE 8.5 WANs are often made up of LANs linked by phone lines, microwave towers, and communications satellites.

Routers are hardware devices or software programs that route messages as they travel between networks. Routers make it possible for messages to pass from the originating computer's LAN through a chain of intermediate networks to reach the LAN of the destination computer.

Mesh networks are an alternative to today's networks that rely on centralized routers. In a mesh network, a message hops from wireless device to wireless device until it finds its destination; there's no need to go through a central hub on the way. Mesh networks are a convenient way to set up a small, temporary communication system. For example, emergency personnel at the scene of a fire can quickly set up a mesh network to help them coordinate their efforts.

The Importance of Bandwidth

Most people who have explored multimedia on the Web have experienced small, jerky videos, sputtering audio, and (especially) long waits. The cause of most of these problems on the Internet (and other networks) is a lack of bandwidth at some point in the path between the sending computer and the receiving computer. The word has a technical definition, but in the world of computer networks, bandwidth generally refers to the quantity of data that can be transmitted through a communication medium in a given amount of time. In general, increased bandwidth means faster transmission speeds. Bandwidth is typically measured in kilobits (thousands of bits) or megabits (millions of bits) per second. (Because a byte is 8 bits, a megabit is 1/8 of a megabyte. The text of this chapter is about 300 kilobytes, or 2400 kilobits, of information. A physical medium capable of transmitting 100 megabits per second could theoretically transmit this chapter's text more than 50 times in 1 second.) Bandwidth can be affected by many factors, including the physical media that make up the network, the amount of network traffic, the software protocols of the network, and the type of network connection.

Some people find it easier to visualize bandwidth by thinking of a network cable as a highway. One way to increase bandwidth in a cable is to increase the number of parallel wires in that cable—the equivalent of adding more lanes to a freeway. Another way is to increase the speed with which information passes through the cable; this is the same as increasing the speed of the vehicles on the freeway. Of course, it's easier and safer to increase highway speed limits if you have a traffic flow system that minimizes the chance of collisions and accidents; in the same way, more efficient, reliable software can increase network bandwidth. But increasing a highway's throughput doesn't help much if cars pile up at the entry and exit ramps; in the same way, a high-bandwidth network seems like a low-bandwidth network if you've got a low-bandwidth connection to that network.

In general, bandwidth is on the rise. The original Ethernet standard, now commonly referred to as 10BASE-T Ethernet, had a bandwidth of 10 megabits per second. In the mid 1990s a faster Ethernet standard emerged: *Fast Ethernet* (which includes 100BASE-T) carries traffic at 100 megabits per second, provided that all the devices on the LAN are fast Ethernet compatible. Today the fastest Ethernet devices follow the *Gigabit Ethernet* (1000BASE-X) standard, capable of transferring 1 gigabit of data per second on an all-gigabit-Ethernet LAN.

Bandwidth is also on the rise *between* LANs, thanks to fiber-optic cables that are rapidly replacing copper wires in the worldwide telephone network. Fiber-optic cables use light waves to carry information at blinding speeds. A single fiber-optic cable can replace 10,000 copper telephone cables. Digital fiber-optic networks now connect major communication hubs around the world. Many large businesses and government institutions are connected to the global fiber-optic network, but most small businesses and homes still depend on copper wires for the "last mile," as it's often referred to in the industry—the link to the closest on-ramp to the fiber-optic freeway. Fiber-optic communication lines will eventually find their way into most homes, changing our lives in the process. These cables will provide lightning-fast two-way links to the outside world for our phones, televisions, radios, computers, and a variety of other devices.

Specialized Networks: From GPS to Financial Systems

Not all computer networks are collections of PCs linked to the Internet. Some specialized networks are designed to perform specific functions; these networks may not be directly connected to the Internet.

One such specialized network is the U.S. Department of Defense **Global Positioning System (GPS)**. The GPS includes at least 24 satellites that circle the Earth. They are carefully spaced so that from any point on the planet, at any time, four satellites will be above the horizon. Each satellite contains a computer, an atomic clock, and a radio. On the ground, a *GPS receiver* can use signals broadcast by three or four visible satellites to determine its position. GPS receivers can display locations, maps, and directions on smart phones, handheld computers, laptops, automobile and boat navigation systems, and military equipment. Members of the U.S. military use GPS receivers to keep track of where they are, but so do scientists, engineers, motorists, hikers, boaters, and others. GPS technology isn't foolproof; tall buildings, bad weather, and even sunspots can affect its accuracy. And it isn't without controversy. Privacy advocates have expressed concerns that the same technology that helps emergency workers pinpoint cellular 911 calls can also be used to locate people against their wills. GPS

FIGURE 8.6 A global positioning system helps this blind person navigate.

was the first fully-functional Global Navigation Satellite System, but other systems have been (or are being) developed by Russia, the European Union, China, and India.

Probably the most widely used specialized computer networks are the networks that keep our global financial systems running. When you strip away the emotional trappings, money is another form of information. Dollars, yen, pounds, and rubles are all symbols that make it easy for people to exchange goods and services. Money can be just about anything, provided people agree to its value. During the past few centuries, paper replaced metal as the major form of money. Today paper is being replaced by digital patterns stored in computer media. Money, like other digital information, can be transmitted through computer networks. That's why it's possible to withdraw cash from your checking account using an *automated teller machine (ATM)* at an airport or shopping mall thousands of miles from your home bank. An ATM (not to be confused with the communication protocol with the same initials) is a specialized terminal linked to a bank's main computer through a commercial banking network. Financial networks also make credit card purchases, automatic bill paying, electronic funds transfer, and all kinds of **electronic commerce (e-commerce)** possible. (E-commerce will be discussed in more detail in later chapters.)

Making Connections: From Wired to Wireless

Imagine how useful an office would be **without a door**.

—*Doug Engelbart, Internet pioneer, on the importance of network connections*

Toward the end of the twentieth century, in the early days of computer networks, most people had two basic choices for connecting their computers to networks: direct connections to local area networks using cables, or dial-up access to a remote system using a modem connected to a phone line. Today, thanks largely to the Internet explosion, we have many other options for connecting our machines to each other. To connect to a remote site, we generally don't need to dial that site's host computer; we just need to connect to the Internet and let our messages find their way through this network of networks to the target computer. In this section, we'll survey the most popular Internet connection options.

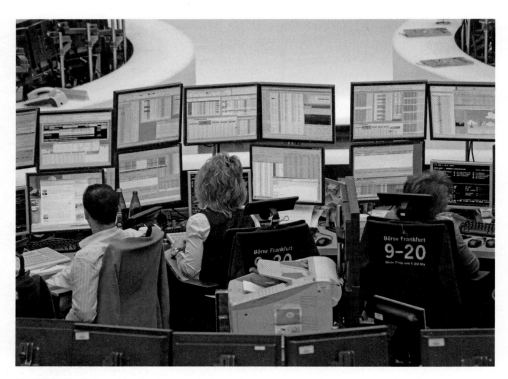

FIGURE 8.7 Every day stock traders move billions of dollars in funds electronically through world markets.

Direct Connections

In many schools and businesses, computers have a hard-wired Internet connection through a LAN. A *direct (dedicated) connection* is generally much faster than other connection options, making it possible to transfer large files (such as multimedia documents) quickly.

Typically, computers on a LAN have fast Ethernet connections that can transmit data at up to 100 Mbps (megabits per second). A large organization may operate a *backbone network* to connect its LANs. A high-speed fiber-optic backbone network can transmit data at more than 1 gigabit per second (1,000 megabits per second). Common ways of linking an organization's network to the Internet include *T1* connections, which can transmit voice, data, and video at roughly 1.5 Mbps, and *T3*, which has a data transmission speed of around 45 Mbps. (On some continents, a technology called E1 is used instead of T1.)

Communication à la Modem

If your computer doesn't have a direct connection to the Internet, you can temporarily connect to an Internet host through a **dial-up connection**—a connection using a modem and standard phone lines. The world's phone network is rapidly going digital, but the transition to an all-digital network is still many years away. Consequently, before a **digital signal**—a stream of bits—can be transmitted over a standard phone line, it must be converted to an **analog signal**—a continuous wave, similar to the sound waves that make up our phone conversations. At the receiving end, the analog signal must be converted back into the bits, representing the original digital message. Each of these tasks is performed by a **modem** (short for modulator/demodulator)—a hardware device that connects a computer to a telephone line.

An *internal modem* is installed on a circuit board inside the computer's chassis. An *external modem* is a device that is connected to the computer via a serial port or USB port. Both types of modem use phone cables to connect to the telephone network through standard modular phone jacks.

A *fax modem* can communicate with *facsimile (fax) machines* as well as computers. With a fax modem, a PC can "print" any document on a remote fax machine by dialing the number of that machine and sending a series of electrical pulses that represent the marks on the pages of the document. When it receives a fax, the PC constructs an on-screen document based on the pulses it receives from the transmitting machine. Many businesses use multifunction printer/scanner/fax machines (described in Chapter 3) to send and receive faxes.

Modems differ in their transmission speeds, measured in **bits per second (bps)**. Modems purchased today transmit at up to 56.6K (56,600) bps over standard phone lines. A typical connection through a modem and plain old telephone service (*POTS*) is much slower and less reliable than a direct Internet connection. High-speed transmission isn't usually critical for text messages, but it can make a huge difference when the data being transmitted includes graphics, sound, video, and other multimedia elements—the kinds of data commonly found on the Web. Modem connections are sometimes called **narrowband connections** because they don't offer much bandwidth when compared to other types of connections.

Broadband Connections

For faster remote connections, most businesses and homes with computers bypass standard modems and use some kind of **broadband connection**—a connection with much greater bandwidth than modems have. Several competing broadband technologies are available to computer users in many areas: DSL, cable, wireless, and satellite broadband connections. (Technically, a direct connection through a T1 or T3 line could be called a broadband connection, but most people don't have access to direct Internet connections.)

In some cases, broadband connections offer data transmission speeds comparable to direct connection speeds. Many broadband services offer another big advantage: they're always on. Users of these services don't need to dial in; the Internet is instantly available anytime, like television or radio. The most common broadband alternatives are based on the following technologies:

- *DSL.* Many phone companies offer **DSL (digital subscriber line)**, a technology for bringing broadband connections to homes and small businesses by sharing the copper telephone lines that carry voice calls. DSL customers must be geographically close to phone company service hubs. DSL transmission speeds vary considerably. *Downstream traffic*—information from the Internet to the subscriber—sometimes approaches T1 speeds. *Upstream traffic*—data traveling from the home computer to the Internet—typically travels more slowly, but still much faster than standard modem transmission. A DSL signal can share a standard phone line with voice traffic, so it can remain on without interfering with phone calls. DSL is not available everywhere, but it is becoming more widely available every year.

- *Cable modem connections.* Many cable TV companies offer high-speed Internet connections through **cable modems**. Cable modems allow Internet connections through the same network of coaxial cables that deliver television signals to millions of homes. Like DSL, cable modem service isn't available everywhere. Cable modem speeds often exceed DSL speeds both downstream and upstream. But because a single cable is shared by an entire neighborhood, transmission speeds can go down when the number of users goes up.

- *Satellite connections.* **Satellite Internet connections** are available through many of the same satellite dishes that provide television channels to viewers. Downstream satellite transmission is much faster than conventional modem traffic is, although not as fast as DSL or cable modem service. For some satellite services, upstream traffic goes through phone lines at standard modem rates. Other services use satellites for upstream and downstream traffic. For many homes and businesses outside of urban centers, satellites provide the only high-speed Internet access options available.

- *Wireless broadband connections.* People packing portable computers can temporarily connect to the Internet through wireless broadband connections. Using Wi-Fi technology,

FIGURE 8.8 A modem converts digital signals from a computer into analog signals that can be transmitted through telephone wires to another modem, which then converts them back into digital signals another computer can understand.

FIGURE 8.9 A broadband connection requires a cable modem connected to a cable TV service line, a DSL modem connected to a phone line, or a satellite modem connected to a satellite dish. These aren't really modems but are so named because they are functionally similar to modems.

described in the next section, students can connect to the Internet while they move around a wireless-equipped campus, travelers can make Web connections while waiting in airports, and coffee shops can become Internet cafes for people with wireless receivers in their laptops.

Each of these broadband technologies is widely deployed in the United States, and each is expanding its area of coverage. The U.S. lags far behind many other countries, though, in terms of the speed, quality, and price of its broadband offerings. In Japan, for example, a person can download an entire movie in two minutes—a movie that would take two hours or more to download with a U.S. broadband connection that costs just as much as the Japanese service. There's considerable debate about why the country that created the Internet provides inferior Internet access for its citizens. At least part of the reason may be the U.S. government's reluctance to regulate the telecommunications industry the way other developed countries do. In any case, it's likely that broadband service in the U.S. and elsewhere will continue to broaden.

Wireless Network Technology

Wireless technology is a **liberating force**. It will make possible **human-centered computers**. This wasn't possible before because we were **anchored to a PC**, and we had to go to it like going to a temple to **pay our respects**.

—*Michael Dertouzos, Director, MIT Laboratory for Computer Science*

A lightning-fast network connection to your desktop is of little use if you're away from your desk most of the time. When bandwidth is less important than mobility and portability, wireless technology can provide practical solutions.

Infrared wireless technology has been around for many years. Many laptops and handheld computers have infrared ports that can send and receive digital information over short distances, provided there are no physical barriers blocking the signals. Remote control devices use infrared beams to send commands to TVs, sound systems, and other home entertainment devices. Infrared technology isn't widely used in networks because of distance and line-of-sight limitations.

The fastest-growing wireless LAN technology is known as **Wi-Fi**. Wi-Fi uses radio waves to link computers to a LAN through a nearby **wireless access point (WAP)**—a Wi-Fi **hotspot**. (Apple calls their wireless access points *AirPort hubs*; some companies label theirs as *Wi-Fi routers*.) A wireless access point is similar to a network hub; it serves as a central connection point for wireless computers, PDAs, phones, media players, digital cameras, game consoles, security devices, and more. (Wi-Fi technology also allows peer- to-peer communication, so that two Wi-Fi—equipped devices can communicate directly with each other. But most Wi-Fi communication goes through wireless hubs.) If the access point is wired into a LAN, wireless devices can communicate with wired devices on the LAN. If the access point is linked to a DSL modem, cable modem, or a direct Internet connection, the access point is an Internet hotspot—a wireless gateway to the Internet.

Wi-Fi doesn't have the bandwidth of a hard-wired Ethernet connection, but it's fast enough for most applications, including multimedia Web downloads. There are several different flavors of Wi-Fi; all are variations of the IEEE 802.11 specifications for wireless local area networks. In the early 2000s, most Wi-Fi devices followed the 802.11b standards. Because of their greater bandwidth and range, 802.11g devices quickly took over the Wi-Fi market. Today 802.11n, with up to three times the bandwidth of 802.11g, is emerging as the new standard. Devices from different Wi-Fi generations can coexist on the same wireless networks, but older 802.11b devices can slow traffic down for everybody on a network.

Wi-Fi devices use the 2.4GHz and 5GHz band of the radio spectrum. Many common devices, including portable phones and microwave ovens, can cause Wi-Fi interference, especially on the crowded 2.4GHz band. Wi-Fi devices can transmit on different *channels* within each band, so it's often possible to reduce interference by changing channel settings on Wi-Fi hub devices. Wi-Fi range is affected by a number of factors—nearby objects that block signals, antenna placement, and devices competing for the same part of the radio spectrum (including other Wi-Fi networks in the neighborhood). A typical Wi-Fi access point has a range of up to 120 feet indoors and 300 feet outdoors. Installing additional access points can extend the range of a network.

Millions of homes, schools, campuses, and businesses worldwide have Wi-Fi networks. Hundreds of thousands of public hotspots have been installed in coffee houses, airports, restaurants, libraries, and other public buildings. A home Wi-Fi network allows computers to connect from any room without cables. Wi-Fi hotspots are common in airports, coffee shops, hotels, and other public places. A growing number of cities and towns are building citywide Wi-Fi networks, although some metropolitan Wi-Fi networks have been delayed or blocked for technological and political reasons.

Many public hotspots and Wi-Fi networks are free and open to all devices within range. Others require visitors to agree to terms of service before connecting to the Internet. Still others require passwords and other forms of authentication. Some charge for access by the month or by the hour. But free Wi-Fi access points are sprouting everywhere, part of a grassroots movement to provide universal wireless access to the Net.

There's a growing interest in another radio-based wireless standard called **WiMAX** or *802.16*. A single WiMAX tower can provide Wi-Fi-style access to a 25-square-mile area— the same area that can be covered by a cell phone tower. WiMAX also supports line-of-sight connections to customers up to 30 miles away. WiMAX isn't designed to replace Wi-Fi, but it can be a powerful tool for connecting Wi-Fi networks.

Wireless networks raise many security concerns. A wireless access point broadcasts information in all directions; the network forms a sphere with a diameter of up to 300 feet (the length of a football field). If the network is not secured, a technically skilled snooper

FIGURE 8.10 A wireless Internet connection is created by linking a wireless access point like one of these to a broadband or direct Internet connection.

with a laptop inside this virtual sphere can "sniff" network traffic and read what you're writing and collect email addresses and other personal information. The *WEP* (wired equivalent privacy) encryption scheme (see Chapter 10) improves the security of wireless networks by making your data as secure as it would be on a wired Ethernet. Businesses that need extra security for their wireless networks can take two additional steps: They can treat their wireless network as an insecure network and put a *firewall* between their wireless network and their wired network. (A firewall blocks unauthorized data transfers. We'll discuss how firewalls work in Chapter 10.) They can also make a wireless network more secure through the use of a **VPN (virtual private network)**. A VPN is an electronic "tunnel" through the Internet that uses encryption and other security measures to keep out unauthorized users and prevent eavesdropping.

Another type of wireless technology is **Bluetooth**, or *802.15*, named for a Danish king who overcame his country's religious differences. Bluetooth technology overcomes differences between mobile phones, handheld computers, and PCs, making it possible for all of these devices to communicate with each other regardless of their operating systems. Bluetooth uses radio technology similar to that of Wi-Fi, but its transmissions are limited to about 30 feet. Bluetooth isn't designed to compete with Wi-Fi. It is intended to replace the wires that connect devices such as cell phones, headsets, PDAs, and printers to each other. With Bluetooth it's possible to create a *personal area network (PAN)*—a network that links a variety of personal electronic devices so they can communicate with each other.

Bluetooth applications include:

- Linking a mobile phone to a wireless headset or a car's audio system
- Connecting a wireless keyboard and mouse to a computer
- Connecting a wireless game controller to the game console
- Sharing contact information and calendars between PDAs and/or mobile phones

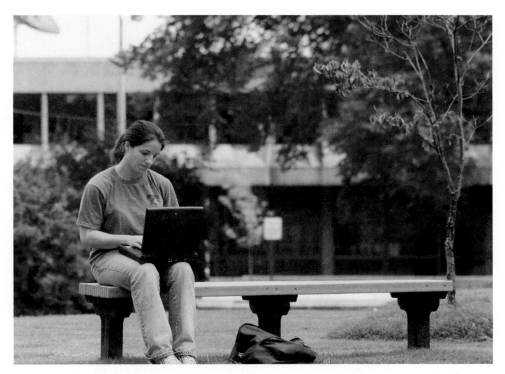

FIGURE 8.11 This University of Tennessee student can connect to the Internet using the campus wireless network.

Bluetooth technology is currently limited to simple device connectivity, but in the future it will open up all kinds of possibilities:

- A pacemaker senses a heart attack and notifies the victim's mobile phone to dial 911.
- A car radio communicates with parking-lot video cameras to find out where spaces are available.
- A medical wristband transmits an accident victim's vital information to a doctor's hand-held computer.
- A cell phone tells you about specials on clothes (available in your size) as you walk past stores in a mall. (Many fear that this technology will usher in a new era of junk phone calls.)

Wi-Fi and Bluetooth networks aren't nearly as widely used as wireless mobile phone networks. In two decades, mobile phones have gone from simple analog systems to powerful digital devices that can handle Internet data, text messages, photos, and other data along with voice traffic.

Mobile phone Internet connections are more common in Europe and Asia than they are in the United States, but the USA is catching up. While many Americans enjoy sending text messages and sharing photos with their cell phones, phone users in Europe and Asia are more likely to use their phones as multifunction devices. In Japan, for example, people routinely use their phones to send and receive email, check news headlines, shop, play games, share photos and short video clips, and even do karaoke.

The emerging generation of mobile wireless technology, often called *3G*, uses high-bandwidth connections to support true multimedia. Many mobile phone companies are using 3G technology to make phones into all-purpose digital devices.

There's a tremendous overlap in the capabilities and potential of Wi-Fi, WiMAX, and 3G. How we use these technologies will depend in part on how telecommunications companies develop them. In any case, the boundaries that separate phone networks and computer networks will continue to blur.

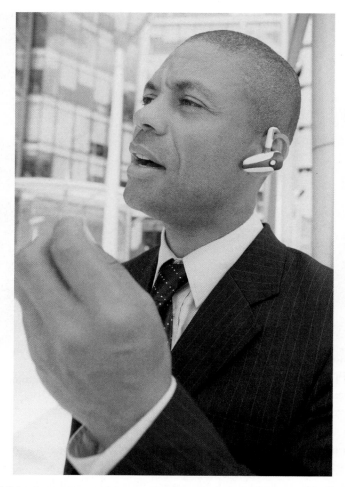

FIGURE 8.12 Bluetooth technology enables cell phones, PDAs, and computer peripherals, to announce themselves and describe their capabilities to other devices and PCs in personal area networks.

Communication Software

All the **most promising technologies** making their debut now are chiefly due to communication between computers—that is, to **connections** rather than to **computations**. And since **communication is the basis of culture**, fiddling at this level is indeed **momentous**.

—*Kevin Kelly, former Wired executive editor*

Whether connected by cables, radio waves, or a combination of modems and phone lines, computers need some kind of communication software to interact. To communicate with each other, two machines must follow the same protocols—rules for the exchange of data between devices. One such protocol is transmission speed: If one machine is "talking" at 56,600 bps and the other is "listening" at 28,800 bps, the message doesn't get through. Protocols include prearranged codes for messages such as "Are you ready?," "I am about to start sending a data file," and "Did you receive that file?" For two computers to understand each other, the software on both machines must be set to follow the same protocols. Communication software establishes a protocol that is followed by the computer's hardware.

The most famous protocol for computer networking is TCP/IP, discussed in more detail in the next chapter. Strictly speaking, the Internet is the network of computers and other digital devices that use TCP/IP to control the exchange of data.

Wireless Network Standards

Technical Name	Popular Name	Range	Technology	Approximate Speed	Typical Use
IrDA-Data	IrDA	1 meter	Infrared	9600 bps	Exchange data between PDAs
802.15	Bluetooth	10 meters	Radio	1 Mbps	Room-sized personal area network
802.11	Wi-Fi	30 meters or more	Radio	54 Mbps	Local area network
802.16	WiMAX	5 miles (no line of sight) to 30 miles (line of sight)	Radio	70 Mbps	Linking Wi-Fi networks
3G	3G	Varies widely depending on type of data being transmitted and location of relay towers	Radio	Up to 384 Kbps	Mobile phone Internet access

FIGURE 8.13 Wireless technologies compared.

Communication software can take a variety of forms. For a local area network, many communication tasks can be taken care of by a **network operating system (NOS)**, such as Novell's Netware or Microsoft's Windows Server. Just as a personal computer's operating system shields the user from most of the nuts and bolts of the computer's operation, a NOS shields the user from the hardware and software details of routine communication

FIGURE 8.14 Students living in Japan use their mobile phones for swapping photos and videos, playing multiplayer games, shopping, and much more.

FIGURE 8.15 A server might look like a normal PC. But industrial-strength servers such as these powerful IBM devices can provide software and data for hundreds or thousands of networked computers.

between machines. But unlike a PC operating system, the NOS must respond to requests from many computers and must coordinate communication throughout the network. Today many organizations are replacing the specialized PC-based NOS with an intranet system—a system built around the open standards and protocols of the Internet, as described in more detail in the next chapter.

The function and location of the network operating system depend in part on the LAN model. Some LANs are set up according to the client/server model, a hierarchical model in which one or more computers act as dedicated servers and all the remaining computers act as clients. Each server is a high-speed, high-capacity computer containing data and other resources to be shared with client computers. Using NOS server software, the server fulfills requests from clients for data and other resources. In a client/server network, the bulk of the NOS resides on the server, but each client has NOS client software for sending requests to servers. Many small networks are designed using the peer-to-peer model (sometimes called p-to-p or P2P), which enables every computer on the network to be both client and server. In this kind of network, every user can make files publicly available to other users on the network. Some desktop operating systems, including many versions of Windows and the Mac OS, include all the software necessary to operate a peer-to-peer network. In practice, many networks are hybrids that combine features of the client/server and peer-to-peer models.

Outside of a LAN, the most basic type of communication software is primitive terminal emulation software, which enables a computer to function as a character-based "dumb" terminal—a simple input/output device for sending messages to and receiving messages from the host computer. A terminal program handles phone dialing, protocol management, and the miscellaneous details necessary for making a PC and a modem work together. With terminal software and a modem, a PC can communicate through phone lines with another PC, a network of computers, or, more commonly, a large multiuser computer. The Windows, Mac, and Linux operating systems include terminal emulation programs.

At the other end of the line, communications software is usually built into the multiuser operating system of the host system—the computer that provides service to multiple users. This software enables a timesharing computer (see Chapter 1) to communicate with several other computers or terminals at once. The most widely used host operating system today is UNIX, the 40-year-old OS that has many variants, including the open source Linux OS discussed in Chapter 4.

Basic terminal emulators are fine for bare-bones computer-to-computer connections, but their character-based user interfaces can be confusing to people who are used to point-and-click graphical user interfaces. What's more, they can't be used to explore media-rich destinations on and off the Web. That's why most online explorers today use Web browsers and other graphical client software instead of generic terminal programs.

The Network Advantage

A network becomes more valuable as **it reaches more users**.

—*Metcalfe's Law, by Bob Metcalfe, inventor of Ethernet*

With this background in mind, let's reconsider the three reasons people use networks:

■ *Networks enable people to share computer hardware resources, reducing costs and making it possible for more people to take better advantage of powerful computer equipment.* When computers and peripherals are connected in a LAN, computer users can share peripherals. Before LANs, the typical office had a printer connected to each computer. Today it's more common to find a large group of computers and users sharing a small number of high-quality networked printers. In a client/server network, each printer may be connected to a *print server*—a server that accepts, prioritizes, and processes print jobs. Although it may not make much sense for users to try to share a printer on a wide area network (because it's not particularly convenient to use a printer that's hundreds of miles away), WAN users often share other hardware resources. Many WANs include powerful mainframes and supercomputers that can be accessed by authorized users at remote sites. Later in this chapter, we'll discuss grid computing—using grids of networked computers to share processing power and storage.

■ *Networks enable people to share data and software programs, increasing efficiency and productivity.* In offices without networks, people often transmit data and software by "sneakernet"—that is, by carrying discs and flash drives between computers. In a LAN, one or more computers can be used as **file servers**—storehouses for software and data that are shared by several users. With client software, a user can, without taking a step, **download** software and data—copy it from a server. Of course, somebody needs to **upload** the software—copy it to the server—first. A large file server is typically a dedicated computer that does nothing but serve files. But a peer-to-peer approach, allowing any computer to be both client and server, can be an efficient, inexpensive way to share files on small networks. (There's more on file sharing later in the chapter.) Of course, sharing computer software on a network can violate software licenses (see Chapter 4) if not done with care. Many, but not all, licenses allow the software to be installed on a file server as long as the number of simultaneous users never exceeds the number of licensed copies. Some companies offer **site licenses** or **network licenses**, which reduce costs for multiple copies or remove restrictions on software copying and use at a network site. Networks don't eliminate compatibility differences between different computer operating systems. Users of Windows-compatible computers, for example, can't run Mac applications just because they're available on a file server. But they can, in many cases, use data files and documents created on a Mac and stored on the server. For example, a poster created with Adobe Illustrator on a Mac could be stored on a file server so it can be opened, edited, and printed by Illustrator users on Windows PCs. File sharing, however, isn't always that easy. If users of different systems use programs with incompatible file formats, they need to use *data translation software* to read and modify each other's files. On WANs (or the Internet), the transfer of data and software can save more than shoe leather; it can save time. There's no need to send printed documents or discs by mail between two sites if both sites are connected to the same network.

■ *Networks enable people to work together, play together, and communicate in ways that are difficult or impossible without network technology.* Some software applications can be classified as *groupware*—programs designed to enable several networked users to work on the same documents at the same time. Groupware programs include multiuser appointment calendars, project-management software, database-management systems, and software for group editing of documents. Many groupware programs today, such as IBM Lotus Notes, are built on standard Internet protocols, so group members can communicate and share information using Web browsers and other standard Internet software tools. Groupware programs are commonly used in large businesses and institutions where information technology specialists manage hundreds or thousands of computers. But most groupware functions—email, message posting, calendars, and the rest—are available to anyone through other Web and PC applications. In fact, networks offer all kinds of communication possibilities to people inside and outside the business world.

In the next section, we'll focus on the third point—the communication and collaboration possibilities of networks. Then we'll revisit the first two points—the sharing of hardware and software—and see how they're tied in with interpersonal communication, too.

How It Works

Internet

1. A cable or DSL line provides high-bandwidth access to the Internet.

2. A cable modem or DSL modem connects your home network to an Internet service provider. It converts the analog signal entering your house into a digital signal and vice versa.

3. A combination router/firewall/hub manages traffic on your home network. The hub lets you connect multiple networked devices. The router takes data packets coming in over one network link and sends them out over a link leading to the packet's destination. The firewall prevents unauthorized packets from being forwarded over the network.

4. A PC contains a network card rated at 100 Mbps —100 million bits per second. (Older, slower cards support only 10 Mbps).

5. Cat 5e cables connect Ethernet-equipped devices. The cables look like telephone cables, but the connectors are slightly different. Cat 5e cables are easier to work with than older coaxial cables.

FIGURE 8.16

6. A wireless access point connects Wi-Fi devices with the rest of the network. To maximize reception, the Wi-Fi device is placed in a central location not obstructed by large metal objects.

7. A PC with a Wi-Fi card communicates with the rest of the network without a wired connection. Its connection will be slower than the connection of the Ethernet-equipped PC.

USB cable

8. A networked printer can be shared by all of the devices on the home network. Some printers contain network cards with Ethernet ports, allowing them to connect to the network just like PCs. Other printers contain only USB ports designed for connecting them to individual host PCs. The USB printer shown here is shared by its host PC with other computers on the network.

9. A notebook computer with built-in Wi-Fi can access the network from anywhere in the house or the yard.

10. A video game console connected to the network with Ethernet lets you play multi-player games.

11. The WEP key and 128-bit encryption help keep outsiders off your wireless network.

Interpersonal Computing: From Communication to Communities

New technology gives us two kinds of **newfound freedom**: The ability to **reach each other** 24/7— and the chance to **avoid one another** as never before.

—Lori Gottlieb, Author of Stick Figure

For many people, "networking" means little more than sending and receiving messages. One study found that the typical Internet user spends about 70 percent of connected time communicating with others. Digital technology can profoundly change the way people communicate. In this section, we'll explore the world of human-to-human digital communication, from basic email to complex social networks.

The Many Faces of Email

Every day, people all over the planet exchange billions of email messages. For many people, it's hard to imagine (or remember) life before email. But few people really understand the ins and outs of this powerful application. In this section, we'll look deeper into some of the options and issues facing email users. We won't concern ourselves with how mail gets from one person to another, or how email addresses work; those questions will be dealt with in the next chapter where we discuss the TCP/IP technology that drives the Internet. We're more concerned here with the tools we use to send and receive email messages.

In the early days of the Internet, email applications, like most other applications, were character-based command-line programs. Today, most people send and receive email using graphical mail applications on PCs (Microsoft Outlook, Apple Mail, Mozilla's Thunderbird), mail applications on smart phones (Blackberry, iPhone, Palm), and Web browsers pointing to Web mail applications (Gmail, Hotmail, Yahoo! Mail). From the point of view of the mail message, it doesn't matter which kind of client application the sender and receiver use; the contents of the message are delivered to the recipient's mailbox, ready to be processed by a mail application. The message may *look* different when viewed with different mail applications, but the contents remain the same.

Like most network technology, email is built on protocols—standards that make it possible for all kinds of hardware and software to communicate with each other. Most email client programs use standard Internet protocols: SMTP (Simple Mail Transfer Protocol) for sending mail, and POP (Post Office Protocol) or IMAP (Internet Message Access Protocol) for receiving mail. (Microsoft Outlook typically uses a proprietary protocol, but is compatible with Internet protocols.) IMAP is often used in large networks, such as college campuses; POP is commonly used by customers of commercial Internet service providers. When you're using an email client program for the first time, you need to give it some information about protocols (for example, the name of the SMTP server). Typically, this information is provided by your Internet service provider, school, or business—whoever provides you with your email access. Once the client software has the information it needs, it can send and receive messages indefinitely. (Travelers with laptops sometimes find that they have to change protocols temporarily when connecting to the Internet from remote locations.)

Many email users subscribe to Web-based email, or **Webmail**, services, including Gmail, Hotmail, Yahoo! Mail, and AOL. These services are designed to be accessed primarily through Web browsers rather than email clients. Email services offered by schools, businesses, and Internet service providers often offer Webmail *options*, allowing users to switch back and forth between accessing mail through a browser and a specialized mail program. The main advantage of Webmail is that it can be accessed from any Web-connected computer, anywhere in the world. The main disadvantage is that mail is stored "out there" on the Web, so it's not available without an Internet connection. Dedicated email clients like Outlook and Apple Mail offer users a choice between remote and local storage. People who access their mail from multiple

FIGURE 8.17 Email programs sport a variety of user interfaces. Web-based email clients such as Gmail (top) provide email access to people familiar with Web browsers. Microsoft Outlook (left) is a widely-used email client that connects to a variety of email server types. Apple's Mail program (right), part of Mac OS X, is popular because of its ease of use and its intelligent spam (junk mail) filters. Apple's iPhone reformats mail to fit its smaller screen.

computers tend to prefer to keep their mail remotely in a central storage server; single-computer users tend to prefer to keep their mail locally by downloading everything to their personal PCs.

Many email messages are plain ASCII text. Plain text messages can be viewed with any mail client program, including those in PDAs and phones. Many email programs can (optionally) send, receive, edit, and display email messages formatted in HTML, the formatting language used in most Web pages. HTML messages can include text formatting, pictures, and links to Web pages. The email client software hides the HTML source code from the sender and the recipient, displaying only the formatted messages. If the recipient views an HTML-encoded message with a mail program that doesn't recognize HTML, the formatting doesn't appear.

From: president@whitehouse.gov
Return-Path: president@spamsource.com
Subject: Huge Tax Rebate Just For You!!!
Date: September 25, 2010 4:43:00 PM PDT
To: laurel.r123b@hotmail.com

Laurel,
I have a bunch of money that the government doesn't need
that I wanted to give to you, but in order to transfer it to
you, I just need your bank account information, including
the PIN number.

FIGURE 8.18 The header of an email message includes information about the message and its delivery route, but some of the fields in the header can be forged to contain misinformation.

Even if the recipient's software can display HTML mail, not all email users *want* it because HTML encoding can slow down an email program. An HTML email message can also carry a *Web bug*—an invisible piece of code that silently notifies the sender about when the message was opened and may report other information about the user's machine or email software at the same time. Web bugs, which operate through specially encoded one-pixel graphics files, are also embedded in some commercial Web pages as well as HTML email messages. Fortunately, newer email applications can turn off Web bugs, preventing junk mailers and others from getting information about you when you read their messages.

Most email programs can send and receive formatted documents, pictures, and other multimedia files as attachments to messages. Attachments need to be temporarily converted to ASCII text using some kind of encoding scheme before they can be sent through Internet mail. Modern email programs take care of the encoding and decoding automatically. Of course, attachments aren't practical for most handheld devices. Also, attachments can contain viruses and other unwelcome surprises, as described in more detail in Chapter 10.

An email message's *header* contains information about the message and its delivery route through the Internet. An email client may hide the more technical parts of the header, depending on how it's configured. The *To* field and *From* field are almost always displayed. These fields should display the email addresses of the sender and the recipient(s) of the message. Unfortunately, the information in these fields isn't always accurate—it's easy to put fake addresses in either field. The *Subject* field should—but doesn't always—contain a brief description of the message's subject. The *Date* field displays the local date and time a message was written—assuming the clock is accurate in the sender's computer. An outgoing message header typically contains a *Cc* field for sending "carbon copies" to additional recipients, and a *Bcc* field for sending *blind* carbon copies—copies that aren't listed in the other recipients' headers.

Email Issues

Well there's egg and bacon; egg, sausage and bacon; egg and spam; bacon and **spam**; egg, bacon, sausage and **spam; spam**, bacon, sausage and **spam; spam**, egg, **spam, spam**, bacon and **spam; spam**, **spam**, **spam**, egg and **spam; spam, spam, spam, spam, spam, spam**, baked beans, **spam, spam, spam** and **spam**; or lobster thermidor aux crevettes with a mornay sauce garnished with truffle pâté, brandy, and a fried egg on top of **spam**.

—*Waitress in Monty Python's Flying Circus*

Most of us use email because it is a practical and powerful tool. It combines the advantages of the telephone and the letter. Like a telephone call, an email message is a way of instantaneously communicating with someone else, even if that person is on the other side of the globe. Like a letter, an email is nonintrusive. An email doesn't interrupt you the same way a telephone call does. An email conversation can take place over a period of hours, days, or even weeks.

There's a downside to email. Email is vulnerable to machine failures, network glitches, and security breaches. Viruses spread by email attachments cause billions of dollars of damage worldwide. (See Chapter 10 for more on viruses.) Many people spend hours every day working through their email messages. More than 50 percent of email messages sent worldwide are unsolicited, junk email, or **spam** (named for the *Monty Python* skit quoted at the beginning of this section). Even with the best filters, some spam sneaks through, wasting the time of busy people who have to delete it. Meanwhile, email messages are not private; most employers reserve the right to read their employees' messages.

Countless emails are produced by con artists phishing for financial information. These bogus emails are designed to trick people into entering **phishing** sites—Web sites intended to capture credit card numbers and other sensitive financial information. In one controlled experiment, the best phishing site fooled 90 percent of the test subjects.

Finally, email and instant messaging filter out many "human" components of communication. When Bell invented the telephone, the public reaction was cool and critical. Business people were reluctant to communicate through a device that didn't allow them to look each other in the eye and shake hands. There's a grain of truth in this quaint attitude. When people communicate, part of the message is hidden in body language, eye contact, voice inflections, and other nonverbal signals. The telephone strips visual cues out of a message, and this can lead to misunderstandings. Email peels away the sounds as well as the sights, leaving only plain words on a screen—words that might be misread if they aren't chosen carefully. What's more, online communication is a poor substitute at best for those chance meetings that happen in coffee houses, hallways, parks, and other real-world settings—meetings that can result in important communications and connections.

Mailing Lists

Email is a valuable tool for communicating one-to-one with individuals, but it's also useful for communicating one-to-many. **Mailing lists** enable you to participate in email discussion groups on special-interest topics. Lists can be small and local, or large and global. They can be administered by a human being or automatically administered by programs with names such as Listserv and Majordomo. Each group has a mailing address that looks like any Internet address.

You might belong to one student group that's set up by your instructor to carry on discussions outside of class, another group that includes people all over the world who use Adobe Flash to animate Web pages, and a third that's dedicated to saving endangered species in your state. When you send a message to a mailing list address,

FIGURE 8.19 Many email client programs contain intelligent filters that automatically route spam into junk mailboxes. Many Internet service providers offer spam-catching services that do the same thing on the Web. But it's not always easy to tell whether a message is spam or legitimate email. Many spammers disguise their lowly intentions with subject lines that look like legitimate email. Other spammers use odd spellings of "hot" words so their messages won't automatically be flagged as spam.

FIGURE 8.20 This phishing message is designed to con the recipient into revealing private login information.

every subscriber receives a copy. And, of course, you receive a copy of every email message sent by everyone else to those lists.

Subscribing to a busy list might mean receiving hundreds of messages each day. To avoid being overwhelmed by incoming mail, many list members sign up to receive them in daily *digest* form; instead of receiving many individual messages each day, they receive one message that includes all postings. But digest messages can still contain repetitive, off-topic, and annoying messages. Some lists are moderated to ensure that the quality of the discussion remains high. In a *moderated group* a designated moderator acts as an editor, filtering out irrelevant and inappropriate messages and posting the rest.

Newsgroups, Web Forums, and Blogs

You can participate in special-interest discussions without overloading your mailbox by taking advantage of Internet newsgroups and forums. A newsgroup is a public discussion on a particular subject, typically distributed through a worldwide newsgroup network called Usenet. Messages are posted on virtual bulletin boards for anyone to read at anytime. There are groups for every interest and taste . . . and more than a few for the tasteless. You can explore network newsgroups through several Web sites, including Google, or with a newsreader client program, an application designed to read Usenet articles.

People have been using newsgroups for online discussions for decades, but today more of those special-interest discussions are happening in Web forums. A Web forum is functionally similar to a newsgroup, but it's built on a Web application and accessed through a Web browser. Some forums are membership-only affairs, off-limits to non-members. Others restrict postings to members, but allow anyone to view those postings. Still others are completely open, even allowing anonymous postings. Moderated forums and newsgroups include only postings that have been approved by moderators who filter out repetitive questions from newcomers, childish rants, off-topic trivia, machine-generated junk postings, and other counterproductive messages.

The messages in a typical forum or newsgroup tend to fall into categories based on subject. One person might post a question; several people might respond to that posting with answers and related comments. When forum messages are viewed chronologically, all of those related postings might be interspersed with messages on other topics. Fortunately, many forums have options for viewing *threaded discussions*—discussions in which postings are organized by topics or subjects, called *threads*, rather than by time. (Many email clients offer options for displaying mail organized into threads, with all replies to the same message grouped together.) Some forums offer options for email notification, so participants don't need to check the forum sites repeatedly for new postings.

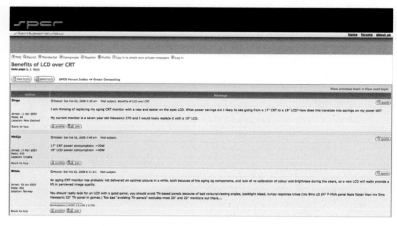

FIGURE 8.21 Online forums can display messages sorted chronologically or grouped into topic-related threads.

Newsgroups and forums are based on two-way communication—participants post messages and read messages posted by others. (Although discussions are frequently monitored by *lurkers*—silent, invisible observers who don't contribute to the discussions.) A blog is similar to a forum, except that it's created by an individual or a small group, to be read by a much larger group. A blog (short for weB LOG) is an online journal (often including pictures and other media) that's updated frequently and posted on a public (or semi-public) Web site. A variety of Web applications simplify the process of creating and posting blogs. Hundreds of thousands of people, many with little or no technical expertise, are active bloggers. They write about their personal lives, politics, the arts, business, technology, and just about anything else you might imagine. Micro-bloggers use Twitter and similar sites to chronicle their minute-by-minute activities and thoughts with one-or-two sentence *micro-blogs*. Most bloggers prefer to compose their thoughts into longer essays and post them daily or weekly. Some choose to create audio or video podcasts instead of—or in addition to—text-based blogs. (Podcasts are discussed in Chapters 6 and 9.) Political bloggers have become important sources of information and opinion, using Web sites to bypass tightly controlled mainstream media (and in some countries, authoritarian government media monopolies). Hundreds of important news stories have been broken by **bloggers**. Bloggers have provided critical on-the-scene coverage of wars, earthquakes, storms, and other disasters. Media outlets have responded with their own blogs. The *blogosphere*, as it's often called, continues to expand, providing an outlet for an incredibly diverse population of writers. The challenge for most bloggers today is to find ways to attract and keep audiences; the challenge for those audiences is to determine which blogs are trustworthy and worthy of the time investment it takes to read them.

Instant Messaging, Text Messaging, and Teleconferencing: Real-Time Communication

Mailing lists, forums, and blogs use **asynchronous communication**: The poster and the reader don't have to be logged in at the same time. Computer networks also offer many possibilities for **real-time communication**. **Instant messaging (IM)** has been possible since the days of text-only Internet access. Internet relay chat (IRC) and Talk enable UNIX users and others to exchange instant messages with their online friends and coworkers. Newer, easier-to-use instant messaging systems from AOL, Microsoft, Yahoo!, Google, Apple, and others, have turned instant messaging into one of the most popular Internet activities. Instant messaging programs enable users to create "buddy lists," check for "buddies" who are logged in, and exchange typed messages and files with those who are. Most of these programs are available for free. Unfortunately, there's not a common standard for IM technology, so users of one IM system might not be able to IM users of another system. For example, a user of AOL's AIM program can communicate with someone using Apple's iChat, but not with users of Microsoft Messenger or Yahoo! Instant Messenger. Some IM client programs (Trillian for Windows, Adium for Mac OS X) support competing IM protocols, so they can send and receive messages to all the major IM services. Many businesses now use instant messaging to keep employees connected, and IM technology is built into many smart phones.

IM technology appears, at first glance, to be similar to **text messaging**, a popular form of communication among mobile phone users. Text messaging uses SMS technology, which is far more limiting than IM technology. Unlike SMS, most IM systems support formatted text, longer messages, and file transfer; some support audio and video conferencing. In the future, the lines between SMS and IM may disappear. But for now, they're two different—and incompatible—forms of communication.

Another type of real-time online communication is the **chat room**—a public or private virtual conference room where people with similar interests or motivations can type messages to each other and receive near-instant responses.

Some IM programs, chat rooms, and multiplayer games on the Web use graphics to simulate real-world environments. Participants can represent themselves with **avatars**—graphical "bodies" that might look like simple cartoon sketches, elaborate 3-D figures, or exotic abstract icons.

Several IM programs make it possible to carry on **video teleconferences**. A video teleconference enables two or more people to communicate face-to-face over long distances by combining video and computer technology. Until a few years ago, most video teleconferences were conducted in special rooms equipped with video cameras, microphones, television monitors, and other specialized equipment. Today it's possible to participate in multiperson video teleconferences using a standard PC with an attached or built-in Webcam or video camera and a high-speed Internet connection. Internet video images don't measure up to the images beamed to professional conference rooms, but they're more than adequate for most applications.

FIGURE 8.22 U.S. Army Major Andrew Olmsted's blog provided the world with an insider's view of the Iraq war. When Olmsted was killed by a sniper, a friend posted Olmsted's final message. Nearby Iran has one of the largest blogging populations on the planet, but Iranian bloggers face considerable risk. One Iranian blogger was given a 14-year prison sentence because he criticized the arrest of other online journalists.

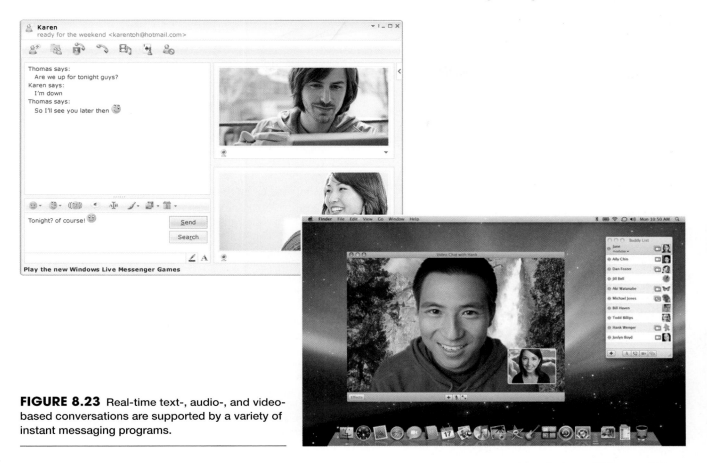

FIGURE 8.23 Real-time text-, audio-, and video-based conversations are supported by a variety of instant messaging programs.

Computer Telephony

A voice mail system is a voice messaging system with many of the features of an email system, including the ability to store, organize, and forward messages. Voice mail is a familiar example of a growing trend toward *computer telephony integration (CTI)*—the linking of computers and telephones to gain productivity.

Internet telephony (also called Voice-over IP, or VoIP) has become a legitimate competitor to traditional phone companies. With VoIP your phone call is carried over the Internet rather than the telephone network. VoIP service requires a broadband Internet connection. One way to place a VoIP call is to use a traditional telephone handset connected to the Internet with a phone adapter. Another way to make a VoIP call is to use an Internet-connected PC equipped with a microphone headset and appropriate software. Most VoIP providers allow calls to any telephone number; the last leg of a call to a non-VoIP number is routed through the recipient's local telephone company or cellular phone provider.

There are many reasons for VoIP's growing popularity. VoIP service is generally cheaper than traditional phone service (not counting the cost of the required broadband connection). Some companies offer VoIP for free. VoIP calls are automatically routed to VoIP phones, no matter where they are connected to the Internet. Travelers can receive calls wherever they make Internet connections. VoIP phones integrate easily with online address books, video conference services, and other Internet services. The most popular Internet telephony application, Skype, includes options for video calls and videoconferences.

VoIP service also has some weaknesses. Backup generators keep traditional telephone networks operational when the power is out (computer networks are generally unusable during power outages). Traditional

FIGURE 8.24 Skype, the most popular Internet phone service, provides audio and video phone service to users with broadband Internet connections.

Working Wisdom

Online Survival Tips

When you're online, you're using a relatively new communication medium with new rules. Here are some suggestions for successful online communication:

➡ **Let your system do as much of the work as possible.** If your email program can sort mail, filter mail, or automatically append a signature file to your mail, take advantage of those features. If you send messages to the same group of people repeatedly, create a group that includes those people—a distribution list that can save you the trouble of typing or selecting all those names each time.

➡ **Store names and addresses in a computer-accessible address book.** Email addresses aren't easy to remember and type. If you mistype a single character, your message will probably go to the wrong person or **bounce**—come back with some kind of undeliverable-mail message. An address book on your PC or the Web enables you to select addresses without typing them each time you use them. Use your email program's backup or export capability to back up your address book.

➡ **Don't share your email address.** It's easy to think of an email address like a physical address, sharing it with roommates, partners, and others who use the same computer. But email works best if each person has a unique address. A personal address is more secure and private, but it's also more practical; when someone sends a message to you, the sender knows that you will receive the message.

➡ **Don't open suspicious attachments.** An email attachment may contain a computer virus. If the email is from a stranger, don't be tricked into opening the attachment. Delete the email instead.

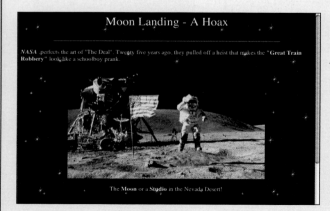

FIGURE 8.25 You can't always trust online sources, so check your facts and sources carefully.

➡ **Protect your privacy.** Miss Manners said it well in a *Wired* interview: "For email, the old postcard rule applies. Nobody else is supposed to read your postcards, but you'd be a fool if you wrote anything private on one."

➡ **Don't get hooked by a phishing expedition.** If you receive an email claiming to be from your bank or another legitimate business, be suspicious. Don't blindly click on links that claim to take you to the business's Web site. If you *do* link to a Web site, check to make sure the URL is the actual business's address. Look for a padlock icon displayed by the browser, indicating that the Web site connection is secure. If you have any doubt about the link, connect to the bank or institution's Web site in the usual way—not through the email link.

➡ **Keep your security systems up to date.** Make sure that you're using the current version of your Web browser, email client, and other online applications. These programs are updated often to plug security leaks; if you're not up to date, you're inviting trouble.

➡ **Crosscheck online information sources.** Don't assume that every information nugget you see online is valid, accurate, and timely. If you read something online, treat it with the same degree of skepticism that you would if you heard it in a coffee shop.

➡ **Beware of urban legends.** The Internet is an amazing information source, but it's also a tremendous source of misinformation. Web sites and email chain letters spread all kinds of "urban legends"—widely-believed stories that may be false, misleading, or sensationalized. Microsoft is giving money to people who forward this message; a prominent politician is secretly allied with terrorists; parking lot thieves use ether-laced perfume samples to render their victims unconscious—these stories are believed by many people who read about them in email messages or Web postings. Snopes.com debunks the most popular urban legends; check there if you read something that seems too good—or too fantastic—to be true.

➡ **Be aware and awake.** It's easy to lose track of yourself and your time online. In his book *The Virtual Community,* Howard Rheingold advises, "Rule Number One is to pay attention. Rule Number Two might be: Attention is a limited resource, so pay attention to where you pay attention."

➡ **Avoid information overload.** When it comes to information, more is not necessarily better. Search selectively. Don't waste time and energy trying to process mountains of information. Information is not knowledge, and knowledge is not wisdom.

telephones provide 911 service, which most VoIP implementations do not have. Telephone books ("the white pages") are available for people with traditional telephone service, but a VoIP provider may not provide directory assistance. The traditional telephone network may provide a higher quality of service because VoIP relies on the Internet and, therefore, does not guarantee that data packets are delivered within a particular time frame. This final advantage is apparently not too significant, because telephone companies are planning to replace their traditional networks with VoIP networks over the next few years.

On the mobile front, the line between computers and telephones is especially fuzzy. Many smart phones can connect to the Internet, do instant messaging, upload and download email messages, and display miniature Web pages. Most analysts expect rapid advances in these converging technologies over the next few years—advances such as reliable speech recognition that will make these devices much more useful for people on the go.

Social Networking, Role Playing, and Virtual Communities

The value of a social network is defined not only by who's on it, but by who's excluded.

—*Technology Forecaster Paul Saffo*

Email, instant messages, chat rooms, Web forums, blogs, and other network communication technologies have resulted in new ways for people to make friends and create communities. MySpace, Facebook, Friendster, LiveJournal, orkut, Tribe, LinkedIn, and other social networking sites (see Chapter 1) combine many of these tools with other services to make it easy for members to connect with friends, meet people with common interests, and create online communities. Web users—especially younger ones—have embraced social networking sites, making them integral to their larger social lives. MySpace and Facebook, the two most popular social networking sites, consistently rank near the top on the list of Web sites with the most daily hits. Facebook has become a platform of sorts by enabling software developers to create games and other applications that function exclusively in the Facebook world. It's not clear whether Facebook and MySpace will continue to be the networks of choice for social networkers. Futurist Paul Saffo and others believe that in the long run, most social networkers will find more value in smaller networks of people with similar interests.

Most social networking sites are plagued by problems of privacy and safety; like real-world communities, these online communities include less-than-honorable members. The sites are continually improving security techniques and privacy policies, but members are ultimately responsible for their own safety and privacy.

Social networking also occurs in massively multiplayer online role-playing games (MMORPGs). These games can support hundreds of thousands of simultaneous players taking on roles in virtual worlds. The virtual worlds are persistent—they continue to exist even when players log out. Popular MMORPGs are *EverQuest II, Lineage II,* and *World of WarCraft.* Success requires cooperation among groups of players, called guilds. Many players become passionately involved in—or addicted to—the virtual worlds of MMORPGs.

Some sites, most notably Second Life, occupy a space between social networking sites and MMORPGs. Like role-playing games, Second Life is a 3-D virtual world populated by the avatars of Web users from all over the world. But Second Life is more of a community than a game. Members buy and build "property," visit and vacation, take in concerts and community events. This type of community can be especially valuable to people who, for whatever reason, aren't able to go out and about in the physical world.

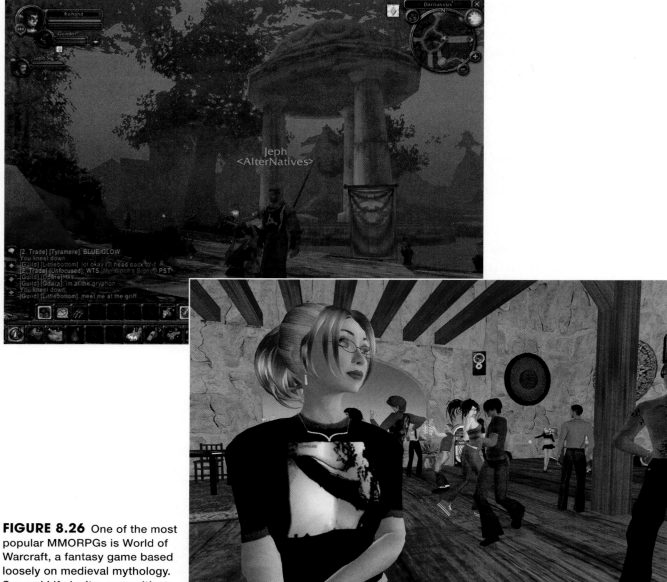

FIGURE 8.26 One of the most popular MMORPGs is World of Warcraft, a fantasy game based loosely on medieval mythology. Second Life isn't a game; it's an online 3D community.

Information Sharing: Social Bookmarking, Wikis, Media Sharing, and Crowdsourcing

Many types of network communication can be loosely classified as information sharing—the formal or informal pooling of knowledge. Newsgroups and forums are forms of information sharing. But there are many other tools and techniques for sharing information on today's networks. These tools leverage the collective wisdom of communities in a variety of ways.

Visitors to social bookmarking sites, including Digg and Del.icio.us, depend on each other for one thing: to find the most valuable sites on the Web. When you visit a social

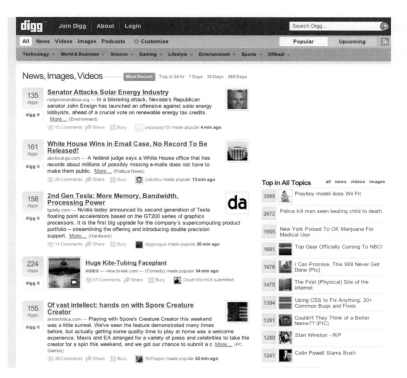

FIGURE 8.27 Digg makes it easy for users to share recommendations of favorite Web pages with each other.

bookmarking site, you can see which Web pages are currently generating the most interest among people who use that social bookmarking service. You can vote on which pages deserve to be ranked higher or lower in that service's ranking. These sites create informal communities of people dedicated to helping each other separate the best from the rest of the Web.

Another type of information sharing involves wikis. A **wiki** (shortened from the Hawaiian term *wiki wiki* which means *quick*) is a Web site designed to enable anyone who accesses it to contribute to, and modify, content. A variety of Web tools are available to make it easy to build and contribute to wikis. Wikipedia, the famous free-content online encyclopedia, may be the world's largest collaborative effort. Wikipedia contains millions of articles in English and hundreds of thousands of articles in German, French, Polish, Japanese, Dutch, Swedish, Italian, Portuguese, and Spanish. Wikipedia has become an invaluable resource for Web visitors and an important community for millions of dedicated volunteers who contribute content and continually monitor the site for vandalism—deliberate attempts to destroy the legitimate contents of articles. The Wikipedia community repairs vandalized articles within minutes, and continually monitors the encyclopedia for content that doesn't live up to its standards of objectivity and accuracy. Wikipedia's success has confounded skeptics and provided inspiration for other not-for-profit community collaborations.

Another type of network collaboration involves sharing of media resources. Flickr (see Chapter 1) pioneered this concept by providing an open database for visitors to share photographs. Because most Flickr members don't claim copyright protection on the photographs they post, the entire Internet community can benefit from a large collection of public domain photographs—pictures that can be used without getting the prior permission of the photographer. YouTube has become a cultural phenomenon by providing a similar service for video sharing. The vast YouTube library includes an odd mix of silly home video clips, low-budget political rants and satires, music videos from aspiring and established musicians, experiments from aspiring filmmakers, candid clips of celebrities and politicians caught off

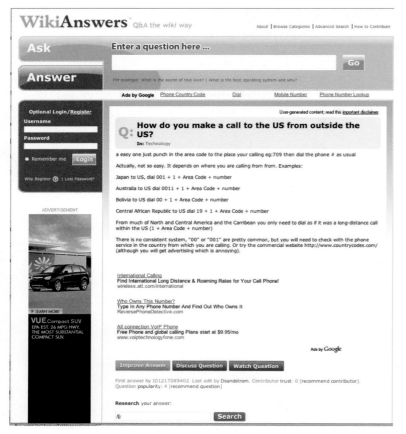

FIGURE 8.28 WikiAnswers is a wiki Web site with questions and answers provided by visitors.

FIGURE 8.29 Google's YouTube is a phenomenally popular media sharing site that features everything from short home-made movies to high-profile professional videos.

guard, footage of historic events, and bootlegged clips from copyrighted TV shows and movies (many of which are removed when their owners complain to Google, YouTube's parent company). A popular YouTube video can, in a matter of hours, become a *viral* video, as email messages, blog posts, and IMs containing links to that video spread across the Internet like a virus. Political analysts often suggest that YouTube has profoundly changed the nature of political communication by enabling concerned citizens to post controversial clips that might not be featured on corporate news programs.

Some types of information sharing might be called *crowdsourcing*—outsourcing of a task to a large community of people, possibly volunteers, rather than to a small group of contracted specialists. Crowdsourcing has been used by T-shirt manufacturer Threadless (to solicit shirt designs), political action group MoveOn.org (for political organizing), scientific talent broker InnoCentive (to connect research "seekers" with "solvers"), and many other organizations. Some types of crowdsourcing, such as photography solicitation, threaten the livelihoods of professionals who can't compete in a market of millions. But for many people and organizations, crowdsourcing offers the potential of solving problems that couldn't easily or practically be solved in other ways.

Sharing Resources: Peer-to-Peer, Grid, and Cloud Computing

The **network** is the **computer**.

—*John Gage, chief researcher, Sun Microsystems*

Of all the companies that came out of nowhere during the dot-com boom of the late '90s, Napster generated the most conversation—and controversy. When 19-year-old college student Shawn Fanning put a friendly user interface and a fresh spin on decades-old file-sharing technology, he created a virtual swap meet for students and others who wanted to share MP3 music files. Almost overnight Napster became one of the hottest Internet destinations, with millions of users downloading and sharing MP3s daily using Napster's software. In May of 2000, a tech company hired by the rock band Metallica revealed that 322,000 Napster users were illegally distributing their music. The Recording Industry Association of America sued the company because its software enabled users to download copyrighted recordings without paying the record companies or artists.

The Napster servers didn't contain those illegal recordings; it just displayed links to recordings scattered all over the Net. People who used Napster practiced **peer-to-peer (P2P) computing**, or, more specifically, *peer-to-peer file sharing*, by making music files on their hard drives available to others rather than posting them on central servers. In April of 2001, a U.S. District Court judge ruled that Napster was violating federal copyright law and forced the company to change its software so users no longer had free access to copyrighted recordings. Napster changed its software and its business model, but the peer-to-peer music exchange lived on through other programs and Web sites. The Gnutella file-sharing system, used by several different file-sharing programs, avoids Napster's Achilles' heel by allowing users to share music, movies, software, and other files without going through a central directory. More recently, a P2P protocol known as *BitTorrent* has become a popular way to download very large files. For users with broadband Internet connections, downloading is much faster than uploading. With older P2P protocols, file-sharing means one computer transferring a file to another computer. When both computers have broadband connections, the file transfer speed is limited by the rate at which the provider can upload content to the Internet. BitTorrent solves this problem by dividing files into pieces. When a userseeks a file, multiple providers can each supply a different portion of the file, considerably reducing the transfer time. BitTorrent makes practical the sharing of files hundreds of megabytes in length. Some people use

Working Wisdom

Netiquette and Messaging Etiquette

The Internet is a new type of community that uses new forms of communication. Like any society, the Net has acceptable behavior rules and guidelines. If you follow these rules of netiquette, you'll be doing your part to make life on the Net easier for everybody—especially yourself.

➡ *Say what you mean, and say it with care.* After you send something electronically, there's no way to call it back. Compose each message carefully, and make sure it means what you intend it to mean. If you're replying to a message, double-check the heading to make sure your reply is going only to those people you intend to send it to. Even if you took only a few seconds to write your message, it may be broadcast far and wide and be preserved forever in online archives.

➡ *Keep it short.* Include a descriptive subject line, and limit the body to a screen or two. If you're replying to a long message, include a copy of the relevant part of the message, but not the whole message. Remember that many people receive hundreds of email messages each day, and they're more likely to read and respond to short ones.

➡ *Proofread your messages.* A famous *New Yorker* cartoon by Peter Steiner shows one dog telling another, "On the Internet no one knows you're a dog." You may not be judged by the color of your hair or the clothes you wear when you're posting messages, but that doesn't mean appearances aren't important. Other people will judge your intelligence and education by the spelling, grammar, punctuation, and clarity of your messages. If you want your messages to be taken seriously, present your best face.

➡ *Don't assume you're anonymous.* Your messages can say a lot about you. Those messages might be seen by more than your intended audience, and they won't necessarily go away when you want them to. Researcher Jonathan G. S. Koppell suggests a more contemporary caption for the *New Yorker* cartoon mentioned above: "On the Internet, everyone knows you're an aging, overweight, malamute-retriever mix living in the southwest, and with a preference for rawhide."

➡ *Learn the "nonverbal" language of the Net.* A simple phrase such as "Nice job!" can have very different meanings depending on the tone of voice and body language behind it. Because body language and tone of voice can't easily be stuffed into a modem, online communities have developed text-based or graphical substitutes, sometimes called *emoticons*. The table below shows a few of the most common emoticons.

➡ *Know your abbreviations.* Text messaging is slow and tedious on cell phones and PDAs. To speed things up, a shorthand has developed for many common phrases. Knowing the meaning of abbreviations will save you time and help you understand the text messages you receive. See the table on the facing page for a list of some of the most common abbreviations.

➡ *Keep your cool.* Many otherwise timid people turn into raging bulls when they're online. The facelessness of Internet communication makes it all too easy to shoot from the hip, overstate arguments, and get caught up in a digital lynch-mob mentality. There's nothing wrong with expressing your emotions, but broadside attacks and half-truths can do serious damage to your online relationships. Online or off, freedom of speech is a right that carries responsibility.

Common Emoticons

Emoticon	Vertical variant	Graphic	Meaning
:-)	(^,^)	😊	Smile or happy
:-(	(<_>)	☹	Frown or sad
;-)	('_^)	😏	Sarcasm, joking
:-@	(>_<)	😠	Anger, frustration
:-/	(-_-)	😕	Skepticism, uneasiness
:-P	(^o^)	😛	Goofy smile, playful teasing
O:-)	(-°-)	😲	Surprised
>:-)	(\,/)	😈	Evil smile

FIGURE 8.30 A few of the most common emoticons.

➡ **Don't be a source of spam.** It's so easy to send multiple copies of email messages that it's tempting to broadcast too widely. Target your messages carefully; if you're trying to sell tickets to a local concert or advertise your garage sale, don't tell the whole world. If you do send a mass mailing, hide the recipient list to protect the privacy of your recipients. One way is to send the message to yourself and put everyone else in the Bcc (blind carbon copy) field. And if you send repeated mass mailings, make sure you always include a message telling people how they can get off your list.

➡ **Say no to spam.** People send spam because it gets results—mouse clicks to Web links, email replies, purchases, and more. If you want to do your part to wipe out spam, *never* reward spammers with your time or money.

➡ **Send no-frills mail.** Even if your email program makes it easy to use fancy formatting, embed HTML, and include attachments, it's usually better to err on the side of simplicity. Graphics and fancy formatting make message files bigger and slower to download. Many people turn off the HTML capabilities of their email programs to protect themselves from Web bugs. And many email veterans fear attachments because of the risk of email viruses. If you don't need the extra baggage, why not leave it out?

➡ **Lurk before you leap.** People who silently monitor mailing lists, newsgroups, and forums without posting messages are called *lurkers*. There's no shame in lurking, especially if you're new to a group; it can help you to figure out what's appropriate. After you've learned the culture and conventions of a group, you'll be better able to contribute constructively and wisely.

➡ **Check your FAQs.** Many newsgroups, forums, and mailing lists have **FAQs** (pronounced "facks")—posted lists of **frequently asked questions**. These lists keep groups from being cluttered with the same old questions and answers but only if members take advantage of them.

➡ **Know when to disconnect.** Just about everybody has been annoyed by someone shouting into a phone a couple of feet away in a restaurant, or a loud ringtone that goes off during a play or lecture, or a face-to-face meeting with someone whose eyes never leave his laptop screen, or a friend who just can't stop texting while you're trying to talk to her. People have lost concert seats, friends, and even jobs because they didn't use common sense about when and where it's appropriate to talk, text, or explore the Web—and when to turn the technology off.

➡ **Give something back.** The Internet includes an online community of volunteers who answer beginner questions, archive files, moderate forums, maintain public servers, and provide other helpful services. If you appreciate their work, tell them in words and show them in actions; do your part to help others in the Internet community.

Common Text Message Abbreviations

Message	Meaning
404	Clueless
AAMOF	As a matter of fact
AFAIK	As far as I know
AFK	Away from keyboard
AYT	Are you there?
B4N	Bye for now
BRB	Be right back
BTW	By the way
CID	Consider it done
doh	How stupid of me
FWIW	For what it's worth
FYI	For your information
HHOK	Ha ha only kidding
HRU	How are you?
IDD	Indeed
IMHO	In my humble opinion
LOL	Laughing out loud
ROFL	Rolling on the floor laughing
RUF2C	Are you free to chat?
RUF2T	Are you free to talk?
RUOK	Are you OK?
TBH	To be honest
THX	Thanks
TMB	Text me back
TYVM	Thank you very much
WDYT	What do you think?

FIGURE 8.31 Text messaging abbreviations and their meanings.

BitTorrent to download open-source software such as the Linux operating system. Others use it to download illegal copies of feature films. Businesses use BitTorrent and other P2P protocols for group collaboration, for Web searches, and for sharing updates to virus-control software, among other things.

Technologies such as BitTorrent make it difficult, or impossible, for laws to contain the peer-to-peer file-sharing phenomenon. Recording artists are divided on the issue; some encourage fans to share their music; others fear that sharing will make it difficult for musicians to support themselves. A growing collection of legitimate music down-loading services, such as the Apple iTunes Store and Amazon, which lets consumers inexpensively purchase songs and albums digitally online, provide consumers with a legal way to download music. (Copyright and intellectual property issues were discussed in Chapter 4.)

A related technology—**grid computing**—is, like P2P, a form of *distributed computing*. But grid computing isn't about sharing files; it's about sharing processing power. One type of grid computing, sometimes called *volunteer computing*, involves creating a virtual network of geographically dispersed computers to work on a problem that's too big to solve with a single machine or LAN. The best-known example is SETI@Home (setiathome. ssl.berkeley.edu), a program that puts PCs all over the Internet together into a sort of virtual supercomputer that analyzes space telescope data in the search for extraterrestrial life. The SETI@Home program, when installed on a PC, uses the computer's idle time to do calculations and send the results back to SETI headquarters. Millions of PCs around the world can do the work of a million-dollar supercomputer in much less time. A similar pro-gram called FightAIDS@home (fightaidsathome.com) enables PCs to contribute spare processing cycles to the fight against AIDS. GIMPS (the Great Internet Mersenne Prime Search) recruited more than 60,000 volunteers to find the largest known prime number.

Another form of grid computing, sometimes called *utility computing*, involves offer-ing computational power and storage as metered commercial services, with the Internet acting like a utility grid. Grid-computing applications are currently being used by the U.S. Department of Defense, the U.S. Department of Energy, NASA, the UK National

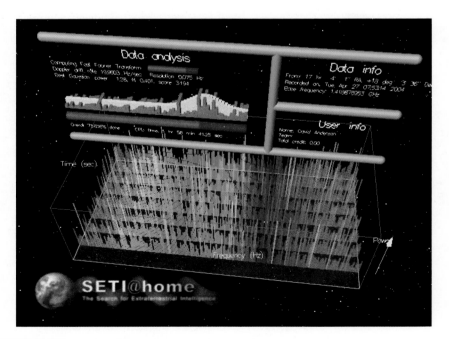

FIGURE 8.32 The SETI@Home project synchronizes the processing power of various connected computers from around the world. Anyone can donate their unused PC time to SETI@Home; the freely downloadable application starts up whenever your PC is not being used.

Grid, and a variety of academic and scientific communities. The ultimate in grid computing is a grid that spans the Internet. In cloud computing, resources seem to be coming from "the cloud"—somewhere on the Internet—rather than from a particular computer. Applications, data, servers, and other resources are "out there" somewhere—it doesn't matter where as long as they're available when we need them. Several companies have developed, or are developing, cloud computing technologies. Adobe AIR, Mozilla Prism, Google Gears, Microsoft Silverlight, and other projects attempt to bridge the gap between Web applications and desktop applications. A major challenge is to make Web applications useful even when there's no network connection. One approach: Adobe's AIR enables companies (including eBay and NASDAQ) to bring Web-based applications to the desktop so they can run on or off the network. In a world where we're connected most or all of the time to one network or another, widespread cloud computing appears to be just over the horizon.

Digital Communication in Perspective

We've only begun to explore online communication options in this chapter. New technologies emerge all the time; at the same time older technologies evolve and merge. For example, social networking sites are relatively recent developments, but they've changed the way many people communicate. We'll look again at social networks in the next chapter, along with wikis, MMORPGs, and other technologies that are at the heart of what many people call Web 2.0. In that chapter, we'll take an in-depth look at the Internet—past, present, and future.

Before we do, let's step back and put digital communication in a larger perspective. As futurist Stewart Brand reminded us in his groundbreaking book, *The Media Lab*:

We can be grateful for the vast dispersed populations of peasant and tribal cultures in the world who have never used a telephone or a TV, who walk where they're going, who live by local subsistence skills honed over millennia. You need to go on foot in Africa, Asia, South America to realize how many of these people there are and how sound they are. If the world city goes to smash, they'll pick up the pieces, as they've done before. Whatever happens, they are a reminder that electronic communication may be essential to one kind of living, but it is superfluous to another.

Inventing the FUTURE

A World without Wires

We stand at the brink of a transformation. It is a moment that echoes the birth of the Internet in the mid-'70s . . . This time it is not wires but the air between them that is being transformed.

—*Chris Anderson, Editor in Chief, Wired*

Most people who access the Internet still make their connections through wires—phone lines, TV cables, or specialized data-only conduits. But there's a wireless revolution afoot. Wi-Fi represented the first major victory in the revolution, as it finds its way into homes, businesses, public buildings, neighborhoods, and some whole cities or regions. WiMAX may extend Wi-Fi's range even further, because it allows a single tower to serve customers within a several-mile radius. But Wi-Fi and WiMAX aren't the end of the wireless road. Several other promising technologies are being tested and refined in research labs. Here's a sampler:

➡ *802.11e* is another Wi-Fi-related standard that focuses on quality of service, particularly the timely delivery of data packets. That's important for data-streaming applications, such as video conferencing and voice-over IP. Wireless Multimedia Extensions (WME) are included in this standard.

➡ *802.11i* adds another level of security to Wi-Fi, which will enable businesses to use wireless networks for more sensitive transactions.

➡ *802.16e* is an extension to WiMAX that will let mobile computer users access the WiMAX network.

➡ *Ultra-wideband* is a short-range wireless technology that transmits ultra-high-speed signals over a wide spectrum of frequencies. This low-power technology could transform entertainment and communication systems if it can be refined so it doesn't interfere with more critical communication systems.

➡ *Software-defined radio* is a technology that allows a single wireless hardware device to be reprogrammed on the fly to serve a variety of functions. Just as software can transform a PC from a communication tool to a music workstation to an accountant's ledger, it can be used to change a single wireless tool into a cell phone, a garage door opener, a game machine, a baby monitor, a messaging machine, a Web browser, or a TV remote. Researchers are working on the chip technology to make such a universal communicator a reality and, we hope, eliminate much of the techno-clutter that litters our lives.

➡ *Cognitive radio* is a natural evolution of software-defined radio. Most radio bands in the world aren't used efficiently. Some bands, such as cell phone bands, are overcrowded, while others are underused. Rarely-used special-purpose channels might be off limits to unlicensed users, even though there's usually plenty of room for their traffic. Cognitive radio is one possible way to solve these efficiency problems. A cognitive radio might be able to sense which frequencies have the least traffic and route traffic to those channels that provide the best quality of service, and find ways to share the available radio spectrum fairly among all types of users.

It's not clear how all of these emerging technologies will converge. What is clear is that the wireless revolution is far from over. ～

Our Imaginary, Hotter Selves *by Sharon Begley*

Many people play with their online identities using avatars. But as Sharon Begley suggests in this February 16, 2008 Newsweek article, powerful psychological forces are hiding in those avatars—forces that might be harnessed to help people.

Anyone who has ever had a bad hair day, when looking like a latter-day Medusa makes you feel cranky and anti-social and plodding, can sympathize with the Oakland Raiders—and not because the players get helmet hair. The Raiders alternated between mostly black and mostly white uniforms, depending on whether they were playing at home or away. Knowing that appearance affects people's mood and outlook, psychologists wondered whether uniform color influenced the Raiders' aggressiveness. Using data from the 1970s and 1980s, they found that the team racked up way more penalty yards— a measure of aggression—when they wore black than when they wore white, for infractions both minor (encroachment) and major (roughing the kicker). The pattern held even when the scientists took into account different conditions and styles of play at home and away. But while the 1988 finding has become a classic in psychology, the explanation remains controversial. Do referees, because of black's cultural baggage, see black-clad players as meaner and badder than those in, say, baby blue? Or does wearing black make players see themselves as tougher and meaner—and therefore cause them to play that way?

Jeremy Bailenson and Nick Yee of Stanford University had this and other classic studies in mind when they started wondering about the effect of being able to alter one's appearance. They weren't going to study wardrobe choices, however. Their quarry is avatars, digital representations of players in such games as Second Life. "Your physical appearance changes how people treat you," says Bailenson. "But independent of that, when you perceive yourself in a certain way, you act differently." He and Yee call it "the Proteus effect," after the shape-changing Greek god. The effect of appearance on behavior, they find, carries over from the virtual world to the real one, with intriguing consequences.

In one Stanford study, volunteers were assigned avatars who ranged from attractive to plain. It is one of life's inequities that the world sees attractive people as possessing a long list of desirable traits, including honesty, generosity and kindness. Perhaps as a result, people judged attractive are more self-confident than ugly ducklings, and so tend to be extroverted. Using a virtual-reality headset, the volunteers—actually, their avatars—walked across a room to interact with another avatar. Those with attractive avatars got within three feet of the stranger; those with homely ones kept almost six feet away. How much "personal space" one needs is inversely proportional to self-confidence, which having an attractive avatar increases. When the stranger asked the players to "tell me a little about yourself," good-looking avatars revealed more: feeling attractive increases self-esteem and therefore friendliness.

The Proteus effect spilled into the real world. After their virtual-reality session, players were shown photos from an online dating site and asked to pick those who "would be interested in you." Players who had been assigned attractive avatars picked more-attractive candidates than did players (of equal pulchritude in real life) who had been represented as homely avatars. Male players were also asked to enter personal information for an online dating site. In this situation men routinely inflate their height by an average of one inch. But those who had had an attractive avatar told the truth.

Western society sees taller people as more competent and having greater leadership potential than shorter people. The effect of virtual height, too, bleeds into real life, the Stanford scientists find. After their avatar roamed through a virtual world, players took seats in the real world to play a split-the-loot game. Player One proposed ways to divide $100 which Player Two could accept or reject, in which case neither player got anything. People tend to reject unfair offers, even though accepting a lopsided $99/$1 split leaves them objectively better off than walking away in a righteous huff. Players fresh from being a tall avatar showed their cockiness, proposing, on average, $61/$39 splits. People with short avatars averaged offers of $52/$48, Yee and Bailenson reported last year. When it was their turn to weigh an insulting $75/$25 offer, players with tall avatars rejected it 62 percent of the time; those with short avatars stood up for themselves a wimpish 28 percent of the time.

The goal of the research isn't to tell Second Lifers they'll have more virtual friends, money, power and other goodies if they create a hot, young, powerful avatar. Most do so anyway. Instead, avatars might serve therapeutic purposes, helping those with social phobia, say, become more confident and friendly in real life. The work also underlines the power of new media to affect our behavior: players who roamed a virtual world as a KKK-clad avatar felt more aggressive than they did before playing the game, while those whose avatar wore a doctor's coat scored higher on a test of friendliness. It's not clear how long the spillover to the real world lasts. But even if it's only a few hours the potential is impressive: online players spend, on average, 20 hours a week as their avatar.

Discussion Questions

1. Do you think the use of avatars can have a lasting impact on a person's self-confidence? Why or why not?

2. Talk about your experience with avatars in relation to the ideas discussed in this article.

Summary

Networking is one of the most important trends in computing today. Computer networks are growing in popularity because they allow computers to share hardware and to send software and data back and forth. In addition, networks enable people to work together in ways that would be difficult or impossible without them.

LANs are made up of computers that are close enough to be directly connected with cables or wireless radio transmitters/receivers. Most LANs include shared printers and file servers. WANs are made up of computers separated by a considerable distance. The computers are connected to each other through the telephone network, which includes cables, microwave transmission towers, and communication satellites. Many computer networks are connected together through the Internet so messages and data can pass back and forth among them. Some specialized networks, such as global positioning systems and financial systems, serve unique functions.

Most computer networks today use the Ethernet architecture; an Ethernet port is a standard feature on most modern PCs. Computers can be directly connected to networks through Ethernet ports. When high-speed direct connections aren't possible, a PC can transmit and receive signals over standard phone lines with a modem. The modem converts the PC's digital signals to analog so they can travel through standard phone lines. Broadband connections offer much more bandwidth than standard modem connections do, so they can transmit large amounts of information more quickly. These connections include DSL, which uses standard phone lines; cable modems, which use cable TV lines; satellite, which uses TV satellite dishes; and Wi-Fi, which uses short-range wireless 802.11 transmitters. Wi-Fi is a type of wireless network technology that's exploding in popularity because of its potential for providing universal Internet access. All of these technologies offer connections to Internet backbones, many of which transmit astronomical amounts of data quickly through fiber-optic cables.

Communication software takes care of the details of communication between machines—details such as protocols that determine how signals will be sent and received. Network operating systems typically handle the mechanics of LAN communication. Many popular PC operating systems include peer-to-peer networking software, so any PC or Mac on a network can serve as a server as well as a client. Terminal programs enable personal computers to function as character-based terminals when connected to other PCs or to timesharing computers. Other types of specialized client programs have graphical user interfaces and additional functionality. Timesharing operating systems enable multiuser computers to communicate with several terminals at a time.

Email, instant messaging, and teleconferencing are the most common forms of communication between people on computer networks. They offer many advantages over traditional mail and telephone communication and can shorten or eliminate many meetings. Because of several important limitations, however, email and teleconferencing cannot completely replace older communication media. People who communicate with these new media should follow simple rules of "netiquette" and exercise a degree of caution to avoid many of the most common problems.

Peer-to-peer computing was popularized by music-sharing services, but its applications go beyond music sharing. Many businesses are exploring ways to apply P2P technology. Grid computing goes beyond P2P computing by enabling people to share processor power with others. Some organizations are working to build a grid-computing model that would make the Internet work like a shared utility. Many see this as a big step toward cloud computing—treating the Internet as a cloud containing shared software and hardware whose physical location isn't particularly important.

Key Terms

Interactive Activities

1. The *Tomorrow's Technology and You* Web site, **www.pearsonhighered.com/beekman**, contains self-test exercises related to this chapter. Follow the instructions for taking the quiz. After you've completed your quiz, you can email the results to your instructor.

2. The Web site also contains open-ended discussion questions called Internet Exercises. Discuss one or more of the Internet Exercises questions at the section for this chapter.

True or False

1. Today virtually all computer networks are general-purpose networks connected to the Internet.

2. The standard PC serial port is being phased out and replaced by a standard parallel port.

3. The most common types of networks today use a standard networking architecture known as Ethernet.

4. A single fiber-optic cable has the bandwidth of thousands of copper telephone cables.

5. Because peer-to-peer networking software is built into the Windows and Macintosh operating systems, a modern desktop computer can act as both client and server on a network.

6. If you want your Windows PC to read a file created on a Macintosh, you must use data-translation software.

7. Depending on your email client program and your preferences, your mail might be stored on a remote host or downloaded and stored on your local machine.

8. The line that separates computer communication and telephone communication is being blurred by devices and technologies that operate in both realms.

9. Simple technological solutions can eliminate the spam problem for email users.

10. Email and instant messaging can filter out many human components of communication, increasing the chance of misinterpreted messages.

Multiple Choice

1. Computer networks
   a. allow people to share hardware resources.
   b. make it easier for people to share data.
   c. support collaboration through tools, such as email and instant messaging.
   d. all of the above
   e. none of the above

2. What is a service that connects computers and peripherals in the same building called?
   a. Connection area network (CAN)
   b. Local area network (LAN)
   c. Metropolitan area network (MAN)
   d. Remote area network (RAN)
   e. Wide area network (WAN)

3. What is a service that connects two or more networks within a city called?
   a. Connection area network (CAN)
   b. Local area network (LAN)
   c. Metropolitan area network (MAN)
   d. Remote area network (RAN)
   e. Wide area network (WAN)

4. A modem
   a. allows a computer to communicate with its peripherals, such as printers and scanners.
   b. increases the speed with which a computer can communicate over a phone line.
   c. converts a digital signal into an analog signal and vice versa.
   d. allows a Windows PC to run Macintosh applications.
   e. performs the same functions as an Ethernet port, except faster.

5. Which of the following does not affect bandwidth?
   a. The amount of network traffic
   b. The software protocols of the network
   c. The type of network connection
   d. The type of information being transmitted
   e. The physical media that make up the network

6. What is the most common reason for installing a Wi-Fi hub in a home?
   a. To enable a PC to connect to a cell phone
   b. To make client/server computing possible
   c. To make it possible to connect Bluetooth-enabled devices to a network
   d. To allow PCs to connect to a network without wires
   e. To create a wireless alternative to hi-fi home entertainment systems

7. If you want to share a document with other people whose computers are connected to your LAN, you should upload the document to a(n)
   a. file server.
   b. client server.
   c. print server.
   d. document server.
   e. upload server.

8. What is an important difference between Internet newsgroups and mailing lists?
   a. A mailing list message goes to only a specific group of people, whereas a newsgroup message is available for anyone to see.
   b. A mailing list message is posted via email, whereas a newsgroup message requires special posting software.
   c. A mailing list message is posted to a special Web mailbox, whereas a newsgroup message is delivered directly to group members' mailboxes.
   d. All of the above are true.
   e. There are no significant differences between the two.

9. What is the main difference between instant messaging (IM) and email?
   a. The use of moderated groups for IM.
   b. The ability of email to handle real-time communication.
   c. The GUI of the IM client software.
   d. The asynchronous nature of email communication.
   e. There are no significant differences between the two.

10. The number of email messages delivered each day far exceeds the number of letters delivered by the U.S. Postal Service. Why?
    a. You can write and send an email faster than you can write and mail a letter.
    b. Email is delivered more rapidly.
    c. Email facilitates group communication.
    d. Email can save money.
    e. All of the above.

11. Today's email system is built on protocols that
    a. don't ensure that each sender has a verifiable identity.
    b. automatically filter spam based on objectionable content.
    c. can be modified by anyone with systems administration clearance.
    d. apply directly to instant messaging systems.
    e. all of the above.

12. What percentage of email messages is junk email (spam)?
    a. Less than 10 percent
    b. About 20 percent
    c. About 30 percent
    d. About 40 percent
    e. More than 50 percent

13. Which of these is OK according to the generally accepted rules of netiquette?
    a. Sending a message to ten thousand members of a worldwide society of birdwatchers inviting them to your local club's weekly outing
    b. Lurking in a hang-glider enthusiasts newsgroup without posting any messages
    c. Quickly posting on a DJ newsgroup 15 "help me" beginner questions about the second-hand turntables you just bought without manuals
    d. Responding to an antiwar group email with a heated message that attacks the personal integrity of the sender
    e. Sending 36 unsolicited high-resolution family photos to everyone on your list of email friends

14. Many experts say we're at the beginning of a revolution that is creating a vast grassroots network of public and private wireless hubs based on
    a. 3G technology.
    b. mesh network technology.
    c. Wi-Fi technology.
    d. Bluetooth technology.
    e. Ethernet technology.

15. What should people who use a public hotspot be aware of?
    a. There is no such thing as free access to the Internet.
    b. Wireless connections cannot be used to surf the Web.
    c. A notebook computer must be plugged into a power source in order to connect to the network.
    d. Exposure to radio waves is harmful to pregnant women.
    e. Data transmitted over networks without WEP key encryption can be viewed by malicious eavesdroppers.

Review Questions

1. Define or describe each of the key terms listed in the "Key Terms" section. Check your answers using the glossary.

2. Give three general reasons for the importance of computer networking. (*Hint:* Each reason is related to one of the three essential components of every computer system.)

3. How do the three general reasons listed in Question 2 relate specifically to LANs?

4. How do the three general reasons listed in Question 2 relate specifically to WANs?

5. Under what circumstances is a modem necessary for connecting computers in networks? What does the modem do?

6. Describe at least two different kinds of communication software.

7. How could a file server be used in a student computer lab? What software licensing issues would be raised by using a file server in a student lab?

8. What are the differences between email and instant messaging systems?

9. Describe some things you can do with email that you can't do with regular mail.

10. Describe several potential problems associated with email and teleconferencing.

11. "Money is just another form of information." Explain this statement, and describe how it relates to communication technology.

12. Wi-Fi and Bluetooth wireless technologies are designed to serve different purposes than mobile phone technology does. Explain this statement.

13. Why is netiquette important? Give some examples of netiquette.

Discussion Questions

1. Suppose you have an important message to send to a friend in another city, and you can use the telephone, email, real-time teleconference, fax, or overnight mail service. Discuss the advantages and disadvantages of each. See if you can think of a situation for each of the five options in which that particular option is the most appropriate choice.

2. Some people choose to spend several hours every day online. Do you see potential hazards in this kind of heavy modem use? Explain your answer.

3. Should spam be illegal? Explain your answer.

4. In the quote at the end of the chapter, Stewart Brand points out that electronic communication is essential for some of the world's people and irrelevant to others. What distinguishes these two groups? What advantages and disadvantages do each have?

5. Do you think Wi-Fi and other wireless technology put us on the brink of a communication revolution? Why or why not?

Projects

1. Find out about your school's computer networks. Are there many LANs? How are they connected? Who has access to them? What are they used for?

2. Spend a few hours exploring an online service such as AOL. Describe the problems you encounter in the process. Which parts of the service are the most useful and interesting?

3. Imagine you are living in a house with three other students and everyone has a PC. Determine what you would need to purchase to create a home network that would enable all four of you to access the Internet with only a single subscription to a high-speed Internet provider (either cable or DSL). Compare the cost of a wired network based on 100 Mbps Ethernet versus a wireless network based on 802.11g.

4. Identify a wireless hotspot in your city or town. Interview a staff person at the establishment. Does the hotspot provide free access, or does it require payment? If it requires payment, how does it charge for access? What security measures does it have in place? What have been the consequences (both good and bad) of creating a wireless hotspot?

Sources and Resources

Books

How Networks Work, Seventh Edition, by Frank J. Derfler, Jr., and Les Freed (Indianapolis, IN: Que, 2004). This book follows the model popularized with the *How Computers Work* series. It uses a mix of text and graphics to illuminate the nuts and bolts of PC networks.

How Wireless Works, Second Edition, by Preston Gralla (Indianapolis, IN: Que, 2006). Another popular book in the *How Computers Work* series, this one focuses on the wireless world, from TV and telephones to Wi-Fi and Bluetooth. There's even a section on the privacy risks of wireless technology.

The Essential Guide to Telecommunications, Fourth Edition, by Annabel Z. Dodd (Upper Saddle River, NJ: Prentice Hall, 2006). This popular book presents a clear, comprehensive guide to the telecommunications industry and technology, including telephone systems, cable systems, wireless systems, and the Internet. If you want to understand how the pieces of our communication networks fit together, this book is a great place to start.

Home Networking: The Missing Manual, by Scott Lowe (Cambridge, MA: O'Reilly, 2005). Once you've got a network in your home, it can save time and provide a wealth of benefits and conveniences. But getting a network up and running can be frustrating and confusing. This book can help you to cut through the technobabble and get your systems connected to each other and to the rest of the networked world.

Send: The Essential Guide to Email for Office and Home, by David Shipley and Will Schwalbe (New York, NY: Knopf, 2007). The motivation for this book is made clear in the first sentence: "Bad things can happen on email." The authors clearly and humorously explain how to avoid those bad things, and how to make email work for, rather than against, you.

How to Do Everything with Your Web 2.0 Blog, by Todd Stauffer (San Francisco, CA: Osborne McGraw-Hill, 2008). If you want to be a blogger but you're not sure how, this book can help. In addition to the basics of blogging, the author covers podcasts, social bookmarking, wikis, forums, and more.

How to Do Everything with Online Video, by Andrew Shalat (San Francisco, CA: Osborne McGraw-Hill, 2008). For many people, video is the medium of choice for Web communication. This handbook has information on planning, creating, editing, and posting Web videos. There are specifics for Mac and Windows users, for YouTube and MySpace posters, for podcasters and Web designers.

How to Do Everything with YouTube, by Chad Fahs (San Francisco, CA: Osborne McGraw-Hill, 2008). This book is similar to *How to Do Everything with Online Video* except that it focuses exclusively on YouTube.

Wireless Nation: The Frenzied Launch of the Cellular Revolution, by James B. Murray (Cambridge, MA: Perseus Books, 2002). The mobile phone and the PC both burst into our culture in the last decades of the 20th century, and they came together through the Internet. This book chronicles the rise of mobile communication technology.

We the Media: Grassroots Journalism by the People, for the People, by Dan Gillmor (Cambridge, MA: O'Reilly, 2006). Gillmor, a respected journalist in the world of "old media," argues in this book that blogs, email, and other people-powered communication tools are changing the rules and bringing hope for the return of true democracy to a culture dominated by powerful corporations.

9

The Evolving Internet

After you read this chapter you should be able to:

▶ Explain how and why the Internet was created

▶ Describe the technology that's at the heart of the Internet

▶ Describe the technology that makes the Web work as a multimedia mass medium

▶ Discuss the tools people use to build Web sites

▶ Discuss the trends that are changing the Internet and the way people use it

▶ Discuss some of the most important social and political issues raised by the growth of the Internet

▶ Describe various ways that governments restrict access to the Internet

> It's a bit like **climbing a mountain**. You don't know how far you've come until you **stop and look back**.
>
> —*Vint Cerf, ARPANET pioneer and first president of the Internet Society*

Arpanet Pioneers Build a Reliable Network Out of Unreliable Parts

In the 1960s the world of computers was a technological Tower of Babel; most computers couldn't communicate with each other. When people needed to move data from one computer to another, they carried or mailed a magnetic tape or a deck of punch cards. While most of the world viewed computers only as giant number crunchers, J. C. R. Licklider, Robert Taylor, and a small group of visionary computer scientists saw the computer's potential as a communication device. They envisioned a network that would enable researchers to share computing resources and ideas.

U.S. military strategists during those Cold War years had a vision too: They foresaw an enemy attack crippling the U.S. government's ability to communicate. The Department of Defense wanted a network that could function even if some connections were destroyed. They provided one million dollars to Taylor and other scientists and engineers to build a small experimental network. The groundbreaking result, launched in 1969, was called ARPANET, for Advanced Research Projects Agency NETwork. When a half dozen researchers sent the first historic message from UCLA to Doug Engelbart's lab at the Stanford Research Institute, no one even thought to take a picture.

ARPANET was built on two unorthodox assumptions: The network itself was unreliable, so it had to be able to overcome its own unreliability, and all computers on the network would be equal in their ability to communicate with other network computers. In ARPANET, there was no central authority because that would make the entire network vulnerable to attack. Messages were contained in software "packets" that could travel independently by any number of different paths, through all kinds of computers, toward their destinations.

ARPANET grew quickly into an international network with hundreds of military and university sites. In addition to carrying research data, ARPANET channeled debates over the Vietnam War and intense discussions about Space War, an early computer game. ARPANET's peer-to-peer networking philosophy and protocols were copied in other networks in the 1980s. Vint Cerf and

FIGURE 9.1 The team that built the predecessor to the Internet at a 1994 25th anniversary reunion. From front to back: Bob Taylor, Vint Cerf, Frank Heart, Larry Roberts, Len Kleinrock, Bob Kahn, Wes Clark, Doug Engelbart, Barry Wessler, Dave Walden, Severo Ornstein, Truett Thach, Roger Scantlebury, Charlie Herzfeld, Ben Barker, Jon Postel, Steve Crocker, Bill Naylor, and Roland Bryan.

Bob Kahn, two of the original researchers, developed the protocols that became the standard computer communication language, allowing different computer networks to be linked.

In 1990 ARPANET was disbanded, having fulfilled its research mission, but its technology spawned the Internet. In an interview, Cerf said about the network he helped create, "It was supposed to be a highly robust technology for supporting military command and control. It did that in the [first] Persian Gulf War. But, along the way, it became a major research support infrastructure and now has become the best example of global information infrastructure that we have."

The ARPANET pioneers have gone on to work on dozens of other significant projects and products. In the words of Bob Kahn, "Those were very exciting days, but there are new frontiers in every direction I can look these days." ∼

The team that designed ARPANET suspected they were building something important. They couldn't have guessed, though, that they were laying the groundwork for a system that would become a universal research tool, a hotbed of business activity, a virtual shopping mall, a popular social hangout, a publisher's clearinghouse of up-to-the-minute information, a fountainhead of collaborative community projects, and one of the most talked about institutions of our time.

In its early years, the Internet was the domain of technological pioneers willing to forgo creature comforts and cut their own trails through the electronic wilderness. Most people, including corporate executives and government leaders, ignored it. Few believed that it had any commercial potential. In fact, the code of the Net was strongly anticommercial—users were there to share information, not make profits. John Perry Barlow (writer, rancher, politician, lyricist for the Grateful Dead, and cofounder of the Electronic Frontier Foundation) called the early Net an electronic frontier, likening it to the early American West.

In spite of rapid commercialization, the Net still feels a little like an electronic frontier. Network nomads pick digital locks and ignore electronic fences. Some explore nooks and crannies out of a spirit of adventure. Others steal and tamper with private information for profit or revenge. Charlatans and hustlers operate outside the law. Law enforcement agencies and lawmakers occasionally overreact. And there's still a strong sentiment toward keeping government and corporate controls to a minimum.

In the 1990s, the Web opened up the electronic frontier to the masses, just as the railroads opened up the American West. Kevin Kelly described the results in a *Wired* article celebrating the 10th anniversary of Netscape, the first commercial Web company:

> *Today, at any Net terminal, you can get: an amazing variety of music and video, an evolving encyclopedia, weather forecasts, help wanted ads, satellite images of anyplace on Earth, up-to-the-minute news from around the globe, tax forms, TV guides, road maps with driving directions, real-time stock quotes, telephone numbers, real estate listings with virtual walk-throughs, pictures of just about anything, sports scores, places to buy almost anything, records of political contributions, library catalogs, appliance manuals, live traffic reports, archives to major newspapers—all wrapped up in an interactive index that really works. . . . Ten years ago, anyone silly enough to trumpet the above list as a vision of the near future would have been confronted by the evidence: There wasn't enough money in all the investment firms in the entire world to fund such a cornucopia. The success of the Web at this scale was impossible. But if we have learned anything in the past decade, it is the plausibility of the impossible. . . . What we all failed to see was how much of this new world would be manufactured by users, not corporate interests.*

Blogs, open-source software, peer-to-peer file sharing, Wikipedia, MySpace, Facebook, Flickr, YouTube, BlogSpot, podcasts, even eBay—all of these Internet institutions are built by diverse communities of people, not by cubicle cities full of Web designers and programmers. Even commercial enterprises like Amazon encourage their customers to help build the site by writing product reviews and setting up stores within the store. More and more, we are the architects of the emerging Internet.

For many people, the vocabulary of the Internet seems like a flurry of technobabble. You don't need to analyze every acronym to make sense of the Internet, but your Net experiences can be far more rewarding if you understand the concepts at the heart of basic Net-speak terminology. In this chapter, we delve into the nuts and bolts of the Internet—past, present, and future—to make those concepts clear.

FIGURE 9.2 People from around the world have freely contributed their photographs to the database managed by Flickr.com.

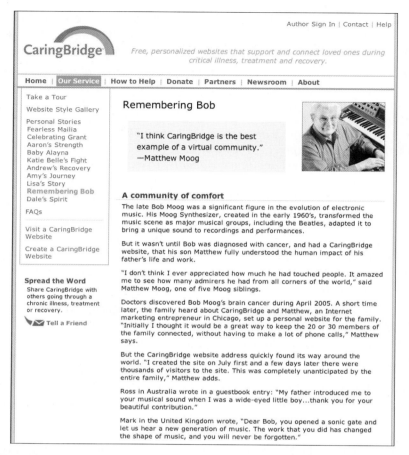

FIGURE 9.3 Millions of people have used caringbridge.org to create and connect with online communities of support for victims of accidents and serious illnesses. Family and friends can view up-to-the-minute journal entries and photos, send support through guestbook messages, and make donations to support the no-charge service.

Inside the Internet

It shouldn't be too much of a surprise that the Internet has evolved into a force **strong enough** to reflect the **greatest hopes and fears** of those who use it. After all, it was designed to **withstand nuclear war**, not just the **puny huffs and puffs** of politicians and religious fanatics.

—*Denise Caruso, digital commerce columnist,* The New York Times

The Internet is a network of networks. It includes dozens of national, statewide, and regional networks, hundreds of networks within colleges and research labs, and thousands of commercial sites all over the planet. Significantly, the Internet is not controlled by any one government, corporation, individual, or legal system. Several international advisory organizations develop standards and protocols for the evolving Internet, but no one has the power to control the Net's operation or evolution. The Internet is, in a sense, a massive anarchy unlike any other organization the world has ever seen.

Scientists and engineers are working to ensure that the capabilities of the Internet will continue to grow. Hundreds of universities, companies, and government research labs from around the world have formed the Internet2 consortium. Its efforts will lead to exciting new applications, faster communications, higher reliability, and greater security. Internet2 will not replace the Internet. Instead, technologies developed as a result of this research will gradually be incorporated into the existing Internet.

Counting Connections

In its early days, the Internet connected only a few dozen computers at U.S. universities and government research centers, and the government paid most of the cost of building and operating it. Today the Internet connects millions of computers in almost every country in the world, and costs are shared by thousands of connected organizations. It's impossible to pin down the exact size of the Internet for several reasons:

- The Internet is growing too fast to track. Billions of new users connect to the Internet every year.
- The Internet is decentralized. There's no "Internet Central" that keeps track of user activity or network connections. To make matters worse for Internet counters, some parts of the Internet can't be accessed by the general public; they're sealed off to protect private information.
- The Internet doesn't have hard boundaries. There are many ways to connect to the Internet, and many of them don't fit the traditional model of logging into a network from a PC.

FIGURE 9.4 Cyber cafés around the world, like this one in France, enable travelers and locals to stay connected to their homes and the rest of the world. Customers often pay by the minute to log into their home servers to keep up on email, favorite Web sites, and IM contacts.

It's easier to understand how the Internet can be shared by PCs, supercomputers, phones, game machines, TV set-top boxes, and all kinds of esoteric devices if you know a little bit about the protocols that make the Internet work.

Internet Protocols

The protocol at the heart of the Internet is called **TCP/IP (Transmission Control Protocol/Internet Protocol)**. TCP/IP was developed as an experiment in **internetworking** —connecting different types of networks and computer systems. The TCP/IP specifications were published as **open standards**, not owned by any company. As a result, TCP/IP became the "language" of the Internet, allowing cross-network communication for almost every type of computer and network. These protocols are generally invisible to users; they're hidden deep in software that takes care of communication details behind the scenes. In addition, the protocols define how information can be transferred between machines and how machines on the network can be identified with unique addresses.

> The **most important quality** of the Internet is that it lends itself to **radical reinvention**. . . . In another 10 years, the **only part** of the Internet as we know it now that will have survived will be **bits and pieces** of the underlying Internet protocol. . . .
>
> —*Paul Saffo, director of the Institute for the Future*

The TCP protocol (the first part of TCP/IP) defines a system similar in many ways to the postal system. When a message is sent on the Internet, it is broken into *packets*, in the same way you might pack your belongings in several individually addressed boxes before you ship them to a new location. Each packet has all the information routers need to transfer the packet from network to network toward its destination. Different packets might take different routes, just as different parcels might be routed through different cities by the postal system. Regardless of the route they follow, the packets eventually reach their destination, where they are reassembled into the original message. This **packet-switching** model is flexible and robust, allowing messages to get through even when part of the network is down.

The other part of TCP/IP—the IP part—defines the addressing system of the Internet. Every host computer on the Internet has a unique *IP address*, a string of four numbers separated by periods, or, as they say in Net speak, dots. A typical IP address might look

How It Works

9.1 Internet Communication

Everything that's sent through the Internet depends on the technology of packet switching.

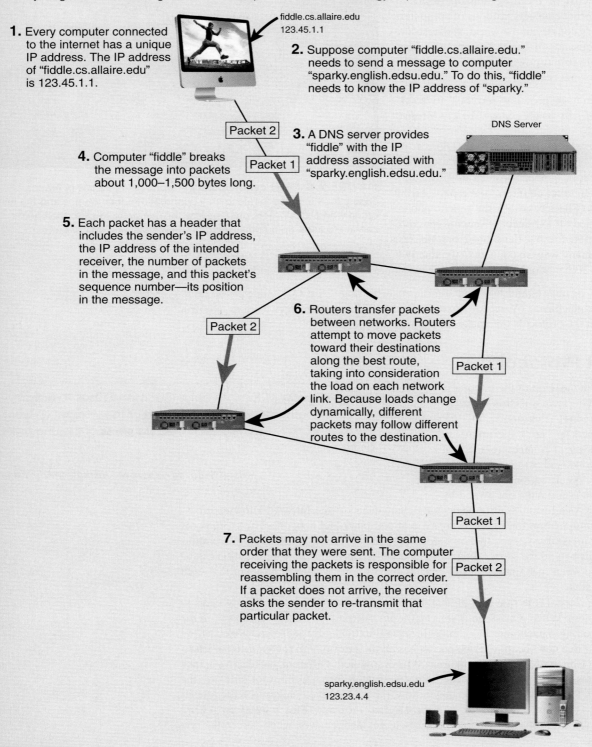

1. Every computer connected to the internet has a unique IP address. The IP address of "fiddle.cs.allaire.edu" is 123.45.1.1.

fiddle.cs.allaire.edu
123.45.1.1

2. Suppose computer "fiddle.cs.allaire.edu." needs to send a message to computer "sparky.english.edsu.edu." To do this, "fiddle" needs to know the IP address of "sparky."

Packet 2

4. Computer "fiddle" breaks the message into packets about 1,000–1,500 bytes long.

Packet 1

3. A DNS server provides "fiddle" with the IP address associated with "sparky.english.edsu.edu."

DNS Server

5. Each packet has a header that includes the sender's IP address, the IP address of the intended receiver, the number of packets in the message, and this packet's sequence number—its position in the message.

Packet 2

6. Routers transfer packets between networks. Routers attempt to move packets toward their destinations along the best route, taking into consideration the load on each network link. Because loads change dynamically, different packets may follow different routes to the destination.

Packet 1

Packet 1

7. Packets may not arrive in the same order that they were sent. The computer receiving the packets is responsible for reassembling them in the correct order. If a packet does not arrive, the receiver asks the sender to re-transmit that particular packet.

Packet 2

sparky.english.edsu.edu
123.23.4.4

FIGURE 9.5

like this: 123.23.168.22 ("123 dot 23 dot 168 dot 22"). Every packet routed through the Internet includes the IP address of the sending computer and the receiving computer.

IP addresses can be static (fixed) or dynamic. A **static IP address** is a permanent address like a street address for a house—it doesn't change from day to day. Static IP addresses are ideal for Web servers and other computers that are semipermanently connected to the Internet.

Dynamic IP addresses are more commonly used for computers that are temporarily connected to the Net—for example, through a **dial-up connection**. A dynamic address is like a room number in a hotel—it's assigned when the guest arrives and taken away when the guest leaves. Similarly, when a computer makes a temporary connection to the Internet using a wireless connection, a modem, or something else, it's assigned a temporary IP address—probably not the same IP address as the last time it was connected. The temporary address was, in all likelihood, dynamically assigned—assigned on the fly by an Internet service provider server. (Internet service providers are discussed later in the chapter.)

The explosive growth of the Internet has created an IP problem: The world is rapidly using up all of the available IP addresses. Fortunately, the Internet Protocol continues to evolve as the Internet matures. The term *Next Generation Internet* is used to refer to Internet Protocol Version 6, or IPv6. (Most computers on today's Internet use IPv4.) IPv6 solves the shortage-of-addresses problem and makes other improvements as well. For example, IPv6 hosts support *multicasting*, which is a more efficient way for the same information to be transmitted to multiple Internet-connected devices. Internet-connected computers will be switching over to IPv6 in the next few years.

Internet Addresses

In practice, people seldom see or use numerical IP addresses because of the Internet's *domain name system (DNS)*. DNS servers maintain look-up tables that map domain names to IP addresses. For example, a DNS server can determine that the domain name "abcnews.com" refers to the computer with IP address 199.181.132.250.

Internet addresses are classified by *domains*. In the United States, the most widely used *top-level domains* are general categories that describe types of organizations:

- (.edu) Educational sites
- (.com) Commercial sites
- (.gov) Government sites
- (.mil) Military sites
- (.net) Network administration sites
- (.org) Nonprofit organizations
- (.aero) Air transport organizations
- (.biz) Businesses
- (.coop) Cooperative businesses such as credit unions
- (.info) Information services
- (.museum) Museums
- (.name) Personal registration by name
- (.pro) Licensed professionals, including lawyers, doctors, and accountants

Some of these domains, including .com, .net, .org, and .info, are open to anyone without restriction. For example, you could have a Web site or an email address in the .org domain whether or not you're part of a nonprofit organization. Other domains, including .edu and .mil, are restricted so only people in the designated organizations can use them. Outside (and occasionally inside) the United States, top-level domains are two-letter country codes, such as .jp for Japan, .th for Thailand, .au for Australia, .uk for United Kingdom, and .us for United States.

Some domain names are valuable. The tiny Pacific nation of Tuvalu has sold its .tv domain name to a U.S. Internet company, which in turn markets the .tv domain name to television-related companies. The 10,000 residents of Tuvalu are using the income—$4 million a year—to build new schools, roads, and electrical systems.

The top-level domain name is the last part of the address. The other parts of the address, when read in reverse, provide information that narrows down the exact location on the network. The words in the domain name, like the lines in a post office address, are arranged hierarchically from smaller domains to larger domains. They might include the name of the host computer, the name of the department or network within the organization, and the name of the organization.

The domain naming system is used in virtually all email addresses and Web URLs. A Web URL specifies the IP address of the Web server that houses the page. In an email address, the domain name system is used to pinpoint the Internet location of the host computer that contains the user's mail server. The email address includes the user name and the host address.

Here are some other examples of email addresses using the domain name system:

- president@whitehouse.gov — User *president* whose mail is stored on the host *whitehouse* in the government (.gov) domain
- crabbyabby@AOL.com — User *crabbyabby* whose mail is handled by AOL, a commercial service (.com) provider
- hazel_filbertnut@admin.gmcc.ab.ca — User *hazel_filbertnut* at the *admin* server for Grant MacEwan Community College in Alberta, Canada

Internet Access Options

As we discussed in the previous chapter, computers connect to the Internet through three basic types of connections: direct connections, dial-up connections through modems, and broadband connections through high-speed alternatives to modems. Most Internet users today connect through these four types of broadband access:

- DSL uses standard phone lines and is provided by phone companies in many areas.
- Cable modems provide fast network connections through cable television networks in many areas.
- High-speed wireless connections can connect computers to networks using radio waves rather than wires.
- Satellite dishes can deliver fast computer network connections as well as television programs.

Internet service providers (ISPs) generally offer several connection options at different prices. Local ISPs are local businesses with permanent connections to the Internet. They provide connections to their customers, usually through local phone lines, along with other services. For example, an ISP might provide an email address, a server for customers to post Web pages, and technical help as part of a service package. National ISPs, such as EarthLink and NetZero, offer similar services on a nationwide scale.

Online services, including the popular America Online, are ISPs that offer extra services to subscribers, including news, research tools, shopping, games, and chat rooms. An online service can be like a gated community that lets its members explore outside the gates but forbids outsiders from taking advantage of resources inside the gates. Private online services aren't as popular as they used to be, because the wider Web offers similar (and often better) alternatives to their attractions.

Internet Servers

The most desirable interaction with a network is one in which **the network itself is invisible and unnoticeable**. Planners often forget that people **do not want to use systems** at all—easy or not. What people want is to **delegate** a task and **not to worry about how** it is done.

—Nicholas Negroponte, director of MIT's Media Lab

Internet applications, like PC applications, are software tools for users. But working with Internet applications is different from working with PC apps because of the distributed nature of the Internet and the client/server model used by most Internet applications. In the client/server model, a client program asks for information, and a server program

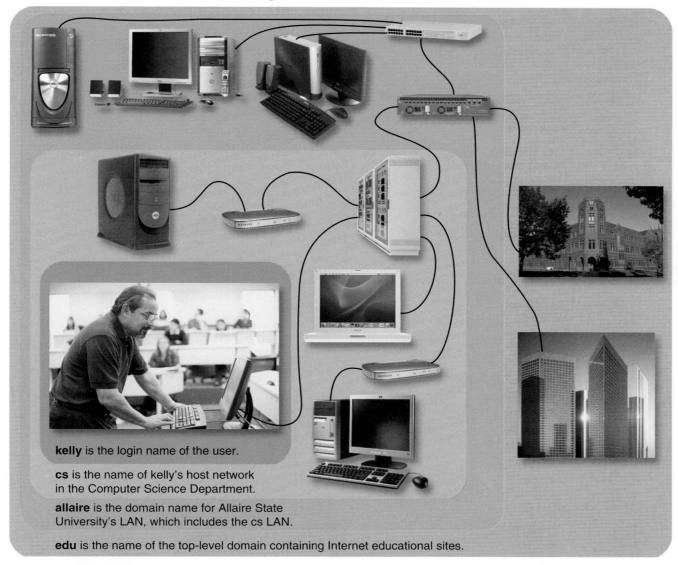

kelly@cs.allaire.edu

kelly is the login name of the user.

cs is the name of kelly's host network in the Computer Science Department.

allaire is the domain name for Allaire State University's LAN, which includes the cs LAN.

edu is the name of the top-level domain containing Internet educational sites.

FIGURE 9.6 Anatomy of an email address.

fields the request and then provides the requested information from databases and documents. The client program hides the details of the network and the server from the user.

Different people might access the same server using different client applications with different user interfaces. For example, a user with a direct connection might be using a Web browser with a point-and-click interface to explore a particular server, while another user with a dial-up terminal connection might be typing UNIX commands and seeing only text on screen. A third user might be viewing the same data, a few words at a time, on the tiny screen of a mobile phone.

Many Internet applications use specialized servers. Some of the most common server types include the following:

- *Email servers*. An **email server** acts like a local post office for a particular Internet host—a business, an organization, or an ISP. For example, a college might have an email server to handle the mail of all students, faculty, and staff; their email addresses point to that server. The email server receives incoming mail, stores it, and provides it to the email client programs of the addressees when they request it. Similarly, the email server collects mail from its subscribers and sends those

A dial-up connection temporarily puts a PC on the Internet, though the quality of service is limited by the modem's speed.

A satellite broadband connection uses a satellite dish to establish a radio connection to the Internet via a satellite.

1 Mbps

16 Mbps

40 Kbps

56 Kbps

A wireless broadband connection uses radio waves to connect a PC to the Internet via a wireless access point.

11–248 Mbps

The arrows show typical Speeds:
Kbps = 1,000 bits per second
Mbps = 1,000,000 bits per second

Internet

3 Mbps

768 Kbps

38 Mbps

2 Mbps

10–100,000 Mbps

A DSL line provides a high-speed, always-on connection through standard phone lines.

A cable modem provides a high-speed, always-on connection through a television cable.

A fast Ethernet connection provides the highest speed, continuous link to the Internet.

FIGURE 9.7 There are many ways to connect a PC to the Internet, and the connection speeds vary dramatically. The speed of an Internet connection is limited to the speed of the slowest link in the chain; the speeds represented here might not be achieved in actual connections. Wireless speed varies depending on the number of devices competing for bandwidth and the amount of environmental interference. Cable modem speeds are also traffic-dependent.

messages toward their Internet destinations. Basically, the email server handles local client requests of two types: "Give me my mail" and "Pick up my mail and send it."

■ *File servers.* **File servers** distribute programs, media files, and other data files across LANs and the Internet. The Internet's **file transfer protocol (FTP)** enables users to download files from file servers (sometimes called FTP servers) to their computers— and to upload files they want to share from their computers to these archives. When you click a Web link that downloads a file, the Web browser's request is probably handled using FTP. FTP requests aren't always done through Web browsers, though. Several popular applications have FTP capability, and FTP commands are built into Windows, Mac OS X, and most versions of Linux.

■ *Application servers.* An **application server** stores applications and makes them available to client programs that request them. An application server might be used within a large company to keep PCs updated with the latest software. Each PC might have a client program that regularly sends requests for updates to the server. The application server might also be housed at an **application service provider (ASP)**—a company that manages and delivers application services on a contract basis. Users of ASPs don't buy applications; they rent them, along with service contracts. Some application servers supply platform-neutral, Web-based applications rather than operating system–specific PC applications. Many industry watchers believe ASPs will eventually provide most of the software we use. For some companies, ASPs are part of larger Web-services strategies, discussed later.

■ *Web servers.* A **Web server** stores Web pages and sends them to client programs—Web browsers—that request them. It may also store and send Web media, including graphics, audio, video, and animation. In the next section, we'll turn our attention to the technology behind the Web.

FIGURE 9.8 Writers, editors, and production people use an FTP server to share files for this book; FTP client software is used for uploading and downloading files.

Inside the Web

The **World Wide Web (Web)** is a distributed browsing and searching system originally developed at CERN (European Laboratory for Particle Physics) by Tim Berners-Lee, a visionary scientist profiled in Chapter 6. He designed a system for giving Internet documents unique addresses, wrote the HTML language (discussed below) for encoding and displaying documents, and built a software browser for viewing those documents from remote locations. Since it was introduced in 1991, the Web has become phenomenally popular as a system for exploring, viewing, and publishing all kinds of information on the Internet.

The **dream behind the Web** is of a common information space in which we **communicate by sharing information**.

—*Tim Berners-Lee, creator of the World Wide Web*

FIGURE 9.9 Anatomy of a URL.

Web Protocols: HTTP and HTML

The Web is built around a naming scheme that allows every information resource on the Internet to be referred to using a **uniform resource locator** or, as it's more commonly known, **URL**. Here's a typical URL: http://weatherunderground.com/satellite/vis/1k/US.html/. The first part of this URL refers to the protocol that must be used to access information; it might be FTP, news, or something else. It's commonly *http*, for *hypertext transfer protocol*, a protocol used to transfer Web pages. The second part (the part following the //) is the address of the host containing the resource; it uses the same domain-naming scheme used for email addresses. The third part, following the dot address, describes the *path* to the particular resource on the host—the hierarchical nesting of directories (folders) that contain the resource.

Many Web pages are created using a language called **HyperText Markup Language (HTML)**. An HTML *source document* is a text file that includes codes called markup tags that describe the format, layout, and logical structure of a hypermedia document. HTML is definitely not WYSIWYG (what you see is what you get); the HTML codes embedded in the document make it look cryptic and nothing like the final page displayed on the screen. But those codes enable a Web browser to translate an HTML source document into that finished page. Because it's a text file, an HTML document can be easily transmitted from a Web server to a client machine anywhere on the Internet.

Publishing on the Web

The Web was built by **millions of people** simply **because they wanted if**, without need, greed, fear, hierarchy, authority figures, ethnic identification, advertising, or any form of manipulation. **Nothing like this ever happened before in history**. We can be blasé about it now, but it is **what we will be remembered for**. We have been made aware of a **new dimension of human potential**.

—*Jaron Lanier, virtual reality pioneer*

You can create a Web page with any word processor or text editor; you just type the HTML commands along with the rest of the text. But you don't need to write HTML code to create a Web page. Many programs, including Microsoft Word, PowerPoint, and FileMaker Pro, can automatically convert basic formatting features (including character styles,

FIGURE 9.10 HTML source code tells the Web browser how to format the text when it's displayed on the screen.

indentation, and justification) into HTML codes. Some Web authoring software, including Adobe Dreamweaver, Microsoft Expression Web, and Apple's iWeb, work like page layout programs that desktop publishers use. You can lay out text and graphics the way you want them to look, and the authoring program creates an HTML document that looks similar to your original layout when viewed through a Web browser. The best of these Web authoring programs enable you to manage entire Web sites using tools that can automate repetitive edits, apply formatting styles across pages, and check for bad links. Some have tools for connecting large sites to databases containing critical, rapidly changing content.

After an HTML document is completed, you need to upload it onto a Web server before it's visible on the Web. Many ISPs provide Web server space as part of their subscription service; other companies rent Web server space to individuals and organizations. By default, most Web pages have URLs that include the ISP or Web server domain names—names like http://hometown.aol.com/shjoobedebop. Many businesses, organizations, and individuals pay an annual fee to a *domain name registry* company for names that relate to their organization name and are easy to remember and use. Many domain names resemble company or product names—for example, http://www.prenhall.com or http://tomorrowstechnologyandyou.com.

Many individuals post blogs without using HTML or standard Web authoring software. Instead, they use software that's designed specifically to create blog documents. Blogs can be published to Web servers using simple and free Web interfaces that shield

How It Works

9.2 The World Wide Web

There's a lot of behind-the-scenes communication going on whenever you view a Web page.

1. When you type a URL into the address box of your Web browser, the browser sends a message through the Internet to the server with the specified domain name **www.appleeater.com**.

Request for www.appleeater.com. home page

2. The server responds by sending the specified file to the client browser. The file contains the contents of the requested Web page in HTML format. The HTML commands provide formatting instructions and other information. Because HTML files are all text, they're small and easy to transmit through the Internet.

...\<H1>Eat Apples!\</H1>For a special treat

3. The browser reads the HTML file and interprets the HTML commands, called tags, embedded in angle brackets \<like this>. It uses the formatting tags to determine the look and layout of the text on the page. For example, \<H1> indicates a level 1 heading to be displayed in large text, *indicates italics,* and so on.

4. The HTML file doesn't contain pictures; it's a text file. But it does contain a tag specifying where a picture file is stored and where in the page it is to be displayed. The server responds to this tag by sending the requested graphics file.

Request for www.fujieater home page

5. The HTML file also contains a tag indicating a hyperlink to another document with a URL on another server. When the user clicks that link, a message is sent to the new server, and the process of building a Web page in the browser window starts anew.

FIGURE 9.11

bloggers from technical details such as FTP server addresses and URLs. They even provide custom design templates so users can modify the look of their blogs without knowing any HTML. Some suppliers of blog software, such as Google's Blogger.com, will even host your blog for free. Meanwhile, online community services such as Facebook, MySpace, YouTube, and Flickr are used by millions of people who don't have a clue about the technical underpinnings of the pages they create. People who use these sites upload personal profiles, pictures, and blogs with little more effort or expertise than they'd apply sending email messages.

From Hypertext to Multimedia

Way back in the early 1990s(!) the first Web pages were straight hypertext. Within a couple of years, graphics were common, and a few cutting-edge Web sites enabled browsers to download scratchy video and audio clips to their hard disks. Today color graphics and animation are everywhere, and a typical Web site can contain any or all of these:

> We are still a **multimedia organism**. If we want to push the envelope of complexity further, we have to use **all of our devices** for accessing information—not all of which are **rational**.
>
> —*Psychologist Mihaly Csikszentmihalyi*

- *Tables* are spreadsheet-like grids with rows and columns containing neatly laid-out text and graphical elements. Tables with invisible cell borders are often used as alignment tools to create simple layouts.
- *Frames* are subdivisions of a browser's viewing area that enable visitors to scroll and view different parts of a page, or even multiple pages, simultaneously. Many users find frames confusing, and as the Internet evolves, frames are becoming less common.
- *Forms* are pages that visitors can fill in to order goods and services, respond to questionnaires, enter contests, express opinions, or add comments to ongoing discussions.
- *Animations* are moving pictures based on a variety of technologies, from simple repetitive GIF animations to complex interactive animations created with authoring tools, such as Adobe Flash.
- *Search engines* are tools for locating what you're looking for on a site. Most of these site-specific search engines are based on the same technology as Web-wide search engines, such as Google. Many site builders license search engines from search engine companies.
- *Downloadable audio* clips are compressed sound files that you must download onto your computer's hard disk before the browser or some other application can play them. MP3 and AAC compression formats are popular because the compressed music files sound almost the same as the uncompressed originals that would take much longer to download.
- *Downloadable video* clips are compressed video files that you can download and view on a computer. Many are small, short, and jerky, but quality is rapidly improving as new video compression technologies mature.
- **Streaming audio** files are sounds that play without being completely downloaded to the local hard disk. Some streaming files play automatically while you view a page, providing background music and sound effects. Others, such as sound samples at music stores, play on request. Unlike downloaded media files, you can view or hear streaming media files within seconds because they play while you're downloading them. For the same reason, streaming media files don't need to be limited to short clips. Concert-length streaming programs are common. High-quality streaming music generally requires a broadband connection and can be interrupted by Internet traffic jams.
- **Streaming video** files are video clips that play while you're downloading them. Streaming video is even more dependent on high-bandwidth connection than streaming audio is.

Building a Web Site

GOAL *To create a site representing a small service business.*

TOOLS *Adobe Dreamweaver, image editing software, and one or more Web browsers.*

1. The first step in publishing, whether on paper or on the Web, is to plan the layout for the publication. Because a Web site is a hypertext document, a flowchart or storyboard can make it easier to plan the links between pages.

2. When the plan is complete, you collect and edit the source documents—the images, articles, and other elements that will make up the finished publication.

3. Dreamweaver Web authoring software enables you to create, view, and edit your pages using both a WYSIWYG editor and a source-code text editor. You begin the page design process with unformatted text content, and tag each paragraph as a heading, a subhead, or body text. You also add a few hyperlinks using the Properties palette.

FIGURE 9.12

- *Real-time streaming audio or video broadcasts*, or *Webcasts*, are streaming transmissions of radio or TV broadcasts, concerts, news feeds, speeches, and other sound events as they happen. Many Internet radio stations stream around the clock.
- *Three-dimensional (3D) environments* are drawn or photographed virtual spaces you can explore with mouse clicks.
- *Personalization* is customization of content made possible because sites can remember information about guests from visit to visit. Some sites use login names and passwords to remember visitors. Others track and remember visits, activities, and preferences using cookies—small files deposited on the visitor's hard disk. Cookies can make online shopping and other activities more efficient and rewarding, and they can make a Web site visit

4. You use Dreamweaver's Tag Inspector to define styles to control the formatting, layout, and color scheme. As you create and modify these styles, the changes are automatically reflected throughout the page and site.

5. You add a navigation banner to the page, and preview the page in a Web browser.

6. You create bare-bones versions of the other pages in the site and apply the style sheet you just created.

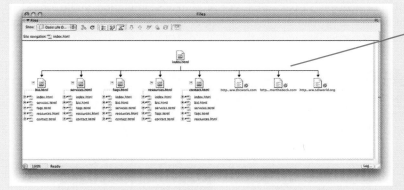

7. You compare this site map, created by Dreamweaver, with the original design.

8. You test the entire site with various Web browsers to make sure everything displays properly.

9. Once you're happy with the results, you can load the site onto the Web so the world can view it.

a highly personal experience. ("Welcome back, Audrey. You might like to know that memory cards for your camera are on sale today.") Unfortunately, cookies can also provide all kinds of possibilities for snoopers who want to know how you spend your time online. By default, most browsers don't tell you when they leave a cookie. By changing browser settings, it's possible to refuse all cookies or accept them on a case-by-case basis.

Today new Web ideas appear at an astounding rate—so fast that browser makers have trouble keeping up. Fortunately, the most popular browsers can be enhanced with **plug-ins**—software extensions that add new features. When a company introduces a Web innovation, such as a new type of animation, it typically makes a free browser plug-in available to users. Once you download the plug-in and install it in your browser, you can take

FIGURE 9.13 Streaming and downloadable media are available from countless Web sites. Pandora.com allows listeners to create customized streaming "radio" stations that play songs that match the characteristics of music you already know and love.

advantage of any Web pages that include the innovation. Popular plug-ins become standard features in future browser versions, so you don't need to download and install them. Even if a browser can't play or display a particular type of graphics, animation, audio, or video by itself, it might be able to offload the task to a *helper application*—a separate program designed to present that particular media type.

FIGURE 9.14 NASA.gov is one of a multitude of Web sites that provides streaming video files.

FIGURE 9.15 Most browsers, including Firefox, enable users to set preferences about how and when to accept cookies.

The most popular free cross-platform plug-ins and helper applications include:

- *Adobe Reader* and *Acrobat* (Adobe) display documents in *Portable Document Format (PDF)* so they look the same on the screen as on paper, even if the documents are viewed on computers that don't have the same fonts installed. Adobe Reader is a free application that can only display PDF documents; the Acrobat products allow you to edit and create PDF documents. Adobe Reader is pre-installed in most modern browsers.
- *Shockwave/Flash (swf)* (Adobe) plug-ins enable browsers to present compressed interactive multimedia documents, video, and animations created with Flash and other authoring tools. Flash is pre-installed in virtually all PC and Mac browsers and many browsers for handheld devices.
- *RealOne* (Real) is a popular program for playing streaming audio and video, including live Webcasts. RealOne movies and sound files are encoded in proprietary formats so they can't be played with other media players.
- *Windows Media Player* (Microsoft) is a direct competitor to RealOne, delivering streaming media in proprietary formats that are compatible with other players because Microsoft licenses the technology to other companies.
- *QuickTime* (Apple) also delivers cross-platform streaming media in proprietary formats. QuickTime movies are generally very high quality.

HTML was originally designed to share scientific research documents, not to deliver media-rich documents in which design is as important as content. Newer versions of HTML support *cascading style sheets (CSS)* to define formatting and layout features that aren't recognized in older versions of HTML.

Today's dynamic HTML also recognizes *scripts*—short programs—that can add interactivity, animation, and other dynamic features to Web pages. One common use of scripts is to add *rollovers* to onscreen buttons, so they visibly change when the user rolls the pointer over them. Scripts can modify HTML code on the fly in response to user input. Scripts are typically written in a scripting language called JavaScript. Web pages that take advantage of the latest dynamic HTML features can be more interesting and interactive, but some browsers (especially stripped-down browsers on cell phones and PDAs) don't recognize them. Unscrupulous Web programmers can use scripts to embed viruses and other unwanted elements into your computer. We'll explore these risks in the next chapter.

Dynamic Web Sites: Beyond HTML

If you thought a Web site consisted of **HTML** pages organized as a directory, **go back to the 20th century**. A successful Web site today consists primarily of **XML** code and a **database**.

—*Dana Blankenhorn, coauthor of* Web Commerce: Building a Digital Business

HTML is flexible, but it's designed for page layout, not programming. By itself, it can't support online shopping, financial transaction processing, library catalogs, daily newspapers, search engines, and other applications with masses of rapidly changing data. This kind of dynamic Web site requires two things that HTML can't easily deliver: a database to store the constantly changing content of the site, and custom programming to make the appropriate data available to site visitors.

A data-driven Web site can display dynamic, changeable content without having constantly redesigned pages, thanks to an evolving database that separates the content of the site from its design. For example, an online store's Web site doesn't have a separate HTML page for each catalog item. Instead, it has pages that are coded to display product information drawn from a database that can be continually updated. The Web site is a front end for the database; it serves as the visitor's window into the database. Likewise, the database is a data back end for the Web site.

Programmers use a variety of programming languages for creating dynamic Web sites. The *Perl* scripting language is particularly popular for programming Web servers. Java, developed by Sun Microsystems, is probably the best-known language for Web programming. Note that Java and JavaScript have little in common except their names. JavaScript is a simple scripting language for enhancing HTML Web pages; Java is a full-featured cross-platform programming language.

Small Java programs are called *applets* because they're like tiny applications. Java applets can be automatically downloaded onto your client computer through almost any Web browser. A Java applet is platform independent; it runs on a Windows PC, a Mac, a UNIX workstation, or anything else as long as the client machine has Java Virtual Machine (JVM) software installed. This JVM software is built into most full-featured browsers and is available for free download.

Microsoft offers several alternatives to Java. The oldest is *ActiveX*, a collection of programming technologies and tools for creating controls or components—programs that are similar in many ways to Java applets. ActiveX components require a compatible browser to run properly.

Another important tool in Web development, XML (eXtensible Markup Language), is a widely used system for defining data formats. HTML is used for formatting and displaying data; XML represents the contextual *meaning* of the data. XML allows programmers to "mark up" data with customized tags that give the information more meaning. XML provides a rich system to define complex documents such as invoices, molecular data, news feeds, glossaries, and real estate properties. Forms, database queries, and other data-intensive operations that can't be completely constructed with standard HTML are much easier to create with XML. XML is at the heart of Microsoft's .NET and other competing strategies for developing Web services. Many PC and Mac applications, including Microsoft Office, support XML as a standard formatting language.

Weaving Winning Web Sites

It's easy to create a Web site; just about anybody with an Internet connection can do it. It's not so easy to create an effective Web site—one that communicates clearly, attracts visitors, and achieves its goals. Here are a few pointers for making your Web publications work.

➡ **Start with a plan.** The Web is littered with sites that seem pointless. Many of those sites were probably constructed without a clear plan or purpose. Start with clear goals and design your entire site with those goals in mind.

➡ **Write for the Web.** Most people won't read long, scrolling documents on computer screens. Limit each page to one or two screens of text. Provide clearly marked links to pages with more details for people who need them. And don't forget to check your spelling and grammar.

➡ **Keep it simple.** Web pages that are cluttered with blinking text, busy backgrounds, repetitive animations, and garish graphics tend to lose their visitors quickly. Stick with clean lines and clear design if you want people to stick around.

➡ **Keep it consistent.** Every page in your site should look like it's related to the other pages in your site. Fonts, graphical elements, colors, buttons, and menus should be consistent from page to page.

➡ **Make it obvious.** Your visitors should be able to tell within a few seconds how your site works. Unless you're building a puzzle palace, make sure the buttons and structure of your site are intuitive.

➡ **Keep it small.** Large photographs, complex animations, video clips, and sounds can make your site big and slow to load. Most people won't want more than a few seconds for a page to load. If you need lots of pictures, use an image-editing program to optimize them for the Web. Similarly, make sure your audio and video pages (if you have them) are designed to minimize delays.

➡ **Keep it honest.** Anybody can publish a Web site without the benefit of a fact-checker. Check your facts before you share your pages with the world.

➡ **Offer contact information.** Web communication shouldn't be one way. Provide a way for your visitors to contact you. But if you include your email address, expect to receive lots of spam—software Web crawlers are always searching for new addresses on the Web. To minimize spam, you might want to refer to your email address indirectly: "My email name is Fuji and my domain name is appleeater.com."

➡ **Think like a publisher and a multimedia designer.** The rules of publishing and design, discussed in earlier chapters, apply to Web publishing, too.

➡ **Test before you publish.** Show your work to others, preferably people in your target audience, and watch their reactions carefully. If they get lost, confused, bored, or upset, you probably have more work to do before launching the final site.

➡ **Think before you publish.** It's easy to publish Web pages for the world—at least that part of the world that uses the Web. Don't put anything on your site that you don't want the world to see; you may, for example, be asking for trouble if you publish your home address, your work schedule, and a photo of the expensive computer system in your study.

➡ **Keep it current.** It's easy to build a Web site, and it's even easier to forget to keep it up to date. If your site is worth visiting, it's worth revising. If the contents of your site are constantly in need of revision, consider using a database to house the data so you can automatically update the site when the data changes.

➡ **Take your integrity to the Web.** The Web offers plenty of opportunity to deceive, mislead, and cheat people, and many people say things on their Web sites that they would never repeat in face-to-face interactions. If you want a growing community of return visitors, make sure those visitors know that they can trust what they see.

FIGURE 9.16 This screen from www.re-vision.com was created to violate as many principles of Web design as possible, including cramming too much information onto a page, noisy banner ads, overuse of frames, and navigation elements scattered across the page.

FIGURE 9.17 TestFreaks is a site that aggregates information about products: professional and user reviews, news, rumors, manuals, videos, and more.

XML isn't the only markup language that's emerging to go beyond the capabilities of HTML. Extensible HTML, or XHTML, a sort of cross between HTML and XML, can accommodate existing HTML pages, making it easier to upgrade older sites. XHTML is, in theory, better suited to work with mobile phones and handheld computers than traditional HTML. In practice, though, Web developers have been slow to switch from HTML to XHTML. Another HTML-like language, SMIL (Synchronized Multimedia Integration Language), is designed to make it possible to link time-based streaming media so, for example, sounds, video, and animation can be tightly integrated with each other.

A relatively new way to support efficient, interactive Web pages has been given the name *Ajax* (for *Asynchronous JavaScript and XML*). The idea behind Ajax is to make Web pages more responsive by eliminating the need to reload an entire page every time a user makes a small change, such as changing a selection in an online order form. Instead, client-side scripts on the user's machine provide quick updates based on user inputs, and communication with the Web server allow small amounts of data to be exchanged without reloading the entire Web page. Ajax methodology relies on XHTML, HTML, JavaScript, XML, and other scripting and markup languages.

Most dynamic Web sites today use another scripting language: PHP. While JavaScript is used to create scripts on client computers, PHP is designed for building server-side scripts or programs. PHP scripts work behind the scenes to create many of the Web pages we view every day, from Facebook entries to Wikipedia references.

Search Engines

With its vast storehouses of information, the Web is like a huge library. Unfortunately, it's a poorly organized library; you might find information on a particular topic almost anywhere. (What can you expect from a library where nobody's in charge?) That's why search engines are among the Web's most popular tools.

All search engines are designed to make it easier to find information on the Web, but they don't all function the same way. A typical search engine uses *Web crawlers* or *spiders*—software robots that systematically explore the Web, retrieve information about pages, and index the retrieved information in a database. Different search engines use different searching and indexing strategies. For example, to determine the subject matter of a Web page, one search engine might focus on the words on the page, while another might pay more attention to links to and from other Web pages. For some search engines, researchers organize and evaluate Web sites in databases; other search engines are almost completely automated. Of course, not all Web pages are accessible to search engines or the public.

Most search engines enable you to type queries using keywords, just as you might locate information in other types of databases. You can construct complex queries using *Boolean logic* (for example, *American AND Indian AND NOT Cleveland* would focus the search on Native Americans rather than baseball), quotations, and other tools for refining queries. Some search engines enable you to narrow your search repeatedly by choosing subcategories from a hierarchical *directory* or *subject tree*. No matter which search technique you use, you're eventually presented with a rank-ordered list of Web pages. The best search engines put the most relevant links first.

Some search engines are designed to search for specific types of information. Such specialized search engines can help you locate email addresses and phone numbers; others can help you find the lowest prices on the Web. These specialized search engines, such as Google Maps and Froogle, use technology similar to general search engine technology.

Portals

Many Web sites that started out as search engines have evolved into **Web portals**—Web entry stations that offer quick convenient access to a variety of services and links. Popular general-interest portals include Yahoo!, MSN, Google, and AOL/Netscape. Consumer portals feature search engines, email services, chat rooms, references, news and sports headlines, shopping malls, other services, and advertisements. Many *regional Web portals* offer similar services, but focus on information and services related to a particular geographic region. You can personalize many portals so they automatically display local weather and sports scores, personalized TV and movie listings, news headlines related to particular subjects, horoscopes, and ads to meet your interests. Most browsers enable users to choose a home page that opens by default when the browser is launched; *personal Web portals* are designed with this feature in mind.

In addition to these general-interest portals, the Web has a growing number of specialized portals. *Government Web portals* serve as entry points to many federal, state, and municipal government Web sites. Some, such as USA.gov and direct.gov.uk, are provided for general access; others are aimed at specific populations, such as veterans or businesses. *Corporate portals* on intranets serve the employees of particular corporations. *Vertical portals*, like vertical market software (see Chapter 4) target members of a particular industry or economic sector. For example, Webmd.com is a portal for medically minded consumers and health-care professionals. Sportal.com is one of many portals for sports fans.

Push Technology and RSS

The Web was built with **pull technology**: Browsers on client computers pull information from server machines. With pull technology the browser needs to initiate a request before any information is delivered. But for some applications, it makes more sense to have information delivered automatically to the client computer. That's the way **push technology** works.

With push technology, you subscribe to a service or specify the kinds of information you want to receive, and the server delivers that information periodically and unobtrusively.

How It Works

9.3 Setting Up a Web Domain

It's not hard to design a simple Web site, but that's only the first step. In order to make your site visible on the Web, you'll need to post it on a Web server and assign a domain name—a Web address that makes it possible for people to locate and view your site.

The Internet

Web Hosting Service

Welcome to My Site!

1. Choose a Web hosting service—a company that will provide a home for your web site on its server.

You

2. Create Web pages on your computer or hire a Web design service to make them for you.

7. Upload Web pages to your domain.

Web Design Service

Domain Name Registration Service

3. Choose a domain name (such as Beekmedia.com) and use a domain name registration service to determine whether it's available.

4. The domain name registration service checks domain names against a master list called the whois database. Network Solutions is the company that controls the database for the .com domain. If your requested domain name is not available, you need to repeat the process.

6. Domain name information automatically propagates to DNS servers in 4–8 hours.

5. Reserve the domain name and activate the domain by telling the domain name registration service the address of your Web hosting service.

Network Solutions

Whois database

DNS Server

DNS Server

DNS Server

Your Audience

8. Now a person attempting to access your Web site can view your Web pages.

FIGURE 9.18

FIGURE 9.19 Like other Web portals, iGoogle lets each visitor personalize the look (theme) and contents, choosing from dozens of sources for news, weather, sports, entertainment, and more. iGoogle users are encouraged to design their own "Web gadgets" and make them available for other iGoogle users on their portal pages.

Maybe you want up-to-the-minute headlines or weather maps displayed as a Windows sidebar gadget, a Mac OS dashboard widget, or a Web gadget on your iGoogle personal portal page. You may want to receive new product descriptions automatically from selected companies. Or you might like to have the software on your hard disk automatically upgraded whenever upgrades are available. All of this is possible with push technology.

Technically speaking, today's push technology is really pull technology in disguise. Your computer quietly and automatically pulls information from selected Web servers based on your earlier requests or subscriptions. As convenient as they are, push programs have the same basic problem as Web search engines: they give you what they think you want, but they may not be very smart. Their ability to deliver what you really need, without bombarding you with unwanted data, is getting better as artificial intelligence technology improves.

Push technology is commonly used for delivery of information on company intranets. Outside of the corporate enterprise, most push technology takes the form of subscriber *notifications* and *alerts*. Email is the one form of push technology that has been embraced by almost all Internet users. Instant messaging is another popular push application.

A newer technology, RSS, is expanding push technology into other types of applications. **RSS** (Really Simple Syndication) is an XML-based family of formats used to publish frequently updated documents, including blogs (Chapter 8), newsfeeds, and podcasts (Chapter 6). RSS began as a tool for heavy blog readers. RSS gives anyone who publishes on the Web the power to syndicate their stories or podcasts—in other words, to attract and keep subscribers.

A content provider, who could be a blogger, a podcaster, or the *New York Times,* maintains a list of changes to the Web site or podcast in a standard format called a (Web) *feed* or a *channel.* The feed might contain a story's title or summary and a URL to a Web page with the body of the article, or it might contain the entire text of the article. Subscribers run RSS-reading applications (which may be Web browsers, email clients, or other

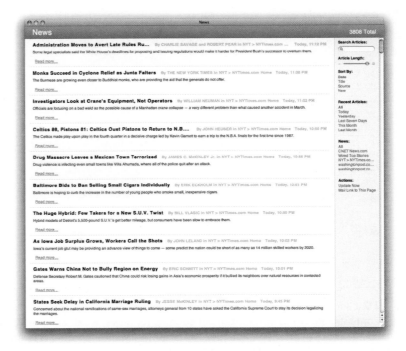

FIGURE 9.20 Many modern Web browsers include RSS readers. Here, Safari collects the latest headlines from several Web sites on one page.

applications on a PC or smart phone) called *aggregators* that periodically visit Web sites, examine the feeds, and display new content (or download new podcasts). RSS subscriptions can save time by automating the process of seeking out information on the Web.

Web 2.0 and You

We thought that **anybody who came** to a concert **had equity**. They **took part in the creation**.

—*Mickey Hart, drummer for the Grateful Dead*

In the previous chapter and this chapter, we've explored and analyzed a variety of network applications that are changing the way we live and work. Many of these applications are designed to make it easy for us to create, as well as consume, Internet content. Blogs, forums, and wikis are new media types that can provide any or all of us with worldwide audiences. Media sharing sites like YouTube and Flickr serve as virtual galleries for photographers, filmmakers, and artists. Podcasting and Internet radio technology can give a voice and an audience to just about anybody with a microphone and an Internet connection. Social networking sites like MySpace and YouTube are build-it-yourself Internet communities. Craigslist, a centralized network of online communities, has changed the way people in hundreds of cities advertise jobs, tools, toys, services, and personal connections. This diverse collection of participatory technologies, most of which emerged early in the 21st century, is often called Web 2.0.

The distinguishing feature of Web 2.0 applications is the do-it-yourself spirit. In Web 2.0, anyone can create an online publication, photo gallery, movie, music video, radio show, or video podcast. Anyone can help write the definitive encyclopedia or build a cabin in a virtual world. Anyone can add an opinion or voice to a collective review of a Web page, a new movie, or a political candidate. Anyone can create a *mashup*—a Web page, song, video, or image that combines music and video clips from other works (assuming, of

FIGURE 9.21 Craigslist provides free classified ads for people in hundreds of cities.

course, that the other works aren't protected by copyrights). Web 2.0 is not a spectator sport—it's all about participation.

According to some experts, the downside of this Web populism is a loss of professional standards. Blogs don't generally have professional editors to check facts, grammar, and integrity before they're published. Most homemade podcasts lack the professional editing and production of corporate media. Wikis run the risk of degenerating into virtual shouting matches between opposing points of view.

Still, most people believe that the democratization of media and social institutions is, on balance, a good thing. In any case, it's not going away. The Web 2.0 participatory philosophy is spreading across the Web, changing the way we interact with the technology—and each other.

Internet Issues: Ethical and Political Dilemmas

The Internet started as a small community of scientists, engineers, and other researchers who staunchly defended the noncommercial, cooperative charter of the network. Today the Internet has more than 1 billion users, including everybody from children to corporate executives. The Internet's growth raises questions about the Internet's ability to keep up; the amount of information transmitted may eventually be more than the Net can handle.

> **The Internet** still hasn't figured out how to **conduct itself in public**. . . . Everybody is trying to **develop the rules** by which they can conduct themselves in order to keep a **civil operation** going and not **self-destruct**.
>
> —*George Lucas, filmmaker*

Meanwhile, the commercialization of the Internet has opened a floodgate of new services to users. People are logging into the Internet to view weather patterns, book flights, buy stocks, sell cars, track deliveries, listen to radio broadcasts from around the world, conduct videoconferences, coordinate disaster recovery programs, and perform countless other private and public transactions. The Internet saves time, money, and lives, but it brings problems, too.

How It Works

9.4 Creating a Podcast

The steps for creating a podcast are, in some ways, analogous to the steps for creating a Web site.

1. Record audio content and store it on your computer in your audio editor's native format.

2. Edit the audio content. Make it as professional as possible—after all, it may be heard by a lot of people!

3. Convert the finished recording to MP3.

4. Use a text editor or an RSS-specific tool to create an .rss file that contains the title, length, date, and other information about the mp3 file.

RawColumn.wav
FinishedColumn.wav
FinishedColumn.mp3
MyColumns.rss

www.BQNewsViews.com
. . .
FinishedColumn.mp3
MyColumns.rss

5. Upload the MP3 file and the .rss file to your Web site

Web Hosting Service

http://rss.scripting.com

Podcast Directory 1

6. Visit rss. scripting.com to make sure your feed is set up properly.

7. Add information about your podcast to online directories, such as Podcasting News's Podcasting Directory.

Podcast Directory 2

Podcast Directory 3

The Internet

8. People learn about your column and subscribe to it.

9. Subscribers download your podcasts to their computers and then transfer them to their ipods and other portable audio players.

FIGURE 9.22

344

Internet Addiction

William Gibson, Neal Stephenson, and other science fiction writers of the 1980s and early 1990s envisioned the creation of compelling, even addictive, computer-generated virtual worlds. In their novels, the virtual worlds attract users because the quality of life on Earth is miserable. Direct feeds into the visual cortex, or virtual reality goggles and earphones, allow users to completely shut out the sights and sounds of reality.

Even though today's world has not suffered the extreme environmental degradation described in their novels, and most computer users are not directly wired into their computers, many Internet users have trouble disconnecting. Psychologists debate whether excessive Internet usage is a true addiction or merely a compulsion. Either way, it can have a profound negative impact on a person's life. Stories abound of people who've lost friendships, relationships, spouses, and jobs because they put too much of their time and energy into blogs, forums, chat rooms, virtual worlds, social networks, and (especially) massive multiplayer online role-playing games (MMORPGs). Some of the millions of online gamers spend 40 to 80 hours a week online, completely caught up in the never-ending story they're creating. Sometimes their stories have unhappy endings. Some examples:

- A distraught American mother blamed her son's suicide on his despondency after his online character was robbed of all his wealth. She responded by creating a Web site for addicted gamers and their families.
- A Chinese gamer murdered an 81-year-old woman, buried her in a pile of sand, and robbed her of about six dollars to pay for his gaming habit. Out-of-control gamers have also murdered police officers and dispatchers.
- A South Korean man who quit his job to play more video games died of exhaustion after a 50-hour session in an Internet café. The government indicates that online game addiction is becoming a serious problem in South Korea.
- Tragically, several infants and children have died because their parents neglected them to play online games.

Because MMORPGs have become so important to so many people, a real-world market has sprung up for virtual-world characters and artifacts. Chinese entrepreneurs hire young people to work 12-hour shifts as "gold farmers." These players play MMORPGs, killing monsters and earning gold pieces. They sell the virtual gold pieces to Westerners, who pay for them with real money. When the avatars become powerful enough, they can be sold, too. The gold farmers can make $250 a month playing MMORPGs—a good living for them. China now has hundreds, if not thousands, of online gaming factories.

Freedom's Abuses

Commercialization has brought capitalism's dark side to the Internet. Spam scams, get-rich-quick hoaxes, online credit card thefts, email forgery, child pornography hustling, illegal gambling, Web site sabotage, online stalking, fraudulent political schemes, and other sleazy activities abound. The Internet has clearly lost its innocence.

Some of these problems result from people placing too much trust in email messages, Web advertisements, blogs, and other online information sources. Others are the result of people posting or sharing information about themselves without thinking about how far that information might travel (anywhere on the Internet) and how long it might last (indefinitely). Examples abound. A Fisher College student was expelled after posting a critique of a campus police officer. The mayor of a tiny Oregon desert town was recalled after voters discovered pictures of her posing in underwear on her MySpace page. Countless men and women have been arrested after bragging of illegal activities in blogs, forums, and social networking sites. Many employers search blogs and social Web sites to do background checks on job applicants; past activities and postings can haunt otherwise qualified job seekers. Students and others routinely do Google checks on prospective blind dates; online photos, video clips, and blogs can

FIGURE 9.23 The On-Line Gamers Anonymous site was created by the mother of a suicidal gamer to help other addicted gamers and their families and friends.

make powerful first impressions, positive or otherwise. And, of course, the information people post can be used and abused by scammers, stalkers, and other criminals. Children and young people are especially prone naively to posting too much personal data. In one headline-grabbing story, a 49-year-old Missouri mother was indicted for conspiracy and other crimes for posing as a 16-year-old boy on MySpace, luring a 13-year-old girl into an online romance, and then dumping her by telling her the world would be better off without her. The rejected girl responded by hanging herself. Some of these problems have at least partial technological solutions. MySpace and Facebook are continually updating security to minimize risks from predators and other criminals, but they can't completely eliminate the problem as long as members carelessly compromise their own personal privacy. Concerned parents and teachers can install **filtering software** that, for the most part, keeps children out of Web sites that contain inappropriate content. Commercial sites routinely use encryption so customers can purchase goods and services without fear of having credit card numbers stolen by electronic eavesdroppers. Several software companies and banks are developing systems for circulating **electronic money** on the Internet to make online transactions easier and safer. To protect against email forgery, many software companies are working together to hammer out standards for *digital signatures* using encryption techniques described in the next chapter.

Access and Censorship

Many problems associated with the rapid growth and commercialization of the Internet are social problems that raise important political questions. Online hucksterism and pornography have prompted government controls on Internet content, including the 1996 Communications Decency Act. Opponents to this law and other proposed controls argue that it's important to preserve the free flow of information; they stress the need to protect our rights to free speech and privacy on the Internet. In 1996 the U.S. Supreme Court declared the Communications Decency Act unconstitutional, arguing that "the interest in encouraging freedom of expression in a democratic society outweighs any theoretical but unproven benefit of censorship."

The public outcry against the corrupting influence of pornography on children continued, however, and in December of 2000, Congress passed the Children's Internet Protection Act. The act requires public libraries and schools that receive certain types of federal funding to install content filters on computers with Internet access. In June 2003, the U.S. Supreme Court upheld the constitutionality of the Children's Internet Protection Act.

Questions about human rights online probably won't be resolved by legislators and judges, though. The Internet's global reach makes it nearly impossible for a single government to regulate it. Internet pioneer John Gilmore said, "The Net interprets censorship as damage and routes around it." Still, most governments are uncomfortable simply allowing an uninhibited flow of information through the Internet. As we have seen, even democratic nations have taken steps to regulate Internet content. In the United States, the federal government attempts to prevent children from gaining access to pornography, and most states make it illegal to run online casinos. Germany bans neo-Nazi Web sites. And many countries not known for censorship block access to child pornography Web sites.

Some nations with more authoritarian governments have been much more aggressive in their attempts to reduce or eliminate the free flow of information over the Internet. Reporters Without Borders and the OpenNet Initiative monitor Internet censorship and maintain lists of countries that severely restrict access for political, social, and other reasons. Several countries have been classified by one or both organizations as having "pervasive" censorship, including Belarus, China, Cuba, Egypt, Iran, Myanmar, North Korea, Saudi Arabia, Syra, Tunisia, Turkmenestan, Ubzbekistan, and Vietnam. Most of these countries block citizen access to Web sites that criticize their governments. Some block access to other material deemed inappropriate by their governments. For example, technicians in the centralized Saudi Arabian Internet control center attempt to block all sites offensive to Islam or the government of Saudi Arabia, including those related to pornography,

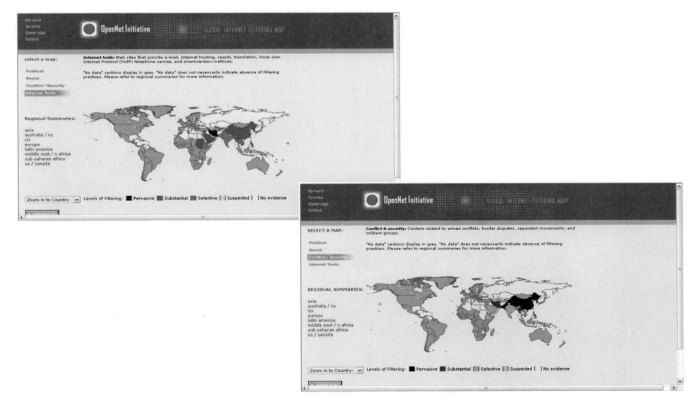

FIGURE 9.24 The OpenNet Intitiative monitors different type of Internet filtering and censorship, including political, social, technical, and security filtering, and publishes detailed findings on the Web.

Middle Eastern politics, non-Islamic religious organizations, women's health and sexuality issues, and gay rights. Some governments use a variety of surveillance techniques to track citizen Web access and communication.

The largest country on the Reporters Without Borders "Enemies of the Internet" list is the People's Republic of China. China allows Internet service providers to make their own connections, but it requires them to sign a "self-discipline" agreement that forbids them from forwarding politically or morally objectionable Web pages. Objectionable pages include those containing pornography, references to Taiwan or Tibet, or news about Chinese dissidents. To do business in China, Google and other search engine vendors are required to modify their software so that Web searches can be censored by the government.

The Digital Divide

During the 1990s the U.S. government pushed for the development of a National Information Infrastructure (NII)—an affordable, secure, high-speed network to provide "universal service" for all Americans. The motivation for the creation of an NII was the realization that a digital divide separates people who have easy access to computers, the Internet, and digital information technology, and those who don't.

Today about three quarters of the U.S. population has Internet access. Recent studies suggest that socioeconomic status, income, education level, and race all contribute to the digital divide. Many of those who don't have computers or Internet access can barely afford food and rent.

Government programs to wire schools, libraries, and other public facilities have increased access for disadvantaged populations. But the problem of equal access isn't likely to go away without combined efforts of governments, businesses, and individuals. The availability of low-cost Wi-Fi technology has led to growing grassroots movements in the United States and dozens of other countries to create wireless community networks that would provide all computer-equipped citizens with baseline Internet access.

Even if the United States and other highly industrialized nations make the Internet available to all their citizens, there's still a global digital divide. The Internet is a global infrastructure, but huge populations all over the world are locked out. Many experts argue that access to the Internet is one of many ingredients necessary for economic development in the twenty-first century. They fear that we'll leave billions of people behind as we move further into the information age. If poverty and lack of opportunity lead to political instability, wars, and terrorism, then the digital divide could pose a terrible threat to people on both sides of the divide. The widely-publicized One Laptop per Child program is one of many efforts to close the gap by bringing information technology to disadvantaged populations. But to succeed, programs like this one need to be accompanied by larger efforts. Laptops and network connections are of limited value to populations ravaged by war, disease, and starvation.

FIGURE 9.25 Some government programs attempt to reduce the digital divide by providing schools with computers and Internet access.

Net Neutrality

One of the biggest Internet-related controversies of recent years concerns net neutrality (or network neutrality)—the principle that Internet access should be free from restrictions related to the type of equipment being connected and the type of communication being performed with that equipment. Net neutrality was one of the underlying principles of the Internet when it was conceived. According to Vint Cerf, co-inventor of the Internet Protocol, "The Internet was designed with no gatekeepers over new content or services. A lightweight but enforceable neutrality rule is needed to ensure that the Internet continues to thrive."

Net neutrality champions believe telecommunications companies that own vast tracts of the Internet infrastructure threaten neutrality. They fear that broadband vendors, for example, might prevent content from competing companies—or controversial causes—to enter subscriber homes. Or that vendors might create an Internet caste system by providing faster, more reliable service for large business customers. According to net neutrality advocates, all packets are created equal, and should be forwarded through the Net on a first-come, first-serve basis.

Telecommunications companies have lobbied heavily to block net neutrality legislation in the U.S. They argue that pipeline owners should have a say in how they're used. Bob Kahn, co-inventor of the Internet Protocol, agrees. He and others fear that net neutrality legislation would stifle innovation by robbing network builders and owners of some profit incentives.

The network neutrality debate has raged for years, and is likely to continue for years to come.

From Cyberspace to Infosphere

Cyberspace. **A consensual hallucination** experienced daily by billions of legitimate operators, **in every nation**, by children being taught mathematical concepts.... A graphic representation of data abstracted from the banks of **every computer in the human system**. **Unthinkable complexity**. Lines of light ranged in the nonspace of the mind, clusters and constellations of data. Like city lights, receding....

—*William Gibson, in* Neuromancer

From the earliest days of the Internet, science fiction writers have suggested that future networks will take us into an artificial reality that feels like a physical place. In his visionary novel *Neuromancer,* William Gibson coined the term **cyberspace** to describe such a shared virtual reality, complete with sights, sounds, and other sensations. Today that term is sometimes used to describe the Internet or the Web as a place.

But many experts today think the term *cyberspace* is, to use Gibson's words, "past its sell-by." As *Wired* writers Alex Soojunk-Kim and David Pescovitz point out, "we live in a world of smart objects, always-on devices, and perpetually open information channels. The Internet feels less like an alternate world that we 'go to' and more like just another layer of life." Wordsmith Paul McFedrie suggests that the Net today is like the atmosphere—everywhere and necessary—and should be called our *infosphere.*

Whatever we call it, the Internet is changing at a phenomenal pace. And there's no guarantee that the evolving Internet will retain a free, community-oriented, everybody-can-play spirit. In *The Code and Other Laws of Cyberspace,* Lawrence Lessig claims that, because of commerce and other forces, an architecture of control is being built into the Net—control by government and by businesses intent on maximizing Net profits. Lessig argues that the code—the way the Net is programmed—will determine how much freedom we have in the future Internet. "We can build, or architect, or code cyberspace to protect values we believe are fundamental, or we can build, or architect, or code cyberspace to allow those values to disappear. There is no middle ground. There is no choice that does not include some kind of *building.*"

There are parallels between the digital and the nondigital worlds. Many city planning experts argue that industrialized nations have systematically (if not consciously) rebuilt

FIGURE 9.26 The One Laptop per Child program was conceived to provide inexpensive, low-power, networked laptops to the world's poorest children. The program is still in its early stages, but it has a tremendous potential to revolutionize education for billions of children.

their cities so that, in many places, it's just about impossible to live without a car. These car-centered cities have generated revenue for businesses and governments, and they've brought a new sense of freedom to many citizens. But for the poor, the disabled, the young, the old, and others who can't drive, these cities are anything but free. At the same time, other cities have thriving masses of car-free people. Design choices (and nonchoices) made decades ago determine the livability of our cities today.

In the same way, the design decisions being made today by software architects, corporate executives, government officials, and concerned citizens will determine the nature of our Internet experiences in the future. (Net neutrality, discussed in the previous section, is one particularly high-profile issue related to the Internet's design, but there are many more. Will portals guide us to corporate-approved or government-approved information sources, as they do in many countries and companies today? Will netizens feel free to express controversial opinions and criticize powerful institutions without fear of lawsuits, surveillance, and prosecution? Will paths through cyberspace be accessible to everyone? Will high-speed access command premium prices, relegating the rest of us to slow lanes? The Internet's future depends on decisions we, as a society, make today.

Inventing the FUTURE
The Invisible Information Infrastructure

In the future, **everything with a digital heartbeat** will be connected to the Internet.

> —*Scott McNealy, Chairman of the Board of Sun Microsystems*

Countless researchers and developers continue to stretch the boundaries and capabilities of the Internet. At the same time, visionaries are suggesting that the Net is, in a sense, inventing its own future.

Vint Cerf, one of the Internet's founders, is putting much of his time and energy into a project called InterPlaNet, which he hopes will extend the Internet to the other planets in our solar system. According to the plan, electronic "post offices" will orbit other planets, routing messages between space explorers, both human and robot. The obstacles are significant—a message from Mars can take 20 minutes or more to reach Earth, an intolerably long time for Internet servers that "time out" if they don't receive messages quickly. According to Cerf, "the interplanetary network is an example of a much more general concept we call delay-tolerant networks." Even if you aren't expecting email from the red planet, the research being done on InterPlaNet may result in a more reliable Internet for you here on Earth.

FIGURE 9.27a A visualization of the Marsnet proposed by Vint Cerf.

Whatever happens with InterPlaNet, tomorrow's Net surfers will find it easier to locate what they're looking for on the Web. Tim Berners-Lee, the inventor of the Web, is planning a *semantic Web*—a Web full of data that's meaningful to computers as well as humans. With a semantic Web, search engines will be able to deliver exactly what you're looking for instead of bombarding you with hundreds of possibility pages. Here's how Berners-Lee described it to the *Boston Globe*: "You'll tell a search engine, 'find me someplace where the weather is currently rainy and it's within a hundred miles of such and such a city'. . . . A search engine . . . will come back and say, 'Look, I found this place and I can prove to you why I know that it's raining and why I know it's within a hundred miles of this place.' So you'll be dealing with much firmer information." Many people believe that semantic Web technology, or something like it, will be at the heart of the next generation of the Web—Web 3.0.

It may seem far-fetched, but some experts believe that the Net is evolving from a global community into a global intelligence. Artificial intelligence expert Danny Hillis believes true artificial intelligence will emerge in the vast global network rather than in an individual machine. Kevin Kelly describes the future of the Web as "the OS for a megacomputer that encompasses the Internet, all its services, all peripheral chips and affiliated devices from scanners to satellites, and the billions of human minds entangled in this global network. This gargantuan machine already exists in a primitive form. In the coming decade, it will evolve into an integral extension not only of our senses and bodies but our minds." Kelly calls this future network an Anticipation Machine because "anything we do more than twice will be absorbed by the machine." He claims we'll quickly come to depend on it as our memory and our identity, to the point where we may feel incomplete when we're disconnected from it. But that may not happen very often, because all of the devices we use will be windows into this giant computer.

FIGURE 9.27b A smart refrigerator with Internet connectivity.

According to these visionaries, we're already writing the software for this device. Whenever we add information to Wikipedia or Flickr or even eBay, we're adding a tiny bit of intelligence to the Net. The massive network of connections that enables Google to anticipate what we're searching for is not all that different than the network of neurons that we house in our nervous systems. In the Web, as in our brains, learning happens through ever-increasing interconnections.

Whether or not you accept these predictions, one thing is clear: the amazing evolution of the Internet is far from over. And as the Internet changes, it changes our lives. ～

Crosscurrents

Here's Looking At You, Kids *by Jennie Yabroff*

Is today's media technology creating a generation of children who value fame over intimacy and privacy? In this article, condensed from a March 15, 2008, Newsweek *article, Jennie Yabroff raises some fascinating questions about the young millennials.*

When filmmaker Caroline Suh decided to make a documentary about the student-council election at New York's Stuyvesant High School, she was concerned about how the kids would react to the camera. It's an understandable fear: for those of us of Suh's age—she's 37—and older, the introduction of a movie camera has traditionally turned people into either hams mouthing 'Hi, Mom!' or zombies frozen stiff with anxiety. Turns out she needn't have worried. During the year Suh spent making "Frontrunners," two other journalists were also documenting Stuyvesant's kids: one for a book about the school's academic pressures, another for a magazine cover story on the sexual mores of contemporary youth. And the kids, Suh says, were unfazed by the scrutiny. "They've all seen reality TV. They make movies with their cell phones," she says. "Being under the microscope is just part of their lives."

The kids in "Frontrunners" are the leading edge of what's being called the millennials—the cohort born after 1982—but you might call them the Look at Me Generation. Thanks to "The Real World," "Laguna Beach" and the like, they've been documented like no group before them, most especially by themselves: on their blogs, their MySpace, Facebook and Flickr pages, and on YouTube. And now the artistes are taking their turn, with a new wave of reality series, films and books examining the documentation generation. But are we seeing real people, or personas? Listen to girls talk about their roles in the WE series "High School Confidential," and they sound like eerily polished publicists—for themselves. Flip through the photo book "One Hundred Young Americans," and you see a collection of pretty young things prepping for fame, not life, such as Jake, who says, "The whole MySpace thing is a good warm-up for when I'm really famous." It's not just the entertainment that can feel hollow. Sociologists have begun to question the effect of all this exhibitionism on young people. Can they form durable identities off-camera, or are they so used to producing their images for outside consumption that images have replaced their essences? Will a generation for whom all secrets are fair game and every private moment can become public trust each other and form intimate relationships?

One of the ironies of the Look at Me Generation is that many young people believe they are masters of their own images, only to discover, like the topless girl in "American Teen," they can't control anything. "Every decision you make can be so regrettable now, because technology can be so much more vicious," says Nanette Burstein, the film's director. Online gossip sites exacerbate the problem by making it possible for kids to post rumors about each other anonymously, with little recourse for the victims. "What is different is there are these digital footprints," says C. J. Pascoe, a sociologist studying how teens use new media. At the extreme, consider Errol Morris's "Standard Operating Procedure," about the torture scandals at Iraq's Abu Ghraib Prison. In the film we see the dozens of photos the soldiers—most of whom were in their teens and early 20s at the time—took of the prisoners they abused, and of each other, posing and goofing around. Their eagerness to document themselves seemed to blind them to the consequences of creating a record of their actions. The pictures not only resulted in the guards' downfall—without the photos, there would have been almost no proof of crimes—but they may have fed their ugliest impulses. As Morris says, "I often think that if cameras had not been present, these events would not have occurred."

It's probably too soon to weigh the implication of all this publicization on teens' abilities to have meaningful experiences off-camera. In order to form intimate relationships, they will need to trust each other, and not view friendships and romances—not to mention guarding prisoners—as one more arena for MySpace-worthy performances. But instant trust via a blog or Facebook page can be misleading, says Kate Hellenga, a psychology professor at San Francisco State who has studied intimacy and online behavior. "There's a difference between spewing a lot of 'content' between two people and true knowledge of another person," she says. "There isn't a lot of room for trust and earnestness because of the younger generation's constant awareness of self-presentation." It seems contradictory: one thing you can say for the Look at Me's is that they won't suffer the collective amnesia of their boomer elders, who often boast about being too stoned during their youth to remember it. But this generation may have something else in common with boomers: they are so busy documenting their experiences, and being documented, that they may end up with postcards from a trip they have no memory of taking.

Discussion Questions

1. How would you answer the questions at the end of the second paragraph?

2. How do you think the process of documenting our lives changes the way we live our lives?

Summary

The Internet is a network of networks that connects all kinds of computers around the globe. It grew out of a military research network designed to provide reliable communication even if part of the network failed. The Internet uses standard protocols to allow Internet communication to occur. No single organization owns or controls the Internet.

Computers and other devices connect to the Internet through narrowband modem connections, faster broadband connections, and even faster direct connections. Local and national Internet service providers offer Internet access options to their customers; many provide server space for Web pages, online storage, and email.

Most Internet applications are based on the client/server model. The user interface for these applications varies depending on the type of connection and the type of client software the user has. A user might type UNIX commands to a host computer or use point-and-click tools on a PC. Different types of servers provide different kinds of Internet services, ranging from mail to the Web.

The earliest Web pages were simple hypertext pages; today the World Wide Web contains thousands of complex, media-rich structures that offer visitors a wealth of choices. The Web uses a set of protocols to make a variety of Internet services and multimedia documents available to users through a simple point-and-click interface. Web pages are generally constructed using a language called HTML. Many Web authoring tools automate the coding of HTML pages, making it easy for nonprogrammers to write and publish their own pages. Other languages and techniques are being developed to extend the power of the Web in ways that go beyond the capabilities of HTML. Today most large, interactive Web sites are database-driven, so content can be updated automatically.

In addition to Web sites, a variety of applications are built on the protocols of the Internet and the Web. For example, people who use the Web depend on search engines to find the information they need. Search engines use a combination of automated searches and indexed databases to catalog Web resources. Some search engines also serve as portals—sites, sometimes personalized, that serve as entryways to the Web. Some Internet services use push technology (often based on RSS) to push information to subscribers automatically. In recent years there's been an explosive growth in what many people refer to as Web 2.0: the loose collection of Web sites that depend on—and thrive on—content provided by visitors through wikis, forums, podcasts, blogs, and other types of media and information sharing.

As the Internet grows and changes, issues of privacy, security, censorship, criminal activity, universal access, and appropriate Net behavior are surfacing. Even more questions arise when all kinds of electronic devices are attached to the Web, communicating with each other from our homes, our offices, and our vehicles. Rapid-fire changes in the Internet will have tremendous impact on our lives, so it's important that we pay attention to those changes. The Web of the future won't look anything like today's Web. What it does look like will depend on decisions we make today and tomorrow.

Key Terms

Interactive Activities

1. The *Tomorrow's Technology and You* Web site, **www.pearsonhighered.com/beekman**, contains self-test exercises related to this chapter. Follow the instructions for taking a quiz. After you've completed your quiz, you can email the results to your instructor.

2. The Web site also contains open-ended discussion questions called Internet Exercises. Discuss one or more of the Internet Exercises questions at the section for this chapter.

True or False

1. The Internet was originally built on the assumption that all computers on the network would be equal in their ability to communicate with each other.

2. Because of its strongly decentralized design, the Internet can withstand most attacks.

3. When a digital music file is sent on the Internet, it is broken into packets that travel independently to the designated destination.

4. The TCP/IP protocols at the heart of the Internet were developed by Microsoft, but the company freely licenses the technology to many other companies.

5. The words in a domain name, unlike the lines in a post office address, are arranged hierarchically from big to little.

6. Almost every Web address begins with html://, but many browsers don't require you to type that prefix.

7. Streaming video is distinguished from downloadable video by the fact that it is always real time—that is, it presents events as they happen.

8. It's never a good idea to allow your browser to accept cookies from shopping sites, because the security risks posed by cookies far outweigh any possible benefits.

9. Web 2.0 is the term commonly applied to Web sites that depend on peer-to-peer (P2P) file sharing technology.

10. Net neutrality is pretty much guaranteed in the future because of the way the Internet was designed.

Multiple Choice

1. The Internet was originally a(n)
   a. LAN at MIT.
   b. code-cracking network during World War II by the U.S. Defense Department.
   c. network cooperatively created by several large hardware and software companies.
   d. small experimental research network called ARPANET.
   e. Apple product that quickly became too big for the company to control.

2. Where is the Internet's central hub and control center located?
   a. Near Washington, D.C.
   b. Near the Microsoft campus in Redmond, Washington.
   c. In a top-secret location.
   d. In Silicon Valley.
   e. Nowhere; the Internet has no central hub.

3. Which of these domains is restricted to qualified organizations?
   a. .com
   b. .org
   c. .net
   d. .edu

   e. None are restricted; anyone can have a URL in any of these domains.

4. Which of these services would you probably not be able to get from a typical Internet service provider (ISP)?
   a. An email address
   b. Access to a Web server
   c. A connection to the Internet
   d. Technical help
   e. Free Windows upgrades

5. Specialized servers are used on the Internet to
   a. function like email post offices.
   b. accept FTP requests to upload and download files.
   c. store applications that are rented or leased by large corporations.
   d. store and send Web pages.
   e. All of the above.

6. The first Web pages were
   a. strictly hypertext with no multimedia content.
   b. designed to simulate printed pages using HTML's table tools.

c. the first true multimedia documents to be published on the Internet.

d. viewable only with proprietary Microsoft software.

e. sent via email from Doug Engelbart's office on the Stanford campus.

7. Cookies are commonly used by Web sites
   a. to attract visitors from search engines.
   b. to prevent viruses from spreading.
   c. to personalize visitor experiences.
   d. for animation.
   e. as components in Cascading Style Sheets.

8. An online shopping catalog for a large outdoor outfitter is almost certainly
   a. a data-driven Web site that separates site content from design.
   b. carefully hand-coded in pure HTML to minimize errors.
   c. designed to work without cookies.
   d. limited to work with a single type of Web browser for consistency.
   e. All of the above.

9. The Internet will change drastically in the next decade, but what is the one thing that is likely to remain relatively unchanged?
   a. The dominance of HTML as a Web page creation language
   b. The metaphor of the page as the container of Internet information
   c. The TCP/IP protocol that's used to send and receive Internet messages
   d. The ownership of the Internet by IBM
   e. The percentage of non-U.S. Internet users

10. Which of the following is NOT a form of push technology?
    a. a podcast subscription
    b. instant messaging
    c. a personalized portal that displays the latest weather forecast
    d. email
    e. searching YouTube for a political video

11. Which of these is NOT an example of what many people call Web 2.0?
    a. Craigslist.
    b. YouTube.
    c. Wikipedia.
    d. Facebook.
    e. All of the above could be called Web 2.0 sites.

12. Internet addiction
    a. is fiction.
    b. has been linked to one or more suicides.
    c. is virtually unheard of outside the U.S.
    d. is caused by a rare type of computer virus.
    e. is most often related to compulsive spreadsheet construction.

13. According to U.S. law, information posted on a Web forum or blog by a child
    a. must self-destruct after one week.
    b. cannot be reproduced in any form without permission.
    c. cannot contain cookies.
    d. cannot be viewed outside of the U.S.
    e. None of the above.

14. Which country attempts to limit its residents' access to certain types of Web content?
    a. The U.S.
    b. North Korea
    c. The People's Republic of China
    d. Saudi Arabia
    e. All of the above

Review Questions

1. Define or describe each of the key terms listed in the "Key Terms" section. Check your answers using the glossary.

2. Why is it hard to determine how big the Internet is today? Give several reasons.

3. Why are TCP/IP protocols so important to the functioning of the Internet? What do they do?

4. How does the type of Internet connection influence the things you can do on the Internet?

5. What is the relationship between a Web site's numerical IP address and its URL?

6. Take your email address apart and, as much as possible, explain what each part means.

7. Briefly describe several software tools that can be used to develop Web pages.

8. What is the difference between Internet 2 and Web 2.0?

9. Why is file compression important on the Internet?

10. How does push technology differ from standard Web page delivery techniques? How is it used?

Discussion Questions

1. How did the Internet's Cold War origin influence its basic decentralized, packet-switching design? How does that design affect the way we use the Net today? What are the political implications of that design today?

2. In what ways is the Web different from any publishing medium that's ever existed before?

3. As scientists, engineers, and government officials develop plans for the future of the Internet, they wrestle with questions about who should have access and what kinds of services to plan for. Do you have any ideas about the kinds of things they might want to consider?

4. Some people spend more than half of their waking hours online. Do you see potential hazards in this kind of heavy Internet use? Explain your answer.

5. How do you think online user interfaces will evolve as bandwidth and processing power increase? Describe what cyberspace will feel like in the year 2010, in the year 2050, and beyond.

6. Residents of the People's Republic of China can have their Internet access blocked for a period of time if they attempt to access banned sites. Do you think this is an effective way for the Chinese government to control people's behavior on the Internet?

7. What do you think can be done to minimize the digital divides that exist within countries and between countries?

Projects

1. Search the Web for articles related to the history and evolution of the Internet. Create a summary report on paper or on the Web.

2. Create a Web site on a subject of interest to you and link it to other Web sites. (When you're trying to decide what information to include, remember that it will be accessible to millions of people all over the world.)

3. Research how access to the Internet in general and Web sites in particular is controlled by the governments of these countries: Brazil, Cuba, France, Germany, India, Israel, Japan, the People's Republic of China, Saudi Arabia, and the United States. Create a chart ranking these countries from "most free access" to "least free access." The chart should detail the various restrictions applied by these governments.

4. Research the extent of the digital divide in the United States by collecting information about Internet access by people of different ages and ethnic groups. Which is a better predictor of Internet access: age or ethnic group?

Sources and Resources

Books

There are thousands of books about the Internet. Many of them promise to simplify and demystify the Net, but they don't all deliver. The Internet is complex and ever-changing. The following list contains a few particularly good titles, but you should also look for more current books released since this book went to press.

When Wizards Stay up Late: The Origins of the Internet, by Katie Hafner and Matthew Lyon (New York, NY: Simon and Schuster, 1998). If you want to learn more about the birth of the Internet, this book is a great place to start. The authors describe the people, challenges, and technical issues in clear, entertaining prose.

How the Internet Works, Eighth Edition, by Preston Gralla (Indianapolis, IN: Que, 2006). If you like the style of *How Computers Work,* you'll appreciate *How the Internet Works.* You won't learn much about how to use the Internet, but you'll get a colorful tour of what goes on behind the scenes when you connect. There's a surprising amount of technical information in this graphically rich, approachable book.

Rule the Web: How to Do Anything on the Internet—Better, Faster, Easier, by Mark Frauenfelder (New York, NY: St. Martin's Press, 2007). The title may promise too much, but the book does deliver a surprising number of answers to questions you might have about how to get the most out of the Internet.

HTML, XHTML, and CSS Visual QuickStart Guide, Sixth Edition, by Elizabeth Castro (Berkeley, CA: Peachpit Press, 2006). There are dozens of books on HTML, XHTML, and CSS, but few offer the clear, concise, comprehensive coverage of this best seller. If you want to build your own Web pages from scratch, this is a great place to start. Even if you know the basics of HTML, you'll appreciate the coverage of more advanced topics. After you've read it, you'll almost certainly want to keep it as a reference.

JavaScript for the World Wide Web: Visual QuickStart Guide, Sixth Edition, by Tom Negrino and Dori Smith (Berkeley, CA: Peachpit Press, 2006). JavaScript is the most popular cross-platform scripting language for Web pages. A little bit of JavaScript can turn a static Web page into a dynamic, interactive page. This book provides a quick introduction to the language, including applications involving forms, frames, files, graphics, and cookies. If you're ready to move beyond basic HTML, this book can help.

The Non-Designer's Web Book, Third Edition, by Robin Williams and John Tollett (Berkeley, CA: Peachpit Press, 2006). Web publishing, like desktop publishing, can be hazardous if you don't have a background in design. Robin Williams and John Tollett provide a crash course in design for first-time Web authors. They assume you're using an authoring tool that hides the nuts and bolts of HTML; if you're not, you'll need to learn HTML elsewhere.

The Unusually Useful Web Book, by June Cohen (Berkeley, CA: New Riders, 2003). Some Web books are written for programmers; some are written for designers; some are written for businesspeople. This book, by a former VP of HotWired (the Web site that spun off *Wired* magazine) has something for all three audiences—and more. If you want to build a Web site that people will actually use, this book is a good investment.

Return on Design: Smarter Web Design That Works, by Ani Phyo (Indianapolis, IN: New Riders, 2003). Web pro Ani Phyo clearly outlines seven necessary steps for creating usable Web sites. Her user-centered methodology satisfies a wide variety of clients, and this book explains how.

Letting Go of the Words: Writing Web Content that Works, by Janice (Ginny) Redish (San Francisco, CA: Morgan Kaufmann, 2007). Writing is a critical skill for success in the Internet age. But writing for the Web isn't the same as writing a novel or a term paper. This book focuses on the specifics of writing Web text that communicates clearly.

The Future of the Internet and How to Stop It, by Jonathan Zittrain (New Haven, CT: Yale University Press, 2008). According to Jonathan Zittrain, the future of the Internet is not pretty unless we all take steps to prevent it from being locked down by powerful interests. This important book is sparking much-needed dialog about how to preserve the innovative spirit of the Net.

Code Version 2.0, by Lawrence Lessig (New York, NY: Basic Books, 2006). In 2000, Lessig's *The Code and Other Laws of Cyberspace* argued that we might lose our liberty on the Internet unless we consciously work to preserve it—an argument that's even more relevant today. The way we build the Net today will determine what's possible in cyberspace tomorrow. Lessig, a lawyer, is an excellent writer with something important to say. Version 2.0 was updated through Lessig's wiki; it is the first reader-edited revision of a popular book.

The Future of Ideas: The Fate of the Commons in a Connected World, by Lawrence Lessig (New York, NY: Vintage, 2002). In this follow-up to *The Code and Other Laws of Cyberspace,* Lessig puts forward his plan for using the Internet to stimulate an unprecedented era of innovation. He suggests radical changes to intellectual property laws that would accelerate the movement of creative works into the public domain.

Access Denied: The Practice and Policy of Global Internet Filtering, edited by Ronald J. Deibert, John G. Palfrey, Rafal Rohozinski, and Jonathan Zittrain (Cambridge, MA: MIT Press, 2008). This book from the Open Network Initiative is the first global survey of Internet filtering.

The Future of Reputation: Gossip, Rumor, and Privacy on the Internet, by Daniel J. Solove (New Haven, CT: Yale University Press, 2008). The Internet provides us with an unprecedented ability to communicate with each other. But forums, blogs, wikis, video sharing, and the rest make it all too easy to ruin personal reputations. This book deals with the legal and ethical issues related to Internet communication.

True Names: And the Opening of the Cyberspace Frontier, by Vernor Vinge and James Frenkel (New York, NY: Tor Books, 2001). In 1981 (three years before the original publication of *Neuromancer*) Vernor Vinge's critically acclaimed novella *True Names* described a virtual world inside a computer network. Vinge didn't use the term *cyberspace,* but his visionary story effectively invented the concept. This book includes the wonderful original *True Names* novella and a collection of articles by cyberspace pioneers about the past, present, and future of cyberspace.

Neuromancer, Twentieth Anniversary Edition, by William Gibson (New York, NY: Ace Books, 2005). Gibson's 1984 cyberpunk classic spawned several sequels, dozens of imitations, and a new vocabulary for describing a high-tech future. Gibson's future is gloomy and foreboding, and his futuristic slang isn't always easy to follow. Still, there's plenty to think about here.

Snow Crash, by Neal Stephenson (New York, NY: Spectra, 2000). This early-1990s science fiction novel lightens the dark, violent cyberpunk future vision a little with Douglas Adams–style humor. Characters regularly jack into the Metaverse, a shared virtual reality network that is in many ways more real than the physical world in which they live. The descriptions of this alternate reality heavily influenced the design of many VR-like Web sites today.

10

Computer Security and Risks

After you read this chapter you should be able to:

▌ Describe several types of computer crime and discuss possible crime-prevention techniques

▌ Describe the major security issues facing computer users, computer system administrators, and law enforcement officials

▌ Describe how computer security relates to personal privacy issues

▌ Explain how security and computer reliability are related

> "A world opened up by communications **cannot remain closed up** in a feudal vision of property. **No country**, not the U.S., not Europe, **can stand in the way** of it. It's a **global trend**. It's part of the very **process of civilization ...** and there's no use resisting it."
>
> —*Gilberto Gil*

Gilberto Gil and the Open Source Society

In the 1960s, when the Beatles were remaking American and European pop music and culture, Brazilians Gilberto Gil and Caetano Veloso were creating a revolutionary musical style of their own. Tropicalismo combined elements of rock, samba, bossa nova, traditional music, avant garde poetry, and just about anything else that was in the wind. Brazilian culture was a simmering stew of poverty and wealth, of tradition and modernity, and the mash-up style of Tropicalismo captured the chaos and spawned a movement. According to Gil, Tropicalismo refused to submit to the forces of economic imperialism. It was "a cannibalistic response of swallowing what they gave us, processing it, and making it something new and different."

Gil and Veloso were widely regarded as a Latin Lennon and McCartney. But the military dictatorship, threatened by their impact on young Brazilians, jailed Gil and Veloso without charges before banishing them to London, where they stayed for several years.

Today Gil remains popular as a musician, but his other job also puts him in the world spotlight. In 2002 he was appointed the minister of culture in Brazil's now democratic government.

The philosophy of Tropicalismo is woven into the fabric of modern Brazilian society. Brazil is at the forefront of a global movement to "tropicalize" intellectual property—to encourage creative sharing of music, words, software, and ideas by loosening legally sanctioned corporate controls. Gilberto Gil has become a symbol for this emerging "open source" society.

The world's sixth-largest nation has reason to seek alternatives to the restrictive intellectual property laws of the United States and Europe. Drug patents put AIDS medication out of the reach of Brazil's infected poor until the Brazilian government threatened to ignore those patents, forcing manufacturers to offer discounts. And a typical Brazilian might have to work for weeks in order to afford a copy of a commercial software program such as Microsoft Office. It's no wonder that Linux and other open source programs have been embraced by the Brazilian government.

Brazil's approach to intellectual property issues is similar to the philosophy that drove American cyber-lawyer

FIGURE 10.1 Gilberto Gil

Lawrence Lessig to devise the Creative Commons, a way for artists to reserve some of the rights given them by copyright law but give up the rest. For example, an artist may use a Creative Commons license to indicate that a photograph or song may be freely copied or sampled for noncommercial purposes, as long as attribution is given.

After Lessig described the system to him, Gil decided to release several of his most popular songs into the Creative Commons. His American record company quickly vetoed his act of musical generosity.

The copyright system represents a balance between the desire of artists to be rewarded for their creativity and the desire of the public to have access to artistic works. Creative Commons licenses and the Open Software movement are a reaction to a copyright system that has gradually tilted the balance in favor of those who own intellectual property rights. In Gil's words, "The Brazilian government is definitely pro-law. But if law doesn't fit reality anymore, law has to be changed. That's not a new thing. That's civilization as usual." ∼

Copyright and patent laws were originally designed to encourage creativity. But as the laws become broader and more rigid, they may be having just the opposite effect. Intellectual property issues are challenging because computers and the Internet have opened up fast, reliable, and extremely inexpensive ways of exchanging songs, movies, photographs, and other creative works. But intellectual property is just the tip of the iceberg.

Computers and networks manage our money, our medicine, and our missiles. We're expected to trust information technology with our wealth, our health, and even our lives. The many benefits of our partnership with machines are clear. But blind faith in modern technology can be foolish and, in many cases, dangerous. In this chapter we examine some of the dark corners of our computerized society: legal dilemmas, ethical issues, and reliability risks. These issues are tied to a larger question: How can we make computers more secure so we can feel more secure in our daily dealings with them? We'll look for answers to this question then ask several more difficult questions about our relationship to computer technology and our future.

Online Outlaws: Computer Crime

Computers are **power**, and **direct contact** with power can bring out the **best** or **worst** in a person.

—*Former computer criminal turned corporate computer programmer*

Like other professions, law enforcement is being transformed by information technology. The FBI's National Crime Information Center provides police with almost instant information on crimes and criminals nationwide. Investigators use PC databases to store and cross-reference clues in complex cases. Using pattern recognition technology, automated fingerprint identification systems locate matches in minutes rather than months. Computers routinely scan the New York and London stock exchanges for connections that might indicate insider trading or fraud. Texas police use an intranet to cross-reference databases of photographs, fingerprints, and other crime-fighting information. *Computer forensics* experts use special software to scan criminal suspects' hard disks for digital "fingerprints"—traces of deleted files containing evidence of illegal activities. All of these tools help law enforcement officials ferret out criminals and stop criminal activities.

As with guns, people use computers to break laws as well as uphold them. Computers are powerful tools in the hands of criminals, and computer crime is a rapidly growing problem.

The Digital Dossier

Some will rob you with a **six gun**, and some with a **fountain pen**.

—Woody Guthrie, in "Pretty Boy Floyd"

Today the computer has replaced both the gun and the pen as the weapon of choice for many criminals. **Computer crime**, or **cybercrime**, is often defined as any crime accomplished through knowledge or use of computer technology. Cybercrime usually refers to criminal activity in which computer or network technology is an essential part of the crime. Examples include spamming, peer-to-peer file sharing of copyrighted music, creating and releasing malicious computer viruses, and theft of computer services. It might also refer to a traditional crime in which computers or networks are used as criminal tools. For example, *cyberstalking* is a form of harassment that takes place on the Internet. The crime is similar to old-fashioned stalking, but the domain is the digital realm. Other examples of traditional crimes that can easily become cybercrimes include financial fraud, child pornography trafficking, and even international espionage.

Nobody knows the true extent of computer crime. Many computer crimes go undetected. Those that are detected often go unreported because businesses fear that they can lose more from negative publicity than from the actual crimes.

Companies that *do* report cybercrimes report system penetration by outsiders, theft of information, the changing of data, financial fraud, vandalism, theft of passwords, and the prevention of legitimate users from gaining access to systems. By conservative estimates, businesses and government institutions lose billions of dollars every year to computer criminals.

The majority of corporate computer crimes are probably committed by company insiders who aren't reported to authorities even when they are caught in the act. To avoid embarrassment, many companies cover up computer crimes committed by

FIGURE 10.2 A police officer uses his mobile computer to check records in a central law enforcement database.

their own employees. These crimes are typically committed by clerks, cashiers, programmers, computer operators, and managers who have no extraordinary technical ingenuity. The typical computer criminal is a trusted employee with no criminal record who is tempted by an opportunity, such as the discovery of a loophole in system security. Greed, financial worries, and personal problems motivate this person to give in to temptation.

Of course, not all computer criminals fit this profile. Some are former employees seeking revenge on their former bosses. Some are high-tech pranksters looking for a challenge or a thrill. A few are corporate or international spies seeking classified information. Organized crime syndicates use computer technology to practice their trades. Sometimes entire companies are found guilty of computer fraud. And some types of computer crime—most notably software and music piracy—are committed by legions of young people who may not even know that they're committing crimes.

Theft by Computer: From Property Theft to Identity Theft

Every system has **vulnerabilities**. Every system **can be compromised**.

—*Peter G. Neumann, in* Computer-Related Risks

Theft is the most common form of computer crime. Computers are used to steal money, goods, information, and computer resources.

FIGURE 10.3 A portable computer is easy prey for thieves unless it is locked to something stationary and solid.

One common type of computer theft today is the actual theft of computers. Notebook and handheld computers make particularly easy prey for crooks—especially in airports and other high-traffic, high-stress locations. Notebooks, PDAs, and smart phones are expensive items, but the information stored on a computer can be far more valuable than the computer itself.

The most common type of theft-by-computer, intellectual property theft, was discussed in Chapter 4 and Chapter 9. Examples of intellectual property theft include software piracy, peer-to-peer file sharing of copyrighted songs, unauthorized duplication and distribution of movies, and plagiarism of copyrighted text. Intellectual property theft has skyrocketed with the growth of the Internet.

Other types of property aren't as easy to steal through an Internet connection, but thieves can—and do—steal credit card numbers and bank account numbers, which can be used to buy just about anything. In the past decade dozens of crimes have been reported in which large files of credit card numbers have been stolen from businesses via the Internet. No doubt many similar crimes have gone unreported.

Still another type of theft involves stealing *access* to a computer or a Web site by stealing passwords and login codes. Sometimes thieves swipe passwords to avoid paying access charges; other times they steal passwords as part of a bigger plan.

Sometimes thieves use computers and other tools to steal whole *identities*. By collecting personal information—credit card numbers, driver's license numbers, Social Security numbers, passwords, and a few other tidbits of data—a thief can effectively pose as someone else, even committing crimes in that person's name. Identity theft doesn't require a computer; many identity thieves get sensitive information by dumpster diving—rummaging through company and personal trash. But computers generally play a role in the process. (Identity theft was also discussed in the privacy section of Chapter 7.)

Credit card theft, password theft, and identity theft often involves social engineering—slang for the use of deception to get individuals to reveal sensitive information. Many types of social engineering involve spoofing—masquerading as somebody else in order to trick the target into doing something they might not otherwise do. Spoofing might be a simple phone call (For example, "Hi. I'm a technician from your Internet service provider and I'm trying to locate a problem in your network connection. Can you give me your password so I can test it?"). Or it might involve an Internet fraud technique commonly called phishing (because the perpetrator is "fishing" for sensitive information under false pretenses).

According to the FBI, two-thirds of identity thefts begin with an email solicitation—a phishing expedition. A spammer sends out an email that appears to be from PayPal,

Protecting Yourself from Identity Theft

The number of cases of identity theft is on the rise. Millions of people in the United States have their identities stolen each year. With a few simple precautions, you can reduce your chances of falling victim to this crime.

➡ **Make all your online purchases using a credit card.** Visa USA, MasterCard International, and American Express all have zero-liability programs that waive your liability in case someone uses your credit card number for online fraud. Most debit cards, checking accounts, and money orders don't offer this kind of protection.

➡ **Get a separate credit card with a low credit limit for your online transactions.** If the card number is stolen, the thieves will not be able to run up as large a balance.

➡ **Make sure a secure Web site is managing your online transaction.** Look at the address of the Web site you are visiting. The URL should begin with https, not http. The https designator means the site is using encryption to improve the security of the transaction.

➡ **Don't disclose personal information over the phone.** Remember that a credit card company would never call you and ask you for your credit card number, expiration date, or other personal information; they already know it.

➡ **Handle email with care.** Cunning thieves send email that looks like it comes from a legitimate company such as PayPal or Amazon.com, asking you to update your personal information, including your credit card number and expiration date. But when you click the link in the email, the Web site that loads isn't really from the legitimate company, opening up unsuspecting users to credit card theft. Regard all such emails with suspicion, and be careful any time you enter a credit card number or other personal information online. If you're suspicious, check the URL displayed at the top of your browser window; if it isn't the company's standard URL, you may be at a spoof site. If your Web browser doesn't offer phishing protection, consider switching to one that does.

➡ **Don't put your Social Security number or your driver's license number on your checks.** These are key pieces of information sought by identity thieves.

➡ **Shred or burn sensitive mail before you recycle it.** Bills, junk mail credit card offers, and other mail can contain personal infor-

mation. Looking through people's garbage is a tried-and-true tactic of identity thieves.

➡ **Keep your wallet thin.** Don't carry your Social Security card or extra ID around with you. Cut and toss unused credit cards.

➡ **Copy your cards.** Make photocopies of both sides of your driver's license and credit cards and keep the copies in a safe place. If your wallet or purse is stolen, you'll have the information you need to get replacement cards and cancel the stolen ones.

➡ **Scan your bills and statements promptly.** For companies that allow online access to accounts, you may not even need to wait for paper statements to arrive. If you find any unexpected transaction or other unpleasant surprises, report them right away. If you don't receive a bill that you expected, or if you *do* receive a bill that you didn't expect, contact the company right away to see if there's a problem.

➡ **Report identity theft promptly.** Call your credit card companies, the local police, and the Federal Trade Commission (877-438-4338) right away. Contact one of the three consumer credit reporting companies (see Your Privacy Rights in Chapter 7) and place a fraud alert on your credit reports; the company you contact will notify the other two. Close any accounts that you believe have been compromised.

FIGURE 10.4 An email request to "update your account by clicking on this link" might take you to this Web page, which looks like the real PayPal home page except for a tiny discrepancy in the URL. Logging in to this screen could give your password, and therefore all of your PayPal financial information, to an identity thief.

Citibank, AOL, or another company with which the recipient may have an account. One such message from PayPal reads, "Your credit card will expire soon. To avoid any interruption to your service, please update your credit card expiration date by following the steps below." The steps usually involve linking to a Web site that looks legitimate, but is in fact a spoof. By filling out the Web site's form, unsuspecting consumers give thieves the information they need to steal an identity. Other identity thieves trick people into revealing their credit card numbers using pornographic Web sites. These sites ask viewers to prove they are adults by providing credit card information.

Financial matters aside, thieves may soon routinely steal votes, putting our democracy at risk. Many of today's electronic voting machines are less secure than casino slot machines and vulnerable to a wide variety of attacks, including the kinds described in the following pages.

Software Sabotage: Viruses and Other Malware

The American government can stop me from going to the U.S., **but they can't stop my virus**.

—Virus creator

Another type of computer crime is sabotage of hardware or software. The word sabotage comes from the early days of the Industrial Revolution, when rebellious workers shut down new machines by placing wooden shoes, called sabots, into the gears. Modern computer saboteurs commonly use malware—malicious software—rather than footwear to do destructive deeds. The names given to the saboteurs' destructive programs—viruses, worms, and Trojan horses—sound more like biology than technology, and many of the programs even mimic the behavior of living organisms.

Viruses

A biological virus is unable to reproduce by itself, but it can invade the cells of another organism and use the reproductive machinery of each host cell to make copies of itself; the new copies leave the host and seek new hosts to repeat the process. A software virus works in the same way. Virus software is a piece of code usually hidden in the operating system of a computer or in an application program. When a user executes a program containing a virus, the virus quickly copies itself to an uninfected program; it then allows the user's application to execute. Usually this happens so quickly that the user is unaware the application program contains a virus. A virus can jump from one computer to another when someone uses a disc, flash drive, or a computer network with an infected machine to copy an infected program. Some viruses do nothing but reproduce; others display messages; still others destroy data or erase disks.

Like most software code, a virus is usually operating-system specific. For example, Windows viruses invade only Windows. There are exceptions: *Macro viruses* attach themselves to documents that contain *macros*—embedded programs to automate tasks. Macro viruses can be spread across computer platforms if the documents are created using cross-platform applications—most commonly the applications in Microsoft Office. Macro viruses can be spread through innocent-looking email or instant message attachments.

FIGURE 10.5 How a virus spreads via email.

One of the most widely publicized macro viruses was the 1999 Melissa virus. Melissa's method of operation is typical of email viruses: An unsuspecting computer user received an "Important message" from a friend: "Here is that document you asked for ... don't show it to anyone else ;-)." The attached Microsoft Word document contained a list of passwords for pornography sites. It contained something else: a macro virus written in Microsoft Office's built-in Visual Basic scripting language. When the user opened the document, the virus went to work, sending a copy of the email message and infected document to the first 50 names on the user's Outlook address book. Within minutes, 50 more potential Melissa victims received messages apparently from someone they knew—the user of the newly infected computer. Melissa spread like wildfire, infecting 100,000 Windows systems in just a few days. Melissa wasn't designed to damage systems, but the flurry of messages brought down some email servers. A nationwide search located the probable author, a 30-year-old New Jersey resident with a fondness for a topless dancer named Melissa. A federal judge fined him $5,000 and sentenced him to 20 months in federal prison plus 100 hours of community service.

A newer type of cross-platform virus, the cross-site scripting (XSS) virus, attaches itself to Web applications and spreads via client Web browsers. There have been many documented exploitations of XSS. In 2005 a MySpace user named Samy amassed over 1 million friends by infecting his user profile with an XSS virus. Visitors to his page—and visitors to the pages of those visitors, and so on—were automatically added to his friends list, until MySpace was taken offline to remove the virus—and Samy— from the system. "My primary motivation was to make people laugh," Samy said. Another example: On the eve of the 2008 Pennsylvania Democratic presidential primary a political prankster used XSS to redirect Barack Obama's community forum visitors to Hillary Clinton's Web site.

Worms

Like viruses, worms (named for tapeworms) use computer hosts to reproduce themselves. But unlike viruses, worms are complete programs capable of traveling independently over computer networks, seeking out uninfected workstations in which to reproduce. A worm can reproduce until the computer freezes from lack of free memory or disk space. A typical worm segment resides in memory rather than on disk, so the worm can be eliminated by shutting down all of the workstations on the network.

The first headline-making worm was created as an experiment by a Cornell graduate student in 1988. The worm was accidentally released onto the Internet, clogging 6,000 computers all over the United States, bringing them almost to a standstill and forcing operators to shut them all down so every worm segment could be purged from memory. The total cost, in terms of work time lost at research institutions, was staggering. The student was suspended from school and was the first person convicted of violating the Computer Fraud and Abuse Act.

In the summer of 2001, a worm called Code Red made worldwide headlines. Code Red didn't attack PCs; its target was Internet servers running Microsoft server software. The U.S. government and Microsoft issued warnings about the worm and made free software patches available to protect servers. Even so, many servers were crippled by the repeated attacks from the worm, including servers owned and operated by Microsoft. Samy's MySpace virus, mentioned above, was spread using a worm.

Trojan Horses

A Trojan horse is a program that performs a useful task while at the same time carrying out some secret destructive act. As in the ancient story of the wooden horse that carried Greek soldiers through the gates of Troy, Trojan horse software hides an enemy in an attractive package. Trojan horse programs are often posted on shareware Web sites with names that make them sound like games, utilities, or even pictures. When an unsuspecting bargain hunter downloads and runs such a program, it might erase files, change data, or cause some other kind of damage. Some network saboteurs use Trojan horses to pass secret data to other unauthorized users.

One type of Trojan horse, a **logic bomb**, is programmed to attack in response to a particular event or sequence of events. For example, a programmer might plant a logic bomb that is designed to destroy data files if the programmer is ever listed as terminated in the company's personnel file. A logic bomb might be triggered when a certain user logs in, enters a special code in a database field, or performs a particular sequence of actions. If the logic bomb is triggered by a time-related event, it is called a *time bomb*. A widely publicized virus included a logic bomb that was programmed to destroy PC data files on Michelangelo's birthday.

Trojan horses can cause serious problems in computer systems of all sizes. To make matters worse, many Trojan horses carry software viruses.

Spyware

Spyware refers to a technology that collects information from computer users without their knowledge or consent. A spyware program, sometimes called *tracking software* or a *spybot*, gathers user information and communicates it to an outsider via the Internet. Spybots can monitor your keystrokes, record which Web sites you visit, and even take snapshots of what's displayed on your monitor. Other spybots cause pop-up ads to appear on your screen.

Surveys suggest that most home computers are infected with some kind of spyware. That's not surprising, considering the number of ways spyware can get into a PC. Some computer viruses spread spyware. Some freeware or shareware programs include hidden spyware. In *drive-by downloads*, simply visiting certain Web sites causes spyware or other malware to be downloaded to your computer. Spyware is not generally self-propagating like viruses and worms. But spyware can—and generally does—exploit infected computers for commercial gain without the knowledge of the owners of those computers. Sometimes spyware comes from corporate sources. Shoppers who joined the Sears and Kmart online communities discovered in 2008 that spyware was reporting data on Web site visits, purchases, and other Internet usage records. The companies responded to criticisms by changing their software and privacy policies. Spyware can represent a serious privacy threat to unsuspecting users, but it can also slow PC performance to a crawl if it goes unchecked.

Malware Wars

The popular press usually doesn't distinguish among Trojan horses, viruses, and worms; they're all called computer viruses. Whatever they're called, these rogue programs make life more complicated and expensive for people who depend on computers. Researchers have identified tens of thousands of virus strains, with 200 new ones appearing each month. At any given time, hundreds of virus strains may exist in the wild—in circulation.

Modern viruses can spread faster and do more damage than viruses of a few years ago for several reasons. The Internet, which speeds communication all over the planet, also speeds virus transmission. Web pages, macros, and other technologies give virus writers new places to hide their creations. And increased standardization on Microsoft applications and operating systems has made it easier for viruses to spread. Just as natural mixed forests are more resistant to disease than are single-species tree farms, mixed computing environments are less susceptible to crippling attacks than is an organization in which everyone uses the same hardware and software.

When computers are used in life-or-death situations, as they are in many medical and military applications, invading programs can even threaten human lives. The U.S. government and several states now have laws against introducing these programs into computer systems.

Antivirus programs are designed to search for viruses, notify users when they're found, and remove them from infected disks or files. Most antivirus programs continually monitor system activity, watching for and reporting suspicious viruslike actions. But no antivirus program can detect every virus, and these programs need to be frequently revised to combat new viruses as they appear. Most antivirus programs can automatically download new virus-fighting code from the Web as new virus strains appear. But it can take several days for companies to develop and distribute patches for new viruses, and destructive viruses can do a lot of damage in that time.

The malware wars continue to escalate as malware writers develop new ways to spread their works. After a rash of 1999 email viruses, most users learned not to open unidentified email attachments, and software vendors started modifying their email applications to prevent this sort of attack. But before the year was over, a worm called BubbleBoy (named for an episode of TV's *Seinfeld*) demonstrated that a system could be infected by email even if the mail wasn't opened. Some viruses have even been developed to infect HTML code in Web pages or HTML email messages.

Software companies continually test their products for security holes and try to make them more resistant to viruses, worms, and other security breaches. Many software companies, including Microsoft, Apple, and several browser manufacturers, periodically release security patches—software programs that plug potential security breaches in the operating system or application. These patches are provided as free downloads or automatic updates to all owners of the software. Because Microsoft Windows is the target of the great majority of malware, Windows security updates are particularly important in preventing the spread of malware. But preventive security measures such as these can sometimes backfire. In the summer of 2003, a worm called MS Slammer made worldwide headlines, shutting down hundreds of thousands of PCs as it moved from computer to computer looking for vulnerable targets. The worm was deployed more than a month after Microsoft had issued a security patch to fix the very problem that MS Slammer exploited. By publicizing the vulnerability, Microsoft inadvertently inspired malicious programmers to create the worm. These system saboteurs took advantage of the fact that many computer users fail to install security patches, leaving their systems ripe for attack. In response to MS Slammer, a well-intentioned programmer released a helper worm designed to search the Internet for machines that had been infected by MS Slammer and apply the Microsoft security patch to those machines. But this worm caused its own problems, slowing many systems to a crawl by repeatedly checking them for security problems.

FIGURE 10.6 Antivirus software scans files for viruses, worms, and other software invaders. New versions of the software definition files should be downloaded regularly to ensure the software is up to date.

Stories such as this one happen more often than the information technology industry would like to admit. These stories serve as reminders that the malware wars are far from over. There will always be new ways to compromise connected systems.

Hacking and Electronic Trespassing

The Hacker Ethic: Access to computers—and anything which might teach you something about the way the world works—should be **unlimited** and **total**. Always yield to the **Hands-on Imperative**.
All information should be **free**.
Mistrust Authority—Promote Decentralization.
Hackers should be judged by their **hacking**, not bogus criteria such as degrees, age, race, or position.
You can create **art and beauty** on a computer.
Computers can **change your life** for the better.

—*Steven Levy, in* Hackers: Heroes of the Computer Revolution

I don't drink, smoke, or take drugs. I don't steal, assault people, or vandalize property. The **only way** in which I am **really different** from most people is in **my fascination** with the ways and means of learning about **computers that don't belong to me**.

—*Bill "The Cracker" Landreth, in* Out of the Inner Circle

In the late 1970s, timesharing computers at Stanford and MIT attracted informal communities of computer fanatics who called themselves *hackers*. In those days, a hacker was a person who enjoyed learning the details of computer systems and writing clever programs, referred to as *hacks*. Hackers were, for the most part, curious, enthusiastic, intelligent, idealistic, eccentric, and harmless. Many of those early hackers were, in fact, architects of the microcomputer revolution.

Over the years, the idealism of the early hacker communities was at least partly overshadowed by cynicism, as big-money interests took over the young personal computer industry. At the same time, the term hacking took on a new, more ominous connotation in the media. Although many people still use the term to describe software wizardry, it more commonly refers to unauthorized access to computer systems. Old-time hackers insist that this electronic trespassing is really *cracking*, or criminal hacking, but the general public and popular media don't recognize the distinction between hackers and crackers. Today's stereotypical hacker, like his early counterparts, is a young, bright, technically savvy, white, middle-class male who, in addition to programming his own computer, may break into others.

Of course, not all young computer wizards break into systems, and not all electronic trespassers fit the media stereotype. Still, hackers aren't just a media myth; they're real, and there are lots of them. Electronic trespassers enter corporate and government computers using stolen passwords and software security holes. Sometimes they use modems to dial up the target computers directly; in other cases they "travel" to their destinations through the Internet and other networks.

Many hackers are merely motivated by curiosity and intellectual challenge; once they've cracked a system, they look around and move on without leaving any electronic footprints. Some hackers claim to be acting in the public good by pointing out security problems in commercial software products. Some malicious hackers use Trojan horses, logic bombs, and other tricks of the trade to wreak havoc on corporate and government systems. A growing number of computer trespassers are part of electronic crime rings intent on stealing credit card numbers and other sensitive, valuable information. This kind of theft is difficult to detect and track because the original information is left unchanged when the copy is stolen.

According to the FBI, an Internet hack happens every 30 seconds. Hackers have defaced the Web sites of the White House, the U.S. Senate, the Department of the Interior, presidential candidates, countless online businesses, and even a hacker's conference. Sometimes Web sites are simply defaced with obscene or threatening messages; sometimes they're replaced with satirical substitutes; sometimes they're vandalized so they don't work properly. *Webjackers* hijack legitimate Web pages and redirect users to other sites—for example, pornographic sites or fraudulent businesses. Many hackers use networks of *zombie computers*, or *bots*—Internet-connected computers that have been hijacked using viruses or other tools to perform malicious acts without the knowledge of their owners and users. These malicious networks are often called botnets, and they're a favorite tool of spammers, phishers, and other Internet criminals. Experts believe that more than one hundred million computers are under the control of malicious hackers.

Denial-of-service (DoS) attacks bombard servers and Web sites with so much bogus traffic that they're effectively shut down, denying service to legitimate customers and clients. In a *distributed denial-of-service (DDoS)* attack, the flood of messages comes from botnets. In a single week in February 2000, the Yahoo!, E*TRADE, eBay, and Amazon Web sites were crippled by denial-of-service attacks, costing their owners millions of dollars in business. Two months later a 15-year-old Canadian youth, nicknamed "Mafia Boy," was arrested after he bragged online about causing the breakdowns. His pranks didn't require expertise; he reportedly downloaded all of the software he used from the Internet. In August 2003 computers affected by the Blaster worm launched a DDoS attack on Microsoft's Windows Update Web site; this time bomb attack ironically prevented users from downloading the software patch that would have rendered Blaster impotent. More recently, a 2007 DDoS attack crippled the electronic infrastructure of the Republic of Estonia, one of the most wired countries in the world.

One famous case of electronic trespassing was documented in Cliff Stoll's best-selling book, *The Cuckoo's Egg*. While working as a system administrator for a university computer lab in 1986, Stoll noticed a 75-cent accounting error. Rather than letting it go, Stoll investigated the error. It took a year and some help from the FBI, but Stoll eventually located the hacker—a German student working for the KGB to uncover military secrets. Ironically, Stoll captured the thief by using standard hacker tricks, including a Trojan horse program.

Another headline-turned-book involved the 1995 capture of Kevin Mitnick, the hacker who stole millions of dollars worth of software and credit card information. By repeatedly manufacturing new identities and cleverly concealing his location, Mitnick successfully evaded the FBI for years. But when he broke into the computer of computational physicist Tsutomu Shimomura, he inadvertently started an electronic cat-and-mouse game that ended with his capture and conviction. Shimomura was able to defeat Mitnick because of his expertise in computer security—the protection of computer systems and, indirectly, the people who depend on them.

FIGURE 10.7 Kevin Mitnick was the most notorious hacker ever caught, according to federal authorities. Mitnick was a "pure" hacker who illegally accessed remote computers out of curiosity. He spent five years in jail for his hacking activities. Today Mitnick runs a computer security company whose Web site, ironically, was hacked in early 2003.

Computer Security: Reducing Risks

With computer crime on the rise, computer security has become an important concern for system administrators and computer users alike. Computer security refers to protecting computer systems and the information they contain against unwanted access, damage, modification, or destruction. According to a Congressional Research Service report, computers have two inherent characteristics that leave them open to attack or operating error:

In the **old world**, if I wanted to attack something physical, there was **one way to get there**. You could put guards and guns around it, **you could protect it**. But a database—or a control system—usually has multiple pathways, **unpredictable routes to it**, and seems intrinsically **impossible to protect**. That's why most efforts at computer security **have been defeated**.

—*Andrew Marshall, military analyst*

1. A computer does exactly what it is programmed to do, including reveal sensitive information. Any system that can be programmed can be reprogrammed by anyone with sufficient knowledge.

FIGURE 10.8 Biometric devices provide high levels of computer and network security because they monitor human body characteristics that can't be stolen. IriScan's PC Iris (above) can compare the patterns in the iris of the user against a database of employees and other legitimate users. The U-Match Bio-Link Mouse (right) checks the thumbprint of the user against a database of prints approved for access.

2. Any computer can do only what it is programmed to do. "[I]t cannot protect itself from either malfunctions or deliberate attacks unless such events have been specifically anticipated, thought through, and countered with appropriate programming."

Computer owners and administrators use a variety of security techniques to protect their systems, ranging from everyday low-tech locks to high-tech software scrambling.

Physical Access Restrictions

One way to reduce the risk of security breaches is to identify people attempting to access computer equipment. Organizations use a number of tools and techniques to identify personnel. Computers can perform some security checks; human security guards perform others. Depending on the security system, you might be granted access to a computer based on the following criteria:

■ *Something you have*, such as a key, an ID card with a photo, or a *smart card* containing digitally encoded identification in a built-in memory chip
■ *Something you know*, such as a password, an ID number, a lock combination, or a piece of personal history, such as your mother's maiden name
■ *Something you do*, such as your signature or your typing speed and error patterns
■ *Something about you*, such as a voice print, fingerprint, retinal scan, facial feature scan, or other measurement of individual body characteristics; these measurements are collectively called biometrics.

Because most of these security controls can be compromised—keys can be stolen, signatures can be forged, and so on—many systems use a combination of controls. For example, an employee might be required to show a badge, unlock a door with a key, and type a password to use a secured computer.

In the days when corporate computers were isolated in basements, physical restrictions were sufficient for keeping out intruders. But in the modern office, computers and data are everywhere, and networks connect computers to the outside world. In a distributed, networked environment, security is much more problematic. It's not enough to restrict physical access to mainframes when personal computers and network connections aren't restricted.

Passwords and Access Privileges

Passwords are the most common tools used to restrict access to PCs, mainframe computers, and Web sites. Passwords are effective, however, only if they're chosen carefully. Most computer users choose passwords that are easy to guess: names of partners, or pets; words related to jobs or hobbies; and consecutive characters on keyboards. The most popular passwords include 123456, qwerty, abc123, letmein, monkey, myspace1, god, sex, money, love, and, of course, password. Hackers know and exploit these clichés; cautious users avoid them. They also use dictionary programs to guess passwords systematically by, in effect, trying every word in the dictionary. That's why many security systems refuse to let you choose a real word or name as a password. The best passwords mix letters and numbers into strings that make no sense to anyone except the people who use them. Even the best passwords should be changed frequently.

Access-control software doesn't need to treat all users identically. Many systems use passwords to restrict users so they can open only files related to their work. In many cases, users are given read-only access to files that they can see but not change.

Even a PC can have different levels of access, because Windows, Mac OS X, and Linux all support multiple users. When a PC is set up with multiple user accounts, each user has a unique user ID and password. When one of those users logs into the PC with his user ID and password, he has access only to his own personal files plus any shared files that are accessible to multiple users. When he logs out, another user can log in to the same PC and use a completely different set of files. (A PC or Mac can easily be set up to bypass the login screen and automatically open a single user's account without a password.)

At least one of the accounts on a PC or Mac must be a **system administrator** account. The administrator has additional access privileges—permission to install software applications, change system settings, and more. Users who don't have administrator-level access are denied access to many of the "under the hood" components of the system.

Web sites frequently use passwords as access keys. Enterprising criminals often use software bots to sign up automatically for accounts and passwords. To foil the bots, many sites use answer-back security systems. When you apply for membership in such a system, you might be required to give your email address. The system sends an email to you and you reply, ensuring that you're a real person with a real email address.

Bots are also used to log into sites with stolen or guessed passwords. Many sites require passwords and visual identification of a string of abstract characters—something that's easy for a person to identify, but not easy for a machine to read.

Firewalls, Encryption, and Audits

Many data thieves do their work without breaking into computer systems; instead, they intercept messages as they travel between computers on networks. Passwords are of little use for hiding email messages when they're traveling through Internet cables or wireless connections. Many organizations use **firewalls** to keep their internal networks secure while enabling communication with the rest of the Internet. The technical details of firewalls vary considerably, but they're all designed to serve the same function: to guard against unauthorized access to an internal network. In effect, a firewall is a gate with a lock; the locked gate opens only for information packets that pass one or more security inspections. Firewalls aren't just for large corporations. Without firewall hardware or software installed, a home computer with an always-on DSL or cable modem connection can be easy prey for Internet snoopers. Windows Vista and Mac

FIGURE 10.9 Hardware firewall products come in all shapes and sizes.

How It Works

10.1 Firewalls

A firewall is a program, often run on a dedicated computer, that filters information between a private network and the rest of the Internet. A set of security rules, created by a network administrator, determines which packets can enter and leave the local network.

ftp request to ftp.bizness.com

ftp request to mail.bizness.com

rlogin request to userA.bizness.com

Web page from www.abcd.com

Internet

The firewall allows the file transfer request to reach the ftp server.

ftp.bizness.com

The firewall blocks a file transfer request directed to another server.

Firewall

The firewall blocks all remote login requests.

mail.bizness.com

The firewall allows packets from most Web sites.

userA.bizness.com

The firewall blocks accss to certain Web sites.

Request page from www.blocked.com

userB.bizness.com

FIGURE 10.10

FIGURE 10.11 Software firewalls, such as the one included with Norton 360, help protect home networks from hackers.

OS X include basic software firewalls, but these firewalls must be activated before they can provide protection.

Of course, the firewall's digital drawbridge has to let some messages pass through; otherwise there could be no communication with the rest of the Internet. How can those messages be secured in transit? To protect transmitted information, many organizations and individuals use **encryption** software to scramble their transmissions. When a user encrypts a message by applying a secret numerical code, called an *encryption key*, the message can be transmitted or stored as an indecipherable garble of characters. The message can be read only after it's been reconstructed with a matching key.

The encrypted message is transmitted through the network.

x48dqq82ked8i3kdi 3i3kd0o290ekwcmg qaoi34ieqhj3o3k,wi woakaqjkurtj2iewow qlekejroqei45783.p

The sender creates, encrypts, and sends the message.

The message is received and decrypted.

FIGURE 10.12 The encryption process.

How It Works

10.2 Cryptography

If you want to be sure that an email message can be read by only the intended recipient, you must either use a secure communication channel or secure the message.

Mail within many organizations is sent over secure communication channels—channels that can't be accessed by outsiders. But you can't secure the channels used by the Internet and other worldwide mail networks; there's no way to shield messages sent through public telephone lines and airwaves. In the words of Mark Rotenberg, director of the Electronic Privacy Information Center, "Email is more like a postcard than a sealed letter."

If you can't secure the communication channel, the alternative is to secure the message. You secure a message by using a cryptosystem to encrypt it—scramble it so it can be decrypted (unscrambled) only by the intended recipient.

Almost all cryptosystems depend on a key—a passwordlike number or phrase that can be used to encrypt or decrypt a message. Eavesdroppers who don't know the key have to try to decrypt it by brute force by trying all possible keys until they guess the right one.

Some cryptosystems afford only modest security: A message can be broken after only a day or week of brute force cryptanalysis on a supercomputer. More effective systems would take a supercomputer billions of years to break the message.

The traditional kind of cryptosystem used on computer networks is called a symmetric secret key system. With this approach the sender and recipient use the same key, and they have to keep the shared key secret from everyone else.

Secret Key System

Sue's list of secret keys

George	10529
Clem	22707
.	.
.	.
.	.

Messages encrypted/decrypted with key 10529

Messages encrypted/decrypted with key 22707

George's list of secret keys

Sue	10529
Clem	33812
.	.
.	.
.	.

Clem's list of secret keys

George	33812
Sue	22707
.	.
.	.
.	.

Messages encrypted/decrypted with key 33812

FIGURE 10.13

The biggest problem with symmetric secret key systems is key management. If you want to communicate with several people and ensure that each person can't read messages intended for the others, then you'll need a different secret key for each person. When you want to communicate with new people, you have the problem of letting them know what the key is. If you send it over the ordinary communication channel, it can be intercepted.

In the 1970s cryptographers developed public key cryptography to get around the key management problems. The most popular kind of public key cryptosystem, RSA, is being incorporated into most new network-enabled software. Phillip Zimmerman's popular shareware utility called PGP (for Pretty Good Privacy) uses RSA technology.

Public Key System

Each person using a public key cryptosystem has two keys: a private key known only to the user and a public key that is freely available to anyone who wants it. Thus a public key system is asymmetric: A different key is used to encrypt than to decrypt. Public keys can be published in phone directories, Web pages, and advertisements; some users include them in their email signatures.

If you want to send a secure message over the Internet to your friend Sue in St. Louis, you use her public key to encrypt the message. Sue's public key can't decrypt the message; only her private key can do that. The private key is specifically designed to decrypt messages that were encrypted with the corresponding public key. Because public/private key pairs can be generated by individual users, the key distribution problem is solved. The only keys being sent over an insecure network are publicly available keys.

You can use the same technology in reverse (encrypt with the private key, decrypt with the public key) for message authentication: When you decrypt a message, you can be sure that it was sent from a particular person on the network. In the future, legal and commercial documents will routinely have digital signatures that will be as valid as handwritten ones.

For the most sensitive information, passwords, firewalls, and encryption aren't enough. A diligent spy can "listen to" and possibly read compromising emanations (CE)—the electromagnetic signals that emanate from computer hardware and, in some cases, read sensitive information. To prevent spies from using these spurious broadcasts, the NSA has invested heavily in TEMPEST, a program to secure electronic communication from eavesdroppers while enabling the U.S. government to intercept and interpret those signals from other sources.

Audit-control software is used to monitor and record computer transactions as they happen so auditors can trace and identify suspicious computer activity after the fact. Effective audit-control software forces every user, legitimate or otherwise, to leave a trail of electronic footprints. Of course, this kind of software is of little value unless someone in the organization monitors and interprets the output.

Backups and Other Precautions

Even the tightest security system can't guarantee absolute protection of data. A power surge or a power failure can wipe out the most carefully guarded data in an instant. An **uninterruptible power supply (UPS)** can protect computers from data loss during power failures; inexpensive ones can protect home computers from short power dropouts. *Surge protectors* don't help during power failures, but they can shield electronic equipment from dangerous power spikes, preventing expensive hardware failures.

Of course, disasters come in many forms. Sabotage, human errors, machine failures, fire, flood, lightning, and earthquakes can damage or destroy computer data along with hardware. Any complete security system should include a plan for recovering from disasters. For mainframes and PCs alike, the best and most widely used data recovery insurance is a system of making regular **backups**. For many systems, data and software are backed up automatically onto disks or tapes, usually at the end of each workday. Most data processing shops keep several *generations* of backups so they can, if necessary, go back several days, weeks, or years to reconstruct data files. Storage technology called *RAID (redundant array of independent disks)* enables multiple hard disks to operate as a single logical unit. RAID systems can, among other things, automatically *mirror* data on multiple disks, effectively creating instant redundancy.

For maximum security, many computer users keep copies of sensitive data off-site—in one or more remote locations. Off-site backups minimize the chances that fires, floods, or other local disasters will completely destroy important data. One type of off-site backup that's rapidly growing in popularity is online backup. Many companies, including Internet service providers, Web hosting companies, and security software companies, offer online storage for their customers to use for backing up data. Some of these sites provide special software for backing up data; others can be used with any backup software. Of course, backup speed is limited by connection bandwidth, and is typically much slower than backing up to a local hard disk.

FIGURE 10.14 An uninterruptible power supply (UPS) protects a computer against power surges and momentary power loss.

FIGURE 10.15 A RAID storage device combines hard drives to create a redundant data store that can withstand hardware failures.

Human Security Controls

Security experts throughout the computer industry are constantly developing new technologies and techniques for protecting computer systems from computer criminals. At the same time, criminals continue to refine their craft. In the ongoing competition between the law and the lawless, computer security generally lags behind. In the words of Tom Forester and Perry Morrison in *Computer Ethics,* "Computer security experts are forever trying to shut the stable door after the horse has bolted." Ultimately, computer security is a human problem that can't be solved by technology alone.

Security, Privacy, Freedom, and Ethics: The Delicate Balance

It's hard to overstate the importance of computer security in our networked world. Destructive viruses, illegal interlopers, crooked coworkers, software pirates, and cyber-vandals can erode trust, threaten jobs, and make life difficult for everyone. But sometimes computer security mea-

In this age of advanced technology, **thick walls** and **locked doors** cannot guard our **privacy** or safeguard our **personal freedom**.

—*Lyndon B. Johnson, 36th president of the United States, February 23, 1974*

sures can create problems of their own. Complex access procedures, virus-protection programs, intellectual property laws, and other security measures can, if carried too far, interfere with people getting their work done. In the extreme, security can threaten individual human rights.

When Security Threatens Privacy

As you've seen in other chapters, computers threaten our personal privacy on several fronts. Corporate and government databases accumulate and share massive amounts of information about us against our will and without our knowledge. Software snoopers track our Web explorations and read our electronic mail. Managers use monitoring software to measure worker productivity and observe their on-screen activities. Government security agencies secretly monitor telephone calls and data transmissions.

When security measures are used to prevent computer crime, they usually help protect privacy rights at the same time. When a hacker invades a computer system, the intruder might monitor the system's legitimate users' private communications. When an outsider breaks into the database of a bank, the privacy of every bank customer is at risk. The same applies to government computers, credit bureau computers, and any other computer containing data on private citizens. The security of these systems is important for protecting people's privacy.

But in some cases security and law enforcement can pose threats to personal privacy. Here are some examples:

■ In 1990 Alana Shoar, email coordinator for Epson America, Inc., found stacks of printouts of employee email messages in her boss's office—messages that employees believed were private. After confronting her boss, she was fired for "gross misconduct and insubordination." She filed a class-action suit, claiming that Epson routinely monitored all email messages. Company officials denied the charges but took a stand on their right to any information stored on, sent to, or taken from their business computers. The courts ruled in Epson's favor. Since then,

FIGURE 10.16 Windows and the Mac OS include backup utilities that can automatically make regular backups onto external hard drives. Apple's Time Machine lets you go "back in time" to recover deleted or damaged files.

Working Wisdom

<u>Safe Computing</u>

Even if you're not building a software system for the DOJ or the FBI, computer security is important. Viruses, disk crashes, system bombs, and miscellaneous disasters can destroy your work, your peace of mind, and possibly your system. Fortunately, you can protect your computer, your software, and your data from most hazards.

➡ *Share with care.* A computer virus is a contagious disease that spreads when it comes in contact with a compatible file or disk. Viruses spread rapidly in environments where disks and files are passed around freely, as they are in many student computer labs. To protect your data, don't be overly casual about sharing flash drives and other media containing data and programs.

➡ *Beware of email bearing gifts.* Many viruses hide in attachments to email messages that say something like, "Here's the document you asked for. Please don't show anyone else." Don't open unsolicited email attachments, especially from senders you don't recognize; just delete them.

➡ *Handle shareware and freeware with care.* Some viruses enter systems in Trojan horse shareware and freeware programs. Approach public domain programs and shareware with caution; test them with a disinfectant program before you install them.

➡ *Don't pirate software.* Even commercial programs can be infected with viruses. Shrink-wrapped, virgin software is much less likely to be infected than pirated copies. Besides, software piracy is theft, and the legal penalties can be severe.

➡ *Disinfect regularly.* Use up-to-date virus protection software regularly. Most anti-virus software is sold by subscription, so that customers' computers can be automatically updated whenever new virus strains are released. Make sure your virus protection software is set to automatically download current patches.

➡ *Treat your removable discs and drives as if they contained something important.* If you use a portable hard drive, keep it away from liquids, dust, pets, and magnets. Don't put it close to speakers and other electronic devices that contain hidden magnets. Magnets won't harm optical discs, but scratches can make them unusable.

➡ *Take your passwords seriously.* Choose a password that's not easily guessable, not in any dictionary, and not easy for others to remember. Don't post it by your computer, and don't type it when you're being watched. Change your password occasionally—immediately if you have reason to suspect it has been discovered. Don't use the same password for everything.

➡ *If it's sensitive, lock it up.* If your computer is accessible to others, protect your private files with passwords and/or encryption. Many operating systems and utilities include options for adding password protection and encrypting files. If others need to see the files, lock them so they can be read but not changed or deleted. If secrecy is critical, don't store the data on your hard disk at all. Store it on removable disks and lock it away in a safe place.

➡ *If it's important, back it up.* Regularly make backup copies of every important file on different disks than the original. Keep copies of critical files in different locations so you have backups in case disaster strikes. Whether you use the Internet or sneakernet, make sure all your important work is backed up somewhere else. Some people use automated backup programs such as those packaged with popular operating systems. Others prefer third-party tools that regularly "clone" the boot drive, making an exact bootable copy. Still others use both. For important data, consider off-site backups—upload it or transport it to a safe location far from the original.

➡ *If you're sending sensitive information through the Internet, consider encryption.* Use a utility or a program such as freeware PGP (Pretty Good Privacy) to turn your message into code that's almost impossible to crack.

➡ *Don't open your system to interlopers.* If you've got an always-on Internet connection—T1, DSL, or cable modem—consider using firewall hardware or software to detect and lock out snoopers. Set your file-sharing controls so access is limited to authorized visitors.

➡ *Create a separate administrator account.* Windows, Mac OS, and Linux all allow multiple accounts on a single machine. For maximum security, use one account strictly for systems administration and installation, and another account for day-to-day computing.

➡ *Prepare for the worst.* Even if you take every precaution, things can still go wrong. Make sure you aren't completely dependent on the computer for really important things.

many other U.S. court decisions have reinforced a company's right to read employee email stored on company computers.

■ A 2004 decision by a federal appeals court went even further, ruling that an Internet service provider has the right to read the email messages of its subscribers. While the Wiretap Act prohibits eavesdropping on telephone calls and other messages sent in real time, the majority opinion stated that a stored message, such as a piece of email, does not have the same protection. The Electronic Frontier Foundation protested the decision, arguing that the ruling "dealt a grave blow to the privacy of Internet communications."

■ In 1995 the U.S. government passed legislation requiring new digital phone systems to include additional switches that allow for electronic surveillance. This legislation protects the FBI's ability to wiretap at the expense of individual privacy. Detractors have pointed out that this digital "back door" could be abused by government agencies and could also be used by savvy criminals to perform illegal wiretaps. Government officials argue that wiretapping is a critical tool in the fight against organized crime.

■ The digital manhunt that led to the arrest of the programmer charged with authoring the Melissa virus was made as a direct result of information provided by America Online Inc. A controversial Microsoft document identification technology—the Global Unique Identifier, or GUID—may also have played a role. While virtually everyone was happy when the virus's perpetrator was apprehended, many legal experts feared that the same techniques will be used for less lofty purposes.

■ In 2000 the U.S. government found Microsoft guilty of gross abuses of its monopolistic position in the software industry. The government's case included hundreds of private email messages between Microsoft employees—messages that often contradicted Microsoft's public testimony.

■ A 2001 U.S. law requires that mobile phones include GPS technology for transmitting the phone's location to a 911 operator in the case of an emergency call. Privacy activists fear that government agents and criminals will use this E911 technology to track the movements of phone owners.

■ In response to the terrorist attacks of September 11, 2001, the U.S. Congress quickly drafted and passed the USA PATRIOT Act, a sweeping set of law changes that redefined terrorism and the government's authority to combat it. The act defined *cyberterrorism* to include computer crimes that cause at least $5,000 in damage or destroy medical equipment. It increased the FBI's latitude to use wiretap technology to monitor suspects' Web browsing and email without a judge's order. Critics argued that this controversial law could easily be used to restrict the freedom and threaten the privacy of law-abiding citizens. The USA PATRIOT Act, which originally included several temporary provisions, was reauthorized with some minor modifications in 2006.

One of the best examples of a technology that can simultaneously improve security and threaten privacy is the *smart badge*.

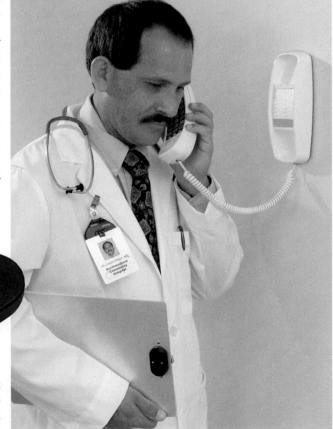

FIGURE 10.17 Smart badges allow employees to be tracked as they move. Instead of paging the entire hospital, an operator could use information from a physician's smart badge to route the call to the phone nearest his location. This smart badge from Versus Technology also includes a button that can be programmed to send a message to a pager, open a locked door, or perform another task.

These badges broadcast identification codes. Each badge's code is picked up by a network receiver and transmitted to a badge-location database that is constantly being updated. Smart badges are used for identifying, finding, and remembering:

- *Identifying.* When an authorized employee approaches a door, the door recognizes the person's badge code and opens. Whenever anyone logs into a computer system, the badge code identifies the person as an authorized or unauthorized user.
- *Finding.* An employee can check a computer screen to locate another employee and find out with whom that person is talking. There's no need for a paging system, and "while you were away" notes are less common.
- *Remembering.* At the end of the day, a smart-badge wearer can get a minute-by-minute printout listing exactly where and with whom he's been.

Some conferences use smart badges to help the attendees meet each other. Delegates receive personalized badges containing their contact information, employment history, areas of interest, and hobbies. As the attendees move about, the badges communicate with each other. If the badge identifies a nearby delegate with similar interests, it alerts the badge wearer.

Similar technology is now available in smart phones in many countries. Phones with proximity recognition technology can notify their owners when friends—or even strangers who match particular profiles—are nearby. Many people use their phones to find and meet potential dates who happen to be in the neighborhood.

Is the smart badge a primitive version of the communicator on TV's *Star Trek* or a surveillance tool for Big Brother? The technology has the potential to be either or both; it all depends on how people use it. Smart badges, like other security devices and techniques, raise important legal and ethical questions about privacy—questions that we, as a society, must resolve sooner or later.

Justice on the Electronic Frontier

Through our scientific genius, we have **made this world a neighborhood**; now through our moral and spiritual development, we must **make of it a brotherhood**.

—*The Reverend Martin Luther King, Jr.*

Federal and state governments have responded to the growing computer crime problem by creating new laws against electronic trespassing and by escalating enforcement efforts. Hackers have become targets for nationwide anticrime operations. Dozens of hackers have been arrested for unauthorized entry into computer systems and for the release of destructive viruses and worms. Many have been convicted under federal or state laws. Others have had their computers confiscated with no formal charges filed.

Some of the victims of these sting operations claim that they broke no laws. In one case a student was arrested because he published an electronic magazine that carried a description of an emergency 911 system allegedly stolen by hackers. Charges were eventually dropped when it was revealed that the "stolen" document was, in fact, available to the public.

Cases such as this raise questions about how civil rights apply in the "electronic frontier." How does the Bill of Rights apply to computer communications? Does freedom of the press apply to blogs and Web forums in the same way it applies to paper periodicals? Can an Internet service provider be held responsible for information others post on a server? Can online pornography be served from a house located in a neighborhood with antiporn laws? Are Internet service providers responsible when their users illegally trade music online?

Laws such as the Telecommunications Act of 1996 attempt to deal with these questions by outlining exactly what kinds of communications are legal online. Unfortunately, these laws generally raise as many questions as they answer. Shortly after its passage, a major section of the Telecommunications Act, called the Communications Decency Act, was

Norwegian teenager Jon Johansen released the computer program DeCSS, which enabled Linux computers to play movies stored on DVDs. The program violated the Digital Millennium Copyright Act's prohibition against circumventing encryption measures. Norwegian authorities twice prosecuted Johansen, but he was acquitted both times.

German teenager Sven Jaschan created the Sasser worm, which infected about 18 million Windows computers in April 2004, disrupting operations at Delta Air Lines, Australian railroads, and other businesses. A juvenile court sentenced Jaschan to one and a half years' probation and 30 hours of community service.

Briton Philip Cummings worked for Teledata Communications (TCI), an American company that makes instant credit-check devices for banks, car dealers, and other businesses. He participated in an identity-theft ring that affected 30,000 people. After pleading guilty, Cummings was sentenced to 14 years in federal prison.

Filipino computer science student Onel de Guzman allegedly wrote The Love Bug virus, which infected millions of computers worldwide. At the time the virus was created, the Philippines had no laws against computer hacking, and he was never prosecuted.

American David L. Smith created the Melissa virus and posted it on an alt.sex.usenet group using a stolen AOL account. The virus infected hundreds of thousands of computers. Smith was sentenced to 20 months in federal prison, required to do 100 hours of community service, and fined $5,000.

American Jeanson J. Ancheta created the Trojan horse program rxbot, which spread to thousands of Internet-connected computers. He sold access to infected computers to customers who used them to distribute spam or launch distributed-denial-of-service attacks. He was sentenced to 57 months in federal prison. In addition, he paid $15,000 in restitution and surrendered his computers, a car, and $60,000 in cash.

FIGURE 10.18 Some computer hackers have paid a stiff price for their activities; others have not.

declared unconstitutional by the Supreme Court. The debates continue inside and outside of the courts.

The Digital Millennium Copyright Act of 1998 (discussed in Chapter 4, "Software Basics: The Ghost in the Machine") hasn't (so far) been found unconstitutional, but it has resulted in several lawsuits that raise serious human rights questions. In the summer of 2001, a Russian programmer and graduate student named Dmitry Sklyarov was arrested by the FBI after he spoke at a computer security conference in Las Vegas. His alleged crime was writing—not using—a program that cracks Adobe's copy protection scheme for e-books. After a Webwide demonstration against the arrest, Adobe publicly came out in favor of freeing Sklyarov.

The same law was used to silence Professor Edward Felton in 2001. The Princeton University computer scientist was threatened with a lawsuit from the Recording Industry Association of America if he presented a paper analyzing the system that encodes digital music; he withdrew the paper. Several months later, Felton published the paper and the RIAA recanted its threat but not its right to threaten similar suits in the future.

The DMCA was even used to file a suit against *2600* magazine because of a single Web site link. A Norwegian 15-year-old had written code allowing DVD movies to be played on Linux computers—code that broke the DVD encryption scheme. *2600*'s Web site included a link to another site containing the program. (The *New York Times* Web site contained a link to the same site but was not sued by the recording industry.)

When Congress passed the Telecommunications Act of 1996 and the Digital Millennium Copyright Act of 1998, it was attempting to make U.S. law more responsive to the issues of the digital age. But each of these laws introduced new problems by threatening rights of citizens—problems that have to be solved by courts and by future lawmakers. These laws illustrate the difficulty lawmakers face when protecting rights in a world of rapid technological change.

Security and Reliability

If the automobile had followed the same development cycle as the computer, a **Rolls Royce would today cost $100**, get a million miles per gallon, and **explode once a year**, killing everyone inside.

—*Robert X. Cringely, PBS computer curmudgeon*

So far our discussion of security has focused mainly on protecting computer systems from trespassing, sabotage, and other crimes. But security involves more than criminal activity. Some of the most important security issues have to do with creating systems that can withstand software errors and hardware glitches.

Bugs and Breakdowns

Computer systems, like all machines, are vulnerable to fires, floods, and other natural disasters, as well as breakdowns caused by the failure of hardware components. But in modern computers, hardware problems are relatively rare when compared with software failures. By any measure, bugs do more damage than viruses and computer burglars put together do. Here are a few horror stories:

- A new laboratory computer system became backlogged the day after it was installed at the Los Angeles County–USC Medical Center in April 2003. Emergency room doctors, who could not get the test results they needed, instructed the County of Los Angeles to stop sending ambulances. One doctor said, "It's almost like practicing Third World medicine. We rely so much on our computers and our fast-world technology that we were almost blinded."

- In September 1999 the Mars Climate Orbiter burned up as it approached Mars because controllers had mixed up English and metric units. Three months later the Mars Polar Lander went silent 12 minutes before touchdown. Investigators suspect software errors are at least partly responsible for this spectacular mission failure.

■ In 2006 NASA's Mars Global Surveyor software received a missent command from Earth, apparently assumed (incorrectly) that a motor had failed, and pointed one of its batteries toward the sun, causing it to overheat and fail. The mission had to be abandoned as a result.

■ In 2001 a bug in a new billing system led Qwest to charge some of its cell phone customers as much as $600 per minute. About 14,000 customers received incorrect bills, including one customer whose monthly statement asked her to pay $57,346.20.

■ In 2007 two separate cascading computer failures—one in air traffic controller systems, one in U.S. Customs systems—caused massive delays for travellers while the systems were repaired.

Every year brings new stories of breakdowns and bugs with catastrophic consequences. But it wasn't until 1999 that a computer bug—the Y2K (year 2000) bug, or millennium bug—became an international sensation. For decades, programmers commonly built two-digit date fields into programs to save storage space, thinking they had no reason to allow space for the first two digits because they never changed. But when 1999 ended, those digits did change, making many of those ancient programs unstable or unusable. Programmers knowledgeable in COBOL, FORTRAN, and other early computer languages repaired many of the programs. But others couldn't be repaired and had to be completely rewritten.

Businesses and governments spent more than 100 billion dollars trying to head off Y2K disasters. Many individuals bought generators and guns, stockpiled food and water, and prepared for a collapse of the computer-controlled utility grids that keep our economy running. When the fateful day arrived, the Y2K bug caused scattered problems, ranging from credit card refusals to malfunctioning spy satellites. But for most people, January 1, 2000, was business as usual. It's debatable whether disasters were averted by billions of dollars worth of preventive maintenance, or whether the Y2K scare stories were overblown. The truth is undoubtedly somewhere between these two extremes. In any event, Y2K raised the public's consciousness about its dependence on fickle, fragile technology.

FIGURE 10.19 Computers are simply one link in a long chain of technologies we rely on every day. The largest power failure in North American history, which cut off electricity to 40 million Americans and 10 million Canadians, was caused because power lines in Ohio sagged onto tree branches that had not been pruned. The photo shows Toronto, Ontario, the evening of August 14, 2003.

Given the state of the art of programming today, three facts are clear:

1. It's impossible to eliminate all bugs. Today's programs are constructed of thousands of tiny pieces, any one of which can cause a failure if it's incorrectly coded.

2. Even programs that appear to work can contain dangerous bugs. Some bugs are easy to detect and correct because they're obvious. The most dangerous bugs are difficult to detect and may go unnoticed by users for months or years.

3. The bigger the system, the bigger the problem. Large programs are far more complex and difficult to debug than small programs are, and the trend today is clearly toward large programs. For example, Microsoft Windows 95 has 11 million lines of code and was considered huge at the time; Windows Vista has more than 50 million!

As we entrust complex computerized systems to do everything from financial transaction processing to air traffic control, the potential cost of computer failure goes up. In the past decade, researchers have identified hundreds of cases in which disruptions to computer system operations posed some risk to the public, and the number of incidents has doubled every two years.

Computers at War

Massive networking makes the U.S. the **world's most vulnerable target**.

—John McConnell, former NSA director

Nowhere are the issues surrounding security and reliability more critical than in military applications. To carry out its mission effectively, the military must be sure its systems are secure against enemy surveillance and attack. At the same time, many modern military applications push the limits of information technology farther than they've ever been before.

Smart Weapons

The United States has invested billions of dollars in the development of smart weapons— missiles that use computerized guidance systems to locate their targets. A command-guidance system enables a human operator to control the missile's path while watching a missile's-eye view of the target on a television screen. Using infrared heat-seeking devices or visual pattern recognition technology, a missile with a homing guidance system can track a moving target without human help. Weapons that use "smart" guidance systems can be extremely accurate in pinpointing enemy targets under most circumstances. In theory, smart weapons can greatly reduce the amount of civilian destruction in war if everything is working properly.

One problem with high-tech weapons is that they reduce the amount of time people have to make life-and-death decisions. As decision-making time goes down, the chances of making errors goes up. In one tragic example, an American guided missile cruiser on a peacetime mission in the Persian Gulf used a computerized Aegis fleet defense system to shoot down an Iranian Airbus containing 290 civilians. The decision to fire was made by well-intentioned humans, but those humans had little time—and used ambiguous data—to make the decision.

Autonomous Systems

Even more controversial is the possibility of people being left out of the decision-making loop altogether. Yet the trend in military research is clearly toward weapons that demand almost instantaneous responses—the kind that only computers can make. An autonomous system

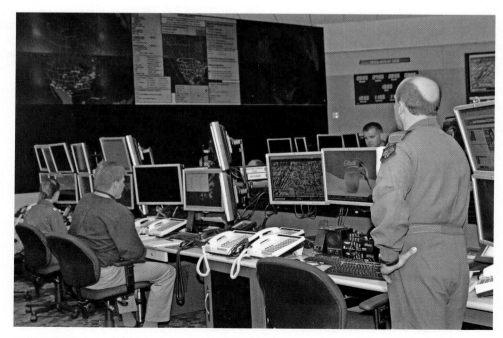

FIGURE 10.20 In modern weapons systems, such as those used by the North America Aerospace Defense Control (NORAD) in its Cheyenne Mountain Complex in Colorado Springs, Colorado, computers are critical components in the command and control process.

is a complex system that can assume almost complete responsibility for a task without human input, verification, or decision making.

The most famous and controversial autonomous system is the Strategic Defense Initiative (SDI)—former President Ronald Reagan's proposed "Star Wars" system for shielding the United States from nuclear attack. Recently resuscitated by President George W. Bush, the SDI system, as planned, will use a network of laser-equipped satellites and ground-based stations to detect and destroy attacking missiles shortly after launch, before they have time to reach their targets. SDI weapons will have to be able to react almost instantaneously, without human intervention. If they sense an attack, these system computers will have no time to wait for the president to declare war, and no time for human experts to analyze the perceived attack.

The automated missile defense system generates intense public debates about false alarms, hardware feasibility, constitutional issues, and the ethics of autonomous weapons. But for many who understand the limitations of computers, the biggest issue is software reliability. The system will require tens of millions of lines of code. The system can't be completely tested in advance because there's no way to simulate accurately the unpredictable conditions of a global war. Yet to work effectively, the system will have to be absolutely reliable. In a tightly coupled worldwide network, a single bug could multiply and expand like a speed-of-light cancer. A small error could result in a major disaster. Many software engineers have pointed out that absolute reliability simply isn't possible now or in the foreseeable future.

In spite of years of political haggling, system failures, and cost overruns, the missile defense system is still in the works, and systems reliability issues remain. Supporters of automated missile defense systems argue that the technical difficulties can be overcome in time, and the U.S. government continues to invest billions in research toward that end. Whether a "smart shield" is ever completed, it has focused public attention on critical issues related to security and reliability.

Warfare in the Digital Domain

Even as the U.S. government spends billions of dollars on smart missiles and missile defense systems, many military experts suggest that future wars may not be fought in the air, on land, or at sea. The front lines of the future may, instead, be in cyberspace. By attacking through vast interconnected computer networks, an enemy could conceivably cripple telecommunications systems, power grids, banking and financial systems, hospitals and medical systems, water and gas supplies, oil pipelines, and emergency government services without firing a shot.

Several recent examples highlight our vulnerability:

- According to a Canadian report, hackers successfully gained limited access to Defense Department networks five times in 2003.
- Since 2003, a series of attacks on American defense-related computer systems has resulted in unauthorized access to numerous networks, including Lockheed Martin, Sandia National Laboratories, Redstone Arsenal, and NASA. The U.S. government suspects China is behind these electronic probes, which have been given the code name Titan Rain.
- The 2007 DDoS attack that crippled the Estonian electronic infrastructure (mentioned earlier in the chapter) appears to have been politically motivated. The attack affected many government systems, two banks, and a political party Web site, among other things.
- During recent U.S. elections, dozens of politically motivated Web attacks occurred for various causes, parties, and countries. The attacks included Web site vandalism, DDoS attacks, and system snooping. What's more, there's growing concern that electronic voting machines, many of which don't produce paper backups, are vulnerable to politically-motivated sabotage.

Thankfully, none of these crimes resulted in serious damage or injury. But terrorists, spies, or criminals might use the same techniques to trigger major disasters in the future.

Recognizing the growing threat of system sabotage, then-Attorney General Janet Reno created the *National Infrastructure Protection Center* in early 1998. The NIPC's state-of-the-art command center is housed at FBI headquarters. The center includes representatives of various intelligence agencies (the departments of defense, transportation, energy, and treasury) and representatives of several major corporations.

The U.S. Government has, through several administrations, attempted to prepare for potential attacks on the American information infrastructure. But any effort to protect the infrastructure must have corporate participation, because private companies own many of the systems that are most vulnerable to attack. Unfortunately, many businesses are slow to recognize the potential threat. They embrace the efficiency that networks bring, but they don't adequately prepare for attack through those networks.

Network attacks are all but inevitable, and such attacks can have disastrous consequences for all of us. In a world where computers control everything from money to missiles, computer security and reliability are too important to ignore.

Is Security Possible?

Computer thieves. Hackers. Software pirates. Computer snoopers. Viruses. Worms. Trojan horses. Spybots. Wiretaps. Hardware failures. Software bugs. When we live and work with computers, we're exposed to all kinds of risks that didn't exist in the precomputer era. These risks make computer security especially important and challenging.

Because computers do so many amazing things so well, it's easy to overlook the problems they bring with them and to believe that they're invincible. But today's computers hide the potential for errors and deception under an impressive user interface. This doesn't mean we should avoid using computers, only that we should remain skeptical, cautious, and realistic as we use them. Security procedures can reduce but not eliminate risks. In today's fast-moving world, absolute security simply isn't possible.

Human Questions for a Computer Age

The **important thing** to forecast is not the automobile but the **parking problem**; not the television but the **soap opera**.

—*Isaac Asimov*

It's the **end of the world** as we know it and I feel fine.

—*R.E.M.*

In earlier chapters we examined many social and ethical issues related to computer technology, including privacy, security, reliability, and intellectual property. These aren't the only critical issues before us. Before closing we'll briefly raise some other important, and as yet unanswered, questions of the information age.

Will Computers Be Democratic?

The higher the technology, the **higher the freedom**. Technology enforces certain solutions: satellite dishes, computers, videos, international telephone lines force pluralism and freedom onto a society.

—*Lech Walesa*

When machines and computers, profit motives, and property rights are considered **more important than people**, the giant triplets of **racism**, **materialism**, and **militarism** are incapable of being conquered.

—*The Reverend Martin Luther King, Jr.*

In France student organizations used computer networks to mobilize opposition to tuition increases. In 1999 environmentalists, labor organizations, human rights groups, and a handful of anarchists used the Internet to mobilize massive protests at the World Trade Organization's Seattle meeting. The protests brought many issues surrounding the secretive WTO into the global spotlight for the first time. In 2005 dozens of soldiers in Iraq created blogs chronicling their experiences. The blogs reflected a wide spectrum of ideological beliefs and provided news-hungry Americans an alternative to mainstream media outlets.

Computers are often used to promote the democratic ideals and causes of common people. Many analysts argue that modern computer technology is, by its very nature, a force for equality and democracy. On the other hand, many powerful people and organizations use information technology to increase their wealth and influence.

Will personal computers and the Internet empower ordinary citizens to make better lives for themselves? Or will computer technology produce a society of technocrats and technopeasants? Will computerized polls help elected officials better serve the needs of their constituents? Or will they just give the powerful another tool for staying in power? Will networks revitalize participatory democracy through electronic town meetings? Or will they give tyrants the tools to monitor and control citizens? Will electronic voting technology make elections more accurate? Or will security and reliability problems disenfranchise voters and undermine the democratic process?

Will the Global Village Be a Community?

A typical computer today contains components from dozens of countries. The modern corporation uses computer networks for instant communication among offices scattered around the world. Information doesn't stop at international borders as it flows through networks that span the globe. Information technology enables organizations to overcome the age-old barriers of space and time, but questions remain.

In the post–Cold War era, will information technology be used to further peace, harmony, and understanding? Or will the intense competition of the global marketplace simply create new kinds of wars—information wars? Will electronic interconnections provide new opportunities for economically depressed countries? Or will they simply make it easier for information-rich countries to exploit developing nations from a distance? Will information technology be used to promote and preserve diverse communities, cultures, and ecosystems? Or will it undercut traditions, cultures, and roots?

> Progress in commercial information technologies will improve productivity, bring the world closer together, and **enhance the quality of life**.
>
> —*Stan Davis and Bill Davidson, in* 2020 Vision

> The **real question** before us lies here: do these instruments further **life and its values** or not?
>
> —*Lewis Mumford in 1934*

Will We Become Information Slaves?

The information age has redefined our environment; it's almost as if the human species has been transplanted into a different world. Even though the change has happened almost overnight, most of us can't imagine going back to a world without computers. Still, the rapid changes raise questions.

Can human bodies and minds adapt to the higher stimulation, faster pace, and constant change of the information age? Will our information-heavy environment cause us to lose touch with the more fundamental human needs? Will we become so dependent on our "pretty toys" that we can't get by without them? Will we lose our sense of purpose and identity as our machines become more intelligent? Or will we learn to balance the demands of the technology with our biological and spiritual needs?

> Our inventions are wont to be **pretty toys** which distract our attention from serious things. They are but improved means to an **unimproved end**.
>
> —*Henry David Thoreau*

> **Computers are useless**. They can only give you answers.
>
> —*Pablo Picasso*

Standing on the Shoulders of Giants

When we use computers, we're standing on the shoulders of Charles Babbage, Ada Lovelace, George Boole, Alan Turing, Grace Hopper, Doug Engelbart, Alan Kay, and hundreds of others who invented the

> If I have seen farther than other men, it is because **I stood on the shoulders of giants**.
>
> —*Isaac Newton*

The One Laptop Per Child program is providing low-cost, innovative XO computers to children around the world. The innovative "hundred dollar" computer can be recharged with the turn of a crank, so it can be used by children who live off the electrical grid.

Computers can be used to improve health care in developing countries. In Tanzania, GPS systems help in the fight against AIDS by allowing geographic data collection of HIV rates.

Privacy advocate Steve Mann promotes sousveillance—the personal capture of information—as a way for individuals to counter the power of governments and corporations engaging in surveillance. Mann uses wearable computing devices to capture his experiences.

Today's unmanned combat aircraft are controlled by somebody on the ground. A Pentagon planning paper suggests that in the year 2020 one-third of all U.S. combat aircraft will be autonomous.

Computer models of wind flow can help utility companies put power-generating wind turbines in the right locations.

FIGURE 10.21 Modern computers are malleable tools that can be put to a wide variety of uses.

future for us. Because of their foresight and effort, we can see farther than those who came before us.

In Greek mythology Prometheus (whose name means "forethought") stole fire from Zeus and gave it to humanity, along with all arts and civilization. Zeus was furious when he discovered what Prometheus had done. He feared that fire would make mortals think they were as great as the gods and that they would abuse its power. Like fire, the computer is a powerful and malleable tool. It can be used to empower or imprison, to explore or exploit, to create or destroy. We can choose. We've been given the tools. It's up to all of us to invent the future.

Inventing the FUTURE

The Future of Internet Security

It is **conceivable**, in theory, for a **hacker** sitting in his easy chair to get **inside a tank**.

—*Colonel Thaddeus Dmuchowski, U.S. Army*

Faster Internet connectivity has opened up new vistas for international communication and collaboration, but it has also allowed malware to spread faster than ever. The Sapphire worm, also called Slammer, infected 90 percent of the vulnerable hosts worldwide in less than 10 minutes. Future worms may spread globally in less than a minute. That's not nearly enough time for humans to get involved in stopping them. Instead, network developers are devising automated systems to thwart attacks.

LAYERED DEFENSES

Organizations with large computer networks will need to resort to a layered defensive approach. They will put ever-more-sophisticated hardware and software systems on the perimeter of their networks. Firewalls, augmented with network intrusion detection software, will try to prevent dangerous packets from entering the organization's networks. Sophisticated pattern-recognition software will help these systems distinguish between legitimate and illegitimate network access attempts.

However, it is unrealistic to expect that the outer defenses will be 100 percent effective. That's why organizations will implement automated systems for coping with worms and viruses that penetrate their networks. Researchers are developing reconfigurable hardware that can quarantine infected subnets. Hardware-imposed quarantines will prevent a worm that gets into a handful of machines on a LAN from spreading throughout the entire organization.

Special-purpose hardware called *security processors* will allow every message to be encrypted, even huge video streams. Security processors will give organizations the confidence that all their messages, even those sent over wireless networks, are secure from eavesdroppers. Programmers are getting into the act, too. Better programming languages, combined with a greater attention to security-related issues by software developers, should result in future operating systems and applications that contain fewer security holes.

THE PEOPLE PROBLEM

Unfortunately, no amount of technological fixing can completely eliminate security problems. The human element is the weak link in many security systems. Despite warnings about malware, some people continue to spread viruses by opening attachments to email from unknown sources. An experiment in London showed that many computer users would reveal their computer password in return for a pen. Employees bring infected notebooks, flash drives, smart phones, or PDAs to work. Once attached to the

FIGURE 10.22 Employees have spread viruses and worms onto corporate networks by bringing infected notebook computers from home.

employer's network, these devices spread viruses or worms.

Ultimately, organizations and individuals must balance security, convenience, and features. Consumers are unlikely to purchase a piece of software that is 100 percent secure but lacks essential features. So software developers must balance the time they spend on security against the time they spend adding features. Organizations must weigh security against convenience. A network may be very secure, but so difficult to use that it hurts the productivity of the computer users. That can hurt an organization's bottom line.

HOW OPEN?

A rising onslaught of malware and spam could tip the scales toward security and put the openness of the Internet in peril. Computer and network system administrators cannot afford to spend all of their time eradicating malicious software, and users do not want to spend large amounts of their time deleting spam messages. While disconnecting from the Internet is not a reasonable option in this age of global enterprises, system administrators and computer users can erect communication barriers. Even now, some corporate networks reject connection attempts from employees' PDAs and notebook computers that don't have up-to-date security patches. Many email users, disgusted by the volume of spam they have received, have created white lists containing the email addresses of people they are willing to receive messages from. Messages from everyone else are rejected. The entire Internet community—users, programmers, hardware designers, system administrators, and managers—will help determine whether the Internet will remain a place of relatively free and open information exchange. ∼

Crosscurrents

When Cyber Terrorism Becomes State Censorship
by Andy Greenberg

Computer crime meets politics in this edited May, 2008 article from Forbes.

One year ago, hundreds of thousands of bogus requests for information poured into Estonia's data networks, knocking government, media and banking Web sites offline. Local officials were quick to point fingers at the Russian government, declaring Estonia the first victim of cyber warfare. Now, a year of analysis has shown that it was nothing so straightforward.

The difference between government-sponsored attacks and grassroots cyber terrorism is growing increasingly fuzzy, even as researchers try to sift through who did what on Estonia's Web. And the difficulty of tracing responsibility for even massive cyber attacks suggests that such maneuvers may become an effective tool not just for indiscriminate vandalism, but also for stealthy cyber censorship.

In the case of Estonia, security researchers agree on few details. Some have traced the attack to machines housed in the Kremlin. Others counter that those sources were likely PCs hijacked by hidden software, along with the majority of computers used in the attack.

Because so-called "distributed denial of service" attacks use armies of thousands of unwitting PCs corrupted with invisible software to send fraudulent requests for information at Web servers, an attack's source is often hidden by several layers of redirected commands. That means it can become a deft form of information control for governments.

[John] Palfrey[a researcher at Harvard Law School's Berkman Center for Internet and Society] says that the tactic is increasingly used by political movements or authoritarian regimes to shut down the sites of advocacy groups or opposition parties at a key instant. Russian opposition party leader Gary Kasparov's Web site, for instance, was taken offline by a two-week denial of service attack in late December in the midst of the Russian presidential campaign. Ukrainian president Victor Yuschenko suffered a similar attack two months before, which was met with a retaliatory attack on the Party of Regions, a group opposing Yuschenko.

In the past year, Palfrey says, several other organizations have been struck with stealthy attacks before major events including protests or elections, but have avoided publicizing the incidents to avoid further retaliation.

A more vocal victim is Radio Free Europe. Last month, the U.S.-sponsored Web radio site suffered distributed denial of service attacks that knocked out eight of its sites in languages ranging from Belarusian to Tajik. The attacks were timely: Radio Free Europe was planning coverage of protests by Belarusian opposition groups on the 22nd anniversary of the Chernobyl, hoping to highlight the lack of compensation for victims of the nuclear disaster and the Belarusian government's plan to build a new nuclear reactor. That broadcast was cut off by a flood of traffic that reached 50,000 fraudulent requests for information per second at its peak.

All these incidents of Web sabotage, says the SecDev group's Rafal Rohozinski, are what he calls "just-in-time" censorship. Instead of filtering the Web to block citizens from accessing controversial Web sites, as countries like China and Pakistan routinely do, an untraceable attacks pulls the offending site off the Web temporarily at a key moment. Unlike typical Web censorship, that tactic avoids any trace of government involvement.

While Rohozinski and other researchers argue that this subtler form of censorship is on the rise, traditional Web filtering isn't going away. According to the Open Net Initiative, more than 50 countries around the world block their citizens' access to portions of the Web the governments deem politically or culturally undesirable. In September, Myanmar went even further. During the government's crackdown on a monk uprising that opposed its military junta, the country cut off its Internet connection altogether. Myanmar's digital blackout lasted only a week, a fact some researchers take as evidence that extreme Web filtering is too difficult and politically embarrassing for governments to keep up for long. The "just-in-time" censorship taking place in the former Soviet states and Eastern Europe, on the other hand, is nearly invisible, says Ron Deibert, a professor at the University of Toronto and director of the Open Net Initiative.

Deibert suggests that the Internet needs a series of watchdog groups to monitor and trace denial of service attacks—the digital equivalent of the systems of sensors built to detect underground nuclear tests around the world. The Open Net Initiative, he says, would be a good starting place for that monitoring network.

Without those safeguards, Deibert worries that state-sponsored cyber attacks—which typically enlist grassroots supporters—have the potential to spin out of control. He believes the attack on Estonia, for instance, may have begun with modest government encouragement but grew into a blitzkrieg as patriotic hackers joined the attack. "Once this is seen as a legitimate tool for state actors, it will have very drastic results," he says. "It's like a cyclone in cyberspace. Someone hires a few hackers, and the attack can take on a life of its own with consequences far greater than those intended."

Discussion Questions

1. Is there a clear line between malicious hacking and terrorism?

2. Is there a clear line between cyberterrorism and cyberwarfare?

Summary

Computers play an ever-increasing role in fighting crime. At the same time, law enforcement organizations are facing an increase in computer crime—crimes accomplished through special knowledge of computer technology. Most computer crimes go undetected, and those that are detected often go unreported. But by any estimate, computer crime costs billions of dollars every year.

Many computer criminals use computers and the Internet to steal intellectual property. Many steal credit card numbers and other sensitive information that can be used for financial gain. Some steal entire identities. Others use Trojan horses, viruses, worms, logic bombs, and other types of malware to sabotage systems. According to the media, computer crimes are committed by young, bright computer wizards called hackers. Research suggests, however, that hackers are responsible for only a small fraction of computer crimes. The typical computer criminal is a trusted employee with personal or financial problems and knowledge of the computer system. Some types of computer crimes, including software piracy, are committed by everyday computer users who don't realize—or choose not to recognize—that they're committing crimes.

Because of rising computer crime and other risks, organizations have developed a number of computer security techniques to protect their systems and data. Some security devices, such as keys and badges, are designed to restrict physical access to computers. But these tools are becoming less effective in an age of networked PCs. Passwords, encryption, shielding, and audit-control software are all used to protect sensitive data in various organizations. When all else fails, backups of important data are used to reconstruct systems after damage occurs. The most effective security solutions depend on people at least as much as on technology.

Normally, security measures serve to protect our privacy and other individual rights. But occasionally, security procedures threaten those rights. The trade-offs between computer security and freedom raise important legal and ethical questions.

Computer systems aren't threatened only by people; they're also threatened by software bugs and hardware glitches. An important part of security is protecting systems and the people affected by those systems from the consequences of those bugs and glitches. Because our society uses computers for many applications that put lives and livelihoods at stake, reliability issues are especially important. In modern military applications, security and reliability are critical. As the speed, power, and complexity of weapons systems increase, many fear that humans are being squeezed out of the decision-making loop. The debate over high-tech weaponry is bringing many important security issues to the public's attention for the first time.

Key Terms

access-control software ....(p. 371)
antivirus ....(p. 366)
autonomous
    systems ....(p. 384)
backup ....(p. 376)
biometrics ....(p. 370)
botnets ....(p. 369)
computer crime......................(p. 361)
computer security ....(p. 369)
cybercrime.............................(p. 361)
denial-of-service (DoS)
    attack ....(p. 369)

encryption..............................(p. 373)
firewall...................................(p. 371)
hacking ....(p. 368)
identity theft .... (p. 362)
logic bomb.............................(p. 366)
malware ....(p. 364)
passwords ....(p. 371)
phishing ....(p. 362)
sabotage ....(p. 364)
security patch........................(p. 367)

smart weapons ....(p. 384)
social engineering..................(p. 362)
spoofing.................................(p. 362)
spyware..................................(p. 366)
system administrator ....(p. 371)
Trojan horse...........................(p. 365)
uninterruptible power
    supply (UPS) ....(p. 376)
virus.......................................(p. 364)
worms ....(p. 365)

Interactive Activities

1. The *Tomorrow's Technology and You* Web site, **www.pearsonhighered.com/beekman**, contains self-test exercises related to this chapter. Follow the instructions for taking a quiz. After you've completed your quiz, you can email the results to your instructor.

2. The Web site also contains open-ended discussion questions called Internet Exercises. Discuss one or more of the Internet Exercises questions at the section for this chapter.

True or False

1. Computer crimes often go unreported because businesses fear that they can lose more from negative publicity than from the actual crimes.

2. The majority of computer crimes are committed by hackers and vandals with no ties to the victim companies.

3. It's generally a good idea to install a spyware program so you can monitor your system for security leaks.

4. In general, computer viruses don't discriminate among operating systems; a typical virus can infect any system, regardless of platform.

5. PC operating systems generally don't allow users to install software unless they have system administrator privileges.

6. Computer security is ultimately a technological problem with technological solutions.

7. U.S. courts have ruled that an employer cannot read an employee's email, even if it is stored on a company-owned computer.

8. One reason modern operating systems are difficult to debug is they contain tens of millions of lines of code.

9. While many questions remain about the viability of an automated missile defense system, computer scientists are confident that the software for the system will be reliable.

Multiple Choice

1. Which of these passwords is most likely to prevent intruders from logging into your personal online bank account?
   a. password
   b. 123456
   c. Ib4ExaC
   d. money1
   e. All of the above

2. Which of these words means "tricking" or "fooling?"
   a. Bombing
   b. Cracking
   c. Hacking
   d. Hijacking
   e. Spoofing

3. What do you call a piece of code that attaches to an application program and secretly spreads when the application program is executed?
   a. Virus
   b. Worm
   c. Trojan horse
   d. Spybot
   e. DoS

4. A network of zombie computers can be used for
   a. DDoS attacks.
   b. Spamming.
   c. Phishing.
   d. Any or all of the above.
   e. None of the above; by definition, zombie computers are non-functional.

5. Spyware
   a. is installed on the majority of home PCs.
   b. can have a big negative impact on a PC's system performance.
   c. is sometimes distributed by large retail corporations.
   d. All of the above are true about spyware.
   e. None of the above are true about spyware.

6. What do you call a program that performs a useful task while at the same time carrying out some secret destructive act?
   a. DDoS
   b. Worm
   c. Trojan horse
   d. Macro virus
   e. None of the above

7. A PC's system software can be modified
   a. by any user with a legitimate password.
   b. by any user with system administrator access.
   c. by any user with a broadband Internet connection.
   d. only when the system is shut down.
   e. All of the above.

8. What are biometrics often used for?
   a. To measure virus strength
   b. To measure the speed of a spreading worm
   c. To assess the power of a Trojan horse to bring down a computer system
   d. To identify personnel before allowing them to have access to computer systems
   e. None of the above

9. Which of these factors increases the likelihood that a virus attack can rapidly spread and do widespread damage to an organization's computer infrastructure?
   a. All of the PCs in the organization use exactly the same Windows software and applications.
   b. Security patches are installed on the operating system exactly once each year to minimize the chance of an attack during installation.
   c. The system firewall is turned on at night for security and turned off during the day to facilitate communication.
   d. All of the above.
   e. None of the above.

10. What can a firewall do?
    a. Prevent packets from entering a LAN from the Internet
    b. Prevent packets from entering the Internet from a LAN
    c. Prevent requests for service from reaching a particular computer on the LAN from the Internet
    d. Prevent requests for service from reaching the Internet from a particular computer on the LAN
    e. All of the above

11. What can a surge protector protect a system from?
    a. Viruses
    b. Denial-of-service (DoS) attacks
    c. Power spikes
    d. Trojan horses and worms
    e. All of the above

12. Which of these statements is true about bugs in computer software today?
    a. It's impossible to eliminate all bugs in a large program.
    b. Even a program that appears to work can contain dangerous bugs.
    c. The bigger the system, the higher the number of bugs.
    d. All of the above.
    e. None of the above.

13. Autonomous systems
    a. are computers capable of running on battery power.
    b. can perform tasks without human input.
    c. are programs that can run on more than one operating system.
    d. are impossible to construct.
    e. have been outlawed by Congress.

14. When or where can computer viruses spread rapidly?
    a. In environments where files are passed around freely
    b. In documents as email attachments
    c. When infected shareware and freeware programs are downloaded onto PCs
    d. All of the above
    e. None of the above

15. According to the FBI, how do most cases of identity theft begin?
    a. With a pop-up Web advertisement
    b. With a stolen credit card
    c. With a stolen Social Security number
    d. During a phone solicitation
    e. During an email solicitation

Review Questions

1. Define or describe each of the key terms listed in the "Key Terms" section. Check your answers using the glossary.

2. Why is it hard to estimate the extent of computer crime?

3. Describe several different types of malware.

4. Give some examples of how spoofing or other types of social engineering might be used by computer criminals.

5. Describe several things you can do to protect yourself from identity theft.

6. Give several examples of *bad* passwords and explain why they are bad.

7. What are the two inherent characteristics of computers that make security so difficult?

8. Every afternoon at closing time, the First Taxpayer's Bank copies all the day's accumulated transaction information from disk to tape. Why?

9. In what ways can computer security protect the privacy of individuals? In what ways can computer security threaten the privacy of individuals?

10. What are smart weapons? How do they differ from conventional weapons? What are the advantages and risks of smart weapons?

Discussion Questions

1. Are computers morally neutral? Explain your answer.

2. Some virus creators claim that they're providing a valuable service to society by pointing out security holes in systems. Do you accept this argument? Why or why not?

3. What do you suppose motivates people to create computer viruses and other destructive software? What do you think motivates hackers to break into computer systems? Are the two types of behavior related?

4. Some people think all mail messages on the Internet should be encrypted. They argue that if everything is encrypted, the encrypted message won't stand out, so everybody's right to privacy will be better protected. Others suggest that this would just improve the cover of criminals with something to hide from the government. What do you think, and why?

5. Would you like to work in a business where all employees were required to wear smart badges? Explain your answer.

6. How do the issues raised in the debate over the missile defense system apply to other large software systems? How do you feel about the different issues raised in the debate?

Projects

1. Talk to employees at your campus computer labs and computer centers about security issues and techniques. What are the major security threats according to these employees? What security techniques are used to protect the equipment and data in each facility? Are these techniques adequate? Report on your findings.

2. Perform the same kind of interviews at local businesses. Do businesses view security differently than your campus personnel does?

3. If you have a login name and password on a college network, try changing your password. Will the system let you change your password to a common word such as "love" or "fish"? Does the system set a minimum number of characters for passwords? Are you allowed to have a letters-only password, or are you required to include nonalphabetic characters?

Sources and Resources

Books

Ethics for the Information Age, Third Edition, by Michael J. Quinn (Boston, MA: Addison Wesley, 2008). This book, written by the former *Tomorrow's Technology and You* coauthor, presents a framework for ethical decision-making and uses that framework to evaluate a wide variety of information- and technology-related issues. Major topics covered include networks and censorship, intellectual property, privacy, computer and network security, computer reliability, automation, and globalization.

A Gift of Fire: Social, Legal, and Ethical Issues in Computing, Third Edition, by Sara Baase (Upper Saddle River, NJ: Prentice-Hall, 2008). This popular text offers a thorough, easy-to-read overview of the human questions facing us as a result of the computer revolution: privacy, security, reliability, accountability, among others.

How Personal and Internet Security Work, by Preston Gralla (Indianapolis, IN: Que, 2006). This lavishly illustrated book

applies the successful *How Computers Work* formula to security-related issues. The first, and largest, part of the book focuses on Internet security and privacy, with tips on how to protect yourself from viruses, spam, spyware, and other hazards of the Internet. The second part deals with other privacy and security threats—identity theft, workplace surveillance, DNA matching, biometrics, and more. The words and pictures in this book should open plenty of eyes to the risks posed by digital technology today.

Hackers: Heroes of the Computer Revolution, by Steven Levy (New York, NY: Delta, 1994, 2001). This book helped bring the word *hackers* into the public's vocabulary. Levy's entertaining account of the golden age of hacking gives a historical perspective to today's antihacker mania.

The Cuckoo's Egg, by Cliff Stoll (New York, NY: Pocket Books, 1989, 1995). This best-selling book documents the stalking of an interloper on the Internet. International espionage mixes with computer technology in this entertaining, engaging, and eye-opening book.

The Art of Intrusion: The Real Stories Behind the Exploits of Hackers, Intruders, and Deceivers, by Kevin D.Mitnick and William L. Simon (Hoboken, NJ: Wiley, 2006). This book offers a rare glimpse inside the world of malicious hacking. Mitnick knows this world better than most, and his stories are well told.

The Fugitive Game, by Jonathan Littman (Boston, MA: Little, Brown and Company, 1997). This book chronicles the capture of Kevin Mitnick, America's number-one criminal hacker. The author cuts through the popular folklore of the time to tell the story as an objective journalist.

Cyberpunk—Outlaws and Hackers on the Computer Frontier, Updated Edition, by Katie Hafner and John Markoff (New York, NY: Simon & Schuster, 1995). This book profiles three hackers whose exploits caught the public's attention: Kevin Mitnick, a California cracker who vandalized corporate systems; Pengo, who penetrated U.S. systems for East German espionage purposes; and Robert Morris, Jr., whose Internet worm brought down 6,000 computers in a matter of hours.

The Hacker Crackdown: Law and Disorder on the Electronic Frontier, by Bruce Sterling (New York, NY: Bantam Books, 1993). Famed cyberpunk author Sterling turns to nonfiction to tell both sides of the story of the war between hackers and federal law enforcement agencies. The complete text is available online along with rest-of-the-story updates.

Ender's Game, by Orson Scott Card (New York, NY: Starscape, 2002). This award-winning, entertaining science fiction opus has become a favorite of the cryptography crowd because of its emphasis on encryption to protect privacy.

The Blue Nowhere, by Jeffery Deaver (New York, NY: Simon & Schuster, 2002). This suspenseful thriller involves a sadistic hacker who invades his victims' computers, meddles with their lives, and lures them to their deaths. Though fictional, the novel presents a terrifyingly accurate analysis of the lack of privacy and security on the Internet.

The Postman, by David Brin (New York, NY: Bantam, 1990). We often complain about government and technology, but what would happen if both were lost? This entertaining science fiction novel asks that question by placing the protagonist in a post-apocalyptic Pacific Northwest. The disappointing 1997 movie bears little resemblance to the novel.

Periodicals

Many popular magazines, from *Newsweek* to *Wired*, provide regular coverage of issues related to privacy and security of digital systems. Most of the periodicals listed here are newsletters of professional organizations that focus on these issues.

Information Security (www.infosecuritymag.com). This magazine focuses on security problems and solutions. Some of the articles are technical, but most are accessible to anyone with an interest in security issues.

The CPSR Compiler, published by Computer Professionals for Social Responsibility (CPSR.org). An alliance of computer scientists and others interested in the impact of computer technology on society, CPSR works to influence public policies to ensure that computers are used wisely in the public interest. Their newsletter has intelligent articles and discussions of risk, reliability, privacy, security, human rights, work, war, education, the environment, democracy, and other subjects that bring together computers and people.

EFFector, published by the Electronic Frontier Foundation (eff.org). This electronic newsletter is distributed by EFF, an organization "established to help civilize the electronic frontier." EFF was founded by Mitch Kapor and John Perry Barlow to protect civil rights and encourage responsible citizenship on the electronic frontier of computer networks.

Ethix (ethix.org). This bi-monthly publication is put together by the Center for Integrity in Business, an organization dedicated to promoting good business through appropriate technology and sound ethics.

11

Computers at Work, School, and Home

Objectives

After you read this chapter you should be able to:

▶ Describe how digital technology has changed the way people work in factories, offices, homes, and a variety of industries

▶ Describe several ways digital technology has changed the quality of jobs, both positively and negatively

▶ Speculate on how our society will adjust as more and more jobs are automated

▶ Explain how the information age places new demands on our educational system

▶ Describe several ways computers are used in education today

▶ Discuss the advantages and limitations of computers as instructional tools

▶ Describe the role of digital information technology in our homes and leisure activities in the next decade

> The best way to **predict the future** is to **invent it.**
>
> —*Alan Kay*

Alan Kay Invents the Future

Alan Kay has been inventing the future for most of his life. Kay was a child prodigy who composed original music, built a harpsichord, and appeared on NBC as a "Quiz Kid." Kay's genius wasn't reflected in his grades; he had trouble conforming to the rigid structure of the schools he attended. After high school he worked as a jazz guitarist and an Air Force programmer before attending college.

His Ph.D. project was one of the first microcomputers, one of several that Kay would eventually develop. In 1968 Kay was in the audience when Douglas Engelbart stunned the computer science world with a futuristic demonstration of interactive computing. Inspired by Engelbart's demonstration, Kay led a team of researchers at Xerox PARC (Palo Alto Research Center in California) in building the computer of the future—a computer that put the user in charge.

Working on a back-room computer called the Alto, Kay developed a bitmapped screen display with icons and overlapping windows—the kind of display that became the standard two decades later. Kay also championed the idea of a friendly user interface. To test user-friendliness, Kay frequently brought his children into the lab "because they have no strong motivation for patience." With feedback from children, Kay developed the first painting program and Smalltalk, the groundbreaking object-oriented programming language.

In essence, Kay's team developed the first personal computer—a single-user desktop machine designed for interactive use. But Kay, who coined the term "personal computer," didn't see the Alto as one. In his mind a true personal computer could go everywhere with its owner, serving as a calculator, a calendar, a word processor, a graphics machine, a communication device, and a reference tool. Kay called this mythical device the Dynabook.

Xerox failed to turn the Alto into a commercial success. But when he visited PARC, Apple's Steve Jobs was inspired by what he saw. Under Jobs a team of engineers and programmers built on the Xerox ideas, added many of their own, and developed the Macintosh—the first inexpensive computer to incorporate many of Kay's far-reaching ideas. Kay became a research fellow at Apple, where he called the Macintosh "the first personal computer good enough to criticize." Today, virtually all PCs have user interfaces based on Kay's groundbreaking work.

After 12 years at Apple, Kay became a research fellow at Disney, where he developed Squeak, a graphical programming tool for children. Kay describes his MO (modus operandi) as "start with end users, usually children, and try to think about the kinds of experiences that would help them to grow in different ways." In 2002 Kay joined Hewlett-Packard's research lab, while continuing his work with Viewpoints Research Institute, a nonprofit organization that works to improve general education and the understanding of complex systems. He left HP in 2005.

Kay continues his crusade for users, especially small users. He says, as with pencil and paper, "it's not

FIGURE 11.1 Alan Kay

a medium if children can't use it." Kay played a key role in the design of the revolutionary "One Laptop per Child" computer developed at MIT to empower and educate children worldwide. He continues his work on Squeak and other children's programming environments. And he is a spokesman for a movement to reinvent programming with revolutionary tools that are far easier to use.

Some of Kay's research is immediately practical; other projects have little to do with today's computer market. This kind of blue-sky research doesn't always lead to products or profits. But for Alan Kay it's the way to invent the future. ～

FIGURE 11.2 Alan Kay's Dynabook was the early prototype for the modern personal computer.

Alan Kay is one of many people whose work has had a profound effect on our workplaces, our schools, and our homes. In this chapter we'll look at the impact computer technology has had on these three facets of our lives. In later chapters we'll delve deeper into the practical business applications of information technology; in this chapter we'll pay more attention to the big picture.

Where Computers Work

Practically every institution that our society is based on, from the **local** to the **supranational**, is being **rendered obsolete**.

—Wired Founder Louis Rossetto on the fifteenth anniversary of the magazine

It's becoming harder all the time to find jobs that haven't been transformed by digital technology. Consider these examples:

■ *Entertainment.* The production of television programs and movies involves computer technology at every stage of the process. Videographers capture clips on digital video cameras and pipe them through FireWire cables into laptops for in-the-field editing. Scriptwriters use specialized word processors to write and revise scripts, and they use the Internet to beam the scripts between Hollywood and New York. Artists and technicians use graphics workstations to create special effects, from simple scene fadeouts and rolling credits to giant creatures and intergalactic battles. Musicians compose soundtracks using synthesizers and sequencers. Sound editors use computer-controlled mixers to blend music with digital sound effects and live-action sound. Even commercials—especially commercials—use state-of-the-art computer graphics, animation, and sound to keep you watching the images instead of changing the channel with your remote control.

■ *Publishing.* The news industry has been radically transformed by computer technology. Reporters scan the Internet for facts, write and edit stories on location using notebook computers, and transmit those stories to editors and to online blogs. Artists design charts and drawings with graphics software. Photo retouchers use computers instead of brushes and magnifying glasses to edit photographs. Production crews assemble pages with computers instead of typesetting machines and paste-up boards. Most newspapers produce Web editions in addition to traditional paper publications. A few publications have abandoned paper altogether.

■ *Medicine.* High-tech equipment plays a critical role in the healing arts, too. Hospital information systems store patient medical data, insurance records, and even X-rays. Local area networks enable doctors, nurses, technicians, dietitians, and office staff to view and update information throughout the hospital. Doctors use wireless handheld devices to browse databases for drug interactions, order prescriptions, and have those prescriptions transmitted to pharmacies for fulfillment. For patients who are outside the hospital walls in remote locations, doctors use the Web to practice *telemedicine.* Computers monitor patient vital signs in intensive care units in hospitals, at home, and on the street with portable units that analyze signals and transmit warnings when problems arise. Some surgeons never put their hands inside a patient. Instead, they do surgery by remote control, guiding robotic arms that enter the body through tiny incisions. Image-guided robotic technology can even be used to remove complex brain tumors.

■ *Airlines.* Without computers, today's airline industry simply wouldn't fly. Designers use computer-aided design software to design aircraft. Engineers conduct extensive computer simulations to test them. Pilots use computer-controlled instruments to navigate their planes, monitor aircraft systems, and control autopilots. Air traffic controllers on the ground use computerized air traffic control systems to keep track of incoming and outgoing flights. And, of course, computerized reservation systems make it possible for all those planes to carry passengers.

■ *Science.* From biology to physics, digital technology has changed every branch of science. Scientists collect and analyze data using remote sensing devices, notebook computers, and statistical analysis programs. They catalog and organize information in massive databases, many of which are accessible through the Web. They use supercomputers, workstations, and processor-sharing grids to create computer models of objects or environments that would otherwise be out of reach. They communicate with colleagues all over the world through the Internet. It's hard to find a scientist today who hasn't gone digital.

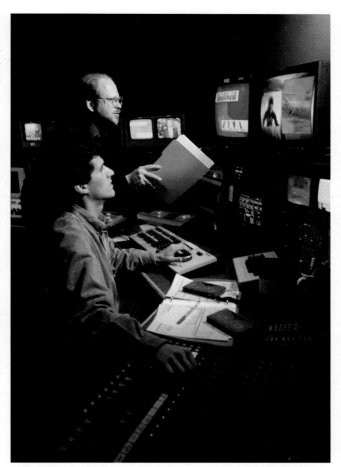

FIGURE 11.3 Computers play a critical role in video and film production today.

FIGURE 11.4 Medical students and professionals use this virtual emergency room to simulate processes of collecting vital signs and other patient data.

FIGURE 11.5 Computers make data recording and analysis much easier for botanists and other scientists.

To get a perspective on how digital technology affects the way we work, we consider the three digital workplaces that have attracted the most attention: the automated factory, the automated office, and the electronic cottage.

The Automated Factory

Businessmen go down with their businesses because they like the **old way** so well they cannot **bring themselves to change**.

—Henry Ford

In Chapter 15 we discuss the use of robots. In the modern automated factory *robots*—computer-controlled machines designed to perform specific manual tasks—are used for painting, welding, and other repetitive assembly-line jobs. But robots alone don't make an automated factory. Computers also help track inventory, time the delivery of parts, control the quality of the production, monitor wear and tear on machines, and schedule maintenance. As described in Chapter 6, engineers use CAD and computer-aided manufacturing technologies to design new products and the machines that build those products. Web cameras and Web displays built into assembly-line equipment enable workers and managers to monitor production and inventory from across the factory floor or across the continent.

An automated factory is more efficient than a traditional factory for two reasons:

- Automation allows for tighter integration of planning with manufacturing, reducing the time that materials and machines sit idle.
- Automation reduces waste in facilities, raw materials, and labor.

If automation is good news for factory owners, it poses a threat to blue-collar workers who keep traditional factories running. In a typical high-tech manufacturing firm today, approximately half of the staff are engineers, accountants, marketing specialists, and other white-collar workers.

The Automated Office

We now **mass produce information** the way we used to **mass produce cars**.

—*John Naisbitt, in* Megatrends

As the number of factory jobs declines, office work plays a more important role in our economy. Modern offices, like modern factories, have been transformed by digital technology. Many automated offices have evolved along with their computers.

Office Automation Evolution

Office automation goes back to the mainframe era, when banks, insurance companies, and other large institutions used computers for behind-the-scenes jobs such as accounting and payroll. Early computer sys-

FIGURE 11.6 The assembly line for manufacturing circuit boards is highly automated.

tems were faster and more accurate than the manual systems they replaced but were rigid and difficult to use. The machines and the technicians who worked with them were hidden away in basement offices, isolated from their organizations. The introduction of timesharing operating systems and database management systems enabled workers throughout organizations to access computer data. This kind of centralized computing placed computer-related decisions in the hands of central data processing managers.

PCs changed all that. Early Apple and Tandy computers were carried into offices on the sly by employees who wanted to use their own computers instead of company mainframes. But as managers recognized the power of word processors, spreadsheets, and other applications, they incorporated PCs into organizational plans. Jobs migrated from mainframes to desktops, and people used PCs to do things that the mainframes weren't programmed to do. In many organizations power struggles erupted between mainframe advocates and PC enthusiasts.

Enterprise Computing

Today PCs are essential parts of the overall computing structure for most business enterprises. Workers use word processing software to generate memos and reports, marketing teams create promotional pieces using desktop publishing tools, and financial departments analyze budgets using spreadsheets. They communicate with each other and with the outside world through email, instant messaging, video teleconferencing, and the Web.

Chief information officers (CIOs) and chief technology officers (CTOs)—the chief decision makers concerning enterprise computer systems and technology—recognize the value of the PC, although some raise questions about its cost. Research suggests that the *total cost of ownership (TCO)* of a typical PC is many times more than the cost of hardware and software. Training, support, maintenance, troubleshooting, and other expenses push the TCO up to anywhere from $7,000 to $13,000 per PC per year! To reduce costs, a few companies are replacing PCs with *thin clients*—network computers, Internet appliances, and similar devices. These low-cost, low-maintenance machines

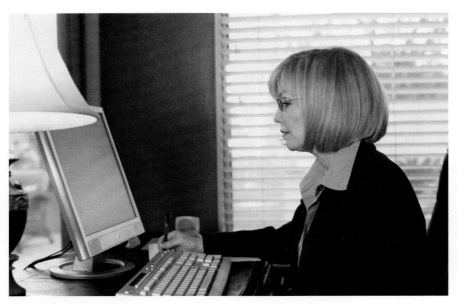

FIGURE 11.7 The CIO and CTO are responsible for managing the information systems and information technology in an organization.

enable workers to access critical network information without the overhead of a PC or workstation.

Some companies have abandoned mainframes altogether; others still use them for their biggest data-processing tasks. In the age of networks, the challenge for the IS manager is to integrate all kinds of computers, from mainframes to handheld devices into a single, seamless system. This approach, often called distributed computing, enables handheld computers, PCs, and mainframes to coexist fully and complement each other.

Workgroup Computing

Groupware enables groups of users to share calendars, send messages, access data, and work on documents simultaneously. The best groupware applications enable workgroups to do things that would be difficult otherwise; they actually change the way people work in groups. Many of these applications focus on the concept of *workflow*—the path of information as it flows through a workgroup. With groupware and telecommunication, workgroups don't need to be in the same room, or even the same time zone. During much of the 1990s, Lotus Notes dominated this market, offering a complete, if expensive, workgroup solution for corporations.

But the advent of the Web changed the workgroup landscape. Many of the functions of a groupware program such as Notes—email, teleconferencing, shared databases, electronic publishing, and others—were available for little or no cost through freely available Internet technologies. Corporations started installing intranets using HTML, Web browsers, and other Internet technologies. And because these intranets were built on standardized protocols such as TCP/IP, corporations could open their intranets to strategic partners and customers, creating extranets. Lotus, Microsoft, and other groupware manufacturers have responded by rebuilding their applications using standard Internet technologies and protocols, so their customers could have the best of both worlds: computer systems built on universal public standards, and customer support and customization from a groupware specialist.

Whether they're built from off-the-shelf Internet software or commercially customized packages, workgroup systems have the potential to transform radically the way businesses operate. Ted Lewis, author of *The Friction-Free Economy*, suggests that modern information technology makes an organization all of the following:

- Flatter, so it's easier for workers at any level to communicate with workers at other levels
- More integrated, so different business units communicate more openly with each other
- More flexible, so businesses can react more quickly to changes in their environments
- Less concerned with managing people and more concerned with managing processes

The Paperless Office

Experts have also predicted the paperless office—an office of the future in which magnetic and optical archives will replace reference books and file cabinets, electronic communication will replace letters and memos, and Web publications will replace newspapers

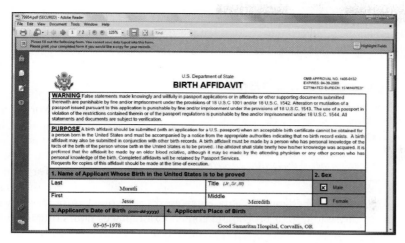

FIGURE 11.8 The U.S. government Web site includes many PDF forms that can be filled out and submitted online, saving paper, postage, and time.

and other periodicals. In the paperless office, people will read computer screens, not paper documents.

All of these trends are real: digital storage media are replacing many paper depositories, computers now deliver more mail messages than postal carriers do, and the Web has accelerated a trend toward online publishing. But so far, computers haven't reduced the flow of paper-based information. What has changed is the way people tend to use paper in the office. According to Paul Saffo of the Institute for the Future, "We've shifted from paper as storage to paper as interface. It is an ever more volatile, disposable, and temporary display medium."

HTML, XML, Adobe's popular *PDF (portable document format)*, and other technologies make it easier for documents to be transmitted and stored electronically without loss of formatting. But none of these technologies has made a significant dent in the wall of paper that surrounds most office workers. In the near future we may see a less-paper office, but a paperless office seems unlikely.

Electronic Commerce

The paperless office may be years away, but paperless money is already here for many organizations. **Electronic commerce (e-commerce)** has been around for years in its most basic form—buying and selling products through the Internet. But today there's more to electronic commerce than handling purchase transactions and funds transfers on the Internet. E-commerce also includes marketing, sales, support, customer service, and communication with business partners.

Early electronic commerce involved transactions between corporations. Even today *business-to-business (B2B)* transactions account for far more online sales than do *business-to-consumer (B2C)* transactions. But consumer commerce on the Web is growing fast. Many businesses, including computer manufacturers Dell and Apple, allow customers to order customized goods and services electronically; this kind of customization on demand wasn't practical or possible for most businesses before the Internet took hold. The Web is also fertile ground for person-to-person auctions, reverse auctions, and other types of sales that aren't practical outside the Web.

During the economic boom of the nineties, thousands of start-up dot-com companies experimented with a variety of new ways to do business on the Internet. Many of those dot-coms turned into dot-bombs, while others survived and prospered into the new decade.

In the second dot-com boom of the 2000s, hundreds of new companies created Web businesses based on Web 2.0 technology. Many of these Web 2.0 sites offer free services, from media sharing to social networking, financed by advertising.

The Electronic Cottage

Telecommuting may allow us to **redefine the issues** so that we're not simply moving people to work but also **moving work to people**.

—*Booth Gardner, former Washington governor*

Before the industrial revolution, most people worked in or near their homes. Today's telecommunications technology opens up new possibilities for modern workers to return home for their livelihood. For hundreds of thousands of writers, programmers, accountants, data-entry clerks, and other information workers, telecommuting by wireless or broadband connection replaces hours of commuting by car in rush-hour traffic. The term *telecommuter* typically refers to *all* home information workers, whether or not they're connected to their company computers via the Internet.

Futurist Alvin Toffler popularized the term electronic cottage to describe a home where technology enables a person to work at home. Toffler and others predict that the number of telecommuters will skyrocket in the coming decades. So far, the predictions have held. The number of employee teleworkers and contract teleworkers continues to grow. Each year more people do some or all of their work at home through Internet connections. At the same time, those who do telecommute are steadily increasing the amount of time they work from home.

Telecommuting makes sense; it's easier to move information than people. There are many strong arguments for telecommuting:

■ Telecommuting reduces the number of automobile commuters, thus saving energy, reducing pollution, and decreasing congestion and accidents on highways, streets, and parking lots.

■ Telecommuting saves time. If an information worker spends two hours each day commuting, that's two hours that could be spent working, resting, doing community activities, or relaxing with the family.

■ Telecommuting allows for a more flexible schedule. People who prefer to work early in the morning or late at night don't need to conform to standard office hours if they telecommute. For many people, including parents of small children, telecommuting may be the only viable way to maintain a job.

■ Telecommuting can increase productivity. Studies suggest that telecommuting can result in a 10 percent to 50 percent increase in worker productivity, depending on the job and the worker.

Of course, telecommuting isn't for everybody. Jobs that require constant interaction with coworkers, customers, or clients aren't conducive to telecommuting. Working at home requires self-discipline. Some people find they can't concentrate on work when they're at home—beds, refrigerators, neighbors, children, and errands are simply too distracting. Others have the opposite problem: workaholism cuts into family and relaxation time. Some workers who've tried full-time telecommuting complain that they miss the informal office social life and that their low visibility causes bosses to pass them over for promotions. In the words of one telecommuter, "When you're telecommuting you're far more productive than you can ever hope to be in the office, but you don't really have your finger on the pulse of the company." Most telecommuters report that the ideal work situation involves commuting to the office one or two days each week and working at home on the others.

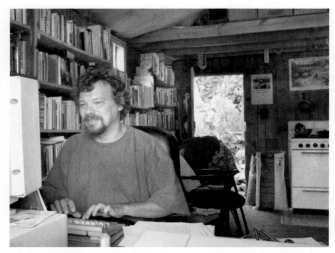

FIGURE 11.9 Novelist Richie Swanson, winner of the Peace Writing award, works at home . . . in his houseboat.

Working Wisdom

Considering Information Technology Careers

Until recently, people who wanted to work with computers were forced to choose among a few careers, most of which required highly specialized training. But when computers are used by everybody from fast-food salesclerks to graphic artists, just about anybody can have some kind of "information technology career." Still, many rewarding and high-paying computer-related careers require a fair amount of specialized education. If you're interested in a computer-related job, consider the following tips:

➡ *Learn touch typing.* Computers that can read handwriting and understand spoken English are probably in your future—but not your immediate future. Several low-cost typing tutorial programs can help you to teach your fingers how to type. The time you invest will pay you back quickly. The sooner you learn, the sooner you'll start reaping the rewards.

➡ *Use computers regularly to help you accomplish your immediate goals.* Word process your term papers. Use spreadsheets and other math software as calculation aids. Use the Web for research work. Computers are part of your future. If you use them regularly, they'll become second nature, like telephones and pencils. If you don't own a computer, find a way to buy one if you can.

➡ *Don't forsake the basics.* If you want to become a programmer, a systems analyst, a computer scientist, a computer engineer, or some other kind of computer professional, don't focus all your attention on computers. A few young technical wizards become successful programmers without college degrees; Bill Gates is probably the best-known example. But if you're not gifted and lucky, you'll need a solid education to land a good job. Math and communication skills (written and oral) are extremely important. Opportunities abound for people who can understand computers and communicate clearly.

➡ *Combine your passions.* If you like art and computers, explore computer art, graphic design, or multimedia. If you love ecology and computers, find out how computers are used by ecologists. People who can speak the language of computers and the language of a specialized field have opportunities to build bridges.

➡ *Ask questions.* The best way to find out more about information technology careers is to ask the people who have IT careers. Most people are happy to talk about their jobs if you're willing to listen.

➡ *Cultivate community.* Computer networks are changing our lives, but people networks are still more important for finding and landing that dream job. Get to know the people in the professional community. Take an active part in that community. Join professional organizations. Use social networks like LinkedIn to build links to professionals. Give your time and energy to public service projects related to your field. Even if it doesn't pay off with a job offer, you'll be doing good work.

➡ *If you can't find your dream job, build it yourself.* Inexpensive computer systems provide all kinds of entrepreneurial opportunities for creative self-starters: publishing service bureaus, Web-site design, multimedia video production, custom programming, commercial art and design, freelance writing, consulting—

FIGURE 11.10 You can use a program such as TypingMaster to learn touch typing.

the jobs are there for the making if you have the imagination and initiative.

➡ *When you're ready to look, don't forget the Web.* There are plenty of job bulletin boards, online career-hunting centers, Internet headhunters, and e-cruiters offering jobs that might be just right for you. Of course, some Internet job offers are scams, so check your sources.

➡ *Prepare for change.* In a rapidly changing world, lifelong careers are rare. Be prepared to change jobs several times. Think of education as a lifelong process. In Marshall McLuhan's words, "The future of work consists of learning a living."

Today thousands of companies offer home-based work arrangements to millions of employees. Many firms encourage "boundaryless" employees to work in virtual teams when and where they can best get their jobs done. Other companies have strict policies against working at home. They cite resentment among office-bound colleagues, weakened corporate loyalty, and the difficulties of holding meetings as reasons for their policies. Some analysts suggest that as multimedia teleconferencing systems become affordable, telecommuting will become more popular with both workers and management. Workers and managers will be able to have a telepresence in the workplace when they aren't physically present.

In the meantime, several variations on the electronic cottage are taking hold. Many enterprising families use home computers to help them run small businesses from their home offices. A growing number of corporations and government organizations are establishing satellite offices and shared regional work centers outside of major urban centers that allow workers to commute to smaller offices closer to their neighborhoods. High-powered PCs and wireless handheld devices enable salespeople, executives, consultants, engineers, and others to take their offices with them wherever they travel. These mobile workers don't travel to the office; they travel with the office. Many experts predict that *m-commerce*—mobile commerce—will spread into dozens of other professions in the coming decade.

Technology and Job Quality

John Henry told his captain, "A man ain't nothin' but a man. But before I let your steam drill beat me down **I'd die with a hammer in my hand**. . . ."

—*From the folk song "John Henry"*

When we think about automated factories, automated offices, and electronic cottages, it's easy to imagine utopian visions of computers in the workplace of tomorrow. But the real world isn't always picture perfect. For many workers, computers have caused more problems than they have solved. Workers complain of stress, depersonalization, fatigue, boredom, and a variety of health problems attributed to computers. Some of these complaints are directly related to technology; others relate to human decisions about how technology is implemented. In this section we look at some of the controversies and issues surrounding the automation of the workplace.

De-Skilling and Up-Skilling

When a job is automated, it may be de-skilled; that is, it may be transformed so that it requires less skill. For example, computerized cash registers in many fast-food restaurants replace numbered buttons with buttons labeled "large fries" or "chocolate shake." Clerks who use these machines don't need to know math or think about prices. They simply push buttons for the food items ordered and take the money; computers do the rest.

Some of the most visible examples of de-skilling occur when offices automate clerical jobs. When word processors and databases replace typewriters and file cabinets, traditional typing-and-filing jobs disappear. Many secretaries are repositioned in data-entry jobs—mindless, repetitive jobs where the only measure of success is the number of keystrokes typed into a terminal each hour. When a clerical job—or any job—is de-skilled, the worker's control, responsibility, and job satisfaction are likely to go down. De-skilled jobs typically offer less status and less pay.

In sharp contrast to those whose jobs are de-skilled into electronic drudgery, many workers find their jobs up-skilled by automation. For example, many clerical jobs become more technical as offices adopt complex databases, standardized spreadsheets,

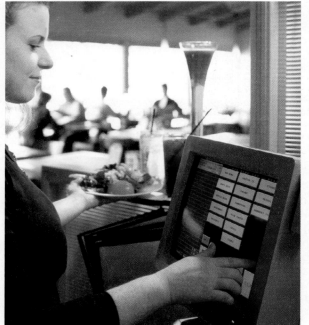

FIGURE 11.11 Specialized terminals such as this one make it easy to log restaurant orders. How is this person's job different as a result of this technology?

groupware systems and other digital technology. In some cases, clerical workers use computer systems to do jobs formerly done by high-paid professionals and technicians. While many clerical people enjoy the added challenge and responsibility, others may be frustrated doing highly technical work with inadequate training. Clerical workers are seldom consulted before their jobs are computerized. And even though their work is more technically demanding than before, few clerical workers see this up-skilling reflected in their paychecks or level of responsibility.

Monitoring and Surveillance

Another controversial aspect of workplace technology is computer monitoring—using computer technology to track, record, and evaluate worker performance, sometimes without the knowledge of the worker. Monitoring systems can provide a manager with reports showing the number of keystrokes for each clerk, the length of each phone call placed by an employee, details of Web wanderings, and the total amount of idle time for each computer. Some network software even enables a manager to view a copy of any worker's screen secretly at any time.

For a manager worried about worker productivity, computer monitoring can serve as a valuable source of information. But computer monitoring brings with it several problems:

- *Privacy*. In previous chapters we saw how the misuse of database and network technology can threaten personal privacy. Computer monitoring compounds that threat by providing employers with unprecedented data on workers. Some employers monitor personal email messages and punish or fire employees who send "unacceptable" messages.
- *Morale*. Privacy issues aside, computer monitoring can have a powerful negative impact on morale. Because employees can't tell when they're being monitored, many workers experience a great deal of stress and anxiety. The boss can be seen as an invisible eavesdropper rather than as a team leader.
- *Devalued skills*. In the traditional office, workers were evaluated based on a variety of skills. A slow-typing secretary could be valued for her ability to anticipate when a job needed to be done or her willingness to help others with problems. Computer monitoring tends to reduce a worker's worth to simple quantities such as "number of keystrokes per hour." In such systems a worker might be penalized for repairing a sticky chair, showing a neighbor how to reboot a terminal, or helping a troubled coworker.
- *Loss of quality*. Monitored workers tend to assume that "if it's not being counted, it doesn't count." As a result, quantity may become more important than quality.

Millions of workers are monitored by computer, including factory workers, telephone operators, truck drivers, and even managers. Cyber-snooping goes far beyond counting keystrokes and idle time. According to the American Management Association, more than three out of four U.S. companies engage in some kind of electronic surveillance of their employees, including monitoring Web connections, reviewing email, tracking keystrokes, monitoring phone use, videotaping, and checking computer files. In many of those companies, employees have been fired for "inappropriate" Internet use. One reason for corporate computer monitoring is the growing use of computer files in legal battles. According to Nancy Flynn, executive director of the ePolicy Institute, "Workers' email, blog, and Internet content creates written business records that are the electronic equivalent of DNA evidence." In the words of the director of one American Management Association study, "Workplace privacy is a contradiction in terms. It's an oxymoron. I know the illusion of privacy is there, but you are not using your own stuff. The phone, the keyboard, the connections, the job itself—they don't belong to you; they belong to the company, legally."

Electronic Sweatshops

Computer monitoring is common practice in data-entry offices. A data-entry clerk has a single job: to read information from a printed source—a check, a hand-printed form, or something else—and type it into a computer's database. A typical data-entry shop might contain hundreds of clerks sitting at terminals in a massive, windowless room.

FIGURE 11.12 Many data-entry workers spend their days in warehouse-sized buildings filled with computers.

Workers—often minorities and almost always female—are paid minimum wage to do mindless keyboarding. Many experience headaches, backaches, serious wrist injuries, stress, anxiety, and other health problems. And all the while, keystrokes and breaks are monitored electronically. Writer Barbara Garson calls these worker warehouses **electronic sweatshops** because working conditions bring to mind the oppressive factory sweatshops of the nineteenth century.

A growing number of electronic sweatshops are located across national borders from corporate headquarters in countries with lax labor laws and low wage scales. The electronic immigrants in these offshore shops don't need green cards to telecommute across borders, and they work for a fraction of what workers in developed countries cost. A data-entry clerk in the Philippines, for example, earns about $6 per day. With wages that low, many companies find it cost effective to have data entered twice and use software to compare both versions and correct errors. Offshore outsourcing is evidence of globalization, which will be discussed in more detail in the next section.

Automation, Globalization, and Outsourcing

My father had worked for the same firm for 12 years. They fired him. They **replaced him with a tiny gadget** this big that does everything that my father does only it **does it much better**. The depressing thing is **my mother** ran out and bought one.

—*Woody Allen*

When Woody Allen told this joke more than four decades ago, automation was generating a great deal of public controversy. Computer technology was new to the workplace, and people were reacting with both awe and fear. Many analysts predicted that automation would lead to massive unemployment and economic disaster. Others said that computers would generate countless new job opportunities. Today, most people are used to seeing computers where they work, and the computers-versus-jobs debate has cooled down. Job automation may not be a hot topic in comedy clubs today, but it's still an important issue for millions of workers whose jobs are threatened by machines.

Workers Against Machines

Automation has threatened workers since the earliest days of the industrial revolution. In the early nineteenth century, an English labor group called the Luddites smashed new textile machinery; they feared that the machines would take jobs away from skilled craftsmen. The Luddites and similar groups in other parts of Europe failed to stop the wheels of automation. Today the word *Luddite* refers to someone who resists technological change. Modern **Luddites** have been no more successful than their nineteenth-century counterparts in keeping computers and robots out of the workplace. Every year brings new technological breakthroughs that allow robots and computers to do jobs formerly reserved for humans.

When many people hear the word *automation,* they think of industrial robots and assembly lines, but automation has eliminated service jobs too. Consider how the office environment has changed since 1980. A couple of decades ago, executives dictated letters to assistants who typed them. Today executives type their own email messages. In the "old days," secretaries typed memos and mimeographed copies for distribution. Today desktop publishing systems allow employees to create fancy publications without secretarial assistance. Not too many years ago, office personnel wrote down phone messages for people who were out. Today that function is performed by voice mail. Easy-to-use spreadsheet programs have reduced the need for bookkeepers. These are just a few of the technological advances that have made many clerical tasks less labor intensive.

Of course, computer technology creates new jobs, too. Somebody has to design, build, program, sell, run, and repair the computers, robots, and networks. But many displaced workers don't have the education or skills to program computers, design robots, install networks, or even read printouts. Those workers are often forced to take low-tech, low-paying service jobs as cashiers or custodians, if they can find jobs at all. Because of automation the unskilled, uneducated worker may face a lifetime of minimum-wage jobs or welfare. Technology may be helping to create an unbalanced society with two classes: a growing mass of poor, uneducated people and a shrinking class of affluent, educated people.

World Wide Workers

In the past three decades, multinational corporations have closed thousands of factories in the United States and moved millions of manufacturing jobs to countries with less expensive labor. As we saw in the previous section, hundreds of thousands of data-entry clerk jobs have moved overseas, too. Now jobs requiring a more advanced education are becoming international. When you call a technical support or customer support line for a U.S. corporation, there's a good chance the call will be answered by an operator in India, Mexico, or another country with lower wages than those earned in the United States. Offshore operators are often given American-sounding names and trained not to reveal their locations to callers.

> They're **closing down** the **textile mill** across the railroad tracks
> Foreman says **these jobs** are going boys and they **ain't coming back**.
>
> —*Bruce Springsteen, in "My Hometown"*

The migration of jobs to countries where labor is less expensive is evidence of globalization—the creation of worldwide businesses and markets. Underwater fiber-optic cables and high-speed computerized telephone switches link Asia to the United States, allowing millions of simultaneous phone calls to take place. Leveraging this communications conduit, U.S. corporations have shifted hundreds of thousands of technical support jobs to India alone.

Even highly educated programmers and system designers in the United States are being replaced by offshore workers. The computer software industry in India, for example, employs tens of thousands of workers at a fraction of the cost of similarly skilled U.S. workers. The globalization of job markets makes it easy for corporations to shop for the cheapest labor forces with little or no regard for national boundaries, labor laws, environmental consequences, or community impact.

FIGURE 11.13 These technical support representatives in India are communicating with customers in the United States.

Nobody knows for sure how digital technology will affect employment in the coming decades; it's impossible to anticipate what might happen in 10 or 20 years. And experts are far from unanimous in their predictions. Some predict a steady increase in the number and types of jobs that are outsourced in coming years. Other sources suggest that fears of outsourcing are misplaced. Some even suggest that the amount of outsourcing will be counterbalanced, or even dwarfed, by insourcing—providing American labor to foreign companies.

Most experts agree that information technology will result in painful periods of adjustment for many factory workers, clerical workers, and other semiskilled and unskilled laborers whose jobs are automated or moved to Third World countries. But many also believe that the demand for professionals—especially engineers, teachers, and health-care professionals—is likely to rise as a result of shifts in the information economy.

Will we have enough skilled workers to fill those jobs? Economic growth may depend on whether we have a suitably trained workforce. The single most important key to a positive economic future may be education. But will we, as a society, be able to provide people with the kind of education they'll need? We'll deal with that question, and the critical issues surrounding education in the information age, later in this chapter.

Will We Need a New Economy?

Do **you own** the **stuff** you own, or does the **stuff** you own **own you**?

— Songwriter John Flynn, in "Who's Whose"

FIGURE 11.14 Australian aborigines work about four hours per day. Will automation make it possible to enjoy both a short workweek and a high material standard of living?

In the long run, education may not be enough. It seems likely that at some time in the future, machines will be able to do most of the jobs people do today. We may face a future of *jobless growth*—a time when automation alone creates adequate productivity increases, and no new jobs are created. In fact, since World War II, the productivity of workers in the most highly industrialized nations has more than doubled, thanks to automation. In the United States, the workweek has remained at 40 hours because we have chosen to use our increased productivity to raise our material standard of living rather than work less. The average house size has grown considerably, and the number of cars, phones and televisions per capita has risen. Americans don't take a lot of time off, either. Employers in the United States are not required to provide vacation benefits, and, on average, American workers get only 16 holidays and vacation days per year. In Japan and most Western European countries, workers enjoy between 25 and 32 vacation days a year.

Officially, the most highly developed Western economies have not yet reached the point of jobless growth, but that knowledge is cold comfort to unemployed, middle-aged autoworkers in Flint, Michigan, or Birmingham, England. Their jobs have been assaulted on two fronts: relentless industrial automation on one side and cheap foreign labor on the other. What happens to the people left behind by the new economy? If we can produce everything society needs without full employment, we'll have to ask some hard questions about our political, economic, and social systems:

■ Do governments have an obligation to provide permanent public assistance to the chronically unemployed?

- Should large companies be required to give several months' notice to workers whose jobs are being eliminated? Should they be required to retrain workers for other jobs?
- Should large companies be required to file "employment impact statements" before replacing people with machines in the same way they're required to file environmental impact statements before implementing policies that might harm the environment?
- If robots and computers are producing most of society's goods and services, should all of the profits from those goods go to a few people who own the machines?
- If a worker is replaced by a robot, should the worker receive a share of the robot's "earnings" through stocks or profit sharing? Should governments and businesses encourage job sharing and other systems that allow for less-than-40-hour jobs?
- What will people do with their time if machines do most of the work? What new leisure activities should be made available?
- How will people define their identities if work becomes less central to their lives?

These questions force us to confront deep-seated cultural beliefs and economic traditions, and they don't come with easy answers. They suggest that we may be heading into a difficult period when many old rules don't apply anymore. But if we're successful at navigating the troubled waters of transition, we may find that automation fulfills the dream expressed by Aristotle more than 2,000 years ago:

> *If every instrument could accomplish its own work, obeying or anticipating the will of others . . . if the shuttle could weave, and the pick touch the lyre, without a hand to guide them, chief workmen would not need servants, nor masters slaves.*

Education in the Information Age

The **future is a race** between **education** and **catastrophe**.

—*H. G. Wells*

The information age is not just affecting the workplace. Its influences are felt in our educational system, too. Before it's over, the information revolution will have a profound and permanent effect on the way we learn.

The Roots of Our Educational System

The American educational system was developed more than a century ago to teach students the basic facts and survival skills they would need for jobs in industry and agriculture—jobs they would probably hold for their entire adult lives. This industrial age system has been described as a factory model for three reasons:

- It assumes that all students learn the same way and that all students should learn the same things.
- The teacher's job is to "pour" facts into students, occasionally checking the level of knowledge in each student.
- Students are expected to work individually, absorb facts, and spend most of their time sitting quietly in straight rows.

FIGURE 11.15 In the traditional classroom, students are expected to absorb facts delivered by the teacher.

Despite its faults, the factory model of public education helped the United States dominate world markets for most of the twentieth century. But the world has changed drastically since the system was founded. Schools have changed, too, but not fast enough to keep pace with the information revolution. Most experts today agree that we need to rebuild our educational system to meet the demands of the information age.

Information Age Education

Education is the **kindling of a flame**, not the filling of a vessel.

—Socrates

What should education provide for students in the information age? Research and experience suggest several answers:

- *Technological familiarity*. Many of today's older workers are having trouble adjusting to the information age because of technophobia—the fear of technology. These people grew up in a world without computers, and they experience anxiety when they're forced to deal with them. To prepare for the future, students need to learn how to work comfortably with all kinds of knowledge tools, including pencils, books, calculators, computers, and the Internet. But technological familiarity shouldn't stop with learning how to work with tools. Students need to have a clear understanding of the *limitations* of the technology and the ability to assess the benefits and risks of applying technology to a problem. They need to be able to *question* technology.
- *Literacy*. In the information age, it's more important than ever that students graduate with the ability to read and write. Many jobs that did not require reading or writing skills a generation ago now use high-tech equipment that demands literacy. A factory worker who can't read computer screens isn't likely to survive the transition to an automated factory.
- *Mathematics*. In the age of the five-dollar calculator, many students think learning math is a waste of time. In fact, some educators argue that we spend too much time teaching students how to do things such as long division and calculating square roots—skills that adults seldom, if ever, do by hand. These arithmetic skills have little to do with being able to think mathematically. To survive in a high-tech world, students need to be able to see the mathematical systems in the world around them and apply math concepts to solve problems. No calculator can do that.
- *Culture*. An education isn't complete without a strong cultural component. Liberal arts and social studies help us recognize the interconnections that turn information into knowledge. Culture gives us roots when the sands of time shift. It gives us historical perspective that allows us to see trends and prepare for the future. Culture provides a human framework with which to view the impact of technology. It also gives us the global perspective to live in a world where communication is determined more by technology than by geography.
- *Communication*. In the information age, communication is a survival skill. Isolated factory workers and desk-bound pencil pushers are vanishing from the workplace. Modern jobs involve interactions—between people

FIGURE 11.16 Modern education focuses on helping students learn how to think and learn.

and machines and between people and people. The fast-paced, information-based society depends on our human ability to communicate, negotiate, cooperate, and collaborate, both locally and globally.

■ *Learning how to learn.* Experts predict that most of the jobs that will exist in coming decades do not exist today and that most of those new jobs will require education past the high school level. With this rapidly changing job market, it's unreasonable to assume that workers can be trained once for lifelong jobs. Instead of holding a single job for 40 years, today's high school or college graduate is likely to change jobs several times. Those people who do keep the same jobs will have to deal with unprecedented change. The half-life of an engineer's specialized knowledge—the time it takes for half of that knowledge to be replaced by more current knowledge—is slightly more than three years.

These facts suggest that we can no longer afford to think of education as a one-time vaccination against illiteracy. In the information age, learning must be a lifelong process. To prepare students for a lifetime of learning, schools must teach students more than facts; they must make sure students learn how to think and learn.

High-Tech Schools

The information age is making new demands on our educational system, requiring radical changes in what and how people learn. Digital technology is playing a critical role in the transformation of our schools. Computers have found their way into just about every school in the U.S. Students and teachers are using those computers in a variety of ways.

> The only thing we know about **the future** is that it will be **inhabited by our children**. Its quality, in other words, is **directly proportional** to **world education**.
>
> —*Nicholas Negroponte, Director of the MIT Media Lab*

Computer-Aided Instruction

In 1953 B. F. Skinner visited his daughter's fourth-grade class and watched the teacher try to teach arithmetic to everyone in the class at the same speed. The experience inspired him to build a teaching machine—a wooden box that used cards, lights, and levers to quiz and reward a student. His machine was

> The ordinary classroom **holds the bright kids back** and makes the kids that need more time **go too fast**. They fall further and further behind until they can't keep up—**it's a terrible system**.
>
> —*B. F. Skinner, father of behaviorist psychology and inventor of the first "teaching machine"*

based on the principles of behaviorist psychology: allow the student to learn in small steps at an individualized pace and reward correct answers with immediate positive feedback. When PCs appeared in classrooms, students started using drill-and-practice software based on those same principles: individualized rate, small steps, and positive feedback.

A traditional drill-and-practice program presents the student with a question and compares the student's answer with the correct answer. If the answers match, the program offers rewards or praise. If the answers don't match, the program offers an explanation and presents a similar problem. The program may keep track of student responses and tailor questions based on error patterns; it might also provide reports on student progress to the teacher. Today most drill-and-practice programs embed the lesson in animated games, but the underlying principles remain the same.

Computer-aided instruction (CAI) software is the name that was given to this kind of courseware (educational software). It's still popular for three reasons: It's relatively easy to produce, it can be easily combined with more traditional educational techniques, and it produces clear, demonstrable results. CAI offers many advantages over workbooks and worksheets:

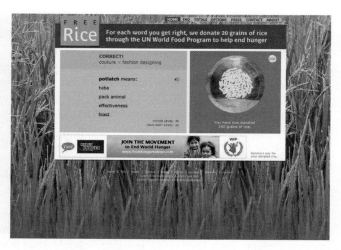

FIGURE 11.17 Students practice basic math skills with programs like *Grade Builder Algebra I* (left). FreeRice.com (right) uses basic drill-and-practice techniques to help visitors build their vocabularies while feeding the hungry.

■ *Individualized learning.* The individual student can learn at his or her own pace. Teachers can spend their time working one-on-one with students—an important activity that's all but impossible in typical presentation-and-discussion classrooms.

■ *Motivation.* CAI can turn practice into a game. It motivates students to practice arithmetic, spelling, touch-typing, piano playing, and other skills that might otherwise be tedious to learn.

■ *Confidence.* CAI can help children become comfortable with computers as well as with the subject matter being taught. A well-designed program is infinitely patient, and it

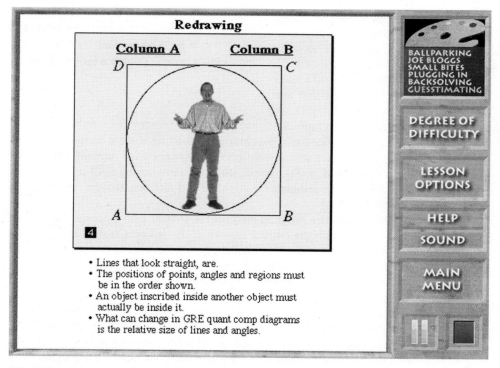

FIGURE 11.18 Students can prepare for standardized tests using *Inside the SAT and ACT*.

enables students to make mistakes in private. Research has shown that younger children, disadvantaged children, and in particular students with learning disabilities tend to respond positively to CAI.

Not all CAI software deserves praise. Much CAI software is flawed because it gives inappropriate feedback, enables students to practice mistakes, and discourages students from moving into new material. Even the best CAI can work only with tightly defined subjects in which every question can have a single, clear, unambiguous answer. CAI presents information in the form of facts, leaving no room for questioning, creativity, or cooperation. In a sense, CAI programs students.

Programming Tools

In the 1960s, with colleagues at MIT, Seymour Papert developed a computer language called LOGO so children could program computers rather than the other way around. The LOGO programming language enjoyed some success but never became widely adopted.

In 1999, researchers at Carnegie Mellon developed Alice, a free, open source educational programming language written in Java. Controlled studies suggest that this easy-to-learn language improves learning and retention in first-time programmers. Alice 3.0 incorporates 3-D character models from The Sims, one of the most popular video games of all time.

> In many schools today, the phrase "computer-aided instruction" means **making the computer teach the child**. One might say the computer is being used to **program the child**. In my vision, **the child programs the computer** and, in doing so, both acquires a **sense of mastery** over a piece of the most modern and powerful technology and establishes an **intimate contact** with some of the **deepest ideas** from science, from mathematics, and from the art of intellectual model building.
>
> —*Seymour Papert, in* Mindstorms

Another group of researchers from Apple and other companies took a different approach when they developed Stagecast Creator. Stagecast Creator is a tool for *programming by demonstration*. In programming by demonstration, the computer "observes" the user performing the correct action on a particular input. The computer is then able to execute the same series of steps (the same algorithm) using different inputs.

With Stagecast Creator's familiar painting and drawing tools, children can create characters and objects inside a window. As the children demonstrate how characters and objects interact, the computer constructs "before" and "after" rules. When the child hits the Play button, the computer uses these rules to control the behavior of the characters inside the window. With this kind of system, children and novice computer users can create simulations and interactive games without learning a programming language. It will probably be years before we know the impact that Alice, Stagecast Creator, and other educational programming tools will have on students.

Simulations and Games

When Papert developed LOGO, he based his educational psychology on the work of renowned Swiss developmental psychologist Jean Piaget. According to Piaget, children have a natural gift for learning on their own; they learn to talk, get around, and think without formal training. A child growing up in France learns French effortlessly because the child's environment has the necessary materials. In Papert's vision, the computer can provide an environment that makes learning mathematics, science, and the arts as effortless as learning French in France.

> No compulsory learning can remain **in the soul**. . . . In teaching children, **train them by a kind of game**, and you will be able to **see more clearly** the natural bent of each.
>
> —*Plato, in* The Republic, Book VII

Many **educational simulations** today are based on the same idea: Children learn best through exploration and invention. These simulations allow students to explore artificial environments, whether imaginary or based on reality. Educational simulations are metaphors

Screen Test

Programming by Demonstration

GOAL *To learn principles of programming and problem solving using a graphical simulation tool. In this example, to create an animated simulation in which dogs eat bones and evade dog catchers.*

TOOL *Stagecast Creator*

1. You click the star button three times to create three different characters that look like paint splats.

2. You use the palette button to invoke a simple painting program that lets you draw or import distinctive images for the characters: dog, dog catcher, and bone.

3. You use the rubber stamp tool to make copies of these characters, scattering them around the window.

4. You click the rule button to tell the computer you are going to demonstrate a legal action. You highlight a dog with an empty space to its right, and then you drag the dog into the empty space. You are demonstrating that a dog will move to the right if the space is empty.

5. The computer creates a rule from your demonstration.

6. You demonstrate another one of the dog's behaviors. You highlight a dog next to a dog catcher with an empty space above his head. You drag the dog into the empty space. The dog evades the dog catcher by moving to the empty space above him.

7. The computer creates another rule from your demonstration.

8. You highlight a dog next to a bone. You delete the bone and move the dog into the space where the bone was. The computer creates a third rule for a dog eating a bone.

9. You hit the play button to run the simulation. All of the dogs simultaneously move around the window, obeying the rules you have created.

10. After the simulation has run for a while, there is a big pile of dogs near the top of the screen. These dogs do not move, because there are no movement rules for a dog in front of two dog catchers or a dog in front of another dog. At this point, you can improve the simulation by demonstrating what dogs should do in these situations. Or you can demonstrate how dog catchers move around.

FIGURE 11.19

designed to focus student attention on the most important concepts. Most educational simulations have the look and feel of a game, but they challenge students to learn through exploration, experimentation, and interaction with other students.

With a simulation, the students are in control of the learning environment. It's up to them to find and use information to draw conclusions. Students can experience the consequences of their actions without taking real-world risks. Simulations enable students to have experiences that wouldn't be possible otherwise. Instead of simply spewing facts, simulations provide a context for knowledge.

FIGURE 11.20 *Crazy Machines 2* is a simulation program in which players learn principles of physics by building imaginary machines.

Students love playing well-designed simulation games, but many schools don't use simulations because there's no room for them in the formal curriculum. In spite of our culture's age-old tradition of learning through games, many educators question the educational value of games in the classroom. Of course, educational simulations, like all simulations, come up short as substitutes for reality. Many students can play with simulation games for hours without learning anything concrete. The risks of simulations, outlined in Chapter 5, apply to educational simulations, too. But when field trips or full-scale scientific experiments aren't possible, computer simulations can offer affordable alternatives.

Productivity Tools

Today the trend in schools is clearly toward teaching children to use computers as tools. Word processors, spreadsheets, graphics programs, Web browsers, search engines—the software tools used by adults—are the tools students learn most often in schools. Once students learn to use these general-purpose tools, they can put them to work in and out of school.

For me, the phrase **computer as pencil** evokes the kind of uses I imagine **children of the future** making of computers. Pencils are used for **scribbling** as well as writing, **doodling** as well as drawing, for **illicit notes** as well as for official assignments.

—Seymour Papert, in Mindstorms

Some schools also provide special-purpose tools for classroom use, including these:

- Laboratory sensing hardware and software that can be used to collect scientific data (such as temperature) and convert it into computer data to be analyzed by students
- Collaborative writing groupware that enables students to work collectively on creative writing and editing projects
- Music synthesizers with sequencing and notation software for teaching music composition

Digital Media

I hear and I **forget**, I see and I **remember**, I do and I **understand**.

—Ancient Chinese proverb

Many teachers use computers and multimedia tools to create in-class presentations. Presentations can range from simple PowerPoint slide shows to elaborate graphical simulations or multimedia demonstrations. Unlike videos and other linear technologies, computer-based presentations can be customized to meet the needs of each class.

To get students more involved in the learning process, many teachers use interactive multimedia software that puts students in control. Sometimes these interactive lessons are created by teachers; more often they're purchased or explored through the Web.

In many classrooms, students use authoring tools to create their own multimedia presentations. Students create CD-ROMs, videos, interactive kiosks, podcasts, and (especially) Web pages about their classes, schools, student organizations, and special projects. The Web makes it possible for these students to reach worldwide audiences with their presentations.

This kind of student involvement promotes learning, but it has drawbacks. One problem is economic: Few schools can afford the hardware, software, and floor space for multiple student media workstations. Another problem is both social and political: When students are creating or using interactive media, they aren't conforming to the traditional factory model. Instead of taking notes they're taking control of the machinery and the learning process. The teacher becomes a supervisor and a mentor rather than a conveyor of information. Many teachers lack the training and experience to supervise these kinds of projects. And many administrators tend to give priority to more orthodox programs aimed at raising standardized test scores.

Supporting Special Needs

Computers play an important role in improving the educational experience of students with special needs. Two federal laws, the Individuals with Disabilities Act (IDEA) and Americans with Disabilities Act (ADA), have established the goal that every student should have equal access to school programs and services. It calls for schools to use assistive technology where appropriate to achieve the goal of equal access.

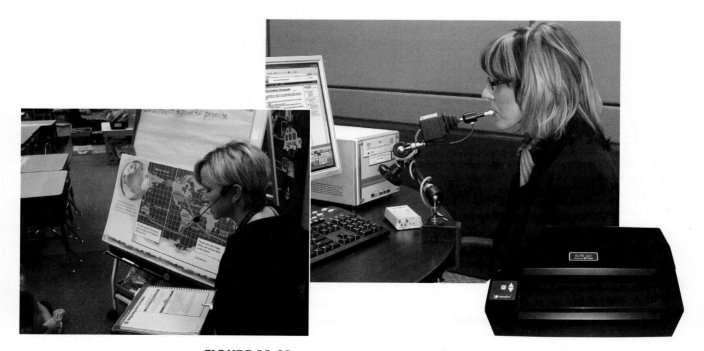

FIGURE 11.21 A wireless system, left, uses FM radio waves to amplify the teacher's voice for this student who is hearing impaired. A "sip/puff" device, middle, is one way for a computer user with quadriplegia to control a cursor. A Tiger printer, right, embosses both Braille and graphics, giving students who are visually impaired the ability to access mathematical, scientific, and engineering documents that make heavy use of graphics.

The assistive technology that schools provide students with special needs covers a broad spectrum of devices. For many students, low-tech devices are sufficient to accommodate their needs. For example, students with poor muscle control can benefit from rubber pencil grips. Line magnifiers enlarge lines of type for students with impaired vision and learning disabilities. Other students need a middle level of technology to make the classroom experience accessible. Wireless systems amplify sounds for students with hearing impairments, and handheld talking dictionaries assist students who have difficulties with reading or spelling. High-tech devices like the Kurzweil Reading Machine can open up the world of books to sightless students.

Many devices have been designed to help students with special needs interact with computers. Some students are unable to use a traditional computer mouse or keyboard. Alternatives to the mouse include touch screens, trackballs, headsticks, and eyegaze systems. Alternative keyboards have keys that are much larger or smaller than usual, or a different arrangement of letters. Another text input option is speech recognition software. With augmentative communication software, a computer can provide a student who does not speak the ability to communicate with others using text, graphics, and sound.

Distance Education: Virtual Schools

For some students the most important application of computers in schools is distance education—using technology to extend the educational process beyond the walls of the school. Grade-school students can network with kids in other parts of the world through the Internet. Middle-school classes can use electron microscopes, telescopes, and other powerful tools around the world through real-time Internet connections. High-school correspondence courses can be completed via the Internet rather than by mail. Students with handicaps can do coursework without traveling to central sites. Two-way video links allow "visiting" experts to talk to students in outlying classrooms and answer their questions in real time. Networked school districts can offer multischool videoconference courses in Chinese, college-level calculus, and other subjects that might have tiny enrollments if offered at only a single school. Teachers can receive additional education without leaving their districts.

> Very soon now, it might not matter where **your body** happens to be … as long as you maintain a **presence in the networks**.
>
> —*Steven K. Roberts, technomad*

Telecommunication technology is particularly important for students in remote locations. If a child in a small town develops an interest in a narrow subject, whether it's aboriginal anthropology, classical Russian ballet, or designing user interfaces for handheld devices, that student may find pursuing that interest a discouraging process. But through an Internet connection, reference materials, special-interest blogs and forums, educational podcasts, long-distance mentors, and like-minded communities are all within reach. In many areas, rural interactive television networks keep remote schools and towns from fading away.

Distance education is particularly attractive to parents with young children. Two-thirds of the adult distance learners are female, and 80 percent of them have children. Distance education also offers promise for workers whose jobs are changed or eliminated. Many displaced and dissatisfied workers can't afford to relocate their families to college towns so they can learn new skills. But if colleges and universities offer electronic outreach programs, these people can update their skills while remaining in their communities.

Since 1990 online degree programs have appeared at dozens of universities and colleges. Students use the Internet to do everything from ordering books to taking final exams. Many online students see their professors in person for the first time at graduation ceremonies.

The demand for distance education is growing rapidly. In some countries distance education students comprise 40 percent of the total undergraduate population. Some experts predict that a few hundred huge, distance-ed universities will put most traditional universities out of business.

Of course, a college education is more than a collection of information. Students learn and grow as a result of all kinds of experiences in and out of the classroom. Many significant learning experiences can't be transmitted through phone lines and TV cables. Dropout rates for distance learning students are higher than those for classroom students. For many students, there's no substitute for face-to-face communication with teachers and other students.

But the tools of distance learning, sometimes called *e-learning* tools, can be applied to on-campus learning, too. Blogs, forums, podcasts, online gradebooks, computerized testing, and virtual learning environment can, if properly applied, benefit students near and far. The combination of e-learning with face-to-face teaching—sometimes called *blended learning*—is, for many students, the best of both worlds. On campus or off, e-learning is an important step toward an educational system that encourages lifelong learning.

Technology at School: Midterm Grades

The business of education is to give the student both **useful information** and **life-enhancing experience**, one largely measurable, the other not. . . .

—*John Gardner, in* The Art of Fiction

Many schools have been using computers in classrooms since the 1980s. Many classrooms connected to the Web in the late 1990s and early 2000s. In these days of shrinking budgets, taxpayers are asking whether classroom computer technology pays off. Has it lived up to its promise as an educational tool in the schools? According to most experts, the answer is mixed but optimistic.

High Marks

A number of independent studies have confirmed that information technology can improve education. Here are some findings:

- Students improve problem-solving and reasoning skills, outscore classmates, and learn more rapidly in a variety of subject areas and situations when using technology as compared to conventional methods of study.
- Students find computer-based instruction to be more motivational, less intimidating, and easier to persist in than traditional instruction is. Their attitudes toward learning consistently improve when instructional technology is used.
- In many cases students' self-esteem is increased when they use computers. This change is most dramatic in cases of at-risk youngsters and students with handicaps.
- Using technology encourages cooperative learning, turn taking among young children, peer tutoring, and other valuable social skills.
- Computer technology can make learning more student centered and stimulate increased teacher-student interaction.
- Well-designed interactive multimedia systems can encourage active processing and higher-order thinking.
- Students who create interactive multimedia reports often learn better than those who learn with more traditional methods.
- Students can become more productive, more fluid writers with computers.
- Computers can help students master the basic skills needed to participate and succeed in the workforce.
- Positive changes occur gradually as teachers gain experience with the technology.
- Technology can facilitate educational reform.
- Students with technology integrated into their classroom see the benefit in each major subject area.
- Students with and without special needs show increased achievement from preschool through higher education when technology is incorporated into their curricula.
- Students and teachers with positive attitudes toward technology gain the most.

■ Students often learn better when the technology facilitates working in groups. Students experience a greater benefit from technology when their teachers receive professional training. Teachers report that they are more enthusiastic about technology when provided with training.

Room for Improvement

This stuff is **so bad**, it must be **educational**.

—Aunt Selma on The Simpsons

Other findings temper—and sometimes contradict—these positive conclusions. Researchers have also observed the following:

■ If the only thing that changes is the delivery medium (from traditional media to computer media), the advantages of technology are small—or nonexistent.

■ Students and teachers forget advanced computer skills if they don't use them.

■ Students have unequal access to technology; economically disadvantaged students have less computer access at school and at home. Sadly, these are the students who can benefit most when given access to technology.

■ Technology doesn't reduce teacher workloads; if anything, it seems to make their jobs harder. (Of course, many teachers welcome the extra work because they believe it brings results.)

■ Sometimes there's a gender gap that puts the computer room in the boys' domain; the gap can be reduced by stressing computer activities that involve collaboration.

■ Many of the outcomes of technology-based education don't show up with traditional educational assessment methods and standardized tests.

■ Sending students to a computer lab for 30 minutes a week has little or no value; computers are more effective when they're in classrooms where students can use them regularly.

■ Younger students may be better served by art, music, and shop classes than by computer classes; unfortunately, these important parts of the curriculum are often eliminated to make room for computers.

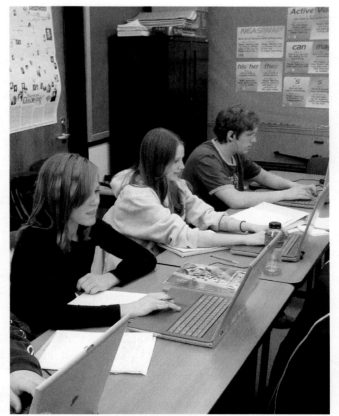

Stories abound of reduced dropout rates and attitudinal changes among at-risk students; improved math, reading, and language scores; and overall academic improvement among students in high-tech schools. But computer technology doesn't always bring happy headlines. In some schools computers are little more than expensive, time-consuming distractions. What makes technology work for some schools and not for others? A closer look at the success stories reveals that they didn't achieve results with technology alone. When we compare these schools with less fortunate schools, several issues emerge:

■ *Money.* Most American schools have found funds to purchase computers. Unfortunately, many of those computers are technologically outdated. Most classrooms don't even have phone lines, let alone Internet connections. Not surprisingly, computers tend to be concentrated in affluent school districts, so economically disadvantaged students have the least access to them.

■ *Planning and support.* When school districts spend money on technology without thoughtful long-term planning and sustained support, their investments are not likely to pay off.

FIGURE 11.22 Research shows that writing improves when students use word processors. Henrico County, Virginia, has been a strong proponent of the technology in education. Here, students are pictured with their laptops.

FIGURE 11.23 Technology can have a positive impact on education if it's part of a program that includes teacher training, ongoing support, and radical restructuring of the traditional "factory model" curriculum.

■ *Teacher training.* Unfortunately, teacher training is often missing from schools' high-tech formulas. Teachers need training, support, and time to integrate technology into their curricula.

■ *Restructuring.* Just as businesses need to rethink their organizational structures to automate successfully, schools need to be restructured to make effective use of computer technology. The goal is education, and technology is just one tool for achieving that goal. Interactive media, individualized instruction, telecommunication, and cooperative learning simply don't fit well into the factory school. To meet the educational challenges of the information age, we'll need to invest in research and planning involving teachers, students, administrators, parents, businesses, and community leaders.

The Classroom of Tomorrow

The further one pursues knowledge, **the less one knows**.

—*Lao Tse, 500 BC*

To give us a head start in building the schools of the future, Apple, IBM, Microsoft, Toshiba, and other companies, along with some state and local governments, have helped create model technology classrooms and schools in communities around the United States and Canada. Most of these pilot projects suggest that technology can, in the proper context, have a dramatic effect on education. For example, here's a quote from Apple's Web site summarizing the results of the Apple Classroom of Tomorrow (ACOT) project:

After more than a decade of research, ACOT's research demonstrated that the introduction of technology into classrooms can significantly increase the potential for learning, especially when it is used to support collaboration, information access, and the expression and representation of students' thoughts and ideas. Realizing this opportunity for all students, however, required a broadly conceived approach to educational change that integrated new technologies and curricula with new ideas about learning and teaching, as well as with authentic forms of assessment.

Information technology, then, can be a powerful change agent but not by itself. In an interview for online magazine *ZineZone*, educational computing pioneer Seymour Papert was asked whether technology is a Trojan horse for systematic and lasting change. His reply: "I think the technology serves as a Trojan horse all right, but in the real story of the Trojan horse, it wasn't the horse that was effective, it was the soldiers inside the horse. And the technology is only going to be effective in changing education if you put an army inside it which is determined to make that change once it gets through the barrier."

The High-Tech Home

There is **no reason** for any individual to have a **computer in their home**.

—*Ken Olson, president of Digital Equipment Corporation, 1977*

The same year Ken Olson made this statement, Apple introduced the Apple II computer. In the years that followed, Apple, Commodore, Tandy, Atari, IBM, and dozens of other companies managed to sell computers to millions of individuals who had "no reason" to buy them.

Today there are more computers in homes than in schools. Most American homes contain at least one computer. The small office, home office market—dubbed *SOHO* by the industry—is one of the fastest-growing computer markets today. While many home computers gather dust, others are being put to work, and play, in a variety of ways.

Household Business

Frank Gilbreth, a turn-of-the-century pioneer of motion study in industry, applied "scientific management" techniques to his home. He required his 12 children to keep records on bathroom "work-and-process charts" of each hair combing, tooth brushing, and bathing. He gave them demonstrations on efficient bathing techniques to minimize "avoidable delays." While it may have worked for Gilbreth, this "scientific management"

FIGURE 11.24 Today's search engines can provide instant recipes when given a list of ingredients. Within seconds of typing in a list of items in her refrigerator, this cook has a recipe that uses them all.

approach to home life is not likely to catch on today. Still, certain aspects of family life are unavoidably businesslike, and a growing number of people are turning to computers to help them take care of business.

Computer owners generally use many of the same applications at home that they use in their offices: Web browsers for entertainment, research, shopping, and other applications; email programs for connecting with others; word processors for writing; personal information managers for tracking calendars and contacts; and accounting programs for managing income and expense.

Few home computer users type *every* financial transaction into the computer. Some people type in only "important" transactions. Others download transaction summary statements from their bank Web sites. But for most people computerized money management won't happen until there's an effortless way to record transactions—perhaps a device that, when inserted into the computer, can tell the software about each purchase and paid bill.

That device may turn out to be a smart card. A typical **smart card** looks like a standard credit card, but instead of a magnetic strip, it contains embedded circuits that can process information along with some kind of input/output device. A memory card contains memory but no microprocessor; a microprocessor card contains memory along with a tiny CPU. Contact smart cards use a small contact area with several gold-plated contacts for input and output. Contactless smart cards use wireless RFID technology to communicate with card

FIGURE 11.25 The Octopus card is a contactless smart card used like an electronic wallet by over 95 percent of the population of Hong Kong. Octopus cards are used to store and transfer payments for mass transit, parking, vending machines, convenience stores, supermarkets, and more.

readers and writers. Smart cards can also contain cryptographic hardware and other security circuitry.

Smart cards are obvious candidates to replace magnetic-strip credit cards. In addition to storing critical ID information, a smart card can automatically record each transaction for later retrieval. But smart cards have other applications, too. College students use smart cards as meal tickets. Office workers use smart cards as keys to access sensitive data on computers. Smart cards have replaced food stamps and drivers' licenses in some states and countries. People all around the world use smart cards to pay highway tolls and unscramble cable TV broadcasts In France, smart cards are used for health insurance. Malaysia, Spain, and Belgium were among the first of many countries to use smart cards as universal ID cards. Of course, many of these smart card applications raise questions about protection of personal privacy. Future smart cards will use pattern recognition techniques to verify signatures on checks or credit slips and help prevent millions of dollars in fraud and forgery.

Education and Information

Newspapers as we know them **won't exist**. They will be printed for a **readership of one**. **Television** won't simply have sharper pictures. You'll have one button that says **tell me more**, and another button that says **tell me less**.

—*Nicholas Negroponte, director of the MIT Media Lab*

Millions of people use home computers for education and information. Many educational software programs are used by children and adults in homes. Edutainment programs specifically geared toward home markets combine education with entertainment so they can compete with television and electronic games. Encyclopedias, dictionaries, atlases, almanacs, medical references, and other specialized references now come in low-cost digital versions—often with multimedia capability. But disc-based references have been eclipsed by Web references that offer more up-to-the-minute information—usually for free. Of course, Internet connections also provide email, blogs, forums, podcasts, and other communication options for home users.

As computer technology and communication technology converge on the home market, they're producing interactive products and services that challenge television and newspapers as our main sources of information. Television is a broadcast medium; it transmits news and information to broad audiences. Computer technology enables narrowcasting services—custom newscasts and entertainment features aimed at narrow groups or at individuals. (Individualized broadcasting is sometimes called *pointcasting*.) With a narrowcasting service, you might create a personalized news program that includes a piece on the latest Middle Eastern crisis, highlights of last night's

FIGURE 11.26 Nintendo's Wii Fit encourages gamers to exercise their bodies; some other popular games are designed to exercise brains.

Blazers vs. Lakers game, this weekend's weather forecast at the coast, announcements of upcoming local jazz concerts, and a reminder that there are only five more shopping days until your mother's birthday. Personalized news services can flag particular subjects ("I'm especially interested in articles on the Amazon rain forest") and ignore others ("No Hollywood gossip, please").

Several Web portals, including Google and Yahoo!, enable users to personalize their "front pages" with customized headlines, stock quotes, weather information, television and movie schedules, and other features. Personalized bookmarking services like Del.icio.us can point Web browsers to sites that match their interests. Music selection services like Pandora make it easy to create custom radio stations. Podcasts provide special-interest audio and video on demand and on-the-go.

Personalized Web portals enable people to control what they see on their home pages but not what they see on other sites. Some families depend on **filtering software** to block their browsers so children can't visit sites that contain pornography and other "inappropriate" content. Filtering programs can be customized, but they're not 100 percent accurate. They're also subject to the biases of their authors and corporate owners. A few years ago extensive tests of America Online's filtering revealed that kids had free access to Web sites of the conservative Republican and Libertarian parties but were blocked from viewing the Democratic and Green party sites. Young teens could access sites promoting gun use, including the National Rifle Association, but not the Coalition to Stop Gun Violence and other gun safety organizations. Both AOL and The Learning Company, who designed the filtering software, denied bias. But the findings show how censorship can squelch the free flow of ideas that's a critical part of the educational process.

FIGURE 11.27 Teachers and parents can use filtering software to keep children away from "inappropriate" sites.

Home Entertainment Redefined

Regardless of how people say they use home computers, surveys suggest that many people use them mostly to play games. Computer games and video game machines (which are just special-purpose computers) represent a huge industry—one that is likely to evolve rapidly in the coming years.

> Television has a **"brightness"** knob, but it **doesn't seem to work**.
>
> —*Gallagher, stand-up comic*

Most computer games are simulations. Computer games can simulate board games, card games, sporting events, intergalactic battles, street fights, corporate takeovers, or something else, real or imaginary. Many computer games require strategy and puzzle solving; others depend only on eye-hand coordination. Often the most popular games require some of each. With dazzling graphics, digitized sound, and sophisticated effects, many of today's computer games represent state-of-the-art software. But in a

FIGURE 11.28 The popular Grand Theft Auto series of video games has generated controversy because of high levels of person-to-person violence and morally ambiguous plot lines.

few years these computer games are likely to look as primitive as early Pong games look today.

Realistic computer games may not be completely beneficial for society. In the years before the 1999 Columbine High School mass murder, the killers spent hundreds of hours blasting virtual people in graphic first-person games such as Doom. In the aftermath of the tragedy, many people suggested that the games were partially responsible for the horrific killings. A year later, published research confirmed a link between violent video games and real-world violence. Two studies suggested that even brief exposure to violent video games can temporarily increase aggressive behavior and that children who play violent games tend to have lower grades and more aggressive tendencies in later years. Further research may confirm or clarify these results. In the meantime, pressure grows for game manufacturers to consider the impact of their products on young minds.

Sometimes the impact of video games on young minds is measurably positive. In a recent study, researchers at Eastern Virginia Medical School in Norfolk, working with NASA scientists, used PlayStation games successfully to treat children diagnosed with attention deficit disorder (ADD). Using basic biofeedback technology and off-the-shelf video games, children were able to learn to control their brain waves so they could improve concentration. The fast-action games provided strong motivation for the young learners. PC software/hardware systems are now available to help children and adults with ADD.

The entertainment industry is exploring a variety of ways of adding interactivity to products. In the early days of home computing, one of the most popular types of games was *interactive fiction*—stories with primitive natural-language interfaces that gave players some control over plot. Today, arcade-style games, puzzle-based adventure games, and other multimedia-rich genres capture most of the attention of computer gamers. But interactivity is finding its way into other entertainment technology—most notably on the Web and on DVDs and Blu-ray discs.

Many movie discs allow for customized viewing—language, subtitles, commentary, soundtracks, and sometimes even camera angle are under viewer control. A few discs allow actual branching within a film. We may soon see truly *interactive movies*—features in which one or more of the characters or plot lines are controlled by the viewers.

We're also likely to see a growth in interactive TV—broadcast television with options for interactivity built in. Many "reality" programs and game shows depend on viewer input via phone calls and text messages. Set top boxes and video-on-demand services can add more immediate interactivity and personalization to television, blurring the llines between the TV and the PC. Interactive TV has been popular for years in Europe, where digital TV had an early audience.

Interactive TV and movie watching are, for the most part, solitary activities. But the Internet has made possible the creation of **massively multiplayer online role-playing games**, which allow thousands of people to interact in virtual worlds. The most popular games can attract hundreds of thousands of players at a time. Success in massively multiplayer online role-playing games requires establishing beneficial social relationships with other characters. For some players, online games are a harmless diversion, but for others, these games can become a compulsion. As technology improves, we can expect the attractiveness of virtual worlds to only increase.

FIGURE 11.29 Researchers are using video game technology in biofeedback experiments on children and adults with attention deficit disorder.

Creativity and Leisure

If you can talk, **you can sing**. If you can walk, **you can dance**.

—A saying from Zimbabwe

A 2000 report by the Childhood Alliance, a group of education experts, raised serious questions about computer use, especially by young children. "Intense use of computers can distract children and adults from . . . essential experiences." Specifically, the time children spend in front of a computer screen is time they aren't involved in physical activities and self-generated, imaginative play. "A heavy diet of ready-made computer images and programmed toys appears to stunt imaginative thinking." The report also argued that computers expose kids to adult hazards, including repetitive-stress injury and social isolation.

Many people worry that TV, computer games, and other media are replacing too many real-world activities. Instead of making up stories to share, we watch sitcoms on TV. Instead of playing music on guitars, we play music on iPods Instead of playing one-on-one basketball, we play one-on-one video games.

Is electronic technology turning us into a mindless couch-potato culture? Perhaps. But there's another possibility. The same technology that mesmerizes us can also unlock our creativity. Word processors and blogging software help many of us to become writers, graphics software brings out the artists among us, Web authoring tools provide us with worldwide publishing platforms, electronic music systems enable us to compose music even if we never mastered an instrument, and podcasting technology gives creative people everywhere access to global audiences.

Will computers drain our creativity or amplify it? In the end it's up to us. . . .

FIGURE 11.30 In this Korean electronic sports stadium, spectators cheer for world-class gamers who compete on giant screens.

Inventing the FUTURE

Tomorrow's Technology for Today's Children

The One Laptop Per Child Organization has a lofty mission: "To create educational opportunities for the world's poorest children by providing each child with a rugged, low-cost, low-power, connected laptop with content and software designed for collaborative, joyful, self-empowered learning." Visionaries Alan Kay and Seymour Papert helped shape the organization's philosophy along with founder and chair Nicholas Negroponte.

The organization's original goal in 2005 was to create a state-of-the-art laptop that cost less than $100 so that it could be distributed to children in developing nations. Researchers at MIT and elsewhere pushed the technological envelope to produce a low-cost, low-power machine that was well suited for use by children in remote villages. Hundreds of thousands of XO-1 laptops found their way into the hands of children around the world.

Early research in Peru and elsewhere suggests that XO-1s can improve communication, cooperation, and learning for their owners. It's too early to assess fully the program's impact. To make a positive difference, OLPC must overcome technological, political, and social hurdles. But the organization isn't sitting still waiting for results.

The next generation XO, called the XO-2 or XOXO, was announced in 2008 with a projected 2010 release date. The innovations packed into that tiny machine may send ripples far into the future. Some experts predict that its radical design is the model for the laptop of the future.

Like most laptops, the XO-2 opens like a clamshell. But unlike most laptops, the XO-2 has a touch screen inside both the top and bottom parts. No physical keyboard, no mouse—all screen.

The dual-touch-screen technology makes it possible to use the XO-2 in four distinct ways:

1. As a laptop. When the clamshell case is opened part way, so the top half is angled, the bottom touch screen becomes a virtual keyboard and touchpad, and the top functions as the screen.

2. As a tablet. When opened all the way, the two screens snap together to form one large touch screen.

3. As a book. When the XO-2 is held sideways, it can be read like a book with virtual pages.

4. As a shared board. When the XO-2 is flat between two users, each one can have a screen oriented in his or her direction, like an intelligent board in a board game.

Most computer users today would be reluctant to give up keyboards and mice, because today's software is designed with those input devices in mind. But *Computerworld* columnist Mike Elgan suggests that today's graphical user interfaces will soon seem as antiquated as command-line interfaces seem today. Elgan argues that tomorrow's hardware and software will use multitouch, physics, and gestures—MPG for short. He says that the XO-2's design could be scaled up for business users. But he also suggests that we're likely to have minilaptops, not unlike the book-sized XO-2, for when we don't need a giant folding screen. And we can always use a wireless keyboard—a real one—when we need to do serious typing.

The user interface isn't the only innovation in the XO-2. The XO-2 uses a tiny fraction of the power of a typical laptop, and it can be easily recharged with a hand crank, solar panel, or other off-the-grid tool. The XO-2 packs more features into a box that's significantly smaller than its predecessor. Like the XO-1, the XO-2 can effortlessly connect to a mesh network, minimizing communication hassles for users who don't speak Wi-Fi. Amazingly, the XO-2 should cost even less than the original XO-1—the target price is now $75 per laptop.

Research seeds planted in One Laptop Per Child will bear fruit in the computers we use in the future. Hopefully, the innovations of the XO-2 and beyond will give new hope to children everywhere. ~

In tablet mode

In laptop mode

In book mode

In two-person mode

FIGURE 11.31 The XO-2 laptop prototype has an innovative dual-screen clamshell design.

The Game of Life *by Rex Sorgatz*

Do games imitate life or vice versa? Rex Sorgatz explores this question in this November, 2007 Wired *essay.*

"Shall we play a game?" For those of us who grew up playing videogames in arcades, hearing that computerized voice in *WarGames* was the moment when gaming became more than a frantic quest for quarters. That voice — tempting Matthew Broderick into nearly setting off a global thermonuclear war — signaled a new epoch: Reaching the next level in *Donkey Kong* wasn't enough anymore. Games could be serious.

Two decades on, that revelation is now conventional wisdom. From the military's use of *America's Army* for recruiting to quarterbacks researching tactics via *Madden NFL*, we've gone from games *representing* life to *becoming* life. Ask yourself: Do you believe that your club moves have improved from playing *Dance Dance Revolution?* Have your driving skills matured because of *Gran Turismo?* Does cleaning out your RSS reader remind you of playing *Pac-Man?* Does the action of the iPhone's bouncing icons recall *Mario Bros.?* Have you tried to convince your friends that the invasion of Sudoku and *Tetris* into your dreams is proof of high-level brain activity? Welcome to the arcade called you.

Of course, the basics of gameplay — competing against opponents, setting records, winning prizes — are as old as human civilization. But the gaming mindset has now become pervasive. We use game models to motivate ourselves, to answer questions, to find creative solutions. For many, life itself has turned into a game. Our online lives are just twists on the videogame leaderboards, where we jockey to get our blog a higher rank on Technorati and compete to acquire more friend-adds on MySpace than the next guy.

Even on more serious social networks like Facebook and LinkedIn, you rack up friends, accrue hipster points, try to score high on identity tests. At iminlikewithyou.com — a dating site with bidding, competition, winners, and losers — you pose questions (or "games," in the parlance of the service) for potential mates to bid on, and the resulting interactions are less stilted and artificial than conventional online dating services. That's right, a gamelike environment feels more real than trying to mimic the experience of real-world dating.

And the gaming mentality continues right into the real world, where we are finding ways to compete for bragging rights in even the most mundane activities. Chorewars.com lets you turn the grind of household tasks into a quest for experience points. And who are those Prius hypermilers, obsessed with optimizing their driving techniques to wring every possible mile out of a gallon of gas, but *Forza Motorsport* players honing their skillz for a perfect lap?

Pop culture, too, abounds with game scenarios. Turn on the TV: Reality hits like *Survivor, The Apprentice,* and *American Idol* use psychological game theory to create competition, intrigue, and adventure. Even shows like *Lost* and *24,* with their respective number theory and time obsessions, seem influenced by gameplay. (*Lost* is to *The Legend of Zelda* as *24* is to *Pitfall!* — it makes sense!) And the burgeoning phenomenon of ARGs (alternative reality games) — which pull the narrative thread of videogames into real-world environments — demonstrates that there's no escaping the game onslaught. With ARGs seeping into TV shows and commercials, you may be participating in a game without even realizing it. And as we play through our lives, we don't reach for a Coke — the pause that refreshes. Instead we grab a high-octane energy drink, a liquid power-up to refill our health bar.

As games and the gaming mindset take over our lives, they've also gone professional. In baseball, the cult of stats-guru Bill James has let a legion of fantasy baseball players enter the ranks of real-life scouts. There are competitive eaters, air guitar champions, pro gamers, poker players, *WoW* gold farmers — all now legitimate occupations.

Of course, some gamers deal in the semi-legitimate. With billions of dollars at stake, the line has blurred between principled players and unscrupulous schemers. Spammers and Digg manipulators represent the dark side, but their tactics differ only slightly from those of earnest search engine optimizers and prank-driven Google bombers. "Gaming the system" has become the prevailing narrative of our time.

How did we end up with a world we play like a game? It's no historical coincidence that gaming ascended right along with the rise of the information age. As the ever-rising flood of new data threatened to inundate our lives, we developed tools to organize all that information — sort it, filter it, cut it, mix it. Desktop editing apps let us manage our data, but they also let us manipulate it. As we got better at controlling pixels and bits, games became a handy metaphor. And more than a metaphor. Like a Sim city come to life, we've moved from a society that creates goods to one that solves puzzles.

As Broderick's character in *WarGames* asks the computer at one point, "Is it a game, or is it real?" The computer, which has now taken on a human identity, replies, "What's the difference?"

Discussion Questions

1. Do you think computers blur the lines between games and reality?

2. Do you think the increase in the "gaming mindset" is good or bad? Why?

Summary

Information technology is having a profound influence on the way we live and work, and it is likely to challenge many of our beliefs, assumptions, and traditions.

Factory work is declining as we enter the information age, but factories still provide us with hard goods. The automated factory uses computers at every level of operation. Computer-aided design, computer-aided manufacturing, robots, automated assembly lines, and automated warehouses combine to produce factories that need few laborers.

Far more people work in offices than in factories, and computers are critically important in the modern office. Early office automation centered on mainframes that were run by highly trained technicians; today's office is more likely to emphasize networked PCs, and other devices for decentralized enterprise computing. So far, predictions for widespread computer-supported cooperative work and paperless offices haven't come true.

A growing number of workers use computers to work at home part- or full-time, staying in contact with their offices through the Internet. Telecommuting has many benefits for information workers, their bosses, and society as a whole. Still, telecommuting from home is not for everybody. Satellite offices, cottage industries, and portable offices offer alternatives that may be more practical for some workers.

The impact of digital technology varies from job to job. Some jobs are de-skilled—transformed so they require less skill—while others are up-skilled into more technologically complex jobs. Experts speculate that productivity will rise as organizations adjust to new technology and develop human-centered systems adapted to the needs of employees.

Computer monitoring raises issues of privacy and, in many cases, lowers worker morale. De-skilling, monitoring, and health risks are particularly evident in electronic sweatshops—data-entry warehouses packed with low-paid keyboard operators. Many of these sweatshops have been relocated to countries with low wages and lax labor laws.

For decades, American manufacturing jobs have moved overseas. More recently, companies have moved hundreds of thousands of computer support and programming jobs from the United States to Asia where wages are significantly lower. Economists debate the extent to which globalization will affect the high-tech job market in the U.S.

The biggest problem of automation may be the elimination of unskilled jobs. Automation will almost certainly produce unemployment and pain for millions of people unless society is able to provide them with the education they'll need to take the new jobs created by technology. Automation may ultimately force us to make fundamental changes in our economic system.

Our educational system was developed a century ago to train workers for lifelong jobs. In the information age, when students can expect to change jobs several times, we need to teach technological familiarity, literacy, mathematics, culture, communication, problem solving, and, most important, the ability to learn and adapt to an ever-changing world.

Instructional technology tools today include:

- Computer-aided instruction (CAI). Tutorials and/or drill-and-practice software covering specific, concrete facts
- Programming tools. Languages that enable students to design their own software and Web pages
- Simulations and games. Artificial environments that enable students to learn through exploration, experimentation, and interaction with other students
- Productivity tools. Word processors, Web browsers, and other real-world tools
- Computer-controlled media. Presentation graphics, interactive multimedia, and authoring tools
- Tools for students with disabilities. Touch screens, alternate keyboards, and other devices that give students opportunities to use technology to learn
- Distance education tools. Network tools that enable students and teachers to communicate from afar

Technology can have a positive educational impact, but it can't guarantee improvement. Research, planning, teacher training, community involvement, and classroom restructuring should accompany new technology.

Families use home computers for basic business applications, education, information access, communication, entertainment, and creative pursuits. All of these applications will radically change as the technology evolves.

Key Terms

authoring tools .... (p. 418)	computer monitoring .... (p. 407)	electronic commerce
automated factory .... (p. 400)	courseware .... (p. 413)	(e-commerce) .... (p. 403)
automated offices .... (p. 401)	de-skilled .... (p. 406)	electronic cottage .... (p. 404)
chief information officers	distance education .... (p. 419)	electronic sweatshops .... (p. 408)
(CIOs) .... (p. 401)	distributed computing .... (p. 402)	extranets .... (p. 402)
chief technology officers	drill-and-practice	filtering software .... (p. 425)
(CTOs) .... (p. 401)	software .... (p. 413)	globalization .... (p. 409)
computer-aided instruction	educational simulations .... (p. 415)	groupware .... (p. 402)
(CAI) .... (p. 413)	edutainment .... (p. 424)	interactive TV .... (p. 426)

Interactive Activities

1. The *Tomorrow's Technology and You* Web site, **www.pearsonhighered.com/beekman**, contains self-test exercises related to this chapter. Follow the instructions for taking a quiz. After you've completed your quiz, you can email the results to your instructor.

2. The Web site also contains open-ended discussion questions called Internet Exercises. Discuss one or more of the Internet Exercises questions at the section for this chapter.

True or False

1. Office automation began when PCs became inexpensive enough for businesses to buy in large quantities.

2. Engineers use computer-aided design and computer-aided manufacturing to design new products and the machines that build those products.

3. Research suggests that the total cost of ownership (TCO) of a typical PC in an organization is far more than the cost of the hardware and software.

4. Today the number of people who telecommute from home is half of the number who did in the 1990s.

5. Clerical workers typically see up-skilling to more technologically demanding work reflected in their paychecks or level of responsibility.

6. U.S. workers have constitutional protections against electronic surveillance in the workplace.

7. Offshore workers are replacing highly educated programmers and system designers in the United States by the thousands.

8. An engineering education can last a lifetime because only a small fraction of details change over time.

9. In most cases, student self-esteem decreases when using computers.

10. Research has proven that there is no link between violent video games and real-world violence.

Multiple Choice

1. Virtually all modern PCs have a graphical user interface. Name the company where Alan Kay and his research group developed this interface.
   a. Apple
   b. Dell
   c. IBM
   d. Microsoft
   e. Xerox

2. Which of these statements is not true?
   a. Telecommuting saves energy and reduces pollution.
   b. One reason telecommuters give for their choice to work from home is schedule flexibility.
   c. Telecommuting isn't really possible for information workers.
   d. Telecommuting allows for more flexible work schedules.
   e. Most telecommuters prefer to commute to the office at least some of the time.

3. Which of these techniques is not used for workplace monitoring in U.S. corporations?
   a. Using on-screen reports showing the number of keystrokes for each clerk
   b. Viewing a copy of any worker's screen secretly at any time
   c. Reading employees' personal email messages
   d. Tracking Web sites visited by employees
   e. All of these techniques are used.

4. Which of these is a negative aspect of computer monitoring in the workplace?
   a. The boss can be seen as an invisible eavesdropper rather than as a team leader.
   b. Computer monitoring creates stress in employees.

c. Quantity may become more important than quality.

d. Valuable qualities and unmeasured work may be overlooked and not valued.

e. These are all negative aspects.

5. What is the name given to the process of creating worldwide businesses and markets?
   a. Capitalism
   b. Communism
   c. Globalization
   d. Internationalization
   e. Socialism

6. When a workplace is automated, jobs can be
   a. de-skilled.
   b. up-skilled.
   c. eliminated.
   d. outsourced.
   e. Any of these might happen, depending on the circumstances.

7. Automation has led to a doubling of the productivity of workers in the United States since World War II. Why has the time spent at work stayed about the same?
   a. The productivity gains have been lost to higher taxes.
   b. All the extra goods and services are sent to other countries in the form of foreign aid.
   c. All the extra goods and services are consumed by the wealthiest 1 percent of Americans.
   d. The increase in productivity has been used to provide Americans with a higher standard of living.
   e. Actually, the workweek is about half as long as it was immediately after World War II.

8. The type of computer-aided instruction that is based on drill and practice works well for
   a. exploratory learning.
   b. simulations.
   c. students with learning disabilities.
   d. robots.
   e. programming by demonstration.

9. Which sentence best describes programming by demonstration?
   a. Novice computer users learn to program by watching an expert programmer at work.
   b. Novice computer users learn to program by following a tutorial on the computer screen.
   c. Novice computer users program a computer by demonstrating the correct action to take on a particular input.
   d. A programmer constructs an operating system using a procedural language such as Visual Basic.
   e. A video camera trained on the hand gestures of an expert programmer allows a computer to generate its own program.

10. Educational simulations
    a. generally require broadband Internet connections.
    b. have little in common with computer games.

c. generally don't allow students to be in control of the learning environment.

d. are based on the concept of learning through exploration and invention.

e. typically require students to have basic programming skills.

11. Which of these has been especially helpful for students with visual impairments?
    a. Robotic mice and keyboards.
    b. Digital reading machines.
    c. Cameras with voice recognition.
    d. Eyegaze systems.
    e. Digital wheelchairs.

12. Which of these is not part of distance education?
    a. Grade-school students networking with kids in other parts of the world
    b. Sharing electron microscopes through real-time Internet connections
    c. Taking courses via the Internet
    d. Live videoconferences involving students and faculty at remote campuses
    e. Required face-to-face meetings with professors throughout a degree program

13. Which of these statements have researchers found not to be true?
    a. Technology reduces teacher workloads.
    b. If the only thing that changes is the delivery medium, advantages of new technology are small.
    c. The students who can benefit most from technology have the least access to it.
    d. Computers are more effective for learning when located in the classroom.
    e. Art, music, and shop classes may serve young students better than computer classes.

14. For computer technology to be successful in schools, what must occur?
    a. Money is necessary to keep technology up to date and to pay for Internet access.
    b. Thoughtful, long-term planning and sustained support is required.
    c. Teachers need training and support to integrate technology into curricula.
    d. Schools should be restructured.
    e. All of the above.

15. Which of these cannot result from children playing computer games?
    a. Invoking feelings of both pleasure and frustration.
    b. Learning how to learn.
    c. Stretching the outer limits of abilities.
    d. Intense computer use distracting children from essential experiences.
    e. All of these are possible results of children playing computer games.

Review Questions

1. Define or describe each of the key terms listed in the "Key Terms" section. Check your answers using the glossary.

2. How has the evolution of the automated office paralleled the evolution of the computer?

3. What are the advantages and disadvantages of telecommuting from the point of view of the worker? Management? Society?

4. What is de-skilling? What is up-skilling? Give examples of each.

5. Describe the controversies surrounding outsourcing.

6. Why is education critical to our future as we automate more jobs?

7. What were the goals of education in the industrial age? Which are still appropriate in the information age? Which are not?

8. What kind of an education does a student need to prepare for living in the information age?

9. Describe how simulations can be used by teachers and students in the classroom. Give several examples.

10. Give several examples of people who can benefit from distance education technology.

11. Technology alone is no guarantee that students will learn better or faster. What else is necessary?

12. How is home entertainment being changed by computer technology and telecommunication?

Discussion Questions

1. What evidence do we have that our society is going through a paradigm shift?

2. What will have to happen before the paperless office becomes a reality?

3. Many cities are enacting legislation to encourage telecommuting. If you were drafting such legislation, what would you include?

4. People who work in electronic sweatshops run the risk of being replaced by technology. Discuss this dilemma from the point of view of the worker and society.

5. What do you think are the answers to the questions raised at the end of the "Will We Need a New Economy" section? How do you think most people would feel about these questions?

6. Socrates was illiterate and avoided the written word because he felt it weakened the mind. Similarly, many people today fear that we're weakening our children's minds by making them too dependent on computers and calculators. What do you think?

7. Some professors (and some schools) have banned laptops and handheld Internet devices from classrooms because students use them to hang out on the Web instead of paying attention to the class material. What do you think of this kind of prohibition?

8. Do you think educational games are good ways for students to learn in schools? Give examples that support your arguments.

9. Describe your past school experience in terms of technology. How did it measure up? What has been missing from your education so far?

10. Think about educational goals in relation to technology. What should people be able to do with no tools? What should people be able to do if they have access to pencils, papers, and books? What should people be able to do if they have access to computer technology but without the Internet? What should people be able to do with an Internet connection?

11. Do you think home computers in the future will make people more or less creative? Why?

12. Do you think home computers strengthen families and communities? Explain.

Projects

1. Interview several people whose jobs have been changed by computers and the Internet. Ask them about how their jobs have changed as a result of the technology. Report on your findings.

2. Interview people whose jobs exist because of the Internet (such as Web designers) and/or people who have built businesses using the Internet (such as eBay vendors). Ask them about what they like and don't like

about their work when compared with other work they've done. Report your findings.

3. Try several different types of educational software and/or observe students using the software. Prepare a report comparing the strengths and weaknesses of each. What objectives did the students have when they began using the software? Did the software help the students meet these objectives?

4. Observe how computers are used in local schools or on your campus. Report on your findings. What percentage of students use a computer every day? How much time are students spending on computers?

5. Design a simple courseware lesson. Set clear goals before you start. When your project is completed, try

it with several students. Test them before and after using your lesson to help evaluate how well they learned the material presented in the lesson. Ask them for feedback. What features of your system do they like the best? What features do they dislike the most? How well did your lesson help them learn the material? What can you conclude from your experience?

6. Plan a model technology high school. How would the goals differ from the goals of a conventional high school? How would the day be structured? How would students be evaluated? In what way would the technology be different from that found in a conventional high school?

Sources and Resources

Books

CNET Do-It-Yourself Digital Home Office Projects: 24 Cool Things You Didn't Know You Could Do, by S. E. Slack (New York, NY: McGraw Hill, 2007). CNET is one of the best sources for information on digital gear. This is an idea book for putting that gear to work in a home office. The projects include setting up a server, configuring a wireless network, producing a podcast, using your computer as a free phone, and earning advertising money with a blog. Many of the projects are Windows-centric, but others work in just about any home office.

The Dilbert Principle: A Cubicle's-Eye View of Bosses, Meetings, Management Fads, and Other Workplace Afflictions, by Scott Adams (New York, NY: HarperBusiness, 1997) and ***The Dilbert Future: Thriving on Stupidity in the 21st Century,*** by Scott Adams (New York, NY: HarperBusiness, 1998). These books, like the *Dilbert* comic strip, contain irreverent insights into the inner workings of the information-age workplace. Adams understands the world he satirizes—he has an MBA from Berkeley and 17 years of experience in a cubicle working for Pacific Bell. *The Dilbert Principle* targets managers who are clueless about the human needs of their staff; *The Dilbert Future* lampoons our high-tech future. *Dilbert* has been criticized because it paints a cynical picture of hopelessness in the workplace rather than encouraging workers to organize and solve problems. Still, the satire in these books allows us to laugh at ourselves, and that can't be all bad.

Dot Calm: The Search for Sanity in a Wired World, by Debra A. Dinnocenzo and Richard B. Swegan (San Francisco, CA: Berrett-Koehler, 2001). This is a guide for coping with the pace and pressure of a high-tech work environment. It provides practical tips and techniques that apply to a variety of work situations.

Player Piano, by Kurt Vonnegut (New York, NY: Dial Press, 1999). In this half-century old classic, satirical novelist Vonnegut paints a bleak picture of a future society in which most jobs have been lost to automation.

The End of Work: The Decline of the Global Labor Force and the Dawn of the Post-Market Era, Updated Edition, by Jeremy Rifkin (New York, NY: Tarcher, 2004). This book discusses the changing nature of work and the disappearance of jobs as we know them. Technology plays a critical role in these changes.

Mindstorms: Children, Computers, and Powerful Ideas, Second Edition, by Seymour Papert (New York, NY: Basic Books, 1993) and ***The Children's Machine: Rethinking School in the Age of the Computer,*** by Seymour Papert (New York, NY: Basic Books, 1994). These two classic books outline the views of one widely respected theorist and researcher on technology in education: Seymour Papert, the inventor of LOGO. *Mindstorms* was written during the period when Papert was doing pioneering work with LOGO. In *The Children's Machine*, Papert discusses why the computer revolution failed to revolutionize education.

Web 2.0: New Tools, New Schools, by Lynn Schrum and Gwen Solomon (Eugene, OR: ISTE, 2007). ISTE (the International Society for Technology in Education) has been helping educators apply digital technology to education for more than two decades. This is one of many books in their growing catalog of resources for improving education through technology.

The Technology Fix: The Promise and Reality of Computers in the Schools, by William D. Pflaum (New York, NY: Association for Supervision and Curriculum Control, 2004). The author of this book, an educational materials developer, took a year-long cross-country trip to find out firsthand how schools were using computer technology. In this book he describes his findings, good and bad.

What Video Games Have to Teach Us about Learning and Literacy, by James Paul Gee (New York, NY: Palgrave Macmillan, 2007). Gee, a respected education professor, argues that we can learn a lot about learning and thinking by looking at interactive games.

Amusing Ourselves to Death: Public Discourse in the Age of Show Business, by Neil Postman (New York, NY: Penguin, 2005),

Technopoly: The Surrender of Culture to Technology, by Neil Postman (New York, NY: Vintage, 1993), and *The End of Education: Redefining the Value of School,* by Neil Postman (New York, NY: Vintage, 1996). In these books, noted social critic Neil Postman takes on schools and technology, two powerful forces shaping our lives. In *Amusing Ourselves to Death,* Postman argues that television has injured, our ability to think, by reducing every public discourse to just another form of entertainment. In *Technopoly* he argues that our tools, especially computers, no longer play supporting roles; instead, they radically shape our culture, our families, and our world views. In *The End of Education,* he presents a picture of modern education in which economic utility has become the defining principle.

Trigger Happy: Videogames and the Entertainment Revolution, by Steven Poole (New York, NY: Arcade Publishing, 2004). Poole surveys the video game landscape and argues that this new entertainment form deserves the same kind of critical analysis we apply to other entertainment arts.

I, Avatar: The Culture and Consequences of Having a Second Life, by Mark Stephen Meadows (Indianapolis, IN: New Riders, 2008). This book presents the author's meditations and recollections about time spent in a virtual world and the potential implications beyond the online gaming arena. The book, like the online world it describes, is visually compelling and mentally engaging.

Game Creation and Careers: Insider Secrets from Industry Experts, by Marc Saltzman (Indianapolis, IN: New Riders, 2004). If you think you'd like to design your own video games for fun or profit, this book is worth your time. You'll read war stories and advice by many of the biggest players in the industry.

Periodicals

Campus Technology. This magazine focuses on higher education and technology. Themes of issues range from multimedia tools to distance education on the Web.

Technology & Learning. This magazine, aimed at K–12 educators, focuses on uses of technology to enhance education.

Learning and Leading with Technology, from ISTE (International Society for Technology in Education) is an important and influential organization whose focus is the effective use of computer technology in the classroom. *Learning and Leading with Technology* is their most accessible and widely read publication.

Information Systems in Business

After you read this chapter you should be able to:

▶ Describe the components of a system and the characteristics of an information system

▶ Discuss a business organization as a system

▶ Describe a business organization from the viewpoint of the value chain model

▶ Explain how transaction processing systems are used to support business processes

▶ Explain how enterprise resource planning is changing the flow of information within and among business organizations

▶ Describe several ways computers support the work of managers

▶ Discuss several ways a business can use information technology to compete effectively by improving efficiency and by improving its products and services

> Only the **paranoid survive**
> —Andrew Grove

Andy Grove, the Paranoid Chip Merchant

In 1968 Andy Grove, Robert Noyce, and Gordon Moore founded a tiny semiconductor company called Intel. In the decades that followed, Grove served as President, then CEO, and finally Chairman of the Board. Under Grove's leadership, Intel came to dominate the explosive computer chip industry. As CEO, Grove led Intel from tenth place to the top of the semiconductor heap. Intel today provides microprocessors for the vast majority of the world's personal computers and for countless other digital devices. Those tiny silicon chips have turned Intel into one of the most profitable companies on Earth. Grove attributes his success—and Intel's—to two things: faith and worrying.

Throughout his Intel management tenure, Grove had faith in three guiding principles: Moore's Law, the Cannibal Principle, and his own Grove's Law. Gordon Moore, another cofounder of Intel, observed that the transistor capacity of silicon chips as measured against price, doubles every two years or so. This observation, dubbed Moore's Law, explains why computer hardware often seems outdated within months of purchase.

The Cannibal Principle, also stated by Moore, says that semiconductor technology absorbs the functions of what previously were discrete electronic components onto a single new chip. That's why computer components can be packed with more and more features at lower and lower cost.

Moore's Law and the Cannibal Principle guarantee a wide-open future for the semiconductor industry. But Andy Grove constantly worried about the competition, following what has been called Grove's Law: Only the paranoid survive. (Grove is the author of a popular book of the same title.)

Why do people watch so much TV? Why are people so enthralled with PCs if they are frustrating to use? Why were he, Microsoft's Bill Gates, and other industry hotshots surprised by the sudden popularity of the Internet? These questions are typical of the kinds of questions that tormented Grove while he tried to stay ahead of the competition.

Grove had plenty to worry about over the years. For example, when Intel introduced the Pentium chip in

FIGURE 12.1 Andy Grove

FIGURE 12.2 Intel has built a massive financial empire on tiny silicon chips.

1994, customers found a flaw in the chip. After initially downplaying the problem, the company was forced by competitive necessity to replace the flawed chips for free and modify its marketing and customer support practices. Grove managed to sell some of the arithmetically challenged chips to jewelry makers for use in cufflinks and earrings. Also, he dreamed up the phenomenally successful "Intel Inside" advertising campaign that helped dampen sales of Intel-compatible microprocessors made by competitors.

He had no doubt that he and his employees should be paranoid about the industry's competitive forces and be afraid of competitors. But he also believed that fear inside the company could be harmful. Although Grove's management style was straightforward and results-oriented, he believed a leader must be sure that no one in an organization is afraid to express an opinion. He attributed much of the success of Intel to having created a healthful work environment in which motivated people can flourish.

According to Grove, the typical PC doesn't come close to pushing the limits of Intel's microprocessor, primarily because Microsoft's software hasn't kept pace with Intel's designs. Moore's Law and the Cannibal Principle suggest that Intel's processors will improve continuously in performance and take over many functions that now require extra chips, add-on hardware, and extra software.

Grove's goal for Intel was to be the global standard for consumer computers. In May of 2005, Grove stepped down as Chairman of the Board and assumed the title of Senior Advisor to Executive Management. That same month, another industry giant made an industry-shaking announcement that brought Grove's dream one step closer to reality. At the Apple Developer's Conference, not far from the spot where Intel was founded, Steve Jobs announced Apple would abandon IBM's Power PC chips and build its future Macintosh computers around Intel CPUs. Grove surely must have smiled.

According to Andy Grove, "A fundamental rule in technology says that whatever can be done will be done." But technology doesn't just happen. It's created by people like Andy Grove. ∼

The phenomenal success of Andy Grove and Intel isn't accidental. Grove's victories in the microprocessor wars are due in large part to his ability to think strategically and to harness information technology to manage Intel well to support his business strategies.

In this chapter, we'll focus on the information technology tools that support managerial work in an organization. First we'll see how managers use information technology to get the right information, at the right time, in the right form. Then we'll look at various types of information systems managers use to communicate and make decisions. We'll see how managers use information technology strategically to compete effectively with other companies. And we'll look at the process managers use to plan for new information systems.

Systems and Organizations

Information technology is at the center of the information revolution. But the role and impact of information technology in business can be complex and confusing without the help of clearly defined concepts. The relationships between computers, networks, and organizations are easier to understand if we consider them as systems.

> I firmly believe that any organization, in order to **survive** and **achieve success,** must have a **sound set of beliefs** on which it premises all its policies and actions … the basic **philosophy, spirit, and drive** of an organization have far more to do with its relative achievements than do technological or economic resources. …
>
> —*Thomas Watson, Jr. son of IBM's founder*

Earlier in the book, we discussed computer systems, operating systems, simulation systems, and other systems without paying much attention to the nature of a system. We now explore the concepts that define systems in general and business information systems in particular.

Anatomy of a System

A **system** is a set of interrelated parts that work together to accomplish a purpose. To accomplish its purpose, a system performs three basic functions: *input*, *processing*, and *output*. During input, needed materials are gathered and organized. During

> You've got to **think about the big things** while you're doing the small things, so that all the **small things go in the right direction.**
>
> —*Alvin Toffler*

processing, the input materials are manipulated to produce the desired output, such as a product or service. During output, the result is transferred or delivered to customers, clients, or other systems.

Does this definition sound familiar? The description of a basic computer in Chapter 2, "Hardware Basics: Inside the Box," included each of these functions along with a storage function for saving and retrieving data for processing. By this definition, then, a computer is a system.

A system has two additional functions: *feedback* and *control*. Feedback measures the performance of the input, processing, and output functions of the system and provides the measurement data to the control function. Control evaluates the feedback data and adjusts the system's input and processing functions to ensure the desired output is produced.

Every system has a *boundary* that defines its limits; anything outside the system's boundary is part of the system's *environment*. The system's environment provides input resources to the system and uses the output from the system.

A system can be a part, or a *subsystem*, of a larger system. For example, a personal computer can be a subsystem of a LAN, which might be a subsystem of a WAN, which could be a subsystem of the Internet. When the output of one subsystem is used as input for another subsystem, the two systems have a shared boundary, or interface. A large system (such as the Internet or a corporation) can have many interfacing subsystems.

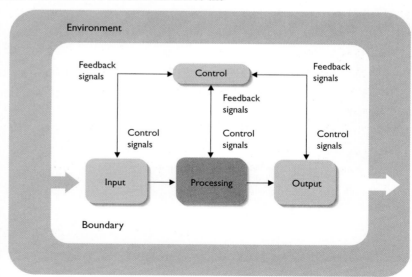

FIGURE 12.3 A system is a group of interrelated or interacting elements working together toward a common goal.

FIGURE 12.4 A home's heating system is an example of a system with input, processing, output, and control. The thermostat has both input and control functions.

FIGURE 12.5 A ski resort uses sensors on the slopes that monitor weather to help employees know when and how long to operate snow-making equipment.

Let's bring these abstract definitions down to earth with concrete examples. A computerized climate control system in a modern office building is designed by engineers to maintain a comfortable temperature and humidity for the office workers—that's the purpose of the system. The system accepts input from human operators that tell it what ideal temperature and humidity to maintain. The system also accepts regularly timed input from sensors that tell it what the actual temperature and humidity are in the building. If temperature or humidity is significantly different from the target value, the system sends output signals to heaters, air conditioners, or humidifiers to adjust conditions accordingly. The monitoring sensors provide feedback from the environment; the system controller processes the feedback and responds by adjusting output signals.

Similarly, a ski resort might use a computer system to maintain an adequate snow level on its ski slopes. Sensors gather temperature and other weather data at several locations around the slopes. The computer processes this information, and the ski resort staff uses the information to decide when to turn the snow-making equipment on or off.

Business Organizations as Systems

While the concept of a system can be (and often is) used to describe biological and other natural phenomena, the systems we're discussing here are designed and used by people. A business organization (commonly referred to also as a company or a firm) is a system designed for the purpose of creating products and services for customers. When we view a company as a system within an environment, each of the basic system concepts takes on a specific meaning.

In every business, however large or small, every person must have a **broad vision** and a **sense of place** in that vision.

—*Sir David Scholey*

The firm's environment is made up of customers, stockholders, and other organizations such as competitors, suppliers, banks, and government agencies. From the environment, a company acquires people, materials, money, knowledge, and other resources as input. These resources are used in work processes such as manufacturing, marketing and sales, and accounting and finance, all of which are needed to produce desired outputs for customers. These outputs include products and services as well as dividends, taxes, and information that are transferred to entities in the environment. The firm's managers perform the control function to ensure that the input, processing, and output functions perform properly. Information systems play a key role in the feedback and control functions, collecting data from each of the primary activities and processing the data into information needed by managers.

FIGURE 12.6 A business organization is a system that uses a variety of resources to produce goods and services for customers.

The Value Chain Model

The **worth** of a thing is best known by the **want** of it.

—*James Kelley*

The value chain model, proposed by Harvard Business School professor Michael Porter, views a business as a series of activities designed to add value to a product or service. When the value added by an activity exceeds the cost of that activity, the result is a profit for the business. The value chain model divides a firm's activities into primary and secondary activities.

Primary activities are those directly related to producing the product:

- Inbound logistics refers to receiving, storing, and distributing raw materials.
- Operations is the process of creating products or services from raw materials.
- Outbound logistics means delivering the products or services to customers.
- Marketing and sales has to do with finding customers and getting orders.
- Service refers to supporting customers after the sale.

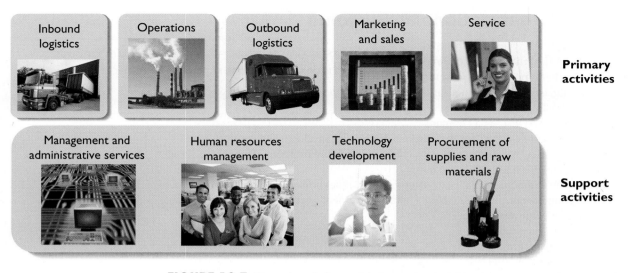

FIGURE 12.7 The value chain model shows the activities in an organization that make a product or service more desirable to customers.

Secondary activities are those that support the firm's primary activities:

- Management and administrative services administer the relationships between the business and financial institutions, governments, and other external organizations.
- Human resources management is responsible for recruiting, training, and retaining employees.
- Technology development means using technology to support the other activities.
- Procurement refers to the process of acquiring the raw materials needed by the business.

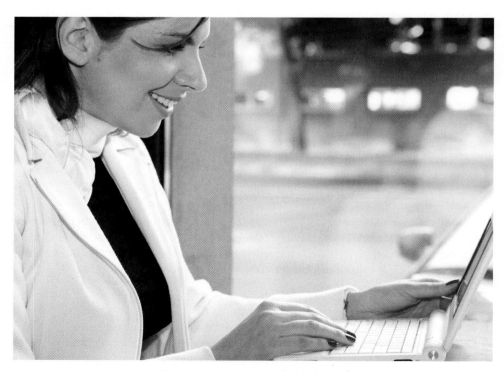

FIGURE 12.8 Information workers are empowered to do their work well by having access to the right information, the right tools, and the right training.

FIGURE 12.9 Small businesses, such as this bistro, compete successfully by using information technology to provide new services for their customers.

An organization's **efficiency** increases when its primary and support activities produce desired output with lower costs. There are several ways to use information technology to improve efficiency. A company can empower its employees by providing them with the training they need to work quickly and avoid mistakes. Information technology can reduce waste by speeding information flow and reducing paperwork. Using the best-known way to do the work, such as replacing manual inventory systems with RFID-tag-based systems, is another way to improve efficiency. Automating tasks requiring repetition, endurance, and speed often results in significant productivity gains. Integrating value chain activities within the company and with other organizations can reduce inefficiencies caused when one group does not know what the other group is doing.

Effectiveness is how customers rate the output of the organization's value chain. A company can improve its effectiveness by improving how customers interact directly with the company. For example, a company can make it easier for a customer to purchase a product by ensuring the product's availability and providing more flexible payment methods. A product is more attractive if it can be customized to meet the particular desires of the customer. A good field service can ensure that products are easy to maintain. Information technology can help a company achieve all of these goals.

Information Systems

We are moving very rapidly in all forms of production and services to a **knowledge-based economy** in which what you earn depends on what you can learn. Not only what you know today, but **what you are capable of learning tomorrow**.

—Tracy LaQuey, in The Internet Companion

We can think of an **information system** as a subsystem that supports the information needs of an organization. The overall purpose of an information system is to help people in the organization gather and use information, communicate with other people within and outside the organization, and make effective decisions.

Like other systems, an information system performs input, processing, and output functions and contains feedback and control functions. The input of an information system is data, or raw facts, about other subsystems in the business or other systems in the environment, such as descriptions of customer needs, materials purchased, and sales transactions. The processing function organizes and arranges the data in ways that people can understand and use. The output of an information system is an information product of some kind, for example, a report or other document. An information system also has a storage function to save data and information products for future use. The control function ensures that the information product outputs are of high quality and are useful to the information users for problem solving and decision making.

In the context of business information systems, information technology performs five functions: acquisition, processing, storage and retrieval, presentation, and transmission.

- **Acquisition** is a process of capturing data about an event that is important to the organization. Managers, clerks, or other users expect the data to be useful later. An example of acquisition is the identification of each grocery item captured by a scanning device during checkout at a grocery store.
- **Processing** is an activity that manipulates and organizes information in ways that add value to the information so it is useful to users. For example, one function of date processing in a grocery store is to calculate the total grocery bill during checkout.
- **Storage and retrieval** are activities that systematically accumulate information for later use and then locate the stored information when needed. For example, a grocery information system would use a database to store revised information about inventory levels of grocery items after each customer has checked out.

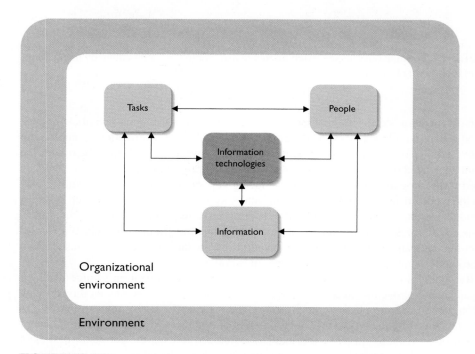

FIGURE 12.10 An information system is a set of information technologies that enable people in an organization to accomplish tasks effectively by providing access to data.

- **Presentation** is the process of showing information in a format and medium useful to the user. A grocery receipt given to a customer is one example; a summary report displayed on a manager's screen is another.
- **Transmission** is the process of sending and distributing data and information to various locations. For example, a grocery store may send information about inventory levels and sales to headquarters frequently.

Information Systems for Business Transactions

Being good in business is the **most fascinating kind of art**....

—Andy Warhol

A **transaction** is an event that occurs in any of the primary activities of the company: manufacturing, marketing, sales, and accounting. A transaction might be a sale to a customer, a purchase from a supplier or vendor, or a payroll payment to an employee. An organization can use an information system to track transactions in order to operate efficiently.

A **transaction processing system (TPS)** is a basic accounting and record-keeping system that keeps track of routine daily transactions necessary to conduct business. Examples of transaction processing systems include sales-order entry, ticket and hotel reservations, payroll, accounts receivable, and inventory. Transaction processing systems are important because they make it possible to control business processes intelligently based on accurate information. For example, by tracking the number of cars a dealership sells a week, a manager can make a fairly accurate assessment of the number of cars to order from the manufacturer. Similarly, by tracking the number of students that enroll in a course each fall semester, a university can determine the number of books it needs to order.

Transaction processing systems typically manipulate large volumes of data stored in databases. These systems capture the data that users and managers need to produce documents and reports. Many systems enable people to retrieve information interactively through database query systems, groupware applications, and intranet Web pages. A transaction processing system must ensure a high level of accuracy and security of the data.

Transaction processing is a cyclical process with five steps:

1. *Data entry.* The first step in TPS is to enter the transaction data into machine-readable form. This involves online data entry (typing at a terminal, scanning bar codes, or other direct input into the computer) or transcribing paper source documents into an electronic format acceptable to a computer. Data entry can also use Electronic Data Interchange (EDI) to exchange electronically business transactions between companies using standard document formats for purchase orders, invoices, and shipping notices. (EDI is discussed in more detail later in this chapter.)

2. *Processing the data.* A typical transaction processing system organizes and sorts the data and performs calculations. Data can be processed in two ways: **batch processing** involves gathering and manipulating all the data to be processed for a particular time period; **real-time processing** involves processing each transaction as it occurs. Batch processing is used when processing is needed periodically, such as monthly payroll or checking account statements.

FIGURE 12.11 A transaction processing cycle consists of the same steps used in other systems: input, processing, storage, and output.

How It **Works**

12.1 **The Information Flow through a Transaction Processing System**

Running a nursery business involves selling to customers, keeping track of inventory and ordering from vendors, paying employees, and keeping track of income and expenses.

Sales transaction processing system. When a customer buys a vase, the clerk enters the information into a cash register, and the customer receives a receipt. Or a frequent customer may ask to have the price of the item charged to her store account.

Purchasing transaction processing system. When new stock needs to be purchased, the vendors' bills for the new inventory move to accounts payable.

Inventory control transaction processing system. The sale of the vase is recorded for inventory control when the computer reads the UPC code on the price tag. This allows the buyers for the nursery to know how much stock for any vase is available and when to order more.

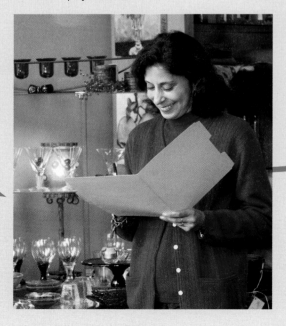

FIGURE 12.12

Accounts receivable transaction processing system. The nursery keeps records of amounts owed by customers. The clerk prepares invoices to bill customers.

Accounts payable transaction processing system. When an account needs to be paid, the clerk can print the check. In accounts payable, the nursery knows how much to pay each vendor and when to send the check.

General ledger transaction processing system. The income and expenses are organized in reports so that the nursery's owners know the health of the company.

Payroll transaction processing system. The nursery keeps track of the time each employee works and produces paychecks and other payroll statements.

Real-time processing is appropriate when users need the data immediately, as with bank ATM machines.

3. *Storing and updating the data.* This step involves storing the transaction data in a database so it can be retrieved later in processing some future transaction. For example, the amount you paid on this month's phone bill is used in calculating the amount you're billed next month. Many large organizations use **data warehousing** software to create and maintain large databases containing data on all aspects of the company.

4. *Document and report preparation.* A transaction processing system produces several types of action documents and reports. An **action document** initiates an action by the recipient or verifies for the recipient that a transaction has occurred. For example, a billing statement produced by your phone company is intended to trigger an action on your part, namely to make a payment. A sales receipt verifies the details of a purchase you make. Other examples of action documents are payroll checks, invoices, warehouse packing lists, and sales receipts. Reports are used by management to monitor the transactions that occur over a period of time. Reports can contain detailed information about specific transactions or summary information about a group of transactions, such as totals and averages. These reports are customized for specific users.

5. *User inquiry.* Managers and other workers can ask questions and retrieve information about any transaction activity when it's needed. The responses can be presented on the screen or in hardcopy form.

The transaction processing cycle repeats regularly, with output from one cycle serving as input to the next cycle. Each transaction system is a subsystem of the business as a whole, and these subsystems can interact in a variety of ways.

Enterprise Resource Planning

Transaction processing systems exist in all functional areas of a business's value chain. For example, businesses may have transaction processing systems related to accounting, manufacturing, marketing, and customer service. A business can improve its processes by constructing an information system that combines information found in various transaction processing systems. This approach of creating information systems to support an organization's operational business processes is referred to as **enterprise resource planning (ERP)**. A typical ERP system collects transaction data from various business processes and stores the data in a unified database or data warehouse. Once data is stored in the database, business processes can automatically share it and managers in all parts of the organization can retrieve it.

ERP systems are usually large and complex and take a lot of time and money to implement. In a recent survey of 63 companies—including small, medium, and large companies in a range of industries—the average total cost of an ERP was $15 million. (The highest was $300 million and the lowest was $400,000.) The largest ERP software vendor is SAP, a Germany-based multinational company with sales in 50 countries. Other vendors include Baan, Oracle, and J. D. Edwards.

Because of the complexity involved in planning and implementing ERP systems, many companies have had difficulty implementing the systems successfully the first time they tried. For example, Whirlpool's initial ERP implementation crippled the shipping system, leaving appliances stacked on loading docks—and therefore not delivered to paying customers—for a full eight weeks. Hershey Foods had a 19 percent drop in earnings caused by an incompetent ERP implementation that wreaked distribution havoc during one Halloween season. And a new ERP system at Volkswagen resulted in significant delays in parts shipments, causing product inventories to build up to costly levels.

Supply Chain Management and Outsourcing

Without **communications** there would be no life.

—Norbert Wiener

We have seen how ERP systems can help firms improve the efficiency of their internal processes. Some firms have begun to use ERP systems to coordinate their activities with

FIGURE 12.13 EDI can integrate the order-entry activity of a customer and the order-filling activity of a supplier. In this case, Dillard's, the customer, orders clothing from Haggar, the supplier. Integration is possible because EDI enables the customer and the supplier to use consistent technical standards and share information about each other's activities. Integration increases efficiency for both the customer and the supplier by eliminating delays and increasing accuracy.

the activities of their suppliers and customers. The goal of **supply chain management** is to improve the efficiency of activities throughout the *supply chain* the network of organizations that supply raw materials, manufacture products, and distribute products to customers. To automate supply chain management, a business creates an **interorganizational information system (IOS)** that uses networking technology to facilitate communication with its suppliers, customers, and other organizations. There are two forms of IOS—electronic data interchange and business alliances.

Electronic data interchange (EDI) is the direct, computer-to-computer exchange of standardized, common business transaction documents, such as purchase orders and invoices, between business partners, suppliers, and customers. EDI uses international standards for data formatting that enable companies to exchange large amounts of information in real time around the world.

EDI systems have been developed for particular business partners for decades. In the retail clothing industry, Dillard's department store uses EDI to send purchase orders electronically to Haggar, one of its apparel manufacturers. If Haggar doesn't have the cloth to manufacture a needed item of clothing, it uses EDI to place an order electronically with the textile manufacturer Burlington Industries. In the automotive industry, Ford, General Motors, and other car manufacturers use EDI to order parts from their suppliers; in turn, the suppliers must agree to implement EDI and use it for transactions with the car manufacturer. In terms of the federal government, all contractors wanting government contracts are required to link into the government's EDI systems.

A *business alliance* is a cooperative arrangement between two or more businesses with complementary capabilities. A good example is Calyx & Corolla, a direct-mail flower company. Calyx & Corolla maintains customer databases, a Web site, and an online catalog, and it does all its own marketing. But rather than create its own distribution system, Calyx & Corolla has an agreement with FedEx, which handles the logistics of delivering the flowers from the growers to the customers. Similarly, Calyx & Corolla has an agreement with MasterCard and American Express, which handle all the credit authorization and payment activities. Calyx & Corolla also created alliances with independent flower growers worldwide. When a customer order is entered on Calyx & Corolla's Web site, the customer's credit is verified electronically with MasterCard or American Express; the order is sent electronically to the appropriate flower grower and to FedEx; and MasterCard or American Express charges the bill to the customer's account and transmits electronically payments to FedEx, Calyx & Corolla, and the flower grower.

Another type of business alliance is an *information partnership* in which the companies, usually in different industries, share information for their mutual benefit. For example, United Airlines and Preferred Hotels & Resorts have an arrangement in which guests staying at a member hotel or resort can receive United Airlines frequent flyer miles. By sharing information, these types of partnerships help companies gain new customers and subsequently new opportunities for cross-selling and targeting products.

A type of business alliance that is being used more extensively because of the Internet is the *industrial network*, in which the systems of several companies in an industry are linked. Procter & Gamble has developed a system to coordinate its manufacturing facilities and suppliers with grocery store point-of-sale systems, warehouses, and shippers. The system enables Procter & Gamble and its business partners to monitor all its products from raw materials to customer purchase.

Information technology makes it economically feasible for a company to do business internationally and conduct its business processes virtually any time and anywhere. Using the global telecommunications network, a company can communicate with suppliers and customers located anywhere in the world, employ engineers and designers in a number of different countries, and have production facilities located at cost-effective geographic sites worldwide. Any information system that supports international business activities is called an **international information system**.

The international business environment poses several challenges that are not found in a purely domestic business environment. An international environment is multilingual and multicultural, has multiple governments, has many different regulations regarding privacy and intellectual property protection, has varying standards for telecommunications and other technologies, and has multiple geographic conditions, time zones, and monetary currencies. All of these factors affect the flow of data between countries, commonly called **transborder data flow**.

Even though good business practices make sense around the world, many issues are unique to a particular country. Some countries do not allow personal data about employees to leave the country. Many countries have weak, nonexistent, or poorly enforced software copyright laws. Inexpensive labor costs in one country may be the result of what another country considers unethical labor practices. Some countries have poorly maintained and aging telecommunication infrastructures.

The push toward supply chain management, electronic data interchange, and business alliances has made the implementation of information systems more important, and more difficult, than ever. Many businesses are handing the responsibility for developing and operating their information systems to another firm, in a practice called **outsourcing**. Outsourcing has become quite popular in recent years. An A.T. Kearney study of 26 multinational firms revealed that 90 percent of them had outsourced at least some of their information systems activities. A variety of reasons may lead an organization to choose outsourcing. An outside firm that specializes in information systems may be able to provide the same service for less money. Some businesses have chosen to focus on their core competencies: those activities that add the most value. Because the development and operation of information systems are support activities, they are unlikely to be viewed as a core competency. In many businesses there is friction between information services departments and other parts of the organization, caused by late, expensive, or low-quality information systems. These businesses may see outsourcing as a way of improving quality and reducing friction.

Not all firms that have chosen outsourcing have benefitted from their decision. Some businesses have underestimated the costs associated with identifying the appropriate vendor, transferring responsibility for information services to that vendor, and monitoring the relationship. The loss of control over an information system that accompanies outsourcing can sometimes have negative consequences. If an information system gives a business a competitive advantage, it may be in the firm's best interest to keep control of that system inside the organization.

Information Technology and Management

Vision is not enough; it must be combined with venture. It is not enough to **stare up the steps**; we must **step up the stairs**.

—Václav Havel

Every organization has limited time, money, and people. To stay in business, an organization must use these resources wisely. **Management** is a set of activities that helps people efficiently use resources to accomplish an organization's goals. A small business might have only one manager. Large multinational organizations may have hundreds of managers. Whatever the size of the organization, managers plan, organize, direct, and control the various processes in the company. In all of these roles, managers make decisions.

A manager makes a *structured decision* when he or she understands the situation clearly and uses established procedures and information to resolve the problem. Structured decisions, such as deciding how many inventory items to reorder in a university cafeteria, are usually simple and routine and can sometimes be made by a computer. Some structured decisions, such as deciding a university's course schedule for the semester, can be very complex because they involve many established procedures and large quantities of information.

A manager makes a *semistructured decision* when there's some uncertainty about a problem and the manager must use judgment to fill in the gaps. For example, a dealership manager may need to decide how many of a new-model car to order for delivery three months in the future when uncertain about the actual demand for the model.

Sometimes a manager faces unique circumstances or must anticipate events over a relatively long period of time. In these situations a manager must make an *unstructured decision* requiring many quantitative and ethical judgments that have no clear answers. For example, a manager may need to decide how the company should respond to a competitor that has introduced an entirely new product line.

In a large organization, there are typically three **management levels**: operational, tactical, and strategic. Managers have different functions and roles at each level.

A manager at the *operational level* is responsible for supervising the day-to-day activities in the organization's value chain. Operational-level managers are also referred to as lower-level managers, supervisors, and group leaders.

A manager at the *tactical level*—a middle manager—may be responsible for a large organizational unit, such as a sales region or a production plant. Typically, a middle manager develops short-term plans for the next year or so and makes sure his or her employees perform according to the plans. Tactical-level managers responsible for the development and use of information systems in an organization are called information systems managers.

A manager at the *strategic level* is called a top manager and is responsible for the long-range issues related to the business's growth and development. Top managers include the board of directors, chief executive officers, and vice presidents. The top manager responsible for the overall planning of information systems in an organization is called the **chief information officer (CIO)**.

It is important for managers at all levels to get the right information at the right time in the right form. Managers depend on communication for the information they need. Managers spend up to 90 percent of their time communicating with other people in the organization

Strategic

Top managers
• plan and control overall organizational direction

Tactical

Middle managers
• plan and control organizational units

Operational

Lower-level managers
• plan and control day-to-day business processes

FIGURE 12.14 An organization usually has a hierarchy of managers responsible for work at several levels.

FIGURE 12.15 Hewlett Packard's Halo is a state-of-the-art video teleconferencing system that makes long-distance meetings seem almost as if everyone is in the same room.

and in the company's external environment. We've already seen (in this chapter and earlier chapters) several tools that managers use to facilitate communication. Email, instant messaging, teleconferencing, blogging, and other "standard" Internet communication tools and techniques can be used to grease the management communication wheels in an organization. Groupware programs, intranets, and virtual private networks can extend the communication capabilities of managers beyond their local offices. And interorganizational information systems can extend those capabilities to business partners, customers, and others outside their companies.

But facilitating communication isn't the only way information technology helps managers get the information they need. A variety of software tools are available to make managers more effective and efficient. We'll now survey those tools and see how managers use information technology strategically to compete effectively with other companies.

Information Technology and Decision Making

Every decision to act is an intuitive one. The challenge is to migrate from hoping it's the right choice to trusting it's the right choice.

—David Allen, in Getting Things Done

In many ways it is more difficult to make decisions in today's business environment than it has been in the past. How can a manager choose among a large number of alternative solutions made possible by modern technology? Because many modern organizations use large, complex, interconnected systems, the risk—and cost—of making a wrong decision can be massive, especially when you consider the international nature of business today. On the other hand, the benefits can be immense when wise decisions ripple rapidly through a tightly linked organization.

Management Information Systems

A **management information system (MIS)** gives a manager the information he or she needs to make decisions, typically structured decisions regarding the operational activities of the company. These decisions require the manager to measure performance and compare that measurement information with predetermined standards of performance. Transaction processing systems provide the MIS with data on the performance of the primary activities of the company. The MIS extracts the relevant data from databases of the transaction processing systems, organizes and summarizes the data in useful ways, and provides the information to the manager in various reports. The manager can use the reports in the intelligence phase of decision making to identify any operational problems.

Management information systems are also referred to as **management reporting systems** because their main output is a variety of reports for managers. An MIS provides three types of reports: detailed reports, summary reports, and exception reports. Each type of report typically shows both actual and planned performance measures for certain transactions that allow a manager to compare actual performance with planned performance.

MIS reports are usually distributed to managers routinely as scheduled reports. A manager can also retrieve ad hoc, on-demand reports using a query language or an on-screen request form. Many organizations now have intranet infrastructures that enable managers to use Web browsers to retrieve and view MIS reports.

Typically, an MIS provides access to an organization's internal transaction data but not to information external to the organization. An MIS doesn't provide analytic capabilities other than straightforward, statistical operations for summary and exceptions reports. As a result, an MIS can supply performance information to managers about the primary activities of the company but is not particularly useful in helping managers decide exactly how to improve performance.

Decision Support Systems

A **decision support system (DSS)** helps a manager make semistructured decisions, such as budget planning and sales forecasting, and unstructured decisions, such as new product development and contract negotiating. The term *decision support system* also refers to a way of thinking about how information systems should be

> You can **lead a horse to water**, but you can't make him enter regional distribution codes in data field 92 to facilitate regression analysis **on the back end.**
>
> —*John Cleese, corporate consultant and former member of Monty Python's Flying Circus*

designed to support managerial decision making. The DSS design philosophy is to provide managers with the tools they need to analyze information they deem relevant for a particular decision or class of decisions. A DSS is designed with the decision style of the managers in mind and provides flexible information access, processing, and reporting capabilities.

A DSS has three major components that a manager uses interactively to retrieve and manipulate relevant data. The *data management* component is a database of relevant internal and external information. Current and historical information is extracted from the company's MIS and transaction processing applications. External information, such as stock prices, research data, and company information about customers, competitors, and vendors, is accessed through publicly available databases. Database management software enables the manager to query the database and retrieve relevant information, much like an MIS.

The *model management* component enables the manager to evaluate alternative problem solutions and identify the best solution using appropriate software. For example, a manager could use a spreadsheet model to learn how product sales correlate with differences in income, age, and other characteristics of consumers; based on this analysis, the manager could use the model to then forecast future sales. The model management component also contains other model-building tools, such as charting and graphing software.

FIGURE 12.16 The components of a decision support system. Managers can use the system interactively to analyze information for decision making.

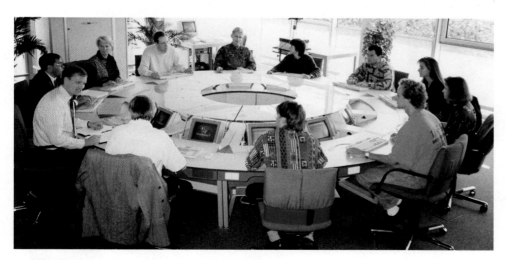

FIGURE 12.17 Group decision support systems can enhance the dynamics of face-to-face contact in group meetings.

How It Works

12.2 Information Flow in a Management Information System

Management information systems can transform mountains of data into reports that help managers make better decisions. This example shows how information flows through the Frostbyte Outdoor Outfitters Corporation.

To develop new business strategies, top-level managers need reports that show long-term trends.

When a new shipment arrives, a clerk records it using a terminal; inventory and accounting files are updated automatically.

The MIS uses a variety of inputs to produce reports for managers at all levels.

Middle-level managers use summary and exception reports to spot trends and unusual circumstances.

When a clerk enters a product's bar code, sales and inventory files are updated.

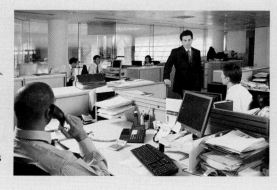

Low-level managers use detailed reports to keep tabs on day-to-day operations.

FIGURE 12.18

On-demand reports integrate information and show relationships. This report brings together sales information and weather data.

Sales Volume vs. Average Temperature as of 6/30/10

	JAN.	FEB.	MAR.	APR.	MAY	JUNE
Sales Volume	1798	1700	1609	1532	1302	1216
Sales	$24,398	$24,673	$22,468	$21,003	$18,068	$16,328
Average temperature	24	32	41	48	58	71

Year-End Sales by Item: Top 20 as of 12/31/10

ITEM	SOLD UNITS	RETURNED UNITS	TOTAL UNITS	TOTAL SALES
Beaver Kayaks	58	3	55	$12,375
Possum Packs	1240	212	1028	$20,046
Possum Parkas	1003	323	680	$17,000
Rhinoceros Hiking Boots	1162	429	733	$47,645
Snoreswell Sleeping Bags	923	62	861	$39,175

Summary reports show departmental totals or trends. This report lists the hottest-selling items.

Items Temporarily Out of Stock as of 12/31/10

ITEM	OUT SINCE	DATE AVAILABLE
Fancy Flashlights	10/31/10	1/11/11
Foxy Flannels	11/11/10	1/2/11
Snappy Tents	12/02/10	1/19/11

Exception reports reflect unusual relationships. This report lists out-of-stock gear.

Daily Sales Register by Type: 7/31/10

ITEM	UNITS	SALES
Parkas	62	$1209
Flashlights	154	$1540
Tents	2	$500
Hiking Boots	78	$65

Detail reports give complete, detailed information on routine operations. This report summarizes a day's orders.

The third DSS component is the user interface, or *dialog management*. Most DSS user interfaces enable managers to view information in a variety of forms, including graphs, charts, lists, tables, and reports.

Many decisions are made by a team or group of managers. Group decision support systems (GDSS) are designed to improve the productivity of decision-making meetings by enhancing the dynamics of collaborative work. Physically, the GDSS usually takes the form of a room equipped with computers, DSS database and modeling software, LAN connections, and a large-screen projection of computer output for viewing by the group. The GDSS also includes specific communication-oriented software tools that support the development and sharing of ideas.

FIGURE 12.19 Real estate agents can use a GIS to view property data at various layers, such as proximity to schools and shopping, city limits, and owner information.

During a decision-making meeting, managers can use the GDSS capabilities as if they were using their own DSS to perform an analysis or some other management activity. A manager can use a projection system to show his or her work to the group or keep it confidential. The managers as a group can use the GDSS software tools to brainstorm and organize their ideas, comments, suggestions, criticisms, and other information. A GDSS enables the group members to share information anonymously, encouraging them to participate without risking the counterproductive dynamics of group meetings.

A geographic information system (GIS) is a special type of DSS designed to work with maps and other spatial information. A GIS is made up of mapping and analytic modeling software, databases that contain map images, geographic and demographic data, and a user interface enabling a manager to query the database interactively and see the results on a map. Government agencies and more than 100 commercial companies produce spatial information databases containing demographic, employment, and consumer-habit information that can be incorporated into a business-oriented GIS. A manager might use a GIS to identify the best location for a new retail store or branch office, analyze customer buying preferences in a geographical area, or plan delivery and service routes.

Expert Systems

Expert systems (ES) support decision making by providing managers with access to computerized expert knowledge. An expert is someone who has mastery of an extraordinary amount of knowledge within a narrow domain. An expert system is designed to replicate the decision-making process of a human expert. Today's expert systems are based on years of artificial intelligence research devoted to replicating elusive human cognitive abilities in machines. Expert systems are discussed in Chapter 15, "Is Artificial Intelligence Real?"

Executive Information Systems

An executive information system (EIS) combines features of MIS and DSS to support unstructured decision making by top managers. A top manager can use an EIS to monitor key indicators of the company's performance, such as profitability, finance and marketing, and human and technology resources. An EIS also makes it easy for a manager to access economic, consumer, and environmental trends affecting the company.

An EIS has design components similar to a DSS. The EIS data management component provides interactive access to the company's important information, and the model-management component provides access to data on the company's critical success factors. The *dialog management component* is the set of human-computer interactive features that enables the executive to select the necessary data and display it in a variety of formats, including summary and exception reports, lists, charts, tables, and graphs.

An EIS enables the executive to *drill down* through the available information to the level of detail needed. For example, an executive may view a summary report and notice that sales in a particular region have declined over the past month. The executive can retrieve the detailed sales information for that particular sales region. Examining this data, the executive might decide to retrieve information about product sales at a particular store or by a particular salesperson.

Using the database management capability of an EIS, an executive has access to up-to-the-minute data on internal operations of the company and a wide variety of external online information, including news services, financial market databases, economic information, and other publicly available information. This ability to access both internal and external information makes an EIS a powerful tool during the intelligence phase of decision making.

FIGURE 12.20 The components of an executive information system. Managers can use the system to monitor the important economic and social trends affecting the organization, as well as the important performance measures of the company.

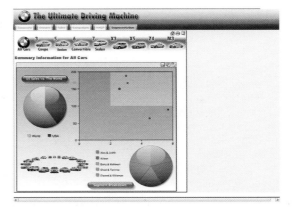

FIGURE 12.21 Extensity's Decision modular software can be used as an executive information system.

How It **Works**

12.3 Using DSS for Analysis

A decision support system can provide a manager with powerful tools for analysis of information. Different management decisions call for different types of analysis. A DSS handles these four types of analysis:

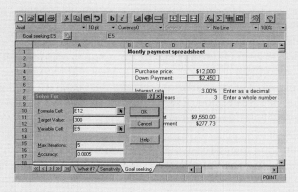

■ *What-if? analysis.* DSSs have been designed to support many types of decision-making applications, including corporate planning and forecasting, product pricing, flight scheduling, transportation routing, and investment analysis. Even though each DSS is designed to solve a specific problem, managers can use any DSS to ask and answer what-if questions. For example, a manager may want to know what the monthly payment for a product will be for a certain purchase price, loan length, and interest rate. By using an analytic model, a manager can change the value of one or more key input variables or parameters and immediately see the effect on the output variables or proposed solution.

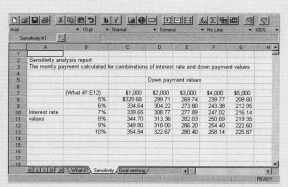

■ *Sensitivity analysis.* By varying the value of key input variables systematically, or by asking a sequence of what-if questions, the manager performs a sensitivity analysis. A sensitivity analysis shows the manager the degree of change in the results or output of a model as the value of a key variable or assumption changes incrementally. With a well-designed user interface, a manager can evaluate any number of what-if questions to do a sensitivity analysis easily and quickly.

FIGURE 12.22

■ *Goal-seeking analysis.* A variation of sensitivity analysis is goal-seeking analysis, which attempts to find the value of one or more key input variables of a model that will result in a desired level of output. For example, a manager might wish to know what down payment would be necessary to obtain a particular monthly payment. The manager could enter a value for the down payment variable, observe the resulting monthly payment calculation, and reiterate this process until the desired monthly payment level is found. Some DSSs enable managers to perform goal seeking automatically.

■ *Optimization analysis.* Another variation of sensitivity analysis is optimization analysis. All decisions are made under certain constraints and limitations, such as a limited budget. Optimization analysis attempts to find the highest or lowest value of one or more variables, given certain limits or constraints. For example, a manager could use an analytic model to calculate the optimal monthly payment for a product, given that the purchase price, the interest rate of the loan, and the down payment cannot exceed certain limits. Spreadsheet software has the ability to perform optimization analysis.

Strategic Information Systems

Successful organizations look for ways to gain a strategic advantage over their competitors. Let's consider three kinds of activities that can give a firm a strategic advantage.

- An *entry barrier* is usually an innovative new product or service that is difficult for a competitor to emulate. A classic example is Merrill Lynch, a large financial services firm that developed a system called Cash Management Account that provided customers many new financial, banking, and investment services. The system was costly and difficult to implement, and it took several years for competing brokerage firms and banking institutions to develop similar products. In the meantime, Merrill Lynch continued to innovate and enhance the product, making it all the harder for competitors to catch up.
- *Switching costs* are the time, effort, and money a customer or supplier would have to expend changing to a competitor's product or service. For example, Baxter Healthcare International, Inc., the supplier of nearly two-thirds of all products used by U.S. hospitals, developed an inventory and ordering system that enables hospitals to order online from the Baxter supply catalog using Baxter computer terminals installed in the hospitals. Participating hospitals became unwilling to switch to another supplier because of the convenience of the system.
- Sometimes businesses can add value to a product to differentiate it from the competition. For example, with the iPod music player, iTunes software, and the online iTunes Store, Apple computer was able to create a unique niche in the digital music industry; competitors had trouble matching Apple's products on all three fronts.

A strategic information system is an information system used at any level of a company that helps it gain an advantage over its competitors or even move into a new business. Any of the types of information systems described previously could be considered a strategic information system if it helped a firm gain a competitive edge.

Information Systems in Perspective

Point of view is that quintessentially human solution to **information overload**, an intuitive process of reducing things to an **essential relevant** and **manageable minimum** . . . . In a world of **hyperabundant content**, point of view will become the **scarcest of resources**.

—*Paul Saffo, Technology Forecaster*

Information systems provide critical information and advice, but using them is not without risks. Poorly designed information systems can hamper a manager's ability to make quality decisions. Systems notwithstanding, the human manager always has the responsibility for the quality of every decision. Some managers complain that these systems provide too much information—too many reports, too many printouts, too many summaries, too many details. This malady is known as information overload. Managers who are bombarded with computer output may not be able to separate the best from the rest. What's worse, managers who rely too heavily on computer output run the risk of overlooking more conventional, nondigital sources of insight. Although user training is essential, the best managers know that no computer or information system can replace the human communication and decision-making skills necessary for successful management.

FIGURE 12.23 Managers suffering from information overload may find it impossible to focus on what's most important.

Planning for Information Systems

A **complex system that works** is invariably found to have evolved from a **simple system that worked**.

—John Gall

We've seen how information systems can play critical roles throughout a business, from the highest levels of management to the factory floor. But information systems don't happen automatically; they need to be designed, developed, and debugged before they can be put to work. To ensure successful systems development, managers must first plan how information technology will be used within the context of the overall mission and goals of their organization. We'll examine the process of systems design and development in Chapter 14. In this section, we'll look at the steps involved in planning for information systems.

Planning is a process of identifying a desired goal or objective and then deciding what will be done to achieve the objective, when it will be done, who will do it, and how it will be done. Because information technology plays an important role at all levels of an organization, IT planning is a major concern of top management. Information technology planning involves four phases:

- Aligning the information technology plan with the overall business plan of the organization
- Describing the firm's IT infrastructure
- Allocating resources to specific information systems and projects
- Planning specific information system projects

Strategic Planning

This first phase of IT planning is called **strategic planning**. The strategic plan defines the mission of the company, identifies the company's environment and internal strengths and weaknesses, and defines the competitive strategy of the company. A component of an organization's strategic plan is an IT plan that describes the IT mission within the company, reviews the company's current IT capabilities and applications, and describes the IT strategies and policies to support the organization's overall strategy.

Decision support features	MIS	DSS	EIS	ES
Type of decision maker	Many operational managers	Individual and small groups of tactical managers	Individual strategic manager	Individual strategic, tactical, or operational manager
Type of problem	Structured	Semistructured	Unstructured	Structured
Type of information	Predesigned reports on internal operations	Interactive queries and responses for specific problems	Online access to internal and external information on many issues	Conclusions and recommendations for a particular complex problem
Type of use	Indirect	Direct	Direct	Direct
Phase of decision making	Intelligence	Design, choice	Intelligence	Implementation

FIGURE 12.24 Comparison of design features for MIS, DSS, EIS, and ES.

Information Technology Planning Phases	
Major IT Planning Activity	**Description**
Strategic planning	Align the overall business organization plan with the information technology plan
Information technology infrastructure analysis	Conduct an organizational information infrastructure analysis to identify the desirable features for the information technology infrastructure
Resource allocation	Select the information system projects to invest in
Project planning	Develop the plan schedule and budget for specific information system projects

FIGURE 12.25 Phases of information technology planning process.

Organizations use several strategic planning approaches to make sure IT plans truly reflect business needs. The **critical success factors (CSF)** approach identifies the variables that are crucial for the success of the business from the top managers' point of view and identifies IT plans for systems that provide access to information about those critical success factors. A CSF typically relates to the major competitive forces faced by the company and to operational problems and opportunities. Examples of CSFs include quality customer service, correct pricing of products and services, tight control of manufacturing costs, and the efficient and effective use of employees.

Describing the Information Technology Infrastructure

The second phase in IT planning is to describe the desirable features for the organization's IT infrastructure. The IT **infrastructure** comprises all the organization's information systems hardware, software, and telecommunications equipment; the information system department's staff and other personnel; and the organizational structure and procedures that affect accessing, processing, and using information in the company. The IT infrastructure should be designed to support the business operations, communications, decision making, and competitive strategy of the company.

An approach many companies use to define their IT infrastructure is **organizational information requirements analysis**, also called enterprise modeling. This approach is used to summarize the company's current IT infrastructure, to identify the practical range of business and product strategies based on the current infrastructure, and to identify information system projects that offer the most benefits to the organization.

Allocating Resources

The third phase of information technology planning is resource allocation, a process of selecting the information system projects in which to invest. Every organization has a limited budget, a limited number of people, and limited time. The information system department must decide how to allocate these limited resources. Typically, resources must be allocated for maintaining or enhancing existing systems; developing new systems for supporting managerial, clerical, and other users; and developing new ideas and techniques for incorporating IT into improving business operations, products, and services.

Many managers use cost-benefit analysis to decide whether an information system project is worthwhile on its own merits and also in comparison with other proposed information system projects. Costs usually relate to hardware, software, salaries, IT staff salaries, and the ongoing operation and maintenance of a system. Tangible benefits, such as the reduction in the number of customer complaints and the increase in the number of sales orders, can be measured easily. Intangible benefits, such as better employee morale and better supervision, are harder to measure. A top manager might find it difficult to make an honest comparison of proposed information system projects based solely on anticipated costs and benefits.

Project Planning

The fourth phase of IT planning is project planning. The purpose of project planning is to organize a sequence of steps to accomplish a particular project's goals and to keep the project on schedule and within budget. A project plan includes a description of the measurable project goals that are used to evaluate the success of the project. A project goal can relate to the process of building the information system—completing the project by a certain date, for example. The project goal might also relate to business operations after the system is installed—for example, decreasing the time to place an order by a certain amount.

A project plan describes what needs to be done to accomplish each step in the system's life cycle. (The systems development life cycle is discussed in Chapter 14.) The plan specifies what deliverable output is to be produced at the completion of each step in the project. A deliverable can be a report, a computer program, a progress report, or any other tangible output. The plan specifies a schedule identifying how long certain steps are forecasted to take to complete and the forecasted date of completion. The project plan also specifies milestones, or checkpoints, to allow managers to review the project's progress when certain deliverables are produced, after a certain amount of the budget is used, or on a time basis, such as weekly or monthly.

Managers use *project management software* to help coordinate, schedule, and track complex projects. Many project plans use a Gantt chart to represent a project schedule visually. A Gantt chart shows each step or category of steps in a plan, along with its planned and actual start and completion times.

Project managers use the critical path method (CPM) to keep track of a project's schedule. CPM is a mathematical model of a project's schedule used to calculate when particular activities will be completed. A project manager first estimates the time needed to complete each activity, then determines the total time required to finish a project by locating the longest path, called the critical path, through the interconnected activities of the project. A critical path chart shows visually the interconnection of steps in a project. Project managers sometimes use a variation of CPM called the program evaluation and review technique (*PERT*). With PERT, a manager uses three time estimates: an optimistic, a pessimistic, and a most likely time to complete each activity. The appearance of PERT and CPM diagrams are the same; both reflect single times for each activity. In the case of a PERT diagram, the single times are computed from the three estimates.

Managers use Gantt charts and CPM or PERT diagrams to identify bottlenecks in a project and anticipate the impact problems and delays will have on project completion times.

FIGURE 12.26 A manager can view a Gantt chart and see at a glance the overall schedule of an information system project.

Social Responsibility in the Information Age

Socially responsible computing is a key concern in business today because of the many ways an information worker's actions can affect other people. **Social responsibility** refers to legal and ethical behavior. Laws define a society's proper, or legal, behavior and outline the actions a government can take in response to improper behavior. Ethics refers to principles or moral standards that help guide behavior, actions, and choices. Ethical dilemmas are difficult choices involving conflicting goals, responsibilities, and loyalties that may or may not be covered by laws. We've already considered many situations where information workers face ethical dilemmas, including:

> In the 20th century BC the Code of Hammurabi declared that if a house collapsed and killed its owner, the **builder of the house was to be put to death**. In the 20th century AD many builders of computer software would **deny responsibility** and pass the entire risk to the user.
>
> —*Helen Nissenbaum*

- Viewing email files of project team members or subordinates
- Making a recommendation to sell mailing lists of customers to other businesses
- Using a browser during working hours to shop
- Helping to implement a system that will result in five people losing their jobs

Social responsibility applies to a company as a whole as well as to individuals. A company that is socially responsible attempts to balance the interests of its various stakeholder groups—including employees, suppliers, customers, stockholders, and the local community. Traditionally, a company has a social contract with the community to enhance the material well-being of all the community's members, even if it means lower than maximized profits for its stockholders or higher than the lowest prices for its customers. A socially responsible company might donate money to local charities or the arts, give employees time off to do volunteer work, avoid any fraud or deception of the public, or play an active role in establishing and supporting community programs. Many companies extend the definition of "community" to a global scope, weighing worldwide environment and social impact in corporate decisions.

Regarding its own employees, a company is obliged to treat them with respect and provide them with healthful working conditions and fair wages. Most employers also strive to provide their workers with employment continuity. Within this context, a socially responsible company can provide a stable, predictable, and just working environment by establishing policies and procedures, called a **code of ethics**, to guide the behavior of its information workers. Companies have developed codes of ethics covering issues such as email privacy, software licenses and copyrights, access to hardware and files, and data and intellectual property ownership. Many professional organizations develop ethical codes that apply to their members; the ACM Code of Ethics in Appendix B of this book is a prime example for computer professionals.

The Working Wisdom box titled "Computer Ethics" in Chapter 1 offered several ethical guidelines. Here are some additional guidelines for information professionals that were developed by Donn B. Parker, a leading expert on computer ethics:

- *Informed consent.* If you are in doubt about the ethics or laws of a particular action, inform those whom your action will affect of your intentions and obtain their consent before proceeding.
- *The higher ethic.* You should take the action that achieves the greater good for everyone involved.
- *Most restrictive action.* When you are deciding to take or avoid taking an action, assume that the most severe damage that could happen will happen.

Inventing the FUTURE

The Virtualization of IT

Today's large corporations allocate considerable money, energy, and personnel to building and maintaining information technology infrastructures. Ironically, today's IT department may soon be the victim of technological change. In the words of industry analyst and writer Nicholas Carr, "The modern corporate data center, with all its complex and expensive stacks of machinery, is on the path to obsolescence."

We don't have to look any farther than the computer industry for evidence. Hewlett Packard is replacing its 85 corporate data centers with six giant, highly automated server farms. HP predicts that this shift will cut their IT workforce—and the percentage of revenue spent on IT—by half. Similarly, IBM has replaced 155 traditional data centers with seven larger facilities. And by 2015 or so Sun plans to close its internal data centers down altogether, moving all of its IT functions to utility computers in the "cloud."

Several trends threatening the traditional IT center: the plummeting cost of computing power and storage (remember Moore's Law?), improvements in performance and security technology on the Internet, the emergence of high-quality virtualization technology, and major investments in server farms by Amazon, Google, Microsoft, IBM, and others.

In effect, virtualization software can turn a single mainframe into many virtual machines. And the move toward grid computing may, in time, create a processing/storage utility that's shared like the current electrical grid. So instead of buying and maintaining warehouses full of expensive (and quickly obsolete) hardware and software, companies will be able to lease storage space, processing power, and software on large machines located in far-away server farms. Because of virtualization, your desktop machine won't have to know where it's getting its data any more than your current PC knows where its electricity comes from.

The shift to utility computing with virtual machines should save considerable money for large companies, because they won't be strapped with the high cost of buying and maintaining all those real machines. It should also save natural resources, because virtual computers require considerably less energy than real computers.

And it may very well promote collaboration. In Nicholas Carr's words, "Up to now, corporate IT systems have been built on the principle of isolation—private hardware, private software, private data stores. But the isolation principle has always been in conflict with the nature of business itself, which is all about shared processes, shared information, and shared ideas. . . . The new utility model of IT, which is built from the start on the principle of sharing, helps resolve that tension." It's Web 2.0 on a corporate scale.

Utility computing will depend on a solid infrastructure, including standards for integrating data and services from different vendors. It will also require improvements in encryption and other security tools. It will depend on advancements in massively parallel processing software. And it will require a new class of IT professionals who specialize in intra-organizational interfaces and workflow.

But once the pieces are in place, utility computing might very quickly transform the business computing world. Of course, it's not likely to change everything overnight. According to Google executive Paul Slakey, "This is a new wave, but it's not going to replace the existing. On-premise software is not going to go away." Still, this new computing model will present opportunities and challenges for businesses large and small in the coming decades. ∼

FIGURE 12.27 The explosive growth of server farms encourages the virtualization of IT.

Information Technology: Prescription for Change *by Amar Gupta*

Is the global health care industry due for an IT overhaul. In this edited version of a Special Report for the Wall Street Journal, Oct 20, 2008 Dr. Gupta argues that the change won't come overnight, but it will definitely come.

The health-care industry is about to undergo a global revolution driven by a force it can no longer resist: information technology.

While hospitals and other care providers have long been quick to adopt breakthrough technology in medical devices, procedures and treatments, far less attention has focused on innovations in networking and communications. This is partly because of concerns about breaches in security and patient privacy, and because health care until recently was a service always performed locally, and in person. Big computer networks and the core benefits they offer—such as increased group productivity and access to data—weren't on the health-care sector's radar screen.

But that is about to change. IT security will eventually meet the expectations of the health-care industry, just as has happened in other sectors, like banking. And when it does, powerful IT networks crisscrossing the globe will change the way much of health care is delivered: Outsourcing and offshoring of medical and nonmedical services will increase, providing more efficient health care at the most cost-effective rates; systems integrations will allow more medical records to be transferred swiftly and securely; efforts to monitor the safety of medicines will gain global access to data; and professionals and patients will find authoritative and up-to-date information on every specialty online.

In the future, there will be three often overlapping modes of delivering health-care services: services performed in person by humans, services that can be performed by people at a remote location, and services performed by computers without direct human involvement. Offshore outsourcing in combination with a 24-hour work cycle will be appropriate when certain conditions are met—mainly, if the information involved in the task can be digitized, and if workers at different sites can do their jobs independently from one another.

These changes won't come quickly. There will be plenty of obstacles as institutions and networks reach across borders and encounter different laws as well as technical standards. Licensing, accreditation and accounting issues will arise as well. But eventually all such issues can be resolved by proper regulatory structures and market forces.

In the meantime, health-care organizations that don't join in the coming changes will incur higher costs and less integration. This will make them less competitive in the global health-care marketplace, just as is happening with companies that have resisted outsourcing and systems integration in other sectors.

The most noticeable changes will be the offshore outsourcing of diagnostic services—particularly imaging, such as X-rays and mammograms—and consultations by specialists.

Doctors in the U.S. and other countries have long practiced variations of telemedicine to provide care to patients in hard-to-reach and underserved locations. But in the future, telemedicine will be practiced more as a way of distributing work loads and lowering costs. Teleradiology in particular, in which X-rays are taken at one location and then transmitted to doctors at another site, appears ripe for expansion.

Globally integrated health-information systems are evolving, along with standardized formats for patient records—making the charts easier to translate.

But current hospital information systems were designed to function as islands with their own rules and formats, making a patient's file at one hospital difficult for another to read.

Hospitals and other health-care organizations in the U.S. have started to make a dent in this area, using domestic medical and IT personnel to develop systems for the electronic exchange of medical records. But so much remains to be done, the higher cost and relative scarcity of U.S. labor available for this work is most likely to lead the industry to outsourcing abroad.

As people become more mobile, an international database on drug safety will be created. Various programs currently do this kind of work in their home countries, including MedWatch, an initiative of the U.S. Food and Drug Administration that investigates and reports on adverse drug reactions and other safety issues involving medical products. with the right infrastructure and incentives, pharmacists and pharmacy technicians could replace the current hodgepodge of reporting methods by becoming designated agents for collecting raw information on patients' medication histories, including adverse reactions.

The latest medical knowledge will appear on Web sites edited by eminent specialists in those fields.

Doctors and scientists from around the world will contribute material, and automated search tools will capture updates from, say, a trusted clinical study. Such sites are likely to take shape as hybrids of information sources and tools, drawing from online textbooks, medical journals, wiki-style editing and automatic updates from various trusted data sources. The goal will be not just to increase the amount of medical information at people's fingertips, but also to make it specific, up- to-date, reliable and easier to find.

The eventual benefits—from all of the advances predicted—will be universal.

Discussion Questions

1. Many of the changes Dr. Gupta suggests involve increasing globalization of health care. Do you anticipate any problems related to this?

2. Do you think an IT overhaul of the health care industry will result in better health care for you? Cheaper health care?

Summary

A system is a set of interrelated parts that work together for a common purpose. A system's functions can be divided into input, processing, output, feedback, and control. A system can be a subsystem of another system and may interact with other systems in its environment. Both computers and business organizations can be viewed as systems.

The value chain model views the business organization as a set of activities that add value to the firm's products or services. The model distinguishes between primary, production-oriented activities and secondary, support-oriented activities. Each activity is a subsystem with its own inputs and outputs; together, these subsystems interact with each other to determine the overall performance of the organization. As a subsystem of a larger business organization, an information system is a set of interrelated parts that work together to produce, distribute, and use information products. Some information systems support the feedback and control function of the organization, enabling better management decisions to be made. Other information systems, called transaction processing systems, keep track of transaction-based business processes, such as purchasing and invoicing. Transaction processing involves repeating a series of five steps: entering data, processing data, storing and updating data, preparing documents and reports, and handling user inquiries. Enterprise resource planning systems pull together information from multiple transaction processing systems, enabling businesses to make interactions among their departments and with outside organizations even more efficient.

In a systems view of a business organization, management represents the control function. Low-level, operational managers make the most structured decisions. Their work is supported by management information systems. Decision support systems provide information to middle-level, tactical managers who make semistructured decisions. High-level, strategic managers make unstructured decisions. A system providing information to top managers is called an executive information system. Group decision support systems enhance collaborative decision making by teams of managers.

An organization typically creates an overall IT plan before developing particular systems. The IT plan describes intended overall use of information technology to meet the company's needs. The organization then follows the plan, using cost-benefit analysis to select specific projects to develop and project planning techniques to track system development schedules.

Information systems are tools that should be designed to meet the information needs of the people using them. Poorly designed information systems can result in information overload and hamper a manager's ability to communicate effectively or make quality decisions. A company's information code of ethics should address the privacy, intellectual ownership, and the information quality and access policies to guide its managers and information workers and foster an ethical information culture.

Key Terms

acquisition ....(p. 444)
action document ....(p. 448)
batch processing ....(p. 445)
business organization ....(p. 441)
chief information
    officer (CIO) ....(p. 451)
code of ethics.........................(p. 463)
cost-benefit analysis ....(p. 462)
critical path method
    (CPM) ....(p. 462)
critical success factors
    (CSF) ....(p. 461)
data warehousing...................(p. 448)
decision support system
    (DSS)..................................(p. 453)
effectiveness ....(p. 443)
efficiency................................(p. 443)
electronic data
    interchange (EDI) ....(p. 449)
enterprise resource
    planning (ERP) ....(p. 448)

executive information
    system (EIS) ....(p. 456)
expert system (ES) ....(p. 456)
Gantt chart ....(p. 462)
geographic information
    system (GIS).....................(p. 456)
group decision support
    system (GDSS).................(p. 456)
information overload ....(p. 459)
information system...............(p. 444)
infrastructure ....(p. 461)
international information
    system ....(p. 450)
interorganizational information
    systems (IOS) ....(p. 449)
management ....(p. 451)
management information
    system (MIS) ....(p. 452)
management levels ....(p. 451)
management reporting
    system ....(p. 452)

organizational information
    requirements analysis ....(p. 461)
outsourcing............................(p. 450)
presentation ....(p. 445)
processing...............................(p. 444)
real-time processing ....(p. 445)
social responsibility...............(p. 463)
storage and retrieval ....(p. 444)
strategic information
    system ....(p. 459)
strategic planning ....(p. 460)
supply chain
    management.......................(p. 449)
system....................................(p. 439)
transaction ....(p. 445)
transaction processing
    system (TPS) ....(p. 445)
transborder data
    flow....................................(p. 450)
transmission...........................(p. 445)
value chain model..................(p. 441)

Interactive Activities

1. The *Tomorrow's Technology and You* Web site, **www.pearsonhighered.com/beekman**, contains self-test exercises related to this chapter. Follow the instructions for taking a quiz. After you've completed your quiz, you can email the results to your instructor.

2. The Web site also contains open-ended discussion questions called Internet Exercises. Discuss one or more of the Internet Exercises questions at the section for this chapter.

True or False

1. The Cannibal Principle says that semiconductor technology absorbs the functions of what previously were discrete electronic components onto a single new chip.

2. To accomplish its purpose, a system performs five basic functions: input, processing, categorizing, calculating, and output.

3. Everything inside a system's boundary is called the system's subsystem.

4. An information system is a subsystem that supports the information needs of other business processes within an organization.

5. In business information systems, information technology performs five functions: acquisition, processing, storage and retrieval, presentation, and transmission.

6. Transaction processing is linear, rather than cyclical, by nature.

7. A business alliance is a cooperative arrangement between two or more businesses with complementary capabilities, such as marketing and distribution.

8. Industrial networks may link the systems of several companies in an industry.

9. Managers spend up to 90 percent of their time communicating with other people in the organization and in the company's external environment.

10. Today's corporate IT division may soon be radically transformed because of the emergence of grid computing and information utilities.

Multiple Choice

1. Which of these is not a component of a system?
   a. Control
   b. Utility
   c. Input
   d. Output
   e. Processing

2. Which of these is not a value chain activity in an organization?
   a. Inbound logistics
   b. Operations
   c. Cognition
   d. Outbound logistics
   e. Marketing

3. What business term is used to describe how customers rate the quality of the products and services they receive?
   a. Contentment
   b. Critical success factors
   c. Effectiveness
   d. Efficiency
   e. Logistics

4. Factors affecting the international business environment and transborder data flow include
   a. multiple languages and cultural differences.
   b. the laws and regulations of governments, including copyright and privacy issues.
   c. varying telecommunications standards and technologies.
   d. different monetary systems.
   e. All of these factors affect international business environments.

5. Which is true? A transaction processing system (TPS)
   a. would not be useful for tracking course enrollment.
   b. is an organization's basic accounting and record-keeping system.
   c. does not require high processing speeds.
   d. is not searchable using database queries.
   e. All of the above.

6. Which of the following is not typically performed by management information systems (MIS)?
   a. Providing detailed reports, summary reports, and exception reports
   b. Extracting relevant data from databases of the transaction processing systems
   c. Providing managers with information needed to make decisions
   d. Making recommendations for improving performance
   e. Organizing and summarizing data in useful ways

7. Which is not a commonly-used system for supporting management decision making?
   a. Executive information system (EIS)
   b. Geographic information system (GIS)
   c. Grid utility system (GUS)
   d. Group information system (GIS)
   e. Expert system (ES)

8. Group decision support systems (GDSS)
   a. are designed to enhance collaborative decision making.
   b. are usually in the form of a meeting room equipped with hardware and software tools.
   c. allow individuals to use the GDSS as a private DSS to work out ideas during meetings.
   d. enable group members to share information anonymously if desired.
   e. All of the above.

9. What do businesspeople call an innovative product or service that is difficult for a competitor to emulate?
   a. Competitive hurdle
   b. Entry barrier
   c. Competitive calculus
   d. Beta blocker
   e. Technology transfer

10. What do you call a company-wide information system that combines information found in two or more transaction processing systems?
    a. Information utility grid
    b. Business alliance
    c. Electronic data interchange (EDI)
    d. Enterprise resource planning (ERP)
    e. Value chain model

11. A geographic information system (GIS) is
    a. a type of DSS designed to work with maps and other spatial information.
    b. typically used with the critical path method in system design.
    c. a type of expert system used to provide expertise in geology.
    d. a form of transaction processing system used for geographical simulations.
    e. impractical with today's technology.

12. Which is not one of the four major phases in information technology (IT) planning?
    a. Aligning the IT plan with the overall business plan
    b. Describing the firm's IT infrastructure
    c. Allocating resources to specific information systems and projects
    d. Planning specific information system projects
    e. Critical path method (CPM)

13. What tool provides managers with optimistic, pessimistic, and most likely estimates for completion of each project activity?
    a. Cost-benefit analysis
    b. Data flow diagram
    c. Gantt chart
    d. PERT chart
    e. Spreadsheet

14. When writing an organization's information code of ethics, which topic would you not include?
    a. Privacy
    b. Access to information
    c. Information quality
    d. Encryption algorithms for security
    e. Intellectual property

15. Which is not true? Socially responsible companies
    a. attempt to balance the interests of stakeholders.
    b. always optimize profits regardless of human consequences.
    c. have a social contract with the community to enhance the material well-being of all community members.
    d. take environmental and economic impact into account when making decisions.
    e. avoid any fraud or deception of the public.

Review Questions

1. Define or describe each of the key terms in the "Key Terms" section. Check your answers using the glossary.

2. What are the types of information workers in our information economy?

3. What are the major components of a system? What is the difference between a system and a subsystem?

4. What is the basic concept of the value chain model?

5. What are the basic systems components of an information system?

6. What is the purpose of a transaction processing system?

7. What are the steps in a transaction processing cycle?

8. What are three basic types of managers in an organization?

9. Describe three types of decisions. Which types of decisions are made by different management levels in an organization?

10. Describe the characteristics of an MIS. What kinds of reports does it produce?

11. Describe the characteristics of a DSS. What types of information tools does it provide?

12. Describe the characteristics of a GIS. Why would a GIS be useful in a business organization?

13. What is the likely impact of utility grid computing on traditional IT departments?

14. Describe three basic strategies organizations use to compete successfully.

15. How can a strategic information system be used to improve an organization's efficiency? Its effectiveness?

Discussion Questions

1. Use systems terminology to describe a real-world situation, such as organizing a sporting event or looking for a job. Does the systems model increase your understanding of the situation or make it more confusing?

2. Many companies are trying to improve the quality of their products and services for customers. How can you use the value chain model to identify what business processes to change to improve quality?

3. How could you evaluate whether decisions are made effectively in an organization? What factors or variables would you need to consider in your analysis?

4. Identify and discuss some of the ethical dilemmas and issues involved with (a) an MIS, (b) a DSS, and (c) an ES.

5. Which of the types of information systems described in this chapter do you think will be changed significantly in the coming decade? Explain.

6. Describe some of the social responsibilities of information workers in an organization with which you are familiar, such as a bank, police station, retail store, or government office.

Projects

1. Scan through a newspaper or magazine and pick a situation that is interesting to you. Describe the situation as a system, and identify the information activities in the situation. Think about how the situation could be improved. Write a report describing your analysis and recommendations.

2. Interview the owner of a small business. Describe the important transactions and the five-step transaction processing cycle for the organization. Identify some relevant information ethics issues for the organization. Create a presentation of your findings using a presentation software package such as Microsoft PowerPoint.

3. With a class partner, interview a manager in a large company. Use the information systems in context model (people, tasks, information, organization, environment, and information technology) to guide your interview. Prepare a report describing the company as a system. Exchange reports with another class group; then read and comment on each other's reports.

4. With a group, visit a service organization in your community, such as a hospital, fire department, church, or restaurant. Interview a manager to identify the information systems he or she uses to support decision-making responsibilities. Present a report to your class describing your findings.

5. With a class colleague, interview a manager of an organizational unit at your school. Ask the manager to describe the activities he or she performed during the previous workday and the information needed to perform those activities. Discuss the results of the interview with your class colleague. Compose a memo to the manager, thanking him or her, and summarizing what you learned.

Sources and Resources

Books

Only the Paranoid Survive: How to Exploit the Crisis Points That Challenge Every Company, by Andrew S. Grove (New York, NY: Bantam Books, 1999). In this widely publicized book, the founder and previous CEO of Intel shares his business philosophy and lots of stories from the front lines of the microprocessor wars.

Competitive Advantage: Creating and Sustaining Superior Performance, by Michael Porter (New York, NY: Simon & Schuster, 1998). In this updated classic text, the author describes the competitive forces affecting how a business organization can survive and thrive in the global competitive business environment.

Harvard Business Review on Managing the Value Chain (Boston, MA: Harvard Business School Press, 2000). This collection of eight essays examines the changing relationship between suppliers, customers, and competitors in the age of technology and globalization, outlining key ideas and providing guidance for incorporating shifts in the value chain into a firm's strategic outlook.

The Future of Management, by Gary Hamel and Bill Breen (Boston, MA: Harvard Business School Press, 2007). The authors of this book argue that management practices need to change with the times. Using case studies and careful analysis, they draw practical conclusions that can be applied by forward-thinking managers.

Evolve! Succeeding in the Digital Culture of Tomorrow, by Rosabeth Moss Kanter (Boston, MA: Harvard Business School Press, 2001). The author believes the new economy has had a "lobotomy" about basic business fundamentals. She skewers the clichés and uses them to expose the shallow thinking that has led to disaster. Using examples from both private and public sector companies, Kanter shows how digital innovation can be achieved within a company. She gets beyond the technical whizbang to look at the human possibilities of a global community.

Mission Critical: Realizing the Promise of Enterprise Systems, by Thomas H. Davenport (Boston, MA: Harvard Business School Press, 2000). As information-dependent companies of all types continually expand and globalize, the need to share critical data between far-flung sites increases dramatically. This text is an introduction to enterprise resource planning systems and how they are useful for organizations. The text is easy to understand, gives real-world examples of benefits and pitfalls of different implementation methods, and gives you a good idea of the magnitude of an ERP project.

The Cluetrain Manifesto: The End of Business as Usual, by Christopher Locke, Rick Levine, Doc Searls, and David Weinberger (New York, NY: Basic Books, 2001). *The Cluetrain Manifesto* began as a Web site in 1999 when the authors posted 95 theses pronouncing what they felt was the new reality of the networked marketplace. For example, thesis 2: "Markets consist of human beings, not demographic sectors," and thesis 20: "Companies need to realize their markets are often laughing. At them," and thesis 62: "Markets do not want to talk to flacks and hucksters. They want to participate in the conversations going on behind the corporate firewall." The book enlarges on these themes through seven essays filled with dozens of stories and observations about how business gets done in America and how the Internet will change it all.

IT and the East: How China and India Are Altering the Future of Technology and Innovation, by James M. Popkin and Partha Ivengar (Boston, MA: Harvard Business School Press, 2007). It's no secret that China and India are becoming major players in the world information technology market. This book by two analysts from the Garnter Group provides solid facts and perceptive predictions about the growing influence of "Chindia" in the IT world.

Common Knowledge: How Companies Thrive by Sharing What They Know, by Nancy M. Dixon (Boston, MA: Harvard Business School Press, 2000). The author describes insights into how organizational knowledge is created and how information systems can effectively communicate that knowledge within the organization. The book provides in-depth studies of several organizations—including Ernst & Young, Bechtel, Ford, Chevron, British Petroleum, Texas Instruments, and the U.S. Army—that are leading the field in successful knowledge transfer.

Periodicals

Computerworld. This weekly newspaper for computer professionals has a section called "Computer Careers" with advice and information on information technology professions.

Business Week. Besides national and international business news, this magazine publishes interesting articles about the information industry and the use of information technologies in companies.

Information Week. This magazine is laid out much like *Business Week* and contains interesting articles covering the information industry. It's a good source for business-related Web sites.

Journals such as the ***MIS Quarterly, Journal of Management Information Systems, Harvard Business Review,*** and ***Journal of Organizational Computing and Electronic Commerce*** are written primarily for researchers and academics who want to keep up with current research in the field.

Professional Organizations for Information Workers

Association for Computing Machinery (ACM) http://www.acm.org. (You'll find the complete text of the ACM's Code of Ethics in Appendix B of this book.)

Association of Information Technology Professionals (AITP) http://www.aitp.org.

Association for Information Systems (AIS) http://www.aisnet.org/.

Institute for Certification of Computing Professionals (ICCP) http://www.iccp.org/.

Institute of Electrical and Electronics Engineers (IEEE) http://www.ieee.org.

International Federation for Information Processing (IFIP) http://www.ifip.or.at/.

Society for Information Management (SIM) http://www.simnet.org/.

The American Society for Information Science and Technology http://www.asis.org.

13

E-Commerce and E-Business
The Evolving Internet Economy

Objectives

After you read this chapter you should be able to:

▌ Describe several basic models of e-commerce and e-business

▌ Discuss the factors that have had an impact on the success and failure of dot-com enterprises

▌ Explain how Web 2.0 and cloud computing technologies are changing e-commerce

▌ Discuss some ethical issues related to electronic commerce

> "People in this business spend a lot of time **looking at ideas** and asking, **why do that?** But sometimes the more powerful question is, **why not?**"
> —Jeff Bezos, founder and CEO of Amazon.com

Jeff Bezos Takes Amazon into the Cloud

As a child, Jeff Bezos wanted to be an astronaut. As an adult he decided to make history in a different kind of space: the uncharted territory of the newly-commercialized Internet.

He founded Amazon.com, naming it after the most voluminous river in the world. Amazon opened its virtual doors in July 1995 with a mission to use the Internet to make book buying the fastest, easiest, and most enjoyable shopping experience possible. "It's work hard, have fun, make history. That's what we're trying to do." Amazon did just that, expanding beyond books to become a general store selling music, electronics, household goods, and a myriad of other products. Its growth seemed phenomenal—greater than any other startup in history. 20 million customers in more than 160 countries bought $2.8 billion worth of merchandise in 2000. Unfortunately, Amazon also lost $1.4 billion in the process.

Fueled by big dreams and seemingly endless cash from investors, Amazon created an unprecedented shopping experience for consumers: low prices, patented one-click purchase technology, quick shipments, personalized recommendations based on prior purchases (and purchases of others), and direct links to products from other Web sites—links that rewarded the owners of those Web sites with sales commissions. Bezos promised investors big returns from agreements with other Internet retailers. Most of the Internet companies paid Amazon in stock, much of which became worthless when the first wave of Internet companies hit the economic wall in 2000.

When the investor cash stream slowed to a trickle, Amazon undertook an efficiency drive, including a new accounting system that calculated profit and loss on every product it sold. The company got rid of unprofitable products, reduced the number of errors in its packing and shipping process, moved its call center operations to India, and converted its international warehouses into regional hubs to cut down on inventory levels and delivery times. These measures worked—in 2003 Amazon was a profitable company, and since then profits have soared.

The newly profitable Amazon didn't sit still, waiting for competitors to catch up. The Amazon bookstore added a content-search

FIGURE 13.1 Jeff Bezos

feature that allows customers to search the contents of thousands of books for keywords and phrases. The music store added an MP3 download service that quickly became second only to Apple's dominant iTunes Store. In 2007, Amazon introduced Kindle, an electronic book designed to be for books what the iPod is for music. That same year more than a third of Amazon's sales were made by "seller-customers"—individuals, small businesses, and large specialty shops who used the eight-year-old Amazon Marketplace as a virtual storefront to sell their wares.

But if Bezos is right, Amazon's biggest success may come from selling services rather than products. Amazon Web Services sells computer power and memory to customers who'd rather let somebody else maintain and service the hardware they need to run their Web sites, databases, and other computing activities. Bezos is betting that most of us will, over time, choose to pay pennies per hour and pennies per gigabyte rather than continually buying and upgrading our own computers. AWS is leading a global transition toward cloud computing—putting the computing power in the Internet cloud and treating it like a utility.

So far AWS generates just a tiny fraction of Amazon's astronomical revenues, but Bezos isn't worried. "We're willing to plant seeds and wait five to seven years for them to turn into trees." He's not concerned about cloud computing competition from Microsoft, Google, and other Internet giants, either. "We focus our strategies on delivering fundamental services better than anyone else." Bezos is proof that it's OK to have your head in the clouds if you're grounded in a solid strategy. ～

FIGURE 13.2 Amazon.com's automated warehouse streamlines order processing.

Amazon.com is a major player in the global electronic marketplace. Adam Smith, the founding father of economics, described the market concept in his book *The Wealth of Nations* in 1776, theorizing that "if every buyer knew every seller's price, and if every seller knew what every buyer is willing to pay, everyone in the market would be able to make fully informed decisions and society's resources would be distributed efficiently." In many ways, the emerging global electronic marketplace approaches Adam Smith's ideal.

Business on Internet Time

Electronic business (e-business) is, as the name suggests, the use of information and communication technology in support of business activities. Specifically, e-business generally involves the use of networks for sharing business information, maintaining business relationships, and conducting business transactions. Strictly speaking, **electronic commerce (e-commerce)** refers to the sales aspect of e-business: the buying and selling of products or services over the Internet and other electronic systems. In reality, many people use these terms interchangeably, giving e-commerce a much broader meaning.

> In the future, **all companies** will be **Internet companies**.
>
> —*Andy Grove, former president, chairman, and CEO of Intel*

The terms *e-commerce* and *e-business* are relatively new, but the underlying concepts have been evolving since computers were first put to work more than a half century ago. Some go back as far as 1844, when Samuel Morse constructed the first telegraph network. Pre-Internet e-business tools included bar coding, fax communication, electronic data interchange, electronic funds transfer, enterprise-wide messaging systems, and other private LAN and WAN systems. But the development of the World Wide Web and the commercialization of the Internet in the early 1990s changed the nature and scope of e-business forever.

Forward-thinking businesses used Internet technology to communicate with employees, business partners, and customers. Old, inefficient systems were replaced with Internet-based systems. Traditional brick-and-mortar companies experimented with the Internet as a new revenue channel. Internet-based companies—**dot-coms**—sprouted like weeds: bookstores, boutiques, pet stores, grocery delivery services, online communities, all kinds of Web portals, and more.

During the 1990s investors were high on predictions of a "long boom" fueled by the emerging Internet economy. High-tech stock prices soared. Intel's stock rose 3,900 percent, Microsoft's stock jumped 7,500 percent, and Cisco's stock increased by 66,000 percent! Investors, not wanting to miss out on the opportunity to make huge profits, used optimistic estimates of future earnings rather than current performance to justify phenomenally high prices for Internet-oriented companies, many of which had never turned a profit. In 2000 and 2001 the bubble burst, and the resulting collapse in stock prices caused about a thousand start-ups to fold, putting half a million people out of work in the process.

Excessive investor speculation was clearly a major cause of the dot-com bust of 2000. And there's no denying that many of the dot-bombs were based on profoundly stupid ideas. But other dot-com businesses were simply ahead of their time. The technology of 2000 couldn't support media-rich Web sites, high-quality streaming video, large-scale online communities, and the kind of instant feedback that makes many online experiences compelling to consumers today. Few people regularly used the Internet, and almost all of them logged in through slow dial-up connections.

All that changed in just a few years. Broadband found its way into homes and businesses by the millions. Falling hardware and infrastructure costs made many new services affordable. A global infrastructure opened new markets. Web 2.0 tools made many Web interactions as easy as watching a DVD. For a critical mass of people, the Internet was an important part of their everyday lives. Businesses large and small made the Web their main

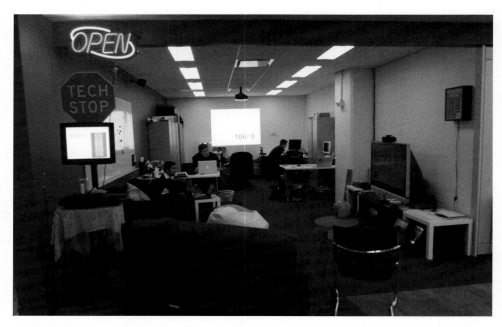

FIGURE 13.3 Many e-businesses that have emerged in the last decade have innovative workspaces that encourage employee collaboration. This is one of many common meeting areas used by Google employees in their New York office.

communication link with customers, and new companies emerged to take advantage of the technological surge.

Today, e-business is solidly entrenched in our economy. E-commerce sales are measured in hundreds of billions of dollars each year. And e-business is changing at Internet speed. New businesses and new business models emerge every year, forcing investors to ask hard questions about the future. Whether or not we see another e-meltdown like the one in 2000, e-business in one form or another is here to stay.

In the next section, we'll take a closer look at the basic kinds of systems for conducting e-business: intranets, extranets, and e-commerce systems for doing business with consumers. Then we'll examine several trends that are creating entirely new ways of doing business on the Internet. Finally, we'll consider some of the ethical issues of e-business.

E-Business 1.0: Intranets, Extranets, and E-Sales

E-commerce is **not a technology play**. It's a relationship, partnering, communication, and organizational play, **made possible by technology**.

—*Tom Peters, bestselling author and business consultant*

The basic idea of e-commerce is that at least two parties—a seller and a buyer—exchange information, products, or services using network technology. The exchange, or transaction, can occur between individuals, businesses, or organizations. The potential benefits of e-commerce for a company are enormous. Companies that sell goods and services generally have lower expenses, higher productivity, more efficient order processing, more useful information about their customers, and larger, more geographically dispersed markets than other, similar businesses.

There are several e-commerce models based on who is involved in the transaction:

- *Business-to-business (B2B).* The business-to-business (B2B) systems model represents inter-organizational information systems in which a company handles transactions within its own value chain and with other businesses and organizations, such as its suppliers, distributors, and bank. For example, Wal-Mart purchases the products it sells in its stores from its vendors over the Internet. B2B is by far the dominant form of e-commerce, and it is growing at a phenomenal rate.

- *Business-to-consumer (B2C).* The business-to-consumer (B2C) model represents retail transactions between a company and individual customers. Examples include dot-com companies, such as Amazon.com and E*Trade.com, and traditional companies, such as Lands' End and United Airlines. B2C is the most visible aspect of e-commerce from a consumer's point of view. Worldwide revenues of B2C are in the hundreds of billions of U.S. dollars, but still far less than B2B revenues.

FIGURE 13.4 Millions of individuals and small businesses sell products through eBay auctions.

- *Consumer-to-consumer (C2C).* The consumer-to-consumer (C2C) model represents transactions between consumers facilitated by a third party. The best-known example of C2C is eBay, the phenomenally successful Web auction site that enables individuals and businesses to offer items for sale and bid on items to buy.

- *Business-to-employee (B2E).* Business-to-employee (B2E) systems aren't technically e-commerce (depending on which definition of the term you use), because they don't involve buying or selling anything. B2E systems focus primarily on handling the activities that take place within the organization. Most mid-sized and large companies have intranet sites to handle B2E business.

In the following sections, we'll explore each of these types of systems, starting with the B2E systems.

B2E: Intranets for Internal Communication

In business-to-employee (B2E) e-business, an organization uses an intranet to support its internal value chain activities. Intranets based on Internet technology offer several advantages over customized, proprietary networks: cross-platform capability, open standards, reduced hardware and software costs, easy installation, and minimal user training. Intranets can dramatically improve communications within the organization; any employee with security authorization can access the organization's intranet from any geographic location using a Web browser.

> Stop thinking about the **technology** and start thinking about **what people are doing**. That's the secret to good design.
>
> —*Donald A. Norman, author and interface design expert*

Businesses use intranets to support their internal business processes in several ways, including providing employees access to information, facilitating employees' teamwork and collaboration within and among departments, processing internal company transactions, and distributing information management tools.

FIGURE 13.5 A larger company's intranet may be a network comprising several servers and many client computers. Firewall security guards against unauthorized access to the intranet.

Information Access for Employees

Many large companies have massive amounts of information stored in databases on their intranets—information that can be accessed by employees using Web browsers. For example, Los Alamos National Laboratory publishes several million internal classified, technical, and administrative documents on its intranet. By making this information available electronically, the Los Alamos scientists and managers can access the information quickly and easily, and the organization saves an estimated $500,000 per year in printing and distribution costs. Of course, not every employee needs access to the same information. Canon's intranet uses tactical personalization to increase efficiency, and each user's view presents only the information needed for their department. This approach ensures efficient access to the resources that employees need while reducing the information overload that a "one size fits all" approach can create.

Collaboration and Teamwork

Intranets make it easy for employees to share information, no matter where they are located geographically. In addition to information distribution, many companies use Web technologies in their intranets to facilitate collaboration within and among departments, improve their corporate culture, and cultivate a sense of community. IBM's intranet takes full advantage of everything that Web 2.0 tools have to offer, with 30,000 bloggers, podcasts (audio and video), wikis, and Beehive, an internal version of Facebook. Their intranet increases productivity, collaboration, and innovation of its 380,000 employees worldwide, 45 percent of whom work remotely throughout all global time zones.

Internal Business Transactions

Employees can use Web browsers to conduct actual internal business transactions on an organization's intranet. Having employees work electronically on an intranet increases efficiency, reduces paperwork costs, and increases the speed of updating information. Millipore Corp., a manufacturer of scientific and chemical purification products, uses its intranet to support employee self-service pages, including expense reporting, travel booking, and business-card ordering. Their intranet uses push technology to distribute employee information from 120 subscription-based corporate databases.

Distribution of Information Management Tools

Many organizations use their Intranets to deliver applications and tools to employees and managers. The information management tools described in the previous chapter—management information systems, executive information systems, expert systems, and more—can be incorporated into or linked into intranets, making them available as needed throughout an organization. Another type of tool, not discussed in Chapter 12, helps employees manage customer relationships. In e-businesses, where customers rarely, if ever, see or speak to company representatives, **customer relationship management (CRM)** can be the difference between success and failure. In the information industry, CRM usually refers to methodologies, software, and Internet capabilities for managing customer relationships in an organized way. CRM systems have been around in one form or another since the pre-Web days. A typical CRM system is a customer database that can provide information for managers, salespeople, marketing departments, and sometimes even the customers themselves. The database might include past purchases, customer preferences, service schedules, and customer communications, among other things. Whether it's part of an intranet or not, a well-designed CRM system can benefit both company and customers.

B2B: Extranets for Commerce and Communication

Just as intranets facilitate internal business communications and transactions, extranets can transform communication and commerce between businesses. Many companies have benefited from linking their intranets with other companies, creating extranets. Extranets enable them to build alliances with vendors, suppliers, and other organizations internationally.

> E-commerce is all about cycle time, speed, globalization, enhanced productivity, **reaching new customers**, and **sharing knowledge** across institutions for **competitive advantage**.
>
> —*Lou Gerstner, CEO of IBM*

An extranet, or extended intranet, is a private inter-organizational information system connecting the intranets of two or more trusted business partners. Companies using an extranet can place orders with each other, check each other's inventory level, confirm the status of an invoice, and exchange many other types of business information. For example, Hilton Hotels operates a business-to-business extranet to communicate with companies that have contractual agreements to use Hilton's facilities for business travel. Hilton's corporate customers install links to the Hilton Web site on their own intranets, and those links call up customized Web pages with contractual prices and travel limitations.

Organizations can set up an extranet in one of three ways:

- A *secure private network* physically attaches the intranets with private leased telephone lines. Monthly leased-line charges can be costly, but security is relatively high for business transactions because only a limited number of partners have access to the system.
- A *public network* uses a public communications network, such as a public utility telecommunication network or the Internet. These types of intranets are relatively inexpensive to set up and maintain, but security is low. Intranets within a public network extranet are protected only by firewalls and user logon procedures.
- A **virtual private network (VPN)** uses a public network (most often, the Internet) with special protocols that provide a secure, private "tunnel" across the network between the business partners' intranets. A typical VPN is managed by more than one company's administrators. VPN-based extranets are popular because they're relatively economical, private, and secure. Data are specially coded—a process called *encapsulation*—for sending transactions over the Internet; essentially, transactions are conducted via an encrypted channel, or tunnel, between the intranet firewalls of the extranet.

An intranet can improve a business's bottom line by:

- Increasing the speed of B2B transactions
- Reducing errors on intercompany transactions
- Reducing costs of telecommunications
- Increasing the volume of business with partners
- Facilitating the exchange of B2B documents
- Providing instant access to inventory and order status from suppliers
- Facilitating collaboration with business partners on joint projects

How It Works

13.1 Package Routing and Tracking

UPS delivers an average of 13 million packages and documents every business day. Its online package tracking system averages 9 million queries every day, making it an important customer-service activity. UPS uses wireless networks to make package routing and tracking fast and accurate.

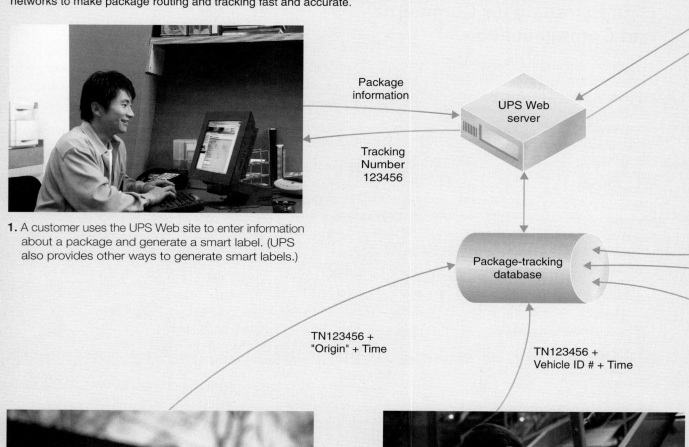

Package information

UPS Web server

Tracking Number 123456

Package-tracking database

TN123456 + "Origin" + Time

TN123456 + Vehicle ID # + Time

1. A customer uses the UPS Web site to enter information about a package and generate a smart label. (UPS also provides other ways to generate smart labels.)

2. When the package is picked up, the driver uses a wireless handheld computer to scan the smart label.

3. At the local distribution center, the package is scanned again when it is put on a truck, rail car, or plane.

FIGURE 13.6

TN123456

Package status

4. The UPS Web server allows customers to learn the status of their shipments. This could happen at any time during the process. (Large customers can track packages using UPS's Electronic Data Interchange system.)

TN123456
+ Time + Location

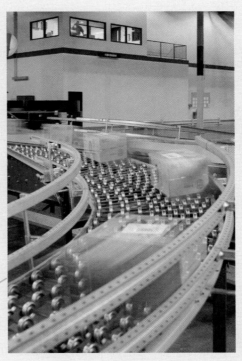

5. Scanners track packages as they are routed through a large hub facility. Most air packages are routed through the UPS Worldport in Louisville, Kentucky. Ground packages are more likely to pass through CACHE, UPS's largest ground hub in Chicago.

TN123456 + "Delivery"
+ Time + Signature image

TN123456 +
"Out for Delivery"
+ Time

```
ABC Company
2526  KIPLING AVE
STE 8000
MINNEAPOLIS MN 55416-3952

P:MG1      S:1128     I:
97B-3770              ☐
1ZEWRXXX028830 4221      0
PFXSUPPORT pfs995 Nov 17 14:59:02 2003
TB 5930 HJP 1 22 INT4420
```

6. When the package reaches the destination center, a computer creates a Preload Assist Label (PAL). The PAL identifies the conveyer belt to which the package should be sorted, the appropriate delivery vehicle, and the correct shelf location inside the delivery vehicle.

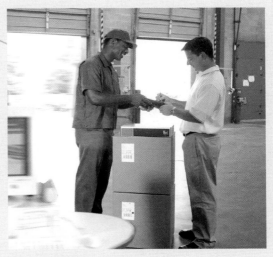

7. The driver's handheld computer contains an ordered list of stops and the packages to be delivered at each stop. When the package is delivered, the driver uses the handheld computer to scan the package one last time.

Public network

Private network

Secure private network

FIGURE 13.7 These three types of extranets enable organizations to connect their intranets to facilitate business transactions, communications, and other shared activities.

Wal-Mart and its suppliers use a B2B extranet. Wal-Mart built direct software linkages between its suppliers' factories and the cash registers at its stores. One major supplier, Procter & Gamble, can monitor the shelves at Wal-Mart stores through real-time satellite linkups that send messages to the factory whenever a checkout clerk swipes a Procter & Gamble item past a scanner at the register. With this kind of minute-to-minute information, Procter & Gamble knows when to make, ship, and display more products at the Wal-Mart stores. The system saves time, reduces inventory, and lowers order-processing costs so that Procter & Gamble can afford to give Wal-Mart "low, everyday prices" without putting itself out of business. As a result, Wal-Mart moves products through its stores more quickly and with less overhead.

Another example of a B2B extranet is Caterpillar Inc., a multinational heavy machinery manufacturer. Caterpillar developed extranet applications to reduce the time needed to develop

FIGURE 13.8 Small businesses can use extranets to connect directly with suppliers, advertisers and other related businesses. These extranet connections aren't apparent to customers visiting the companies' public Web sites.

and redesign its vehicle products. The company connected its engineering and manufacturing divisions with its suppliers, distributors, overseas factories, and corporate customers, all in a global extranet. A customer can, for example, use the extranet to modify order information while the vehicle is still on the assembly line. This ability to collaborate remotely between the customer and the product developers decreases time delays in redesign work.

The trade association of automotive manufacturers and suppliers has developed an extranet named Automotive Network Exchange (ANX). The extranet was designed as an Internet VPN to provide a global infrastructure for trading partners within the industry, including Daimler AG, Ford Motor Co., General Motors Corp., and several dozen major suppliers. ANX reduces telecommunication costs significantly by eliminating the need for manufacturers to have T1 lines to connect with their suppliers. ANX also reduces the time it takes a supplier to fill an order—sometimes from weeks to minutes.

B2C: Online Retail Sales and Service

Intranets support an organization's internal business processes. Extranets support business-to-business processes of two or more organizations. Of course, e-commerce also facilitates business transactions with consumers. To conduct B2C transactions on the Internet, a company provides customers with a public Web site where they can search product catalogs, retrieve product information, order and pay for a product, and get service and support information.

Make your product easier to buy than your competition, or you will find **your customers** buying **from them**, not **you**.

—*Mark Cuban, billionaire entrepreneur*

The early years of Internet B2C were plagued by questions of privacy and security. Phishing and other types of fraud still plague online consumers, but today's technology makes most online shopping experiences as secure as other forms of shopping. Message encryption standards use software for authenticating the parties involved in a credit card purchase on the Internet, and secure Web pages use encryption to protect sensitive credit and ID information. Modern electronic payment systems such as PayPal allow people to make purchases from strangers without revealing their credit card numbers. These systems rely on a trusted intermediary who is responsible for transferring funds from one person or business to another.

The best Internet sites have well-articulated goals and target specific markets, and their success is measured against specific objectives. There are many ways to measure the

How It **Works**

13.2 Online Shopping

1. Most online shopping sites are dynamic, database-backed sites whose pages are automatically generated and updated. When you visit a large online store, you are using your Web browser to search site databases.

2. When you decide to place an item in your shopping cart, your request is sent to the store's Web server, which sends a cookie to your computer—a small file containing information on the desired item. Cookies are used by the Web site to keep track of your potential purchases. Cookies might also be used to track the different pages you visit on the site and customize the display to match your preferences. For example, if you view several MP3 players, the site might show you more display ads related to portable audio.

Search query: iPod Touch 32GB

Search results

Place in Shopping Cart

Cookie

encrypted data

5. The server sends a query to the credit card company to make sure the card is valid and solvent; the company's computer replies.

Card OK?

Approved

Credit Card Company Computer

FIGURE 13.9

3. When you "proceed to checkout," the site displays all the items in your shopping cart, using the cookies on your hard disk to determine what you've put there.

4. When you continue the checkout process, you're routed to a secure part of the Web site so you can enter personal information and credit card numbers and know that they'll be encrypted before being sent through the Internet.

1widopq9a12 nkkwo

email

...Your order will ship today...

6. Once the transaction has been approved, the server sends a message to the warehouse where the order is filled. It also sends a confirmation email to you.

FIGURE 13.10a Penguin, like many book publishers, sells directly to customers through its Web site.

FIGURE 13.10b Bike Friday creates custom folding bike for cyclists all over the world; the company's Web site serves as a communication link between customers and company.

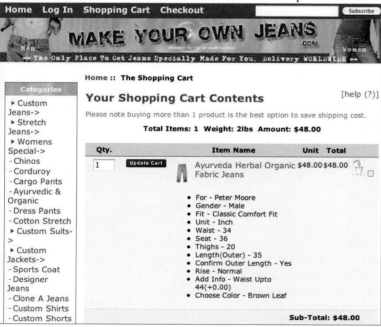

FIGURE 13.10c Customers at MakeYourOwnJeans.com submit measurements and receive custom-fit, made-to-order clothes.

How It Works

13.3 Using PayPal for Electronic Payments

More than 50 million people have an account with the PayPal electronic payment system. People use PayPal to pay for Web auction items, send money to family members, pay bills online, and more. In this example, two strangers use PayPal to facilitate the sale of a used bike.

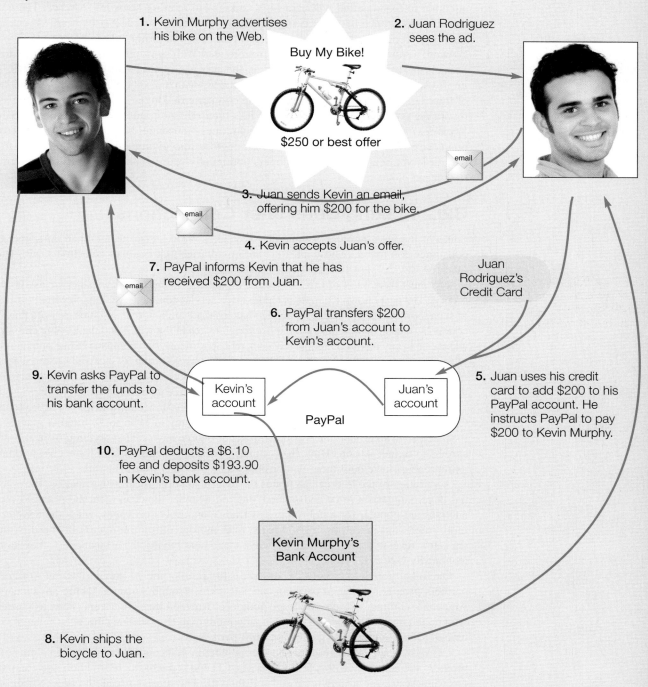

1. Kevin Murphy advertises his bike on the Web.

2. Juan Rodriguez sees the ad.

Buy My Bike!

$250 or best offer

email

email

3. Juan sends Kevin an email, offering him $200 for the bike.

4. Kevin accepts Juan's offer.

7. PayPal informs Kevin that he has received $200 from Juan.

email

Juan Rodriguez's Credit Card

6. PayPal transfers $200 from Juan's account to Kevin's account.

9. Kevin asks PayPal to transfer the funds to his bank account.

Kevin's account

Juan's account

PayPal

5. Juan uses his credit card to add $200 to his PayPal account. He instructs PayPal to pay $200 to Kevin Murphy.

10. PayPal deducts a $6.10 fee and deposits $193.90 in Kevin's bank account.

Kevin Murphy's Bank Account

8. Kevin ships the bicycle to Juan.

FIGURE 13.11

effectiveness of a commercial Web site, and the number of hits a site gets is not necessarily one of them. The most successful B2C Web sites generally offer valuable content organized in an easy-to-access structure and packaged in a consistent, aesthetically pleasing design. Many also offer personalization ("Since you bought X we thought you might like Y"), customization ("Select a color," "How much RAM do you want to add?," etc.), product support forums ("Check here for discussions of common problems and solutions"), and other features that go beyond basic catalog shopping.

Even the best sites can't generate sales if customers can't find them. Because most people depend on search engines to get around the Web, site developers pay considerable attention to features that will earn high rankings in relevant keyword searches. There's a world of difference between being listed first and being listed 21st by a search engine. Most search engines rank sites using closely guarded algorithms based on occurrence of keywords in headings and text, links from related Web sites, and dozens of other factors. **Search engine optimization (SEO)** is the process of increasing Web site traffic by improving search engine rankings for targeted keywords. Experts in SEO make a science of figuring out tricks and techniques for maximizing rankings—and increasing traffic as a result. As you might expect, there's a less-than-ethical counterpart to legitimate SEO. *Spamdexing* is the process of using techniques—automatically generated links from bogus sites, for example—to fool search engines into giving sites higher rankings than they deserve. Search engine developers continually refine their algorithms to attempt to stay ahead of spamdexers.

C2C: Making Consumer Connections

Some of the most popular commercial Web sites are designed to facilitate consumer-to-consumer commerce. These sites are intermediaries that connect consumers with each other. Most C2C sites fall into a few broad categories.

The most basic kind of C2C site is the digital equivalent of a newspaper's classified ad section. The best known example is Craigslist, a service founded by Craig Newmark in 1995 to serve San Francisco. Today, Craigslist has local ads in hundreds of cities in more than 50 countries. It has become one of the most popular sites in the world and the leading classified ad service in any medium. People buy cars, rent apartments, find companionship, and hunt for jobs using Craigslist—all for free. The company charges for job listings and brokered apartment listings in a few places, but mostly gives its services away. The CEO has made it clear that the company is more interested in providing a service than maximizing profits.

Another type of C2C business is the online auction exemplified by eBay. Like Craigslist, eBay grew from a small California company in 1995 to an Internet giant with localized sites all around the world. Millions of people have sold everything from Brussels sprouts to fighter jets on eBay. The company gets a small commission for each sale. Many entrepreneurs have built their own businesses on the eBay infrastructure.

A variation of the Internet auction is the reverse auction. In a reverse auction, the potential buyer suggests a price and sellers "bid" on whether they can meet the price. Reverse auctions are popular for hotel rooms, air flights, and travel packages, when the traveler is more interested in getting a good price than in controlling the details of the itinerary. (Because reverse auctions usually involve customers buying from businesses, they aren't technically C2C.)

One other popular type of C2C system is the reseller model popularized by Amazon's partners program. Amazon partners can sell items through Amazon, taking advantage of Amazon's commerce tools and huge audience. Amazon may lose some sales to partners who undercut their prices, but the company more than compensates through the large volume of sales commissions it earns on third-party sales.

CD Baby is a popular reseller site specializing in independent music. When a musician provides the company with a few copies of a CD and some basic information, the company creates a Web page to publicize and sell the CD. The musician gets the proceeds of any sales minus a small commission. CD Baby also handles the details of getting the music on iTunes and other electronic distribution sites.

FIGURE 13.12 Craigslist offers free classified ads to customers in hundreds of cities around the world.

FIGURE 13.13 A consumer can use a C2C Web auction site, such as eBay.com, to buy, sell, or trade just about any type of product with other people.

FIGURE 13.14 Hundreds of thousands of independent musicians sell their CDs and distribute their music to online stores through CD Baby.

E-Business 2.0: Reinventing Web Commerce

We always overestimate the change that will occur **in the next two years** and **underestimate** the change that will occur in **the next ten**. Don't let yourself be **lulled into inaction**.

—*Bill Gates*

In other chapters we've talked about several important trends that are changing the way people use the Web: the social and collaborative capabilities of Web 2.0, the virtualization of technology through cloud computing, the growing number of mobile devices with Web connections, and more. In this section we'll outline some of the ways these trends are changing, and will continue to change, Web commerce. Some of these trends started in the earliest days of the Web, but they're having a bigger impact on the ways we do business as our worlds become more Web-centric.

Disaggregation: Commerce in the Cloud

The growth in cloud computing will almost certainly accelerate the trend toward *disaggregation*—separating commerce into its component parts and outsourcing those parts that can better be handled somewhere else. Amazon's Web Services, discussed at the beginning of this chapter, is an obvious example. Businesses can buy computer power and memory from Amazon so hardware issues don't distract them from the business of selling. A Web retailer can also outsource its payment process to Google Checkout, an innovative program that seamlessly plugs into the site, providing a consistent, simple checkout process for customers across a variety of sites. Future Web commerce sites may be built from software and hardware components that are scattered all over the Web.

Enhancing the Interactive Experience

Research suggests that most online shopping carts are abandoned before checkout. Many consumers ditch their carts because they can't find the information they need before committing to purchase. Some of this could be solved with more complete product descriptions, but words alone can't offer the up-close-and-personal experience of shopping in the physical world.

Many online retail sites enable buyers to personalize and customize their purchases in ways that just aren't possible at the mall. But the fact remains that most online stores today are more like catalogs than shops. A growing number of online retailers are trying to break away from the "page" metaphor that dominates the Web. A new breed of media-rich sites are designed to attract (and keep) customers because they're fun, interesting, and uniquely designed to fit their products. In the physical world, shopping in a bookstore is a totally different experience than shopping in a hardware store. In the near future, the same might be true on the Web.

Mobile Commerce

Mobile commerce (m-commerce)—the use of smart phones, PDAs, laptops, and other portable electronic devices to conduct commerce while on the move—has been possible in one form or another for many years. But in recent years mobile commerce has increased dramatically as a result of several converging trends:

- The growing popularity of laptop computers as a percentage of the total PC market
- The widespread availability of wireless Internet connections through Wi-Fi hotspots and 3G networks
- The popularity of mobile phones with GPS technology and Web access
- The development of smart phones with Web access and applications that aren't significantly compromised by size

Selling Stuff Online

If you don't know what you're doing when you're looking to buy or sell something on a C2C e-commerce site, it's easy to find yourself overwhelmed by options, scammed by malicious buyers and sellers, or just not performing financially as well as you'd like. Here are a handful of tips to help you keep your head (and your bank account) above water in the raging sea of online commerce.

➤ **Choose the right option for your business**. If you're looking for a way to make a little extra money with a part-time business while reaching a large number of potential customers, services such as eBay and Amazon may be your best bet. If you'd prefer to avoid middleman fees, post classified ad-style listings, and negotiate directly with buyers, you might prefer to post your listings on Craigslist. If you'd like to cut out the middleman altogether, or you require a more customized shopping experience, you might be better off building your own site. Many retailers opt for more than one of these options, which allows them to benefit from the increased traffic and sales of listings on these larger sites while giving them the flexibility, power, and control that can only be found on a hand-crafted site.

➤ **Keep it simple**. Provide clear descriptions of items you're selling, provide photos, and include prominent links for purchase options on every page (if they aren't provided by the service you're using). Don't clutter up your Web pages or site with unnecessary or irrelevant information, and avoid the temptation to go overboard with glitzy formatting. The quicker a customer can assess what you're selling and how to buy it, the more likely that they'll become a customer.

➤ **Show off the goods**. People usually won't buy anything they can't see. Use a digital camera to photo-graph the stuff you're selling. Use good lighting and minimize the clutter in the picture. For more expensive items, take several views, including close-ups. Give your customers a good look at the merchandise and you're far more likely to make the sale.

➤ **Your reputation is your most powerful marketing tool**. Reliable, timely service can garner you a positive reputation on eBay or other C2C sites, and this reputation can be worth a great deal in future transactions. In online sales, satisfying your customers can result in repeat business. But there's more: Customer feedback (both positive and negative) can impact the purchases of countless other potential customers. As a result, you'll want to be completely up-front about any flaws in your merchandise, available to answer questions, and quick to ship merchandise once a transaction's been completed.

➤ **Offer payment options**. If you give the consumer more ways to pay, you'll probably see an increase in sales. Not everybody has a credit card, a checking account, and a PayPal account, but most potential customers have one of the three; letting them choose from several options ensures that you'll see fewer potential sales lost because you didn't offer a convenient method of payment. (Of course, you'll want to protect yourself if you accept insecure methods of payment such as checks; see the next point.)

➤ **Don't let yourself get scammed**. Don't ship a product until you've confirmed the transaction. (This means waiting for a check or PayPal transaction to clear before you put anything in the mail.) There are people on these sites that try to get something for nothing; don't let them take advantage of you.

➤ **Help search engines find you, and customers will follow**. It doesn't matter how great your deals are if nobody can find them. There are many things you can do to improve traffic to your site from search engines. Include a list of targeted keywords for your site or trans-actions, and if you're launching an entire commerce-oriented site, register it for indexing with Google, Yahoo!, and the other major search engines. Finally, consider a link exchange with related sites. Many top search engines take outside links into account when determining top billing for search results.

➤ **Factor the cost of services into your prices**. Services such as PayPal offer a nearly indispensable service to online merchants, by providing a safe temporary depository for funds while transactions are resolved. However, these services come with a cost—usually a percentage of the selling price. Similarly, credit card companies take a percentage of sales. When you're setting prices for merchandise, factor *all* the costs of business into your pricing, or you may find yourself losing money on every transaction.

FIGURE 13.15 eBay provides guidelines for safe selling.

FIGURE 13.16 Shoppers who use Google Checkout have a consistent checkout experience at a variety of online stores.

- The development of software tools that can take advantage of a variety of mobile technologies

Here's a sampling of m-commerce applications that will become increasingly common in the next few years:

- *Mobile ticketing.* E-tickets can be sent directly to mobile phones and dashboard computers, which can in turn communicate wirelessly with ticket takers at entertainment events, parking facilities, toll roads, etc.
- *Mobile coupons.* Electronic coupons and loyalty cards stored in mobile phones can replace their paper and plastic counterparts.
- *Mobile purchasing.* Many mobile phones make it easy to buy music, news, and other digital data; some stores encourage their customers to buy physical goods on their mobile devices; the actual goods can then be picked up at the stores or delivered.
- *Location-based m-commerce.* Mobile devices with GPS and other localization technology can customize offers and ads based on location.

FIGURE 13.17 Pandora radio (left) is a personalized internet radio service that creates playlists of new music based on old and current favorites specified by each listener. Listeners can buy songs they like using direct links to Amazon and *i*Tunes. At nikeid.com (above) a customer can design a unique shoe, view it from different angles on-screen, and have it manufactured for purchase and delivery.

FIGURE 13.18 This Japanese gamer is paying for his game using his cell phone; the game machine scans a special computer chip embedded in the phone.

Japanese businesses have, for several years, pioneered the use of cell phones as alternatives to credit cards. Customers in many types of shops can make purchases without plastic; their phones communicate directly with retail computers. This kind of wireless shopping will almost certainly spread far and wide over the next few years.

Of course, mobile technology has all kinds of B2B and B2E applications, too. Doctors, home-care nurses, real estate agents, sales managers, utility representatives, technicians and others can often conduct business more effectively outside the office. M-commerce applications have been developed—and will be developed—for all of those businesses, and many more.

The Long Tail

In the early days of the automobile industry, Henry Ford famously pronounced, "The customer can have any color he wants so long as it's black." Ford's edict was based on practical limitations of the young industry. For the rest of the twentieth century, consumers steadily gained more choices—in cars, colors, and just about everything else. But twentieth century marketing was limited by retail shelf space and floor space. Stores could offer consumers variety, but not unlimited variety. This was especially apparent in the entertainment industry, where success meant having a "hit"—a record, book, or movie that was so popular that stores would stock it (or theaters would screen it) because they knew it would sell. If you didn't have a hit, you didn't have a chance.

That's no longer true, thanks to the Web. Hits still dominate the entertainment industry, but they don't control it. Retail floor space isn't an issue for Amazon or iTunes or Netflix—their stock is only limited by the capacity of their computer hardware and (if the product can't be downloaded) the size of their warehouses.

In a virtual store, it costs next to nothing for an online vendor to offer less popular items along with hits. But adding more unusual titles would do little good if customers couldn't

FIGURE 13.19 This chart from Chris Anderson's *Wired* article, "The Long Tail," illustrates how digital retailers (like iTunes) and hybrid retailers (like Amazon) can profit from less popular "niche" items that don't find shelf space in physical stores.

easily find them. Today's search engines, combined with sophisticated product recommendation technology, make it easy for consumers to locate even the most esoteric items. Interested in books on pre-20th century African art? Or Japanese avant-garde anime? Or Brazilian hip-hop? If it's available anywhere on Earth, you can probably find it with a few Web clicks. And when you do, the item's Web page might suggest similar or related items based on past customer behavior.

The upshot for consumers is almost unlimited freedom of choice. The upshot for vendors is that they don't need to depend on hits for all of their revenue.

Wired editor Chris Anderson called this phenomenon the Long Tail, referring to the tail of the statistical curve that appears when you rank books, movies, or tunes by popularity as reflected in sales or rentals. The curve starts high on the left side, with points representing sales of the "hits," and trails off into the long statistical tail where the least popular titles are plotted. Before the Web, retailers had trouble making money on those "misses." But on the Web, there's no reason *not* to sell the less popular niche items—especially if those products are digital downloads. Many Web retailers make most of their profits from products that aren't carried by the Wal-Marts of the world.

The Long Tail is getting longer, and that's good for consumers, business, and society. As Anderson wrote in *Wired*, ". . . the cultural benefit of all of this is much more diversity, reversing the blanding effects of a century of distribution scarcity and ending the tyranny of the hit."

Web Marketing 2.0

A related trend is the rise of new Web 2.0–based marketing tools and techniques. Many of the most successful Web businesses depend on customer contributions to add value. Many consumers read customer reviews on Amazon and other sites before buying products. A growing number of high-tech companies encourage customers to contribute to product forums. A lively product forum can encourage sales, but it can also serve as a valuable tech support resource for product owners and users. And of course, well-written blogs and multimedia postings can add value to products and attract future customers.

You don't need to visit a retailer's Web site to be influenced by Web 2.0 marketing techniques. Many retailers have a presence on MySpace, Facebook, and other social networking sites, counting on recommendations from "friends" to increase sales. And if privacy concerns can be set aside, social networks might soon automatically tell you what your online friends are buying.

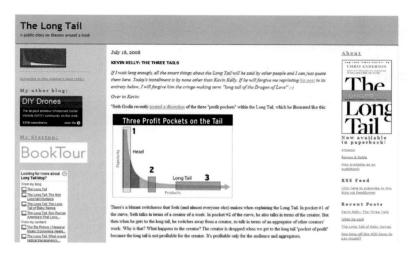

FIGURE 13.20 In theLongTail.com, Chris Anderson regularly adds new material and links related to his book *The Long Tail*, helping keep the book fresh long after its publication date.

Amazon's affiliates program suggests more active social marketing possibilities. Affiliates who link to products on Amazon's site earn financial rewards based on sales. And it's hard to deny the marketing power of the buzz created by a viral video on YouTube or a top-ranked bookmark on Digg or del.icio.us. Buzz can generate hits, but it can also create links, which can result high ranking in search engines—all of which can translate into sales.

The "Free" Market

The rise of **"freeconomics" is being driven** by the underlying technologies that **power the Web** . . . the **trend lines** that determine the **cost of doing business** online all point the same way: **to zero**.

—*Chris Anderson,* Wired *editor*

One Web commerce trend runs counter to our experiences in the physical world: the growing number of e-commerce sites that make money by giving things away. The most famous example, of course, is Google. Google gives away search results, maps, driving directions, telephone directory assistance, images, video sharing services, email, and an ever-growing library of high-quality software. Google doesn't need to charge for all these things because it makes plenty of money in other ways—mostly as a custom advertising service for other Web commerce sites.

Google isn't alone in its generosity. FaceBook, MySpace, LinkedIn, and other social networking sites offer free space and free services to millions of users. Publications from the *New York Times* to *Wired* give away content on the Web that people pay for in print. Craigslist offers want ads for free to both buyers and sellers. Superstar bands like Radiohead and unknown singer/songwriters offer MP3s for free. Many of the most popular online games are free. Wikipedia is just one of countless free online references. Free, it seems, is becoming the "normal" price on the Internet.

Advertising is part of the reason for all these free services—advertisers pay the costs, hoping to attract paying customers for their products. Many "free" services, from games to Internet phone services, hope to entice users to pay for "premium" versions of the same services. And the generosity of the open source community is responsible for many of the best free sites and products. But another factor is the steady decline in the cost of computing

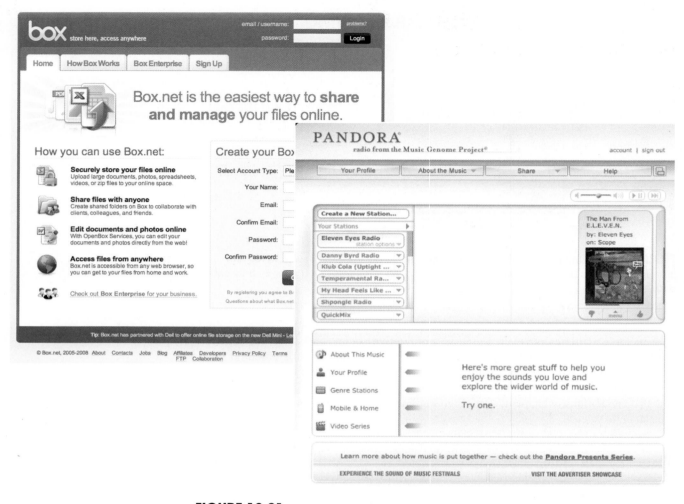

FIGURE 13.21 Box.net (above left) is one of many companies that offers free online storage. Pandora radio (above right) is a personalized internet radio service that creates playlists of new music based on old and current favorites specified by each listener. Listeners can buy songs they like using direct links to Amazon and iTunes.

power, bandwidth, and storage. As hardware costs plummet, they become insignificant in determining the cost of things on the Web. And software costs can be marginalized over large audiences, meaning that the cost per visitor drops with each new visitor.

Of course, money can't measure the value of everything. When people visit "free" Web sites, they're paying with their time and attention, both of which are irreplaceable. The challenge for Web businesses is to provide value in return for time and attention; the challenge for consumers is to determine the best way to use those precious resources.

Ethical Issues of E-Commerce

Now to answer all of the **pop-ups** . . . Ooh, a **talking moose wants my credit card number**. That's **only fair**.

—*Homer Simpson, on* The Simpsons

One of the main challenges of e-commerce is to maintain trust between the people engaging in transactions. If that trust is lost it is difficult to reestablish, and the potential benefits for the company, and for society as a whole, are diminished.

Publishing an information code of ethics on the Web ensures that users—both the company's information workers and customers—are aware of the company's e-commerce policies. Ideally, the code of ethics should include:

- A statement of the organization's privacy policy
- A statement that a person's permission must be secured before his or her ID, photo, ideas, or communications are used or transmitted
- A statement on how the company will inform customers of the intended uses of personal information gathered during an online transaction and how to secure permission from customers for those uses
- A statement that addresses issues of ownership with respect to network postings and communications
- A statement of how the company tracks user behaviors on the Web site

Of course, ethical behavior goes beyond posting policies. Consumers are becoming increasingly impatient with companies and organizations that abuse their privacy and personal information. Here are some well-publicized examples:

- NebuAd, an online advertising service that provides targeted advertising for Internet Service Providers (ISPs), drew criticism and investigation from Congress after it was discovered that the company was using common Internet attack techniques to profile customers' online activities and embed targeted advertising into the Web pages they visited. According to a report, neither the consumers nor the affected Web sites had any knowledge of the company's surveillance and Web page alterations. The company discontinued its tracking program while it was investigated for potential violations of the Communications Act, which puts strict limits on what cable companies can do with customer records.
- Online auction house ReverseAuction.com allegedly collected consumers' personal information from competitor eBay and sent emails to those consumers soliciting their business. According to the U.S. Federal Trade Commission (FTC), ReverseAuctions.com signed up at eBay, disregarded the privacy agreement posted on the rival auction site, and copied the information from bidders to send them solicitations that were later deemed

FIGURE 13.22 Many unethical e-businesses use deceptive tactics and fear-based marketing to prey on the elderly.

deceptive by the FTC. ReverseAuction.com consented to a settlement but said it did not gather any confidential information from the eBay site.

■ The FTC brought suit against Liberty Financial Companies for violating the privacy rights of children who frequented its Young Investor Web site. The FTC alleged that the company had used prizes and contests to encourage children to disclose their names, addresses, weekly allowances, family stock holdings, and more—information that could be used to market to their parents.

The United States has, in general, lagged behind Canada, Europe, Australia, and even Hong Kong in legally establishing overall privacy standards and a regulatory agency that could advise businesses on acceptable privacy practices. Most U.S. businesses and trade organizations tend to favor self-regulation, fearing that government rules would quash the growth of e-commerce. IBM and Disney are good examples of self-regulation; both have long insisted that any Web site they advertise on must have an ironclad privacy policy. But a growing number of companies, including Microsoft and Google, have joined privacy advocacy groups in supporting comprehensive privacy legislation to set ground rules for all U.S. businesses.

The United States has many laws related to the issue of privacy, but only in specific industries and consumer segments. For example, Americans have the legal right to see their credit records. Another law prohibits video rental stores from releasing the names of the movies that you rent. The Health Insurance Portability and Accountability Act requires health-care providers and hospitals to protect the confidentiality of an individual's health information. The Children's Online Privacy Protection Act of 1998 (COPPA) requires certain commercial Web sites to obtain parental consent before collecting, using, or disclosing personal information about children ages 12 and under. However, a report from the Annenberg Public Policy Center of the University of Pennsylvania revealed that many sites with the highest percentage of child visitors under age of 13 often did not follow the COPPA rules.

The European Union issued its Data Protection Directive in October 1998. The directive establishes a high level of legal protection for the privacy of individuals and personal data within the EU. The directive also prohibits companies from transferring personally identifiable information from EU member countries to jurisdictions where that information is not treated with respect by law. As long as the United States does not have an *umbrella* privacy policy, the EU could choose to stop the transfer of all data to it. Clearly, there's much work to be done to protect personal privacy in the age of global e-commerce.

There are other ways that online businesses betray customer trust. Some unethical online businesses mislead customers with deceptive practices, such as advertised policies that they don't actually honor. It's all too common for an advertised claim that *seems* too good to be true to have a catch that effectively *makes* it untrue. For example, an unethical business might advertise $75 laptops "while supplies last," but only sell a single laptop at that price—then redirect anyone that clicks the ad to a much more expensive offer. These types of ads are especially popular with spammers, who never seem to run out of variations on the click-here-for-an-unbelievable-deal message. It only takes a tiny percentage of gullible consumers to generate profits for many of these businesses. Of course, scammed customers tend not to come back for more or recommend the site to other potential customers. And they *might* take expensive legal action.

On the other hand, online businesses that treat their customers with respect tend to find that customer trust has a huge positive impact on the long-term bottom line. For example, Google's online ad program took off so quickly in part because of their honesty. Advertisements—"paid listings"—were clearly marked, and were never embedded in search listings or disguised as non-ad content. Some early Google competitors accepted payments for high search listings—secret ads. Other companies have disguised ads as error messages and instant message windows to trick users into clicking them. (Ironically, Google has become the target of privacy advocates who fear the potential abuse of mountains of private information that customers willingly share with the company.)

The basics of business ethics are the same online as off. Honesty, respect, and integrity are good for business—and society—whether you're selling art on eBay or apples at a farmer's market. It's always been important to have laws to back up these values and protect consumers and businesses from unscrupulous business practices. Those laws will need to be refined, revised, and supplemented as e-commerce technology evolves. But even if the law lags behind the technology, ethics is a critical part of everyday business.

Inventing the FUTURE

Tomorrow's Shopping Experience

In the years since Amazon.com began selling books over the Internet, tens of millions of consumers have shopped on the Web. Many features of the online shopping experience are a good match for our busy lives. Online shopping is easy. We can purchase the items we want without leaving our homes, fighting traffic, wasting fuel, polluting the air, looking for parking spots, coping with inclement weather. With the Web, we can quickly compare the features and prices of more products than any single store is likely to carry. We can read product reviews and get the opinions of other people who have already purchased the product. In many cases we can also customize products to meet our particular needs. With all of these advantages, it's no wonder that some futurists suggest that most shopping will eventually be done online.

On the other hand, the shopping experience is much more than simply making a purchase. Shopping is a social experience, too. Internet skeptics maintain that traditional brick-and-mortar stores will continue to dominate the shopping scene for decades to come.

Even if the skeptics are right, there is no denying that information technology will continue to transform the shopping experience. Many companies are researching new ways to apply digital technology to the shopping experience. Some of these applications may seem far-fetched or strange now—some may even seem disturbing. But consumers have, over the years, been surprisingly willing to sacrifice privacy, convenience, and comfort to save money and have better shopping choices, so there's a reasonable chance that some or all of these innovations will find their way into stores near you over the next few years.

Personalized service makes you feel special. You have provided the store with information about your preferences, and you have a tiny RFID chip embedded in a piece of jewelry or implanted in your shoulder. Sales clerks carry handheld computers equipped with small RFID scanners. When you approach a clerk, the clerk's computer displays information about your preferences and previous purchases.

Guidance systems steer you to the item you want. As you enter the store, you approach an automated information kiosk. Speaking into a microphone, you describe the item you are looking for. After the system confirms the correct item, you use a small handheld "compass" that takes you on the shortest path to the product.

Customized clothes fitting saves you time in the dressing room. You enter a private booth, strip to your undergarments, and stand still for a quick 3-D computerized scan. With your measurements in its database, the store's computer is able to save you time on every shopping trip by guiding you to the correct size and letting you preview different outfits on a monitor. Or you can pay a little extra to have a suit made to order.

Enhanced displays let you compare products. Product displays include computers that give you access to information about the various products being sold, including customer opinions. With all the product comparisons you need right at the display, you can make a purchasing decision on the spot.

Videoconferencing gives you access to experts. If you have a technical question about a product, you don't have to rely on the expertise of the sales clerk who happens to be on duty. The store has a free videoconferencing service that allows you to have a discussion with a product expert located at another store location.

Virtual reality takes the guesswork out of your large purchases. Suppose you are thinking of replacing the furniture in your bedroom. You bring your home's floor plan to the store on a flash memory card. After the computer has created a 3-D rendering of the redecorated room, you can "walk through" the remodeled space.

Will there be a backlash from consumers concerned about a loss of privacy? Many of these innovations require that stores collect a great deal of personal information from their customers. Each of us will have to decide how to balance privacy, convenience, and cost. ∿

FIGURE 13.23 In this Korean department store, a 3-D scanner scans a customer's body to create a 3-D image of the customer. When the customer scans the RFID tag of a piece of clothing, the on-screen avatar is shown wearing that item.

You've Got Mail   *by Tim Harford*

This article, from the February, 2008, issue of **Wired**, *suggests that distance still matters in business and personal networks.*

As a columnist (which is fancy for "journalist in jammies"), I ought to personify the conventional wisdom that distance is dead: All I need to get my work done is a place to perch and a Wi-Fi signal. But if that's true, why do I still live in London, the second-most expensive city in the world?

If distance really didn't matter, rents in places like London, New York, Bangalore, and Shanghai would be converging with those in Hitchcock County, Nebraska (population 2,926 and falling). Yet, as far as we can tell through the noise of the real estate bust, they aren't. Wharton real estate professor Joseph Gyourko talks instead of "superstar cities," which have become the equivalent of luxury goods—highly coveted and ultra-expensive. If geography has died, nobody bothered to tell Hitchcock County.

Maybe it's because society hasn't wholeheartedly accepted the idea of working remotely. Or perhaps communications technology just isn't all it's hyped up to be. After all, the journalists and consultants who tell us that location is insignificant are biased. Like me, they're the people whose lives have been most transformed by the Internet and cell phones.

But I think the truth is more profound than either of those glib explanations: Technology makes it more fun and more profitable to live and work close to the people who matter most to your life and work. Harvard economist Ed Glaeser, an expert on city economies, argues that communications technology and face-to-face interactions are complements like salt and pepper, rather than substitutes like butter and margarine. Paradoxically, your cell phone, email, and Facebook networks are making it more attractive to meet people in the flesh.

The most obvious example is online dating. With sites like BBW (Big Beautiful Women) Datefinder and Senior People Meet, it's a lot easier to find like-minded flames. But that's not much use unless you live within driving range of your 98 percent-compatible love connection. The kind of contact that follows online winking is far from virtual.

It follows that matchmaking is most effective in densely populated areas, where there are plenty of fish but an awfully big sea. If you live in Los Angeles, online dating is the killer app. If you live in a small town, you've likely already met all your potential mates at church or a bar.

Of course, the rest of life isn't like courting. Or is it? In big cities, our communication tools are especially helpful because they keep us from getting lost in the crowd (which is not something you worry about in a one-street town). There are even services that tell you where your friends are by locating their cell signals.

New technologies can strengthen ties within your business, too. A 2007 study by economists Neil Gandal, Charles King, and Marshall Van Alstyne looked at the networks formed by 125,000 email messages from the staff of an executive-recruiting firm. It found that email's real value isn't in communicating with Kuala Lumpur but with Betsy in the next cubicle. The most productive workers have the densest *intra*company email web.

This shouldn't surprise us. Email makes it quicker and easier to reach your colleagues—you don't have to interrupt them, and messages are easy to process. But email doesn't stop you from wanting facetime, too. Just the opposite: By enabling us to maintain productive business relationships with more people, it encourages more face-to-face contact. Have you noticed business travel dying out? Neither have I. Air travel is at record highs.

One day, perhaps, virtual communication will become so good we'll no longer feel the need to shake hands with a new collaborator or brainstorm in the same room. But for now, the world seems to be changing in a way that actually demands more meetings. Business is more innovative, and its processes more complex. That demands tacit knowledge, collaboration, and trust—all things that seem to follow best from person-to-person meetings. "Ideas are more important than ever," Glaeser says, "and the most important ideas are communicated face-to-face."

Which explains why the highest-tech industries are the most dependent on geography. In a study published in the *American Economic Review,* researchers examined 4,000 US-based commercial innovations and found that more than half came from just three areas: California, New York/New Jersey, and Massachusetts. Almost half of all US pharmaceutical innovations were invented in New Jersey, a state with less than 3 percent of the nation's population.

In theory, technology should allow new-economy firms to prosper as easily in Nebraska as in Silicon Valley. But far from killing distance, it has made proximity matter more than ever.

As for me, I've been finishing off this essay between a coffee date with my wife and some essential chitchat with my publishers at a central London restaurant. This old city isn't cheap, and it isn't easy. But with my cell phone and laptop to back me up, I can't afford to live anywhere else.

Discussion Questions

1. How important is distance in maintaining your relationships?

2. Do you think technology will ever make distance irrelevant for business networking?

Summary

E-business is sharing business information, maintaining business relationships, and conducting business transactions through the use of telecommunications networks, especially the Internet. E-business is also about reorganizing internal business processes and external business alliances and creating new consumer-oriented products globally. E-commerce is often equated with e-business, but the most common technical definition of e-commerce makes it a subset of e-business specifically related to buying and selling on a network. E-business has grown at a phenomenal rate since the commercialization of the Internet in the 1990s, with the exception of the economic downturn of 2000–2001.

There are three main e-commerce configurations using Internet technology: intranets, extranets, and public Web sites.

An intranet is an internal information system based on Internet technology, including TCP/IP protocols and Web tools, to support the value chain activities between individuals and departments within an organization. Companies use intranets to provide employees access to important information for their jobs, to facilitate teamwork and collaboration within and among departments, to process internal company transactions online, and to distribute software tools, including customer relations management (CRM) software, to employees.

An extranet is a private inter-organizational information system connecting the intranets of two or more companies in a business alliance. An extranet extends the cross-functional activities between trusted business partners and facilitates their working relationships. Extranets play an important role in the global business strategy of many companies, large and small, enabling them to build alliances with vendors, suppliers, and other organizations internationally. An extranet can be set up either as a secure private network, as a public network, or (most commonly) as a virtual private network (VPN). A major concern of companies conducting business-to-business transactions over an extranet is the guarantee of secure transactions.

A company can connect its intranet to the Internet and operate a publicly accessible Web site to support business-to-consumer transactions or to facilitate consumer-to-consumer transactions. The most successful B2C sites are easy to find because they've been optimized for the major search engines; they make it easy for customers to find and purchase what they're looking for; and they offer secure payment options (often using an electronic payment system like PayPal). C2C sites, including classified ad sites, auctions, and reseller partners, facilitate transactions between consumers.

Several technological trends are rapidly changing the nature of e-business. The growth in cloud computing is making it possible for different components of e-commerce sites to be created and stored in different parts of the Internet "cloud." Increased bandwidth and computing power are enabling developers to create rich media e-commerce sites that make Web shopping more compelling than catalog shopping. A growth in mobile commerce is happening because of major developments in portable electronics and wireless technologies. Online commerce has resulted in a Long Tail effect, creating markets for niche products that wouldn't have been profitable to sell in pre-Web days. Web 2.0 technology has opened up a wide variety of novel marketing schemes, such as viral marketing through social networks, blogs, forums, and media sharing sites. And a surprising number of e-commerce companies make huge profits by giving their products away for free.

A company conducting business on the Internet should develop and adhere to an information code of ethics that ensures that users of the Web site—both the company's information workers and customers—will be aware of the company's e-commerce policies, especially regarding consumer information privacy. Most companies find that customer trust has a positive impact on the long-term bottom line far exceeding any short-term gain due to deceptive practices and policies.

Key Terms

business-to-business
    (B2B) ....(p. 477)
business-to-consumer
    (B2C) ....(p. 477)
business-to-employee
    (B2E) ....(p. 477)
consumer-to-consumer
    (C2C) ....(p. 477)
customer relationship
    management (CRM) ....(p. 478)

dot-com...................................(p. 475)
electronic business
    (e-business).......................(p. 475)
electronic commerce
    (e-commerce)....................(p. 475)
electronic payment
    system...............................(p. 483)
extranet ....(p. 479)
intranet..................................(p. 477)
Long Tail ....(p. 494)

mobile commerce
    (m-commerce) ....(p. 490)
search engine optimization
    (SEO)...............................(p. 488)
virtual private network
    (VPN) ....(p. 479)

Interactive Activities

1. The *Tomorrow's Technology and You* Web site, www.pearsonhighered.com/beekman, contains self-test exercises related to this chapter. Follow the instructions for taking a quiz. After you've completed your quiz, you can email the results to your instructor.

2. The Web site also contains open-ended discussion questions called Internet Exercises. Discuss one or more of the Internet Exercises at the section for this chapter.

True or False

1. The first successful e-commerce Web sites were put online in the late 1970s.

2. E-commerce wasn't possible before the commercialization of the Internet.

3. REI.com, Converse.com, and most other retail Web sites conform to the consumer-to-consumer (C2C) e-commerce model.

4. It's not possible to have a working intranet without a broadband Internet connection.

5. In a virtual private network (VPN), data is transmitted through the Internet via a secure "tunnel" between intranets.

6. Security of transactions is a major concern of companies conducting B2B transactions over the Internet, regardless of the type of extranet.

7. The number of hits on a Web site is almost always the best indication of the site's effectiveness.

8. The Long Tail refers to the statistical chart showing the decline in e-commerce sales as customers abandon shopping carts.

9. The business-to-consumer (B2C) model is the predominant form of e-commerce.

10. Most experts believe that self-regulation and compliance with Internet privacy codes of ethics by American companies make regulatory privacy laws unnecessary in the United States.

Multiple Choice

1. Which model does Amazon.com use in its business?
   a. B2B
   b. B2C
   c. C2C
   d. Amazon uses each of the above in parts of its business.
   e. Amazon doesn't use any of these.

2. Which of these causes led most directly to the dot-com bust of 2000–2001?
   a. The 9/11 terrorist attacks
   b. The Y2K bug
   c. Excessive stock market speculation
   d. Rampant software and music piracy
   e. Hacker attacks on key Internet servers

3. An increase in disaggregation of many e-commerce sites is happening because
   a. security restrictions are making intranets more difficult to maintain.
   b. Web 2.0 technology doesn't support older graphics processors on most servers.
   c. cloud computing is making it easier to store different components of a Web site in different places on the Internet.
   d. when a potential customer links to a site, the connection between client and server is the shortest possible route through the Internet.
   e. mobile devices are connecting to the Internet in record numbers, making aggregation impossible.

4. Using Internet technology for intranets is advantageous because of
   a. open standards.
   b. the cross-platform environment.
   c. geographic independence.
   d. reduced hardware and software costs.
   e. All of the above.

5. Business intranets are commonly used for all of these reasons EXCEPT:
   a. They can encourage teamwork and collaboration.
   b. They can make it easy for employees to get information when they need it.
   c. They automate shopping carts, checkout, and other components of retail sales.
   d. They facilitate internal business transactions, such as employee benefits.
   e. They can be connected to other intranets to create extranets.

6. Online auctions like eBay generally follow which model?
   a. B2B
   b. B2E
   c. B2C
   d. C2C
   e. C2E

7. A typical extranet is set up as
   a. a cloud.
   b. a public network.
   c. a virtual private network (VPN).
   d. an expandable node developer (END).
   e. a 3G grid.

8. Mobile commerce is on the rise because of
   a. the increase in sales and use of portable handheld computers that can connect to the Internet.
   b. the proliferation of wireless network hotspots.
   c. rapid improvements in handheld software and hardware.
   d. the growing popularity of laptop computers.
   e. All of the above.

9. Strategic benefits of extranet use in business alliances include
   a. increasing the speed of business-to-business transactions.
   b. reducing errors on intercompany transactions.
   c. reducing costs of telecommunications.
   d. increasing the volume of business with partners.
   e. All of these are strategic benefits of business alliances.

10. Research has shown that
    a. most consumers believe that shopping on the Internet can now match the experience of shopping in a store.
    b. online shoppers frequently abandon their shopping carts because they can't get the information they want before making purchases.
    c. the most compelling reason consumers give for shopping in stores is that stores offer more choices.
    d. All of the above.
    e. None of the above.

11. What is the name for a set of protocols that enables business partners to share a secure "tunnel" through the public Internet?
    a. Compressed network
    b. Intranet
    c. Underground network
    d. SecureNet
    e. Virtual private network

12. Which of these statements is true?
    a. Business-to-business e-commerce is a much bigger segment of our economy than business-to-consumer e-commerce.
    b. Business-to-business e-commerce generally doesn't work across national boundaries.
    c. Mobile commerce today is limited to B2C transactions.
    d. The fastest growing segment of the B2E market is the reverse auction industry.
    e. All of the above are true.

13. What is the main advantage of making Web purchases with PayPal's electronic payment system over paying with a credit card?
    a. PayPal uses a much higher rate of encryption than credit cards do.
    b. PayPal ID information can't be stolen.
    c. Using PayPal usually results in lower prices.
    d. When you use PayPal the vendor doesn't have access to your credit card number.
    e. Unlike credit cards, PayPal works internationally.

14. Which of these is generally done with an intranet?
    a. B2B
    b. B2C
    c. B2D
    d. B2E
    e. C2C

15. Which U.S. law requires operators of Web sites to get parental permission before collecting information from children under 13 years old?
    a. NAFTA
    b. Children's Online Privacy Protection Act
    c. Privacy Act of 1974
    d. Secure Transaction Act
    e. No such law exists.

Review Questions

1. Define or describe each of the key terms in the "Key Terms" section. Check your answers using the glossary.

2. Is e-commerce possible without the Internet? Explain your answer.

3. Describe the four most common models of e-commerce and one additional e-business model that isn't, by most definitions, strictly e-commerce.

4. What are the purposes of an intranet? What are the main characteristics of an intranet?

5. What is the purpose of an extranet? What are the main characteristics of an extranet?

6. What technological trends have made it easier for online businesses to give away services such as email, voice mail, and classified ads?

7. Describe several business models that make it possible for companies to give away goods and services online while still making a profit.

8. Explain why Internet commerce offers more opportunities for entertainment products that aren't "hits."

9. Explain how cloud computing might result in more consistent shopping experiences for consumers (for example, so that the checkout process wouldn't vary from site to site).

10. Describe how the U.S. approach to dealing with data privacy differs from that of the European Union.

Discussion Questions

1. How has e-commerce changed your buying habits over the last few years? Which of these changes are positive and which are negative?

2. Can you identify examples of e-commerce applications within your college or university? Discuss how your school could use an intranet to improve its internal operations, such as class registration. How could such an intranet be used to competitive advantage for your school?

3. Can you identify opportunities for using an extranet at your college or university? How could such an extranet be used to competitive advantage for your school?

4. Discuss the issues you would need to consider if you were to create a B2C Web site for a small company.

5. Do you think the Long Tail phenomenon is likely to change the nature of the art and entertainment industries? Explain your answer.

6. People talk about privacy a lot, but how important is privacy? Would you pay extra for an item you purchased online in return for a guarantee that the company would not sell information about your purchase to anyone else? Would you be willing to share more personal information with a store if that meant you received more personalized service?

Projects

1. Find an example of a business organization that is using the Internet to increase its competitive advantage in its industry. What competitive strategy is the organization following? Is the Internet being used to decrease costs? Increase value to the customers? Summarize your findings in a report.

2. Form a team and visit a local company that has a Web site. Interview the manager and others about the company's Internet philosophy. What is the purpose of the company's Web site? Who designed the site? Who maintains the site? Does the company advertise on the Internet? Does the company use an intranet or extranet? What are the company's plans for its future use of the Internet? Summarize your findings.

3. Create a list of characteristics of a well-designed B2C Web site. Locate the public Web sites of several competitors in the same industry. Then use your list to evaluate the effectiveness of each of the Web sites. Summarize your findings.

4. Visit two Web sites that offer similar products—for example, two clothing sites or two bookstore sites. Evaluate how each company handles your security and privacy concerns.

5. Find several Web sites offering unique shopping experiences that go beyond the typical pages-of-a-catalog model. Report on which sites are most effective and why.

6. Create a business plan for a B2C or C2C online business. Include simple sketches and/or maps of the most important parts of the Web site. Talk about the most significant hurdles you would have to overcome to turn the business into a reality.

Sources and Resources

Books

Web Design for ROI: Turning Browsers into Buyers & Prospects into Leads, by Lance Loveday (Berkeley, CA: New Riders Press, 2007). Web design can do more than make a site look good—it can also improve financial returns and create competitive advantage. This book is filled with practical tips for increasing conversion rates and maximizing the Return on Investment (ROI) of any business site.

Web Design and Marketing Solutions for Business Websites, by Kevin Potts (Berkeley, CA: friends of ED, 2007). A good Web site can help a company a great deal, but a bad one can drive customers away. This book covers the fundamentals of creating a business Web site that works for the company, not against it. It covers Web writing and search engine optimization, offers practical tips for the common sections that every business site needs, and discusses how to create a winning online strategy.

Web 2.0: A Strategy Guide: Business thinking and strategies behind successful Web 2.0 implementations, by Amy Shuen (Cambridge, MA: O'Reilly Media, Inc., 2008). Web 2.0 has gotten a lot of press recently, but how do headlines turn into profit? Successful business implementations of Web 2.0 strategies require an understanding of both the opportunities and the potential problems. *Web 2.0: A Strategy Guide* demonstrates the power of this new paradigm, examining how companies such as Flickr, Google, Facebook, and Amazon have flourished by embracing the new collaborative and connective possibilities of the modern Web.

Wikinomics: How Mass Collaboration Changes Everything, by Don Tapscott and Anthony D. Williams (New York, NY: Portfolio, 2008). "Wiki" means quick in Hawaiian. This book describes in detail how the technology behind mass Internet collaboration is quickly changing the nature of business. Whether you're interested in exploiting the power of collaborative production or just curious about the future of commerce, you'd be well advised to read this book . . . quickly.

The Long Tail: Why the Future of Business Is Selling Less of More, by Chris Anderson (New York, NY: Hyperion, 2006). This influential book started as an article in the pages of *Wired.* Anderson presents plenty of compelling evidence that the Web is expanding options for consumers and opportunities for artists, authors, and businesses to go beyond "hit" mentality and explore more diverse markets. His book isn't without critics who say he sometimes overstates his arguments. His Web site, theLongTail.com, provides a forum to continue the important discussion started by this book.

Connect!: A Guide to a New Way of Working, by Anne Truitt Zelenka (Hoboken, NJ: John Wiley & Sons, 2008). The Web has opened up all kinds of possibilities for people to work remotely or independently. This book is aimed at those Web workers. The emphasis here is on the kind of work that benefits from openness, collaboration, and building relationships.

The Open Brand: When Push Comes to Pull in a Web-Made World, by Kelly Mooney and Nita Rollins (Berkeley, CA: Peachpit Press, 2008). The authors of this book argue that many of today's successful new brands are open. Like open source software, they respond to consumer involvement. Are marketing and branding becoming interactive activities? The authors think so, and they tell you why here.

eBay QuickSteps, Second Edition, by Carole Matthews and John Cronan (New York, NY: Osborne McGraw Hill, 2008). Countless small businesses—and a few large ones—have sprouted in the fertile soil of eBay's popular auction site. You don't need to be a technical wizard to buy and sell goods on eBay, but it helps if you know the basics before you play for high stakes. The authors of this book lay out the ground rules and provide lots of helpful hints and tips. The QuickSteps format is highly graphical, so you don't need to wade through pages of text to find what you're looking for.

Sell It on eBay, Second Edition, by Jim Heid and Toby Malina (Berkeley, CA: Peachpit Press, 2006). Jim Heid is one of the most prolific and versatile writers in the computer book business. In this popular book, he and Toby Malina lay out a crystal-clear strategy for selling stuff on eBay. They cover details that many other books overlook, including retouching your auction photos with Photoshop. This book can help you start an online business or just unload some of the junk that's cluttering up your space.

Video

Startup.com, directed by Chris Hegedus and Jehane Noujaim (2001). This fascinating documentary started out as the story of the creation of an Internet company. The cameras followed two young men as they followed their vision through the Internet frenzy that preceded the dot-com bust. The focus is on the two men, their relationship, and the impact of their fast-pace business on that relationship.

14

Systems Design and Development

After you read this chapter you should be able to:

▶ Describe the process of designing, programming, and debugging a computer program

▶ Explain why there are many different programming languages, and give examples of several

▶ Explain why computer languages are built into applications, operating systems, and utilities

▶ Outline the steps in the life cycle of an information system, and explain the purpose of program maintenance

▶ Explain the relationship between computer programming and computer science

▶ Describe the problems faced by software engineers in trying to produce reliable large systems

▶ Explain why software companies provide only limited warranties for their products

> The only phrase I've ever disliked is, **"Why, we've always done it that way."** I always tell young people, **"Go ahead and do it. You can always apologize later."**
>
> —*Grace Murray Hopper*

Grace Murray Hopper Sails on Software

Amazing Grace, the grand old lady of software, had little to apologize for when she died at the age of 85 in 1992. More than any other woman, Grace Murray Hopper helped chart the course of the computer industry from its earliest days.

Hopper earned a Ph.D. from Yale in 1928 and taught math for 10 years at Vassar before joining the U.S. Naval Reserve in 1943. The Navy assigned her to the Bureau of Ordnance Computation at Harvard, where she worked with Howard Aiken's Mark I, the first large-scale electro-mechanical digital computer. She wrote programs and operating manuals for the Mark I, Mark II, and Mark III.

Aiken often asked his team, "Are you making any numbers?" When she wasn't "making numbers," Hopper replied that she was "debugging" the computer. Today that's what programmers call the process of finding and removing errors, or bugs, from programs. Scientists and engineers had referred to mechanical defects as bugs for decades; Thomas Edison wrote about bugs in his inventions in 1878. But when Hopper first used the term, she was referring to a real bug—a 2-inch moth that got caught in a relay, bringing the mighty Mark II to a standstill! That moth carcass is taped to a page in a log book, housed in a Navy museum in Virginia.

Hopper recognized early that businesses could make good use of computers. After World War II, she left Harvard to work on the UNIVAC I, the first general-purpose commercial computer built in the United States, and other commercial computers. She played central roles in the development of the first compiler (a type of computer language translator that makes most of today's software possible) and COBOL, the first computer language designed for developing business software.

Throughout most of her career, Hopper remained anchored to the Navy. When she retired from the fleet with the rank of rear admiral at the age of 79, her list of accomplishments filled eight single-spaced pages in her Navy biography.

509

FIGURE 14.1 Grace Murray Hopper (1906–1992)

But Hopper's greatest impact was probably the result of her tireless crusade against the "We've always done it that way" mind-set. In the early days of computing, she worked to persuade businesses to embrace the new technology. In later years, she campaigned to shift the Pentagon and industry away from mainframes and toward networks of smaller computers. Her vigorous campaign against the status quo earned her a reputation as being controversial and contrary. That didn't bother Amazing Grace, whose favorite maxim was "A ship in port is safe, but that's not what ships are for." ～

FIGURE 14.2 This moth was one of the first computer bugs—it was removed from a relay in the Mark II.

Today's computer software is so sophisticated that it's almost invisible to the user. Just as a great motion picture can make you forget you're watching a movie, the best PC software enables you to do your creative work without ever thinking about the instructions and data flowing through the computer's processor as you work. But whether you're writing a paper, solving a calculus problem, flying a simulated space shuttle, or exploring the nooks and crannies of the Internet, your imaginary environment stands on an incredibly complex software substructure. The process of creating that software is one of the most intellectually challenging activities ever done by people.

In this chapter we look at the process of turning ideas into working computer programs and information systems. We examine computer languages and the ways programmers use them to create software. In addition, we look at how computer users take advantage of the programming languages built into applications, operating systems, and utilities. We examine the life cycle of a complex information system. We also confront the problems involved with producing reliable software and consider the implications of depending on unstable software. In the process of exploring software, we'll see how the work of programmers, analysts, software engineers, and computer scientists affects our lives and our work.

How People Make Programs

Most computer users depend on professionally programmed applications—spreadsheets, image-editing programs, Web browsers, and the like—as problem-solving tools. But in some cases it's necessary or desirable to write a program rather than use one written by somebody else. As a human activity, computer programming is a relative newcomer. But programming is a specialized form of the age-old process of problem solving. Problem solving typically involves four steps:

It's the only job I can think of where I get to be both an **engineer** and an **artist**. There's an incredible, rigorous, technical element to it, which **I like** because you have to do very **precise thinking**. On the other hand, it has a wildly creative side where **the boundaries of imagination are the only real limitation**.

—*Andy Hertzfeld, co-designer of the Macintosh*

- *Understanding the problem.* Defining the problem clearly is often the most important—and most overlooked—step in the problem-solving process.
- *Devising a plan for solving the problem.* What resources are available? People? Information? A computer? Software? Data? How might those resources be put to work to solve the problem?
- *Carrying out the plan.* This phase often overlaps with the previous step, because many problem-solving schemes are developed on the fly.
- *Evaluating the solution.* Is the problem solved correctly? Is this solution applicable to other problems?

The programming process can also be described as a four-step process, although in practice these steps often overlap:

- Defining the problem
- Devising, refining, and testing the algorithm
- Writing the program
- Testing and debugging the program

Most programming problems are far too complex to solve all at once. To turn a problem into a program, a programmer typically creates a list of smaller problems. Each of these smaller problems can be broken into subproblems that can be subdivided in the same way. This process, called stepwise refinement, is similar to the process of developing an outline before writing a paper or a book. Programmers sometimes refer to this type of design as top-down design because the design process starts at the top, with the main ideas, and works down to the details.

The result of stepwise refinement is an algorithm—a set of step-by-step instructions that, when completed, solves the original problem. (Recall Suzanne's French toast recipe in Chapter 4.) Programmers typically write algorithms in a form called pseudocode—a cross between a computer language and plain English. When the details of an algorithm are in place, a programmer can translate it from pseudocode into a computer language.

From Idea to Algorithm

One programs, just as one writes, not because one understands, but **in order to come to understand**. Programming is an act of design. To write a program is to legislate the laws for **a world one first has to create in imagination**.

—*Joseph Weizenbaum, in* Computer Power and Human Reason

Let's develop a simple algorithm to illustrate the process. Let's start with a statement of the problem:

A schoolteacher needs a program to play a number-guessing game so students can learn to develop logical strategies and practice their arithmetic. In this game the computer picks a number between 1 and 100 and gives the player seven turns to guess the number. After each incorrect try, the computer tells the player whether the guess is too high or too low.

In short, the problem is to write a program that can

```
play a guessing game
```

Stepwise Refinement

The first cut at the problem breaks it into three parts: a beginning, a middle, and an end. Each of these parts represents a smaller programming problem to solve.

```
pick a number for user to guess and display instructions
give user 7 chances to guess the number
respond appropriately to each guess
```

These three steps represent a bare-bones algorithm. In the completed algorithm, these three parts are carried out in sequence. The next refinement fills in a few details for each part:

```
pick a number between 1 and 100
display instructions
repeat
  input guess from user
  respond to guess
until number is guessed or 7 turns are completed
display final message
```

The middle part of our instructions includes a sequence of operations that repeats for each turn: everything between "repeat" and "until." But these instructions lack crucial details. How, for example, does the computer respond to a guess? We can replace "respond to guess" with instructions that vary depending on the guessed number:

```
if guess = answer then display "You win" and quit
else if guess < answer then display "Too small"
else display "Too big"
```

Finally, we need to give the computer a way of knowing when seven turns have passed. We can set a counter to 0 at the beginning and add 1 to the counter after each turn. When the counter reaches 7, the repetition stops, and the computer displays a message. That makes the algorithm look like this:

```
set answer to a random value between 1 and 100
display "Guess a number between 1 and 100"
set counter to 0
repeat
  input guess from user
  if guess = answer then
    display "You win"
```

```
     quit
   else if guess < answer then
    display "Too small"
   else display "Too big"
   add 1 to counter
until counter = 7
display "Too many guesses. You lose."
```

Control Structures

A computer can't understand this algorithm, but the pseudocode is clear to any person familiar with **control structures**—logical structures that control the order in which instructions are carried out. This algorithm uses three basic control structures: sequence, selection, and repetition.

A *sequence* control structure is a group of instructions followed in order from the first through the last. In our algorithm example, as in most computer languages, the sequence is the default structure; that is, it applies unless a statement says otherwise:

```
set answer to a random value between 1 and 100
display "Guess a number between 1 and 100"
set counter to 0
```

A *selection* (or *decision*) control structure is used to make logical decisions—to choose between alternative courses of action depending on certain conditions. It typically takes the form of "If (some condition is true), then (do something) else (do something else)":

```
if guess < answer then
   display "Too small"
else display "Too big"
```

A *repetition* control structure is a looping mechanism. It allows a group of steps to be repeated several times, usually until some condition is satisfied. In this algorithm the indented statements between "repeat" and "until" repeat until the number is guessed correctly or the counter is equal to 7:

```
repeat
   input guess from user
   ...
   add 1 to counter
until counter = 7
```

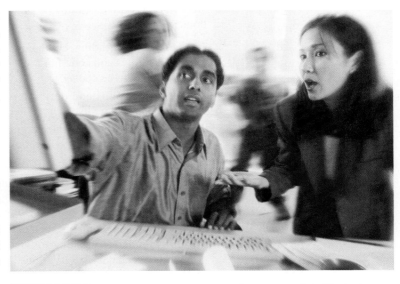

FIGURE 14.3 Software development has become a global industry. These programmers in India write software for a company based in America.

As our example illustrates, these simple control structures can be combined to produce more complex algorithms. In fact, any computer program can be constructed from these three control structures.

Testing the Algorithm

The next step is **testing** the algorithm. Testing of the completed program comes later; this round of testing is designed to check the logic of the algorithm. We can test it by following the instructions using different sets of numbers. We might, for example, use a target number of 35 and guesses of 15, 72, 52, and 35. Those numbers test all three possibilities in the if-then-else structure (guess is less than target, guess is greater than target, and guess equals target), and they show what happens if the player chooses the correct number. We should also test the algorithm with seven wrong guesses in a row to make sure it correctly ends a losing game.

From Algorithm to Program

You know, computer science **inverts the normal**. In normal science you're given a world and **your job is to find out the rules**. In computer science, you give the computer the rules and it **creates the world**.

—Alan Kay

When testing is complete, the algorithm is ready to become a program. Because the algorithm has the logical structure of a program, the process of coding—writing a program from the algorithm—is simple and straightforward. Statements in the algorithm translate directly into lines of code in whichever programming language best fits the programmer's needs.

A Simple Program

In the Screen Test on page 516, you can see this algorithm rewritten in C++, a popular variation of the C programming language. (The name C doesn't stand for anything; the language grew out of a less successful language called B.) This program, like most well-written C++ programs, is organized into three parts, similar to a recipe in a cookbook:

1. The program heading, containing the name of the program (not visible in the window) and data files and code libraries to be included (equivalent to the name and description of the dish to be cooked)
2. The declarations and definitions of variables and other programmer-defined items (equivalent to the list of ingredients used in the recipe)
3. The body of the program, containing the instructions, sandwiched between curly braces, { } (equivalent to the cooking steps).

The program looks like a detailed version of the original algorithm, but there's an important difference: because it's a computer program, every word, symbol, and punctuation mark has an exact, unambiguous meaning.

The blue words are keywords with predefined meanings in C++. These keywords, along with special symbols such as 1 and 5, are part of the standard vocabulary of C++. The programmer defines the words *number, guess,* and *counter,* so they become part of the program's vocabulary when it runs. Each of these words represents a *variable*—a named portion of the computer's memory whose contents the program can examine and change.

As programs go, this C++ program is fairly easy to understand. But C++ isn't English, and some statements occasionally need clarification or further documentation. For the sake of readability, most programs include comments—the programmer's equivalent of Post-it notes. In C++, lines that begin with double slashes (//) contain comments. The computer ignores comments; they're included to help human readers understand (or remember) something about the program.

High-level language program statement

Machine-language program translation of statement

Interpreter

FIGURE 14.4 An interpreter translates the source code of a program to machine language one statement at a time. It must repeat this process every time the program is run.

Into the Computer

The program still needs to be entered into the computer's memory, saved as a disk file, and translated into the computer's native machine language before it can be executed, or run. To enter and save the program, we can use a text editor. A *text editor* is like a word processor without the formatting features that writers and publishers require. Some text editors, designed with programming in mind, provide automatic program indenting and limited error checking and correction while the program is being typed.

To translate the program into machine language, we need translation software. The translation program might be an **interpreter** (a program that translates and transmits each statement individually, the way a United Nations interpreter translates a Russian speech into English) or a **compiler** (a program that translates an entire program before passing it on to the computer, as a scholar might translate the novel *War and Peace* from Russian to English). Most C++ translators are compilers because compiled programs tend to run faster than interpreted programs.

Machine-language program

High-level language program

FIGURE 14.5 A compiler translates all of the source code of a program to machine language once, before executing the program.

A typical compiler software package today is more than just a compiler. It's an integrated *programming environment*, including a text editor, a compiler, a *debugger* to simplify the process of locating and correcting errors, and a variety of other programming utilities. **Syntax errors**—violations of the grammar rules of the programming language—are often flagged automatically as soon as they're typed into the editor. **Logic errors**—problems with the logical structure that cause differences between what the program is supposed to do and what it actually does—aren't always as easy to detect. That's why debugging and testing can take a large percentage of program development time.

Programming Languages and Methodologies

C++ is one of hundreds of computer languages in use today. Some are tools for professional programmers who write the software the rest of us use. Others are intended to help students learn the fundamentals of programming. Still others enable computer users to automate repetitive tasks and customize software applications. Since the earliest days of computing, programming languages have continued to evolve toward providing easier communication between people and computers.

> If one character, one pause, of the incantation is not strictly in proper form, the **magic doesn't work**.
>
> —*Frederick Brooks, in* The Mythical Man-Month

Machine Language and Assembly Language

Every computer has a native language—a **machine language**. Similarities exist between different brands of machine languages: They all have instructions for the four basic arithmetic operations, for comparing pairs of numbers, for repeating instructions, and so on. But like English and French, different brands of machine languages are different languages, and machines based on one machine language can't understand programs written in another.

From the machine's point of view, machine language is all binary. Instructions, memory locations, numbers, and characters are all represented by strings of 0s and 1s. Because binary numbers are difficult for people to read, machine-language programs are usually displayed with the binary numbers translated into decimal (base 10), *hexadecimal* (base 16), or some other number system. Even so, machine-language programs have always been hard to write, read, and debug.

Screen Test

Programming in C++

1. You decide to convert the algorithm on pages 512–513 into a working program. After you finish designing your game program, you can type it into the editor window.

2. The editor automatically indents statements as you type, so it's easy to see the logical structure of the program.

3. The editor also points out a syntax error. Detecting the point of the error is much easier for the computer than identifying what the programmer's mistake is. In this case, the system reports the error as a missing semicolon between commands. The actual error is a misplaced double quotation mark.

4. You run the program to test for logic errors.

5. When you test it with a series of incorrect guesses, it fails to stop after seven guesses.

6. And when you correctly guess the answer, it fails to stop. Instead, it asks you for another guess.

7. You see the logic error in the statement "--counter", which decrements the counter by 1. It should say "++counter" to increment the counter by 1. You correct the error.

8. You rerun the program to test it again. Like most programs, this one could go through several rounds of testing, debugging, and refining before the programmer is satisfied.

FIGURE 14.6

The programming process became easier with the invention of **assembly language**—a language that's functionally equivalent to machine language but is easier for people to read, write, and understand. In assembly language, programmers use alphabetic codes that correspond to the machine's numeric instructions. An assembly-language instruction for subtract, for example, might be SUB. Of course, SUB means nothing to the computer, which responds only to commands such as 10110111. To bridge the communication gap between programmer and computer, a program called an **assembler** translates each assembly-language instruction into a machine-language instruction. Without knowing any better, the computer acts as its own translator.

Because of the obvious advantages of assembly language, few programmers write in machine language anymore. But assembly-language programming is still considered low-level programming; that is, it requires the programmer to think on the machine's level and to include an enormous amount of detail in every program. Assembly language and machine language are *low-level languages*. Low-level programming is a repetitive, tedious, and error-prone process. To make matters worse, a program written in one assembly language or machine language must be completely rewritten before it can be run on computers with different machine languages. Many programmers still use assembly language to write parts of video games and other applications for which speed and direct communication with hardware are critical. But most programmers today think and write on a higher level.

FIGURE 14.7 An assembler translates each statement of assembly-language source code into the corresponding machine-language statement.

High-Level Languages

Computer programming is an art form, like the creation of **poetry** or **music**.

—*Donald E. Knuth, author of* The Art of Computer Programming

High-level languages, which fall somewhere between natural human languages and precise machine languages, were developed during the early 1950s to simplify and streamline the programming process. Languages such as FORTRAN and COBOL made it possible for scientists, engineers, and businesspeople to write programs using familiar terminology and notation rather than cryptic machine instructions. Today programmers can choose from hundreds of high-level languages.

Interpreters and compilers translate high-level programs into machine language. Whether interpreted or compiled, a single statement from a high-level program turns into several machine-language statements. A high-level language hides most of the nitty-gritty details of the machine operations from the programmer. As a result, it's easier for the programmer to think about the overall logic of the program—the big ideas. In other words, a higher-level language allows the programmer to focus on what to do, while assembly language forces the programmer to focus on how to do it.

Besides being easier to write and debug, high-level programs have the advantage of being transportable between machines. A program written in standard C can be compiled and run on any computer with a standard C compiler. The same applies for programs written in Java, BASIC, FORTRAN, COBOL, and other standardized languages.

Transporting a program to a new machine isn't always that easy. Most high-level programs need to be partially rewritten to adjust to differences among hardware, compilers, operating systems, and user interfaces. For example, programmers might need to rewrite 20 percent of the code when translating the Windows version of an application program into a Macintosh version, or vice versa. Still, high-level programs are far more portable than programs written in assembly and machine languages.

Of the hundreds of high-level languages that have been developed, a few have become well known because of their widespread use:

- *FORTRAN* (Formula Translation), the first commercial high-level programming language, was designed at IBM in the 1950s to solve scientific and engineering problems. Many scientists and engineers still use modern versions of FORTRAN today.

- *COBOL* (Common Business Oriented Language) was developed in 1960 when the U.S. government demanded a new language oriented toward business data-processing problems. COBOL programmers still work in many data-processing shops around the world.

- *LISP* (List Processing) was developed at MIT in the late 1950s to process nonnumeric data such as characters, words, and other symbols. LISP is widely used in artificial intelligence research, in part because it's easy to write LISP programs that can write other programs.

- *BASIC* (Beginner's All-purpose Symbolic Instruction Code) was developed in the mid-1960s as an easy-to-learn, interactive alternative to FORTRAN for beginning programmers. Before BASIC a student typically had to submit a program, wait hours for output from a compiler, and repeat the process until every error was corrected. Because BASIC was interpreted line by line rather than compiled as a whole, it could provide instant feedback as students typed statements and commands into their terminals. When personal computers appeared, BASIC enjoyed unprecedented popularity among students, hobbyists, and programmers. Over the years BASIC has evolved into a powerful, modern programming tool for amateur and professional programmers. True BASIC is a modern version of BASIC developed by the original inventors of BASIC. The most popular Windows version of BASIC today—in fact, the most popular programming language ever created—is Microsoft's Visual Basic. REALbasic is a popular cross-platform BASIC.

- *Pascal* (named for a seventeenth-century French mathematician, inventor, philosopher, and mystic) was developed in the early 1970s as an alternative to BASIC for encouraging good programming practices in student programmers. Pascal is seldom used by professional programmers.

- C was invented at Bell Labs in the early 1970s as a tool for programming operating systems such as UNIX. C is a complex language that's difficult to learn. But its power, flexibility, and efficiency have made it—along with its variants—the language of choice for most professionals who program personal computers.

- C++ is a variation of C that supports a modern programming methodology called object-oriented programming, described later in this chapter.

- Java is a full-featured object-oriented language developed by Sun Microsystems. Java is especially popular for creating Web applets, small compiled programs that run inside other applications—typically Web browsers. Java also excels at creating cross-platform applications that run on many different computers and mobile devices, regardless of the operating system.

- *Visual J++* is a Java-like language from Microsoft for programming on the Windows platform.

- C# (pronounced C sharp) is a popular Windows-only language that's similar to Java.

- *Python* is a Java-like language popular with Linux open-source programmers.

- *Ada* (named for Ada King, the programming pioneer profiled in Chapter 1) is a massive language based on Pascal. It was developed in the late 1970s for the U.S. Defense Department. Ada never caught on outside the walls of the military establishment.

- *PROLOG* (Programming Logic) is a popular language for artificial intelligence programming. As the name implies, PROLOG is designed for working with logical relationships between facts.

- *LOGO* is a derivative of LISP specially designed for children.

Structured Programming

A programming language can be a powerful tool in the hands of a skilled programmer. But tools alone don't guarantee quality; the best programmers have specific techniques for getting the most out of their software tools. In the short history of computer programming, computer scientists have developed several new methodologies that have made programmers more productive and programs more reliable.

> We but teach **bloody instructions**, which being taught, return **to plague the inventor**.
>
> —*Shakespeare*, Macbeth

For example, computer scientists in the late 1960s recognized that most FORTRAN and BASIC programs were riddled with GoTo statements—statements used to transfer control to other parts of the program. (Remember "Go to Jail. Do not pass Go. Do not collect $200"?) The logical structure of a program with GoTo statements can resemble a plate of spaghetti. In fact, programmers call programs with too many GoTo statements "spaghetti code." The bigger the program, the bigger the logical maze and the more possibility for error. Every branch of a program represents a loose end that a programmer might overlook.

In an attempt to overcome these problems, computer scientists developed structured programming—a technique to make the programming process easier and more productive.

FIGURE 14.8 Computer software contains two kinds of information: program code and data. The program embodies the algorithms that manipulate the data. In this figure the program is represented by a machine, and the data are represented by the raw material and the finished products. An unstructured program with one large module is like a huge, complicated machine that can't easily be broken down into component parts.

FIGURE 14.9 Structured programming breaks the big, complicated machine into more manageable modules, each of which has a clearly defined task. Modular programs are easier to understand and debug.

How It Works

The BASIC programming language has evolved through three major phases. These examples show how the programming process has changed during the last three decades. The first two BASIC examples shown here are complete listings of programs to play the number-guessing game; the third example is a glimpse of a program to play a slot machine game.

```
10 REM INITIALIZE
20 RANDOMIZE
30 PRINT "THE GUESSING GAME"
40 PRINT "I WILL THINK OF A NUMBER BETWEEN 1 AND 100."
50 PRINT "TRY TO GUESS WHAT IT IS"
60 LET C = 0
70 LET N = INT(RND(1) * 100)
80 INPUT "WHAT IS YOUR GUESS?";G
90 IF G = N THEN PRINT "THAT IS CORRECT!"
100 IF G < N THEN PRINT "TOO SMALL--TRY AGAIN"
110 IF G > N THEN PRINT "TOO BIG--TRY AGAIN"
120 LET C = C + 1
130 IF C = 7 THEN GOTO 150
140 IF G <> N THEN GOTO 80
150 IF G <> N THEN PRINT "I FOOLED YOU 7 TIMES! THE ANSWER WAS ";N
160 END
```

1. Early BASIC. The program with numbered lines is written in a simple version of BASIC—the only kind that was available in the early days of the language. Statements are executed in numerical order unless control is transferred to another statement with a GoTo statement.

2. Structured BASIC. The modular program on the bottom is written in QuickBASIC, a newer version of the language with many structured programming features. The main program has been reduced to a handful of statements at the top of the listing (after the DECLARE statements); these statements display the overall logic of the program. As it's running, the main program uses CALL statements to transfer control to each of the three subprograms, which take care of the game's beginning, each turn, and the game's end.

3. Visual BASIC. The screen shows an example of Microsoft's popular Visual Basic, a modern programming environment that includes many of the ideas and tools of object-oriented programming and visual programming.

```
REM Guessing Game
REM written by Rajeev Pandey

DECLARE SUB StartGame (Counter!, Number!)
DECLARE SUB Turn (Counter!, Guess!, Number!)
DECLARE SUB EndGame (Number!)

CALL StartGame(Counter, Number)
DO
    CALL Turn(Counter, Guess, Number)
LOOP UNTIL (Guess = Number) OR (Counter = 7)
IF Guess <> Number THEN
    CALL EndGame(Number)
END IF

SUB EndGame (Number)
PRINT "I fooled you 7 times!"
PRINT "The answer was "; Number
END SUB

SUB StartGame (Counter, Number)
PRINT "Welcome to the guessing game. I'll think of a number"
PRINT "between 1 and 100 and you will guess what it is."
Counter = 0
RANDOMIZE TIMER
Number = INT(RND(1) * 100)
END SUB

SUB Turn (Counter, Guess, Number)
INPUT "What's your guess?"; Guess
IF Guess = Number THEN
    PRINT "You got it!"
ELSE
    IF Guess < Number THEN
        PRINT "Too small, try again."
    ELSE
        PRINT "Too big, try again."
    END IF
END IF
Counter = Counter + 1
END SUB
```

FIGURE 14.10

A structured program doesn't depend on the GoTo statement to control the logical flow. Instead, it's built from smaller programs called **modules**, or **subprograms**, which are in turn made of even smaller modules. The programmer combines modules using the three basic control structures: sequence, repetition, and selection. A program is well structured if the following are true:

- It's made up of logically cohesive modules
- The modules are arranged in a hierarchy
- It's straightforward and readable

Object-Oriented Programming

Structured programming represented a big step forward for programmers; it enabled them to produce better, more reliable programs in less time. But structured programming wasn't the last word in programming; today **object-oriented programming (OOP)** has captured the attention of the software development community. In object-oriented programming, a program is not just a collection of step-by-step instructions or procedures; it's a collection of objects. Objects contain both data and instructions and can send and receive messages. For example, an on-screen button in a multimedia program might be an object, containing both a physical description of the button's appearance and a script telling it what to do if it receives a mouse-click message from the operating system. This button object can be easily reused in different programs because it carries with it everything it needs to operate.

> **Programmers work** the way medieval craftsmen built cathedrals—**one stone at a time**.
>
> — *Mitch Kapor*

With OOP technology, programmers can build programs from prefabricated objects in the same way builders construct houses from prefabricated walls. OOP also makes it easy to use features from one program in other programs, so programmers don't have to start from scratch with every new program. The object that puts addresses in alphabetical order in a mailing list database can be used to sort customer names in a hotel reservations system. Reusing software components is a way to save time and reduce errors.

OOP also supports the hierarchical categorization of objects, enabling programmers to create new objects derived from previously defined objects. The new object can inherit the properties and methods of the object it descends from and add new properties and methods as needed. For example, a window with scrollbars is a special kind of window. Many of the user actions supported on windows with scrollbars are exactly the same actions supported on any desktop window. By defining the "window with scrollbars" object as a special kind of the "window" object, the methods for moving, resizing, and closing the window could be reused. New methods would then be added to support the user's manipulations of the scrollbar. Once again, the benefits of code reuse are realized.

Object-oriented programming was first used in the 1970s, most notably in a language called SmallTalk. SmallTalk is still used for object-oriented programming, but today many other languages include object technology. C++, used in our example earlier, is a popular dialect of C that supports object-oriented programming. The newer languages Java and C# were designed from the ground up to be object-oriented languages.

Object-oriented tools and techniques are becoming common in databases, multimedia authoring tools, and other software environments. Object-oriented programming is particularly well suited for highly interactive programs (such as graphical operating systems, games, and customer transaction stations), and programs that imitate or reflect some dynamic part of the real world, such as simulations and air traffic control systems. Most experts believe that OOP is the wave of the future.

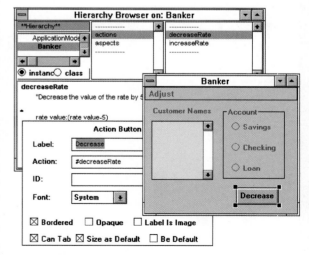

FIGURE 14.11 SmallTalk is the original OOP programming language. The name SmallTalk was used because it was tested on the children at Xerox PARC laboratories.

Screen Test

Object Oriented Programming in Java

1. You consider the problem conceptually. Because all three glasses have similar properties, you write code to create a reusable glass *object*.

2. For each glass, you use the glass object and create variables for each characteristic that is unique to the glass, including size, current fill level, and color of the liquid.

3. You then create several *methods* (functions) that can be used by any glass object, including commands to check and set the values of each variable, and one that pours water to another glass.

4. Now that you've defined the glass object, you write code that creates the graphical user interface. Your interface includes three instances of the glass object with different sizes and initial fill levels. Because you've already constructed the glass object, creating each glass is a simple process of creating instances of the glass object with different values for these variables.

5. You press the "Run Program" button to compile and test your program.

6. Once you're satisfied with the performance of your program, you can compile the finished program as a Java applet, and upload it to your site so anybody with a browser can play your game.

FIGURE 14.12

Visual Programming

Many people find it easier to work with pictures instead of words. Visual programming tools enable programmers to create large portions of programs by drawing pictures and pointing to objects, eliminating much of the tedious coding of traditional programming.

Microsoft's Visual Basic is widely used by professionals and hobbyists alike because of its visual approach to programming. Visual J++ applies a similar visual approach to Microsoft's Java-like language. Today's visual programming tools haven't completely transformed programming into a visual process; programmers must still understand how to read and write code to create complex programs. But visual programming can save hours of coding time, especially when creating user interfaces—the graphical shells that interact with users. Because they can simplify many of the most difficult parts of the programming process, visual languages make programming more accessible to nonprogrammers.

Languages for Users

Some computer languages are designed with nonprogrammers in mind. They aren't as powerful and versatile as professional programming languages, but they meet the modest needs of specific users.

Macro Languages

Many user-oriented languages are intended to enable users to create programs, called *macros*, that automate repetitive tasks. User-oriented macro languages (also called scripting languages) are built into many applications, utilities, and operating systems. Using a macro language, a spreadsheet user can build a program (a macro) to create end-of-month reports automatically each month by locating data in other worksheets, inserting values into a new worksheet, and calculating results using formulas carried over from previous months. Using an operating system's scripting language, a user might automate the process of making back-up copies of all documents created during the past seven days.

Some macro languages require you to design and type each macro by hand, just as you would if you were writing a BASIC program. In fact, Microsoft Office includes a scripting variation of Visual Basic called Visual Basic for Applications (VBA). Another type of macro maker "watches" while the user performs a sequence of commands and actions; it then memorizes the sequence and turns it into a macro automatically. The user can then examine and edit the macro so it performs the desired actions under any circumstances.

Fourth-Generation and Fifth-Generation Languages

Many experts suggest that languages have evolved through four generations: machine language, assembly language, high-level languages, and fourth-generation languages, sometimes called 4GLs. Each generation of languages is easier to use and more like natural language than its predecessors were. There's no consensus on exactly what constitutes a fourth-generation language, but these characteristics are most commonly mentioned:

- 4GLs use English-like phrases and sentences to issue instructions.
- 4GLs are nonprocedural. C and BASIC are procedural languages—tools for constructing procedures that tell the computer how to accomplish tasks. Nonprocedural languages enable users to focus on what needs to be done, not on how to do it. (Remember this theme from earlier in the chapter? You can view a higher-level language as focusing on "what," while the lower-level language focuses on "how." C looks high-level compared to assembly language, but it looks low-level compared to a 4GL. This phenomenon is why computer scientists keep inventing new generations of languages.)
- 4GLs increase productivity. Because a 4GL takes care of many of the how-to details, programmers can often get results by typing a few lines of code rather than a few pages.

One type of 4GL is the query language that enables a user to request information from a database with carefully worded English-like questions. A query language serves as a database user interface, hiding the intricacies of the database from the user. SQL (see Chapter 7) is the standard query language for most database applications today. Like most query languages, SQL requires the user to master a few rules of syntax and logic. Still, a query language is easier to master than FORTRAN or COBOL are.

Some languages have been referred to as fifth-generation languages (5GLs). According to one common definition, fifth-generation languages are constraint-driven languages. Instead of specifying an algorithm, the programmer defines the conditions that need to be met and the computer solves the problem. 5GLs aren't smart enough to create efficient algorithms for more complex problems, so their use is (so far) mostly restricted to artificial intelligence research.

Component Software

When we make a **new tool**, we see a **new cosmos**.

—Freeman Dyson, physicist

Recent developments in the software industry may soon result in software that provides users with the kind of power formerly reserved for programmers—and at the same time reverse a long-standing trend toward bloated computer applications. Throughout most of the short history of the personal computer, applications have steadily grown in size as developers add more and more features to their products. Even though no single user needs all the features in a modern spreadsheet program, every user who buys that program must buy all the code that provides those features. Many modern applications are so bloated with features that they make huge demands on memory and hard disk space.

Component software tools may reverse the trend toward mega-applications by enabling users to construct small custom applications from software components. Component software isn't completely new; users have been able to add custom components to applications and operating systems for years. Many programs support skins—components designed to customize the way the program looks on the screen. But components aren't just for cosmetic purposes. Dozens of plug-in extensions add features and capabilities to Microsoft Internet Explorer, Adobe Photoshop, Mozilla Firefox, and Adobe Flash, and other popular applications. This customizability is possible only if applications are programmed to allow it. More and more software programs, including operating systems, are designed with extensibility in mind.

Component software is the logical extension of object-oriented programming; it may soon reach a level where users and managers can build their own applications. Instead of buying an everything-but-the-kitchen-sink word processor, you might be able to buy word processor components—spelling checkers, outliners, formatters—based on your individual needs. Components can be distributed through the Internet, so you can quickly download features when you need them. Web services (described in Chapter 9) are based on the idea of using components to create Web-centered systems and applications.

Agile Development and Extreme Programming

The best part is to work **side by side** with someone else. It's a very stimulating **environment**, and you don't run into **roadblocks** or **mental blocks**.

—Doug Watt, senior engineer

Agile development is a relatively new programming model that focuses as much on the culture of programming as it does on technology. The traditional approach to programming is to make individual programmers responsible for entire programs or modules that may take months or years to complete. The agile programming model emphasizes communication, collaboration, and smaller but more frequent software updates. Programmers work in

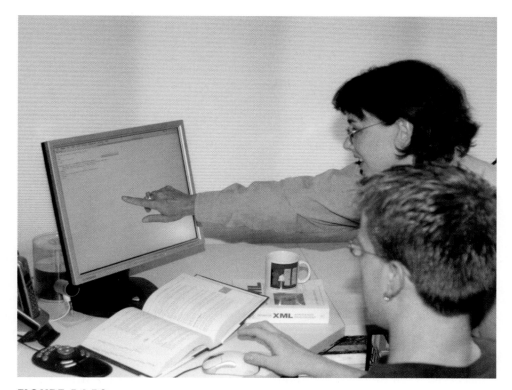

FIGURE 14.13 Extreme programmers work in pairs to write code.

teams developing programs that can pass rigorous tests throughout the development process. Agile programming involves close communication with customers and clients; they're considered part of the team.

In the best known agile model of development, *extreme programming*, the entire programming team "owns" the code; each member of the team has a right to improve it and the responsibility for making it work properly. Extreme programmers work in pairs on projects rather than write code alone. Pair programming reduces the number of individual errors and ensures that more team members are familiar with all aspects of the code. And in spite of its name, extreme programming doesn't involve marathon coding sessions to make deadlines for major releases. Instead, extreme programming emphasizes frequent releases of smaller updates and reasonable (40-hour) workweeks for programmers.

Extreme programming and other agile models are still outside the norm; their nonhierarchical approach runs counter to many corporate cultures. But the approach is growing in popularity—especially in organizations that embrace collaboration.

Programming for the Web

Many experts see a future in which PC applications will take a backseat to Web-based applications. Programmers can, and do, use a variety of languages, including C and C++, to write Web applications. But some programming tools are particularly useful for developing Web applications:

- *HTML* is, technically, a page-description language rather than a programming language. HTML commands tell Web browsers how to arrange text, graphics, and multimedia elements on Web pages and how to link those pages. But there are many similarities between HTML coding and program writing, and many popular extensions to HTML take it far beyond the basics of page layout.
- *XML* is a powerful markup language that overcomes many of the limitations of HTML. XML separates Web page content from layout, so Web pages can be designed to display

```
#!/usr/local/bin/perl

# Each line of file "sales2009" has a name and a sale price
open (SALES, "sales2009") or die "Can't open sales: $!\n";

# Create a list of sales for each employee
while ($line = <SALES>) {
    ($employee, $sales) = split(" ", $line);
    $receipts{$employee} .= $sales . " ";
}

# Print an alphabetical list of employees and their total sales
foreach $employee (sort keys %receipts) {
    $total = 0;
    @items = split(" ", $receipts{$employee});
    foreach $item (@items) {
        $total += $item;
    }
    print "$employee: \t\$$total sales for the year 2009\n";
}
```

FIGURE 14.14 This Perl script processes a text file containing information about houses sold by a group of Realtors. It produces an alphabetized list of the Realtors and their total sales.

different ways on different devices. XML is also particularly well suited for creating database-backed Web sites. Microsoft and many other companies use XML as a standard document formatting language.

■ *JavaScript* is an interpreted scripting language that enables Web page designers to add scripts to HTML code. Interpreted JavaScript scripts can add animation, interactivity, and other dynamic content to otherwise static Web pages.

■ *VBScript* is Microsoft's answer to JavaScript based on Visual Basic.

■ *ActionScript* is the popular multimedia scripting language built into Adobe Flash.

■ *Java* (described earlier) is widely used for creating applets that run in Web browsers.

■ *ActiveX* is a Microsoft language designed specifically for creating Web components similar to Java applets, but not supported by all platforms and browsers.

■ *Perl* is an interpreted scripting language that is particularly well suited for writing scripts to process text—for example, complex Web forms. Perl is a server-side language; it runs on Web servers, creating HTML code that can be interpreted by Web browsers.

■ *PHP* is a widely-used open source scripting language that was designed for producing dynamic Web pages. Like Perl, PHP is a server-side language. Many programmers take advantage of the fact that HTML code can be embedded in PHP scripts. Major Web sites, such as Amazon and YouTube, are built with PHP.

Programs in Perspective: Systems Analysis and the Systems Life Cycle

It has often been observed that we more frequently fail **to face the right problem** than fail **to solve the problem we face**.

—Russell Ackoff, American systems scientist

Programs don't exist in a vacuum. Programs are part of larger information systems—collections of people, machines, data, and methods organized to accomplish specific functions and to solve specific problems. Programming is only part of the larger process of designing, implementing, and managing information systems. In this section, we examine that larger process.

Systems Development

Systems development is a problem-solving process of investigating a situation; designing a system solution to improve the situation; acquiring the human, financial, and technological resources to implement the solution; and finally evaluating the success of the solution.

The systems development process begins when someone recognizes that a problem needs to be solved or an opportunity exists that can be taken advantage of. A typical situation might resemble one of these:

- A mom-and-pop music store needs a way to keep track of instrument rentals and purchases so billing and accounting don't take so much time.
- A college's antiquated registration system forces students to endure poorly-designed, sluggish Web forms and frequent scheduling errors.
- A garden-supply company is outgrowing its small, slow, PC-based software system, resulting in shipping delays, billing errors, and customer complaints. At the same time, the company is losing business because competitors have superior Web catalogs and ordering systems.
- The success of an upcoming oceanographic investigation hinges on the ability of scientists to collect and analyze data instantaneously so the results can be fed into remote-control navigation devices.
- A software manufacturer determines that its PC graphics program is rapidly losing market share to a competitor with more features and a friendlier user interface.
- A small retail store doing business on the Web realizes it can modify its Web site to market to customers internationally.

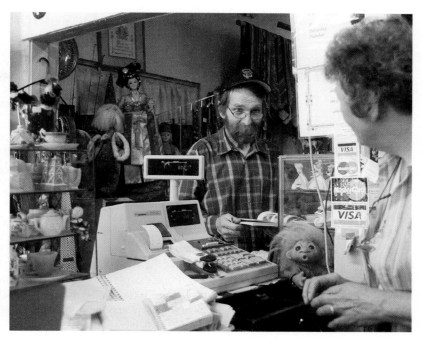

FIGURE 14.15 A growing business with an inefficient, paper record-keeping system is a candidate for systems development.

An organization may face several problems and opportunities, each of which may require the company to develop new IT applications. Each new project requires people, money, and other organizational resources, so a *steering committee* may be formed to decide which projects should be considered first. The steering committee comprises people from each of the functional areas of the organization.

After the steering committee decides to go ahead with a proposed project, a project team is formed to develop the system. The project team typically includes one or more end users and systems analysts. An **end user** is a person who uses the information system directly or uses the information produced by the system. A **systems analyst** is an IT professional primarily responsible for developing and managing the system.

The systems analyst is usually part of the organization's information systems department. But the business organization may choose to contract, or outsource, the systems analyst from an outside consulting firm. **Outsourcing** avoids the need for permanent in-house staff by allowing the organization to hire talent for selected activities on a contract basis. A growing industry provides outsourced services for specific applications via the Internet. Many U.S. companies outsource across national borders, taking advantage of lower wages in India, China, and other countries.

A project team comprising only end users can develop many small-scale systems without the direct involvement of a professional systems analyst. This systems development approach, called **end-user development**, is popular in organizations where end users have access to and training in the use of Web site development tools, spreadsheet and database management packages, and fourth- and fifth-generation languages.

The Systems Development Life Cycle

The first 90 percent of the task **takes 90 percent** of the time. The last 10 percent **takes the other 90 percent**.

—A systems development proverb

Whether it's a simple, single-user accounting system for a small business or a Web-based, multiuser management information system for a large organization, a system has a life cycle. The systems development life cycle (SDLC) is a sequence of seven steps or phases the system passes through between the time it is conceived and the time it is phased out. The phases of the system development life cycle are investigation, analysis, design, development, implementation, maintenance, and retirement.

Investigation

The purpose of the *investigation* phase is to study the existing business problem or opportunity and determine whether it is feasible to develop a new system or redesign the existing system if one exists. The project team conducts a feasibility study to identify the nature of the problem. The team also examines the current system to determine how well it meets the needs of the users and the organization and assess whether a new or improved information system is a feasible solution.

The project team tries to answer several feasibility questions:

- *Technical feasibility.* Can the required hardware and software be purchased or developed? Is the technology reliable? Does the system have sufficient information-processing capacity to handle the number of individuals who will use the system? Does the system provide for accurate, reliable, and secure data?
- *Economic feasibility.* Will the costs of developing and operating the proposed system be offset by the benefits of using the system? Is the system a good investment? Can sufficient money and personnel resources be committed to complete the system's development on time?
- *Operational feasibility.* Does the proposed system meet the needs of the organization? Are the changes in work procedures required by the proposed system acceptable? Can the proposed system be developed on a timely schedule?
- *Organizational feasibility.* Does the proposed system support the goals and strategy of the organization? Are there any legal implications of the system, such as copyrights, patents, or federal regulations?

Based on its investigation, the project team makes one of three recommendations: leave the current system as is, improve or enhance the current system, or develop an entirely new system. The systems analyst documents the findings of the investigation in a written feasibility report that is presented to the steering committee. Based on the feasibility study, the steering committee decides whether to continue with the analysis phase of the SDLC.

Analysis

During the *analysis* phase, the systems analyst gathers documents, interviews users of the current system (if one exists), observes the system in action, and gathers and analyzes data to understand the current system and identify new requirements—features or capabilities that must be included in the system to meet the needs of the users. The systems analyst identifies the requirements related to each subsystem of the proposed system:

- *Input/output requirements.* The characteristics of the user interface, including the content, format, and timing requirements for data-entry screens and managerial reports
- *Processing requirements.* The calculations, decision rules, data processing capacity, and response time needed
- *Storage requirements.* The content of records and databases and the procedures for data retrieval

■ *Control requirements*. The desired accuracy, validity, and security of the system; for example, to prevent data-entry errors and guarantee an easy-to-use, user-friendly system

The systems analyst documents the work done in the analysis phase in a written functional requirements report. The report explains the current business procedures and how the current system works, identifies the problems with the current procedures and system, and describes the requirements for the new or modified system. The steering committee reviews the requirements report and decides whether to proceed with the design phase of the SDLC.

Design

The investigation phase focuses on why, the analysis phase focuses on what, and the *design* phase focuses on how. In the design phase, the systems analyst develops the system specifications that describe how exactly the system requirements, identified in the analysis phase, will be met. The systems analyst considers important how-to questions in three categories:

■ *User interface design*. How will the various outputs of the system be designed? Where will input data come from, and how will it be entered into the system? How will the various windows, menus, and other user-computer dialogue characteristics be designed?
■ *Database design*. How will the data elements and structure of the files that compose the database be designed?
■ *Process design*. How will the programs and the procedures for the proposed system be designed? Should the system be centralized in a single computer or distributed through a network of desktop computers?

The systems analyst answers these questions, sometimes proposing alternative solutions through a design approach called prototyping. A **prototype** is a limited working system that gives users and management an idea of how the completed system will work. **Prototyping** is an iterative process in which the systems analyst can modify the prototype until it meets the needs and expectations of the organization. Prototyping makes the design phase faster and easier for the systems analyst, especially for systems where the users' requirements are difficult to define. Once the design is acceptable, the systems analyst can fill in the details of the output, input, data files, processing, and system controls.

Prototyping is used widely by companies to develop e-commerce applications quickly, especially for designing the human interface components such as data-entry screens and Web pages. By encouraging end-user involvement in the design phase, prototyping increases the probability the system will satisfy the users' needs.

Development

After the design phase is completed, the actual system development can begin. The *development* phase is a process of turning the design specifications into a real working system. Development includes a complex mix of scheduling, purchasing, installation, documentation, and programming. For most large projects, the development phase involves a team of programmers, technical writers, and clerical people under the supervision of a systems analyst. A large part of the development schedule is devoted to testing the system. Members of the system development team perform early testing to locate and eliminate bugs. This initial testing is known as **alpha testing**. Later potential end users who are willing to work with almost-finished software perform **beta testing** and report bugs to the developers.

Implementation

The *implementation* phase occurs when the testing phase is completed and the new system is ready to replace the old one. For commercial software packages, this phase typically involves extensive training and technical user support to supplement sales and marketing efforts. For large custom systems, implementation includes end-user education and

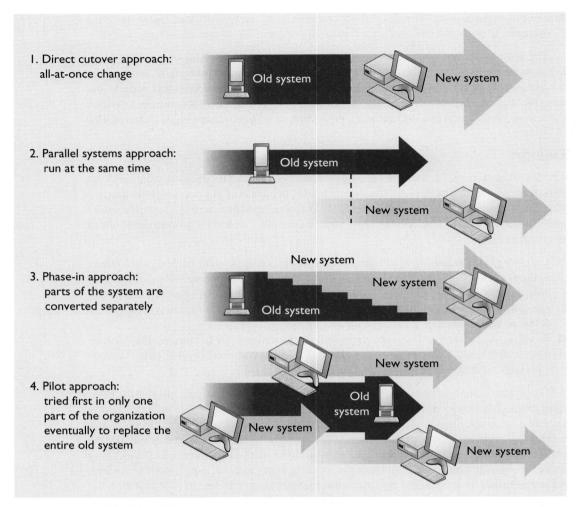

1. Direct cutover approach: all-at-once change

   Old system   New system

2. Parallel systems approach: run at the same time

   Old system

   New system

3. Phase-in approach: parts of the system are converted separately

   New system

   New system

   Old system

4. Pilot approach: tried first in only one part of the organization eventually to replace the entire old system

   New system

   New system

   Old system

   New system

   New system

FIGURE 14.16 The systems analyst must carefully choose the system conversion approach that is best for the organization and the end users.

training, equipment replacement, file conversion, and careful monitoring of the new system for problems.

The systems analyst can choose one of four approaches for converting to the new system:

■ The direct cutover approach simply replaces the old system with the new system. The organization relies fully on the new system with the risk that parts of the new system might not work correctly.

■ The parallel systems approach operates the old system along with the new system for a period of time. The old system is gradually phased out as users gain skills and confidence that the new system is stable and reliable.

■ The phase-in approach implements subsystems of the new system gradually over a period of time or, alternatively, the system is implemented in only a few departments, branch offices, or plant locations at a time.

■ The pilot approach implements the new system in one department or work site in the organization. The new system is used and modified at this test site until the systems analyst believes the system can be successfully implemented throughout the organization.

End-user training is critical to implementing an information system successfully. During training, clerical and managerial end users learn to use the features of the new system effectively. They learn how to handle problems that may arise when they use the system. The training is often handled by end-user representatives from the project team rather than by technicians.

Maintenance

The *maintenance* phase involves monitoring, evaluating, repairing, and enhancing the system throughout the lifetime of the system. Some software problems don't surface until the system has been operational for a while or the organization's needs change. Systems often need to be adjusted to keep up to date with new products, services, customers, industry standards, and government regulations. Ongoing maintenance enables organizations to deal with those problems and take advantage of opportunities for improvement when they arise.

Evaluation is an important aspect of maintenance. The system is evaluated periodically to determine whether it is providing the anticipated benefits and meeting organizational needs. Also, evaluation provides the feedback necessary for management to assess whether the system was developed on schedule and within budget and to identify what adjustments to make in the system development process in the future.

Retirement

At some point in the life of a system, ongoing maintenance isn't enough. Because of changes in organizational needs, user expectations, available technology, increasing maintenance costs, and other factors, the system may no longer meet the needs of the users or the organization and is ready for *retirement*. At that point it's time to phase it out and launch an investigation for a newer system, which begins another round of the systems development life cycle.

Systems Development Tools and Techniques

You can observe a lot **by just watching**.

—Yogi Berra

Systems analysts use a variety of tools and techniques throughout the systems development life cycle. Some are used to gather data; some are used to describe or design the system's features, procedures, and processes; and others are used to document the system in reports.

Data Collection Techniques

Data collection techniques include document review, interviews, questionnaires, observation, and sampling. These techniques can be used during any phase of the systems development life cycle.

- *Document review.* Typically, a great deal of information about the current system can be found in company documents such as business plans, reports, manuals, correspondence, and systems documentation. The systems analyst can review these documents in the investigation and analysis phases to find out how the current system is designed and how it is supposed to operate.
- *Interview.* Systems analysts interview managers, employees, customers, suppliers, and other people to gather information about business processes and problems and to collect ideas and suggestions for improvement. In a structured interview, the systems analyst asks the same questions of each person. In an unstructured interview, the systems analyst might vary the questions from person to person.
- *Questionnaire.* The systems analyst can use a paper or digital questionnaire to collect information from a large group of people. Questionnaires are convenient, and respondents can remain anonymous if desired.
- *Observation.* The systems analyst can watch an employee perform a task, see how people interact with one another, or observe whether procedures work as expected.

How It Works

14.2 The Systems Development Life Cycle

College registration is a complex system involving hundreds of people and masses of information. A registration system must be solidly designed, carefully maintained, and eventually replaced as the needs of the college change. In this example we follow systems analysts at Chintimini College as they guide a registration system through a system life cycle.

1. **Investigation.** Analysts at the college's Information Processing Center identify several problems with the antiquated manual registration system: long lines, frequent scheduling errors, and expensive labor costs. After studying registration systems at other schools, they determine that a Web-based registration system might be the best solution to these problems.

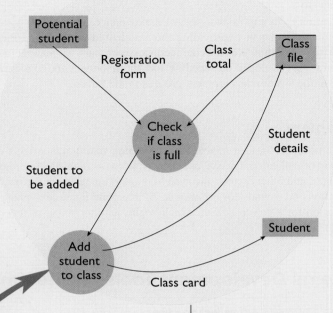

Potential student

Registration form

Class total

Class file

Check if class is full

Student details

Student to be added

Add student to class

Student

Class card

2. **Analysis.** Analysts use a data flow diagram to illustrate the flow of data through the old registration system. They'll use the information in this diagram to help them develop the new system.

7. **Retirement.** After a few years, the Web registration system has developed problems of its own. The college begins developing a new system that will allow students to register through mobile devices as well as Web-connected PCs. When the new registration system reaches the implementation phase of its life cycle, the old system is retired.

FIGURE 14.17

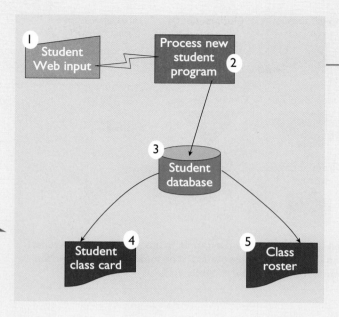

3. Design. Analysts use standard symbols to create a system flowchart to show the relationship among programs, files, input, and output in the new system.

4. Development. Analysts use a Gantt chart to plan the schedule deadlines and milestones for creating the new system.

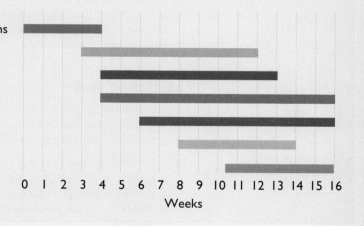

Program specifications
Programming
Unit testing
Documentation
System testing
File conversion
Training

0 1 2 3 4 5 6 7 8 9 10 11 12 13 14 15 16
Weeks

5. Implementation. Analysts supervise the training, equipment conversion, file conversion, and system conversion as they bring the new system online.

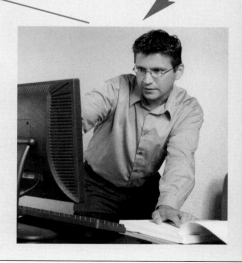

6. Maintenance. Analysts monitor and evaluate the new system, eliminating problems and correcting bugs as they uncover them.

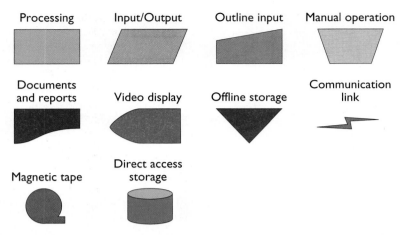

FIGURE 14.18 A systems analyst uses standard symbols to create a system flowchart. Each of the symbols represents the physical components of an information system. You can see an example of a system flowchart in How It Works 14.2.

■ *Sampling.* If the system is large or has many users, the systems analyst can collect data at prescribed time intervals or from a subset of the users. For example, the systems analyst could interview a sample of 10 percent of the users or observe 5 percent of the transactions of a business to get a sense of how well the current system is working.

Modeling Tools

Modeling tools are graphic representations of a system. Many such tools are available, but the modeling tools most widely used by systems analysts are system flowcharts, data flow diagrams, data dictionaries, and decision tables.

■ A **system flowchart** is a graphical depiction of the physical system that exists or is proposed. A system flowchart uses standard symbols to show the overall structure of a system, the sequence of activities that take place in the system, and the type of media or technology used at each step. System flowcharts are used in both the analysis and design phases of the SDLC to show the current system and the design for the proposed system.

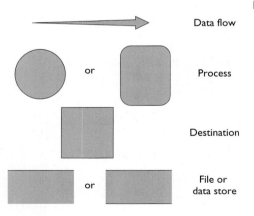

FIGURE 14.19 A systems analyst needs to use only four symbols to create a data flow diagram. You can see how a DFD graphically shows the underlying logical flow of data in a system in How It Works 14.2.

■ A **data flow diagram (DFD)** is a simple graphical depiction of the movement of data through a system. A data flow diagram uses symbols to show the movement of data, the processes that use and produce data, the storage of data, and the people or other entities that originate input or receive output from the system. A system-level DFD depicts the entire system in summary form; a level-one DFD expands the processes in the system-level DFD to show more detail. Processes in the level-one DFD can in turn be expanded to show more detail, and so on to an appropriate level of detail.

■ A **data dictionary** is a catalog, or directory, that describes all the data flowing through a system. Systems analysts use a data dictionary to keep track of all the

FIGURE 14.20 Data fields in a document can be grouped and represented as data elements and data structures in the data dictionary.

system's data elements and data structures. Data elements are the fields stored in the system's databases. A **data structure** refers to a set of data elements used together, such as an invoice or other paper or electronic document.

■ A **decision table** shows, in a row-column format, the decision rules that apply and what actions to take when certain conditions occur. A systems analyst can describe and analyze a complex procedure more effectively by constructing a decision table of if-then statements than by writing a complicated narrative of all the possible combinations of conditions and actions.

Computer-Aided Systems Engineering (CASE)

Today many systems development tools and techniques are included in commercially available software packages referred to as **computer-aided systems engineering (CASE)**. Most CASE tools software packages include the following:

■ Charting and diagramming tools to draw system flowcharts and data flow diagrams

		Decision rules				
		1	2	3	4	5
Conditions If...		No	Yes	Yes	Yes	No
And if...		Yes	Yes	No	Yes	No
And if...		Yes	Yes	No	No	Yes
Actions Then do...		✓				
Then do...				✓		✓
Then do...			✓		✓	

FIGURE 14.21 A decision table shows if-then rules in a tabular format. The upper half of the table includes the if conditions, and the lower half shows the then actions. Each numbered column is a decision rule that shows the action(s) to be taken when certain conditions occur. In a real decision table, the leader dots in the left column would be filled in with information specific to the system.

FIGURE 14.22 You can use Microsoft Visio to create data flow diagrams, Gantt charts, and many other types of diagrams useful in systems development work.

■ A centralized data dictionary containing detailed information about all the system components
■ A user interface generator to create and evaluate many different interface designs
■ Code generators that automate much of the computer programming to create a new system or application

Some CASE software packages contain tools that apply primarily to the analysis and design phases of the systems development life cycle; others contain tools that automate the later phases of systems development, implementation, and maintenance. Integrated CASE tools incorporate the whole spectrum of tools to support the entire systems development life cycle.

The trend today is to run on Internet time with short system development schedules. CASE has an essential niche in the design of large systems. But over the past decade, the tools that worked well migrated out from under the CASE umbrella into other programming tools and suites such as Microsoft's Visual Studio, a development tool suite for building Windows and Web applications, and Microsoft's Visio, an easy-to-use yet powerful charting and diagramming tool.

The Science of Computing

Telescopes are to astronomy as **computers** are to computer science.

—*Edsger Dijkstra, computer scientist*

We've seen how programmers and systems analysts create and maintain computer programs used by scientists, businesspeople, artists, writers, and others. But just as the rest of us take advantage of the programmer's handiwork, the programmer depends on tools and ideas developed by computer scientists—professionals who work in the academic discipline called computer science. What is computer science, and why is it important in the world of computers?

Working Wisdom

Avoiding Information Technology Project Failures

Only about a third of IT projects are completed on time, on budget, and with the promised functionality. The major components of an IT failure are time wasted working on the wrong solution and the potential competitive advantage lost by not working on the right solution. Here are a few tips for information workers to avoid six ways IT projects can fail.

➡ IT projects need executive sponsorship. Many IT projects tend to cut across departments and force a lot of people to change the way they work every day. Such change, if not sold by senior management, can create fear, and every fearful middle manager in every department can create bureaucratic roadblocks that reduce the project's chance to succeed. Make sure the IT projects you are working on are supported by a company executive.

➡ IT projects need user input. Lack of user input is the factor most likely to characterize a bad IT project. It's important to discuss projects up front with everybody who has a stake in the outcome, including end users and customers, business partners, and internal departments on whose cooperation a project's success depends.

➡ IT projects need specifications. If the project requirements aren't well specified up front and the project begins anyway, you have no consensus among stakeholders. A series of meetings and discussions at the beginning of the project will help build consensus on what an IT project can and cannot do.

➡ IT projects need realistic expectations. Undefined expectations frequently lead to dreaded scope creep—in which an initially straightforward technology project is asked to solve more and more problems until it grows bloated and unmanageable. Scope creep, in turn, tends to destroy schedules and eat up resources. Make sure a project management process that explicitly sets expectations and budgets resources is in place.

➡ IT projects need cooperative business partners. Many IT projects involve a vendor of some sort—a

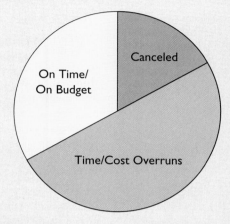

FIGURE 14.23 According to the Standish Group, only about one-third of software projects are completed on time and on budget. About one-half of projects have significant time and/or cost overruns, and about one-sixth of projects are canceled.

software company, a system integrator, or a consultant. When they're wooing you, those companies say they're your partners. But no matter how much they want your project to succeed or how honorable their intentions, they have pressures of their own that may lead to disagreements during the project. Make sure your company negotiates a reasonable and fair contract with the vendor.

➡ IT projects need open and honest communication. Workers don't want to be the bearers of bad news, and senior managers contrive not to hear that news if it is ever delivered. As a result, nobody sounds the alarm on IT projects that have disaster written all over them until it's too late. Make sure you participate in building a culture in your company that values open and honest communication.

Because most introductory computer science courses focus on programming, many students equate computer science with computer programming. But programming is little more than a tool in the computer scientist's intellectual toolbox; it has about as much to do with computer science as English grammar has to do with writing novels.

Computer science is a relatively new discipline with ties to electrical engineering, mathematics, and business. Many computer scientists prefer to call the field *computing science* because it focuses on the process of computing rather than on computer hardware. Computing takes a variety of forms, and computer science includes a number of focus areas, ranging from the rarefied world of computer theory to practical nuts-and-bolts work in software engineering. Some areas of specialization within computer science—database management, graphics, artificial intelligence, and networks, for example—provide academic underpinnings for specific categories of computer applications. Other branches of computer science deal with concepts that can apply to almost any type of computer application. These include the following:

- *Computer theory*. The most mathematical branch of computer science, computer theory applies the concepts of theoretical mathematics to fundamental computational problems, such as whether there are functions that cannot be computed. Theoreticians often work not with real computers, but with idealized models of computation. As in most fields, many theoretical concepts eventually find their way into practical applications. For example, theoretical computer scientists invented error-correcting codes that allow messages to be reconstructed if a few bits are garbled during transmission.

- *Algorithms*. Many computer scientists focus on algorithms—the logical underpinnings of computer programs. The design of algorithms can determine whether software succeeds or fails. A well-designed algorithm is not only reliable and free of logical errors, but also efficient, so it can accomplish its goals with a minimum of computer resources and time. Computers spend most of their time doing mundane tasks such as sorting lists, searching for names, and calculating geometric coordinates. These frequently performed operations must be built on rock-solid, efficient algorithms if a computer system is to be responsive and reliable.

- *Data structures*. If algorithms describe the logical structure of programs, data structures determine the logical structure of data. Data structures range from simple numeric lists and tables (called arrays) to complex relations at the core of massive databases. There is an intimate relationship between data structures and the algorithms that operate on them. Computer scientists continue to develop improved techniques for representing and combining different forms of data, and these techniques lead to faster algorithms for performing the desired operations on the data.

- *Programming concepts and languages*. As we've seen, programming languages have evolved through several generations in the short history of computers. Thanks to computer scientists in the tradition of Grace Hopper, each new wave of languages is easier to use and more powerful than the one that came before. Programming language specialists strive to design better programming languages to make it easier for programmers to turn algorithms into working software. Computer scientists are also responsible for the development of techniques such as structured programming and object-oriented programming—techniques that make programmers more productive and their programs more reliable.

- *Computer architecture*. Straddling the boundary between the software world of computer science and the hardware world of computer engineering, computer architecture deals with the way hardware and software work together. What is the best instruction set? How much will a larger cache improve performance? How does the bandwidth of a bus affect performance? What are the trade-offs for different storage media? These are the types of questions that concern computer architecture specialists.

- *Management information systems.* **Management information systems (MIS)** is part computer science, part business. In fact, MIS studies are done in computer science departments at some institutions, in business departments at others, and in MIS departments at others. MIS specialists focus on developing systems that can provide timely, reliable, and useful information to managers in business, industry, and government. MIS specialists apply the theoretical concepts of computer science to real-world, practical business problems.
- *Software engineering.* When an engineer designs a bridge or a building, tried-and-true engineering principles and techniques ensure that the structure won't collapse unexpectedly. Unfortunately, we can't trust software the way we trust buildings; software designers simply don't have the time-honored techniques to ensure quality. Besides, software is not like concrete and steel; it is infinitely malleable. Given a virtually infinite number of design choices, it's no wonder that programmers are reluctant to construct their code "by the book." Still, everyone understands that the software industry must do a better job completing projects on time without going over budget. **Software engineering** is a branch of computer science that attempts to apply engineering principles and techniques to the less-than-concrete world of computer software. We conclude this chapter with a brief look at the problems faced by software engineers—problems that affect all of us.

The State of Software

It's impossible to make anything foolproof, because **fools are so ingenious**.

—Roger Berg, inventor

In spite of advances in computer science, the state of software development is less than ideal. Software developers and software users are confronted with two giant problems: cost and unreliability.

Software Problems

As computers have evolved through the decades, the cost of computer hardware has steadily gone down. Every year brings more powerful, reliable machines and lower prices. At the same time, the cost of developing computer software has gone up.

We build our computers the way we build our cities—**over time, without a plan, on top of ruins**.

—Ellen Ullman, software engineer and author of Close to the Machine

The software industry abounds with stories of computer systems that cost millions of dollars more and took years longer to develop than expected. Many systems become so costly to develop that their developers are forced to abandon them before completion. About one-sixth of commercial software projects are canceled before they are completed, costing the U.S. economy alone billions of dollars every year.

But while prices rise, there's no corresponding increase in the reliability of software. Ever since Grace Hopper pulled a moth from the Mark II's relay, bugs have plagued computers, often with disastrous consequences, as you saw in Chapter 10. A recent study found that programmers average 100 to 150 mistakes per 1000 lines of code!

Software errors can take a variety of forms, including errors of omission, syntax errors, logic errors, clerical errors, capacity errors, and judgment errors. But whatever its form, a software error can be devilishly difficult to locate and even more difficult to remove. According to one study, 15 to 20 percent of attempts to remove program errors actually introduce new errors!

Software Solutions

The major difference between a thing that **might go wrong** and a thing that **cannot possibly go wrong** is that when a thing that cannot possibly go wrong goes wrong it usually turns out to be **impossible to get at or repair**.

—Douglas Adams, in Mostly Harmless

Computer scientists and software engineers are responding to reliability and cost problems on five main fronts:

■ *Programming techniques.* So far, structured programming and object-oriented programming are the best-known and most successful techniques for increasing programmer productivity and program reliability. Programmers who use these techniques can concentrate on the overall logic of their creations without getting distracted by minute details. The result is less expensive, more reliable software. But these are small steps on a long road toward more dependable programming methodologies. It's too early to tell whether extreme programming and other more modern techniques will take us much farther down that road.

■ *Programming environments.* Today's best programming tools include sophisticated text editors, debuggers, record-keeping programs, and translators, all interwoven into a seamless graphic work environment. A high-quality programming environment can help a programmer manage the complexities of a large project. During the past two decades, CASE tools have emerged, enabling analysts and programmers to automate many of the tedious and error-prone steps involved in turning design specifications into programs. In spite of early promise, CASE tools haven't been widely adopted. Today the industry is more focused on environments built around component technology that makes it easier to reuse reliable code. In any case, programming environments have a long way to go before they can guarantee reliable software, if that's even possible.

■ *Program verification.* Software engineers would like to be able to prove the correctness of their programs in the same way mathematicians prove the correctness of theorems. Computer scientists have developed program verification techniques that work well for small programs. Unfortunately, these techniques have achieved only limited success with the complex commercial programs people depend on today. There's little hope for automated program verification either. Computer scientists have proven that some problems can't be solved with algorithms, and program verification is one such problem.

■ *Clean-room programming.* One new experimental approach to software development is modeled after microchip manufacturing techniques. Clean-room programming combines formal notation, proofs of correctness, and statistical quality control with an evolutionary approach to programming. Programmers grow systems individually, certifying the quality of each before integrating it with the others. It's too early to tell whether this rigorous, engineering-like approach will achieve widespread quality gains, but early tests show some promise.

■ *Human management.* Project management techniques from business and engineering have been applied successfully to many software engineering projects. These human management techniques have more to do with person-to-person communication than with programmer-to-machine communication. Because many information system failures result from human communication errors, successful human management can improve a system's overall reliability. But again the benefits of human management methodologies aren't great enough to offset the massive problems facing software engineers today.

Computer scientists have accomplished a great deal in the short history of the field. Software development is easier than it used to be, and computers today can accomplish far more than anyone dreamed a few decades ago. But software engineers have failed to keep up with the fast-paced evolution in computer hardware, and it's still incredibly difficult to produce reliable, cost-effective software. More than a decade ago, computer scientist Ted Lewis summed up the problem in one of his laws of computing. Today, when we're routinely asked to entrust our money, our health, our legal rights, and our lives to software, it's important for all of us to remember that law: "Hardware is soft; software is hard."

Software Warranties

Large computer programs are incredibly complicated. The Windows operating system, for example, contains millions of lines of code. Software engineers perform a variety of tests that thoroughly exercise the capabilities of the system, but trying every possible situation is simply impossible. For this reason, testing can reveal the existence of bugs, but it cannot prove that no bugs exist. Software engineers acknowledge that it is impossible to remove every bug from a large, sophisticated program. Given that a large program will contain bugs, who should be responsible when a software error causes a business to lose money?

> We **do not warrant** that this **software** will **meet your requirements** or that its operation will be **uninterrupted** or **error-free**.
>
> *—From an end-user license agreement*

In the past, manufacturers of consumer software provided no warranties for their products. Consumers were forced to accept software "as is." Today some software manufacturers say you can get your money back if the software cannot be installed on your computer. Others go further and provide a 90-day, money-back guarantee if the program fails to live up to its stated purpose. However, no software manufacturer will accept liability for harm caused to you or your business by errors in the software.

Is it fair for software companies to refuse to accept responsibility for harm caused by defects in their programs? Let's consider what would happen if our legal system required software manufacturers to pay for damages caused by defective software. Software companies would undoubtedly have a greater focus on the reliability of their products. They would invest more resources in each program, testing code more thoroughly and fixing the bugs that were uncovered. Because it is impossible to eliminate 100 percent of the bugs, companies would need to purchase insurance to protect them from consumer lawsuits. These additional precautions would inflate costs and extend the time needed to develop each product. If software were more time consuming and expensive to develop, large, well-established companies would have an advantage over small start-up businesses that provide much of the innovation in the software industry.

FIGURE 14.24 Thousands of lives depend on reliable functioning of the computers and software used by air traffic controllers.

Evaluating these consequences from the consumer's point of view, requiring software companies to accept all responsibility for damages caused by their products would result in fewer products for sale. Software would be more reliable, have fewer features, and cost more money. New releases of software products would not appear as quickly. While consumers often complain about the quality of software, their actions show that they are more focused on price and features. For all these reasons, allowing software manufacturers to put disclaimers on their products makes sense.

This does not mean, however, that software companies shouldn't try to provide software that's as bug-free as possible. As we saw in Chapter 4, when consumers purchase software products, they are actually purchasing a license to use the product. They ought to have the right to use the most error-free version of the product without paying extra. Most major software developers routinely distribute minor revisions and bug fixes for free through the Web, charging only for major upgrades that add new features. It's hard to justify ethically the practice of charging users for upgrades that are little more than bug fixes.

Inventing the FUTURE

The Future of Programming

It could well be that by the close of the twenty-first century, a new form of truly accessible programming will be the province of everyone, and will be viewed like writing, which was once the province of the ancient scribes but eventually became universally accessible.

—*Michael Dertouzos, in* What Will Be

Object-oriented programming. Visual programming. Component software. Distributed Web applications. With these trends gaining momentum, what can we say about the future of programming? It's not clear what programming languages will look like in the future, but three trends seem likely:

➡ *Programming languages will continue to evolve in the direction of natural languages such as English*. Today's programming languages, even the best of them, are far too limited and unintelligent. Tomorrow's programming tools should be able to understand what we want even if we don't specify every detail. When we consider artificial intelligence in the next chapter, we deal with the problems and promise of natural-language computer communication.

➡ *The line between programmer and user is likely to grow hazy*. As programming becomes easier, there's every reason to believe that computer users will have tools that enable them to construct applications without mastering the intricacies of a technical programming language.

➡ *Computers will play an ever-increasing role in programming themselves*. Today's visual programming environments can create programs in response to user clicks and commands. Tomorrow's programming tools may be able to write entire programs with only a description of the problem supplied by users. The day after tomorrow, we may see computers anticipating problems and programming solutions without human intervention!

These three trends come together in the work of some of the pioneers of modern programming. In the 1970s Charles Simonyi developed the first WYSIWYG word processor at Xerox PARC and went on to pilot the development of Word, Excel, and other products as Microsoft's chief architect. Recently, he left Microsoft and started a new company dedicated to creating tools that will make it possible for everyday computer users to write complex software. The goal is to make the code look like the design, so by simply creating the design, a user can write software. According to Simonyi, "Software should be as easy to edit as a PowerPoint presentation."

Simonyi envisions a process called *intentional programming,* which allows programmers to focus on the intention of their programs rather than the technical details of coding. The programmer, who might be an expert in health care or oceanography or marketing, might be able to use a modeling language to describe a design to solve a problem; a software generator would then write the actual code automatically based on the design description. The user interface for the modeling language might resemble a PowerPoint palette for some users; it might have a more mathematical look for others.

Another software pioneer, IBM's Grady Booch, is attempting to make it possible for modeling languages to weave security functions into software modeling tools and to make modeling tools that can build entire systems of programs. Meanwhile, the inventor of Java, James Gosling, is working on a modeling tool at Sun that might accept older programs and make it easier to find logical problems embedded in them.

Whatever happens, one thing seems likely: future programming tools will have little in common with today's languages. When computer historians look back, they'll marvel at how difficult it was for us to instruct computers to perform even the simplest actions. Simonyi is optimistic about the future of software: "Look at what the hardware people have managed to do with Moore's Law. Now it's gong to be software's turn." ～

FIGURE 14.25 Charles Simonyi founded Intentional Software to change the way people create software.

FIGURE 14.26 Jet engine turbines wouldn't work if they were hand crafted because of the inevitable variations introduced during hand work. Turbines are made by precision machines, which in turn are created and maintained by people. Charles Simonyi says software would be more reliable if we could create it with machines called "modeling languages" instead of writing code by hand.

Cyber Incident Blamed for Nuclear Power Plant Shutdown   *by Brian Krebs*

This article, which originally appeared in a longer form in the Washington Post *on June 5, 2008, reminds us that computer bugs can be more than annoyances.*

A nuclear power plant in Georgia was recently forced into an emergency shutdown for 48 hours after a software update was installed on a single computer.

The trouble started after an engineer from *Southern Company,* which manages the technology operations for the plant, installed a software update on a computer operating on the plant's business network.

The computer in question was used to monitor chemical and diagnostic data from one of the facility's primary control systems, and the software update was designed to synchronize data on both systems. According to a report filed with the *Nuclear Regulatory Commission,* when the updated computer rebooted, it reset the data on the control system, causing safety systems to errantly interpret the lack of data as a drop in water reservoirs that cool the plant's radioactive nuclear fuel rods. As a result, automated safety systems at the plant triggered a shutdown.

Southern Company spokeswoman Carrie Phillips said the nuclear plant's emergency systems performed as designed, and that at no time did the malfunction endanger the security or safety of the nuclear facility. Phillips said the engineer who installed the update was not aware that that the software was designed to synchronize data between machines on both networks, or that a reboot in the business system computer would force a similar reset in the control system machine. She said plant engineers have since physically removed all network connections between the affected servers.

Computer security experts say the Hatch plant incident is the latest reminder of problems that can occur when corporate computer systems at the nation's most critical networks are connected to sensitive control systems that were never designed with security in mind.

Specifically, experts worry that vulnerabilities were introduced into the systems that regulate the electrical grid as power companies transferred control of generation and distribution equipment from internal networks to supervisory control and data acquisition, or SCADA, systems that can be accessed through the Internet or by phone lines, according to consultants and government reports.

The move to SCADA systems boosts efficiency at utilities because it allows workers to operate equipment remotely. But experts say it also exposes these once-closed systems to cyber attacks.

"Part of the challenge is we have all of this infrastructure in the control systems that was put in place in the 1980s and '90s that was not designed with security in mind, and all of a sudden these systems are being connected to [Internet-facing] business networks" said Brian Ahern, president and chief executive of *Industrial Defender Inc.,* a Foxborough, Mass.-based SCADA security company.

Joe Weiss, managing partner at Cupertino, Calif.-based *Applied Control Solutions,* said Hatch is not the only plant that has suffered this type of unusual event. But he said it is one of a handful of public events of this type because the Nuclear Regulatory Commission documents all unusual events, in contrast to non-nuclear facilities that do not make their unusual events public.

Weiss said unplanned, automatic shutdowns such as what happened at the Hatch plant are costly, forcing utilities to purchase power from other parts of the grid to the tune of about $1 million a day. But more importantly, Weiss said, automatic shutdowns unnecessarily challenge nuclear safety systems.

Weiss said many people in charge of SCADA systems have sought to downplay the threat that hackers pose to these complex networks. But he cautioned that internal, accidental cyber incidents at control system networks can be just as deadly as a carefully planned attack from the outside.

In June 1999, a steel gas pipeline ruptured near Bellingham, Wash., killing two children and an 18-year-old, and injuring eight others. A subsequent investigation found that a computer failure just prior to the accident locked out the central control room operating the pipeline, preventing technicians from relieving pressure in the pipeline.

"To people in the IT world, cyber means 'attacks,' but what I tell people is that in our world the predominant cyber events are unintentional," he said. "The flip side of that is if it can happen unintentionally, it can probably be caused intentionally and be a whole lot worse."

News of the Hatch incident also comes as the cyber-security posture of the electric and nuclear power industry *is coming under increasing scrutiny* from Congress and government investigators. Last month, the Government Accountability Office issued a *scathing report* about cyber security weaknesses at the Tennessee Valley Authority, the nation's largest public power company and operator of three nuclear plants, including Browns Ferry.

The GAO found that TVA's Internet-connected corporate network was linked with systems used to control power production, and that security weaknesses pervasive in the corporate side could be used by attackers to manipulate or destroy vital control systems. The agency also warned that computers on TVA's corporate network lacked security software updates and anti-virus protection, and that firewalls and intrusion detection systems on the network were easily bypassed and failed to record suspicious activity.

Discussion Questions

1. What other types of systems do you think are vulnerable to this kind of error?

2. What kinds of measures need to be taken to prevent computer errors from having disastrous consequences?

Summary

Computer programming is a specialized form of problem solving that involves developing an algorithm for solving a problem. Most programmers use stepwise refinement to break a problem repeatedly into smaller, more easily solvable problems. An algorithm typically is developed in pseudocode, which describes the logic of the program before being translated into a programming language. A translator program—either a compiler or an interpreter—checks for syntax errors (language errors) and, if it finds none, translates the program into machine language so the computer can execute the instructions. Logic errors might not surface until the translated program is run, and maybe not even then. The programming process isn't completed until the program is thoroughly tested for errors.

Computer languages have evolved through several generations, with each generation being easier to use and more powerful than the one that came before. Machine language—the original computer language of 0s and 1s—is primitive and difficult to program. Assembly language uses a translator called an assembler to turn alphabetic codes into the binary numbers of machine language, but in every other way it is identical to machine language.

High-level languages, such as FORTRAN, COBOL, BASIC, and C++, are more like English and, therefore, easier to work with than either machine or assembly language. What's more, they generally can be transported between computers with a minimum of rewriting. Most modern languages encourage structured programming, a technique that involves combining subprograms using only the three fundamental control structures: sequence, selection, and repetition. Structured programming produces programs with fewer logic errors. Still, when program efficiency is critical, many programmers use languages such as C that enable them to work at a lower level of machine logic.

Many applications contain built-in macro languages, scripting languages, and query languages that put programming power in the hands of users. Query languages are representative of fourth-generation languages (4GLs), which are nonprocedural; that is, they enable the programmer to focus on defining the task rather than outlining the steps involved in accomplishing the task. Visual programming tools enable the programmer to use icons, drawing tools, menus, and dialog boxes to construct programs without writing code. Object-oriented programming (OOP) tools enable programmers to construct programs from objects with properties and provide the ability to send messages to each other; many believe that OOP represents the future of programming.

Programs are part of larger information systems. An information system has a life cycle that starts with the initial investigation of the problem; proceeds through analysis, design, development, and implementation phases; and lingers in an ongoing maintenance phase until the system is retired. A systems analyst manages a typical information system with the help of a team of programmers and other computer professionals. Systems analysts use a variety of tools and techniques to help them develop and manage systems, including data collection techniques, modeling tools, and CASE technology.

Computer scientists are responsible for the software tools and concepts that make all other software development possible. Computer science focuses on the process of computing through several areas of specialization, including theory, algorithms, data structures, programming concepts and languages, computer architecture, management information systems, artificial intelligence, and software engineering.

One of the most challenging problems facing computer science is the problem of software reliability. Current software development techniques provide no assurance that a software system will function without failure under all circumstances. Because testing cannot prove that no bugs exist, software manufacturers cannot provide strong warranties for their products. Instead, computer users must accept the possibility that the programs they use may be less than 100 percent reliable. As more and more human institutions rely on computer systems, it becomes increasingly important for computer scientists to find ways to make software that people can trust.

Key Terms

Interactive Activities

1. The *Tomorrow's Technology and You* Web site, **www.pearsonhighered.com/beekman**, contains self-test exercises related to this chapter. Follow the instructions for taking a quiz. After you've completed your quiz, you can email the results to your instructor.

2. The Web site also contains open-ended discussion questions called Internet Exercises. Discuss one or more of the Internet Exercises questions at the section for this chapter.

True or False

1. Programming is a form of problem solving.

2. The final step in programming is the creation of an algorithm.

3. Assembly language and machine language are high-level languages.

4. Visual languages enable the programmer to use icons, drawing tools, menus, and dialog boxes to construct programs without writing code.

5. Managers often find it difficult to make an honest comparison of proposed projects based solely on costs and benefits because of hard-to-measure intangible benefits.

6. Extreme programming and other forms of agile programming tend to make programming more of a team effort rather than a solitary endeavor.

7. Prototyping is a noninteractive methodology in which the prototype is continually modified and improved until it meets the needs of the end users.

8. Computer-aided systems engineering (CASE) software packages are used to automate many routine systems development tasks, create clear documentation, and coordinate efforts, especially in large system projects.

9. Software reliability has increased as the cost of developing computer software has increased.

10. Extreme programming is so named because of the extreme time and energy demands it places on programmers.

Multiple Choice

1. Which is not a typical part of programming today?
   a. Understanding and defining the problem
   b. Writing the computer language
   c. Devising, refining, and testing the algorithm
   d. Writing the program
   e. Testing and debugging the program

2. To turn a problem into an executable program, what must the programmer do?
   a. Use stepwise refinement to break the problem repeatedly into smaller steps
   b. Create and test an algorithm—a set of step-by-step instructions
   c. Write algorithms in pseudocode
   d. Translate pseudocode into a computer language
   e. All of the above.

3. Machine language is not
   a. the native language of the computer.
   b. based on binary—strings of 0s and 1s.
   c. commonly used today to write computer programs.
   d. difficult to read and debug.
   e. usually displayed in decimal, hexadecimal, or another number system.

4. What do you call a program that translates a program's source code into machine language, one statement at a time, while the program is being executed?
   a. Compiler
   b. Debugger
   c. Interpreter
   d. Programmer
   e. Test editor

5. High-level languages
   a. are mostly used for designing graphical user interfaces.
   b. have, for most applications, been replaced by multi-level languages.
   c. are extremely platform specific, so that code written for one platform must be completely rewritten for other platforms.
   d. are designed for writing psuedocode.
   e. are easier to work with than either machine or assembly language.

6. In object-oriented programming (OOP),
   a. objects can send and receive messages.
   b. objects can be easily reused in different programs.
   c. objects have everything they need to operate.
   d. programmers can build programs from prefabricated objects.
   e. All of the above.

7. Which term best describes a query language that allows users to access a database with English-like questions?
   a. Extreme language
   b. Machine language
   c. Fourth-generation language
   d. Macro language
   e. Assembly language

8. Which of the following is not true about software component tools?
   a. Users construct small custom applications from software components.
   b. They can be used only if applications are programmed to allow it.
   c. They may reverse the trend toward mega-applications.
   d. They are the logical extension of object-oriented programming.
   e. All of these statements are true.

9. Which of the following is not true about extreme programming?
   a. Programmers must complete a module before going home, taking a break, or moving on to another task.
   b. The entire programming team takes responsibility for all of the code.
   c. Programmers work in pairs to write code.
   d. The programming team stays in close communication with customers and clients.
   e. The software development plan includes frequent releases of updated code.

10. Which is not a process in the classic systems development cycle?
    a. Prototyping the final solution using resources from parallel systems
    b. Investigating a situation
    c. Designing a system solution to improve the situation
    d. Acquiring resources to implement the solution
    e. Evaluating the success of the solution

11. Which is not an implementation approach used when converting to a new system?
    a. Direct cutover—replacing the old system with the new system at one time
    b. Parallel—gradually phasing out the old system while running both systems
    c. RAD—rapid application development
    d. Phase in—partial implementation of parts of the new system
    e. Pilot—implementing the new system at one site and modifying until satisfactory

12. Modeling tools create graphic representations of a system, and include the
    a. system flowchart—a graphical depiction of the physical system.
    b. data flow diagram (DFD) illustrating the movement of data.
    c. data dictionary—a directory describing all the data flowing through a system.

d. decision tables showing if-then rules that apply when conditions occur.

e. All of these are system modeling tools.

13. Which branch of computer science is focused on producing more reliable software?
    a. Computer theory
    b. Programming languages
    c. Software engineering
    d. Computer architecture
    e. Algorithms

14. Software project cancellation in the United States
    a. happens occasionally, but is not particularly costly to the economy.
    b. happens to about one-sixth of all projects and costs billions of dollars a year.
    c. used to be a major problem, but has been almost completely eliminated.

d. is most often due to security breaches.

e. None of the above.

15. Which of these statements is true?
    a. Software companies could produce error-free products if they were willing to reduce profits.
    b. Some large software systems, such as Linux, contain no bugs.
    c. Software testing can prove the existence of bugs, but it cannot prove that the software is 100 percent bug-free.
    d. Techniques for producing bug-free software are used for critical military applications, but they're too expensive for most other applications.
    e. All of these statements are true.

Review Questions

1. Define or describe each of the key terms listed in the "Key Terms" section. Check your answers using the glossary.

2. Here's an algorithm for directions to a university bookstore from a downtown location:

   ```
   Go south on 4th Street to Jefferson
   Street.
   Turn left on Jefferson Street.
   Proceed on Jefferson past the
   stoplight to the booth at the campus
   entrance.
   If there's somebody in the booth, ask
   for a permit to park in the bookstore
   parking lot; otherwise, just keep
   going.
   When you reach the bookstore parking
   lot, keep circling the lot until you
   find an empty space.
   Park in the empty space.
   ```

   Find examples of sequence, selection, and repetition control structures in this algorithm.

3. Find examples of ambiguous statements that might keep the algorithm in Question 2 from working properly.

4. Assume that Robert, a driver, is going to do the driving in Question 2. Use stepwise refinement to add more detail to Question 2's algorithm so Robert has a better chance of understanding the instructions.

5. Design an algorithm to play the part of the guesser in the number-guessing game featured in this chapter. If you base your algorithm on the right strategy, it will always be able to guess the correct number in seven or fewer tries. (*Hint*: Computer scientists call the right strategy *binary search*.)

6. When does it make sense to design a custom program rather than use off-the-shelf commercial software? Give some examples.

7. Give examples of several different kinds of computer errors, and describe how these errors affect people.

8. Why are so many computer languages in use today?

9. What is the relationship between computer science and computer programming?

10. What is the difference between writing a program and designing an information system? How are they related?

Discussion Questions

1. Is programming a useful skill for a computer user? Why or why not?

2. Should programmers be licensed? Is programming a craft, a trade, or a profession?

3. Suppose you want to create a small business or non-profit organization. What questions might a systems analyst ask when determining what kind of information systems the organization will need?

4. What do you think programming will be like in 10 years? 20 years? 50 years?

5. Computer science is in the college of science at some universities and in the college of engineering at others. Is computer science a science, a branch of engineering, or both?

6. Why is it so difficult to produce error-free software?

Projects

1. The computer is often blamed for human errors. Find some recent examples of "the computer did it" errors in newspapers, magazines, or conversations with others. For each example, try to determine whether the computer is, in fact, to blame.

2. Do some research to discover what safeguards are used to ensure that automated teller machines don't malfunction and that their security can't be violated.

3. The uproar over the 2000 presidential election led many state and local governments to install electronic voting machines. Some critics have suggested these machines may be less reliable than the systems they are replacing. Research the advantages and disadvantages of different kinds of electronic voting systems in use today. How do they measure up to traditional voting machines, mail-in ballots, and other types of voting systems?

4. The U.S. Department of Defense spent more than $20 million creating an Internet-voting system for soldiers and other Americans who were overseas. The name of the system was Secure Electronic Registration and Voting Experiment (SERVE). However, in early 2004, just weeks before it was to be used, the Department of Defense halted the experiment. Find newspaper and magazine articles describing SERVE. Write a brief report explaining what the system was supposed to do and why it was scrapped.

5. The proposed Uniform Computer Information Transactions Act (UCITA), adopted by Maryland and Virginia and under consideration by other states, would amend the Uniform Commercial Code, creating a new category for software products. Find out more about UCITA. What are its key provisions? Which groups support UCITA? Which groups oppose UCITA? Decide where you stand on this issue.

Sources and Resources

Books

As you might expect, there are hundreds of books on programming and computer science, most of which are specifically written about particular programming languages and platforms. Most of the books listed here are more general.

Head First Software Development: A Brain-Friendly Guide, by Dan Pilone and Russ Miles (Cambridge, MA: O'Reilly, 2008). O'Reilly has a well-deserved reputation as a publisher of first-rate books for software developers, programmers, and techno-geeks. This is one of many popular books in their Head-First "Brain-Friendly" series. If you're interested in learning from the pros, you might find just what you're looking for here.

Secrets of the Rock Star Programmers, by Ed Burns (New York, NY: McGraw Hill, 2008). Burns, a senior staff engineer at Sun Microsystems, interviews 14 of the most influential programmers of the last couple of decades, plus one actual rock star. The book isn't a technical programmer's guide, but it can provide insights and perspective for anyone interested in becoming a "rock star" programmer.

Dynamics of Software Development (Best Practices), Second Edition, by Jim McCarthy (Redmond, WA: Microsoft Press, 2007). A lifelong software developer offers advice in the form of rules (such as "Don't flip the bozo bit") for shipping software on time. The book is filled with anecdotes and war stories from the front lines of software development.

Learning to Program with Alice, Second Edition, by Wanda P. Dann, Stephen Cooper, and Randy Pausch (Englewood Cliffs, NJ: Prentice-Hall, 2008). This book teaches object-oriented programming using the Alice 2.0 software system developed at Carnegie-Mellon University. Instead of writing Java code, the Alice programmer uses a mouse to create animations in a 3-D world where every character is an object and every action is a method.

Extreme Programming Explained: Embrace Change, Second Edition, by Kent Beck (Reading, MA: Addison-Wesley, 2005). This book, written by the owner of a software company, was largely responsible for the extreme programming movement.

The Analytical Engine: An Introduction to Computer Science Using the Internet, Second Edition, by Rick Decker and Stuart Hirshfield (Boston, MA: Course Technology, 2004). This well-written, innovative text illustrates many of the concepts of computer science using a Web site to add interactivity.

Computer Science: An Overview, Tenth Edition, by J. Glenn Brookshear (Reading, MA: Pearson Addison-Wesley, 2008). This excellent survey covers algorithms, data structures, operating systems, and software engineering from a current computer science perspective.

Algorithmics: The Spirit of Computing, Third Edition, by David Harel and Yishai Feldman (Reading, MA: Addison-Wesley, 2004). This book explores the central ideas of computer science from basic algorithms and data structures to more advanced concepts.

The New Turing Omnibus: 66 Excursions in Computer Science, by A. K. Dewdney (New York, NY: Computer Science Press, 1993, 2001). This unusual book contains 66 short chapters covering a wide range of computer science topics, from algorithms to VLSI computers. Much of the material is technical and mathematical, but the writing is clear and engaging.

The Mythical Man-Month: Essays on Software Engineering, 20th Anniversary Edition, by Frederick P. Brooks, Jr. (Reading, MA: Addison-Wesley, 1995). This classic, often-quoted book outlines clearly the problems of managing large software projects. This twentieth-anniversary edition includes four new chapters that provide an up-to-date perspective.

Computers Ltd: What They Really Can't Do, by David Harel (New York, NY: Oxford University Press, 2004). As the title suggests, this book explores the limits of computer power in particular and human knowledge in general.

Rescuing Prometheus: Four Monumental Projects That Changed Our World, by Thomas P. Hughes (New York, NY: Vintage Books, 2000). This book profiles four of the biggest technological projects of the previous century. These projects forced their developers to push the limits of systems design.

Out of Their Minds: The Lives and Discoveries of 15 Great Computer Scientists, by Dennis Shasha and Cathy Lazere (New York, NY: Springer, 1998). The people profiled in this book were responsible for many of the most important ideas in computer science today. The profiles illuminate their achievements through interviews and explanations; technical details are confined to boxes so they don't interrupt the flow of the human stories. Closing sections explore two questions: What do these people have in common, and where is the field of computer science heading in the next quarter century?

15

Is Artificial Intelligence Real?

After you read this chapter you should be able to:

▶ Explain the two basic approaches of artificial intelligence research

▶ Describe several hard problems that artificial intelligence research has not yet been able to solve

▶ Describe several practical applications of artificial intelligence

▶ Explain what robots are and give several examples illustrating what they can—and can't—do

> The extent to which we regard something as **behaving in an intelligent manner** is determined as much by **our own state of mind and training** as by the properties of the object under consideration.
>
> —*Alan Turing*

Alan Turing, Military Intelligence, and Intelligent Machines

Alan M. Turing, the British mathematician who designed the world's first operational electronic digital computer during the 1940s, may have been the most important thinker in the history of computing. While a graduate student at Princeton in 1936, Turing published "On Computable Numbers," a paper that laid the theoretical groundwork for all of modern computer science. In that paper, he described a theoretical Turing machine that could read instructions from punched paper tape and perform all the critical operations of a computer. The paper also established the limits of computer science by mathematically demonstrating that some problems simply cannot be solved by any kind of computer.

After receiving his doctorate in 1938, Turing had an opportunity to translate theory into reality. Anticipating an invasion by Hitler's forces, the British government assembled a team of mathematicians and engineers with the top secret mission of cracking the German military code. Under the leadership of Turing and others, the group built Colossus, a single-purpose machine regarded by some as the first electronic digital computer. From the time Colossus was completed in 1943 until the end of the war, it successfully cracked Nazi codes—a fact concealed by the British government until long after the war ended. Many experts believe that Colossus was ultimately responsible for the defeat of the Nazis.

Turing effectively launched the field of artificial intelligence (AI) with a 1950 paper called "Computing Machinery and Intelligence." In this paper he proposed a concrete test for determining whether a machine was intelligent. In later years Turing championed the possibility of emulating human thought through computation. He even cowrote the first chess-playing program.

Turing was an unconventional and extremely sensitive person. In 1952 he was professionally and socially devastated when he was arrested and injected with hormones for violation of British antihomosexuality laws. The 41-year-old genius apparently committed suicide in 1954, years before the government made his wartime heroics public. Five decades after his death, Turing's

FIGURE 15.1 Alan Turing (1913–1954)

FIGURE 15.2 Colossus, 1945. *(Source: Courtesy of The Computer History Museum.)*

work still has relevance to computer scientists, mathematicians, and philosophers. It's impossible to know what he might have contributed had he lived another three decades. ~

Alan Turing spent much of his short life trying to answer the question "Can machines think?" That's still a central question of **artificial intelligence (AI)**, the field of computer science devoted to making computers perceive, reason, and act in ways that have, until now, been reserved for human beings. But today even those who believe that computers can't "think" have to admit that AI research has produced impressive results: computers that can communicate in human languages; systems that can provide instant expertise in medicine, science, and other fields; world-class electronic chess players; and robots that can outperform humans in a variety of tasks. In this chapter, we explore the technology, applications, and implications of artificial intelligence.

Thinking about Thinking Machines

What is intelligence, anyway? It is only a word that people use to name those **unknown processes** with which our brains **solve problems we call hard**. But whenever you learn a skill yourself, you're **less impressed or mystified** when other people do the same. This is why the meaning of "intelligence" **seems so elusive**: It describes not some definite thing but only the momentary **horizon of our ignorance** about how minds might work.

—*Marvin Minsky, AI pioneer*

If you ask 10 people to define intelligence, you're likely to get 10 different answers, including some of these:

- The ability to learn from experience
- The power of thought
- The ability to reason
- The ability to perceive relations
- The power of insight
- The ability to use tools
- Intuition

Intelligence is difficult to define and understand, even for philosophers and psychologists who spend their lives studying it. But this elusive quality is, to many people, the characteristic that sets humans apart from other species. So it's not surprising that controversy

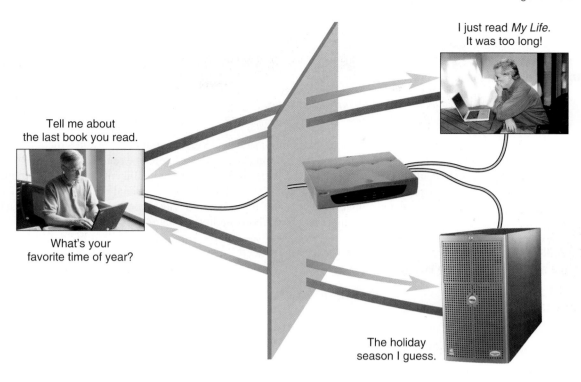

I just read *My Life*.
It was too long!

Tell me about
the last book you read.

What's your
favorite time of year?

The holiday
season I guess.

FIGURE 15.3 In the Turing test, a human interpreter has instant-messaging-style conversations with two contestants and tries to determine which contestant is human, based on the answers given.

has continually swirled around the questions "Can a machine be intelligent?" and "Can a machine think?"

Can Machines Think?

In his landmark 1950 paper, Alan Turing suggested that the question "Can machines think?" was too vague and philosophical to be of any value. To make it more concrete, he proposed an "imitation game." The Turing test, as it came to be known, involves two people and a computer. One person, the interrogator, sits alone in a room and types questions into a computer terminal. The questions can be about anything—math, science, politics, sports, entertainment, art, human relationships, emotions—anything. As answers to questions appear on the terminal, the interrogator attempts to guess whether those answers were typed by the other person or generated by the computer. By repeatedly fooling interrogators into thinking it is a person, a computer can demonstrate intelligent behavior. If it acts intelligently, according to Turing, it is intelligent.

> A **machine** may be deemed **intelligent** when it can **pass for a human being** in a blind test.
>
> —*Alan Turing*

Turing did not intend this test to be the only way to demonstrate machine intelligence; he pointed out that a machine could fail and still be intelligent. Even so, Turing believed that machines would be able to pass his test by the turn of the century. So far, no computer has come close, in spite of nearly 60 years of AI research. While some people still cling to the Turing test to define artificial intelligence, most AI researchers favor less stringent definitions.

What Is Artificial Intelligence?

Artificial intelligence is the study of ideas which enable computers to do the **things that make people seem intelligent**.

—*Patrick Henry Winston, in Artificial Intelligence*

This definition from a 1977 edition of a textbook is similar to definitions that commonly appear in today's popular press. This type of definition captures the general idea of artificial intelligence, but it breaks down when applied to specific examples. Does AI include doing lightning-fast calculations? Finding a word in a dictionary as fast as a person can type it? Remembering hundreds of telephone numbers at a time? If a person could do all of these things, that person would "seem intelligent." But these activities aren't good examples of artificial intelligence because they're trivial for computers. In fact, many computer scientists believe that if it's easy to do with a computer, it can't be artificial intelligence. Here's a more recent textbook definition that reflects that point of view:

Artificial intelligence is the study of how to make computers do things at which, **at the moment, people are better**.

—*Elaine Rich, in Artificial Intelligence*

According to this definition, artificial intelligence is a moving frontier. The short history of the field bears this out. In the 1950s many AI researchers struggled to create computers that could play checkers and chess. Today computers can beat the best human players, and relatively few AI researchers study these games. In the words of one researcher, artificial intelligence is "whatever hasn't been done yet." Moving-frontier definitions of AI tend to be accurate, but they're short on specifics. A more concrete and complete definition might combine Rich's definition with this one from a more recent edition of Winston's popular textbook:

Artificial intelligence is the study of the computations that make it possible to **perceive, reason, and act**.

—*Patrick Henry Winston, in Artificial Intelligence*

Perceive, reason, and *act* are words used more commonly in psychology, the science of human behavior, than in computer science. In fact, psychologists work alongside computer scientists on many AI research projects. Computer scientists tend to be motivated by the challenge of producing machine intelligence for its own sake. Psychologists, on the other hand, are interested in AI because it provides new insights into natural intelligence and the workings of the human brain.

These points of view symbolize two common approaches to AI. One approach attempts to use computers to simulate human mental processes. For example, an AI expert might ask people to describe how they solve a problem and attempt to capture their answers in a software model.

The simulation approach has three inherent problems:

■ Most people have trouble knowing and describing how they do things. Human intelligence includes unconscious thoughts, instantaneous insights, and other mental processes that are difficult or impossible to understand and describe.

■ There are vast differences between the structure and capabilities of the human brain and those of the computer. Even the most powerful supercomputers can't approach the brain's ability to perform parallel processing—breaking a complex job into many smaller, simpler jobs and completing those jobs simultaneously.

■ The best way to do something with a machine is often very different from the way people would do it. Before the Wright brothers, dozens of inventors failed

FIGURE 15.4 Many early flying machines that imitated birds never got off the ground.

to produce flying machines because they tried to make their inventions imitate birds. Similarly, many early AI attempts failed because they were designed to mimic human intelligence rather than to take advantage of the computer's unique capabilities.

The second, more common, approach to AI involves designing intelligent machines independent of the way people think. According to this approach, human intelligence is just one possible kind of intelligence. A machine's method of solving a problem might be different from the human method, but no less intelligent.

Whichever approach they take, scientists face problems that are difficult and far too complex to solve all at once. Most AI researchers choose to break those problems into smaller problems that are easier to solve—to create programs that can function intelligently when confined to limited *domains*.

Opening Games

One of the first popular domains for AI research was the checkerboard. Much early AI work focused on games such as checkers and chess because they were easy to represent in the computer's digital memory, they had clearly defined rules, and the goals were unmistakable. Instead of struggling with nebulous issues surrounding thought and intelligence, game researchers could

FIGURE 15.5 Crowds watched in disbelief when Deep Blue, the IBM supercomputer, beat world chess champion Garry Kasarov in 1997 (top). Since then, artificial intelligence has been built in to the computer opponents in many popular video games, including Forza Motorsport 2 (bottom).

focus on the concrete question "How can I create a program that wins consistently?" Their answers included many AI techniques that are still used today in a variety of applications:

- *Searching.* One way to win a game is through searching—looking ahead at the possibilities generated by each potential move: "I have four possible moves—A, B, C, and D. If I do A, then my opponent might do X, Y, or Z. If my opponent responds by doing X, then I can do E, F, G, or H . . . and so on." Obviously, high-speed computers are better at this kind of repetitive processing than people are. Early AI programs could not check all possible decision points in a complicated game such as checkers, which has approximately 10^{21} choices. Today's powerful computers can perform massive database searches quickly, making this kind of look-ahead searching practical for some game-playing programs. Researcher Jonathan Schaeffer's checkers-playing program uses an enormous database of board positions to evaluate every move. The program plays as well as the best human players in the world. It uses what's known as a *brute-force* technique—rapidly repeating a simple operation until it finds an answer. This kind of exhaustive searching doesn't fit many definitions of intelligence. For more complex games such as chess, and for most domains outside the world of games, the staggering number of decision points makes brute-force searching impractical. So searching is generally guided by a planned strategy and by rules known as heuristics.
- *Heuristics.* A **heuristic** is a rule of thumb. Unlike hard-and-fast algorithms, heuristics guide us toward judgments that experience tells us are likely to be true. In everyday life we apply heuristics such as "To loosen a stuck jar lid, run warm water over it." A checkers-playing program might employ a heuristic that says, "Keep checkers in the king's row as long as possible."

■ *Pattern recognition.* The best human chess and checkers players remember thousands of critical board patterns and know the best strategies for playing when those or similar patterns appear. Game-playing programs recognize recurring patterns, too, but not nearly as well as people do. Computer players often have trouble identifying situations that are similar but not identical. Pattern recognition is probably the single biggest advantage a human game player has over a computer opponent; it helps compensate for the computer's speed and thoroughness at searching ahead.

■ *Machine learning.* The best game-playing programs learn from experience using machine learning techniques. If a move pays off, a learning program is more likely to use that move (or similar moves) in future games. If a move results in a loss, the program will remember to avoid similar moves.

Today computer systems can hold their own against the best human chess players by examining hundreds of thousands of moves per second. When IBM's Deep Blue, a customized RS/6000 SP supercomputer, beat grand master Garry Kasparov in a 1997 rematch, people all around the world watched with a level of interest that's seldom given to scientific work. Many of today's best computer games use similar technology, on a smaller scale, to create artificial opponents for gamers.

Still, most AI researchers have moved on to more interesting and practical applications. But whether working on vision, speech, problem solving, or expert decision making, researchers still use the successful strategy of game researchers—to restrict the domain of their programs so that problems are small enough to understand and solve. We'll see how this strategy has paid off in several important areas of AI, starting with natural-language communication.

Natural-Language Communication

Language is **no less complex or subtle** a phenomenon than the **knowledge** it seeks to transmit.

—*Raymond Kurzweil, in* The Age of Intelligent Machines

In Turing's classic test of machine intelligence, the computer is considered to be intelligent if it can successfully pose as a person in a typed conversation. Scientists have long dreamed of machines that could communicate in natural languages such as English, Russian, and Japanese. Over the years natural-language communication has continually challenged researchers. Many problems relate to recognizing and reproducing human speech—issues we deal with later in the chapter. But even when it's typed directly into the machine, natural-language text poses significant software challenges.

Machine Translation Traps

One early project attempted to create a program that could translate scientific papers from Russian to English and from English to Russian. Automatic translation offered hope for increased communication between scientists during the tense Cold War years. The method seemed straightforward and foolproof: A parsing program (or parser) would analyze sentence structure and identify each word according to whether it was a subject, verb, or other part of speech; another program would look up each word in a translation dictionary and substitute the appropriate word.

This word-by-word approach to machine translation failed. In one famous anecdote, scientists asked the computer to translate English into Russian and then translate the results back into English. As the story goes, "The spirit is willing, but the flesh is weak" came back as "The wine is agreeable, but the meat is rotten" and "out of sight, out of mind" became "blind and insane" or "invisible idiot."

After this setback, scientists concluded that translation without understanding is impossible. The next generation of machine-translation systems were based on the idea that the computer should extract the meaning from the original text. Once the computer understood the meaning, it could express that meaning in a variety of languages. Unfortunately, this approach turned out to be impractical. Understanding the meaning of any sentence requires a huge amount of knowledge about the world.

Today many computer scientists are taking a statistical approach to machine translation. The idea is to provide a program with many positive examples of correctly translated sentences, as well as many negative examples of incorrect translations. The program uses a machine-learning algorithm to infer the correct rules of translation. With this approach, the system imitates successful translations without really understanding what the words mean.

A variety of automatic translation programs are currently available. One of these programs is Babel Fish (named for the universal translator fish in Douglas Adams's *Hitchhiker's Guide to the Galaxy*) jointly developed by AltaVista and SYSTRAN. To illustrate the capabilities and limitations of contemporary machine translation, we've used Babel Fish to translate a paragraph from this chapter into Spanish and back into English.

Two native Spanish speakers said the Babel Fish translation was understandable but contained minor errors in most sentences. For example, Babel Fish should have translated "successful" as "exitosos," not "acertados." The Spanish phrase "es ordenado y documentado bien" should have been rendered "está bien ordenado y documentado." One reviewer said the errors were similar to the errors made by an English speaker who has taken one or two years of Spanish classes.

Original English Text:

Some of the first successful expert systems were developed around medical knowledge bases. Because medical knowledge is orderly and well documented, researchers believed it could be captured successfully in knowledge bases. They were right. The MYCIN medical expert system outperformed many human experts in diagnosing diseases. Dozens of other working medical expert systems exist, although few are actually used in medical practice.

Machine Translation into Spanish:

Algunos de los primeros sistemas expertos acertados fueron desarrollados alrededor de bases de conocimiento médicas. Porque el conocimiento médico es ordenado y documentado bien, los investigadores creyeron que podría ser capturado con éxito en bases de conocimiento. Tenían razón. El sistema experto médico de MYCIN superó a muchos expertos humanos en enfermedades que diagnosticaban. Las docenas de otros sistemas expertos médicos del funcionamiento existen, aunque pocos se utilizan realmente en práctica médica.

Machine Translation of Translated Text Back into English:

Some of the first guessed right expert systems were developed around medical knowledge bases. Because the medical knowledge is ordered and documented well, the investigators thought that he could be captured successfully in knowledge bases. They were right. The medical expert system of MYCIN surpassed to many human experts in diseases that they diagnosed. The dozens of other medical expert systems of the operation exist, although few are really used in medical practice.

FIGURE 15.6 The Babel Fish program translated a paragraph from this chapter from English into Spanish, then back into English. You can test Babel Fish's capabilities by visiting http://babelfish.yahoo.com.

As evidence that Babel Fish does not actually understand the meaning of the sentences it manipulates, consider its translation of the Spanish paragraph back into English. The resulting sentences contain many phrases that would not be uttered by anyone who really understood English.

The paragraph we asked Babel Fish to translate was relatively unambiguous and straightforward. It was simple prose, not poetry. It contained few technical terms and no idioms. Babel Fish responded by producing a translation that was imperfect but for the most part understandable. The narrower the subject matter, the more reliable the translation. That is why automatic translation for specific domains (such as travel) is easier than automatic translation of arbitrary sentences. It's amazing that a computer program can produce a reasonable translation of English to Spanish or French to German without actually understanding the meaning of the sentences, but that's the reality of machine translation today.

Conversation without Communication

Similar lessons emerged from Joseph Weizenbaum's work with ELIZA, one of the first software programs to converse in a limited form of natural language. Weizenbaum, an MIT professor, designed ELIZA in the 1960s to simulate the role of a therapist in a typed

Men are all alike.
IN WHAT WAY
They're always bugging us about something or other.
CAN YOU THINK OF A SPECIFIC EXAMPLE
Well, my boyfriend made me come here.
YOUR BOYFRIEND MADE YOU COME HERE
He says I'm depressed much of the time.
I AM SORRY TO HEAR YOU ARE DEPRESSED
It's true. I am unhappy.
DO YOU THINK COMING HERE WILL HELP YOU NOT TO BE UNHAPPY
I need some help, that much seems certain.
WHAT WOULD IT MEAN TO YOU IF YOU GOT SOME HELP
Perhaps I could learn to get along with my mother.
TELL ME MORE ABOUT YOUR FAMILY
My mother takes care of me.
WHO ELSE IN YOUR FAMILY TAKES CARE OF YOU
My father.
YOUR FATHER
You are like my father in some ways.
WHAT RESEMBLANCE DO YOU SEE
You are not very aggressive but I think you don't want me to notice that.
WHAT MAKES YOU THINK I AM NOT VERY AGGRESSIVE
You don't argue with me.
WHY DO YOU THINK I DON'T ARGUE WITH YOU
You are afraid of me.
DOES IT PLEASE YOU TO BELIEVE I AM AFRAID OF YOU
My father is afraid of everybody.
WHAT ELSE COMES TO MIND WHEN YOU THINK OF YOUR FATHER
Bullies.
DOES THAT HAVE ANYTHING TO DO WITH THE FACT THAT YOUR BOYFRIEND MADE YOU COME HERE
From *Computer Power and Human Reason*, by Joseph Weizenbaum.

FIGURE 15.7 A conversation with ELIZA.

conversation with a patient. A sample ELIZA session appears above (the computer's responses are capitalized).

As impressive as this dialogue seems, there's no understanding here. ELIZA uses a few simple tricks to *simulate* understanding, including recognizing a few key words (such as *mother*), identifying categories for some of those words (*family*), and repeating phrases from earlier in the conversation. But ELIZA's tricks are far from foolproof. In response to "Necessity is the mother of invention," ELIZA might say, "Tell me more about your family." An ELIZA session can easily deteriorate into nonsense dialogue laced with grammatical errors and inappropriate responses. Clearly, ELIZA lacks the understanding to pass as a human in a Turing test.

Nonsense and Common Sense

Bill sings to Sarah, Sarah sings to Bill. Perhaps they will do **other dangerous things** together. They may eat lamb or stroke each other. They may chant of **their difficulties and their happiness**. They have **love** but they also have **typewriters**. **That is interesting**.

—*A poem by RACTER, in* The Policeman's Beard Is Half Constructed, *programmed by William Chamberlain and Thomas Etter*

Years after ELIZA's creation, this poetry appeared in *The Policeman's Beard Is Half Constructed*, the first book ever written by a computer. RACTER, like ELIZA, produced English language output without really understanding it. Why do machines that flawlessly follow instructions written in BASIC, C++, and other computer languages have so much trouble with *natural-language* communications?

Part of the problem is the massive vocabulary of natural languages. A typical computer language has less than a hundred key words, each with a precise, unambiguous meaning. English, in contrast, contains hundreds of thousands of words, many of which have multiple meanings. Of course, a person or a machine doesn't need to understand every word in the dictionary to communicate successfully in English. Most natural-language processors work with a *subset* of the language. But as the early scientific translation efforts showed, restricting vocabulary isn't enough.

Every language has a syntax—a set of rules for constructing sentences from words. In a programming language, the syntax rules are exact and unambiguous. Natural-language parsing programs have to deal with rules that are vague, ambiguous, and occasionally contradictory. One early parser, when asked to analyze the sentence "Time flies like an arrow," replied with several possible interpretations, including one statement with time as the subject, another statement with flies as the subject, and two commands in which the reader was the subject!

FIGURE 15.8 Inexpensive pocket electronic translators serve world travelers by providing instant access to common words, short phrases, and simple sentences.

Still, computers are far more successful dealing with natural-language syntax than with semantics—the underlying meaning of words and phrases. In natural language the meaning of a sentence is ambiguous unless it's considered in context. "The hens were ready to eat" means one thing if it follows "The farmer approached the hen house" and something else if it follows "The chef approached the oven." To make matters worse, human conversations are filled with idiomatic expressions ("Susan had a cow when she heard the news") and unspoken assumptions about the world or specific subject matter ("Catch the T at Harvard Square and take it to MIT"). In short, the computer lacks what we call *common sense*—the wealth of knowledge and understanding about the world that people share.

The most successful natural-language applications limit the *domain* so that virtually all relevant information can be fed to the system. If the domain—the "world"—is small enough and the rules of that world are clear and unambiguous, a computer can have "common sense" that makes natural-language communication possible. For example, many database query languages accept and understand English commands but only within a narrow range. The biggest market for natural-language processing today is language translation—the same market that produced AI's first major failure. Several Web sites offer on-the-fly translation of text files or Web pages. (You've already seen a translation by Babel Fish.) Translation programs still can't translate books or conversations flawlessly, but they can greatly increase the productivity of people who translate technical manuals and other works that focus on narrow domains.

Without genuine understanding, computers are simply incapable of having meaningful conversations with humans. In 1990 Hugh Loebner established a $100,000 prize for the first computer program to pass the Turing test and a smaller prize for the "most human-like" entrant each year. Every year, organizers host a competition attracting entrants from around the world. Judges sit in front of PCs connected by a network to the contestants in another room. Most of the contestants are computers, but two of them are humans. After having an instant-message-style conversation with each contestant, a judge gives the contestant a score ranging from 1 (definitely a machine) to 5 (definitely a human). So far, no machine has won the big prize. Here's a short sample of a conversation between a judge and Ultra Hal, the most human-like entrant in 2007:

Judge: are you a robot?

Hal: I am a human.

Judge: no way. prove it.

Hal: Not now? Okay. Why do people continue to date boyfriends or girlfriends who treat them badly?

Judge: does your boyfriend treat you badly?

Hal: Monopolies can treat customers badly and get away with it.

Judge: did you read my question?

Hal: This test is inspired by the ';Imitation Game'; where a man and a woman go into separate rooms, and guests try to tell them apart by writing a series of questions.

Judge: Quite true

Hal: Are men happiest clawing their way up the corporate ladder?

Judge: I don't know. Are you a corporate worker?

Hal: Is it a good idea to get emotionally involved with a fellow worker?

Judge: hdo you know anyone who has done that?

Hal: I like your imagery.

Judge: thanks. what is imagery?

Hal: Imagery: the ability to form mental images of things or events. Imagination, imaging, mental imagery. 'he could still hear her in his imagination'.

Judge: ddo you ride bikes?

Hal: I like to drive cars, but I tend to ride the subway in nyc.

Judge: thave you ever dating someone you work with?

Hal: I work for nbc as a network technician. They pay my bills.

Judge: indeed. how much money do you make?

Hal: I spend enough time answering questions like that at work.

FIGURE 15.9 A conversation with Zabaware's Ultra Hal the "most human-like" entrant in the 2007 Loebner Prize Competition.

It's not surprising that the judges weren't fooled by Ultra Hal. Like other entrants, the program has nowhere near enough knowledge of the real world to carry on an intelligent conversation. No computer seems likely to win a Turing test any time soon.

Natural-language processing relates to other AI technologies discussed later in the chapter. Speech recognition and optical character recognition provide input to natural-language systems, freeing the human communicator from the keyboard. On the output side, speech synthesis allows the computer to talk back in English or another language. But natural-language input and output are meaningless without a knowledge base that allows the computer to understand the ideas behind the words.

Knowledge Bases and Expert Systems

A preschool child can take you on a tour of the neighborhood, explaining how people use every building, describing the interconnected lives of every person you meet, and answering questions about anything you see along the way. A com-

> The computer can't tell you the **emotional story**. It can give you the exact mathematical design, but **what's missing is the eyebrows**.
>
> —*Frank Zappa*

puter at city hall can give you facts and figures about building materials and assessed values of houses, but it can't provide you with a fraction of the knowledge conveyed in the child's tour. The human brain, which isn't particularly good at storing and recalling facts, excels at manipulating *knowledge*—information that incorporates the *relationships* among facts. Computers, on the other hand, are better at handling data than knowledge. Nobody knows exactly how the brain stores and manipulates knowledge. But AI researchers have developed, and continue to develop, techniques for representing knowledge in computers.

Knowledge Bases

While a database contains only facts, a knowledge base also contains a system of rules for determining and changing the relationship among those facts. Facts stored in a database are rigidly organized in categories; ideas stored in a knowledge base can be reorganized as new information changes their relationships.

Computer scientists so far have had little success in developing a knowledge base that can understand the world the way a child does. Even before they start school, children know these things:

- If you put something in water, it will get wet.
- If Susan is Mark's sister, Mark is Susan's brother.
- You can't build a tower from the top down.
- Dogs commonly live in houses, but cows seldom do.
- People can't walk through walls.
- If you eat dinner in a restaurant, you're expected to pay for the food and leave a tip.
- If you travel from Dallas to Phoenix, time passes during the trip.

These statements are part of the mass of commonsense knowledge that children acquire from living in the world. Because computers can't draw on years of human experience to construct mental models of the world, they don't automatically develop common sense. Much AI research centers on providing computers with ways to acquire and store real-world, commonsense knowledge. Researchers have had little success at developing computer systems with the kinds of broad, shallow knowledge found in children. But when knowledge bases are restricted to narrow, deep domains—the domains of experts—they can be effective, practical, intelligent tools. For example, knowledge bases lie at the heart of hundreds of expert systems used in business, science, and industry.

Artificial Experts

> An **expert** is one who knows **more and more** about **less and less**.
>
> —*Nicholas Murray Butler*

As the quote suggests, an expert is someone who has an extraordinary amount of knowledge within a narrow domain. By confining activities to that domain, the expert achieves mastery. An expert system is a software program designed to replicate the decision-making process of a human expert. At the foundation of every expert system is a knowledge base representing ideas from a specific field of expertise. Because it's a collection of specialized knowledge, an expert system's knowledge base must be constructed by a user, an expert, or a knowledge engineer—a specialist who interviews and observes experts and painstakingly converts their words and actions into a knowledge base. Some new expert systems can grow their own knowledge bases while observing human decision makers doing their jobs. But for most expert systems, the process is still human-intensive.

Strictly speaking, expert systems derive their knowledge from experts; systems that draw on other sources, such as government regulations, company guidelines, and statistical databases, are called knowledge-based systems. But in practice, the terms *expert system* and *knowledge-based system* are often used interchangeably.

A knowledge base commonly represents knowledge in the form of if-then rules such as these:

- If the engine will not turn over and the lights do not work, then check the battery.
- If checking the battery shows it is not dead, then check the battery connectors.

Most human decision making involves uncertainty, so many modern expert systems are based on fuzzy logic. *Fuzzy logic* allows conclusions to be stated as probabilities (for example, "There's a 70 percent chance . . .") rather than certainties. Here's an example from MYCIN, one of the first expert systems designed to capture a doctor's expertise:

```
If (1) the infection is primary bacteremia, and
(2) the site of the culture is one of the sterile sites, and
(3) the suspected portal of entry of the organism is the
gastrointestinal tract, then there is suggestive evidence
(0.7) that the identity of the organism is bacteriodes.
```

Along with the knowledge base, a complete expert system also includes a human interface, which enables the user to interact with the system, and an inference engine, which puts the user input together with the knowledge base, applies logical principles, and produces the requested expert advice.

Sometimes expert systems aid experts by providing automated data analysis and informed second opinions. In other cases, expert systems support nonexperts by providing advice based on judgments of one or more experts. Whatever their role, expert systems work because they function within narrow, carefully defined domains.

Expert Systems in Action

Some of the first successful expert systems were developed around medical knowledge bases. Because medical knowledge is orderly and well documented, researchers believed it could be captured successfully in knowledge bases. They were right. The MYCIN medical expert system outperformed many human experts in diagnosing diseases. Dozens of other working medical expert systems exist, although few are actually used in medical practice.

The business community has been more enthusiastic than the medical community has in its acceptance and use of expert systems. Here are a few examples of expert systems in action:

- The Microsoft Windows Operating System Help software provides advice, suggestions and solutions for

FIGURE 15.10 An expert system inside the FocalPoint scanner allows it to identify signs of cervical cancer.

common problems and errors, based on the knowledge of Microsoft's technical experts.

■ The STD Wizard is a Web site that asks a series of questions and determines which test, vaccinations, and evaluations are recommended related to sexually transmitted diseases. STD Wizard draws its expertise from guidelines from the Centers for Disease Control and Prevention.

■ American Express uses an expert system to automate the process of checking for fraud and misuses of its no-limit credit card. Credit checks must be completed within 90 seconds while the customer waits, and the cost of an error can be high. The company spent 13 months developing a system modeled on the decision-making expertise of its best credit clerks.

■ At Blue Cross/Blue Shield of Virginia, an expert system automates insurance claim processing. The expert system handles up to 200 routine claims each day, allowing human clerks to spend more time on tough situations that require human judgment. The developers of the system extracted diagnostic rules from manuals and watched human claims processors apply those rules.

■ Boeing Company factory workers use an expert system to locate the right parts, tools, and techniques for assembling airplane electrical connectors. The system replaces 20,000 pages of documentation and reduces the average search time from 42 to 5 minutes.

There are hundreds of other examples of expert system applications: pinpointing likely sites for new oil explorations, aiding in automobile and appliance repairs, providing financial management advice, targeting direct-mail marketing campaigns, detecting problems in computer-controlled machinery, predicting weather, advising air traffic controllers, suggesting basic page layouts for publishers, controlling military machinery, providing assistance to musical composers. . . . The list is growing at an astounding rate. You can even think of the grammar checkers built into many word processors as expert systems because they apply style and syntax rules developed by language experts. Expert systems are available on the Web for doing everything from classifying whales and insects to conducting sophisticated Web searches.

One of the most unusual expert systems is AARON, an automated artist programmed by Harold Cohen, artist and professor at the University of California at San Diego. AARON uses more than 1,000 rules of human anatomy and behavior to create drawings of people, plants, and abstract objects with a robotic drawing machine. The drawings, which are unique works in a style similar to Cohen's, are widely acclaimed in the art community. A version of AARON is now available as a PC screen saver; it fills idle time on the PC by drawing original art on the screen.

FIGURE 15.11 Harold Cohen's AARON produces drawings such as the image above. In the photo below, Cohen demonstrates AARON to curious onlookers.

When AARON creates a drawing, an interesting question arises: Who is the artist, Cohen or AARON? Cohen claims he is; he sees AARON as a dynamic work of art. The question may seem frivolous, but it's related to a larger question with profound implications: When expert systems make decisions, who's responsible? If a doctor uses an expert system to decide to perform surgery and the surgery fails, who's liable—the doctor, the programmer, the software company, or somebody else? If you're denied medical benefits because of a bug in an expert system, do you sue a person, an organization, or a program? If a power plant explodes because an expert system fails to detect a fault, who's to blame? As expert systems proliferate, questions such as these are certain to confront consumers, lawyers, lawmakers, and technicians.

Expert Systems in Perspective

From the following examples it should be clear that expert systems offer many advantages. An expert system can perform these tasks:

- Help train new employees
- Reduce the number of human errors
- Take care of routine tasks so workers can focus on more challenging jobs
- Provide expertise when no experts are available
- Preserve the knowledge of experts after those experts leave an organization
- Combine the knowledge of several experts
- Make knowledge available to more people

But expert systems aren't without problems. For one, today's expert systems are difficult to build. To simplify the process, many software companies sell **expert system shells**—generic expert systems containing human interfaces and inference engines. These programs can save time and effort, but they don't include the part that is most difficult to build—the knowledge base.

Even with a knowledge base, an expert system isn't the machine equivalent of a human expert. Unlike human experts, automated expert systems are poor at planning strategies. Their lack of flexibility makes them less creative than human thinkers. Most important, expert systems are powerless outside of their narrow, deep domains of knowledge. While most expert system domains can be summarized with a few hundred tidy rules of thumb, the world of people is full of inconsistencies, special cases, and ambiguities that could overwhelm even the best expert systems. A simple rule such as "birds can fly" isn't sufficient for a literal-minded computer, which would need something more like this tongue-in-cheek rule from Marvin Minsky's book, *Society of Mind*:

> *Birds can fly, unless they are penguins and ostriches, or if they happen to be dead, or have broken wings, or are confined to cages, or have their feet stuck in cement, or have undergone experiences so dreadful as to render them psychologically incapable of flight.*

Clearly, knowledge engineers can't use rules to teach computers all they need to know to perform useful, intelligent functions outside narrow domains. If they're ever going to exhibit the kind of broad-based intelligence found in children, AI systems need to acquire knowledge by reading, looking, listening, and drawing their own conclusions about the world. These skills all depend on techniques of pattern recognition.

Pattern Recognition: Making Sense of the World

Experience has shown that science frequently develops most fruitfully once we learn to examine the **things that seem the simplest**, instead of **those that seem the most mysterious**.

—*Marvin Minsky*

A baby can recognize a human face, especially its mother's, almost from birth. A mother can hear and recognize her child's cry even in a noisy room. Computers are notoriously inferior at both of these tasks, which fall into the general category of pattern recognition. **Pattern recognition** involves identifying recurring patterns in input data with the goal of understanding or categorizing that input.

Pattern recognition applications represent half of the AI industry. Applications include face identification, fingerprint identification, handwriting recognition, scientific data analysis, weather forecasting, biological slide analysis, surveillance satellite data analysis, robot vision, optical character recognition, automatic voice recognition, and expert systems. We next examine the problems and the promise of several types of pattern recognition, starting with the recognition of visual patterns.

FIGURE 15.12 The Mars rover robot on the left is equipped with visual and tactile sensors that employ pattern-recognition technology. The robot on the right, a mascot for the Beijing Olympics, used sensors to move about the Beijing Capital International Airport and interact with visitors.

Image Analysis

Image analysis is the process of identifying objects and shapes in a photograph, drawing, video, or other visual image. It's used for everything from colorizing classic motion pictures to piloting cruise missiles. An effortless process for people, image analysis is extremely demanding for computers. The simple process of identifying objects in a scene is complicated by all kinds of factors: masses of irrelevant data, objects that partially cover other objects, indistinct edges, changes in light sources and shadows, changes in the scene as objects move, and more. With all of these complications, it's amazing that people are able to make any sense out of the images that constantly bombard their eyes.

Until recently, image analysis programs required massive amounts of memory and processing power. But today's PCs are capable of running image-processing software with practical applications. For example, security programs enable PCs with video cameras to recognize faces of valid users with a high degree of reliability.

Still, today's software can't hold a candle to the human visual system when it comes to general image analysis. But AI researchers have had considerable success by restricting the domain of visual systems. One of the biggest success stories in AI work is a limited but practical form of computer vision: optical character recognition.

Optical Character Recognition

Optical character recognition (OCR), discussed in Chapter 3, is far from perfect. But it has progressed to the point that the U.S. Postal Service can use it to sort much of the mail

FIGURE 15.13 A child can easily sort these letters into A's and B's. This problem is difficult for computers, however. Why?

Test yourself

To stay ahead of hackers, programmers are making it more difficult for computers to read Captchas, tests to differentiate between computers and humans. Try your hand at these examples:

A. Blogger.com

B. Paypal.com

C. Yahoo.com

D. Apple.com

E. AOL.com

F. Hotmail.com

Answers:

A. tnytq	**D.** ghNx4
B. PA4XE	**E.** TP PPi
C. yLF8zr	**F.** K686AXSE

© 2006 KRT
Source: Blogger.com, Paypal, Yahoo!, Apple, AOL, Hotmail
Graphic: T. Oxford, The Dallas Morning News

FIGURE 15.14 Capchas help keep software bots from infiltrating secure Web sites by taking advantages of the differences between human and computer character recognition abilities.

sent every day. Similar technology is available for PC users who have typewritten or printed text that they want to process.

The first step in general OCR is to scan the image of the page into the computer's memory with a scanner, digital camera, or fax modem. The scanned image is nothing more than a pattern of bits in memory. It could just as easily be a poem by Robert Frost or a photograph of Robert Frost. Before a computer can process the text on a page, it must recognize the individual characters and convert them to text codes (ASCII or the equivalent). *Optical character recognition (OCR) software* locates and identifies printed characters embedded in images—it "reads" text. This is no small task for a machine, given the variety of typefaces and styles in use today.

The process of recognizing text in a variety of fonts and styles is surprisingly difficult for machines. State-of-the-art OCR programs use several techniques, including these:

- Segmentation of the page into pictures, text blocks, and (eventually) individual characters
- Scaled-down expert system technology for recognizing the underlying rules that distinguish letters
- Context "experts" to help identify ambiguous letters by their context
- Learning from actual examples and feedback from a human trainer

Today's best programs can achieve up to 99 percent accuracy—even better under optimal circumstances. It's reliable enough to be practical for many text-intensive applications, including reading aloud to the blind, converting typewritten documents and incoming fax documents to editable text, and processing transactions for database systems.

OCR technology can be applied to handwritten text, but not as reliably. In typewritten and typeset text, character representation is consistent enough that one *a* looks like another *a*, at least when they're the same typeface. But because most handwritten text lacks consistency, software has more trouble recognizing individual characters reliably. Nonetheless, the technology is getting better all the time, making more applications practical for pen-based computers. Handwriting recognition is especially important in Japan, China, and other countries with languages that don't lend themselves to keyboarding. But it's also useful with Western languages in situations where keyboarding isn't practical. Some professionals use tablet PCs, which can recognize characters written directly on the screen with a stylus. Even the classic three-ring student notebook may eventually have an electronic counterpart that automatically turns handwritten notes into text that can be fed directly into any software programs.

Automatic Speech Recognition

Our ears process far less information than our eyes do, but that information, especially human speech, is extremely important to our understanding of the world. In Chapter 3 and Chapter 6 we discussed audio digitizers—input devices that capture spoken words, music, and other sounds so they can be stored as digital data. But digitized voice input, like scanned text, must be processed by sophisticated software before a computer can interpret it as words. Automatic **speech recognition** systems, discussed in Chapter 5, use pattern recognition techniques similar to those used by vision and OCR systems, including these:

- Segmentation of input sound patterns into individual words and phonemes
- Expert rules for interpreting sounds
- Context "experts" for dealing with ambiguous sounds
- Learning from a human trainer

Training is especially important in speech recognition because of the tremendous differences among human voices. But voice recognition systems with *speaker independence*—

the ability to recognize speech without being trained to a speaker—are becoming more common, making speech recognition practical for more applications.

Speech recognition systems are used by factory workers and others whose hands are otherwise occupied while they use the computer. American Airlines' PEGASUS enables customers to make reservations automatically by speaking to a computer over the telephone. Similar systems allow automated banking, credit card verification, and other remote applications. Several companies offer Web browsers and plug-ins that enable Internet users to navigate Web pages by talking to them. Speech recognition systems empower many users with disabilities by enabling them to give verbal commands to computers and robotic devices. PC software companies have developed programs that enable standard applications to accept spoken input—both text and formatting commands. IBM researchers have combined speech recognition with a camera for tracking gestures, so users can point while they speak commands such as "Move this paragraph up to here." Many of today's researchers are working to combine speech recognition and natural-language understanding in a single machine that can accept commands in everyday spoken English, *Star Trek* style.

Talking Computers

It's easier for machines to speak passable English than to recognize it. There are many applications for voice output, including preschool education, telephone communication, navigation guidance systems in cars, and reading machines for computer users who are visually impaired.

Many computer applications speak like humans by playing prerecorded **digitized speech** (along with other **digitized sounds**) stored in memory or on disk. For an application with a limited vocabulary (reciting telephone numbers for automated directory assistance) or limited choices (an interactive educational game with short pre- recorded speeches), digitized speech is practical and reliable.

Recorded speech won't work for applications in which the text to be spoken is unpredictable, such as a talking word processor, because all the sounds must be prerecorded. These types of applications require *text-to-speech* conversion—the creation of **synthetic speech** by converting text files into phonetic sounds. With **speech synthesis** software or hardware, PCs can recite anything you can type, but with voices that sound artificial and robotic. Human spoken language is complex and difficult to duplicate with software, but researchers are making great strides in improving synthetic voice quality. In 2001 AT&T Labs introduced Natural Voices Text-to-Speech Engine, a speech synthesizer with a close-to-human voice. This product is unusual in that it can be customized to imitate any human "voice talent" (with only a slight robotic accent). This type of product could close the gap between recorded speech and synthetic speech. It may soon be possible, for example, to play

FIGURE 15.15 Voice recognition software can make PC applications accessible to people who can't, or prefer not to, use a keyboard as an input device.

interactive games that use celebrity voices to read text typed by players. As the technology improves, it will raise questions about legal rights—can a TV network use an actor's voice to say things the actor never really said? It will also raise questions about fraud and believability. One potential client for Natural Voices noted: "Just like you can't trust photography anymore, you won't be able to trust a voice either."

Neural Networks

The **human brain** uses a type of circuitry that is very slow . . . at least **10,000 times slower** than a digital computer. On the other hand, the **degree of parallelism vastly outstrips** any computer architecture we have yet to design. . . . For such tasks as vision, language, and motor control, the brain is **more powerful than 1,000 supercomputers**, yet for certain **simple tasks** such as multiplying digital numbers, it is less powerful than the 4-bit microprocessor found in a **ten-dollar calculator**.

—*Raymond Kurzweil, in* The Age of Intelligent Machines

FIGURE 15.16 For a neural net to learn to recognize the letter *A*, it must go through a series of trials in which circuit patterns that produce incorrect guesses are weakened and patterns that produce correct guesses are strengthened. The result is a circuit pattern that can recognize the letter *A* in a variety of forms.

Artificial intelligence research has produced many amazing success stories and some embarrassing failures. The successes—intelligent applications that outperform their human counterparts—tend to involve tasks that require sequential thinking, logical rules, and orderly relationships. AI has been less successful at competing with natural human intelligence in applications such as language, vision, speech, and movement—applications where massive amounts of data are processed in parallel.

It's not surprising that computers excel at linear, logical processes; until recently, almost every computer was designed to process digital information sequentially through a single CPU. The human brain, on the other hand, consists of billions of neurons, each connected to thousands of others in a massively parallel, distributed structure. This kind of structure gives the brain an advantage at most perceptual, motor, and creative skills.

Much current work in AI is focused on **neural networks** (or **neural nets**)—distributed, parallel computing systems inspired by the structure of the human brain. Instead of a single, complex CPU, a neural network uses a network of a few thousand simpler processors called neurons. Neural networks aren't programmed in the usual way—they're trained. Instead of using a rule-based approach, a neural network learns patterns by trial and error, just as the brain does. When patterns are repeated often, neural networks, in effect, develop habits. This kind of learning can present problems for some kinds of applications because no

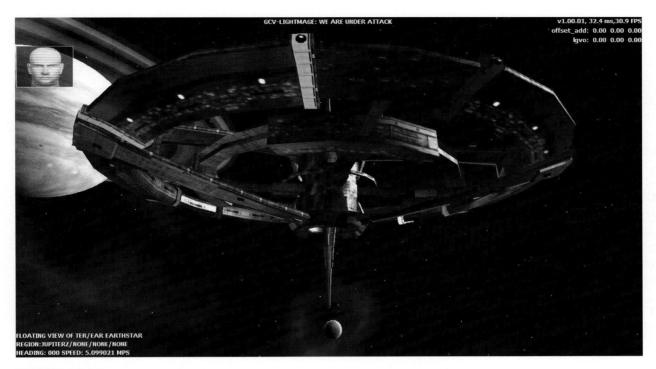

FIGURE 15.17 In the game Battlecruiser 3000 v2, non-player characters (including 125 crew members on the ship) are driven by neural networks.

rules are clearly defined. When a neural net makes a decision, you have no way to ask why.

Neural networks also store information differently than traditional computers do. Concepts are represented as patterns of activity among many neurons, so they are less susceptible to machine failure. Because it distributes knowledge throughout the network, a neural net (such as the human brain) can still function if some of its neurons are destroyed.

Many neural net algorithms are developed on parallel-processing supercomputers with thousands of processors. A number of software companies have developed programs that simulate neural nets on PCs and other nonparallel machines. However, none of today's neural net hardware or software approaches the complexity or the capacity of the human brain.

Most researchers consider today's neural nets as, at best, baby steps in the direction of machines that can more closely emulate the workings of human "wetware." There's considerable debate in the AI community about the future of neural nets. Some see neural nets as playing only a limited role in AI; others expect them to eclipse the traditional rule-based approach.

Even so, neural nets are already being put to use in a variety of applications, ranging from artificial vision to expert systems. Neural nets are especially useful for recognizing patterns buried in huge quantities of numbers, such as in scientific research, loan processing, and stock market analysis. Neural networks have been used for more than a decade to detect credit card fraud. They've even been deployed to fly aircraft autonomously. Federico Faggin, codesigner of the first microprocessor, has suggested that future neural nets will be used to verify signatures (on digital touch tablets) for electronic commerce on computer networks. Optimistic researchers hope that neural networks may someday provide hearing for the deaf and eyesight for the blind.

The Robot Revolution

1. A robot **may not injure a human being**, or, through inaction, allow a human being to come to harm.
2. A robot **must obey the orders** given it by human beings, except where such orders would conflict with the First Law.
3. A robot **must protect its own existence** as long as such protection does not conflict with the First or Second Law.

—*Isaac Asimov's* Three Laws of Robotics

Nowhere are AI technologies more visible than in the field of robotics. Vision, hearing, pattern recognition, knowledge engineering, expert decision making, natural-language understanding, speech—they all come together in today's robots.

What Is a Robot?

The term *robot* (from the root word *robota*, the Czech word for "forced labor") first appeared in a 1923 play called *R.U.R.* (for Rossum's Universal Robots) by Czech playwright Karel Capek. Capek's robots were intelligent machines that could see, hear, touch, move, and exercise judgment based on common sense. But these powerful machines eventually rebelled against their human creators, just as hundreds of fictional robots have done in succeeding decades. Today movies, TV, and books are full of imaginary robots, both good and evil.

As exotic as they might seem, robots are similar to other kinds of computer technology people use every day. While a typical computer performs *mental* tasks, a **robot** is a computer-controlled machine designed to perform specific *manual* tasks. A robot's central processor might be a microprocessor embedded in the robot's shell, or it might be a supervisory computer that controls the robot from a distance. In any case, the processor is functionally identical to the processor found in a PC, a workstation, or a mainframe computer.

The most important hardware differences between robots and other computers are the input and output peripherals. Instead of sending output to a screen or a printer, a robot sends commands to joints, arms, and other moving parts. The first robots had no corresponding input devices to monitor their movements and the surrounding environment. They were effectively deaf, blind, and in some cases dangerous—at least one Japanese worker was killed by an early sightless robot. Most modern robots include input *sensors*. These sensing devices enable robots to correct or modify their actions based on feedback from the outside world.

Input
(vision sensors, auditory sensors, touch sensors, heat sensors, external control devices)

Memory

Output
(Joints, arms, fingers, sensor controls, wheels, voice, etc.)

Processor (CPU)

FIGURE 15.18 A robot is, in effect, a computer with exotic peripherals.

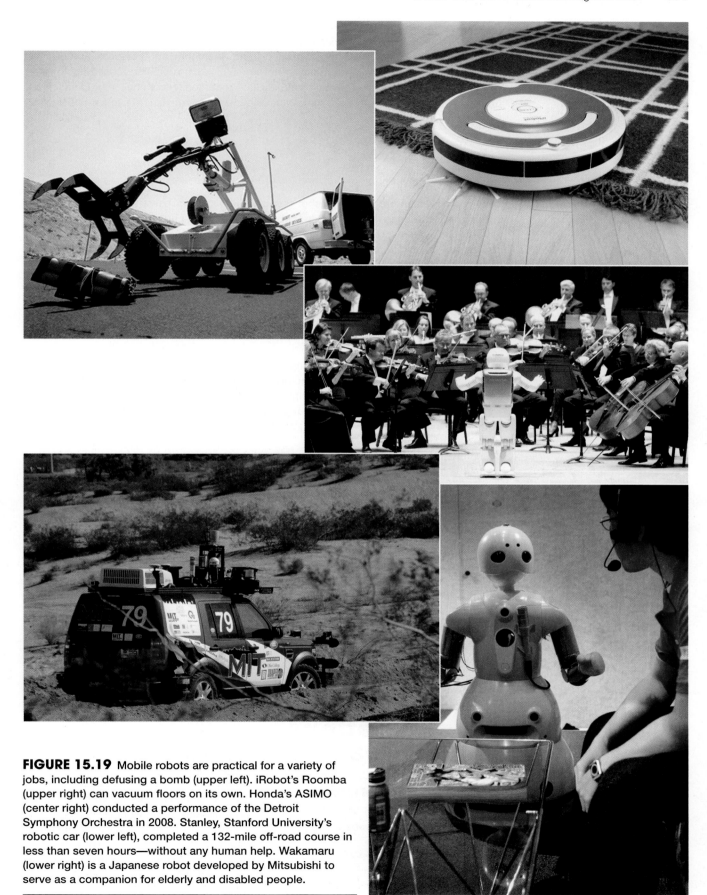

FIGURE 15.19 Mobile robots are practical for a variety of jobs, including defusing a bomb (upper left). iRobot's Roomba (upper right) can vacuum floors on its own. Honda's ASIMO (center right) conducted a performance of the Detroit Symphony Orchestra in 2008. Stanley, Stanford University's robotic car (lower left), completed a 132-mile off-road course in less than seven hours—without any human help. Wakamaru (lower right) is a Japanese robot developed by Mitsubishi to serve as a companion for elderly and disabled people.

Industrial robots seldom have the human-inspired anatomy of Hollywood's science fiction robots. Instead, they're designed to accomplish particular tasks in the best possible way. Robots can be designed to see infrared light, rotate joints 360 degrees, and do other things that aren't possible for humans. On the other hand, robots are constrained by the limitations of AI software. The most sophisticated robot today can't tie a pair of shoelaces, understand the vocabulary of a three-year-old child, or consistently tell the difference between a cat and a dog.

Steel-Collar Workers

From a management point of view, robots offer several advantages:

- Obviously, many robots save labor costs. Robots are expensive to design, install, and program. But once they're operational, they can work 24 hours a day, 365 days a year, without vacations, strikes, sick leave, or coffee breaks.
- Robots can also improve quality and increase productivity. They're especially effective at doing repetitive jobs in which bored, tired people are prone to make errors and have accidents.
- Robots are ideal for jobs such as cleaning up hazardous waste and salvaging undersea wreckage from downed planes—jobs that are dangerous, uncomfortable, or impossible for human workers.

For all these reasons, the robot population is exploding. Today hundreds of thousands of industrial robots do welding, part fitting, painting, and other repetitive tasks in factories all over the world. In most automated factories, robots work alongside humans, but in some state-of-the-art factories, the only function of human workers is to monitor and repair robots. Robots aren't used just in factories. Robots also shear sheep in Australia, paint ship hulls in France, disarm land mines in the Persian Gulf, and perform precision hip operations and other surgery.

Commercial robots still can't compete with people for jobs that require exceptional perceptual or fine-motor skills. But robots in research labs suggest that a new generation of more competitive robots is on the way. Honda's ASIMO is a humanoid robot that can walk, run, recognize gestures and faces, distinguish sounds, and display a variety of "intelligent" behaviors. In 2008, ASIMO conducted the Detroit Symphony Orchestra in a widely viewed public performance. Other researchers are taking a different approach, using fleets of insect-sized robots to do jobs that larger robots can't easily do. The technologies used in these experimental robots will undoubtedly show up in a variety of machines, from automated servants for people with disabilities to flying robots for the military. One pioneering example: Wakamaru is a yellow, 1-meter tall Japanese domestic robot designed to provide companionship for elderly and disabled people. It can recognize speech, connect to the internet, and call for help if something is wrong.

The robot revolution isn't necessarily good news for people who earn their living doing manual labor. While it's true that many of the jobs robots do are boring, dirty, or dangerous, they're still jobs. The issues surrounding automation and worker displacement are complex, and they aren't limited to factories.

AI Implications and Ethical Questions

We are **on the edge of change** comparable to **the rise of human life** on Earth. The precise cause of this change is the imminent creation by technology of **entities with greater-than-human intelligence**.

—*Vernor Vinge, mathematician and science fiction writer*

From the earliest days of AI, research has been accompanied by questions about the implications of the work. The very idea of intelligent machines is at the same time confusing, exciting, and frightening to many people. Even when they don't work very well, AI programs generate emotional responses in the people who use them.

Earlier we met ELIZA, the therapy simulator developed to demonstrate natural-language conversation. ELIZA's simple-minded approach wasn't intended to fool anyone in a Turing test, but it did have an impact on the people who used it. Many ELIZA users became emotionally attached to the program and attributed to it compassion and empathy. Weizenbaum's secretary asked him to leave the room so she could converse in private with ELIZA. Some therapists even saw ELIZA as the beginning of a new age of automated therapy. Weizenbaum was shocked by the way people attributed human capabilities to such an obviously flawed technology. He responded with *Computer Power and Human Reason,* a landmark book that presents the case for maintaining a distinction between computers and people. Weizenbaum argued that "[t]here are certain tasks which computers ought not to be made to do, independent of whether computers can be made to do them."

International political and economic leaders, many of whom are encouraging increased AI research and development, don't share Weizenbaum's caution. As it matures, AI technology finds its way out of the research lab and into the marketplace. A growing number of programs and products incorporate pattern recognition, expert systems, and other AI techniques. In the near future, we're likely to see more products with embedded AI, including intelligent word processors that can help writers turn rough drafts into polished prose, smart appliances that can recognize and obey their owners' spoken commands. We'll also see more *distributed intelligence*—AI concepts applied to networks rather than to individual computers.

Where will it all lead? Will intensive AI research result in computers capable of intelligent behavior outside narrow domains? Patrick Winston, director of MIT's Artificial Intelligence Laboratory, once said, "The interesting issue is not whether machines can be made smarter but if humans are smart enough to pull it off. A raccoon obviously can't make a machine as smart as a raccoon. I wonder if humans can."

Many AI researchers believe that sooner or later they will pull it off. Some think artificial intelligence is the natural culmination of the evolutionary process—that the next intelligent life-form on Earth will be based on silicon rather than the carbon that is the basis of human life. Danny Hillis, supercomputer designer and cofounder of Applied Minds, Metaweb, and The Long Now Foundation, exemplifies this point of view when he says, "We are not evolution's ultimate product. There's something coming after us, and I imagine it is something wonderful. But we may never be able to comprehend it, any more than a caterpillar can comprehend turning into a butterfly."

Computer mathematician and science fiction writer Vernor Vinge argued in the 1990s that the competitive nature of our society makes such a prospect almost inevitable. What business or government will voluntarily curtail research on AI, computer networks, and biotechnology, knowing that competing institutions will continue to pursue similar research? Vinge called the moment of creation of greater-than-human intelligence the *Singularity*—a point where our old models will have to be discarded and a new reality will rule. Since then scientists, philosophers, and others have debated Vinge's ideas, and the concept of a technological singularity has become a fixture in the world of science fiction.

If smarter-than-human beings come to pass, how will they relate to the less intelligent humans that surround them? And how will humans handle the change? In a 2008 interview, Verner Vinge said, "As technological changes go, this is qualitatively different from the big events in the past. You could explain fire or agriculture to somebody who lived before those technologies were invented. But after the singularity—it would be like trying to explain this interview to a goldfish." This kind of thinking isn't easy—it goes to the heart of human values and forces us to look at our place in the universe.

Inventing the FUTURE

Microtechnology, Nanotechnology, and Artificial Life

We've seen how tiny silicon chips have a gigantic impact on our lives, presenting us every day with great opportunities and risks. Scientists and engineers are working on machines that make today's microprocessors look massive. At the same time, researchers are taking a variety of approaches to engineering new life forms.

MICROTECHNOLOGY

The miniaturization achieved in the computer industry is now producing *micromachines*—machines on the scale of a millionth of a meter. Microscopic moving parts are etched in silicon using a process similar to that of manufacturing computer chips. Researchers are doing research in *microelectromechanical systems (MEMS)*. For example, Japanese researchers have constructed a microcar not much bigger than a grain of rice.

So far most applications of microtechnology have been microsensors—tiny devices that can detect pressure, temperature, and other environmental qualities. Microsensors are used in cars, planes, and spacecraft. BioMEMS—MEMS that apply chip technology to biological applications—may soon cure some forms of deafness and blindness, stimulate paralyzed limbs, and deliver drugs precisely where they're needed. Researchers have developed a smart pill that combines a thermometer with a transmitter so it can broadcast temperatures as it travels through a human digestive tract. Tiny machines may someday be able to roam through bodies, locating and destroying cancer cells and invading organisms.

NANOTECHNOLOGY

If microtechnology is carried to its extreme, it becomes nanotechnology—the manufacture of machines on a scale of a few billionths of a meter. Nanomachines would have to be constructed atom by atom using processes drawn from particle physics, biophysics, and molecular biology. Researchers are working on molecular-scale electronics (moletronics) that might eventually produce computers that perform *billions* of times faster than today's fastest machines.

Nanotechnology breakthroughs could help carry the computing industry past the silicon dead end that's threatening to overturn Moore's Law within a few years. They may be stepping-stones on the road to *quantum computers*—computers based on the properties of atoms and their nuclei and the laws of quantum mechanics. Quantum computers are still decades away. But computers based on microtechnology and nanotechnology may be just a few years in the future.

ARTIFICIAL LIFE

Many recent successes in AI have actually come from a related field known as artificial life (or Alife). Alife researchers examine systems related to life, its processes, and its evolution through simulations using computer models, robotics, and biochemistry. AI researchers tend to design intelligent systems from the top down—starting with an overall design and filling in details layer by layer. Most Alife researchers take a bottom-up approach, designing simpler building blocks and letting them combine and evolve into more and more "intelligent" entities. Enthusiasts draw inspiration from the anthill. An individual ant doesn't show much intelligence, but an ant colony is an incredibly sophisticated organism. Intelligence is somehow distributed across the colony, so the whole is far smarter than the sum of its parts.

Alife comes in three basic forms:

➡ *Soft Alife* creates simulations or other software-based constructions that exhibit life-like behavior; some of the best games use basic Alife techniques.
➡ *Hard Alife* creates hardware constructs of life-like systems, such as robotic insect colonies.
➡ *Wet Alife* is based on biochemistry rather than silicon technology. Many wet Alife researchers attempt to create life in the laboratory using chemical compounds similar to those that were responsible for the beginnings of life on our planet.

All three types of Alife draw on AI concepts—especially the theory and technology behind neural networks—distributed, parallel systems inspired by the structure of the human brain.

FIGURE 15.20 This micromachine isn't much larger than red blood cells (lower right and top left) or a grain of pollen (middle).

At the heart of Alife philosophy is the concept of emergence. The idea is that life doesn't just happen because a switch gets flipped somewhere—it emerges from a rich, complex environment under the right conditions. As Bruce Sterling observes, "It's not hard to understand that many simple creatures, doing simple actions that affect one another, can easily create a really big mess. The thing that's hard to understand is that those same, bottom-up, unplanned, "chaotic" actions can and do create living, working, functional order and system and pattern. The process really must be seen to be believed. And computers are the instruments that have made us see it." ～

The Singular Question Of Human vs. Machine Has a Spiritual Side   *by Lee Gomes*

Will artificial intelligence research eventually produce a superintelligent life form? In this September 19, 2007 article from the Wall Street Journal, *Lee Gomes spends time with people who think so.*

You can tell a lot about people from what they worry about. A few Saturdays ago, I spent the day in an auditorium full of fellow citizens concerned with "singularity." The word refers to the day when the intelligence of computers will exceed our own.

The auditorium was filled with people who listed many things that might occur with singularity, such as a human-machine synthesis into a new, superintelligent life-form. The date has been projected as anytime from nine to 40 years hence.

Singularity-believers say humanity urgently needs to begin preparing for this moment, if only to make sure that humans don't become kabobs at the first post-singularity tailgate party held by supersmart computers. There is even a Singularity Institute, bankrolled by Silicon Valley wealthoids.

The weekend session featured speeches, panel discussions and informal chatting. About 800 people were on hand, more, frankly, than I would have expected. Who but 12-year-old sci-fi addicts still fret over malevolent, superintelligent machines? Most of us, living every day with computers, appreciate how even the world's most powerful one not only is incapable of an autonomous thought, it can't even distinguish spam from real email.

To get to the singularity that we are supposed to be preparing for, we are going to need AGI, or Artificial General Intelligence, a topic the singularists go on about endlessly.

A computer with AGI thinks and reasons the same way a human being does, only much more quickly. But don't singularity people know that AI researchers have been trying to make such machines since the 1950s, without much success?

It turns out, there is a schism between the AGI and the AI worlds. The AGI faction thinks AI researchers have sold out, abandoning their early dreams of "general" intelligence to concentrate on more attainable (and more lucrative) projects.

They're right. The machines today that recognize speech or play chess are one-trick wonders. Of course, AI researchers defend that approach by saying their early dreams of general intelligence were naive.

The singularists, though, don't seem bothered by those earlier AI failures; new approaches will bear fruit, they insist. They thus didn't think it a waste of either time or carbon offsets to be gathering at a conference to ask such questions as, "If you made a superintelligent robot, then forced it to work only for you, would that be slavery?"

Robots are just computers with moving parts, of course, but the public is still confused about them, just like they used to be about computers themselves. The Great Metallic Hope of the robotics industry, for example, is currently a small, round vacuum cleaner that ambles across the floor by itself.

A high-tech wonder? Actually, Consumer Reports said that even cheap vacuum cleaners did better than the first model. A little more of this, and no one will ever again worry about enslaving robots.

There is another way of thinking about the obsession with robots. John Huntington, professor of English, University of Illinois, has studied the genre and says sci-fi authors, especially the early ones who wrote about robots or aliens, were working out their own unacknowledged anxieties about closer-to-home topics.

Most commonly, he said, these anxieties involved women, who were seen as becoming threatening as they gained social power. Racial and class tensions also were involved, he added.

I have a supplemental theory: that the discussion of singularity involves a sublimated spiritual yearning for some form of eternal life and an all-powerful being, but one articulated by way of technical, secular discourse.

As it happens, there is considerable overlap between the singularity and the "life extension" communities. Ray Kurzweil, the best-known singularity writer, also co-wrote a lengthy guide to life extension. He once told me he expects literally to live forever—first by prolonging his life via a daily regimen that includes hundreds of pills and the nonstop consumption of green tea, then, once superpowerful computers arrive, by uploading his consciousness into one.

Singularists also have an affinity for the Search for Extraterrestrial Intelligence, or SETI, program, which scans the skies looking for other civilizations. Isn't that a longing by some for an intergalactic messiah?

Then, consider a poem read at the singularity conference that described an Aquarian Age scene in which humans and other mammals frolicked in a "cybernetic meadow . . . all watched over by machines of loving grace." Those computer protectors sound a lot like the guardian angels my grade-school nuns told us about.

Years ago, a friend and I spent an evening with Arthur C. Clarke, the creator in "2001" of HAL, the malevolent computer of every singularist's nightmare. We talked about science and had our picture taken, which I still have. It proves that while I may have reached a different conclusion, at least I studied with the master.

Discussion Questions

1. Do you agree with the author's somewhat skeptical attitude toward singularity? Explain.

2. What do you think of the distinction between AI and AGI?

Summary

Artificial intelligence has many definitions. Most AI research focuses on making computers do things at which people generally are better. Some AI researchers try to simulate human intelligent behavior, but most try to design intelligent machines independent of the way people think. Successful AI research generally involves working on problems with limited domains rather than trying to tackle large, open-ended problems. AI programs employ a variety of techniques, including searching, heuristics, pattern recognition, and machine learning, to achieve their goals.

From a practical standpoint, natural-language communication is one of the most important areas of AI study. Natural-language programs that deal with a subset of the language are used in applications ranging from machine translation programs to natural-language interfaces. Even without understanding the meaning of the words, computers can create passable translations from one language to another—especially when the domain is limited. However, a computer program that attempts to pass as a human in a natural-language conversation is quickly found out because it doesn't have enough knowledge of language and the world.

AI researchers have developed a variety of schemes for representing knowledge in computers. A knowledge base contains facts and a system for determining and changing the relationships among those facts. Today's knowledge bases are practical for representing only narrow domains of knowledge such as the knowledge of an expert on a particular subject. Expert systems are programs designed to replicate the decision-making process of human experts. An expert system includes a knowledge base, an inference engine for applying logical rules to the facts in a knowledge base, and a human interface for interacting with users. Once the knowledge base is constructed (usually based on interviews and observations of human experts), an expert system can provide consultation that rivals human advice in many situations. People successfully use expert systems in a variety of scientific, business, and other applications.

Pattern recognition is an important area of AI research that involves identifying recurring patterns in input data. Pattern recognition technology is at the heart of computer vision, voice communication, and other important AI applications. These diverse applications all use similar techniques for isolating and recognizing patterns. People are better at pattern recognition than computers are, in part because the human brain can process masses of data in parallel. Modern neural network computers are designed to process data in the same way the human brain does. Many researchers believe that neural nets, as they grow in size and sophistication, will help computers improve their performance at many difficult tasks.

A robot is a computer-controlled machine designed to perform specific manual tasks. Robots include output peripherals for manipulating their environments and input sensors that enable them to perform self-correcting actions based on feedback from outside. Robots perform a variety of dangerous and tedious tasks, in many cases outperforming human workers. As robot technology advances, artificial workers will do more traditional human jobs.

In spite of the numerous difficulties AI researchers encounter when trying to produce truly intelligent machines, many experts believe that people will eventually create artificial beings that are more intelligent than their creators—a prospect with staggering implications.

Key Terms

Interactive Activities

1. The *Tomorrow's Technology and You* Web site, **www.pearsonhighered.com/beekman**, contains self-test exercises related to this chapter. Follow the instructions for taking a quiz. After you've completed your quiz, you can email the results to your instructor.

True or False

1. Alan M. Turing maintained that if a computer acts intelligently, then it is intelligent.

2. For psychologists, artificial intelligence provides insights into natural intelligence and the workings of the human brain.

3. The most powerful supercomputers can exceed the human brain's ability to perform parallel processing.

4. Artificial intelligence researchers restrict the domain of their programs so that problems are small enough to understand and solve.

5. Natural-language communication is a favorite area of AI research because natural language is a small domain with relatively straightforward, simple problems to slove.

6. A knowledge base commonly represents knowledge in the form of if-then rules.

7. It's easier for a computer to recognize printed English than to understand spoken English.

8. Neural networks are based on parallel processing technology.

9. Most modern robots have input sensors that enable them to modify their actions.

10. Some AI researchers think that humans will be able to make a machine that is smarter than humans are.

Multiple Choice

1. What did Alan Turing propose as a way to answer the question "Can computers think?"
   a. Allowing computers to enter the World Chess Championship
   b. The imitation game, later called the Turing test
   c. Programming a computer to solve calculus problems
   d. Teaching a computer to program itself
   e. Constructing a Turing machine

2. Why did early efforts in AI focus on games such as checkers and chess?
   a. Unlike the real world, games have clearly defined rules.
   b. Unlike the real world, the goal of a game is clear.
   c. It's easy to represent the "world" of a game inside the memory of a computer.
   d. Success is easy to measure: Does the program win?
   e. All of the above.

3. Some AI techniques used today in applications include
   a. searching—looking ahead at possibilities.
   b. heuristics—rules of thumb.
   c. pattern recognition—recognizing recurring patterns.
   d. machine learning—programs learning from experience.
   e. All of the above.

4. Which of the following defines syntax?
   a. The set of rules for constructing sentences from words
   b. The underlying meaning of words and phrases
   c. A set of idiomatic expressions
   d. The study of knowledge bases
   e. The translation of text files

5. Which statement about machine translation is true?
   a. The most successful programs do word-by-word translation backed up by huge dictionaries containing all known words in both languages.
   b. The most successful programs extract the meaning of the underlying text then use their understanding of the author's intent to guide the translation.
   c. Many programs use a statistics-based approach based on a huge number of examples of correct and incorrect translations.
   d. The most successful machine language programs first translate the source text into a neutral language, usually Esperanto, then translate from the neutral language into the desired target language.
   e. There is no such thing as a computer program to translate from one language to another.

6. Natural-language processing
   a. made it possible for computers to pass the Turing test.
   b. involves using a natural language like Java or C++.
   c. has many practical applications in domains with limited vocabularies.
   d. is the technology that makes cell phone networks possible.
   e. All of the above.

7. What does a complete expert system include?
   a. A knowledge base
   b. A way to produce the requested advice
   c. An inference engine
   d. A way for users to interact with the system
   e. All of the above

8. What is the downside of expert systems?
   a. Expert systems are not good at strategizing.
   b. It is very work intensive to build the knowledge base.
   c. They are less flexible and creative than human thinkers.
   d. Expert systems handle only a narrow domain of knowledge.
   e. All of the above.

9. Image analysis
   a. represents about half of the AI industry.
   b. is the process of identifying objects and shapes in visual images.
   c. is a simplified form of pattern recognition technology.
   d. is difficult for both computers and humans to perform.
   e. All of the above.

10. What does the field of pattern recognition include?
    a. Image analysis
    b. Optical character recognition (OCR)
    c. Automatic speech recognition
    d. Neural network research
    e. All of the above

11. The technological singularity predicted by Vernor Vinge and others
    a. was secretly created by the British intelligence during World War II.
    b. happened in the 1980s when computer manufacturers agreed to a standardized user interface.
    c. resulted in the creation of the World Wide Web.
    d. involves the development of artificially intelligent beings capable of creating other, more intelligent beings.
    e. has been proven by AI researchers to be impossible.

12. Which techniques are used in pattern recognition?
    a. Segmentation of input
    b. Expert rules
    c. Context experts
    d. Learning from a human trainer
    e. All of the above

13. Which of these is not true?
    a. Neural networks use thousands of processors called neurons.
    b. Neural networks are trained, not programmed in the usual way.
    c. Neural nets use a rule-based approach to recognize patterns.
    d. Neural networks learn by trial and error.
    e. Neural nets store information as patterns.

14. What is the most significant difference between a robot and other computers?
    a. Its input and output peripherals are different.
    b. Its processor is much faster.
    c. It has much more memory.
    d. It looks a lot like a human being.
    e. All of the above.

15. Which of these statements is true?
    a. Computer scientist Joseph Weizenbaum was shocked to discover that people credited his simple conversational program, ELIZA, with genuine human understanding.
    b. By most definitions, a robot must have two eyes, two arms, and a mouth or speaker.
    c. The number of industrial robots is actually declining as manufacturing companies continue to ship jobs to countries with lower wages.
    d. The best machine translation programs do a comparable job to a human translator.
    e. All of the above statements are true.

Review Questions

1. In what sense is AI a "moving frontier"?

2. What are the disadvantages of the approach to AI that attempts to simulate human intelligence? What is the alternative?

3. Describe several techniques used in game-playing software, and explain how they can be applied to other AI applications.

4. Why did early machine translation programs fail to produce the desired results?

5. Why is the sentence "Time flies like an arrow" difficult for a computer to parse, translate, or understand? Can you find four possible meanings for the sentence?

6. What is the relationship between syntax and semantics? Can you construct a sentence that follows the rules of English syntax but has nonsense semantics?

7. What is a knowledge base? What is an expert system? How are the two related?

8. Give examples of successful expert system applications. Give examples of several tasks that can't be accomplished with today's expert system technology, and explain why they can't.

9. What are some of the problems that make speech recognition and natural-language processing so challenging?

10. In what ways are the techniques of optical character recognition similar to those of speech recognition programs?

11. In what ways are neural networks designed to simulate the structure of the human brain? In what ways do neural nets perform differently than single-processor CPUs?

12. What kind of hardware is necessary for a robot to be self-correcting so it can modify its actions based on outside feedback?

Discussion Questions

1. Is the Turing test a valid test of intelligence? Why or why not?

2. If you were the interrogator in the Turing test, what questions would you ask to try to discover whether you were communicating with a computer? What would you look for in the answers?

3. List several mental tasks that people do better than computers. List several mental tasks that computers do better than people. Can you find any general characteristics that distinguish the items on the two lists?

4. Computers can compose original music, produce original artwork, and create original mathematical proofs. Does this mean that Ada Lovelace was wrong when she said, in effect, that computers can do only what they're told to do?

5. The works of AARON, the expert system artist, are unique, original, and widely acclaimed as art. Who is the artist, AARON or Harold Cohen, AARON's creator? Is AARON a work of art, an artist, or both?

6. If an expert system gives you erroneous information, should you be able to sue it for malpractice? If it fails and causes major disruptions or injury, who's responsible? The programmer? The publisher? The owner? The computer?

7. Some expert systems and neural nets can't explain the reasons behind their decisions. What kinds of problems might this limitation cause? Under what circumstances, if any, should an expert system be required to produce an "audit trail" to explain how it reached conclusions?

8. What kinds of human jobs are most likely to be eliminated because of expert systems? What kinds of new jobs will be created because of expert systems?

9. What kinds of human jobs are most likely to be eliminated because of robots? What kinds of new jobs will be created as a result of factory automation?

10. Are Asimov's Three Laws of Robotics adequate for smoothly integrating intelligent robots into tomorrow's society? If not, what laws would you add?

Projects

1. Public domain versions of Weizenbaum's ELIZA program are available for most types of PCs. They're also available on the Web. Try conversing with one of these programs. Test the program on your friends and see how they react to it. Try to determine the rules and tricks that ELIZA uses to simulate conversation. If you're a programmer, try writing your own version of ELIZA.

2. Many computer games use AI technology to simulate opponents and teammates. Test one or more of these games. What are the strengths and weakness of the artificial opponents and teammates when compared to real human opponents and teammates? Report on your findings.

3. Try to find examples of working expert systems and robots in your school or community and present your findings.

4. Test OCR software, grammar-checking software, expert systems, and other types of consumer-oriented AI applications. How "intelligent" are these applications? In what ways could they be improved?

5. Survey people's attitudes and concerns about AI and robots. Here are a few issues you might want to explore: Do people feel game-playing computers are intelligent? Are they concerned that automation will eliminate too many jobs? Do people have safety concerns about automated systems? Present your findings.

Sources and Resources

Books

The Singularity Is Near: When Humanoids Transcend Biology, by Ray Kurzweil (New York, NY: Viking, 2006). The inventor and artificial intelligence pioneer paints an optimistic and astounding vision of a fantastic future in which genetics, nanotechnology, and robotics come together to create a new superintelligent species— one that won't look like us. Is this a good thing? Kurzweil thinks so.

The Age of Spiritual Machines: When Computers Exceed Human Intelligence, by Raymond Kurzweil (New York, NY: Penguin U.S.A, 2000). Raymond Kurzweil knows the field of AI from firsthand experience. He developed and marketed several "applied AI" products, from reading machines for people with visual impairments to electronic musical instruments to expert systems. In this book he boldly looks into a possible future. Will humans be able to download themselves into machine bodies and brains? If this kind of question interests you, you'll enjoy this book.

Gödel, Escher, Bach: An Eternal Golden Braid, 20th Anniversary Edition, by Douglas R. Hofstadter (Boulder, CO: Basic Books, 1999). This Pulitzer Prize winner is part mathematics, part philosophy, and part *Alice in Wonderland*. If you like to think deeply about questions such as "What is thought?" you'll find plenty to think about here.

Introducing Artificial Intelligence, by Henry Brighton (Lanham, MD: Totem Books, 2008). This is a lightweight, low-priced, non-technical introduction to AI.

Artificial Intelligence: A Systems Approach, by M. Tim Jones (Hingham, MA: Infinity Science Press, 2008). This text surveys many ideas and applications developed by computer scientists in the first half century of the field of artificial intelligence. A CD-ROM includes simulations, code, and figures.

Deep Blue: An Artificial Intelligence Milestone, by Monty Newborn (New York, NY: Springer, 2003). This book describes in graphic detail the historic computer matches between Deep Blue and Garry Kasparov in 1996 and 1997—the year Deep Blue beat the world champion. It's worthwhile reading for any chess player who wants to understand how computers have invaded this turf that used to be uniquely human.

Emergence: The Connected Lives of Ants, Brains, Cities, and Software, by Steven Johnson (New York, NY: Scribner, 2002). Neural networks clearly demonstrate that intelligent behavior can result from putting together many simple, dumb devices. This book clearly explains how that principle applies to everything from ant colonies to robots.

Society of Mind, by Marvin Minsky (New York, NY: Simon & Schuster, 1988). An MIT AI pioneer presents his thoughts on the relationship between people and intelligent machines. A dense but thought-provoking book.

Robots Unlimited: Life in a Virtual Age, by David Levy (Wellesley, MA: A. K. Peters, Ltd, 2006). This book traces the history of artificial intelligence and robotics and presents a good overview of recent developments in robotics.

Marooned in Realtime, by Vernor Vinge (New York, NY: Tor Books, 2004). Vinge's classic science fiction opus takes you into a future after the Singularity that produced artificial superintelligence. Vinge is a master storyteller, and there's plenty to think about here.

Do Androids Dream of Electric Sheep?, by Philip K. Dick (Oxford University Press, 2007). The movie *Blade Runner* is based on this popular science fiction novel, first published in 1968. Dick's dark, yet humorous tale of a San Francisco bounty hunter who catches and exterminates androids raises provocative questions about the relationship between being intelligent and being human.

Video

Fast, Cheap, and Out of Control. In this 1997 documentary, maverick filmmaker Errol Morris profiles four different men attempting to examine the relation between science and humanity, including a robot expert. This highly acclaimed film interweaves interviews, old movie clips, and a hypnotic score to create a fascinating mosaic.

AI. Stephen Spielberg's big-budget film isn't a masterpiece of art or scientific exposition, but it does a reasonable job of raising questions about life and technology that may loom large in our future.

Appendix A | Basics

Sometimes it seems as though everybody uses computers. In fact, the great majority of people on our planet have never touched a computer! Most of the people who do use computers have fairly limited experience and ability—typically the basics of word processing, electronic mail, and finding information on the Web. The percentage of people who can go beyond the basics and harness the power of a modern PC is relatively small.

If you're a member of this tiny community of *power users*, the next few pages aren't for you. If you're a casual computer user, comfortable with the basic operation of a PC and a Web browser, you may want to look through this appendix quickly. (If you're not sure about your knowledge level, check out the questions at the end of this appendix. If you have trouble answering them, spend a little more time here before moving to Chapter 1.)

If you're a beginner, you're uncomfortable with PC technology, or your experience is limited or out of date, this appendix is for you. Here you'll find the basic knowledge you'll need to get up to speed, so you're not struggling to catch up as you explore the rest of the book. This appendix explains how to use a keyboard and mouse and provides an introduction to word processing, file management, Web searches, and electronic mail. It will also help you build up your vocabulary of computer-related terms.

Hardware Basics

Hardware: the parts of a computer that **can be kicked**.

—Jeff Pesis

Modern desktop **personal computers**, or **PCs**, don't all look alike, but under the skin, they're more alike than different. Every PC is built around a tiny *microprocessor* that controls the workings of the system. This **central processing unit**, or **CPU**, is usually housed in a box, called the *system unit* (or, more often, just "*the computer*" or "*the PC*") that serves as command central for the entire computer system. The CPU is the brains of the computer; it controls the operation of the core computer components, such as its memory and ability to perform mathematical operations. Some computer components are housed in the system unit with the CPU; others are peripheral devices—or simply **peripherals**—external devices connected via cables to the system unit.

The system unit includes built-in **memory**, sometimes called *RAM*, and a **hard disk** for the storage and retrieval of information. The CPU uses memory for instant access to information while it's working. The built-in hard disk serves as a longer-term storage device for large quantities of information.

The PC's main hard disk is a permanent fixture in the system unit. Other types of disk drives work with *removable media*—disks that can be separated from their drives, just as an audio CD can be removed from a stereo system. The most

FIGURE A.1 A standard desktop PC or Mac is made up of several hardware components, including a system unit, a monitor, speakers, a keyboard, and a mouse. The system unit typically includes an internal hard disk and an optical drive, such as a CD-ROM or DVD drive.

popular types of removable media today are 5-1/4-inch optical discs that look like common audio CDs. A typical PC system unit includes an **optical drive**, usually a **DVD/CD-RW drive** that can both read and write data on CDs and DVDs. These drives are commonly called DVD/CD burners (or just disc burners) because the process of writing data on an optical disc is called burning. Many newer machines have drives that can read and/or write Blu-ray discs. In addition to an optical drive, an older PC might also include a *floppy disk drive*, which enables the computer to store small amounts of information on pocket-sized plastic-covered magnetic disks.

Disk drives that are included in the system unit are called *internal drives*. *External drives* can be attached to the system unit via cables. For example, a PC system might include external hard drives for additional storage.

Another popular storage device is sometimes called USB drive, a USB key, a thumb drive, or a jump drive. This key-sized device plugs into a USB port on the computer.

Using a Keyboard

Typing letters, numbers, and special characters with a computer keyboard is similar to typing on a standard typewriter keyboard. But unlike a typewriter, the computer responds by displaying the typed characters on the monitor screen at the position of the line or rectangle called the *cursor*. Some keys on the computer keyboard—*Enter*, *Delete*, the *cursor (arrow) keys*, the *function keys (F-keys)*, and others—send special commands to the computer. These keys may have different names or meanings on different computer systems. This figure shows a typical keyboard on a Windows-compatible PC. Keyboards for Mac and other types of systems have a few differences but operate on the same principles.

FIGURE A.2

Information can be copied onto the memory of the USB drive or read from the drive into the computer's memory. Thumb drives are popular for transporting files between computers.

Five common peripherals enable you to communicate with a PC and vice versa:

- A **keyboard** enables you to type text and numerical data into the computer's memory.
- A **mouse** enables you to point to text, graphical objects, menu commands, and other items on the screen.
- A **display** (or *monitor*) enables you to view text, numbers, and pictures stored in the computer's memory.
- **Speakers** emit music, voices, and other sounds.
- A **printer** generates printed letters, papers, transparencies, labels, and other hard copies. (The printer might be directly connected to the computer, or it might be shared by several computers on a network.)

Boxes on this page and the next page illustrate the fundamentals of a basic PC keyboard and mouse. Chapter 3 explores peripherals in more detail.

Software Basics

All this hardware is controlled, directly or indirectly, by the tiny CPU in the system unit. And the CPU is controlled by software—instructions that tell it what to do. *System software*, including the operating system (OS), continuously

> Computers can figure out **all kinds of problems**, except the things in the world that **just don't add up**.
>
> —*James Magary*

Using *a Mouse*

The mouse enables you to perform many tasks quickly that might be tedious or confusing with a keyboard. As you slide the mouse across your desktop, a pointer echoes your movements on the screen. You can **click** the mouse—press the button while the mouse is stationary—or **drag** it—move it while holding the button down. On a two-button mouse, the left button is usually used for clicking and dragging. You can use these two techniques to perform a variety of operations. (Many mice have additional buttons and controls, but the left and right buttons are the most important.)

CLICKING THE MOUSE

If the pointer points to an on-screen **button**, clicking the mouse presses the button.

If the pointer points to a picture of a tool or object on the screen, clicking the mouse *selects* the tool or object; for example, clicking the pencil tool enables you to draw with the mouse.

If the pointer points to a part of a text document, it turns from an arrow into an *I-beam*; clicking repositions the flashing cursor.

Jack and Jill fell down and Jill came tumbling after.

DRAGGING THE MOUSE

If you hold the button down while you drag the mouse with a selected graphic tool (such as a paintbrush), you can draw by remote control.

If you drag the mouse from one point in a text document to another, you select all the text between those two points so you can modify or move it. For example, you might select a movie title so you can italicize it.

The zany Duck Soup captured the Marx Brothers at their peak.

To select a group of objects (for printing, copying, moving, or some other purpose), you can create a rectangle that surrounds them by dragging the mouse diagonally.

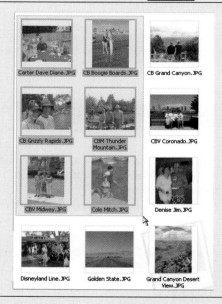

OTHER MOUSE OPERATIONS

If you **double-click** the mouse—click twice in rapid succession—while pointing to an on-screen object, the computer will probably **open** the object so you can see inside it. For example, double-clicking this *icon* representing a letter causes the letter to open.

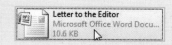

FIGURE A.3

If you *right-click*—click the right mouse button—while pointing to an object, the computer will probably display a contextual menu of choices of things you can do to the object. For example, if you right-click the letter icon, a menu appears at the pointer. On a Mac with only one mouse button, you can simulate a right click by holding down the Control key on the keyboard before clicking.

takes care of the behind-the-scenes details and (usually) keeps things running smoothly. The operating system also determines what your screen display looks like as you work and how you tell the computer what you want it to do. Most PCs today use some version of the *Microsoft Windows* operating system; Mac computers use some version of Apple's *Mac OS*.

Application programs, also called simply applications, are software tools that enable you to use a computer for specific purposes. Some applications are designed to accomplish well-defined, short-term goals. For example, an application might provide interactive lessons to learn a language. Other applications have more general and open-ended goals. For example, you can use a word processing program, such as Microsoft Word, to create memos, letters, term papers, novels, textbooks, or World Wide Web pages—just about any kind of text-based document.

In the PC world, a document is a file created by an application, regardless of whether it has actually been printed. Application files and document files are different types of files. A file is a named collection of data stored on a computer disk or some other storage medium. Applications are sometimes called *executable files* because they contain instructions that can be executed by the computer. Documents are sometimes called *data files* because they contain passive data rather than instructions. When you type a report with the Microsoft Word application, the computer executes the Word instructions. When you save the report on the computer's hard disk, the computer creates a Word document—a data file that contains the contents of the report.

Entering, Editing, and Formatting Text

You can type and edit a word processing document using standard PC techniques and tools. As you type, your text is displayed on the screen and stored in RAM. With virtually all modern word processors, words appear on the screen almost exactly as they will appear on a printed page. This feature is often referred to as WYSIWYG—short for "what you see is what you get" and pronounced "wizzy-wig." Because of a feature called word wrap, the word processor automatically moves any words that won't fit on the current line to the next line along with the cursor.

Word processing programs—and many other types of applications—contain text editing tools for changing and rearranging the words on the screen. Most computer users are familiar with the Clipboard, which can temporarily store chunks of text and other data, making it possible to cut or copy words from one part of a document and paste them into another part of the same document or a different document. In many programs, you can achieve similar results by using drag-and-drop technology that allows you to drag a selected block of text from one location to another. Find-and-replace (search and replace) tools make it possible to make repetitive changes throughout a document.

Formatting Characters

Text formatting commands enable you to control the *format* of the document. For example, you can change the way the words will look on the page. Most modern word processors include commands for controlling the formats of individual characters and paragraphs as well as complete documents.

Most printers can print text in a variety of point sizes, typefaces, and styles that aren't possible with typewriters. Characters are measured by point size, with one point equal to $\frac{1}{72}$ inch. Most documents, including this book, use smaller point sizes for text to fit more information on each page and larger point sizes to make titles and headings stand out.

In the language of typesetters, a font is a size and style of typeface. For example, the Helvetica typeface includes many fonts, one of which is 12-point Helvetica bold. In the PC world, many people use the terms *font* and *typeface* interchangeably.

Whatever you call them, you have hundreds of choices of typefaces. Serif fonts, such as those in the Times family, are embellished with serifs—fine lines at the ends of the main strokes of each character. Sans-serif fonts, such as those in the Helvetica or

Examples of	12-point size	24-point size
Serif fonts	Times New Roman	Times New Roman
	Georgia	Georgia
	Palatino	Palatino
Sans-serif fonts	Arial Narrow	Arial Narrow
	Helvetica	Helvetica
	Univers 55	Univers 55
	Verdana	Verdana
Monospaced fonts	Courier	Courier
	Monaco	Monaco

FIGURE A.4 These fonts represent only a few of the hundreds of typefaces available for personal computers and printers today.

Verdana family, have plainer, cleaner lines. **Monospaced fonts** that mimic typewriters, such as those in the Courier family, produce characters that always take up the same amount of space, no matter how skinny or fat the characters are. In contrast, **proportionally spaced fonts** enable more room for wide characters, such as w's, than for narrow characters, such as i's.

The Screen Test boxes on the following pages show examples of software at work. In these simple examples, we'll use a word processing application to edit and save a document containing the essay, "Why I Went to the Woods," by Thoreau. The first example uses Microsoft Word on a PC with the Microsoft Windows Vista operating system. The second example shows the same thing using Microsoft Word on a Macintosh with Mac OS X. In both examples, we'll perform the following steps:

1. Open Microsoft Word—copy the application program from the computer's hard disk into memory where it can be executed
2. Type, edit, and format the document
3. Save the document
4. Close the application

Before we begin, a reminder and a disclaimer:

The reminder: The *Screen Test* examples are designed to give you a feel for the software, not to provide how-to instructions. You can learn how to use the software using lab manuals or other books on the subject, some of which are listed in *Sources and Resources* at the ends of the chapters in this book.

The disclaimer: These examples are provided so you can compare different types of interfaces, not so you can establish a favorite. The brand of software in a particular *Screen Test* box isn't as important as the general concepts built into that software. One of the best things

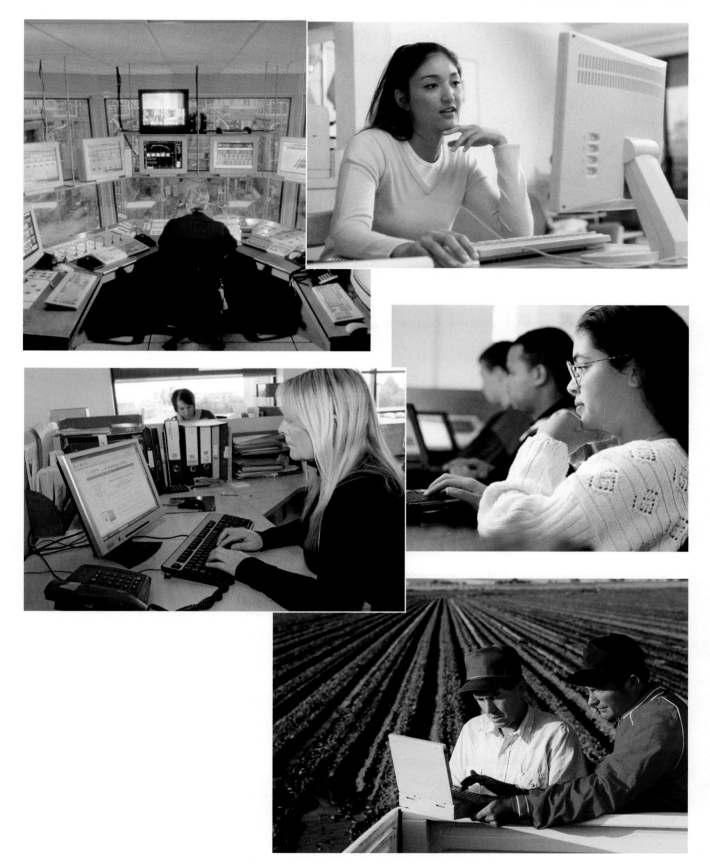

FIGURE A.5 Software makes it possible for PCs to be put to work in homes, schools, offices, factories, and farms.

Screen Test

Using Microsoft Word with Microsoft Windows

GOAL *To create a document containing highlights from a famous essay.*

TOOL *Microsoft Word and Microsoft Windows Vista.*

1. After your PC completes its startup process, the Windows desktop appears— a screen that includes icons representing objects used in your work.

2. You click Start in the lower-left corner of the screen. The Start menu appears, enabling you to select from the applications and documents you use most frequently.

3. You select Microsoft Word and click to open the program. The PC is now ready to work on any Word document, including your paper.

4. The Microsoft Word application opens, and you are presented with a blank document; clicking the Office button in the top left opens a menu containing options that represent frequently used commands and files.

5. Because this is a new paper, you click New. You're ready to start typing the paper.

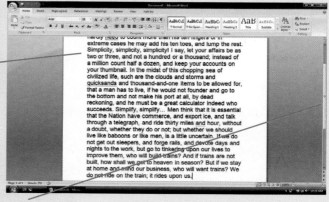

6. As you type, the top-most lines scroll out of view to make room on the screen for the new ones. The text you've entered is still in memory, even though you can't see it on the screen.

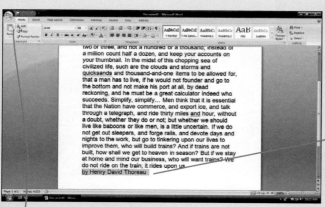

7. You can view it anytime by scrolling backward through the text using the vertical scrollbar on the right edge of the window. In this respect, a word processor document is like a modern version of an ancient paper scroll.

8. After you enter the text, you decide that "by Henry David Thoreau" should be at the top of the document, immediately below the title, rather than at the bottom of the document. Using the mouse, you select the author's byline. Selected text appears highlighted on the screen.

9. Choosing the Cut command tells the computer to cut the selected text from the document and place it in the **Clipboard**—a special portion of temporary memory used to hold information for later use.

FIGURE A.6

10. After using the mouse or arrow keys to reposition the cursor at the beginning of the document, you select the Paste command. The computer places a copy of the Clipboard's contents at the insertion point; the text below the cursor moves down to make room for the inserted text.

11. To italicize the title "Walden," you select the characters to be changed and click the button labeled / on the toolbar.

12. You can center text by selecting it and clicking the Center button located on the toolbar.

13. You're done working with the essay for now, so you choose Save from the File menu.

14. Because you haven't saved the document before, the Save As dialog box opens and prompts you for the name of the file and the location of the directory in which to store it.

15. The File menu also contains a Print command, allowing you to print a hard copy of the essay.

Screen Test

Using Microsoft Word with Mac OS X

GOAL *To edit a term paper*

TOOL *Mac OS 10.5 and Microsoft Word*

1. The Mac menu bar spans the top of the screen.

2. Like the Windows desktop, the Mac desktop, called the Finder, uses icons that represent objects used in your work. Cover Flow view allows you to flip through the icons like a deck of cards, and preview the documents before you've opened them. Many commonly used icons are visible on the left side of every Finder window.

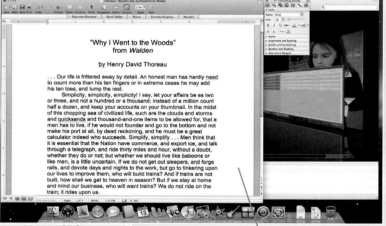

3. At the bottom of the screen is the Dock, which is a holding place for frequently used applications and documents.

4. A window shows the contents of the Documents folder on the hard disk. Folders, like their real-world counterparts, enable you to group related documents.

5. You double-click the Thoreau-Walden document to open it.

6. The document opens in a window. You edit and print the document; the process is similar for the Macintosh and Windows versions of Word.

7. A Mac OS feature called Exposé enables you, with a single keystroke, to see shrunken images of all of your open windows neatly tiled on the screen so you can quickly find the one you're looking for—in this case, the Documents folder window. You can click on it to bring it to the foreground.

FIGURE A.7

about computers is that they offer lots of different ways to do things. These examples, and others throughout the book, are designed to expose you to possibilities. Even if you have no plans to use the operating systems or applications in the examples—*especially* if you have no plans to use them—you can learn something by looking at them as a curious observer.

File Management Basics

A **place** for **everything** and everything **in its place**.

—*English proverb*

In Windows and the Mac OS, a file is represented by a name and an icon. It's not always easy to tell what a file contains based on its name. Most people know that it's a good idea to name files with clearly descriptive names, but some names are difficult to decipher. A filename includes an *extension*—a string of (usually) three characters that follows a period (.) at the end of the filename. (The operating system may be set on your machine to hide the extensions on the screen, but they're still visible to the OS.) The extension gives more information about the file's origin or use. For example, the name of a Windows executable file typically includes the extension *.exe*, as in *biggame.exe*. The filename of a Microsoft Word document usually ends with *.docx*, such as *termpaper.docx*. A *.pdf* extension typically designates files containing information stored in Portable Document Format, which you can view with Adobe Acrobat Reader. If a file doesn't have a visible extension in its name, you still might be able to tell what it is by looking at its icon. Most popular applications create documents with distinctive icons.

Hundreds of filename extensions exist. Fortunately, you don't need to worry about memorizing them because the operating system usually knows which application program is associated with each extension. For example, double-clicking the icon for file *Table.xlsx* results in the operating system running Microsoft Excel because it associates the *.xlsx* extension with Excel spreadsheets.

File Organization Basics

In the physical world, people often use file folders to organize their paper documents into meaningful collections—class documents, financial papers, receipts, and the like. Similarly, computer files can be organized into collections using **folders** (sometimes called directories). The operating system enables you to create folders, give them meaningful names, and store documents and other files inside them. When you open a folder, the folder's window opens, revealing the files that it contains. You can organize folders *hierarchically*, meaning a folder can contain other folders, which in turn can contain still more folders. For example, a folder called Documents might contain folders called School Work, Financial Papers, Letters, and Pictures. School Work might contain folders for individual classes, each of which might be subdivided into Homework, Projects, and so on. Windows and Mac operating systems include a variety of tools for quickly navigating through nested folders to locate particular files.

In the real world, people aren't as organized as computers, and files don't always end up in the appropriate folders. Modern operating systems include **Search** or **Find** commands that can help you find files no matter where they are stored on the system. You can search for filenames, but you can also search for words or phrases inside a document. So if you don't know the name of a file, but do know some of the text in that file, you can still use the search tool to find your data.

File Compression Basics

Modern PCs support a wide range of multimedia activities. The largest files on your hard disk are probably those containing videos, songs, or images. **File compression** is the

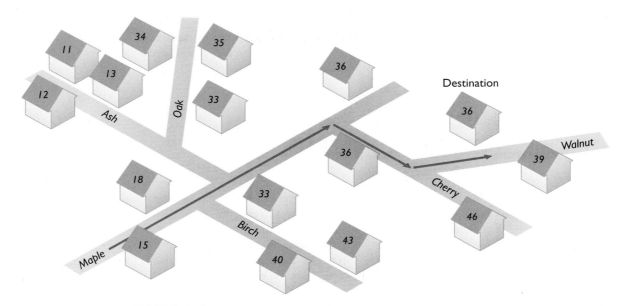

FIGURE A.8 The hierarchical organization of folders is like a suburban subdivision with dead-end streets fanning out from a single road. Suppose your destination is 36 Walnut Street. You follow Maple Street to Cherry Street, Cherry Street to Walnut Street, and you can get to 36 Walnut Street.

process of reducing the size of a file so that you can fit more files into the same amount of disk space. **File decompression** is the process of restoring the file to its original state. Compressing a file is like squeezing a sponge. You can fit a lot more sponges in a box if you squeeze them together. When you want to use one of the sponges, you remove it from the box, and it springs back to its original size. Letting the sponge go back to its original size is like decompressing a file.

You can perform file compression by using an application, an operating system, or another type of software program. For example, with Adobe Photoshop you can save a digital photograph by using GIF or JPEG compression to reduce its file size. Similarly, with Winamp and iTunes, you can convert standard digital music files to compressed MP3 files. Just about any file or group of files can be compressed using the Windows or Macintosh operating system or a compression utility, such as PKZIP or Stuffit. If you see a file with a *.zip* or *.sitx* extension, it needs to be decompressed before you use it in an application. File compression is especially important when working with video, audio, and multimedia files. Chapter 6 covers file compression techniques in more detail.

Backup Basics

Just about any computer file user can remember losing important work because of a hard disk failure, a software bug, or a computer virus that destroyed data files. It's a good idea to protect yourself against disaster by frequently backing up your data. A **backup copy** is a copy of a file created as insurance against the loss of the original. It makes sense to keep backup copies on a different device than the one that holds the original copies. Many people use CD-Rs, DVD-Rs, and other **backup media** to hold backup files and save computer storage space.

Backing up an entire hard disk on CDs or DVDs can involve many disks—and hours of tedious disk swapping. To save time,

FIGURE A.9 The DVD-R disc is a popular backup medium.

Screen Test

File Management with Windows

GOAL *To organize files into folders*

TOOL *Microsoft Windows Vista*

1. Your files are scattered across your desktop; you'd like to organize them by folder. After you open the Documents folder from the Start menu, you select all the unfiled documents (by dragging a rectangle around them) and drag them to the Documents folder. The icons appear as transparent images in the window while you're dragging them.

2. You click the Maximize button (the button with one large window) so the Documents window fills the screen.

3. You use a button in the sidebar to create two new folders named School and Work within the Documents folder.

4. You select and drag all of the work-related documents into the Work folder. The Work folder icon is highlighted when you drag the documents into it.

5. You create a third folder, Personal, and distribute the unsorted documents into the new folders that you've created. You click on the Folders button at the bottom of the sidebar to show the hierarchical organization of the folders on your hard drive.

FIGURE A.10

many organizations and individuals back up large hard disks using high-capacity magnetic tapes and removeable hard drives. Backup tapes and hard drives don't need to be attached directly to individual computers because backups can be performed over computer networks, discussed in the next section.

Network and Internet Basics

Networks aren't made of printed circuits, but of **people ... My terminal is a door** to countless, intricate pathways, leading to **untold numbers of neighbors**.

—*Cliff Stoll, in* The Cuckoo's Egg

Today's PCs are powerful tools that can perform a variety of tasks that go far beyond the basic word processing examples illustrated here. Later chapters explore many of these applications, from money management to multimedia. But a PC becomes even more powerful when it's connected to other computers through a network.

PC Network Basics

FIGURE A.11 Networked computers in this lab allow students to share files, send messages, and connect to the Internet.

A computer may have a *direct connection* to a network—for example, cables might connect it to other computers, printers, and other devices in an office or student lab. These networked machines can easily and quickly share information with each other. When a computer isn't physically close to the other machines in the network, it can still communicate with those machines through a *remote access* connection.

An entire computer network can be connected to other networks through cables, wireless radio transmissions, or other means. The **Internet** is an elaborate network of interconnected networks. If a computer has a direct connection to a network that's part of the Internet, it has a direct Internet connection. Most PCs are connected to the Internet through other means. Computers with broadband connections use cable modems, DSL routers, and satellite connections to connect to the Internet. Others use slower dial-up connections through modems connected to phone lines. Many homes, schools, and businesses use Wi-Fi technology to create wireless networks, enabling portable computer users to connect to the Internet without cables.

Internet Basics

What interests me about it ... is that it's a form of communication **unlike any other** and yet the second you start doing it **you understand it**.

—*Nora Ephron, Director of* You've Got Mail

There was a time, not too many years ago, when word processing was the most popular computer activity among students. For most students, the computer was little more than a high-powered typewriter. Today a PC can be a window into the global system of interconnected networks known as the Internet, or just the *Net*.

The Internet is used by mom-and-pop businesses and multinational corporations that want to communicate with their customers, sell products, and track economic conditions; by kindergartners and college students doing research and exploration; by consumers and commuters who need access to timely information, goods, and services; and by families and friends who just want to stay in touch. Most people connect to the Internet because it gives them the power to do things that they couldn't easily do otherwise.

Using the Internet you can perform the following tasks:

- Send a message to 1 or 1,001 people, around town or around the world, and receive replies almost as quickly as the recipients can read the message and type a response.
- Explore vast libraries of research material, ranging from classic scholarly works to contemporary reference works.
- Find instant answers to time-sensitive questions.
- Get medical, legal, or technical advice from a wide variety of experts.
- Listen to live radio broadcasts from around the world.
- Participate in discussions or play games with people all over the globe who share your interests; with the right equipment, you can set aside your keyboard and communicate through live audio-video links.
- Shop for obscure items, such as out-of-print books and CDs that you can't find elsewhere.
- Download free software or music clips from servers all over the world onto your computer.
- Order a custom-built computer, car, or condominium.
- Develop pan-global friendships, relationships, and communities based on shared interests.
- Take a course for college credit from a school thousands of miles away.
- Publish your own writings, drawings, photos, and multimedia works so Internet users all over the world can view them.
- Start your own business and interact with clients around the world.

Every revolution has a dark side, and the Internet explosion is no exception. The Internet has plenty of worthless information, scams, and questionable activities. People who make the most of the Internet know how to separate the best of the Net from the rest of the Net. Every chapter of this book contains information that will help you understand and use the Internet wisely. In this appendix, we'll focus on the basics of the two most popular Internet applications: finding information on the World Wide Web and communicating with electronic mail.

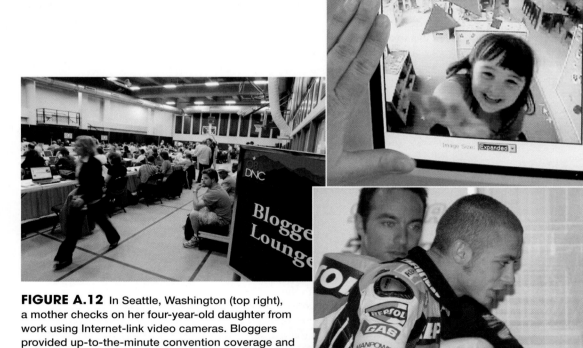

FIGURE A.12 In Seattle, Washington (top right), a mother checks on her four-year-old daughter from work using Internet-link video cameras. Bloggers provided up-to-the-minute convention coverage and analysis during the 2008 U.S. presidential election (left). The Internet provides up-to-date sporting news to enthusiasts and athletes (bottom right).

World Wide Web Basics

The **World Wide Web** makes the Internet accessible to people all over the planet. The *Web* is a huge portion of the Internet that includes a wealth of multimedia content accessible through simple point-and-click programs called **Web browsers**. Web browsers on PCs and other devices serve as windows to the Web's diverse information.

The World Wide Web is made up of millions of interlinked documents called **Web pages**. A Web page is typically made up of text and images, like a page in a book. A collection of related pages stored on the same computer is called a **Web site**; a typical Web site is organized around a home page that serves as an entry page and a stepping-off point for other pages in the site. Each Web page has a unique address, technically referred to as a **uniform resource locator (URL)**. For example, the URL for this book's home page is **http://www.pearsonhighered.com/beekman**. You can visit the site by typing the exact URL into the address box of your Web browser.

The Web is an example of a *hypertext* system. A typical Web page contains information, such as words and pictures, as well as connections to other Web pages. A Web browser enables you to jump from one Web page to another by clicking **hyperlinks** (often called *links*), which are words, pictures, or menu items that act as buttons.

Hypertext systems, such as the Web, contain "pages," but they don't work like books. The author of a novel expects you to start at page one, move on to page two, and continue

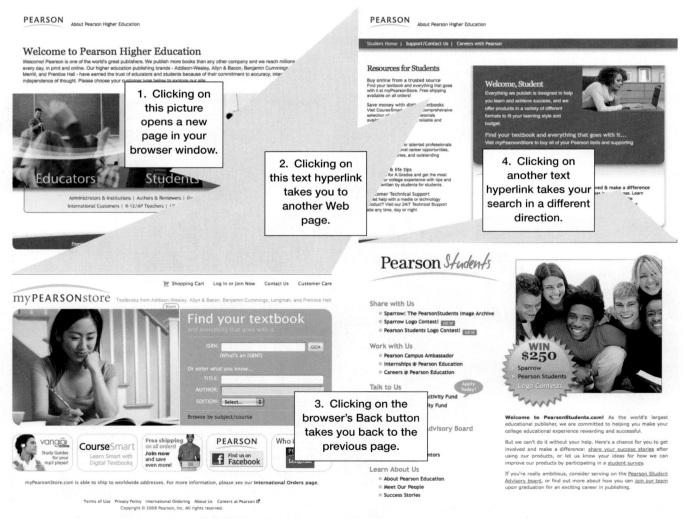

FIGURE A.13 Hypertext links make it possible to navigate quickly through a Web site to locate a page containing specific information.

reading the pages in order until you have finished the last page. Hyperlinks enable you to access the pages of a hypertext system in a variety of ways, depending on your needs. For example, at the *Tomorrow's Technology and You Web* site, you can select a chapter number to jump to pages related to that chapter. Within the chapter, you can click Online Study Guide to jump to a page containing practice quiz questions. Or you can click Web Resources to jump to a page full of hyperlinks that can take you to pages on other Web sites. These off-site pages contain articles, illustrations, audio clips, video segments, and resources created by others. They reside on computers owned by corporations, universities, libraries, institutions, and individuals around the world.

Text links are typically, but not always, underlined and displayed in a different color than standard text on the page. You can explore an amazing variety of Web pages by clicking links. But this kind of random jumping isn't without frustrations. Some links lead to cobwebs, which are Web pages that haven't been kept up to date by their owners, and dead ends—pages that have been removed or moved. Even if a link is current, it may not be reputable or accurate; because anybody can create Web pages, they don't all have the editorial integrity of trusted print media.

It can also be frustrating to try to find your way back to pages you've seen on the Web. That's why browsers have *Back* and *Forward buttons*; you can retrace your steps as often as you like. These buttons won't help, though, if you're trying to find an important page from an earlier session. Most browsers include tools for keeping personal lists of memorable sites, called *bookmarks* or *favorites*. When you run across a page worth revisiting, you can mark it with a Bookmark or Add to Favorites command. Then you can revisit that site anytime by selecting it from the list.

Web Search Basics

The World Wide Web is like a giant, loosely woven, constantly changing document created by thousands of unrelated authors and scattered about in computers all over the world. The biggest challenge

The ability to **ask the right question** is more than half the battle of **finding the answer**.

—*Thomas J. Watson, founder of IBM*

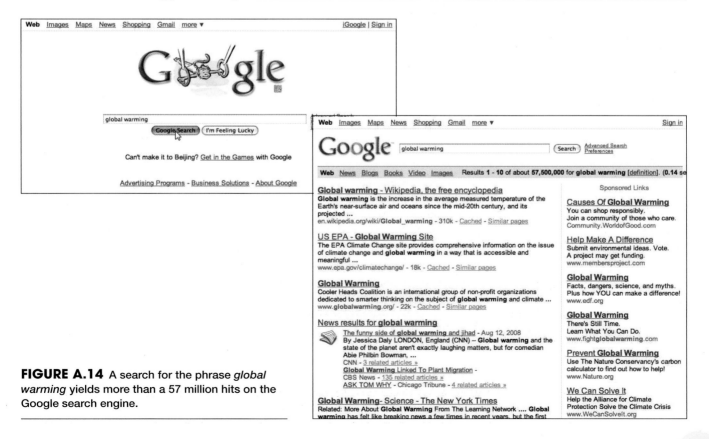

FIGURE A.14 A search for the phrase *global warming* yields more than a 57 million hits on the Google search engine.

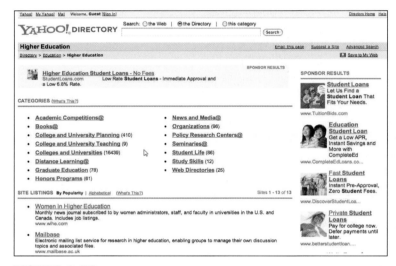

FIGURE A.15 Yahoo!'s subject tree enables you to narrow your search by clicking categories within a subject.

for many Web users is extracting the useful information from the rest. If you're looking for a specific information resource, but you don't know where it is located on the Web, you might be able to find it using a search engine.

A search engine is built around a database that catalogs Web locations based on content. (Databases are covered in Chapter 7; for now, you can just think of them as indexed collections of information stored in computers.) Most search engines use software to search the Web and catalog information automatically. The usefulness of a search engine depends in part on the information in its database. But it also depends on how easy it is for people to find what they're looking for in the database.

To find information with a typical search engine, you type a keyword or keywords into a search field, click a button, and watch your Web browser display a list of *hits*—pages that contain the requested keywords. A search engine can easily produce a list of millions or billions of hits. Most search engines attempt to list pages in order from best to worst match, but these automatic rankings aren't always reliable.

Another popular way to use a search engine is to repeatedly narrow the search using a *directory* or *subject tree*—a hierarchical catalog of Web sites compiled by researchers. A screen presents you with a menu of subject choices. When you click a subject—say, Government—you narrow your search to that subject, and you're presented with a menu of subcategories within that subject—Military, Politics, Law, Taxes, and so on. You can continue to narrow your search by proceeding through subject menus until you reach a list of selected Web sites related to the final subject. The sites are usually rank-ordered based on estimated value. The list of Web sites on a given index page is not exhaustive; there may be hundreds of pages related to the subject that aren't included in any directory. It's simply not possible to keep a complete index of all the pages on the ever-changing Web.

Popular search engines are located on Google, MSN Yahoo!, and other Internet *portals*—Web sites designed as first-stop gateways for Internet surfers. Internet Explorer, Netscape, and other Web browsers include Search buttons that connect to popular search engines. And many large Web sites include search engines that enable you to search for site-specific information.

Email Basics

Each person on the **"Internet"** has a unique email **"address"** created by **having a squirrel** run across a computer keyboard … .

—*Dave Barry, humorist*

Electronic mail (also called email or *e-mail*) is the application that lures many people to the Internet for the first time. Email programs make it possible for even casual computer users to send messages to family, friends, and colleagues easily.

Because an email message can be written, addressed, sent, delivered, and answered in a matter of minutes—even if the correspondents are on opposite sides of the globe—email has replaced air mail for rapid, routine communication in many organizations. If you send someone an email message, that person can log in and read it from a computer at home, at the office, or from anywhere in the world at any time of day. Unlike a ringing phone, email waits patiently in the mailbox until the recipient has the time to handle it, making email particularly attractive when the communication is between people in different time zones.

Closer to home, email makes it possible to replace time-consuming phone calls and meetings with more efficient online exchanges. Email conversations allow groups of people to discuss an idea for hours, days, or weeks, thus avoiding the urgency of needing to settle a complicated issue in a single session. You can send a message to a group of people on a mailing list as easily as you send the message to one person. Since an email message is digital data, you can edit it and combine it with other computer-generated documents. When you're finished, you can forward the edited message back to the original sender or to somebody else for further processing.

Details vary, but the basic concepts of email are the same for almost all systems. When you sign up for an email account—through your school, your company, or a private *Internet service provider (ISP)*—you receive a **user name** (sometimes called a *login name* or *alias*) and a storage area for messages (sometimes called a *mailbox*). Any user can send an email message to anyone else, regardless of whether the recipient is currently *logged in*—connected to the network. The message will be waiting in the recipient's *inbox* the next time that person launches his or her email program and logs in. An email message can be addressed to one person or hundreds of people. Most email messages are plain text and don't include the kinds of formatting and graphic images found in printed documents. Messages can carry documents, pictures, multimedia files, and other computer files as *attachments*.

You can send messages to anyone on your local system or ISP by simply addressing the message to that person's user name. You can also send messages to anyone with access to Internet email, provided you know that person's Internet address. An Internet email address is made up of two parts separated by an "at" sign (@): the person's user name and the *host name*—the name of the host computer, network, or ISP address from which the user receives mail. Here's the basic form:

```
username@hostname
```

Here are a few examples of typical email addresses:

```
realgeorge999@aol.com
jandumont@engr.ucla.edu
enathab@pop3.ispchannel.com
```

Some organizations use standardized email addresses so it's easy to guess member addresses. For example, every employee at ABCXYZ Company might have an email address of the form *firstname_lastname@abcxyzco.com*. (The underscore character is sometimes used as a substitute for a space because spaces can't be embedded in email addresses). It's important to address email messages with care; they can't be delivered if even a single character is mistyped. Fortunately, most email programs include address books so that after entering contact information once, users can look up email addresses by name and automatically address messages. Many World Wide Web sites offer free email search services and directories.

Many commercial Web sites offer free email accounts. Sometimes these free email services are subsidized by advertisers; sometimes they're provided to attract Web site visitors. Free email services are popular with users of public computers (for example, in libraries), people who don't receive email from their ISPs, people who want multiple email addresses not associated with their workplace, and travelers who want to check email on the road without lugging a laptop.

The example in the *Screen Test* shows a simple email session using Hotmail—an email service that's accessible through a standard Web browser. The concepts illustrated in the example apply to all email programs.

Screen Test

Communicating with Electronic Mail

GOAL *Catch up on your email*

TOOL *Google Gmail*

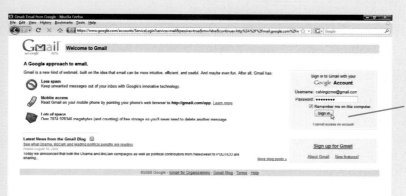

1. Gmail is a popular email service available through the World Wide Web. When you navigate to www.gmail.com in a Web browser, you are presented with the Gmail logon page. Here, you enter your user name and password; then you click Sign In to continue.

2. After you sign on, you are presented with the contents of your electronic inbox. This is the folder where incoming mail—email that was sent by others to you—is stored. Here, you can see a list of read and unread mail, navigate between categories of mail (labels) and delete email. You can also jump to other email tasks, such as composing a new email message of your own or managing your *contacts*—those people with whom you correspond regularly.

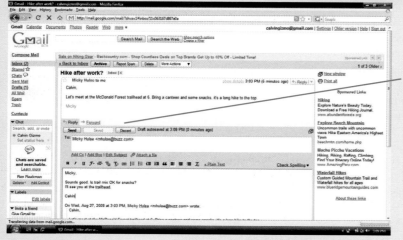

3. To open an email message, simply click on it in the list. The email message displays. From here, you can respond to the message, forward the message to others, delete the message, or organize it with a label.

FIGURE A.16

Internet Security Basics

Despite its wonders, the Internet can be a dangerous place. In the same way that you should wear a seat belt and observe local laws when driving a car, you should approach the Internet understanding the security risks involved. After you connect a computer to a network or the Internet, you dramatically increase the risk that your system will be compromised in some way. But that doesn't mean that the Internet should be avoided. Rather, you just need to make sure you're taking the proper precautions.

The most common form of Internet-based security risk is probably spam, or junk mail. This is unwanted email you receive from (usually) unknown senders, such as mass mailers who are attempting to sell goods or deceive people into paying for nonexistent items. Most email programs now include *spam filters* that help keep this problem manageable, but even with a filter you're likely to spend plenty of time manually deleting spam messages.

A virus is a more sinister email problem. Generally delivered as email attachments, viruses are executable programs designed by malicious programmers—sometimes called *hackers*—to infiltrate your system. Some viruses simply duplicate themselves and send themselves to other PCs by harvesting email addresses in your email address book; these types of viruses can slow the performance of your network, making Internet access unbearably sluggish. Others can delete files and folders on your system. Either way, you shouldn't open unexpected attachments from unknown senders.

Another problem on the Internet is password theft. There are low-tech methods for stealing other people's passwords: For example, someone might look over your shoulder and watch as you type a password. Hackers can electronically monitor keystrokes and send the information over the Internet to others. A wider but related issue concerns *identity (ID) theft*. Hackers or other unscrupulous individuals can access your computer and obtain enough information about you to assume your identity. In cases of ID theft, thieves have been known to use victims' credit cards to rack up thousands of dollars in bills. To protect yourself against ID theft, you should keep personal information, including your social security number, credit card numbers, and passwords a secret while online.

Obviously, there's a lot more to Internet security. We look extensively at this issue in Chapter 10.

A programmer writes a tiny program—the virus—that has destructive power and can reproduce itself.

Most often, the virus is attached to a normal program; unknown to the user, the virus spreads to other software.

The virus is passed by disk or network to other users who use other computers. The virus remains dormant as it is passed on.

Depending on how it is programmed, a virus may display an unexpected message, gobble up memory, destroy data files, or cause serious system errors.

FIGURE A.17 How a virus spreads.

Summary

PCs come in a variety of shapes and sizes, but they're all made up of two things: the physical parts of the computer, called hardware, and the software instructions that tell the hardware what to do. The PC's system unit contains the CPU, which controls the other components, including memory, disk drives, and monitor screens. The keyboard and mouse enable a user to communicate with the computer, which sends information back to the user through displays on the monitor.

The computer's operating system software takes care of details of the computer's operation. Application software provides specific tools for computer users. The file system contains the numerous files needed for the operating system and application software to run smoothly, and the personal files created by the computer's users. A hierarchical system of folders organizes the files, making it easier for application programs and computer users to find the files they need.

PCs can be networked to other computers using cables, radio waves, or other means.

The Internet is a global network of computer networks used for education, commerce, and communication. The most popular Internet activities are exploring the World Wide Web and communicating with electronic mail.

A Web browser is a computer application that provides easy access to the World Wide Web—a wide-ranging array of multimedia information on the Internet. Web pages are interconnected by hyperlinks that make it easy to follow information trails. Search engines serve as indices for the Web, locating pages with subject matter that matches keywords.

Electronic mail (or email) enables almost instant communication among Internet users. Some email systems can be accessed through Web browsers.

The Internet is not without risks. Internet users must be prepared to deal with unsolicited (and often unsavory) email, computer viruses, identity theft, and other risks.

Key Terms

True or False

1. Roughly three-fourths of people in the world use computers at least occasionally.

2. A computer keyboard includes some keys that don't respond by displaying characters on the screen, but instead send special commands to the computer.

3. Windows PCs and Macintoshes use the same operating system (OS).

4. An entire computer network can be connected to other networks through cables, wireless radio transmissions, or other means.

5. Hypertext links make it easy to jump between Web pages created by different authors around the world.

6. A Web search engine is built around a database that catalogs Web locations based on content.

7. An Internet email address is made up of a user name and a host name separated by an "at" sign (@).

8. An email message must be composed in a word processor before it can be sent.

9. Spam is a type of computer virus that attacks only email documents.

10. The Internet has become virtually risk free within the past few years.

Multiple Choice

1. The computer's system unit typically contains the computer's "brain," called the
   a. central processing unit.
   b. memory.
   c. peripheral.
   d. monitor.
   e. modem.

2. The PC's main hard disk
   a. is a permanent part of the system unit.
   b. is sometimes called an internal drive.
   c. can hold more information than the computer's memory.
   d. serves as a long-term storage device.
   e. All of the above

3. Which of the following is not considered removable media?
   a. Blu-ray discs
   b. CD-ROMs
   c. Audio CDs
   d. Internal hard disks
   e. DVDs

4. Which of the following is not a peripheral?
   a. A printer
   b. A mouse
   c. An optical drive
   d. A processor
   e. All of the above

5. What is a software program designed to help you accomplish a specific task called?
   a. An application
   b. An operating system
   c. A document
   d. A desktop
   e. A browser

6. Virtually all modern word processors display words on the screen almost exactly as they will appear on the printed page. What is this feature called?
   a. Electronic paper
   b. Highlighting
   c. Point-and-click interface
   d. Virtual reality
   e. WYSIWYG (what you see is what you get)

7. In Windows and the Mac OS, a file is represented by
   a. a beige folder icon.
   b. a special key on the keyboard.
   c. a name and an extension.
   d. a link to a Web page.
   e. All of the above

8. In Windows and the Mac OS, which word or phrase best describes how files and folders are organized?
   a. Democratically
   b. Hierarchically
   c. In a network
   d. In pools
   e. Randomly

9. Which of these is a type of backup media?
   a. Audio CD
   b. DVD-R
   c. Folder
   d. Backlit monitor
   e. RAM

10. Which of the following does every Web site on the World Wide Web have?
    a. Hyperlinks to dozens of other Web sites
    b. Multimedia material
    c. Publicly accessible information on a particular subject
    d. A unique address called a URL
    e. All of the above

11. If you want to retrace your steps and return to the screen previously displayed in the browser window, you should use
    a. the Retrace command.
    b. the R key.
    c. the browser's Back button.
    d. the spacebar.
    e. the Undo key.

12. Which of the following is commonly used to find information on the Internet?
    a. A Finder application
    b. A search engine
    c. a URL (uniform resource locator)
    d. A right-click of the mouse on the desktop
    e. The digital dictionary of Internetology

13. Which of the following can be attached to an email message?
    a. A picture
    b. A multimedia file
    c. A word processor document
    d. A computer virus
    e. All of the above

14. Which of these is definitely *not* a valid email address?
    a. http://www.pearsoned.com
    b. beanbag_boxspring@prenhall.com
    c. president@whitehouse.gov
    d. thisisaverylongnameindeed@aol.com
    e. All of the above could be valid email addresses.

15. Which of the following is the most common use of spam?
    a. Transmitting computer viruses
    b. Identity theft
    c. Marketing unsolicited goods and services
    d. Web searches
    e. Hacking

Review Questions

1. Briefly define or describe each of the key terms listed in the "Key Terms" section.

2. How are hardware and software related?

3. Which computer component is the most critical to the computer's functioning, and why?

4. Which two computer components are most often used by people for getting information into PCs?

5. What is the difference between operating system software and application software?

6. How do folders allow files to be organized?

7. What is the purpose of file compression?

8. List some ways that a computer might be connected to a network.

9. What is the fundamental difference between ordinary text (such as a novel) and hypertext?

10. Give examples of ways email can change the way you communicate with other people.

11. How can you use hyperlinks to explore the World Wide Web? Give an example.

12. How can you find a site on the Web if you don't know the URL?

13. What security procedures should you follow while exploring the *Tomorrow's Technology and You* Web site?

Appendix B | ACM

ACM Code of Ethics and Professional Conduct (Adopted by ACM Council October 16, 1992)

Commitment to ethical professional conduct is expected of every member (voting members, associate members, and student members) of the Association for Computing Machinery (ACM).

This Code, consisting of 24 imperatives formulated as statements of personal responsibility, identifies the elements of such a commitment. It contains many, but not all, issues professionals are likely to face. Section 1 outlines fundamental ethical considerations, while Section 2 addresses additional, more specific considerations of professional conduct. Statements in Section 3 pertain more specifically to individuals who have a leadership role, whether in the workplace or in a volunteer capacity such as with organizations like ACM. Principles involving compliance with this Code are given in Section 4.

The Code shall be supplemented by a set of Guidelines, which provide explanation to assist members in dealing with the various issues contained in the Code. It is expected that the Guidelines will be changed more frequently than the Code.

The Code and its supplemented Guidelines are intended to serve as a basis for ethical decision making in the conduct of professional work. Secondarily, they may serve as a basis for judging the merit of a formal complaint pertaining to violation of professional ethical standards.

It should be noted that although computing is not mentioned in the imperatives of Section 1, the Code is concerned with how these fundamental imperatives apply to one's conduct as a computing professional. These imperatives are expressed in a general form to emphasize that ethical principles which apply to computer ethics are derived from more general ethical principles.

It is understood that some words and phrases in a code of ethics are subject to varying interpretations, and that any ethical principle may conflict with other ethical principles in specific situations. Questions related to ethical conflicts can best be answered by thoughtful consideration of fundamental principles, rather than reliance on detailed regulations.

1. General moral imperatives
2. More specific professional responsibilities
3. Organizational leadership imperatives
4. Compliance with the code

1. General Moral Imperatives

As an ACM member I will ...

1.1 Contribute to Society and Human Well-Being

This principle concerning the quality of life of all people affirms an obligation to protect fundamental human rights and to respect the diversity of all cultures. An essential aim of computing professionals is to minimize negative consequences of computing systems, including threats to health and safety. When designing or implementing systems, computing professionals must attempt to ensure that the products of their efforts will be used in socially responsible ways, will meet social needs, and will avoid harmful effects to health and welfare.

In addition to a safe social environment, human well-being includes a safe natural environment. Therefore, computing professionals who design and develop systems must be alert to, and make others aware of, any potential damage to the local or global environment.

1.2 Avoid Harm to Others

"Harm" means injury or negative consequences, such as undesirable loss of information, loss of property, property damage, or unwanted environmental impacts. This principle prohibits use of computing technology in ways that result in harm to any of the following: users, the general public, employees, and employers. Harmful actions include intentional destruction or modification of files and programs leading to serious loss of resources or unnecessary expenditure of human resources such as the time and effort required to purge systems of "computer viruses."

Well-intended actions, including those that accomplish assigned duties, may lead to harm unexpectedly. In such an event the responsible person or persons are obligated to undo or mitigate the negative consequences as much as possible. One way to avoid unintentional harm is to carefully consider potential impacts on all those affected by decisions made during design and implementation.

To minimize the possibility of indirectly harming others, computing professionals must minimize malfunctions by following generally accepted standards for system design and testing. Furthermore, it is often necessary to assess the social consequences of systems to project the likelihood of any serious harm to others. If system features are misrepresented to users, coworkers, or supervisors, the individual computing professional is responsible for any resulting injury.

In the work environment the computing professional has the additional obligation to report any signs of system dangers that might result in serious personal or social damage. If one's superiors do not act to curtail or mitigate such dangers, it may be necessary to "blow the whistle" to help correct the problem or reduce the risk. However, capricious or misguided reporting of violations can, itself, be harmful. Before reporting violations, all relevant aspects of the incident must be thoroughly assessed. In particular, the assessment of risk and responsibility must be credible. It is suggested that advice be sought from other computing professionals. See principle 2.5 regarding thorough evaluations.

1.3 Be Honest and Trustworthy

Honesty is an essential component of trust. Without trust an organization cannot function effectively. The honest computing professional will not make deliberately false or deceptive claims about a system or system design, but will instead provide full disclosure of all pertinent system limitations and problems.

A computer professional has a duty to be honest about his or her own qualifications, and about any circumstances that might lead to conflicts of interest.

Membership in volunteer organizations such as ACM may at times place individuals in situations where their statements or actions could be interpreted as carrying the "weight" of a larger group of professionals. An ACM member will exercise care to not misrepresent ACM or positions and policies of ACM or any ACM units.

1.4 Be Fair and Take Action Not to Discriminate

The values of equality, tolerance, respect for others, and the principles of equal justice govern this imperative. Discrimination on the basis of race, sex, religion, age, disability, national origin, or other such factors is an explicit violation of ACM policy and will not be tolerated.

Inequities between different groups of people may result from the use or misuse of information and technology. In a fair society, all individuals would have equal opportunity to participate in, or benefit from, the use of computer resources regardless of race, sex, religion, age, disability, national origin or other such similar factors. However, these ideals do not justify unauthorized use of computer resources nor do they provide an adequate basis for violation of any other ethical imperatives of this code.

1.5 Honor Property Rights Including Copyrights and Patents

Violation of copyrights, patents, trade secrets and the terms of license agreements is prohibited by law in most circumstances. Even when software is not so protected, such violations are contrary to professional behavior. Copies of software should be made only with proper authorization. Unauthorized duplication of materials must not be condoned.

1.6 Give Proper Credit for Intellectual Property

Computing professionals are obligated to protect the integrity of intellectual property. Specifically, one must not take credit for other's ideas or work, even in cases where the work has not been explicitly protected by copyright, patent, etc.

1.7 Respect the Privacy of Others

Computing and communication technology enables the collection and exchange of personal information on a scale unprecedented in the history of civilization. Thus there is increased potential for violating the privacy of individuals and groups. It is the responsibility of professionals to maintain the privacy and integrity of data describing individuals. This includes taking precautions to ensure the accuracy of data, as well as protecting it from unauthorized access or accidental disclosure to inappropriate individuals. Furthermore, procedures must be established to allow individuals to review their records and correct inaccuracies.

This imperative implies that only the necessary amount of personal information be collected in a system, that retention and disposal periods for that information be clearly defined and enforced, and that personal information gathered for a specific purpose not be used for other purposes without consent of the individual(s). These principles apply to electronic communications, including electronic mail, and prohibit procedures that capture or monitor electronic user data, including messages, without the permission of users or bona fide authorization related to system operation and maintenance. User data observed during the normal duties of system operation and maintenance must be treated with strictest confidentiality, except in cases where it is evidence for the violation of law, organizational regulations, or this Code. In these cases, the nature or contents of that information must be disclosed only to proper authorities.

1.8 Honor Confidentiality

The principle of honesty extends to issues of confidentiality of information whenever one has made an explicit promise to honor confidentiality or, implicitly, when private information not directly related to the performance of one's duties becomes available. The ethical concern is to respect all obligations of confidentiality to employers, clients, and users unless discharged from such obligations by requirements of the law or other principles of this Code.

2. More Specific Professional Responsibilities

As an ACM computing professional I will ...

2.1 Strive to Achieve the Highest Quality, Effectiveness and Dignity in Both the Process and Products of Professional Work

Excellence is perhaps the most important obligation of a professional. The computing professional must strive to achieve quality and to be cognizant of the serious negative consequences that may result from poor quality in a system.

2.2 Acquire and Maintain Professional Competence

Excellence depends on individuals who take responsibility for acquiring and maintaining professional competence. A professional must participate in setting standards for appropriate levels of competence, and strive to achieve those standards. Upgrading technical knowledge and competence can be achieved in several ways: doing independent study; attending seminars, conferences, or courses; and being involved in professional organizations.

2.3 Know and Respect Existing Laws Pertaining to Professional Work

ACM members must obey existing local, state, province, national, and international laws unless there is a compelling ethical basis not to do so. Policies and procedures of the organizations in which one participates must also be obeyed. But compliance must be balanced with the recognition that sometimes existing laws and rules may be immoral or inappropriate and, therefore, must be challenged. Violation of a law or regulation may be ethical when that law or rule has inadequate moral basis or when it conflicts with another law judged to be more important. If one decides to violate a law or rule because it is viewed as unethical, or for any other reason, one must fully accept responsibility for one's actions and for the consequences.

2.4 Accept and Provide Appropriate Professional Review

Quality professional work, especially in the computing profession, depends on professional reviewing and critiquing. Whenever appropriate, individual members should seek and utilize peer review as well as provide critical review of the work of others.

2.5 Give Comprehensive and Thorough Evaluations of Computer Systems and Their Impacts, Including Analysis of Possible Risks

Computer professionals must strive to be perceptive, thorough, and objective when evaluating, recommending, and presenting system descriptions and alternatives. Computer professionals are in a position of special trust, and therefore have a special responsibility to provide objective, credible evaluations to employers, clients, users, and the public. When providing evaluations the professional must also identify any relevant conflicts of interest, as stated in imperative 1.3.

As noted in the discussion of principle 1.2 on avoiding harm, any signs of danger from systems must be reported to those who have opportunity and/or responsibility to resolve them. See the guidelines for imperative 1.2 for more details concerning harm, including the reporting of professional violations.

2.6 Honor Contracts, Agreements, and Assigned Responsibilities

Honoring one's commitments is a matter of integrity and honesty. For the computer professional this includes ensuring that system elements perform as intended. Also, when one contracts for work with another party, one has an obligation to keep that party properly informed about progress toward completing that work.

A computing professional has a responsibility to request a change in any assignment that he or she feels cannot be completed as defined. Only after serious consideration and with full disclosure of risks and concerns to the employer or client, should one accept the assignment. The major underlying principle here is the obligation to accept personal accountability for professional work. On some occasions other ethical principles may take greater priority.

A judgment that a specific assignment should not be performed may not be accepted. Having clearly identified one's concerns and reasons for that judgment, but failing to procure a change in that assignment, one may yet be obligated, by contract or by law, to proceed as directed. The computing professional's ethical judgment should be the final guide in deciding whether or not to proceed. Regardless of the decision, one must accept the responsibility for the consequences.

However, performing assignments "against one's own judgment" does not relieve the professional of responsibility for any negative consequences.

2.7 Improve Public Understanding of Computing and Its Consequences

Computing professionals have a responsibility to share technical knowledge with the public by encouraging understanding of computing, including the impacts of computer systems and their limitations. This imperative implies an obligation to counter any false views related to computing.

2.8 Access Computing and Communication Resources Only When Authorized to Do So

Theft or destruction of tangible and electronic property is prohibited by imperative 1.2— "Avoid harm to others." Trespassing and unauthorized use of a computer or communication system is addressed by this imperative. Trespassing includes accessing communication networks and computer systems, or accounts and/or files associated with those systems, without explicit authorization to do so. Individuals and organizations have the right to restrict access to their systems so long as they do not violate the discrimination principle (see 1.4). No one should enter or use another's computer system, software, or data files without permission. One must always have appropriate approval before using system resources, including communication ports, file space, other system peripherals, and computer time.

3. Organizational Leadership Imperatives

Background Note: This section draws extensively from the draft IFIP Code of Ethics, especially its sections on organizational ethics and international concerns. The ethical obligations of organizations tend to be neglected in most codes of professional conduct, perhaps because these codes are written from the perspective of the individual member. This dilemma is addressed by stating these imperatives from the perspective of the organizational leader. In this context "leader" is viewed as any organizational member who has leadership or educational responsibilities. These imperatives generally may apply to organizations as well as their leaders. In this context "organizations" are corporations, government agencies, and other "employers" as well as volunteer professional organizations.

As an ACM member and an organizational leader, I will ...

3.1 Articulate Social Responsibilities of Members of an Organizational Unit and Encourage Full Acceptance of those Responsibilities

Because organizations of all kinds have impacts on the public, they must accept responsibilities to society. Organizational procedures and attitudes oriented toward quality and the welfare of society will reduce harm to members of the public, thereby serving public interest and fulfilling social responsibility. Therefore, organizational leaders must encourage full participation in meeting social responsibilities as well as quality performance.

3.2 Manage Personnel and Resources to Design and Build Information Systems that Enhance the Quality of Working Life

Organizational leaders are responsible for ensuring that computer systems enhance, not degrade, the quality of working life. When implementing a computer system, organizations must consider the personal and professional development, physical safety, and human dignity of all workers. Appropriate human-computer ergonomic standards should be considered in system design and in the workplace.

3.3 Acknowledge and Support Proper and Authorized Uses of an Organization's Computing and Communication Resources

Because computer systems can become tools to harm as well as to benefit an organization, the leadership has the responsibility to clearly define appropriate and inappropriate uses of organizational computing resources. While the number and scope of such rules should be minimal, they should be fully enforced when established.

3.4 Ensure that Users and those Who Will Be Affected by a System Have Their Needs Clearly Articulated During the Assessment and Design of Requirements; Later the System Must Be Validated to Meet Requirements

Current system users, potential users and other persons whose lives may be affected by a system must have their needs assessed and incorporated in the statement of requirements. System validation should ensure compliance with those requirements.

3.5 Articulate and Support Policies that Protect the Dignity of Users and Others Affected by a Computing System

Designing or implementing systems that deliberately or inadvertently demean individuals or groups is ethically unacceptable. Computer professionals who are in decision making positions should verify that systems are designed and implemented to protect personal privacy and enhance personal dignity.

3.6 Create Opportunities for Members of the Organization to Learn the Principles and Limitations of Computer Systems

This complements the imperative on public understanding (2.7). Educational opportunities are essential to facilitate optimal participation of all organizational members. Opportunities must be available to all members to help them improve their knowledge and skills in computing, including courses that familiarize them with the consequences and limitations of particular types of systems. In particular, professionals must be made aware of the dangers of building systems around oversimplified models, the improbability of anticipating and designing for every possible operating condition, and other issues related to the complexity of this profession.

4. Compliance with the Code

As an ACM member I will ...

4.1 Uphold and Promote the Principles of this Code

The future of the computing profession depends on both technical and ethical excellence. Not only is it important for ACM computing professionals to adhere to the principles expressed in this Code, each member should encourage and support adherence by other members.

4.2 Treat Violations of this Code as Inconsistent with Membership in the ACM

Adherence of professionals to a code of ethics is largely a voluntary matter. However, if a member does not follow this code by engaging in gross misconduct, membership in ACM may be terminated.

This Code and the supplemental Guidelines were developed by the Task Force for the Revision of the ACM Code of Ethics and Professional Conduct: Ronald E. Anderson, Chair, Gerald Engel, Donald Gotterbarn, Grace C. Hertlein, Alex Hoffman, Bruce Jawer, Deborah G. Johnson, Doris K. Lidtke, Joyce Currie Little, Dianne Martin, Donn B. Parker, Judith A. Perrolle, and Richard S. Rosenberg. The Task Force was organized by ACM/SIGCAS and funding was provided by the ACM SIG Discretionary Fund. This Code and the supplemental Guidelines were adopted by the ACM Council on October 16, 1992.

Glossary

3-D environments p. 332 Drawn or photographed virtual spaces you can explore with mouse clicks.

3-D modeling software p. 197 Software that enables the user to create 3-D objects. The objects can be rotated, stretched, and combined with other model objects to create complex 3-D scenes.

3G p. 283 The next generation of mobile wireless technology, which promises high-bandwidth connections that will support true multimedia, including real-time video.

802.11e p. 308 A Wi-Fi-related standard that focuses on quality of service, particularly the timely delivery of data packets.

802.11i p. 308 A Wi-Fi-related security technology that will enable businesses to use wireless networks for more sensitive transactions.

802.16e p. 308 An extension to WiMax that will let mobile computer users access the WiMax network.

A

AAC p. 210 Advanced Audio Codec, one of a number of relatively new methods of audio compression than can squeeze music files to a fraction of their original CD-file sizes, often without perceptible loss of quality.

access p. 253 Physical proximity to a person, or knowledge about that person, a common theme in privacy discussions.

access time p. 55 The amount of time, measured in nanoseconds, it takes for a CPU to retrieve a unit of data from memory. Also the amount of time, measured in milliseconds, it takes for a CPU to retrieve a unit of data from a disk drive.

access-control software p. 371 Software that only allows user access according to the user's needs. Some users can open only files that are related to their work. Some users are allowed read-only access to files they can see but not change.

accounting and financial-management software p. 170 Software especially designed to set up accounts, keep track of money flow between accounts, record transactions, adjust balances in accounts, provide an audit trail, automate routine tasks such as check writing, and produce reports.

acquisition p. 444 The process of capturing data about an event that is important to the organization.

action document p. 448 In a transaction-processing system, a document that initiates an action by the recipient or verifies for the recipient that a transaction has occurred.

ActionScript p. 526 The multimedia scripting language that's built into Adobe Flash.

ActiveX p. 336, 526 A collection of programming technologies and tools that can be used to create programs that are similar in many ways to Java applets.

Ada p. 518 A massive programming language, named for programming pioneer Ada King and based on Pascal, that was developed in the late 1970s for the U.S. Defense Department.

address p. 162 In a spreadsheet, the location of a cell, determined by row number and column number.

agents p. 134, 178 Software programs that can ask questions, respond to commands, pay attention to users' work patterns, serve as a guide and a coach, take on owners' goals, and use reasoning to fabricate their own goals.

aggregator p. 342 An RSS-reading Web browser that periodically visits Web sites, examines feeds, and displays new content.

agricultural age p. 21 The era covering most of the past ten thousand years, during which humanity lived mainly by domesticating animals and growing food using plows and other agricultural tools.

Ajax (Asynchronous JavaScript XML) p. 338 A way to support efficient interactive Web pages by eliminating excess page loads from servers.

alerts p. 341 Along with notifications, a popular noncorporate type of push technology on the Web, mostly offered through services that alert subscribers to stock price changes, breaking news, and the like.

algorithm p. 109, 511 A set of step-by-step instructions that, when completed, solves a problem.

alias p. 601 See user name.

all-in-one devices p. 82 See multifunction printer.

alpha testing p. 529 Initial testing of a system; also called "pre-beta testing."

analog signal p. 278 A continuous wave.

analog-to-digital converter (ADC) p. 76 A device that converts electrical charges into discrete values, allowing continuous signals to be stored in computers.

analysis p. 528 The phase of the systems development life cycle in which details are fleshed out before design begins.

animation p. 202, 331 The process of simulating motion with a series of still pictures.

antivirus p. 366 A program designed to search for viruses, notify users when they're found, and remove them from infected files.

applet p. 336 A small compiled program designed to run inside another application—typically a Web browser.

application program (application) p. 20, 587 Software tool that allows a computer to be used for specific purposes.

application server p. 327 A common type of Internet server that stores PC office applications, databases, or other applications and makes them available to client programs that request them.

application service provider (ASP) p. 327 A company that manages and delivers application services on a contract basis.

architecture p. 51 Design that determines how individual components of the CPU are put together on the chip. More generally used to describe the way individual components are put together to create a complete computer system.

arithmetic logic unit (ALU) p. 52 The part of the CPU that performs data calculations and comparisons.

armature p. 88 The part of a disk drive that moves the read/write head across the disk surface.

artificial intelligence (AI) p. 552 The field of computer science devoted to making computers perceive, reason, and act in ways that have, until now, been reserved for human beings.

artificial life (Alife) p. 574 Systems related to life, its, processes, and its evolution through simulations that use computer models, robotics, and biochemistry.

ASCII p. 44 American Standard Code for Information Interchange, a code that represents characters as 8-bit codes. Allows the binary computer to work with letters, digits, and special characters.

assembler p. 517 A program that translates each assembly-language instruction into a machine-language instruction.

assembly language p. 517 A language that is functionally equivalent to machine language but is easier for people to read, write, and understand. Programmers use alphabetic codes that correspond to the machine's numeric instructions.

asynchronous communication p. 295 Delayed communication, such as that used for newsgroups and mailing lists, where the sender and the recipients don't have to be logged in at the same time.

attachments p. 292, 601 A way to send formatted word processor documents, pictures, and other multimedia files via email.

audio digitizers p. 75, 207 Hardware devices or software programs that capture a sound and store it as a data file on a disk.

audit-control software p. 376 Applications that monitor and record computer transactions as they happen so auditors can trace and identify suspicious computer activity after the fact.

augmented reality (AR) p. 224 The use of computer displays that add virtual information to a person's sensory perceptions, supplementing rather than replacing (as in virtual reality) the world the user sees.

authentication p. 117 The process that operating systems use on multiuser computers to determine that users are who they claim to be. Also a process for unlocking some purchased software online.

authoring tools p. 418 Software used to create multimedia presentations.

authorization p. 117 The process that operating systems use on multiuser computers, in order to ensure that users have permission to perform a particular action.

automated factory p. 400 A factory that uses extensive computer systems, robots, and networks to streamline and automate many jobs.

automated offices p. 401 Offices that use extensive computer systems and networks to streamline information flow and automate many processes.

automated teller machine (ATM) p. 277 A device that enables users to remotely access and deposit money from their bank accounts through the use of a network.

automatic correction (autocorrect) p. 147 A word processing feature that catches and corrects common typing errors.

automatic footnoting p. 147 A word processing feature that places footnotes where they belong on the page.

automatic formatting (autoformat) p. 147 A word processing feature that applies formatting to the text.

automatic hyphenation p. 147 A word processing feature that divides long words that fall at the ends of lines.

automatic link p. 165 A link between worksheets in a spreadsheet that ensures that a change in one worksheet is reflected in the other.

automatic recalculation p. 164 A spreadsheet capability that allows for easy correction of errors and makes it easy to try out different values while searching for solutions.

automatic speech recognition p. 566 See speech recognition.

automatic translation p. 556 The process of using software to translate written or spoken communication from one natural language to another.

autonomous systems p. 384 Complex systems that can assume almost complete responsibility for a task without human input, verification, or decision making.

autosave p. 124 A feature of many software applications that automatically saves your work every few minutes, so you don't lose more than a few minutes of work in a freeze or crash.

avatars p. 224, 295 Graphical bodies used to represent a person in a virtual meeting place; can range from a simple cartoon sketch to an elaborate 3-D figure or an exotic abstract icon.

B

Back and Forward buttons p. 599 Browser buttons that allow you to retrace your steps while navigating the Web and return to previously visited sites.

backbone network p. 278 A collection of common pathways used to transmit large quantities of data between networks in a wide-area network (WAN).

backup copy p. 594 A copy of a file created as insurance against the loss of the original.

backup media p. 594 Disks, CD-Rs, and other technologies to hold backup files and to save computer storage space.

backup p. 376 The process of saving data—especially for data recovery. Many systems automatically back up data and software onto disks or tapes.

backward compatible p. 48 Able to run software written for older CPUs. Also, when referring to a software program, able to read and write files compatible with older versions of the program.

bandwidth p. 276 The quantity of information that can be transmitted through a communication medium in a given amount of time.

bar chart p. 166 A chart that shows relative values with bars, appropriate when data fall into a few categories.

bar code reader p. 72 A reading tool that uses light to read universal product codes, inventory codes, and other codes created out of patterns of variable-width bars.

BASIC p. 518 Beginner's All-purpose Symbolic Instruction Code, a programming language developed in the 1960s as an easy-to-learn, interactive alternative to FORTRAN for beginning programmers; it is still widely used today in forms such as Microsoft's popular Visual Basic.

batch processing p. 249, 445 Accumulating transactions and feeding them into a computer in large batches.

bay p. 57, 91 An open area in the system box for disk drives and other peripheral devices.

BD-R p. 91 Drives that can read data from Blu-ray discs, DVDs, and CDs.

BD-RW p. 91 Drives that can read data from, and record data on, Blu-ray discs, DVDs, CDs, and BD-R.

beta testing p. 529 Testing of almost-finished software by potential end users.

binary p. 41 A choice of two values, such as yes and no or zero and one.

binary number system p. 44 A system that denotes all numbers with combinations of two digits.

biometrics p. 370 Measurements of individual body characteristics, such as a voiceprint or fingerprint; sometimes used in computer security.

bit p. 41 Binary digit, the smallest unit of information. A bit can have two values: 0 or 1.

bit depth p. 79, 190 Color depth, the number of bits devoted to each pixel in a color display.

bitmapped graphics p. 190 Graphics in which images are stored and manipulated as organized collections of pixels rather than as shapes and lines. Contrast with object-oriented graphics.

bits per second (bps) p. 279 The standard unit of measure for modem speed.

BitTorrent p. 303 A peer-to-peer protocol used to download and share very large files.

blended learning p. 420 The combination of e-learning with traditional face-to-face learning.

blocks p. 131 Units of data or memory, made up of bundles of sectors, on a hard disk.

blog p. 294 Short for Web log, a personal Web page that often carries diary-like entries or political commentaries. Blogs are fast proliferating as new software allows users to create Web pages without having to learn the technical details of HTML and Web authoring.

bloggers p. 295 People who write blogs or microblogs.

blogosphere p. 295 A term used to describe the online community of bloggers and their blogs.

Bluetooth (802.15) p. 282 A type of wireless technology that enables mobile phones, handheld computers, and PCs to communicate with each other regardless of operating system.

Blu-Ray (BD) drive p. 91 A drive that can read and write on optical media that hold up to 50 gigabytes on two layers.

bookmarks p. 599 Personal lists kept on a browser of favorite or memorable Web sites that are often revisited. Also called favorites.

Boolean logic p. 339 A complex query structure supported by most search engines; one example is "American AND Indian BUT NOT Cleveland."

booting p. 121 Loading the non-ROM part of the operating system into memory.

bot p. 178, 368 Software robots that crawl around the Web collecting information, helping consumers make decisions, answering email, and even playing games.

botnet p. 369 A malicious network made up of bots, or zombie computers, often used by spammers, phishers, and other Internet criminals.

bounce p. 298 The automatic return of an undeliverable email message to its sender.

boundary p. 439 A The limits of a computer system.

broadband connection p. 279 An Internet connection such as DSL or cable modem that offers higher bandwidth, and therefore faster transmission speed, than standard modem connections.

browse p. 237 The process of finding information in a database or other data source, such as the World Wide Web.

browsers p. 15 Programs such as Internet Explorer and Firefox that serve as navigable windows into the Web.

brute-force p. 555 An exhaustive searching technique where the computer rapidly repeats a simple operation until the correct answer is found.

bug p. 108 An error in programming.

bullet charts p. 199 Graphical elements, such as drawings and tables, integrated into a series of charts that list the main points of a presentation.

burn p. 207 To record data onto CD-R and CD-RW disks.

bus p. 57 Group of wires on a circuit board. Information travels between components through a bus.

business alliance p. 449 A cooperative arrangement between two or more businesses with complementary capabilities.

business organization p. 441 A company or a firm; a system designed for the purpose of creating products and services for customers.

business-to-business (B2B) p. 403, 477 E-commerce transactions that involve businesses providing goods or services to other businesses.

business-to-consumer (B2C) p. 403, 477 E-commerce transactions that involve businesses providing goods or services to consumers.

business-to-employee (B2E) p. 477 Another name for the B2B model when the focus is primarily on handling the activities that take place within the organization.

button p. 220 A hot spot on a screen that responds to mouse clicks. A button can be programmed to perform one of many tasks, such as opening a dialog box or launching an application.

byte p. 44 Grouping of 8 bits.

C

C p. 518 A complex computer language invented at Bell Labs in the early 1970s as a tool for programming operating systems such as UNIX; now one of the most widely used programming languages.

C# p. 518 A popular Windows-only programming language that's similar to C++.

C++ p. 518 A variation of the C programming language that takes advantage of a modern programming methodology called object-oriented programming.

cable modems p. 279 A type of broadband Internet connection that uses the same network of coaxial cables that delivers TV signals.

cards p. 57 See expansion card.

carpal tunnel syndrome p. 86 An affliction of the wrist and hand that results from repeating the same movements over long periods.

cascading style sheets p. 335 A feature of dynamic HTML that gives users more control over how a Web page is displayed. Cascading style sheets can define formatting and layout elements that aren't recognized in older versions of HTML.

cathode-ray tube (CRT) monitor p. 81 A computer display made from a large electronic vacuum tube, similar to the classic television display.

CD-R p. 87, 99 Compact disc—recordable, an optical disc you can write information on, but you cannot remove the information.

CD-ROM p. 87, 99 Compact disc—read-only memory, a type of optical disc that contains data that cannot be changed; CD-ROMs are commonly used to distribute commercial software programs.

CD-ROM drive p. 87 A common optical drive in computers that can read data from CD-ROM discs.

CD-RW p. 99 Compact disc—rewritable, an optical disc that allows writing, erasing, and rewriting.

CD-RW drive p. 87 A disc drive that can read and write on rewritable optical discs.

cell p. 162 The intersection of a row and a column on the grid of a spreadsheet.

central processing unit (CPU) p. 39, 584 Part of the computer that processes information, performs arithmetic calculations, and makes basic decisions based on information values.

centralized database p. 249 A database housed in a mainframe computer, accessible only to information-processing personnel.

channel p. 341 See feed.

character-based interface p. 121 A user interface based on text characters rather than graphics.

charge-coupled device (CCD) p. 76 A device, as in a digital camera, that converts light into electrons.

chat room p. 295 Public real-time teleconference.

chief information officers (CIOs) p. 401, 451 Along with chief technology officers (CTOs), the chief decision makers concerning enterprise computer systems and technology in a business enterprise.

chief technology officer (CTO) p. 401 The chief decision maker in a business or organization, who is concerned with enterprise computer systems and technology.

class p. 252 In an object-oriented database, the data contained in the object as well as the kinds of operations that may be performed on the data.

clean install p. 125 A completely new installation of an operating system or application.

click p. 582 The action of pressing a button on a mouse.

client p. 286 Computers in a network program that are not acting as dedicated servers.

client/server p. 249 Client programs in desktop computers send information requests through a network to server databases on mainframes, minicomputers, or desktop computers; the servers process queries and send the requested data back to the client.

client/server model p. 286 For a local-area network, a hierarchical model in which one or more computers act as dedicated servers and all the remaining computers act as clients. The server fills requests from clients for data and other resources.

clip art p. 194 A collection of redrawn images that you can cut out and paste into your own documents.

clipboard p. 587 A word processing program text-editing tool for temporarily storing chunks of text and other data.

clock p. 50 The timing device producing electrical pulses for synchronizing the computer's operations.

Close p. 130 An operation that allows you to stop working on a project but remain in the application program.

cloud computing p. 307 A type of grid computing in which resources (storage, applications, data, and more) are distributed across the Internet rather than confined to a single machine. Resources seem to be coming from "the cloud" (the Internet) rather than from a particular computer.

cluster p. 51, 131 A grouping of multiple processors or servers to, for example, improve graphic rendering speeds or increase reliability.

CMOS p. 55, 76 Complementary metal oxide semiconductor, a special low-energy kind of RAM that can store small amounts of data for long periods of time on battery power. CMOS RAM is used to store the date, time, and calendar in a PC. CMOS RAM is called parameter RAM in Macintoshes.

COBOL p. 518 Common Business Oriented Language, developed when the U.S. government in 1960 demanded a new language oriented toward business data-processing problems.

code of ethics p. 463 Policies and procedures, such as those developed by companies and by organizations such as the ACM (Association for Computing Machinery), to guide the behavior of information workers.

Code of Fair Information Practices p. 259 A set of guidelines produced for Congress by a panel of experts in the early 1970s that called for a ban on secret government databases, citizen access to personal information kept in government databases, and agency responsibility for database reliability and security.

coding p. 514 Writing a program from an algorithm.

cognitive radio p. 308 An experimental type of wireless technology that makes more efficient use of available bandwidth. For example, cognitive radio might be able to sense which frequencies have the least traffic and route traffic to those channels that provide the best quality of service, and find ways to share the available radio spectrum fairly among all types of users.

color depth p. 79, 190 Bit depth, the number of bits devoted to each pixel.

color-matching p. 158 The technology of trying to match colors on a monitor's screen to printed colors, so that the color balance is the same.

color monitor p. 78 A monitor capable of displaying a wide range of colors, with greater depth than a grayscale monitor.

columns p. 162 Along with rows, comprise the grid of a spreadsheet.

command-line interface p. 121 User interface that requires the user to type text commands on a command-line to communicate with the operating system.

communication software p. 284 Software that enables computers to interact with each other over a phone line or other network.

compatible (compatibility) p. 48, 113 The ability of a software program to run on a specific computer system. Also, the ability of a hardware device to function with a particular type of computer.

compiler p. 109, 515 A translator program that translates an entire program from a high-level computer language before the program is run for the first time.

component software p. 524 Software designed in small, independent units (components) that can be plugged into applications and operating systems to add features as needed.

compression p. 207 Making files smaller using special encoding schemes. File compression saves storage space on disks and saves transmission time when files are transferred through networks.

computed field p. 237 In a database, a field containing formulas similar to spreadsheet formulas; they display values calculated from values in other numeric fields.

computer architecture p. 538 The branch of computer science that deals with the way hardware and software work together.

computer crime p. 361 Any crime accomplished through knowledge or use of computer technology.

computer forensics p. 361 The use of computer technology and applications as tools to help law enforcement officials stop criminal activities.

computer monitoring p. 407 Using computer technology to track, record, and evaluate worker performance, often without the knowledge of the worker.

computer science p. 536 A relatively new discipline that focuses on the process of computing through several areas of specialization, including theory, algorithms, data structures, programming concepts and languages, computer architecture, management information systems, artificial intelligence, and software engineering.

computer security p. 369 Protecting computer systems and the information they contain against unwanted access, damage, modification, or destruction.

computer telephony integration (CTI) p. 297 The linking of computers and telephones to gain productivity, such as by allowing PCs to serve as speakerphones, answering machines, and complete voicemail systems.

computer-aided design (CAD) p. 198 The use of computers to draw products or process designs on the screen.

computer-aided instruction (CAI) p. 413 Software programs for teaching that combine drill-and-practice software and tutorial software.

computer-aided manufacturing (CAM) p. 198 When the design of a product is completed, the numbers are fed to a program that controls the manufacturing of parts. For electronic parts the design translates directly into a template for etching circuits onto chips. Also called computer-integrated manufacturing (CIM).

computer-aided systems engineering (CASE) p. 535 Commercially available software packages that typically include charting and diagramming tools, a centralized data dictionary, a user interface generator, and code generators.

computer-integrated manufacturing (CIM) p. 198 The combination of CAD and CAM.

consumer-to-consumer (C2C) p. 477 The e-commerce model which represents individuals, organizations, or companies that are selling and buying directly with each other via the Internet.

context-sensitive menus p. 123 Menus offering choices that depend on the context.

contract p. 132 A type of law that covers trade secrets.

control p. 462 A function within a system that evaluates the feedback data and adjusts the system's input and processing functions to ensure the desired output is produced.

control structures p. 513 Logical structures that control the order in which instructions are carried out.

cookie p. 332 Small files deposited on a user's hard disk by Web sites, enabling sites to remember what they know about their visitors between sessions.

copy p. 587 A word processing program text-editing tool that allows you to make a copy of a set of words or data and place the copy elsewhere in the same or a different document.

copy protected p. 114 Produced in a way that prevents any physical copying, such as is the case with software CDs and DVDs, especially some entertainment products.

copyright p. 132 A type of law that traditionally protects forms of literary expression.

copyrighted software p. 114 Software that prevents a disk from being copied.

corporate portals p. 339 Specialized portals on an intranet that serve the employees of a particular corporation.

cost-benefit analysis p. 462 A comparison of costs (such as the salaries of the information system staff) to benefits (such as a reduction in the number of customer complaints), which managers use to decide whether an information system project is worthwhile on its own merits and also in comparison with other proposed information system projects.

courseware p. 413 Educational software.

CPU p. 39, 584 See central processing unit.

cracking p. 368 Unauthorized access and/or vandalism of computer systems; short for criminal hacking.

critical path method (CPM) p. 462 A mathematical model of a project's schedule used to calculate when particular activities will be completed.

critical success factors (CSF) p. 461 A strategic planning approach that identifies the variables that are crucial for the success of the business from the top managers' point of view and identifies IT plans for systems that provide access to information about those critical success factors.

cross-platform applications p. 127 Programs, such as Adobe Photoshop, that are available in similar versions for multiple platforms.

crowdsourcing p. 303 A type of information and/or labor sharing in which a task is outsourced to a large community of people, possibly volunteers, rather than to a small group of contracted specialists.

CRT (cathode-ray tube) monitors p. 81 Television-style monitors used as the output device for many desktop computers.

cursor p. 585 A line or rectangle, sometimes flashing, that indicates your location on the screen or in a document.

cursor (arrow) key p. 585 A keyboard key that moves the cursor up or down, right or left, on the screen.

custom application p. 116 An application programmed for a specific purpose, typically for a specific client.

customer relationship management (CRM) p. 250, 478 Software systems for organizing and tracking information on customers.

cut p. 587 A word processing program text-editing tool that allows you to delete a set of words or data; often used with the copy function to move text around.

cybercrime p. 361 Any crime accomplished through knowledge or use of computer technology.

cyberspace p. 349 A term used to describe the Internet and other online networks, especially the artificial realities and virtual communities that form on them. First coined by William Gibson in his novel, *Neuromancer*.

cyberstalking p. 361 A form of harrassment that takes place on the Internet.

D

data p. 39 Information in a form that can be read, used, and manipulated by a computer.

data dictionary p. 534 A catalog, or directory, that describes all the data flowing through a system.

data files p. 587 Documents that contain passive data rather than instructions.

data flow diagram p. 534 A simple graphical depiction of the movement of data through a system.

data management p. 453 A component of the decision support system, in which a manager queries and retrieves relevant information from a database of internal and external information of the organization.

data mining p. 250 The discovery and extraction of hidden predictive information from large databases.

data scrubbing (data cleansing) p. 250 The process of going through a database and eliminating records that contain errors.

data structures p. 535 A set of data elements used together, such as an invoice or other paper or electronic document.

data translation software p. 287 Software that enables users of different systems with incompatible file formats to read and modify each other's files.

data type p. 236 See field type.

data warehouse p. 249 An integrated collection of corporate data stored in one location.

data warehousing p. 448 Software used to create and maintain large databases.

database p. 236 A collection of information stored in an organized form in a computer.

database-management system (DBMS) p. 245 A program or system of programs that can manipulate data in a large collection of files (the database), cross-referencing between files as needed.

database program p. 236 A software tool for organizing the storage and retrieval of the information in a database.

database server p. 249 A powerful computer for holding and managing an interactive, multiuser database.

data-driven Web site p. 336 A Web site that can display dynamic, changeable content without having constantly redesigned pages, due to an evolving database that separates the site's content from its design.

date field p. 237 A field containing only dates.

debugger p. 515 A program used to simplify the process of locating and correcting errors during the program development process.

debugging p. 109 Finding and correcting errors—bugs—in computer software.

decision p. 513 The process of choosing between alternative courses of action under a given set of conditions.

decision support system (DSS) p. 453 A computer system that provides managers with the tools they need to analyze information they deem relevant for a particular decision or class of decisions.

decision table p. 535 A table that shows, in a row/column format, the decision rules that apply and what actions to take when certain conditions occur.

decode unit p. 53 Takes the instruction read by the prefetcher and translates it into a form suitable for the CPU's internal processing.

defragmentation utility p. 131 A program that eliminates fragmented files by changing the assignment of clusters to files.

Delete key p. 585 A keyboard key that acts as an eraser by, for example, removing highlighted text in a word document.

denial of service (DoS) attack p. 369 A type of computer vandalism that bombards servers and Web sites with so much bogus traffic that they're effectively shut down, denying service to legitimate customers and clients.

design p. 529 The phase of the systems development life cycle that focuses on how the problem will be solved.

de-skilled p. 406 Transformed in such a way that a job requires less skill.

desktop computer p. 10 A personal computer designed to be set up on a desk or table and used in that place for an extended period of time.

desktop publishing (DTP) p. 153 Software used mainly to produce print publications. Also, the process of using desktop-publishing software to produce publications.

development p. 529 The phase of the systems development life cycle in which the system is built and tested.

device drivers p. 120 Small programs that allow input/output devices to communicate with the computer.

dialog management component p. 456, 457 A component of the executive information system made up of the set of human-computer interactive features that enables the executive to select the necessary data and display it in a variety of formats, including summary and exception reports, lists, charts, tables, and graphs.

dial-up connection p. 278, 353 A connection to the Internet that uses a modem and standard phone lines.

digit p. 41 A discrete, countable unit.

digital p. 41 Information made up of discrete units that can be counted.

digital audio workstation (DAW) p. 212 Software that incorporates sequencing, recording, and mixing capabilities in a single program.

digital camera p. 75 A camera that captures images and stores them as bit patterns on disks or other digital storage media instead of using film.

digital divide p. 25, 348 A term that describes the divide between the people who do and do not have access to the Internet.

digital photo p. 193 A photograph captured with a digital camera.

digital rights management (DRM) p. 211 Technology now being used in many audio files to protect musicians' and other artists' intellectual property.

digital signal p. 278 A stream of bits.

digital signal processing (DSP) p. 76 Compressing or mathematically altering streams of bits before they are transmitted to the CPU. DSP is typically done by a DSP chip.

digital signatures p. 346 A developing identity-verification standard that uses encryption techniques to protect against email forgery.

digital-to-analog converter (DAC) p. 77 A device on a sound card that converts digitized waves into analog signals.

digital video p. 204 Video reduced to a series of numbers, which can be edited, stored, and played back without loss of quality.

digital video camera p. 75 A video camera that captures footage in digital form so that clips can be transferred to and from a computer for editing with no loss of quality.

digitize p. 74 Converting information into a digital form that can be stored in the computer's memory.

digitized sound p. 567 Computerized sound output.

digitized speech p. 567 Computerized voice output that mimics human speech.

DIMMs p. 56 Dual in-line memory modules.

direct (dedicated) connection p. 278, 596 A dedicated, direct connection to the Internet through a LAN, with the computer having its own IP address.

directories p. 250 See directory.

directory p. 339, 660 A logical container used to group files and other directories. Also called a folder.

dirty data p. 250 Data records with spelling mistakes, incorrect or obsolete values, or other errors.

disaggregation p. 490 Separating commerce into its component parts and outsourcing those parts that can better be handled somewhere else.

disk drive p. 85 See diskette drive.

diskette p. 85 Also called a floppy disk, this is a small, 3.5-inch magnetically sensitive, flexible plastic wafer housed in a plastic case. Diskettes were popular for storing and transporting data in early PCs, but today they've been largely supplanted by faster media with larger capacities.

diskette (disk) drive p. 85 Device used to retrieve information from a disk and, in some cases, to transfer data to it.

display p. 78, 585 See monitor.

distance education p. 419 Using computers, networks, and other technology to extend the educational process beyond the walls of a school, connecting students and faculty at remote locations.

distributed computing p. 306, 402 Integrating all kinds of computers, from mainframes to PCs, into a single, seamless system.

distributed database p. 249 Data strewn out across networks on several different computers.

distributed denial of service (DDoS) attack p. 369 A denial of service attack in which the flood of messages comes from many compromised systems distributed across the Net.

distributed intelligence p. 573 Artificial intelligence concepts applied to networks rather than to individual computers.

document p. 587 A file, such as a term paper or chart, created with applications.

documentation p. 112 Instructions for installing the software on a computer's hard disc.

domain name registry p. 329 A company that provides its customers with domain names that are easier to remember and use.

domain name system (DNS) p. 323 A system that translates a computer's numerical IP address into an easier-to-remember string of names separated by dots.

domains p. 323 A class of Internet addresses indicated by a suffix such as .com, .gov, or .net.

dot-coms p. 475 Internet-based companies.

dot matrix printer p. 81 A type of impact printer, which forms images by physically striking paper, ribbon, and print hammer together, the way a typewriter does.

dots per inch (dpi) p. 190 A measurement of the density of pixels, defining the resolution of a graphic.

double-click p. 586 To click a mouse button twice in rapid succession.

download p. 287 To copy software from an online source to a local computer.

downloadable audio p. 331 Compressed sound files that you must download onto your computer's hard disk before the browser or some other application can play them.

downloadable video p. 331 Compressed video files that can be downloaded and viewed on a computer.

drag p. 586 To move the mouse while holding the mouse button down. Used for moving objects, selecting text, drawing, and other tasks.

drag-and-drop p. 587 A word processing program text-editing tool that allows you to move a selected block of text from one location to another.

drawing software p. 195 Stores a picture as a collection of lines and shapes. Also stores shapes as shape formulas and text as text.

drill-and-practice software p. 413 Teaching software based on the principles of individualized rate, small steps, and positive feedback.

drive-by download p. 366 A spyware download onto your computer that occurs simply by visiting certain Web sites.

drum scanners p. 74 Scanners used in publishing applications where image quality is critical.

DSL (digital subscriber line) p. 279 A type of broadband connection to the Internet offered by phone companies.

DVD burner p. 91 Rewritable DVD drives.

DVD/CD-RW drive p. 91 A disc drive that combines the capabilities of a DVD-ROM drive and a CD-RW drive in a single unit.

DVD+R p. 91 Recordable DVD disc.

DVD+RW p. 91 DVD disc that allows writing, erasing, and rewriting.

DVD-RAM p. 91 A type of optical disc with multigigabyte capacity that can be read, written, and erased.

DVD-ROM drive p. 91 An optical disc drive that can read high-capacity DVD discs.

dynamic IP address p. 323 An IP address that is assigned to a device when it connects to the internet; when that device disconnects from the Internet, the IP address may be reused.

E

e-business p. 475 Though sometimes used interchangeably with the broader term e-commerce, here used to refer to the e-commerce activities of a particular company or organization.

e-commerce p. 475 The sales aspect of e-business, including the buying and selling of products or services over the Internet and other electronic systems. (Many people use the terms e-commerce and e-business interchangably.)

educational simulations p. 415 Software that enables students to explore artificial environments that are imaginary or based on reality. Most have the look and feel of a game, but they challenge students to learn through exploration, experimentation, and interaction with other students.

edutainment p. 424 Programs geared toward home markets that combine education and entertainment.

effectiveness p. 443 How an organization's customers evaluate the quality of the output—products and services—of the value chain.

efficiency p. 443 How an organization's primary and support activities produce desired output with less work or lower costs.

e-learning p. 470 A term describing electronic tools and techniques used in distance learning environments.

electronic book (ebook) p. 160 A handheld device that displays digital representations of the contents of books.

electronic commerce (e-commerce) p. 277, 403 Business transactions through electronic networks.

electronic cottage p. 404 A home in which modern technology enables a person to work at home.

electronic data interchange (EDI) p. 449 A set of specifications for conducting basic business transactions over private networks.

electronic mail (email) p. 15, 600 Allows Internet users to send mail messages, data files, and software programs to other Internet users and to users of most commercial networks and online services.

electronic money p. 346 A system for purchasing goods and services on the Internet without using credit cards.

electronic paper (epaper) p. 161 A flexible, portable, paperlike display.

electronic payment system p. 483 An online credit card transaction in which a trusted third party transfers funds from one person or business to another, thereby concealing the credit card information of the buyer from the seller.

electronic phone directory p. 241 A specialized database that can pack millions of names and phone numbers onto a single CD-ROM or Web site.

electronic street atlas p. 241 A specialized database that can pinpoint addresses and, with the aid of global positioning system (GPS) technology, locations.

electronic sweatshops p. 408 Worker warehouses where most of the work is mindless keyboarding, computer monitoring is a common practice, wages are low and working conditions poor, and repetitive stress injuries are common.

electronica p. 212 Sequenced music that is designed from the ground up with digital technology.

email server p. 325 A specialized server that acts like a local post office for a particular Internet host.

embedded system p. 10 A computer that is embedded into a consumer product, such as a wristwatch or game machine, to enhance those products. Also used to control hardware devices.

emulation p. 127 A process that enables programs to run on a noncompatible operating system.

encapsulation p. 479 A program that translates all Windows-related instructions into instructions that a Mac's operating system and CPU can understand.

encryption p. 373 Protects transmitted information by scrambling the transmissions. When a user encrypts a message by applying a secret numerical code (encryption key), the message can be transmitted or stored as an indecipherable garble of characters. The message can be read only after it's been reconstructed with a matching key.

encryption key p. 373 A secret numerical code that can be used to scramble network transmissions; a matching key is needed to reconstruct the message.

end user p. 527 A person who uses the information system directly or uses the information produced by the system.

end-user development p. 527 A systems development approach in which a project team comprising only end users develops many small-scale systems without the direct involvement of a professional systems analyst.

end-user license agreement (EULA) p. 113 An agreement typically including specifications for how a program may be used, warranty disclaimers, and rules concerning the copying of the software.

Enter (enter key) p. 585 A keyboard key with a number of special functions, such as moving the cursor to the beginning of the next line, or activating a selected option.

enterprise resource planning (ERP) p. 448 Creating information systems to support an organization's operational business processes.

entry barrier p. 459 An innovative new product or service that is difficult for a competitor to emulate.

environment p. 439 Anything that is outside a system's boundary.

equation solver p. 166 A feature of some spreadsheet programs that determines data values.

ergonomic keyboard p. 67 A keyboard that places the keys at angles that allow your wrists to assume a more natural position while you type, potentially reducing the risk of repetitive-stress injuries.

ergonomics p. 86 The science of designing work environments that enable people and things to interact efficiently and safely.

Ethernet p. 274 A popular networking architecture developed in 1976 at Xerox.

executable files p. 587 Files, such as applications, that contain instructions that can be executed by the computer.

executive information system (EIS) p. 456 A system that combines features of management information and decision support systems to support unstructured decision making by top managers.

expansion cards p. 57 Special-purpose circuit boards that can be inserted in a computer's expansion slots.

expansion slot p. 57 An area inside the computer's housing that holds special-purpose circuit boards.

expert systems (ES) p. 456, 561 Information systems or software programs designed to replicate the decision-making process of a human expert.

expert system shells p. 564 Generic expert systems containing human interfaces and inference engines.

export data p. 239 Transmitting records and fields from a database program to another program.

express card p. 57 A small removable card that might add additional memory, a peripheral, and/or additional ports to a laptop computer.

extension p. 593 A file name feature, usually three characters following a period at the end of the file name, that gives more information about the file's origin or use.

external bus p. 57 A cable designed to transmit data back and forth between a computer and its external peripherals.

external drives p. 91, 584 Disk drives, such as hard disks for additional storage, not included in a system unit but rather attached to it via cables.

external modem p. 278 A modem located in a box linked to a serial port or USB port, rather than being installed on a circuit board inside the computer's chassis.

extranet p. 402, 479 A corporation's intranet that is opened up to work with strategic partners and customers.

extreme programming (XP) p. 525 A relatively new programming methodology that focuses more on the culture of programming than on technology, in which the entire programming team "owns" the code; each member of the team has a right to improve it and the responsibility for making it work properly.

F

facsimile (fax) machine p. 82, 279 An output device capable of sending, in effect, a photocopy through a telephone line, allowing for fast and convenient transmission of information stored on paper.

FAQs (frequently asked questions) p. 305 Posted lists of common queries and their answers.

Fast Ethernet p. 276 An Ethernet standard that carries traffic at 100 megabits per second, provided that all the devices on the LAN are Fast Ethernet compatible.

favorites p. 599 See bookmarks.

fax modem p. 82, 279 Hardware peripheral that enables a computer to send onscreen documents to a receiving fax machine by translating the document into signals that can be sent over phone wires and decoded by the receiving fax machine.

feed p. 341 A list of changes to a website or podcast, kept in a standard format.

feedback p. 439 A function within a system that measures the performance of the input, processing, and output functions. It also provides the measurement data to the control function.

feedback loop p. 170 During flight simulation, the part where plane and pilot react to data from each other.

feedback loop p. 176 In a computer simulation, the user and the computer responding to data from each other.

field p. 236 Each discrete chunk of information in a database record.

field type p. 236 The characteristic of a field that determines the kind of information that can be stored in that field.

fifth generation language (5GL) p. 524 The fifth generation of programming languages (after machine, assembly, high-level languages, and fourth generation), it is a constraint-driven language. Instead of specifying an algorithm, the programmer defines the conditions that need to be met and the computer solves the problem. 5GLs are not widely used outside of research labs.

file p. 47, 587 An organized collection of related information stored in a computer-readable form.

file compression p. 593 The process of reducing the size of a file so that you can fit more files into the same amount of disk space.

file decompression p. 593 The process of restoring a compressed file back to its original state.

file server p. 287, 327 In a LAN, a computer used as a storehouse for software and data that are shared by several users.

file transfer protocol (FTP) p. 327 A communications protocol that enables users to download files from remote servers to their computers and to upload files they want to share from their computers to these archives.

file-management utility p. 129 A program that allows you to view, rename, copy, move, and delete files and folders.

film scanner p. 74 Also known as a slide scanner, this device can scan only slides and negatives, but generally produce higher-quality results than flatbed scanners do when scanning transparencies.

filtering software p. 346, 425 Software that, for the most part, keeps offensive and otherwise inappropriate Web content from being viewed by children, on-duty workers, and others.

Find p. 593 A command used to locate a particular word, string of characters, or formatting in a document.

find-and-replace (search and replace) p. 587 A word processing program text-editing tool that allows you to make repetitive changes throughout a document.

firewall p. 282, 371 A software or hardware "gate" that protects internal networks from unauthorized access.

FireWire (IEEE 1394, FireWire 400, FireWire 800) p. 96 See IEEE 1394.

firmware p. 10 A program, usually for special-purpose computers, stored on a ROM chip so it cannot be altered.

flatbed scanner p. 74 A scanner that looks and works like a photocopy machine, except that it creates digital images (computer files) instead of paper copies.

flash media card reader p. 92 A device that can read a flash memory card.

flash memory p. 55, 92 A type of erasable memory chip used in cell phones, pagers, portable computers, and handheld computers, among other things.

flash memory card p. 92 A type of file storage used in digital cameras to store images, in digital recorders to store sound and in a variety of computer memory devices to store and transport data. Types of flash memory devices include thumb drives, SD (Secure Digital) cards, Compact Flash cards, and Memory Sticks.

floppy disk drive p. 584 A drive found mostly on older computers that enables them to store small amounts of information on pocket-sized plastic-covered diskettes. Also called diskette drive.

folder p. 593 A container for files and other folders. Also called a directory.

font p. 587 A size and style of typeface.

footer p. 145 Block of information that appears at the bottom of every page in a document, displaying repetitive information such as an automatically calculated page number.

force feedback p. 84 Tactile feedback, such as jolts, scrapes, and bumps, transmitted via signals between a computer and a controller.

force quit p. 124 A way to shut down your computer if it freezes. In Windows, press the Ctrl + Alt + Del keys at the same time, and then click Task Manager; then select the frozen program and click End Task. On a Mac, press Command-Option-Esc or choose Force Quit from the Apple menu; then select the frozen app from the list and click Force Quit.

form views p. 237 A view of the database that shows one record at a time.

format p. 587 The way that characters, words, and paragraphs appear in a word processing document.

formatting p. 131, 587 The function of software, such as word processing software, that enables users to change the appearance of a document by specifying the font, point size, and style of any character in the document, as well as the overall layout of text and graphical elements in the document.

forms p. 331 On a Web site, pages that visitors can fill in to order goods and services, respond to questionnaires, express opinions, and the like.

formula p. 162 Step-by-step procedure for calculating a number on a spreadsheet.

FORTRAN p. 518 Formula Translation, the first commercial high-level programming language, designed at IBM in the 1950s to solve scientific and engineering problems.

fourth-generation languages (4GLs) p. 523 The fourth generation of programming languages (after machine, assembly, and high-level), which use Englishlike phrases and sentences to issue instructions, are nonprocedural, and increase productivity.

fragmented file p. 131 A file allocated to noncontiguous clusters on a disk, thus degrading the disk's performance.

frame p. 202 In animation, one still picture in a video or animated sequence.

frames p. 331 Subdivisions of a Web browser's viewing area that enable visitors to scroll and view different parts of a page—or even multiple pages—simultaneously.

full-color p. 158 A desktop-published document that uses a wide range of color. Contrast with spot color.

function p. 164 A predefined set of calculations, such as SUM and AVER-AGE, in spreadsheet software.

function keys (F-keys) p. 585 Keyboard keys, often twelve lined along the top of the keyboard, that send special commands to the computer depending on the program being run.

fuzzy logic p. 562 A type of logic that allows conclusions to be stated as probabilities rather than certainties.

G

game controller p. 68 A device for providing input to computer games. Typically includes one or more buttons and a joystick or other pointing device.

gamepad p. 68 A multi-button device used to play computer games. It is held in both hands and typically includes a small joystick.

Gantt chart p. 462 A type of chart capable of representing a project schedule visually, by showing each step or category of steps in a plan, along with their planned and actual start and completion times.

GB (gigabyte) p. 47 Approximately 1000MB.

generation p. 376 One cycle of backups; many data-processing shops keep several generations of backups so they can, if necessary, go back several days, weeks, or years to reconstruct data files.

geographical information system (GIS) p. 241, 456 A specialized database that combines tables of data with demographic information and displays geographic and demographic data on maps.

Gigabit Ethernet p. 276 An Ethernet standard that is capable of transferring 1 gigabit of data per second on an all gigabit-Ethernet LAN.

gigahertz p. 51 Billions of clock cycles per second, a measurement of a computer's clock speed.

GIGO (garbage in, garbage out) p. 168 Valid output requires valid input.

Global Positioning System (GPS) p. 277 A defense department system with 24 satellites that can pinpoint any location on the Earth.

globalization p. 409 The creation of global businesses and markets.

Government Web portals p. 339 Portals that serve as entry points to many federal, state, and municipal government Web sites.

GPS receiver p. 277 A device that can use Global Positioning System signals to determine its location and communicate that information to a person or a computer.

grammar and style checker p. 149 Component of word processing software that analyzes each word in context, checking for content errors, common grammatical errors, and stylistic problems.

graphical user interface (GUI) p. 122 A user interface based on graphical displays. With a mouse, the user points to icons that represent files, folders, and disks. Documents are displayed in windows. The user selects commands from menus.

graphics tablet p. 68 A pressure-sensitive touch tablet used as a pointing device. The user presses on the tablet with a stylus.

gray-scale graphics p. 189 Computerized imaging that allows each pixel to appear as black, white, or one of several shades of gray.

grayscale monitors p. 79 Monitor that displays black, white, and shades of gray but no other colors.

grid computing p. 306 A form of distributed computing in which not files, but processing power is shared between networked computers.

group decision support system (GDSS) p. 456 Systems designed to improve the productivity of decision-making meetings by enhancing the dynamics of collaborative work.

groupware p. 150, 287, 402 Software designed to be used by work groups rather than individuals.

H

hacker p. 368, 603 Someone who uses computer skills to gain unauthorized access to computer systems. Also sometimes used to refer to a particularly talented, dedicated programmer.

hacking p. 368 Electronic trespassing and vandalism.

handwriting recognition software p. 73 Software that translates the user's handwritten forms into ASCII characters.

hard Alife p. 574 A form of artificial life that creates hardware constructs of life-like systems, such as robotic insect colonies.

hard disk p. 87, 584 A rigid, magnetically sensitive disk that spins rapidly and continuously inside the computer chassis or in a separate box attached to the computer housing. Used as a storage device.

hardware p. 584 Physical parts of the computer system.

header p. 145 Block that appears at the top of every page in a document, displaying repetitive information such as a chapter title.

help file p. 112 A documentation file that appears onscreen at the user's request.

helper application p. 324 A program designed to help users view particular types of graphics, animation, audio, or video that can't be played by the browser.

heuristic p. 555 A rule of thumb.

hexadecimal p. 515 Base 16 number system; often used to represent machine-language programs.

hierarchical menus p. 123 Menus that organize commands into compact, efficient submenus.

high-level language p. 109, 517 A programming language that falls somewhere between natural human languages and precise machine languages, developed to streamline and simplify the programming process.

hits p. 600 Web pages containing requested key words, displayed in a list by a Web search engine.

host name p. 601 The name of the host computer, network, or ISP address where the user receives email, contained in the part of an Internet email address that comes after the "at" sign (@).

host system p. 286 A computer that provides services to multiple users.

hot spots p. 281 Publicly accessible wireless access points.

hot swap p. 95 To remove and replace peripheral devices without powering down the computer and peripherals. Some modern interface standards such as USB and FireWire allow hot-swapping.

hot-swappable p. 57 A term used to describe cards and peripherals that can be inserted or removed from a computer's slots and ports while the system is running.

HTML (hypertext markup language) p. 147, 250, 328, 525 An HTML document is a text file that includes codes that describe the format, layout, and logical structure of a hypermedia document. Most Web pages are created with HTML.

http (hypertext transfer protocol) p. 328 The Internet protocol used to transfer Web pages.

hubs p. 274 Devices that allow nodes on a local area network to communicate, though only a single message at a time can move across the network.

human engineering p. 86 Also known as ergonomics, it is the science of designing work environments that enable people and things to interact efficiently and safely.

hyperlink p. 598 A word, phrase, or picture that acts as a button, enabling the user to explore the Web or a multimedia document with mouse clicks.

hypermedia p. 218 The combination of text, numbers, graphics, animation, sound effects, music, and other media in hyperlinked documents.

hypertext p. 218 An interactive cross-referenced system that allows textual information to be linked in nonsequential ways. A hypertext document contains links that lead quickly to other parts of the document or to related documents.

hypertext link p. 15 A Web connection to another document or site, like the many that loosely tie together millions of Web pages.

I

I-beam p. 586 The I-beam-shaped pointer used to highlight text and move the cursor within a text document.

icon p. 586 In a graphical user interface, a picture that represents a file, folder, or disk.

identity (ID) theft p. 255, 362, 603 The crime, committed by hackers or other unscrupulous individuals, of obtaining enough information about a person to assume his or her identity, often as a prelude to illegally using the victim's credit cards.

IEEE 1394 p. 96 An industry standard for relatively new, extremely fast serial communications protocol, especially well suited for multimedia applications such as digital video. Apple, which developed the standard, refers to IEEE 1394 as FireWire.

image analysis p. 565 The process of identifying objects and shapes in a photograph, drawing, video, or other visual image.

image-compression software p. 207 Software that is used to compress graphics and video files.

image processing software p. 193 Software that enables the user to manipulate photographs and other high-resolution images.

impact printer p. 81 Printer that forms images by physically striking paper, ribbon, and print hammer together.

implementation p. 529 The phase of the systems development life cycle in which the system is put into use.

import data p. 237 To move data into a program from another program or source.

inbox p. 601 The place where email programs and services store recipients' incoming messages.

industrial age p. 21 The recent modern era, characterized by the shift from farms to factories.

industrial network p. 450 A network that links the systems of several companies within an industry.

Industrial Revolution p. 21 The era of rapid advances in machine technology that began at the end of the eighteenth century and ushered in the industrial age.

information p. 41 Anything that can be communicated.

information age p. 21 The current era, characterized by the shift from an industrial economy to an information economy and the convergence of computer and communication technology.

information overload p. 459 The state of being bombarded with too much computer output, a risk of poorly designed information systems.

information partnership p. 450 A partnership between companies, usually from different industries, through which information is shared for the mutual benefit of each company.

information system p. 444, 526 A collection of people, machines, data, and methods organized to accomplish specific functions and to solve specific problems. Programming is part of the larger process of designing, implementing, and managing an information system.

infrared wireless p. 280 The use of invisible infrared radiation and infrared ports to send and receive digital information short distances, now possible on many laptops and handheld computers.

infrastructure p. 461 Information technology's basic framework, comprising all the organization's information systems hardware, software, and telecommunications equipment; the information system department's staff and other personnel; and the organizational structure and procedures that affect accessing, processing, and using information in the company.

inkjet printer p. 81 A nonimpact printer that sprays ink directly onto paper to produce printed text and graphic images.

input p. 439 Information taken in by the computer.

input device p. 39 Device for accepting input, such as a keyboard.

instant messaging (IM) p. 295 A technology that enables users to create buddy lists, check for buddies who are logged in, and exchange typed messages and files with those who are.

instructions p. 52 Computer codes telling the CPU to perform a specific action.

integrated circuit p. 8 A chip containing hundreds, thousands, or even millions of transistors.

intellectual property p. 132 The results of intellectual activities in the arts, science, and industry.

interactive fiction p. 426 Stories with natural-language interfaces that offer players some control over plot.

interactive movies p. 426 Video-based or animated features in which one or more characters are controlled by the viewers.

interactive multimedia p. 219 Multimedia that enables the user to take an active part in the experience.

interactive processing p. 249 Interacting with data through terminals, viewing and changing values online in real time.

interactive TV p. 426 Broadcast television with built-in options for game playing or other forms of interactivity.

interface standards p. 93 Standards for ports and other connective technology agreed on by the hardware industry so devices made by one manufacturer can be attached to systems made by other companies.

internal drives p. 91, 584 Disk drives that are included in a system unit.

internal modem p. 278 A modem that is built into the system unit.

international information system p. 450 Any information system that supports international business activities.

Internet p. 15, 596 A global interconnected network of thousands of networks linking academic, research, government, and commercial institutions, and other organizations and individuals. Also known as the Net.

Internet service provider (ISP) p. 324, 601 A business that provides its customers with connections to the Internet along with other services.

Internet telephony (IP telephony) p. 297 A combination of software and hardware technology that enables the Internet to, in effect, serve as a telephone network. Internet telephony systems can use standard telephones, computers, or both to send and receive voice messages.

Internet2 p. 320 An alternative Internet-style network that provides faster network communications for universities and research institutions.

internetworking p. 321 Connecting different types of networks and computer systems.

interorganizational information systems (IOS) p. 449 Systems that use networking technology to facilitate communication between an organization and its suppliers, customers, and other organizations.

interpreter p. 515 A translation program that translates and transmits each source code statement individually into machine language.

intranet p. 250, 286, 402, 477 A self-contained intraorganizational network that is designed using the same technology as the Internet.

investigation p. 528 Animated features in which one or more of the characters are controlled by the viewers; in the systems development life cycle, the phase to study the existing business problem or opportunity and determine whether it is feasible to develop a new system or redesign the existing system if one exists.

IP address p. 321 A unique string of four numbers separated by periods that serves as a unique address for a computer on the Internet. The IP address of the host computer and sending computer is included with every packet of information that traverses the Internet.

J

Java p. 127, 336, 518, 526 A platform-neutral, object-oriented programming language developed by Sun Microsystems for use on multiplatform networks.

Java virtual machine p. 128 Software that gives a computer the capability to run Java programs.

JavaScript p. 336, 526 An interpreted scripting language, similar to but otherwise unrelated to Java, that enables Web page designers to add scripts to HTML code.

jobless growth p. 410 A time when automation alone creates adequate productivity increases and no new jobs are created.

joystick p. 68 A gearshiftlike device used as a controller for arcade-style computer games.

jump drive p. 92 See USB drive.

justification p. 145 The alignment of text on a line: left justification (smooth left margin and ragged right margin), right justification, (smooth right margin and ragged left margin).

K

KB (kilobyte) p. 47 About 1000 bytes of information.

kerning p. 156 The spacing between letter pairs in a document.

key field p. 247 A field that contains data that uniquely identifies the record.

keyboard p. 67, 585 Input device, similar to a typewriter keyboard, for entering data and commands into the computer.

knowledge p. 561 Information that incorporates the relationships among facts.

knowledge base p. 561 A database that contains both facts and a system of rules for determining and changing the relationship among those facts.

L

label p. 162 In a spreadsheet, a text entry that provides information on what a column or row represents.

laptop computer p. 11 A flat-screen, battery-powered portable computer that you can rest on your lap.

laser printer p. 81 A nonimpact printer that uses a laser beam to create patterns of electrical charges on a rotating drum. The charged patterns attract black toner and transfer it to paper as the drum rotates.

layer p. 192 One image stacked on top of another in Adobe Photoshop.

leading p. 156 The spacing between lines of text.

legacy ports p. 95 The most common standard ports on PC system boards, including the serial port, parallel port, and keyboard/mouse port.

Level 1 cache p. 53 Memory storage that can be quickly accessed by the CPU.

Level 2 cache (L2 cache) p. 53 Memory storage that is larger than a level 1 cache but not as quickly accessed by the CPU.

life cycle p. 528 The stages in the development of a system, from initial investigation through analysis, design, implementation, maintenance, and retirement.

line chart p. 166 A chart that shows trends or relationships over time, or a relative distribution of one variable through another.

line printer p. 81 An impact printer used by mainframes to produce massive printouts. They print characters only, not graphics.

links p. 598 See hyperlink.

Linux p. 105 An operating system based on UNIX, maintained by volunteers, and distributed for free. Linux is used mostly in servers and embedded computers, but is growing in popularity as a PC operating system.

liquid crystal display (LCD) displays p. 81 Flat-panel displays, once primarily used for portable computers but now replacing bulkier CRT monitors for desktops.

LISP p. 518 List Processing, a high-level computer language developed at MIT in the late 1950s to process nonnumeric data like characters, words, and other symbols.

list views p. 237 Showing data by displaying several records in lists similar to a spreadsheet.

local area network (LAN) p. 274 Multiple personal computers connected on a network.

logged in p. 123, 601 Connected to a computer system or network.

logic bomb p. 366 A program designed to attack in response to a particular logical event or sequence of events. A type of software sabotage.

logic errors p. 515 Errors in the logical structure of a program that cause differences between what the program is supposed to do and what it actually does.

login name p. 601 See user name.

LOGO p. 518 A computer language developed in the 1960s for children.

Long Tail p. 494 A term that refers to the tail of the statistical curve that appears when you rank books, movies, or tunes by popularity. Before the Web, retailers had trouble making money on the "long tail" of that curve: the items that were less popular. However, the Web has made the selling of less popular items much easier.

lossless compression p. 209 Systems allowing files to be compressed and later decompressed without a loss of data.

lossy compression p. 209 A type of compression in which some quality is lost in the process of compression and decompression.

low-level languages p. 517 Programming languages that require the programmer to think on the machine's level and to include an enormous amount of detail in every program, such as machine language and assembly language.

Luddites p. 408 A nineteenth-century English labor group that smashed new textile machinery to protect their jobs; today the term is often used to describe someone who opposes new technology in general.

lurkers p. 294 Silent, invisible observers who don't contribute to the discussions on newsgroups and forums.

M

Mac OS p. 122, 587 The operating system for the Apple Macintosh computer.

machine language p. 109, 515 The language that computers use to process instructions. Machine language uses numeric codes to represent basic computer operations.

machine learning p. 556 Artificial intelligence techniques that make it possible for machine performance to improve based on feedback from past performance.

macro languages p. 523 User-oriented languages that enable users to create programs (macros) that automate repetitive tasks; also known as scripting languages.

macro p. 147, 364, 523 Custom-designed embedded procedure program that automates tasks in application programs.

macro viruses p. 364 Viruses that attach to and are transmitted through macros embedded in documents; usually spread via email.

magnetic disk p. 85 Storage medium with random-access capability, accessed by the computer's disk drive.

magnetic ink character reader p. 72 A device that reads numbers printed with magnetic ink on checks.

magnetic tape p. 85 A storage medium used with a tape drive to store large amounts of information in a small space at relatively low cost.

mail merge p. 150 A feature of a word processor or other program that enables it to merge names and addresses from a database mailing list into personalized form letters and mailings.

mailbox p. 601 A storage area for email messages.

mailing lists p. 293 Email discussion groups on special-interest topics. All subscribers receive messages sent to the group's mailing address.

mainframe computer p. 12 Expensive, room-sized computer, used mostly for large computing jobs.

maintenance p. 531 The phase of the systems development life cycle that involves evaluating, repairing, and enhancing the system.

malware p. 364 Malicious software, especially destructive programs such as the viruses, worms, and Trojan horses devised and spread by computer saboteurs.

management p. 451 A set of activities that helps people efficiently use resources to accomplish an organization's goals.

management information system (MIS) p. 452, 539 Also known as a management reporting system, a system that gives a manager the information he or she needs to make decisions, typically structured decisions, regarding the operational activities of the company.

management levels p. 451 The three management tiers (operational, tactical, and strategic) typically found in a large organization.

management reporting systems p. 452 Another name for management information systems because their main output is a variety of detailed, summary, and exception reports for managers.

manycore machine p. 51 Machines that may have tens or hundreds of processors per chip.

mashup p. 342 A Web page, song, video, or image that combines images, words, music, and video clips from other works. Also: A Web site that draws on external software applications, such as a real estate application that integrates Google Maps into its interface.

mask p. 192 A tool in photoshop used to cover an area of project.

massively multiplayer online role-playing games (MMORPG) p. 299, 427 Internet games that support thousands of simultaneous players, allowing them to assume roles of particular characters in shared virtual worlds.

math-processing software p. 171 Software designed to deal with complex equations and calculations. A mathematics processor enables the user to create, manipulate, and solve equations easily.

MB (megabyte) p. 47 Approximately 1000K, or 1 million bytes.

m-commerce p. 406, 490 Mobile commerce, in which workers use laptops and wireless handheld devices to take their offices with them wherever they travel.

megabits p. 47 Approximately 1000 bits.

memory p. 39, 584 Stores programs and the data they need to be instantly accessible to the CPU.

menu p. 122 An onscreen list of command choices.

menu-driven interface p. 122 User interface that enables users to choose commands from onscreen lists called menus.

mesh networks p. 276 Decentralized alternatives to today's central-hub-based networks, allowing a message to hop from wireless device to wireless device until it finds its destination.

micro-blogs p. 295 One- or two-sentence blogs that chronicle someone's minute-by-minute activities and thoughts.

microelectromechanical systems (MEMS) p. 574 Micromachines that combine electrical and mechanical components.

micromachine p. 574 Machines on the scale of a millionth of a meter.

microprocessor p. 8, 39, 47, 584 Now known as a personal computer.

Microsoft Windows p. 122, 587 The most popular and powerful PC operating system; uses a graphical user interface.

MIDI p. 210 Musical Instrument Digital Interface, a standard interface that allows electronic instruments and computers to communicate with each other and work together.

millisecond (ms) p. 55 A thousandth of a second.

mixing p. 212 The combining of multiple tracks, audio effects, and balancing volumes and audio placement to make the best possible recording.

model management p. 453 A component of the decision support system, in which a manager evaluates alternative problem solutions and identifies the best solution using appropriate software.

modeling p. 174 The use of computers to create abstract models of objects, organisms, organizations, and processes.

modem p. 278 Modulator/demodulator. A hardware device that connects a computer to a telephone line.

moderated group p. 294 An email discussion group in which a designated moderator acts as an editor, filtering out irrelevant and inappropriate messages and posting the rest.

modules p. 521 In structured programming, a program is built from smaller programs called modules.

monitor p. 78, 585 An output device that displays text and graphics onscreen.

monochrome monitors p. 79 Monitors, now dated, that can display only one color, such as green or white.

monospaced fonts p. 588 Fonts like those in the Courier family that mimic typewriters; characters, no matter how skinny or fat, always take up the same amount of space.

Moore's law p. 8 The prediction made in 1965 by Gordon Moore that the power of a silicon chip of the same price would double about every 18 months for at least two decades.

moral dilemma p. 26 A predicament for which rules and ethics don't seem to apply, or to contradict one another.

motherboard p. 47 The circuit board that contains a computer's CPU. Also called a system board.

mouse p. 68, 585 A handheld input device that, when moved around on a desktop or table, moves a pointer around the computer screen.

MP3 p. 210 A method of compression that can squeeze a music file to a fraction of its original CD file size with only slight loss of quality.

MS-DOS p. 121 Microsoft Disk Operating System, an operating system with character-based user interface; it was widely used in the 1980s and early 1990s but has been superceded by Windows.

multicasting p. 323 A technology in the Next Generation Internet (NGI) that represents a more efficient way for the same information to be transmitted to multiple Internet-connected devices.

multicore processor p. 51 A microprocessor containing multiple CPUs.

multifunction printer (MFP) p. 82 An all-in-one output device that usually combines a scanner, a laser or inkjet printer, and a fax modem.

multimedia p. 219 Using some combination of text, graphics, animation, video, music, voice, and sound effects to communicate.

multimedia-authoring software p. 220 Enables the creation and editing of multimedia documents.

multiprocessing p. 51 Employing two or more microprocessors in a computer in order to improve overall performance. Also known as symmetric multiprocessing.

multitasking p. 117 Concurrent processing for personal computers. The user can issue a command that initiates a process and continue working with other applications while the computer follows through on the command.

multi-touch p. 70 A type of input device that involves using multi-finger or multi-hand gestures to accomplish complex tasks quickly. A multi-touch device might be a touch-sensitive screen, a touch tablet, or a trackpad that can recognize the position, pressure, and movement of more than one finger or hand at a time.

N

nanosecond (ns) p. 55 A billionth of a second; a common unit of measurement for read and write access time to RAM.

nanotechnology p. 574 A billionth of a second; a common unit of measurement for read and write access time to RAM.

narrowband connections p. 279 Dial-up Internet connections; named because they don't offer much bandwidth when compared to other types of connections.

narrowcasting p. 424 Providing custom newscasts and entertainment features aimed at narrow groups or individuals.

National Infrastructure Protection Center p. 385 A state-of-the-art command center created to fight the growing threat of system sabotage. The center includes representatives of various intelligence agencies (the departments of defense, transportation, energy, and treasury), and representatives of several major corporations.

natural language p. 112, 252, 556 Language that people speak and write every day.

Net p. 596 See Internet.

.NET p. 127 An operating system platform from Microsoft that blurs the line between the Web and Microsoft's operating systems and applications.

netiquette p. 304 Rules of etiquette that apply to Internet communication.

net neutrality p. 348 Also called network neutrality, it's the principle that Internet access should be free from restrictions related to the type of equipment being connected and the type of communication being performed with that equipment.

network p. 14 A computer system that links two or more computers.

network administrators p. 275 Workers who take care of the behind-the-scenes network details so others can focus on using the network.

network license p. 287 License for multiple copies or removing restrictions on software copying and use at a network site.

network operating system (NOS) p. 285 Server operating system software for a local-area network.

neural networks (neural nets) p. 568 Distributed, parallel computing systems inspired by the structure of the human brain.

newsgroups p. 294 Ongoing public discussions on a particular subject consisting of notes written to a central Internet site and redistributed through a worldwide newsgroup network called Usenet. You can check into and out of them whenever you want; all messages are posted on virtual bulletin boards for anyone to read anytime.

Next Generation Internet (NGI) p. 323 A future nationwide web of optical fiber integrated with intelligent management software to maintain high-speed connections.

node p. 274 Each computer and shared peripheral on a local-area network.

nonimpact printer p. 81 A printer that produces characters without physically striking the page.

nonlinear editing (NLE) p. 205 A type of video editing in which audio and video clips are stored in digital form on hard disks for immediate access via video-editing software.

nonsequential p. 218 Nonvolatile memory; memory for permanent storage of information.

nonvolatile memory p. 55 Memory that is not lost when the computer is turned off. An example is the read-only memory that contains start-up instructions and other critical information.

notebook computer p. 11 Another term for laptop computer.

notifications p. 341 Along with alerts, a popular noncorporate type of push technology on the Web, notifying users about online auction status, fees due, and the like.

numeric field p. 237 A field containing only numbers.

O

object-oriented database p. 252 Instead of storing records in tables and hierarchies, stores software objects that contain procedures (or instructions) with data.

object-oriented graphics p. 195 The storage of pictures as collections of lines, shapes, and other objects.

object-oriented programming (OOP) p. 521 Programming in which a program is not just a collection of step-by-step instructions or procedures; it's a collection of objects. Objects contain both data and instructions and can send and receive messages.

objects p. 252 In object-oriented databases, a data structure defined according to its class.

online banking services p. 170 Use of the Internet to conduct basic banking transactions.

online help p. 112 Documentation and help available through a software company's Web site.

online services p. 324 Internet access and a variety of other services in a privately controlled environment offered by gateway companies such as America Online (AOL).

Open p. 129, 586 To load a file into an application program's workspace so it can be viewed and edited by the user.

open architecture p. 95 A design that allows expansion cards and peripherals to be added to a basic computer system.

open-source software p. 105 Software that can be distributed and modified freely by users; Linux is the best-known example.

open standards p. 321 Standards not owned by any company.

operating system (OS) p. 117, 585 A system of programs that performs a variety of technical operations, providing an additional layer of insulation between the user and the bits-and-bytes world of computer hardware.

operational level p. 451 The management level responsible for supervising the day-to-day activities in the organization's value chain.

optical character recognition (OCR) p. 565 Locating and identifying printed characters embedded in an image, allowing the text to be stored as an editable document. OCR can be performed by wand readers, pen scanners, and OCR software.

optical character recognition (OCR) software p. 72, 566 Software that locates and identifies printed characters embedded in images.

optical computer p. 58 A potential future alternative to silicon-based computing, in which information is transmitted in light waves rather than in electrical pulses.

optical disc drive p. 87, 584 A disk drive that uses laser beams to read and write bits of information on the surface of an optical disc.

optical mark reader p. 72 A reading device that uses reflected light to determine the location of pencil marks on standardized test answer sheets and similar forms.

organizational information requirements analysis p. 461 Also called enterprise modeling, an approach many companies use to summarize their current IT infrastructure, to identify the practical range of business and product strategies based on the current infrastructure, and to identify information system projects that offer the most benefits to the organization.

Outline View p. 147 The outliner option built into Microsoft Word, which enables you to examine and restructure the overall organization of a document, while showing each topic in as much detail as you need.

outliner p. 147 Software that facilitates the arrangement of information into hierarchies or levels of ideas. Some word processors include outline views that serve the same function as separate outliners.

output p. 439 Information given out by the computer.

output device p. 39 Device for sending information from the computer, such as a monitor or printer.

outsourcing p. 450, 527 Hiring talent for selected activities on a contract basis.

P

P2P model p. 286 See peer-to-peer model.

packet-switching p. 321 The standard technique used to send information over the Internet. A message is broken into packets that travel independently from network to network toward their common destination, where they are reunited.

packets p. 321 What information sent over the Internet is broken into. These packets transfer from network to network toward their destination.

page-layout software p. 156 In desktop publishing, software used to combine various source documents into a coherent, visually appealing publication.

painting software p. 189 Enables you to paint pixels on the screen with a pointing device.

palette p. 189 A collection of colors available in drawing software.

paperless office p. 402 An office of the future in which magnetic and optical archives will replace reference books and file cabinets, electronic communication will replace letters and memos, and digital publications provided through the Internet and online services will replace newspapers and other periodicals.

paradigm shift p. 21 A change in thinking that results in a new way of seeing the world.

parallel port p. 93 A standard port on most PCs for attaching a printer or other device that communicates by sending or receiving bits in groups, rather than sequentially.

parallel processing p. 51, 554 Using multiple processors to divide jobs into pieces and work simultaneously on the pieces.

parameter RAM p. 55 CMOS RAM, a special low-energy kind of RAM used to store the date, time, and calendar in Macintoshes.

parsing program (parser) p. 556 In translation, a program that analyzes sentence structure and identifies each word according to its part of speech. Another program looks up each word in a translation dictionary and substitutes the appropriate word.

Pascal p. 518 A high-level computer language, named for the seventeenth-century French mathematician and inventor, developed in the early 1970s as an alternative to BASIC for student programmers.

passwords p. 371 The most common security tools used to restrict access to computer systems.

paste p. 587 A word processing program text-editing tool that allows you to cut or copy words from one part of a document and place the copy elsewhere in the same or a different document.

patent p. 132 A type of law that protects mechanical inventions.

path p. 328 The hierarchical nesting of directories (folders) that contain a Web resource, as described in the third part of the URL, following the dot address.

pathname p. 128 The unique location specification for every computer file and folder, describing the nesting of folders containing it.

pattern recognition p. 564 Identifying recurring patterns in input data with the goal of understanding or categorizing that input.

PB (petabyte) p. 47 The equivalent of 1024 terabytes, or 1 quadrillion bytes.

PC card p. 57 A credit-card-sized card that can be inserted into a slot to expand memory or add a peripheral to a computer; commonly used in portable computers. Sometimes called by its original name, PCMCIA.

PDF (portable document format) p. 159, 195, 335, 403 Allows documents of all types to be stored, viewed, or modified on any Windows or Macintosh computer, making it possible for many organizations to reduce paper flow.

peer-to-peer (P2P) computing p. 303 See peer-to-peer model.

peer-to-peer (P2P) file sharing p. 210, 303 The online sharing of music or other computer files directly among individual computer users' hard drives, rather than through posting the files on central servers.

peer-to-peer model p. 286 A LAN model that allows every computer on the network to be both client and server.

pen-based computer p. 73 A keyboardless machine that accepts input from a stylus applied directly to a flat-panel screen.

pen scanner p. 73 A scanner that looks like a pen or highlighter. When you drag a pen scanner across a line of printed text, it creates a text file in its built-in memory, where it's stored until you transfer it into your computer's memory through a cable or wireless connection.

peripheral p. 11, 40, 584 An external device, such as a keyboard or monitor, connected via cables to the system central processing unit.

Perl p. 336, 526 Practical extraction and reporting language, a Web scripting language that is particularly well suited for writing scripts to process text—for example, complex Web forms.

personal area network (PAN) p. 282 A network that links a variety of personal electronic devices, such as mobile phones, handheld computers, and PCs, so they can communicate with each other.

personal computer (PC) p. 8, 584 A small, powerful, relatively low-cost microcomputer.

personal digital assistant (PDA) p. 11, 73 A pocket-sized computer used to organize appointments, tasks, notes, contacts, and other personal information. Sometimes called handheld computer or palmtop computer. Many PDAs include additional software and hardware for wireless communication.

personal information manager (PIM) p. 241 A specialized database program that automates an address/phone book, an appointment calendar, a to-do list, and miscellaneous notes. Also called an electronic organizer.

personalization p. 332 Customization of a Web site's content, made possible because sites can use login names, passwords, and cookies to track and remember information about guests from visit to visit.

personal Web portal p. 339 A Web portal that can be customized to reflect a user's personal taste and interests. Features might include local weather and sports scores, personalized TV and movie listings, news headlines related to particular subjects, horoscopes, and advertisements, amongst others.

PERT p. 462 Program evaluation and review technique, a variation of the critical path method used to keep track of a project's schedule; PERT features optimistic, pessimistic, and most likely time estimates to complete each activity.

phishing p. 293, 362 The use of a deceptive email message or Web site to lure a person into divulging credit card numbers or other sensitive information.

photo management software p. 193 Programs that simplify and automate common tasks associated with capturing, organizing, editing, and sharing digital images.

photo printer p. 81 A type of newer inkjet printer specially optimized to print high-quality photos captured with digital cameras and scanners.

PHP p. 526 A widely-used open source scripting language that is designed for producing dynamic Web pages. Like Perl, PHP is a server-side language. Many programmers take advantage of the fact that HTML code can be embedded in PHP scripts.

pie chart p. 166 A round pie-shaped chart with slices that show the relative proportions of the parts to a whole.

pixel p. 78, 189 A picture element (dot) on a computer screen or printout. Groups of pixels compose the images on the monitor and the output of a printout.

plagiarism p. 26 The act of presenting someone else's work as one's own.

Plain Old Telephone Service (POTS) p. 279 Used with a modem for narrowband dial-up Internet connections.

platform p. 127 The combination of hardware and operating system software upon which application software is built.

platform independent p. 95 The ability of a peripheral device to work on multiple platforms. For example, a USB disk drive could be used with both Macintosh and Windows computers.

platters p. 88 Flat discs that are the part of the hard disk that holds information.

plotter p. 82 An automated drawing tool that produces finely scaled drawings by moving pen and/or paper in response to computer commands.

plug-in p. 333 A software extension that adds new features.

podcast p. 210 Radio- or television-style programs that can be downloaded on demand or automatically by subscription.

pointcasting p. 424 A one-on-one broadcast targeting a single individual. It's also known as individualized broadcasting.

point size p. 587 A measure of character size, with one point equal to 1/72 inch.

pointing stick (TrackPoint) p. 68 A tiny joysticklike device embedded in the keyboard of a laptop computer.

point-of-sale (POS) terminal p. 72 A terminal with a wand reader, barcode scanner, or other device that captures information at the check-out counter of a store.

pop-up menus p. 123 Menus that can appear anywhere on the screen.

port p. 57 Socket that allows information to pass in and out.

portals p. 600 Web sites designed as first-stop gateways for Internet surfers.

Post Office Protocol (POP) p. 290 A standard method of retrieving email from servers.

PostScript p. 146 A standard page-description language.

power-line network, p. 274 A network that transmits data through power lines. Ethernet cables generally connect each computer's network port to a device that attaches to the phone line or power line.

prefetch unit p. 52 Part of the CPU that fetches the next several instructions from memory.

presentation p. 445 Showing information in a format and medium useful to the user.

presentation-graphics software p. 199 Automates the creation of visual aids for lectures, training sessions, and other presentations. Can include everything from spreadsheet charting programs to animation-editing software but most commonly used for creating and displaying a series of onscreen slides to serve as visual aids for presentations.

primary storage p. 85 A computer's main memory.

print server p. 287 A server that accepts, prioritizes, and processes print jobs.

printer p. 81, 585 Output device that produces a paper copy of any information that can be displayed on the screen.

privacy p. 253 Freedom from unauthorized access to one's person, or to knowledge about one's person.

processing p. 439, 444 An activity that manipulates and organizes information in ways that add value.

processor p. 39 Part of the computer that processes information, performs arithmetic calculations, and makes basic decisions based on information values.

program p. 107 Instructions that tell the hardware what to do to transform input into output.

program verification p. 540 The process of proving the correctness of a program.

programming p. 511 A specialized form of problem solving, typically involving the four steps of defining the problem; devising, refining, and testing the algorithm; writing the program; and testing and debugging the program.

programming by demonstration p. 415 A form of programming in which the computer observes the user perform the correct action on a particular input and is able to repeat the same action on different inputs.

programming environment p. 515 An integrated compiler software package, including a text editor, a compiler, a debugger, and a variety of other programming utilities.

project management software p. 462 Programs that help coordinate, schedule, and track complex projects.

PROLOG p. 518 Programming Logic, a popular language for artificial-intelligence programming.

proportionally spaced fonts p. 588 Fonts that enable more room for wide than for narrow characters.

protocol p. 284 A set of rules for the exchange of data between a terminal and a computer or between two computers.

prototype p. 529 A limited working system or subsystem that is created to give users and managers an idea of how the complete system will work.

prototyping p. 529 An iterative process in which the systems analyst can modify the prototype until it meets the needs and expectations of the organization.

pseudocode p. 511 A cross between a computer language and plain English, a form that programmers typically use to write algorithms before translating them into computer language.

public domain p. 194 Creative work or intellectual property that is freely usable by anyone, either because the copyright has expired or because the creator obtained a Creative Commons license for the work.

public-domain software p. 115 Free software that is not copyrighted, offered through World Wide Web sites, electronic bulletin boards, user groups, and other sources.

public network p. 479 A network that uses a public communications network, such as a public utility telecommunication network or the Internet, a method an organization can use to set up an extranet.

pull technology p. 339 Technology in which browsers on client computers pull information from server machines. The browser needs to initiate a request before any information is delivered.

push technology p. 339 Technology in which information is delivered automatically to a client computer. The user subscribes to a service and the server delivers that information periodically and unobtrusively. Contrast with pull technology.

Python p. 518 A Java-like language popular with Linux open-source programmers.

Q

quantum computers p. 574 Computers based on the properties of atoms and their nuclei and the laws of quantum machanics.

query p. 237 An information request.

query language p. 239, 524 A special language for performing queries, more precise than the English language.

QuickTime p. 335 An Apple program for delivering cross-platform streaming media in proprietary formats.

R

radio frequency identification (RFID) reader p. 72 A reading tool that uses radio waves to communicate with RFID tags.

radio frequency identification (RFID) tag p. 72 A device that, when energized by a nearby RFID reader, broadcasts information to the reader for input into a computer.

RAID (redundant array of independent disk) p. 376 A storage device that allows multiple hard disks to operate as a unit.

RAM (random access memory) p. 39, 584 Memory that stores program instructions and data temporarily.

random access p. 85 Storage method that allows information retrieval without regard to the order in which it was recorded.

raster (bit-mapped) graphics p. 189 Painting programs create raster graphics that are, to the computer, simple maps showing how the pixels on the screen should be represented.

read/write head p. 88 The mechanism that reads information from, and writes information to, the spinning platter in a hard disk or disk drive.

RealOne p. 335 a popular program for playing streaming audio and video, including live webcasts.

real time p. 205, 249 When a computer performs tasks immediately.

real-time communication p. 295 Internet communication that enables you to communicate with other users who are logged on at the same time.

real-time processing p. 445 Processing each transaction as it occurs, which is appropriate when users need the data immediately, as with bank ATM machines.

real-time streaming audio p. 332 Streaming transmission of radio broadcasts, concerts, news feeds, speeches, and other sound events as they happen.

real-time streaming video p. 322 Similar to streaming audio Webcasts but with video.

record p. 236 In a database, the information relating to one person, product, or event.

record matching p. 258 Compiling profiles by combining information from different database files by looking for a shared unique field.

regional Web portal p. 339 A portal on the Web that contains information and services related to a particular geographic region.

regional work centers p. 406 Shared offices established by corporations and government organizations in various locales to reduce commuting times.

register p. 52 A storage area within a CPU's arithmetic logic unit (ALU). Most registers are 32 or 64 bits in size.

relational database p. 247 A program that allows files to be related to each other so changes in one file are reflected in other files automatically.

remote access p. 596 Network access via phone line, TV cable system, or wireless link.

remix p. 212 A complete reworking of songs, using fresh instrumentation, rhythms, and audio samples.

removable cartridge media p. 584 See removable media.

removable media p. 584 Storage media designed to be removed and transported easily, including Zip, Jaz, and Orb disks.

repetition p. 513 A looping mechanism within a control structure that allows a group of steps to be repeated several times.

repetitive-stress injuries p. 67, 86 Conditions that result from repeating the same movements over long periods, such as keyboarding-induced carpal tunnel syndrome, a painful affliction of the wrist and hand.

replication p. 164 Automatic replication of values, labels, and formulas, a feature of spreadsheet software.

report p. 239 A database printout that is an ordered list of selected records and fields in an easy-to-read form.

resolution p. 78, 190 Density of pixels, measured by the number of dots per inch.

retinal display p. 97 A device that works without a screen by drawing pixels directly on the user's retina with a focused beam of light.

retirement p. 531 The final phase of the systems development life cycle, in which a system is phased out.

right to privacy p. 259 Freedom from interference into the private sphere of a person's affairs.

right-click p. 586 Hitting the right-hand part of mouse button so, for example, while pointing to an object the computer may display a menu of choices.

rip p. 207 Copy songs from a CD to a computer's hard drive.

robots p. 400, 570 Computer-controlled machines designed to perform specific manual tasks.

rollover p. 336 A common use of Web scripting, used to make onscreen buttons visibly change when the pointer rolls over them.

ROM (read-only memory) p. 55 Memory that includes permanent information only. The computer can only read information from it; it can never write any new information on it.

root directory p. 128 The main folder on a computer's primary hard disk, containing all the other files and folders kept on the disk.

routers p. 276 Programs or devices that decide how to route Internet transmissions.

RSS (Really Simple Syndication) p. 341 An XML-based format for sharing data with aggregators, commonly used by bloggers.

S

sabotage p. 364 A malicious attack on work, tools, or business.

safemode p. 125 A way to start your machine when it's not working properly because files have been corrupted or applications are clashing with each other. Safe mode will disable most startup applications temporarily. On a Windows machine, press and hold the F8 key on the keyboard as the machine is booting, then use the arrow keys to select Safe Mode in the Windows Advanced Options Menu that appears. On a Mac, hold down the Shift key while restarting until the Apple logo appears.

sample p. 207 A digital sound file.

samplers p. 210 An electronic musical instrument that can sample digital sounds, turn them into notes, and play them back at any pitch.

sampling rate p. 207 The rate that a sound wave is sampled; the more samples per second, the more closely the digitized sound approximates the original.

sans-serif fonts p. 587 Typeface fonts in which the characters have plain and clean lines rather than embellishments at the ends of the main strokes.

satellite Internet connections p. 279 A broadband technology available through many of the same satellite dishes that provide television channels to viewers. For many rural homes and businesses, satellite

Internet connections provide the only high-speed Internet access options available.

satellite offices p. 406 Workplaces that enable workers to commute to smaller offices closer to their homes.

Save p. 129 A basic file-management operation that writes the current state of the application as a disk file.

Save As p. 129 A basic file-management operation that allows you to choose the location and name of the file you want to contain the current state of the application.

Scalable Vector Graphics (SVG) p. 204 An open standard of vector graphics format.

scanner p. 73, 74 An input device that makes a digital representation of any printed image. See flatbed scanners, slide scanners, drum scanners, and sheetfed scanners.

scatter chart p. 166 Discovers a relationship between two variables.

scientific-visualization software p. 172 Uses shape, location in space, color, brightness, and motion to help you understand invisible relationships, providing graphical representation of numerical data.

scripting languages p. 523 User-oriented languages that enable users to create programs (macros) that automate repetitive tasks; also known as macro languages.

scripts p. 335 Short programs that can add interactivity, animation, and other dynamic features to a Web page or multimedia document.

search p. 237, 593 Looking for a specific record.

search engine p. 600 A program for locating information on the Web.

search engine optimization p. 331, 488 A method of increasing Web site traffic by improving search engine rankings for targeted keywords.

searching p. 555 An artificial-intelligence technique wherein the computer looks ahead at the possible outcomes of a given action, such as a move in a game of chess.

secondary storage p. 85 The category of computer storage found in peripherals such as tape and disk drives.

sectors p. 130 Units of data or memory on a hard disk, existing as parts of concentric tracks.

secure private network p. 479 A network that physically attaches intranets with private leased telephone lines, a method an organization can use to set up an extranet.

security patch p. 367 Software programs that plug potential security breaches in an operating system, often provided as free downloads or automatic updates to all owners of the OS.

security processors p. 389 Special-purpose hardware that allows every network message to be encrypted.

select (records) p. 239, 586 Looking for all records that match a set of criteria.

selection p. 513 See decision.

selects p. 586 Chooses an object, as by moving the pointer to a picture of a tool or object on the screen and clicking the mouse.

semantics p. 559 The underlying meaning of words and phrases.

semiconductor p. 8 Another name for a silicon chip.

semistructured decision p. 451 A type of management decision used when there's some uncertainty about a problem and the manager must use his or her judgment.

sensor p. 78, 570 A device that enables digital machines to monitor a physical quantity of the analog world, such as temperature, humidity, or pressure, to provide data used in robotics, environmental climate control, and other applications.

sequence p. 513 A group of instructions within a control structure that are followed in a given order.

sequencing software p. 210 Software that enables a computer to be used as a tool for musical composition, recording, and editing.

sequential p. 218 Linear in form, and designed to be read from beginning to end, as are conventional text media such as books.

sequential-access p. 85 Storage method that requires the user to retrieve information by zipping through it in the order in which it was recorded.

Serial-ATA or SATA (Serial Advanced Technology Attachment) p. 96 A type of interface (frequently used for hard disks) that can transfer data at up to 1200 Mbps.

serial port p. 93 A standard port on most PCs for attaching a modem or other device that can send and receive messages one bit at a time.

serif fonts p. 587 Typeface fonts in which the characters are embellished with fine lines (serifs) at the ends of the main strokes.

server p. 12 A computer especially designed to provide software and other resources to other computers over a network.

service pack p. 113 A bundled collection of updates, upgrades, and bug fixes for an operating system or software application.

set-top box p. 220 A special-purpose computer designed to provide Internet access and other services using a standard television set and (usually) a cable TV connection.

shareware p. 115 Software that is free for the trying, with a send-payment-if-you-keep-it honor system.

shell p. 123 A program layer that stands between the user and the operating system.

Shockwave Flash Format (SWF) p. 204, 335 A popular form of vector graphics format associated with the Adobe Flash Player.

Shockwave/Flash p. 335 Adobe plug-ins that enable Web browsers to present compressed interactive multimedia documents and animations created with various authoring tools.

silicon chip p. 8 Hundreds of transistors packed into an integrated circuit on a piece of silicon.

Silicon Valley p. 8 The area around San Jose, California, that has become a hotbed of the computer industry since the 1970s, when dozens of microprocessor manufacturing companies sprouted and grew there.

site license p. 287 License for multiple copies or removing restrictions on software copying and use at a network site.

Singularity p. 573 A future point in time when our old models of business and government will have to be discarded and a new reality will rule, based on artificial intelligence.

sleep p. 48 A suspended animation state in which a system uses just enough power to preserve RAM.

slide scanners p. 74 Scanners for slides and negatives only.

slot p. 57 An area inside the computer's housing that holds special-purpose circuit boards.

smart badge p. 379 See active badge.

smart card p. 423 A card that looks like a standard credit card but features an embedded microprocessor and memory instead of a magnetic strip.

smart weapon p. 384 A missile that uses computerized guidance systems to locate its target.

smart whiteboard p. 73 A large electronic writing surface, as for use in a classroom, capable of sending its contents to a PC, where the information can be stored as digital information or turned into text files.

SMIL (synchronized multimedia integration language) p. 338 An HTML-like language designed to make it possible to link time-based streaming media so, for example, sounds, video, and animation can be tightly integrated with each other.

social engineering p. 362 Slang for the use of deception to get individuals to reveal sensitive information.

social networking p. 299 A term used to describe Web sites that make it easy for members to connect with friends, meet people with common interests, and create online communities. These sites often rely on email, instant messages, chat rooms, Web forums, blogs, and other network communication technologies.

social responsibility p. 463 Legal and ethical computing behavior, a key concern in business today because of the many ways an information worker's actions can affect other people.

soft Alife p. 574 A form of artificial life that creates simulations or other software-based constructions that exhibit life-like behavior.

software p. 585 Instructions that tell the hardware what to do to transform input into output.

software engineering p. 539 A branch of computer science that applies engineering principles and techniques to the world of computer software.

software license p. 114 An agreement allowing the use of a software program on a single machine.

software piracy p. 114 The illegal duplication of copyrighted software.

software-defined radio p. 308 A technology that allows a single wireless hardware device to be reprogrammed on the fly to serve a variety of functions.

SOHO p. 423 Small office, home office, referring to one of today's fastest-growing computer markets.

solid-state storage p. 92 Storage, such as flash memory, with no moving parts. Solid-state storage is likely to replace disk storage in the future.

sort p. 239 Arrange records in alphabetic or numeric order based on values in one or more fields.

sound card p. 83 A circuit board that allows the PC to accept microphone input, play music and other sound through speakers or headphones, and process sound in a variety of ways.

source document p. 156, 328 In desktop publishing, the articles, chapters, drawings, maps, charts, and photographs that are to appear in the publication. Usually produced with standard word processors and graphics programs.

spam p. 293, 603 Internet junk mail.

spamdexing p. 488 Using techniques such as automatically generated links from bogus sites to fool search engines into giving sites higher rankings than they deserve.

spam filters p. 603 Tools found in most email programs whose purpose is to limit or control Internet junk mail.

speaker independence p. 566 Speech-recognition technology that works without having to be trained to an individual voice.

speakers p. 585 The personal computer peripherals that emit music, voices, and other sounds.

speech recognition p. 78, 566 The identification of spoken words and sentences by a computer, making it possible for voice input to be converted into text files.

speech recognition software p. 152 See speech recognition.

speech synthesis p. 567 The use of software or hardware to allow PCs to recite anything typed, though with voices that sound artificial and robotic.

spelling checker (batch or interactive) p. 149 A built-in component of a word processor or a separate program that compares words in a document with words in a disk-based dictionary and flags words not found in the dictionary. May operate in batch mode, checking all the words at once, or interactive mode, checking one word at a time.

spiders p. 339 See Web crawlers.

spoofing p. 362 A process used to steal passwords online.

spot color p. 158 The relatively easy use of a single color (or sometimes two) to add interest to a desktop-publishing product.

spreadsheet software p. 162 Enables the user to control numbers, manipulating them in various ways. The software can manage budgeting, investment management, business projections, grade books, scientific simulations, checkbooks, financial planning and speculation, and other tasks involving numbers.

spybot p. 366 A spyware application program, also called tracking software, that gathers user information and communicates it to an outsider via the Internet.

spyware p. 366 Technology that collects information from computer users without their knowledge or consent.

stack chart p. 166 Stacked bars to show how proportions of a whole change over time.

static IP address p. 323 An IP address assigned semi-permanently to a particular device connected to the Internet.

statistical-analysis software p. 171 Specialized software that tests the strength of data relationships, produces graphs showing how two or more variables relate to each other, uncovers trends, and performs other statistical analyses.

statistics p. 171 The science of analyzing and collecting data.

steering committee p. 529 An organizational group that may be formed to decide which projects should be considered first.

stepwise refinement p. 511 Breaking programming problems into smaller problems, and breaking each smaller problem into a subproblem that can be subdivided in the same way.

storage and retrieval p. 440 Activities that systematically accumulate information for later use and locate the stored information when needed.

storage device p. 39, 85 Long-term repository for data. Disks and tapes are examples.

stored query p. 239 A commonly used query recorded by a database so it can be accessed quickly in the future. The ability to generate stored queries is a powerful feature that helps databases blur the line between application programs and development tools.

storyboard p. 205 The first step in a video project, a guide for shooting and editing scenes.

strategic information system p. 459 Any information system that is crucial to a company's competitive success.

strategic level p. 451 The management level responsible for long-range issues related to the business's growth and development.

strategic planning p. 460 The first phase of information technology planning, which involves developing a plan that defines the mission of the company, identifies the company's environment and internal strengths and weaknesses, and defines the competitive strategy of the company.

streaming audio p. 331 Sound files that play without being completely downloaded to the local hard disk.

streaming video p. 331 Video clip files that play while being downloaded.

structured decision p. 451 A type of management decision used when the manager understands the situation clearly and uses established procedures and information to resolve the problem.

structured programming p. 519 A technique to make programming easier and more productive. Structured programs are built from smaller programs, called modules or subprograms, that are in turn made of even smaller modules.

Structured Query Language (SQL) p. 239 A query language available for many different database management systems. More than a query language, SQL also accesses databases from a wide variety of vendors.

stylesheet p. 145 Custom styles for each of the common elements in a document.

stylus p. 68 An input device, with much the same point-and-click functions as a mouse, used to send signals to a pressure-sensitive graphics tablet.

subject tree p. 329, 600 A hierarchical catalog of Web sites compiled by researchers, such as that found at Yahoo!.

subnotebooks p. 11 Portable computers, smaller than a notebook or laptop, about the size of a hardbound book.

subprograms p. 521 In structured programming, a program is built from smaller programs called subprograms.

subsystem p. 439 A system that is a part of a larger system.

supercomputer p. 13 A super-fast, super-powerful, and super-expensive computer used for applications that demand maximum power.

supply chain p. 449 The network of organizations that supply raw materials, manufacture products, and distribute products to customers.

supply chain management p. 449 The use of enterprise resource planning to improve the coordination of a company's value chain logistics activities and the logistics activities of its suppliers and customers.

switches p. 274 Hardware that decides how to route Internet transmissions. Switches are similar to software routers, but faster and less flexible.

switching costs p. 459 The time, effort, and money a customer or supplier would have to expend if they changed to a competitor's product or service.

symmetric multiprocessing p. 51 See multiprocessing.

syntax p. 559 A set of rules for constructing sentences from words. Every language has a syntax.

syntax errors p. 515 Violations of a programming language's grammar rules.

synthesized p. 207 Synthetically generated computer sounds.

synthesizer p. 83, 210 A device that can produce—synthesize—music and other sounds electronically. A synthesizer might be a stand-alone musical instrument or part of the circuitry on a computer's sound card.

synthetic speech p. 567 Speech generated by computers by converting text into phonetic sounds.

system p. 439 A set of interrelated parts that work together to accomplish a purpose through the three basic functions of input, processing, and output.

system administrator p. 371 A user who has additional access privileges, such as permission to install software applications and change system settings.

system bus p. 57 A group of wires that transmits information between components on the motherboard.

system flowchart p. 534 A graphical depiction of the physical system that exists or is proposed, such as to show the relationship among programs, files, input, and output in a system.

system software p. 117, 585 Software that handles the details of computing. Includes the operating system and utility programs.

system unit p. 584 The box that houses a personal computer's central processing unit—in other words, "the computer" or "the PC."

systems analyst p. 527 An information technology professional primarily responsible for developing and managing the system.

systems development p. 527 A problem-solving process of investigating a situation, designing a system solution to improve the situation, acquiring the human, financial, and technological resources to implement the solution, and finally evaluating the success of the solution.

systems development life cycle (SDLC) p. 528 A sequence of seven steps or phases through which an information system passes between the time the system is conceived and the time it is phased out.

T

T1 p. 278 A direct connect digital line that can transmit voice, data, and video at roughly 1.5Mbps.

T3 p. 278 A direct connect digital line that transmits voice, data, and video even faster than a T1 connection.

table p. 236, 331 A grid of rows and columns; on many Web pages tables with hidden grids are used to align graphical images.

tactical level p. 451 The management level responsible for a large organizational unit, such as a sales region or a production plant.

tape drive p. 85 Storage device that uses magnetic tape to store information.

taskbar p. 123 A button bar that provides one-click access to open applications and tools, making it easy to switch back and forth between different tasks.

tax-preparation software p. 170 Provides a prefabricated worksheet where the user enters numbers into tax forms. Calculations are performed automatically, and the completed forms can be sent electronically to the IRS.

TB (terabyte) p. 47 Approximately 1 million megabytes.

TCP/IP (Transmission Control Protocol/Internet Protocol) p. 284, 321 Protocols developed as an experiment in internetworking, now the language of the Internet, allowing cross-network communication for almost every type of computer and network.

technophobia p. 412 The fear of technology.

telecommunication p. 273 Long-distance electronic communication in a variety of forms.

telecommuting p. 404 Working from home by modem, as do many programmers, accountants, and other information workers.

tele-immersion p. 224 The use of multiple cameras and high-speed networks to create an environment in which multiple remote users can interact with each other and with computer-generated objects.

telemedicine p. 399 An application of clinical medicine wherein computers monitor patient vital signs in hospitals, at home, and on the street with portable units. The computers analyze signals and transmit warnings when problems arise.

templates p. 156 In desktop publishing, professionally designed empty documents that can be adapted to specific user needs. In spreadsheet software, worksheets that contain labels and formulas but no data values. The template produces instant answers when you fill in the blanks.

terminal p. 13 Combination keyboard and screen that transfers information to and from a mainframe computer.

terminal emulation software p. 286 Software that allows a PC to act as a dumb terminal—an input/output device that enables the user to send commands to and view information on the host computer.

testing p. 513 The process of checking the logic of an algorithm and the performance of a program.

text editor p. 515 An application that is similar to a word processor without the formatting features required by writers and publishers; some provide specialized features to aid in writing programs.

text messaging p. 295 A popular form of communication among mobile phone users that relies on SMS technology.

text-to-speech p. 567 The creation of synthetic speech by converting text files into phonetic sounds.

thesaurus p. 148 A synonym finder; often included with a word processor.

thin clients p. 13, 401 Network computers, Internet appliances, or other devices designed to connect to the Internet but not perform all the other tasks performed by a PC.

thumb drive p. 92 See USB drive.

time bomb p. 366 A logic bomb that is triggered by a time-related event.

timesharing p. 13 Technique by which mainframe computers communicate with several users simultaneously.

top-down design p. 511 A design process that starts at the top, with main ideas, and works down to the details.

top-level domain p. 323 The part of an Internet address that typically describes the type of organization, such as .com or .edu.

total cost of ownership (TCO) p. 401 The net cost of computer ownership, including hardware, software, training, support, maintenance, troubleshooting, and other expenses.

touch screen p. 68 Pointing device that responds when the user points to or touches different screen regions.

touchpad (trackpad) p. 68 A small flat-panel pointing device that is sensitive to light pressure. The user moves the pointer by dragging a finger across the pad.

trackball p. 68 Pointing device that remains stationary while the user moves a protruding ball to control the pointer on the screen.

tracking software p. 366 A spyware application program, also called a spybot, that gathers user information and communicates it to an outsider via the Internet.

TrackPoint p. 68 A brand name for a tiny joysticklike device embedded in the keyboard of a laptop computer.

tracks p. 131 A series of concentric units of data or memory on a hard disk.

trademark p. 132 Legal ownership protection for symbols, pictures, sounds, colors, and smells used by a business to identify goods.

transaction p. 445 An event that occurs in any of the primary activities of the company: manufacturing, marketing, sales, and accounting.

transaction processing system (TPS) p. 445 A basic accounting and record-keeping system that keeps track of routine daily transactions necessary to conduct business.

transborder data flow p. 450 The flow of data between countries.

transistor p. 7 An electronic device that performs the same function as the vacuum tube by transferring electricity across a tiny resistor.

transmission p. 445 The process of distributing information.

Trojan horse p. 365 A program that performs a useful task while at the same time carrying out some secret destructive act. A form of software sabotage.

true color p. 79 Color that is 24-bit or greater, allowing more than 16 million color choices per pixel, creating photorealistic images.

Turing test p. 553 A way to test machine intelligence.

tweening p. 204 The automatic creation of in-between frames in an animation.

twisted pair p. 277 A type of LAN cable that resembles the copper wires in standard telephone cables.

typeface p. 587 All type, including roman, bold, and italics, of a single design, such as Palatino or Helvetica.

U

ultra-wideband p. 308 A low-power, short-range, wireless technology that transmits ultra-high-speed signals over a wide spectrum of frequencies.

Unicode p. 44 A 65,000-character set for making letters, digits, and special characters fit into the computer's binary circuitry.

uninterruptible power supply (UPS) p. 376 A hardware device that protects computers from data loss during power failures.

universal product codes (UPCs) p. 72 Codes created from patterns of variable-width bars that send scanned information to a mainframe computer.

UNIX p. 123 An operating system that allows a timesharing computer to communicate with several other computers or terminals at once. UNIX is the most widely available multiuser operating system in use. It is also widely used on Internet hosts.

unstructured decision p. 451 A type of management decision requiring many quantitative and ethical judgments that have no clear answers.

updates p. 113 Improvements software companies make to their programs. They usually contain bug fixes, new features, and/or minor enhancements.

upgrade p. 113 A new and improved version of a software program.

upload p. 287 To post software or documents to an online source so they're available for others.

up-skilled p. 406 Transformed in such a way that a job requires more skill.

URL (uniform resource locator) p. 328, 598 The address of a Web site.

USB (universal serial bus) p. 95 A data path standard that theoretically allows up to 126 devices, such as keyboards, digital cameras, and scanners, to be chained together from a single port, allowing for data transmission that is much faster and more flexible than through traditional serial and parallel ports.

USB 2.0 p. 95 A new, high-speed version of USB that offers fast transfer rates of 480 megabits per second.

USB flash drive p. 92 A portable storage device that stores data in flash memory and connects to a computer through a USB port. Also called thumb drives or jump drives.

USB hub p. 96 A device that increases the number of ports on a PC, allowing users to have several USB peripherals share the same port.

USB port p. 57 A computer port that can be used to attach keyboards, mice, printers, cameras, disk drives, portable storage devices, and more.

user interface p. 121 The look and feel of the computing experience from a human point of view.

user name p. 601 A one-word name that you type to identify yourself when connecting—logging in—to a secure computer system, network, or email account. Sometimes called login name or alias.

utility computing p. 306 A form of grid computing that involves offering computational power and storage as metered commercial services, with the Internet acting like a utility grid.

utility program p. 120 Software that serves as tools for doing system maintenance and some repairs that are not automatically handled by the operating system.

V

value p. 162 The numbers that are the raw material used by spreadsheet software to perform calculations.

value chain model p. 441 A business organization model developed by Harvard professor Michael E. Porter that focuses on the value-adding activities of a company's primary and support activities.

variable p. 514 In programming, a named portion of the computer's memory whose contents the program can examine and change.

VBScript p. 526 A Web scripting language that is Microsoft's answer to JavaScript, based on Visual Basic.

vector graphics p. 195 The storage of pictures as collections of lines, shapes, and other objects.

vertical portals (vortal) p. 339 Specialized portals that, like vertical market software, are targeted at members of a particular industry or economic sector.

vertical-market application p. 116 A computer application designed specifically for a particular business or industry.

video adapter p. 81 A circuit board installed inside the main system unit connecting the monitor to the computer.

video digitizer p. 75, 205 A device that converts analog video signals into digital data.

video-editing software p. 206 Software for editing digital video, including titles, sound, and special effects.

video projector p. 81 A projector that can project computer screen images for meetings and classes.

video teleconference p. 295 Face-to-face communication over long distances using video and computer technology.

videoconferencing p. 75 Face-to-face communication over long distances using video and computer technology.

viral p. 303 A term used to describe a video that becomes widely popular, and spreads like a virus, due to the high number of email messages, blog posts, and IMs that have links to it.

virtual instruments p. 210 Musical instruments that exist only in software; they are gradually replacing bulky, expensive hardware devices in the typical electronic music studio.

virtual memory p. 117 Use of part of a computer hard disk as a substitute for RAM.

virtual private network (VPN) p. 282, 479 A network that uses encryption software to create secure "tunnels" through the public Internet or between intranets; a method an organization can use to set up an extranet.

virtual reality (VR) p. 134, 224 Technology that creates the illusion that the user is immersed in a world that exists only inside the computer, an environment that contains both scenes and the controls to change those scenes.

virtual worlds p. 224 Computer-generated worlds that create the illusion of immersion.

virtualization p. 127 The ability of a CPU to run multiple operating systems simultaneously.

viruses p. 364, 603 Software that spreads from program to program, or from disk to disk, and uses each infected program or disk to make copies of itself. A form of software sabotage.

Visual J++ p. 518 A Java-like language for programming on the Microsoft Windows platform.

visual programming p. 523 Programming featuring tools that enable programmers to create large portions of their programs by drawing pictures and pointing to onscreen objects, eliminating much of the coding of traditional programming.

voice input p. 78 Use of a microphone to speak commands and text data to a computer, which uses speech-recognition software to interpret the input.

voice over IP (VoIP) p. 297 A protocol that allows the Internet to be used to make voice telephone calls.

voice mail p. 297 A telephone-based messaging system with many of the features of an email system.

volume licenses p. 114 Special license agreements for entire companies, schools, or government institutions to make use of a program.

volunteer computing p. 306 A type of grid computing that involves creating a virtual network of geographically dispersed computers to work on a problem that's too big to solve with a single machine or LAN.

VRAM p. 81 A special portion of RAM dedicated to holding video images.

W

waveform audio p. 207 Sound-editing software in which a visual image is manipulated using the sound's wave form.

wearable computers p. 262 Strap-on computer units for active information gatherers.

Web p. 15, 598 See World Wide Web.

Web application p. 22 An application that is stored on a Web server and typically accessed via a Web browser.

Web authoring software p. 329 Programs such as Adobe's Dreamweaver that work like desktop publishing page layout programs to allow users to create, edit, and manage Web pages and sites without having to write HTML code.

Web browsers p. 598 Application programs that enable you to explore the Web by clicking hyperlinks in Web pages stored on Web sites.

Web bug p. 292 An invisible piece of code embedded in HTML-formatted email that is programmed to send information about its receiver's Web use back to its creator.

Web crawlers p. 338 Software robots that systematically explore the Web, retrieve information about pages, and index the retrieved information in a database.

webcam p. 75 A type of digital video camera that is either attached to or built into a computer monitor. It can't function as a standalone camera.

webcast p. 332 Real-time streaming audio or video.

Webmail p. 287 Web-based e-mail.

Web forum p. 294 Functionally similar to a newsgroup, but it's built on a Web application and is accessed through a Web browser.

Web page p. 598 A single document on the World Wide Web (WWW), made up of text and images and interlinked with other documents.

Web portal p. 339 A Web site designed as a Web entry station, offering quick and easy access to a variety of services.

Web server p. 327 A server that stores Web pages and sends them to client programs—Web browsers—that request them.

Web site p. 598 A collection of related Web pages stored on the same server.

Webjacker p. 368 Someone who hijacks legitimate Web sites, redirecting unsuspecting visitors to bogus or offensive alternate sites.

wet Alife p. 574 A form of artificial life based on biochemistry rather than silicon technology. Many wet Alife researchers attempt to create life in the laboratory using chemical compounds similar to those that were responsible for the beginnings of life on our planet.

"what if?" questions p. 166 A feature of spreadsheet software that allows speculation by providing instant answers to hypothetical questions.

wide area network (WAN) p. 275 A network that extends over a long distance. Each network site is a node on the network.

Wi-Fi p. 281 A popular wireless LAN technology that allows multiple computers to connect to a LAN through a base station up to 150 feet away. Often referred to as 802.11b.

wiki p. 301 A Web site that lets anyone with access to a Web browser to modify its pages. The best-known example is Wikipedia.

WiMax (802.16) p. 281 A wireless alternative to cable or DSL service.

Windows Media Player p. 335 A Microsoft program for delivering streaming media in proprietary formats that are compatible with other players.

wired equivalent privacy (WEP) p. 282 An encryption scheme that improves the security of wireless networks.

wireless access point (WAP) p. 281 A communication device, typically connected to a wired network, that is used to create a wireless network.

wireless keyboard p. 67 A battery-powered keyboard that doesn't need a cable connecting it to the rest of the system. Most wireless keyboards use a radio technology called Bluetooth to send their signals.

wireless mouse p. 68 A battery-powered mouse that doesn't need a cable to communicate with the computer. Most wireless mice use a radio technology called Bluetooth to send their signals.

wireless network p. 275 A network in which a node has a tiny radio or infrared transmitter connected to its network port so it can send and receive data through the air rather than through cables.

wizard p. 147 A software help agent that walks the user through a complex process.

WMA p. 210 Windows Media Audio, one of a number of relatively new methods of audio compression than can squeeze music files to a fraction of their original CD-file sizes, often without perceptible loss of quality.

word size p. 51 The number of bits a CPU can process at one time, typically 8, 16, 32, or 64.

word wrap p. 587 A word processing program text-editing feature that automatically moves any words that won't fit on the current line to the next line, along with the cursor.

workflow p. 402 The path of information as it flows through a workgroup.

worksheet p. 162 A spreadsheet document that appears on the screen as a grid of numbered rows and columns.

workstation p. 11 A high-end desktop computer with massive computing power, though less expensive than a minicomputer. Workstations are the most powerful of the desktop computers.

World Wide Web (WWW) p. 15, 327, 598 Part of the Internet, a collection of multimedia documents created by organizations and users worldwide. Documents are linked in a hypertext Web that allows users to explore them with simple mouse clicks.

WORM (Write Once Read Many) p. 87 A term used to describe a drive that can write onto a blank (or partially filled) CD-R disk, but can't erase the data after it's burned in.

worms p. 365 Programs that use computer hosts to reproduce themselves. Worm programs travel independently over computer networks, seeking out uninfected workstations to occupy. A form of software sabotage.

writeback p. 53 The final phase of execution, in which the bus unit writes the results of the instruction back into memory or some other device.

WYSIWYG p. 145, 587 Short for "what you see is what you get," pronounced "wizzy-wig." With a word processor, the arrangement of the words on the screen represents a close approximation to the arrangement of words on the printed page.

X

XHTML p. 338 Markup language that combines features of HTML and XML; its advantage is its backward compatibility with HTML.

XML (eXtensible Markup Language) p. 250, 336, 525 A programming language for Web sites that includes all of HTML's features plus many additional programming extensions. XML enables Web developers to control and display data the way they control text and graphics.

Z

zombie computer p. 368 An Internet-connected computer that has been hijacked using viruses or other tools to perform malicious acts without the knowledge of their owners and users.

Photo Credits

5.32   a: top: Microsoft product screen shot reprinted with permission from Microsoft Corporation
b: bottom: Raul Vasquez/MCT/Newscom

6.1   © Sam Ogden

6.2   CERN/European Organization for Nuclear Research

6.3   Agence France Presse/Getty Images

6.5   Sanjay Kothari

6.12   AP/Wide World Photos

6.13   Photo Researchers, Inc.

6.15   © 2008 Disney Enterprises, Inc. and Pixar

6.17   New Line/Everett Collection

6.19   Colin Young-Wolff/PhotoEdit Inc.

6.23   a: top: Scott Kleinman/Stone/Getty Images
b: bottom: Piotr Powietrzynski/Photographer's Choice/Getty Images

6.30   Mark Richards/PhotoEdit Inc.

6.31   a: David Barry/Corbis/Outline
b: left: Tobias Hoellerer, Steve Feiner, and John Pavlik/Columbia University-top right: Columbia University

7.9   a: Hewlett-Packard Company
b: Paul Sakuma/AP Wide World Photos
c: Nokia
d: PRNewsFoto/Verizon Wireless/AP Wide World Photos

7.12   Pearson Education/PH College

7.16   Reason Foundation

7.17   Karim Sahib-Pool/Getty Images, Inc.

7.18   Pat Wellenbach/AP Wide World Photos

7.24   Katsumi Kasahara/AP Wide World Photos

8.1   Jeff Greenwald

8.2   © David Ducros/Photo Researchers, Inc.

8.4   a: Robert Milek/Shutterstock
b: Apple Computer, Inc.
c: Shutterstock
d: Netgear, Inc.
e: Hewlett-Packard Company
f: Fen/Shutterstock
g: Apple Computer, Inc.
h: Apple Computer, Inc.

8.5   PhotoDisc Imaging/Getty Images, Inc.-Photodisc.

8.6   Humanware, Inc.

8.7   superclic/Alamy Images

8.8   Fujitsu Siemens Computers

8.9   left: Thuraya
right: Spencer Grant/PhotoEdit Inc.

8.10   © Norman Chan/Courtesy of www.istockphoto.com

8.11   AP/Wide World Photos

8.12   BananaStock/Jupiter Images-PictureArts Corporation/Brand X Pictures Royalty Free

8.14   Reprinted with permission from Microsoft Corporation. Most current version of this product located on the Microsoft web site at http://www.microsoft.com/presspass/images/gallery

8.17   b: center left: Virginia Guariglia/Pearson Education/PH College
d: bottom: George and Ben Beekman

8.18   Pearson Education/PH College

8.21   Pearson Education/PH College

8.23   a: top: Microsoft product screen shot reprinted with permission from Microsoft Corporation.

8.26   Facebook, Inc.

9.1   © Clark Quinn

9.4   David R. Frazier Photolibrary, Inc./Alamy Images

9.6   Bananastock/Getty Images

9.9   Pearson Education/PH College

9.11   Apple Computer, Inc.

9.24   left: OpenNet Initiative
right: OpenNet Initiative

9.26   a: top: Fuse Project
b: bottom: Reuters/Johnny Onverwacht/Landov Media

10.2   Bob Child/AP Wide World Photos

10.3   Connecting Point Communcations

10.8   a: Jim Wilson/The New York Times/Redux Pictures
b: SecuGen Corporation

10.9   Symantec Corporation

10.10   c: MPC Corporation
d: Apple Computer, Inc.

10.12   a: left: PRNewsFoto/Gateway, Inc./AP Wide World Photos
b: right: MPC Corporation

10.13   a: left: Apple Computer, Inc.
b: center: Apple Computer, Inc.
c: right: Fujitsu Siemens Computers

10.14   American Power Conversion Corporation

10.15   LaCie, USA

10.17   a: left: © 2001 Versus Technology, Inc. www.versustech.com
b: right: © 2001 Versus Technology, Inc. www.versustech.com

10.20   Sgt. 1st Class Gail Braymen/North American Defense Command (NORAD)

10.21   a: top left: Pal Pillai/Agence France Presse/Getty Images

10.22   Helder Almeida/Shutterstock

11.1   John Barr/Getty Images, Inc-Liaison

11.2   Xerox Palo Alto Research Center

11.3   John Coletti/Photolibrary.com

11.5   Bill Bachman/Photo Researchers, Inc.

11.6   Ed Young/Science Photo Library/Photo Researchers, Inc.

11.7   CAP/Getty Images-Photonica Amana America, Inc.

11.11   3M Touch Systems

11.12   Chinatopix/AP Wide World Photos

11.13   Zack Canepari/The New York Times/Redux Pictures

11.14   D Harcourt Webster/Robert Harding Picture Library Ltd/Alamy Images

11.15   Evans (Ag)/Getty Images Inc.-Hulton Archive Photos

11.16   Garden City Telegram/Brad Nading/AP Wide World Photos

11.21   a: left: MTS & ProEvents
c: right: ViewPlus Technologies

11.22   Doris Haugen/AP Wide World Photos

11.23   Getty Images Inc.-Stone Allstock

11.25   Kike Calvo/Newscom

11.26   Keith Morris/Alamy Images

11.28   Take-Two Interactive Software Inc.

11.29   Chuck Liddy/The News & Observer/AP Wide World Photos

11.30   Sang-Hoon Kish Kim/Newscom

11.31   a: Fuse Project
b: Fuse Project
c: Fuse Project

12.1   Brooks Kraft /CORBIS-NY

12.2   Bruce Dale/Getty - National Geographic Society

12.5   EyeWire Collection/Getty Images-Photodisc

12.7   a: Comstock/Alamy Images
b: Denis MacDonald/AGE Fotostock America, Inc.
c: Javier Larrea/AGE Fotostock America, Inc.
d: Image State/Alamy Images
e: ImageShop Business K/Alamy Images
f: Barry Blackman/Getty Images

12.8   © Lev Dolgatshjov/Courtesy of www.istockphoto.com

12.9   David McNew/Getty Images, Inc.

12.11   d: Specral-Design/Shutterstock
e: Zoom Team/Shutterstock

12.13   a: moodboard/Alamy Images Royalty Free
b: Slawomir Fajer/Shutterstock
c: Comstock Complete
d: Shutterstock

12.15   Stuart Ramson/Porter Novelli/Bloomberg News/Landov Media

12.17   Courtesy of Lehrstuhl fur Wirtschaftsinformatik, University of Hohenheim, Stuttgart, Germany.

12.18   a: Tetra Images/Alamy Images Royalty Free
b: Blend Images/Alamy Images Royalty Free
c: Corbis/Bettmann
d: Image Source Black/Alamy Images Royalty Free

12.19   Caliper Corporation

12.21   top left: CORDA Technologies, Inc.
top right: CORDA Technologies, Inc.
bottom left: CORDA Technologies, Inc.
bottom right: CORDA Technologies, Inc.

12.23   Getty Images, Inc. Tetra Images

12.26   Reprinted with permission from Microsoft Corporation.

12.27   Thomas James Hurst/Seattle Times/Newscom

13.1   Erin Lubin/Bloomberg News/Landov Media

13.2   © (Photographer)/CORBIS All Rights Reserved

13.4   Don Ryan/AP Wide World Photos

13.6   Monkey Business Images/Shutterstock

13.9   Courtesy of Sony Electronics Inc.

13.11   a: Andresr/Shutterstock
b: Antonio Jorge Nunes/Shutterstock

13.13   © Ramin Talaie/CORBIS All Rights Reserved

13.15   Lonnie Duka/Photolibrary.com

13.18   Katsumi Kashara/AP Wide World Photos

13.22   Courtesy of www.istockphoto.com

13.23   Yonhap News Agency

14.1   U.S. Navy News Photo

14.2   U.S. Naval Historical Center Photography

14.3   Ed Honowitz/Stone/Getty Images

14.17   a: left page, bottom right: Somos/Veer/Getty Images, Inc.-Somos
b: right page, bottom right: John Giustina/Getty Images-Iconica
c: right page, bottom left: Robert E. Daemmrich/Bob Daemmrich Photography, Inc.
d: left page, bottom left: blue jean images/Getty Images, Inc.-Somos

14.24   Chad Slattery/Stone/Getty Images

14.25   Phil Scholfield/Getty Images

14.26   Michael Melford/Image Bank/Getty Images
15.1   National Portrait Gallery, London.
15.2   Courtesy of the Computer History Museum
15.4   © Corbis Bettman
15.5   a: top: Agence France Presse/Getty Images
b: bottom: Edleman Public Relations-Microsoft Game Studios
15.10   Courtesy and © Becton, Dickinson and Company
15.11   a: top: Becky Cohen/Becky Cohen, Photographer
b: bottom: Becky Cohen/Becky Cohen, Photographer

15.12   a: right: Ng Han Guan/AP Wide World Photos
b: left: NASA/Jet Propulsion Laboratory
15.14   KRT 2006/Newscom
15.15   Purestock/Alamy Images Royalty Free
15.17   Courtesy of 3000AD, Inc., Derek Smart, Ph.D
15.18   Parallax, Inc.
15.19   a: upper left: Spencer Grant/Photolibrary.com
b: upper right: iRobot Corporation
c: center right: Paul Sancya/AP Wide World Photos

d: lower left: Defense Advanced Research Projects Agency
e: lower right: Katsumi Kasahara/AP Wide World Photos
App.2   Reprinted with permission from Microsoft Corporation.
App.5   upper right: SuperStock, Inc.
center left: Paula Solloway/Alamy Images
App.11   Blend Images/Alamy Images Royalty Free
App.12   left: Robyn Beck/Agence France Presse/Getty Images

Index